Russian and Soviet Economic Performance and Structure

The Addison-Wesley Series in Economics

Abel/Bernanke
Macroeconomics

Allen
Managerial Economics

Berndt
The Practice of Econometrics

Bierman/Fernandez
Game Theory with Economic Applications

Binger/Hoffman
Microeconomics with Calculus

Boyer
Principles of Transportation Economics

Branson
Macroeconomic Theory and Policy

Brown/Hogendorn
International Economics: Theory and Context

Browning/Zupan
Microeconomic Theory and Applications

Bruce
Public Finance and the American Economy

Burgess
The Economics of Regulation and Antitrust

Byrns/Stone
Economics

Canterbery
The Literate Economist: A Brief History of Economics

Carlton/Perloff
Modern Industrial Organization

Caves/Frankel/Jones
World Trade and Payments: An Introduction

Cooter/Ulen
Law and Economics

Eaton/Mishkin
Reader to accompany The Economics of Money, Banking, and Financial Markets

Ehrenberg/Smith
Modern Labor Economics

Ekelund/Tollison
Economics: Private Markets and Public Choice

Filer/Hamermesh/Rees
The Economics of Work and Pay

Fusfeld
The Age of the Economist

Ghiara
Learning Economics: A Practical Workbook

Gibson
International Finance

Gordon
Macroeconomics

Gregory
Essentials of Economics

Gregory/Ruffin
Economics

Gregory/Stuart
Russian and Soviet Economic Performance and Structure

Griffiths/Wall
Intermediate Microeconomics

Gros/Steinherr
Winds of Change: Economic Transition in Central and Eastern Europe

Hartwick/Olewiler
The Economics of Natural Resource Use

Hogendorn
Economic Development

Hoy/Livernois/McKenna/Rees/Stengos
Mathematics for Economics

Hubbard
Money, the Financial System, and the Economy

Hughes/Cain
American Economic History

Husted/Melvin
International Economics

Invisible Hand Software
Economics in Action

Jehle/Reny
Advanced Microeconomic Theory

Klein
Mathematical Methods for Economics

Krugman/Obstfeld
International Economics: Theory and Policy

Laidler
The Demand for Money: Theories, Evidence, and Problems

Lesser/Dodds/Zerbe
Environmental Economics and Policy

Lipsey/Courant
Economics

McCarty
Dollars and Sense

Melvin
International Money and Finance

Miller
Economics Today

Miller/Benjamin/North
The Economics of Public Issues

Miller/Fishe
Microeconomics: Price Theory in Practice

Miller/VanHoose
Essentials of Money, Banking, and Financial Markets

Mills/Hamilton
Urban Economics

Mishkin
The Economics of Money, Banking, and Financial Markets

Parkin
Economics

Phelps
Health Economics

Riddell/Shackelford/Stamos
Economics: A Tool for Critically Understanding Society

Ritter/Silber/Udell
Principles of Money, Banking, and Financial Markets

Rohlf
Introduction to Economic Reasoning

Ruffin/Gregory
Principles of Economics

Salvatore
Microeconomics

Sargent
Rational Expectations and Inflation

Scherer
Industry Structure, Strategy, and Public Policy

Schotter
Microeconomics

Sherman/Kolk
Business Cycles and Forecasting

Smith
Case Studies in Economic Development

Studenmund
Using Econometrics

Su
Economic Fluctuations and Forecasting

Tietenberg
Environmental and Natural Resource Economics

Tietenberg
Environmental Economics and Policy

Todaro
Economic Development

Waldman/Jensen
Industrial Organization: Theory and Practice

Zerbe/Dively/Lesser
Benefit-Cost Analysis

Russian and Soviet Economic Performance and Structure

SIXTH EDITION

PAUL R. GREGORY
UNIVERSITY OF HOUSTON

ROBERT C. STUART
RUTGERS UNIVERSITY

ADDISON-WESLEY

An imprint of Addison Wesley Longman, Inc.

Reading, Massachusetts • Menlo Park, California • New York • Harlow, England
Don Mills, Ontario • Sydney • Mexico City • Madrid • Amsterdam

Senior Editor: Denise Clinton
Senior Production Editor: Helen Wythe
Managing Editor: James Rigney
Project Coordination and Text Design: Proof Positive/Farrowlyne Associates, Inc.
Cover Design: Eileen R. Hoff
Manufacturing Supervisor: Hugh Crawford
Marketing Manager: Quinn Perkson

Russian and Soviet Economic Performance and Structure, Sixth Edition

Library of Congress Cataloging-in-Publication Data
Gregory, Paul R.
    Russian and Soviet economic performance and structure / Paul R. Gregory,
Robert C. Stuart.—6th ed.
       p.   cm.
    Rev. ed. of: Soviet and post-Soviet economic structure and performance. 5th ed. c1994
    Includes bibliographical references and index.
    ISBN: 0-321-01427-8
    1. Soviet Union—Economic conditions.   2. Soviet Union—Economic policy.   3. Former
Soviet republics—Economic conditions.   4. Former Soviet republics—Economic policy.
I. Stuart, Robert C., 1938–   .   II. Gregory, Paul R. Soviet and post-Soviet economic
structure and performance.   III. Title.
    HC335.G723 1997
    330.947'0854—dc21
                 97–25648
                 CIP

CONTENTS

PREFACE

Rarely are we offered an opportunity to live in historic times, with great events unfolding and ultimate outcomes uncertain. In the late 1990s we live in such a time, and we hope that this sixth edition of *Russian Soviet Economic Performance and Structure* provides the understanding and insights necessary to appreciate the Soviet past, Russia's present, and to clarify how both will interact to shape the future.

The twentieth century has been an eyewitness to two significant experiments in socioeconomic systems. The first took place in the 1930s, with the creation of the administrative command economy in the Soviet Union. The second is the dismantling of that system, which began with the collapse of the Soviet Union as a political entity in 1991. These two events provide the setting for this book by asking three questions: How did the Soviet economic system work, why did it fail, and what courses will the transition economies take as they emerge from its ashes?

This sixth edition accounts for the full circle of Russian economic history. It begins with the last market economy that existed on Russian territory—the Tsarist market economy—and ends with the difficult task of reestablishing a market economy in that same territory. Our account covers almost 150 years—from the emancipation of the Russian serfs in 1861 to the final years of the twentieth century. Over half of these years were lived under the greatest social science experiment of recorded history, the Soviet experiment with the administrative command economy. It was created by design, unlike the industrial revolution or the globalization of the world economy, which arose spontaneously. The later sections of the text concentrate upon the failure of the Soviet experiment and upon the next great experiment—the transition from the administrative command system back to a market economy.

The changing shape of this book through its various editions mirrors the dramatic changes in Russia since 1974, when the first edition was published. The first three editions were devoted to the Soviet economic system—its origins, how it worked, and how well. Although we noted ongoing reform attempts, we concluded that they would have little significance. We also concluded that the Soviet system was remarkably durable, despite its poor performance. The fourth edition, published in the late 1980s, devoted a great deal of attention to perestroika, which the last Soviet leader described as radical reform. We concluded that Gorbachev's reforms were indeed serious—in fact, they may have gone a long way to destroy the Soviet administrative command system. Nevertheless, we felt that Gorbachev stopped short of transition. He was not going to move from one economic system to another.

The fifth edition was published immediately after the collapse of the Soviet Union. It was too early to assess the new era—the end of the Soviet Union and the emergence of the fifteen Newly Independent States—Russia and fourteen other former Soviet Republics.

It is now 1997. Russia and the other Newly Independent States have experienced almost six years of transition. Now we can examine the collapse of the old order and the emergence of a new. Although the final outcomes are unknown at this point, some clear trends are emerging. Also clear is the fact that Russia's past continues to influence its present and future. For this reason, we continue to examine Russia's past. The Soviet heritage is important for a number of reasons. In order to understand the transition process in Russia and the Newly Independent States, we must understand the fundamental nature of the administrative command experiment and why it failed.

ORGANIZATION

The sixth edition represents the most significant revision of *Russian and Soviet Economic Performance and Structure*. The last edition devoted three-quarters of its space to the Soviet period. In contrast, the main focus of this edition is on the transition of Russia and the Newly Independent States. More than half the space is devoted to the period after the collapse of the Soviet Union. Such a great change in emphasis has required a substantial restructuring of the text. The sixth edition has four parts: Part I describes the origins of the Soviet administrative command economy, Part II covers its operation, Part III describes how well it worked, and Part IV describes the Russian transition and those of the other former Soviet republics.

In Part I, five chapters describe the origins of the Soviet administrative command economy. Chapter 1 gives an overview of the administrative command economy. Chapter 2 looks at the Russia's economic history, up to the October 1917 revolution. Chapter 3 examines the period between the October revolution and 1928, during which time two experimental systems—War Communism and NEP—were attempted. Chapter 4 discusses the Soviet industrialization debate of the 1920s, and Chapter 5 examines the creation of the administrative command economy in the late 1920s and early 1930s.

Part II offers four chapters to explain the workings of the administrative command economy. Chapter 6 looks at Soviet planning in theory and practice. Chapter 7 examines management, labor, and pricing in the administrative command economy. Chapter 8 looks at this economy's more informal side—the Soviet household, the second economy, and agriculture. Chapter 9 describes how the administrative command economy traded with the outside world.

Part III presents two chapters that discuss the performance of the Soviet administrative command economy. Chapter 10 describes various theories of how well an administrative command economy would be expected to perform, and Chapter 11 looks at Soviet growth and productivity performance.

Part IV consists of nine chapters devoted to the transition of Russia and the other Newly Independent States from the administrative command economy to a market system. Chapter 12 begins with the relatively modest attempts at reform, beginning in the 1950s and culminating with Gorbachev's "radical" perestroika reforms in the latter half of the 1980s. Chapter 13 presents the theory of transition—how an administrative command economy makes the transition to a market economy. Chapter 14 describes how Russia has gone about the difficult task of creating the institutions of a market economy, and Chapter 15 examines Russia's economic performance during the first six years of transition.

Chapter 16 shows how Russia has gone about creating a capital market to replace its system of budget finance. Chapter 17 examines Russia's growing integration into the world economy. Chapter 18 looks at Russia's leading and lagging sectors, with particular attention to energy and agriculture. Chapter 19 describes the transition process in the other former Soviet republics, and Chapter 20 speculates about the Russian economy in the twenty-first century.

Prerequisites

The sixth edition of *Russian and Soviet Economic Performance and Structure* uses more concepts of modern economic theory. As Russia and the other Newly Independent States move towards market economic structures, it is more relevant to describe them in terms of standard micro- and macroeconomic terminology. Readers are expected to know common economic themes like the operation of central banks, the relationship between money and inflation, rates of return, monopoly rent-seeking, and nominal versus real interest rates. In all cases, economic terms are used in a straightforward and common-sense way. Key terms are emphasized, and their definitions are provided at the end of each chapter. We believe that students need only a course in principles of economics to understand this book well.

ACKNOWLEDGMENTS

We are gratified that the publication of this sixth edition signifies a more than 20-year run for this text. The sixth edition is a culmination of the previous five editions, and it would be difficult (if not foolhardy) to single out a few individuals whose help and assistance we would like to acknowledge. As in the first edition, however, we would first like to thank our respective teachers, Abram Bergson and the late David Granick, for their guidance during our years of graduate study. We should also like to single out the first generation of scholars whose work has indelibly influenced the way we think about Russia and the Soviet Union, in particular, Joseph Berliner, Gregory Grossman, Robert Campbell, Holland Hunter, Robert Davies, and Eugene Zaleski. We wish to collectively thank all those scholars who have commented on earlier editions of this book. Their work forms the core of the knowledge in this book.

Paul R. Gregory
Robert C. Stuart

PART ONE

The Origins
of the
Soviet Economy

CHAPTER 1

The Administrative Command Economy

THE LEGACY OF THE ADMINISTRATIVE COMMAND ECONOMY

The collapse of the Soviet political and economic system in 1991 was an event of major historical proportions.[1] The Soviet Union (**Union of Soviet Socialist Republics**) had existed as a stable political entity since the Bolshevik revolution of 1917, and the administrative command economy had existed since 1928, implemented by Joseph Stalin after the New Economic Planning era of the 1920s. Thus for over sixty years, the Soviet Union existed as a large, wealthy economic and political entity (Figure 1.1). The adherence to **Marxism-Leninism** as the official ideology was of long standing in the Soviet Union, and few questioned the power of the Communist Party of the Soviet Union (**CPSU**).

With its emphasis on an administrative hierarchy, command planning, state ownership, and collectivized agriculture, the Soviet economic system was very different from the market economies of the Western industrialized and less industrialized nations. Soviet economic objectives often differed from those of market economies, leaving a set of arrangements and results differing significantly from those with which we were familiar. At the same time, the postwar performance of the Soviet economy was frequently seen to be wanting. By most measures, especially rates of economic growth, the Soviet economy significantly declined from the late 1950s

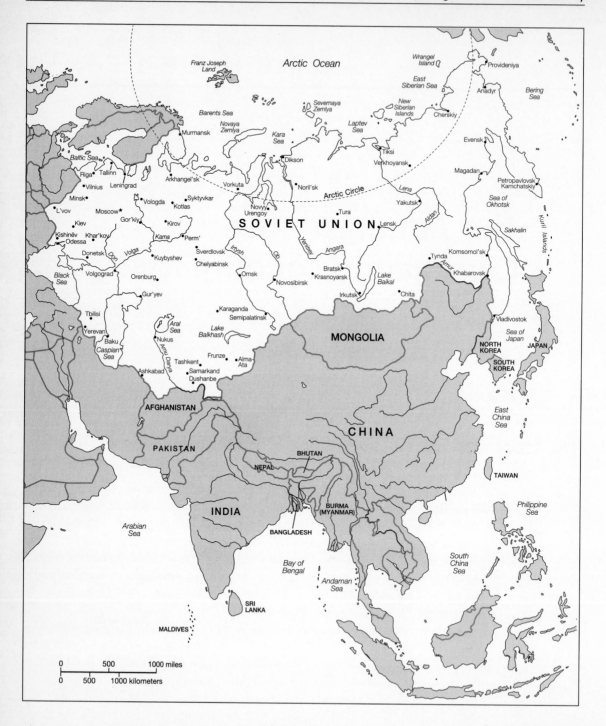

Figure 1.1   The Union of Soviet Socialist Republics   Source: CIA, *World Factbook 1989* (Washington, DC: CIA, 1989).

through the end of the 1980s. Economic reform, the subject of continuing discussion and activity in the post-Stalin era, seemed to have had little if any impact upon the performance of the economy despite promises of quick and easy fixes.[2]

Finally, Mikhail Gorbachev began **perestroika** in 1985 (see Chapter 12) as an attempt to modify the Stalinist command economy from within through radical economic reform. In a sense, Gorbachev seemed to recognize the serious problems facing the Soviet economy, though he sought to find a middle ground that would preserve the basic features of the **administrative command economy,** rather than abandoning it for real market reforms. The major message of the Gorbachev era was the failure of half measures, the inability to bring efficiency to the Soviet form of socialism while the Communist Party retained power as a political entity.

The collapse of the Soviet Union as a political and economic entity has brought unbelievable change in the 1990s—the era of **transition.** However, the story is very much in its early stages. Instead of one story, the Soviet economy, we must now consider fifteen separate and distinct stories, as the fifteen newly independent states **(NIS)** arose from the ashes of the former Soviet Union (Figure 1.2). Due to its size and its legacy, Russia's is the most important story.

While the early stages of the Yeltsin presidency created some rapid changes, the passage of time has demonstrated the difficulty and consequences of implementing sudden change. The transition from an administrative command to a market economy could not be easy, and second best choices had to be made. The macroeconomic system would have to be constructed slowly; the rules for Russian economic engagement in the international arena would have to emerge gradually and sequentially. The process of privatization would be a deeply flawed and perhaps corrupt process that would alienate the average citizen.

Experience has also shown that the newly emerging nations based upon the former Soviet republics would follow widely diverging patterns, varying from the relative success of countries such as the Baltic states versus the much slower and more complicated paths emerging in Georgia, Ukraine, and Central Asia.

The transition of Russia and the other NIS will affect world politics and world economies for the next century. We cannot hope to understand the transition without first understanding the economic system that was abandoned in favor of a market economic system. We cannot understand why one part of the transition (say, price liberalization and currency reform) may prove less difficult than another part, such as privatization and enterprise restructuring. Legacies of the past are major influences on both the present and the future.

WHY STUDY THE ADMINISTRATIVE COMMAND ECONOMY?

Besides simple intellectual curiosity, there are a variety of reasons for studying the Soviet administrative command economy. The Soviet economic system has been alternately described as an *administered* or *planned economy,* and it was the most

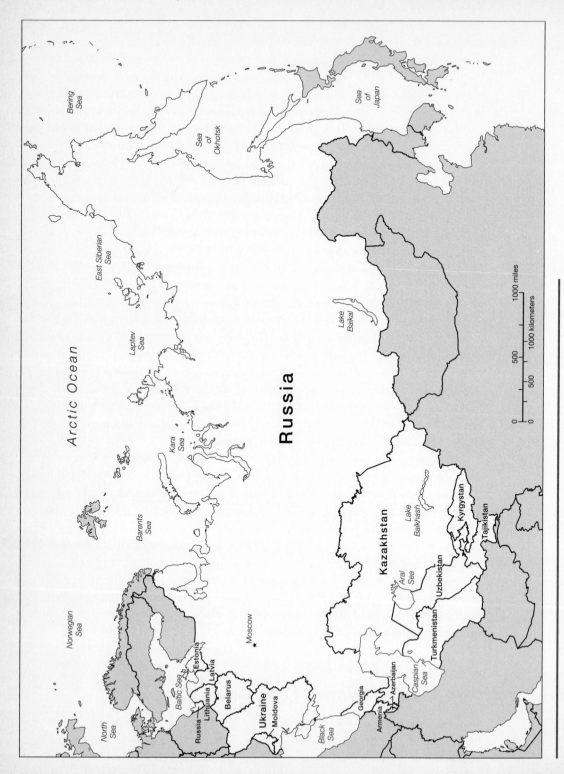

Figure 1.2   Newly Independant States Including Commonwealth States   Source: CIA, Washington DC, 1994.

significant social science experiment of this century. Introduced first in the late 1920s, the Soviet administrative command economy was the first attempt to operate an entire economy by administrative commands rather than by market forces. It therefore behooves us to study how this system worked, with what successes and failures, and why it was abandoned. Was decision making flawed, or were the problems of this system more deeply rooted?

The Soviet economic system was widely copied, partially or fully, in other countries. As we approach the end of the century, the importance of those countries (for example, Cuba and North Korea) has waned, especially given the growing signs of economic failure. However, in major countries such as China, Soviet principles remain operative, albeit with major modifications.

We cannot fully understand transition—and especially variations of transition—without appreciating the legacies and the bases from which the NIS began their transitions. The legacies of the past may be narrow and specific or broad and ill-defined. Thus as Russian privatization continues through the end of the 1990s, the character of Soviet industrial enterprises—large, integrated and technologically outdated—matters. The influence of Soviet arrangements in foreign trade and in agriculture have presented new challenges. At the same time, seventy-five years of Soviet rule created a much less identifiable yet potentially important economic legacy—a different way of thinking about economic issues, a different managerial class, and very different expectations about business objectives. These forces will not change overnight but rather will continue to affect the general course of transition in Russia and the other NIS.

Planning is a very general set of mechanisms for decision making in organizations, whether those organizations be large, as in the case of a national economy, or small, as in the case of a single enterprise. Planning techniques are quite general and of interest as part of more general approaches to decision making. Economists have become increasingly interested in what goes on within a business enterprise, especially highly complex organizations such as large corporations. Does the administrative command economy, probably the most complex hierarchical organization known to man, tell us something about other hierarchical organizations such as large corporations or even government bureaucracies?

As we seek to understand and assess our own past, understanding of the Soviet Union is essential. Whether it be international trade, technology transfer, or the role of the military in the world economy, it would be impossible to understand our past without inclusion of the Soviet Union, our major political and economic adversary for so many years.

Finally, we would be naïve to believe that within Russia and the other NIS, people have eliminated and forgotten the Soviet economic past. We have noted specific and important examples of the past, notably the impact of a peculiar Soviet industrial structure on the course of contemporary privatization. But, there are more general and potentially more important issues. For many Western observers, the significant vote for the Communist Party in the 1996 presidential elections seemed strange and unthinkable. How could the Communist Party attract so many votes after years of repression had been removed and the advantages of the market had begun to unfold?

One of the most obvious features of transition is that the move from administrative command to markets creates winners and losers. The losers outnumber the winners, and in a democracy presumably the loser has the same vote as the winner. For many in the former Soviet Union, the era of transition has been difficult and without significant hope for economic improvement. For example, the market does not provide significant economic benefits for the elderly as small pensions become meaningless in an emerging market economy with galloping inflation, limited job prospects and the end of free if limited medical care. Unquestionably, many feel a nostalgia for the old system, a social contract of the past, and while this nostalgia will doubtless fade over time, our understanding of its sources will help us to understand why many cannot fully embrace the transition era of the present. Understanding the personal costs of transition also provides a framework in which to interpret political events such as the 1996 presidential elections. In fact, knowledge of these costs provides a perspective on the depth of dislike of the communist system. Perhaps the lesson should be the failure of the Communist Party to regain power, despite the enormous costs of transition, rather than the particular number of votes won by the Communist Party.

THE LEGACIES OF THE PAST

The political, economic, and social legacies of the Soviet era are broad and varied. Our initial focus in this book is the Soviet economic system, a fact that simplifies our task. We have described the former Soviet economic system as an "administrative command economy." This phrase has found favor among many observers both inside and outside the former Soviet Union. In fact, it was the phrase used by Mikhail Gorbachev in a disparaging way to describe the Soviet economy. Why have we now settled on this term?

From an ideological perspective, the Soviet Union officially followed the teachings of Marxism-Leninism, suggesting that the Soviet Union had moved beyond capitalism into socialism, with the ultimate goal of developing a communist economic system. While this ideological framework is important and useful for understanding the Soviet system, it is less useful as a model for assessing Soviet economic successes and failures. The more useful paradigm has been that of national economic planning. After all, planning techniques are well specified, generally beyond any particular ideological framework, and were clearly used by the Soviet Union. Many described the Soviet Union as a planned economy that used central directives on resource allocation and translated them at the ministerial level into commands to be implemented by enterprises.

What is wrong with describing the Soviet economy as a "nationally planned economy"? While planning is elegant in theory, Soviet practice was in fact much less elegant. As we shall show, Soviet planning procedures were ad hoc, crude, and far removed from the elegant models of planning theory. Second, the fact that initial plans were rarely achieved and had to be constantly adjusted by state intervention caused some observers to conclude that the Soviet economy was a managed rather than a planned economy.

Cast in the above light, it is understandable that the Soviet economy could be characterized in a variety of ways: a planned economy, a managed economy, a centrally planned economy, a Soviet-type economy, or a planned socialist economy. It is also understandable that the characterization used by Gorbachev—the administrative command economy—would find appeal. Yes, the Soviet Union had a command economy in the sense of centralization and the development of edicts from the center, while at the same time demonstrating considerably less formality in the implementation of decisions, which made the system in a sense an administered economy. The term "command" also captures the crucial role of the Communist Party in creating directives and implementing them.

There may be little to gain by quarreling over the different name tags that we apply to the Soviet economic system. However, these different name tags reflect the fact that we have used a variety of differing paradigms to understand and to judge the Soviet economy. While the Soviet economy may not have been a Marxist-Leninist system nor a full blown planned economy, both paradigms capture essential features of the Soviet system. For convenience, we use the term administrative command economy throughout this book.

Joseph Stalin installed the administrative command economy in the Soviet Union in the 1930s, more than a decade after the Bolsheviks came to power. After the Bolshevik revolution of 1917, the Soviet Union had functioned with two quite different systems—**War Communism** from 1917 to 1921, and the **New Economic Policy** for the rest of the 1920s. While the immediate postrevolutionary economy suffered from major problems, the 1920s was for many observers, a "golden era" of Soviet economic history. Markets reemerged, the economy rebounded, and the focus returned to the pursuit of economic growth and economic development. Cast against this background, it is understandable that the complete change of course begun by Stalin in 1928 and 1929—nationalization, collectivization and the replacement of the market with the plan—was one of the major events of economic history.

Once Stalin's decisions were made, the economic system was changed with astonishing suddenness. Resource allocation was directed in a centralized fashion through a planning apparatus. With rapid and virtually complete nationalization, the state suddenly owned and controlled the enterprises and the farms, and decisions on what to produce and how products would be utilized were made by planners, not by the supply and demand forces of the marketplace. Stalin forcibly collected grain from the countryside, and, through a state monopoly in foreign trade, used the earnings from grain exports to finance the import of intermediate goods and machinery needed to develop industry. The directions of economic development by region and by economic sector were dictated by the state, not through markets. A vast bureaucracy of industrial ministries and state committees became major intermediaries between planners at the upper level and producing units at the local level. Although there is much more to say about the working arrangements of this system, there is little question that markets were abandoned and were replaced by administrative allocation. A vast Communist Party apparatus set objectives, oversaw the economic bureaucracy, controlled executive appointments, and monitored virtually all players from the lowest to the highest levels in the economy.

The Stalinist model oversaw the rapid transformation of the Russian (Soviet) economy from an agricultural, rural-based, light industry-oriented economy to an urbanized industrial economy. It created heavy industry and a military base that was purported in the 1970s and 1980s to rival that of the United States. Between 1928 and 1940, the Soviet Union pursued an industrial transformation that had taken 50 to 100 years in the industrialized West. Thus, after the Soviet Union's impressive victory during World War II (what the Soviets would term "the great patriotic war"), it is not surprising that the West would take the Soviet economic challenge seriously, as Sputnik, the first orbital spaceship, was launched in 1957, and shortly thereafter, Nikita Khrushchev, then Soviet Premier, would announce to the United States "we will bury you."

The administrative command economy that Gorbachev inherited in 1985 was basically the same system that Stalin created in the 1930s. The durability of the administrative command economy did not mean that it worked well in the sense of being efficient. Indeed, from the beginning, it was evident that efficiency levels in this system were well below those in the West. However, in a system where centralized political power allowed Soviet leaders to extract resources and use them for their own ends—for example, for military power at the expense of consumption—major changes could be implemented. But the Soviet system was unable to develop and to implement new ideas on a broad scale. It was unable or unwilling to develop a base for expanding consumption, and its long attempt to socialize consumption—that is, to replace private consumption with social consumption—failed. At the same time, the Soviet Union was unable to create a viable and efficient agriculture, thus missing much of the Green Revolution that was so important in low income countries in other parts of the world. Finally, the state monopoly in foreign trade effectively limited the benefits of foreign trade and prevented the Soviet Union from participating in the globalization of the world economy.

As we approach a new century, the tasks of reformers in the countries of the former Soviet Union are greatly complicated by their Soviet past. For a long span of years, the administrative command economy allocated resources in ways fundamentally different from market economies. The Soviet economic system used institutions suited to administrative command allocation, not to market allocation. Unlike Latin America, where transition requires the privatization of a few state-owned companies, the NIS must privatize virtually all businesses. In other transition settings, prices of certain products must be decontrolled. In the NIS, the state set virtually all prices. In other transition situations, there may be a tradition of private property rights. The NIS are finding it difficult to change fundamentally the nature of property rights in urban and rural societies long dominated by an absence of private property. These countries must create a self-sustaining macroeconomy where none existed. Moreover, consumers must suddenly learn the real cost of everything, whether it be the Moscow Metro or what used to be a heavily subsidized apartment in a large Soviet city. The social contract has changed fundamentally, which is much more acceptable for those in their twenties than for those in their sixties and above.

TRANSITION BLUEPRINTS

The industrialized economies may seem to provide an obvious blueprint for the transition of Russia and the NIS. Actually, the industrialized economies show a desired finishing point but reveal little about the necessary intermediate steps. Russia and the NIS would clearly like to have the political and economic stability of the West along with the sustained economic growth and resulting improvement in standards of living. Having said this, the gap between the former Soviet Union and these industrialized states is great. The task of transition is immense.

As the transition of the NIS and the economies of Eastern Europe moved towards abandoning the old order and replacing it with market arrangements, the initial enthusiasm for a new order was soon replaced by a much more sober assessment. Transition lacked a clear-cut foundation, its implementation turned out to be far more complicated than originally envisioned, and a number of different paths would be tried. While the collapse of the old order was ample evidence of its failure, replacing it would be complex and would be conditioned by many varying factors. For example, in Russia, would its political and economic heritage, so different from that of Eastern Europe, dictate a search for a third way—for example a Swedish-type welfare state—beyond the simplistic alternatives of market or plan?

While reformers have looked to the industrialized market economies for guidance, the usefulness of the messages for very different transition settings has been the subject of substantial controversy in the contemporary scholarly literature. Reformers, while guided by the principles of the market economy, nevertheless looked beyond these principles.

For example, Sweden has been an example of a third way. With high income, a major social safety net, and an egalitarian distribution of income, reformers often admired Sweden. However, it is a case where high income can facilitate a major redistribution of income and can bear the consequences of efficiency losses. High income is not a characteristic of the transition cases. Moreover, as we know, contemporary events have not been kind to the people of Sweden, a system whose viability is now questioned by many.

Russia and the NIS can learn a great deal from former administrative command economies that began their transitions earlier. We now have a wide range of experiences from Eastern Europe, where different countries tried different transition paths, some more successful than others. In fact, three countries of Eastern Europe—Poland, Hungary, and the Czech Republic—seem to have successfully navigated the waters of transition. Why not consider these examples?

Each transition is different. Poland, Hungary and the Czech Republic adopted the administrative command economy only after World War II. All these countries have relatively homogeneous populations, a fact which fosters a commitment to transition. They all had a sense of urgency for transition as a means of protecting themselves against a newly expansive Russia or a revived Soviet Union. Moreover, all were involved in foreign trade in Western markets. Most of these countries were richer than the former Soviet republics, with a geography that places them in central Europe as a part of Europe rather than as a part of Eurasia.

China, onetime Soviet Communist ally, embarked upon its own reform more than two decades ago. The Chinese reforms, begun in the agricultural economy in the late 1970s, have transformed the country from a closed economy to an open economy. Chinese products are traded worldwide, and China has been able to attract foreign capital from the industrialized West. Rates of economic growth have increased significantly under reform, though cyclical instability has been a problem. However, unlike other transition cases, China has maintained basic features of the administrative command economy, and the Communist Party remains the sole political force. Should Russia and the other NIS look to the Chinese example?

TRANSITION: THE TSARIST ECONOMY AS A MODEL

Russia's last experience with a market economy dates back more than 80 years to 1917. Although this is a remote period, it still provides guidance for modern Russian reformers. As contemporary Russian reformers look back to the Tsarist era of Russia, they encounter an economy shrouded in myths and stereotypes. Although some historians have argued that Russia never had a market economy, we will argue in Chapter 2 that this was not the case. Although the Russian state always played an intrusive regulatory role, most property was in private hands and there was no national economic planning per se. Russia had succeeded in attracting large amounts of foreign capital, so much so that the country was the world's largest debtor nation in 1917. Feudal vestiges remained in agriculture, but they had been largely removed by 1917.

A more important issue in looking back to the Tsarist past is the widespread consensus of failure. Soviet historians were constrained by the research agenda set by Lenin in his *Development of Capitalism in Russia*.[3] He was determined to prove that the socialist revolution would occur in Russia, the most economically backward country in Europe. Lenin pictured Russia as a dual economy, combining backward semi-feudal agriculture with enclaves of relatively advanced heavy industry. Lenin argued that this dualism revealed Russia as a colony of the West, whose investments created anomalous pockets of modern industry in a generally backward economy.

Lenin felt that industrial capitalism in Russia was more brutal and concentrated than in the West, where it was restrained by labor unions and progressive legislation. Because it exploited the factory worker more, the Russian factory spawned a revolutionary proletariat more motivated to overthrow the capitalist bosses. Moreover, the Russian factory worker had a natural revolutionary ally—the peasant, burdened by the remnants of feudalism. In Lenin's model, Russia, as the weak link in the capitalist chain, would be the host for the first socialist revolution.

The Leninist interpretation of Russian economic history captivated economic historians both East and West. Lenin painted a picture of capitalism in crisis, bound to be overthrown by a superior economic system. Thus the history of Russia, written in both the East and in the West, focused on the Russian revolution. If the Russian revolution was to be consistent with the Marxian dialectic of an inevitable socialist revolution, then internal contradictions (crises) must have characterized the final stages of capitalism. It is the characterization of these crises—agrarian crises, depressions, stock market collapses, and political unrest—that captured the interest of historians.[4] That the economic performance of the Tsarist economy was unsatisfactory was a foregone conclusion, dictated by the dominant research agenda of the era. Indeed the Russian revolution was itself seen as proof of the failure of capitalism in Russia. Modern Russian reformers have paid very little attention to prerevolutionary Russia for two reasons: First, Russia had not experienced capitalism for more than three quarters of a century, and second, capitalism was presumed to have failed in Russia. Why examine and, most of all, return to a model which spawned crises and ultimately revolution?

We shall reexamine the view of the failure of Russian capitalism in the next chapter. Using standard economic indicators, we will show that the Russian economy had achieved major successes by 1913. In fact, the theory of revolution is only one theory with which to assess the era, and it is a theory with major problems. Just as economists tend to be novices at explaining political phenomena, historians are also novices in understanding and using the tools of economic theory to understand economic history. The link between politics and economics has always been weak and subject to misinterpretation. If Soviet conceptions of the late Tsarist era were effectively constrained by ideological blinders, is it not possible that the NEP era of the 1920s might serve as a model of economic reform?

TRANSITION: THE NEP AS A MODEL

After the Bolshevik revolution in 1917, Lenin first introduced War Communism, an abortive attempt to direct the allocation of resources administratively in the absence of a properly functioning planning system. It was during War Communism that the destruction of capitalist institutions began in earnest, a theme which we develop in Chapter 3. The Land Decree of November 9, 1917, served as the mechanism to distribute the remaining large estates among the peasants. Industry and handicraft enterprises, even those employing only a few workers, were nationalized. Private trade was declared illegal. The hyperinflation that accompanied the civil war destroyed the monetary system, and lead to a barter economy. Peasant agriculture's "surpluses" were requisitioned by force. Although War Communism did allow the Soviet leadership to emerge victorious from the civil war, the program's inconsistencies became increasingly apparent. Industry, agriculture, and transportation virtually collapsed under the inefficiency of War Communism's controls.

Lenin announced the New Economic Policy (NEP) in March of 1921. The state continued to control the commanding heights, namely the major sectors of heavy industry, banking, transportation, and wholesale trade, while markets directed allocation in agriculture, retail trade, and small scale industry. NEP was a compromise blend of market and command.[5] A major monetary reform, completed in 1923, established a stable currency (the **chervonetz**), the Soviet Union's last convertible currency. In agriculture, a proportional tax replaced forced requisitioning of the War Communism era, while peasants were allowed to sell in relatively free agricultural markets.

The NEP system promoted rapid recovery from the ravages of war, revolution, civil war, and the extremes of War Communism. However, in 1928, Stalin brought the NEP era to an end, replacing it with the administrative command economy. Stalin argued that the possibilities for recovery within the NEP system were exhausted, and most important, that peasant agriculture was an unreliable base for further accumulation. However, the NEP era significantly improved the standard of living of the Soviet people. This period of time witnessed the development of a variety of ownership arrangements, with the private sector dominating in agriculture, light industry, and handicrafts. NEP also provided bold experiments with foreign ownership and concessions. Finally, it is important to emphasize that the NEP era was a golden era of economic thought, an era that came abruptly to an end in 1928, after which both economic and political arrangements would change. During the 1920s, as we will see in subsequent chapters, there was widespread discussion of economic issues, especially issues pertaining to the varying paths for economic development. Much of the scholarly literature of this era would have a lasting impact, even though its development and distribution would be (temporarily) silenced by Stalin.

It is not surprising that during the early phases of Perestroika, Soviet reformers looked back to the NEP era. Indeed, there were striking parallels between the NEP era of the 1920s and the era of Perestroika introduced by Mikhail Gorbachev in the mid-1980s. Both sets of reform were initiated at the highest levels, by Lenin in the 1920s and by Gorbachev in the mid-1980s. Both reforms represented a move towards the market, away from the administrative structure of the War Communism era in the 1920s, and away from the rigidities of the administrative command system in the 1980s. In a sense, both experiments sought to sustain a measure of centralized control while at the same time taking advantage of the perceived efficiencies of markets. Both reforms faced strong opposition from factions within the political authority, the Communist Party.

Although some Soviet observers romanticized NEP as a possible reform model, Soviet officialdom continued to present NEP as an economic system that failed.[6] NEP was pictured as a system riddled by crises, failing to provide a viable alternative to collectivization and superindustrialization. The Western interpretation of the NEP era has been strongly influenced by Stalin's interpretation of events.[7] Thus both Soviet and Western literature viewed NEP as inevitably doomed by crisis and unable to serve the needs of economic growth and economic development. In the next chapter, we examine whether these views provide an unwarranted reputation for NEP.

The lessons of NEP are important for understanding change today. The NEP economy revealed the difficulties of combining market and plan. In such a setting, many natural market phenomena, for example the amount of grain offered to the market and speculative behavior, tended to be interpreted as political phenomena. The greater flexibility of the private sector allowed it to bid resources away from the state, incurring the wrath of the Soviet leadership. Moreover, during times of shocks, there is always a tendency to distrust the market, replacing market forces with administrative controls.

THE DIVERSITY OF THE FORMER SOVIET UNION

Unlike the transition cases of Eastern Europe, Russia and the NIS were a single very large country, organized as an administrative command economy under a single dominant Communist party but with significant regional differences. The Soviet Union was comprised of fifteen union republics, each populated by a large number of nationalities (Table 1.1, p. 16). The geographical and ethnic diversity of the Soviet union was itself a consequence of the expansionist policies of the tsars in the nineteenth century as the Tsarist military pushed out the frontiers towards China, Persia, and Turkey. Prior to World War I, the Tsarist empire included most of what later became the Soviet Union, and also included Poland and Finland. Although Poland and Finland achieved their independence during the Russian civil war, following the Bolshevik revolution in 1917, the Soviet Union annexed the Baltic States of Latvia, Lithuania and Estonia in 1940, at the start of World War II.

We must bear in mind the fact that Russia and the other former Soviet republics represent enormous ethnic, political, regional, and historical diversity. These countries include populations of Northern European origin (the Baltic states), which had a relatively brief experience under the administrative command economy; the Slavic peoples of Russia, Ukraine, and Belarus, with their traditions of Russian serfdom

Table 1.1

RUSSIA AND THE NEWLY INDEPENDENT STATES (NIS): 1990

	Population	% Urban	Land Area*	Per Capita GNP**	Ethnicity (%)***
Russia	149,527,000	74	1,707.5	2,650	82
Belarus	10,374,000	65	20.7	2,160	78
Ukraine	51,940,000	67	60.4	1,910	73
Moldava	4,458,000	47	3.4	870	64
Georgia	5,571,000	56	7.0	NA	70
Armenia	3,416,000	68	3.0	680	93
Azerbaidzhan	7,451,000	54	8.7	500	83
Uzbekistan	21,627,000	41	44.8	960	71
Turkmenistan	3,838,000	45	48.8	NA	72
Tadzhikistan	5,680,000	33	14.3	360	62
Kazakhstan	17,104,000	57	271.7	1,160	40
Kirgizstan	4,568,000	38	19.8	630	52
Estonia	1,607,000	72	4.5	2,820	62
Latvia	2,729,000	71	6.5	2,320	52
Lithuania	3,789,000	68	6.5	1,350	80

NA = not available *Million hectares **U.S. Dollars 1994 ***% Russian, Byelarussian, etc. (1991)

Source: CIA, *The World Factbook 1992* (Washington, DC: CIA, 1992); CIA, *Handbook of International Statistics 1992* (Washington, DC: CIA, 1992); CIA, *The Republics of the Former Soviet Union and the Baltic States* (Washington, DC: CIA, 1992); The World Bank, *World Development Report 1996* (Washington, DC: World Bank, 1996).

and Tsarist economic policies; and the predominantly Moslem populations of Central Asia. Although these diversities were largely hidden during the Soviet era, their importance is now evident, as struggles for political independence from Russia have emerged and different countries have embarked upon markedly different transition paths.

Although the primary focus of this book is the former Soviet Union and the successor state of Russia, we now have, in addition to Russia, a real world laboratory of fourteen newly independent states with sharply different levels of economic development and very different political, economic, and regional settings pursuing quite different transitional paths. Insofar as they were all part of the administrative command economy, their experiences should be of major importance both for Russian reformers and for each other.

TRANSITION: LOOKING BACK FROM THE TWENTY-FIRST CENTURY

When we look back from the twenty-first century to the last decade of the twentieth century, we will conclude that the outcome of transition had a major impact in shaping the new century. A successful transition would have created a globalized economy operating according to common economic principles. Russia and the other NIS would have achieved rising standards of living, stable laws, and political and economic institutions capable of reducing the gaps in the standard of living relative to the industrialized West.

A failed transition would place Russia and the NIS in an uncomfortable limbo between the remnants of the administrative command economy and a market economy that had never taken hold. This economic uncertainty could result in political uncertainty and a succession of weak governments or, at the other end of the spectrum, a return to dictatorship. The lack of well developed institutions and law enforcement mechanisms would help to perpetuate the massive rent seeking of entrenched political and business elites and would also strengthen the political and economic power of criminal elements. Chaos and uncertainty would strengthen nostalgia for the stability of the Soviet Union and provide a setting for its restoration.

Those looking back to the 1990s would probably be more realistic in their assessment of the "possibility" of transition. Emerging from many years of the administrative command economy, the institutions of a market economy had to be created in a relatively short time for systems under immense pressure. It would be no surprise for these twenty-first century observers to note emerging systems that were deeply flawed, dominated by rent-seeking behavior, criminal elements, special interests, imperfect protection of property rights, and a continued heavy hand of the state. However, these systems may still be vastly superior to the administrative command systems from which they emerged. They would probably be better able to satisfy consumer needs, to promote innovation and entrepreneurial activity, and to allow productivity to grow. It is unlikely that extremes will emerge; rather, our observer from the next century will look back on a spectrum of emerging systems, some with significant progress, others virtually stagnant.

SUMMARY

Throughout the 1990s, Russia, the republics of the former Soviet Union, and the countries of Eastern Europe have been in transition, replacing the administrative command systems with market economies. In the absence of well-defined paths, transition has proven difficult, with substantial variation from case to case. As Russia moves towards market arrangements, it must do so looking both forward and backward. As it looks backward, it observes a legacy of political and economic events that dominated the Soviet people for almost seventy-five years and served as a defining force in the evolution of East-West relations. The administrative command economy of the Soviet era, often characterized as a planned socialist economy, introduced changes that created an economic system fundamentally different from those in market economies. Moreover, this command system left a substantial legacy of inefficient arrangements in agriculture; overly large, inefficient enterprises in sectors expanded rapidly by state policy directives; and an economy with administratively determined regional development and significant isolation from world market forces. Quite apart from the fact that such issues characterized East-West relations for so long, they also serve as defining constraints in the era of transition, deserving our attention in the 1990s.

Terms and Concepts ───────────────────

Union of Soviet Socialist Republics or **Soviet Union (USSR)**   A socialist state formed in 1917 after the Bolshevik revolution, led by Vladimir Ilich Lenin; overthrew the tsar.

Marxism-Leninism   A body of thought developed by Karl Marx and later modified by Vladimir Ilich Lenin (and others); portrays socioeconomic change as proceeding from class struggle by a revolutionary process from feudalism to capitalism and ultimately through socialism to communism.

CPSU   The Communist Party of the Soviet Union described in the Soviet Constitution of 1977 (Article 6) as "The leading and guiding force of Soviet society and the nucleus of its political system, of all state organizations and public organizations."

perestroika   Literally, reconstruction; a program of economic reform comprising changes in industry, agriculture, and foreign trade; introduced in 1985 by Mikhail Gorbachev, the last leader of the Soviet Union.

administrative command economy   First used by Mikhail Gorbachev in the 1980s, a popular phrase used to describe the Soviet economy; an economy characterized by a complex administrative (bureaucratic) structure and the use of commands from upper levels to lower levels to allocate resources.

transition   Generally interpreted as the replacement of one economic system by another economic system; in the 1990s, the replacement of the planned socialist economic systems of the former Soviet Union and the countries of Eastern Europe with market economies.

NIS   The newly independent states formed from the republics of the Soviet Union.

War Communism (1918–21) The economic system put in place by Lenin immediately following the Bolshevik Revolution of 1917; characterized by state ownership, forced requisitioning of agricultural products, and elimination of money and market relations.

New Economic Policy (NEP) (1921–28) The system put in place after the collapse of War Communism, generally reversing the policies of War Communism by implementing a return to markets, currency stabilization and the extraction of agricultural produce through a proportional agricultural tax on net output.

chervonetz A stable currency introduced in the Soviet Union in 1923.

Selected Bibliography

Gooding, John. *Rulers and Subjects* (New York: St. Martin's Press, 1996).

Kort, Michael. *The Soviet Colossus: History and Aftermath* 4e (Armonk: M.E. Sharpe, 1996).

Ragsdale, Hugh. *The Russian Tragedy: The Burden of History* (Armonk: M.E. Sharpe, 1996).

Remnick, David. *Lenin's Tomb: The Last Days of the Soviet Empire* (New York: Random House, 1993).

Taranovski, Theodore, ed. *Reform in Modern Russian History: Progress or Cycle?* (New York: Cambridge University Press, 1995).

Notes

1. The flag of the Soviet Union was officially lowered at the Kremlin in Moscow on December 25, 1991.
2. Although there is wide variation in terminology, *reform* frequently refers to attempted changes of the economic system from within, leaving the political entity unchanged. *Transition* refers to the replacement of one economic system by another economic system, in the 1990s typically the replacement of plan by market. So defined, we normally think of Soviet economic reform as beginning with a variety of modifications to planning arrangements introduced by Nikita Khrushchev in the 1950s.
3. V. I. Lenin, *The Development of Capitalism in Russia* (Moscow: Foreign Languages Publishing House, 1956).
4. Even the influential writings of Alexander Gerschenkron focus on Russian economic history as a means of explaining revolutionary tendencies. See, for example, A. Gerschenkron, *Backwardness in Historical Perspective* (Cambridge, MA: Harvard University Press, 1962), essay 1.
5. For a discussion of this point, see A. Nove, *An Economic History of the USSR* (London: Penguin, 1969), chs. 3–6; M. Lewin, *Russian Peasants and Soviet Power* (London: Allen & Unwin, 1968); and S. Merl, *Der Agrarmarkt und die Neue Okonomische Politik* [The Agrarian Market and the New Economic Policy] (Munich: Oldenbourg Verlag, 1981).
6. For a discussion of differing assessments of NEP by Soviet reformers, see Y. P. Bokarev, "NEP I problemy perestroiki" [NEP and the Problems of Perestroika], presented at the Soviet-American Conference on Soviet Economic Reform, Houston, Texas, December

1989. For an official assessment of the failures of NEP published shortly after the collapse of the Soviet Union, see G. L. Smirnov, "Vremiia trudnykh voprosov 20–30-x godov I sovremenaia obshchestvennaia mysl" [A Time of Difficult Questions, the History of the 1920s and 1930s in Contemporary Social Thought] *Pravda* (September 30, 1988; October 3, 1988).

7. The work of Maurice Dobb has left a lasting imprint on Western interpretations of the NEP period, even though Dobb fully accepted the Stalinist version of NEP crises. See M. Dobb, *Soviet Economic Development Since 1917,* 5e (London: Routledge & Kegan Paul, 1960), chs. 4–9.

CHAPTER 2

The Economic History of Russia to 1917

The performance of the Russian economy prior to the Bolshevik revolution of 1917 is important for at least two reasons. First, it was Russia's last experience with a market economy before Russia's transition to markets in 1991. If Russia's last market economy can be deemed to have been a success, rather than the failure always suggested by the Soviet leadership, then we have important evidence about the relevance of markets for the post-Soviet era. Second, we cannot judge the performance of the Soviet era without knowing something about the economic base that the Bolsheviks inherited in 1917. Thus, we need to know something about both the level of economic development and the rate of change of the economy in the final decades of the Tsarist era. With an understanding of the late Tsarist era, we will be better able to assess the nature of economic development during the Soviet era and its impact upon transition in the 1990s.

How can Tsarist economic performance be measured? Unfortunately, there is no single or simple answer to this question. We proceed in two general stages. First, we discuss the important economic issues of the period in the Tsarist era that follows the **emancipation** of the serfs in 1861. With better empirical evidence available, we focus on the period after 1880, when Russia demonstrated an ability to generate significant and sustained economic growth. Second, we examine the available evidence using the framework of **Modern Economic Growth** (MEG), suggested by Simon Kuznets.[1] We begin with an examination of developments in industry and agriculture, thereafter examining a variety of key statistical indicators such as GDP (gross domestic product) per capita, the growth of GDP per capita, changes in the sectoral structure of the economy (industry, agriculture and the service sector), and finally demographic characteristics. Why do we choose this framework? The work of Kuznets and other subsequent researchers provides us with a statistical framework, a snapshot if you will, of development patterns in a large number of countries that have experienced varying degrees of economic growth and economic development. We can use this framework and the related statistical evidence to make useful judgments about the Russian experience.

However, some caveats are in order. Both the rate and the level of Russian economic development prior to 1917 are matters of some controversy. First, there are unresolved issues pertaining to data availability and accuracy. Second, much of our thinking has been influenced by questionable stereotypes. Third, from an ideological perspective, controversies abound. From the Soviet perspective, there was always a desire to present the military and industrial power of the Soviet economy exclusively as an achievement of the Soviet era. Yet from a Marxian perspective, one would have expected the development of capitalism in the pre-Soviet era to lay the foundations from which socialism could emerge.

In a sense, then, the question of economic development during the Tsarist era might be presented differently—did capitalism emerge in Russia prior to the Bolshevik revolution of 1917? Lenin proclaimed the backward Tsarist economy, despite its pockets of modernity, as the "weakest link" in the capitalist chain. The official Soviet picture characterized the Tsarist economy as backward, necessitating the sacrifices of the early Stalinist era of the 1930s. Western historians have focused on the rapid industrial growth after 1880, but always emphasized the backwardness of Russian agriculture.[2] We turn now to an examination of the Tsarist economy.

INDUSTRIAL GROWTH UNDER THE TSARS

The reign of Peter the Great (1698–1725) provides us with a convenient starting point from which to understand the Russian economic experience. Because of his experiences during his extensive early travels in Western Europe, Peter the Great was determined to industrialize Russia by looking westward for technology and technicians. While military considerations played an important role in this drive, it nevertheless resulted in the development of an increasingly modern industrial sector by eighteenth century standards. As a result, Russia acquired a nascent industry, which, when combined with its vast natural resources and manpower, enabled it to compete militarily with the West for nearly two centuries, despite a succession of less progressive rulers. Nevertheless, after Peter the Great there emerged a growing gap between Russia and its industrializing European competitors, especially during the nineteenth century.[3] Some of this backwardness may have been intentional. Tsarist authorities feared that the development of railroads would spread egalitarianism and that the growth of factory towns would spawn a rebellious proletariat.[4] One of the ironies of the era was Peter the Great's entrenchment of serfdom, a retrogressive institution, to bolster both the military and the civilian economy.

The Crimean War (1854–56) served as a watershed, beginning a period of increasing recognition of the potential dangers of the economic gap and a resulting resurgence of interest in promoting industrialization. This was especially true under the later leadership of Count Sergei Witte, the Minister of Finance of Russia from 1892 to 1903. The government fostered industrial development in a number of ways. Fostered by state investments, the rail network increased from just over 2,000 kilometers in 1861 to over 70,000 kilometers in 1913 (Table 2.1, p. 24).

In addition to its military significance, this expanded transportation network helped to open up the iron and coal resources of Ukraine, which soon overtook the Ural region as the metallurgical center of the Russian empire. The expanded rail network also facilitated the marketing of wheat (grain output in Russia tripled between 1861 and 1913). A vibrant textile industry grew in Moscow, and metalworking blossomed in St. Petersburg.[5] The state acted as a guarantor of bonds, encouraging the inflow of foreign capital. A generally conservative monetary policy helped to stabilize the ruble exchange rate, which allowed Russia to join the international gold standard in 1897.

The expansion of domestic heavy industry was promoted by a number of state policies, including high protective tariffs, profit guarantees, tax reductions and exemptions, and government orders at high prices to ensure domestic demand. During this period, the Ministry of Finance actively promoted the development of heavy industry as a prime element of Russian military strategy.[6]

In nineteenth century Russia a modern entrepreneurial class began to form, drawn from the civil service as well as the Old Believer sects and Jewish merchants.[7] However, Russian entrepreneurs, like Western entrepreneurs working in Russia, faced a variety of limitations. For example, the tsar's signature was required on the charter of every joint stock company, effectively controlling the development of limited liability corporations. Russian industrialists often got their start in business through state subsidies or preferential state orders. Bribery was one of the routine costs of conducting business in Tsarist Russia, and bureaucratic intervention was commonplace.

Under the leadership of the finance ministry, the Russian economic bureaucracy was ambivalent in its attitude towards capitalist institutions. On the one hand, a succession of able finance ministers understood the need to promote private initiative. On the other hand, the Russian state feared the consequences of unbridled capitalism and attempted to keep the economy under public control and scrutiny. Russian capitalists who banded together into lobbying organizations such as the Association of Southern Coal and Steel Producers and the Association of Industry and Trade shared this ambivalence. They argued for fewer restrictions on their

Table 2.1

BASIC SOCIAL AND ECONOMIC INDICATORS: RUSSIA AND OTHER COUNTRIES, 1861 AND 1913

	Population (millions)	National income in 1913 rubles (millions)	Per capita national income	Infant mortality
1861				
Russia	74	5,269	71	239*
UK	20	6,469	323	148
France	37	5,554	150	190
Germany	36	6,313	175	260
USA	32	14,405	450	NA
Netherlands	3	NA	NA	196
Norway	2	331	166	113
Sweden	4	449	112	124
Italy	25	4,570	183	232
Spain	16	NA	NA	174
Austria-Hungary	35	NA	NA	264
1913				
Russia	171	20,266	119	237
UK	36	20,869	580	108
France	39	11,816	303	112
Germany	65	24,280	374	151
USA	93	96,030	1,033	115
Netherlands	6	2,195	366	91
Norway	2	918	659	64
Sweden	6	2,040	340	70
Italy	35	9,140	261	138
Spain	20	3,975	199	155
Austria-Hungary	50	9,500	190	190

*average 1867–69

NA = not available

Source: P. R. Gregory, *Russian National Income, 1895–1913* (Cambridge: Cambridge University Press, 1982), 155–56.

activities while at the same time relying upon state protection, favorable freight rates, state subsidies, and state credits.

The Russian legal and state system at the turn of the twentieth century was not unusual for a relatively backward country with great economic potential and a firmly entrenched state bureaucracy. Unlike the less well-entrenched British bureaucracy, the Russian bureaucracy found it difficult to sit on the sidelines, leading to more meddling in economic affairs. At the same time, Russia's vast economic potential attracted foreign capital along with the expanding domestic entrepreneurial class.

Much of our interest in Russian economic growth and development in the late Tsarist era focuses on the period after 1880, when there was a significant acceleration of the rate of growth of industrial output. Indeed, interpretation of the events of this era have been the subject of controversy. Arcadius Kahan argued that the upturn in the rate of industrial growth was a natural consequence of market forces, spurred in part by the profit potential of the Russian empire.[8] Kahan and others argued that state activities either hampered (or did not contribute to any degree to) industrial growth, citing the fact that subsidies to industry were quite modest during this period. Others have argued that the acceleration of economic growth was in fact the direct result of state intervention.

Alexander Gerschenkron, the most prominent scholar of Russian economic history, has proposed the idea of **relative backwardness** to explain accelerating economic growth.[9] Gerschenkron argues that when the gap increases between the economic potential of a nation and its economic reality, tension is created, new institutions are substituted for missing preconditions, and a spurt of industrial growth occurs. In Russia, the tension was great, the resulting spurt of industrial growth was significant, and the Russian state, serving as a substitute for missing entrepreneurs and limited demand, acted as an instigator of industrialization. In Table 2.2 (pp. 26–27), we provide evidence of Russian industry and agriculture.

During the last two decades of the nineteenth century, the Russian economy grew rapidly, a growth pattern that has attracted great interest. For example, between the 1860s and the 1880s, the average annual rate of growth of net national product was 1.8 percent, while for the period thereafter up to 1909–13, the rate of economic growth was 3.3 percent.

In terms of the production of critical products such as grain, steel, and coal, the significant expansion of the Russian economy is evident. At the same time, Russia experienced significant population growth, so in per capita terms, on the eve of World War I, Russia still belonged to the group of poor West European countries (Spain, Italy and Austria-Hungary). Moreover, as we shall discover, the rapid growth of industrial output, while a necessary condition for overall growth, is clearly not sufficient alone to conclude that economic development was proceeding rapidly and successfully in prerevolutionary Russia.

RUSSIAN AGRICULTURE UNDER THE TSARS

Examination of the prerevolutionary Russian economic experience would be incomplete without considering the development of agriculture. First, the story of the early stages of economic growth and development is, in large part, the story of struc-

Table 2.2

INDUSTRY AND AGRICULTURE: RUSSIA AND OTHER COUNTRIES, 1861 AND 1913

	Crude steel: 1000 metric tons	Pig iron: 1000 metric tons
1861		
Russia	7	320
UK	334	3,772
France	84	967
Germany	143	592
USA	12	830
Netherlands	NA	NA
Norway	NA	0
Sweden	0	170
Italy	0	27
Spain	NA	67
Austria-Hungary	22	315
1913		
Russia	4,918	4,641
UK	7,787	10,425
France	4,687	5,207
Germany	17,609	16,761
USA	31,800	34,700
Netherlands	NA	NA
Norway	0	NA
Sweden	591	730
Italy	934	427
Spain	242	425
Austria-Hungary	2,611	2,381

NA = not available

(Continued on facing page)

tural transformation. Less developed countries typically begin from an agrarian base and then move towards industrial development, assisted in part by resources from the rural economy. Second, much of the story of the early Soviet period also focuses on the rural economy and its potential support role, most notably the importance of grain output as a contributor to industrial development. From these perspectives, the agrarian sector of Russia under the tsars bears special attention.

Coal: million metric tons	Rail lines: 1000 km	Grain output: 1000 metric tons	Raw cotton: 1000 metric tons
0.38	2.2	41,500	43.0
85.0	14.6	NA	456.0
9.4	9.6	26,220	110.0
18.7	11.5	28,706	74.0
13.3	50.3	39,318	213.0
NA	0.34	292	3.6
NA	0.07	802	NA
0.03	0.57	1,265	7.7
0.03	2.8	6,455	12.0
0.35	2.9	NA	27.0
2.5	3.2	20,745	44.0
36.1	70.2	123,000	424
292.0	32.6	8,948	988
40.8	40.7	30,870	271
277.3	63.4	85,445	478
517.0	400.0	146,000	1,458
1.9	3.2	3,686	36
NA	3.1	1,076	NA
0.36	14.3	4,979	22
0.7	18.9	13,128	202
3.9	15.1	9,025	88
54.2	23.0	38,953	210

Source: P. R. Gregory, *Russian National Income, 1895–1913* (Cambridge: Cambridge University Press, 1982), 155–56.

In general, the agricultural revolution that accompanied the industrialization of Western Europe and England was preceded by the breakdown of **feudalism,** preparing the way for the introduction of modern agricultural institutions and methods. The late development of serfdom in Russia was accompanied by rather odious forms of servitude. Serfs were bound to the soil, could be deported to Siberia, were conscripted into the army virtually for life, and could be sold on the open market by their masters. Depending upon the region of the country, Russian serfs were required to provide labor services on the landlord's land (called **barshchina**) or to make payments in kind from their crops (later on, money) for the use of their allotted land (called **obrok**). In addition, peasant land prior to 1861 was held communally and was periodically redistributed by the village elders, who constituted a form of village self-government.

Russian feudal agriculture provided few incentives for investment, productivity improvements, and better management. Indeed barshchina was frequently termed "all that is done slowly, incorrectly, and without incentive."[10] Even peasants working in town had to pay a large portion of their earnings to their masters and could be ordered to return to their village. This contrasted with the West European practice, in which serfs could gain their freedom by living in the town.

The Emancipation Act of 1861 gave the serfs their juridical freedom (if not economic freedom) and transferred to the peasants about half the land holdings of the landed aristocracy (the gentry). These actions provided a unique opportunity to establish the foundations of a modern Russian agriculture. However, as historians have pointed out, the primary objective of the Russian emancipation was not to create a modern agriculture, but to prevent revolts, to preserve the aristocracy, and to retain state control of agriculture. While the peasants received their juridical freedom, they had to "redeem" their allotted plots of land. The remaining land (over 50 percent) was retained by the gentry, the original owners. Peasant dissatisfaction with the size of land allotments was widespread. These allotments were regarded as too small to provide earnings for redemption payments. Some peasants accepted "beggar's allotments"—small plots of land free of obligations—over larger plots of land that had to be redeemed. As late as 1877, the crown and the treasury still owned almost 50 percent of the land of European Russia. The remainder was split between the gentry and the peasants.

Did the Emancipation Act of 1861 provide the underpinnings for the development of a modern agricultural sector?[11] On the positive side, the large estates that created most of the export surpluses increased, and redemption payments introduced a money economy into the countryside. On the other hand, the act also placed serious constraints upon agricultural development. The emancipation act retained communal agriculture as a form of control through the institution of the **mir** or **obshchina** (two names for Russian village communal organizations). The agricultural commune was held responsible for the debts of individual members. More prosperous commune members were responsible for the defaults of the poorer members, limiting the incentive to accumulate wealth in the commune.[12]

The peasant family could not officially withdraw its land from the commune until the family's debts on the land had been met, and only then with a two-thirds vote of the membership. Moreover, peasants could not leave the land permanently for the city until their land was free of obligations, a system enforced by Russia's internal passport system. Finally, periodic internal redistribution of land within the commune limited the incentive to improve land.

The Emancipation Act of 1861 appeared to make it difficult to create a modern agriculture on peasant lands. Writers, including Gerschenkron, described what they perceived as a growing crisis, not only of peasant agriculture, but of Russian agriculture in general. The aristocracy was wasting its land; peasants were frozen on backward and unproductive communes; tax arrears were rising. As this "agrarian crisis" deepened, so did peasant unrest, a major factor contributing to the Revolution of 1905. The 1905 revolution shocked the Tsarist government into implementing reforms. The **Stolypin reforms** of 1906 and 1910 were significant steps towards weakening communal agriculture and helping to create a class of small peasant proprietors. They allowed peasants to consolidate their parcels of land, canceled peasant debts, and allowed peasants to withdraw from the commune.

The Stolypin reforms would have had a positive effect over a long period of time. However, they came to late. The "agrarian crisis" was simply too deep—mortgaged estates, rising tax arrears, rural poverty, and declining per capita grain output were all causes of the Revolution of 1905.[13] Was this pessimistic view of Russian agriculture justified?

Some scholars have questioned the existence of a deep agrarian crisis. According to more recent evidence, the output and marketing performance of Russian agriculture were much better than believed earlier. Indeed the aggregate figures point to rising peasant living standards, increasing agricultural productivity, and increasing per capita output, all in spite of persistent regional differences. In fact, agriculture's growth during this period was much like that of Western Europe. Internal passport data show that peasant mobility was greater than earlier thought. Peasant tax arrears may not be indicative of exhaustion of the taxpaying capacity of the Russian village. In fact, Russian peasants may have simply adjusted their tax payments automatically, according to harvests and prices, in tune with their sense of social justice.[14] If Russian agricultural performance was in fact better than the agrarian crisis view might suggest, what were the implications for economic growth and economic development during the late Tsarist era? To answer this question, we turn to the framework of modern economic growth and focus on the structural changes of the era.

ECONOMIC GROWTH AND ECONOMIC DEVELOPMENT: THE TSARIST ERA—AN OVERVIEW

We have already presented evidence comparing the Russian economy to its European neighbors (Tables 2.1 and 2.2). Although Russia was a major economic power on the eve of World War I, its relative poverty on a per capita basis is striking. Although the Russian economy was growing, its population was increasing fast enough to temper per capita growth. Moreover, Russia's economic power was concentrated in agriculture. In 1861, Russia produced more grain than any other country and was surpassed by only the United States in 1913. On a per capita basis, however, Russia ranked well behind the major grain-producing countries such as the United States and Germany and was roughly on a par with countries such as France and Austria-Hungary. Russia's industrial base was much less well established. In 1861, Russia was a minor producer of major industrial commodities like coal, iron, and steel, and even though Russia had improved its relative position by 1913, it still lagged far behind the major industrial powers.

The growing relative backwardness of the Russian economy is partially masked by the aggregate figures but is apparent from per capita statistics. Russia began its modern era with a per capita output one-half that of France and Germany, one-fifth that of England, and fifteen percent that of the United States. By 1913, Russia's relative position had deteriorated due primarily to rapid population growth and slow output growth in the years before the 1880s. On a per capita basis, Russia in 1913 was a poor European country ranking well below Spain, Italy, and Austria-Hungary.

THE GROWTH OF PER CAPITA OUTPUT

A distinctive feature of modern economic growth is an accelerated and sustained rate of growth of output per capita. Table 2.3 provides the growth rates of the Russian era. Although there are a variety of problems with such data, we believe that they provide a broadly accurate picture of the era. Although Russian economic growth was slow during the immediate postemancipation era, there was a significant acceleration after 1880. During Russia's "industrialization era" (after 1880), the

Table 2.3

RUSSIAN ECONOMIC GROWTH (PERCENT PER ANNUM)

Time period	Net National Product per Worker (NNP)	Population	Per Capita NNP	Labor Force	NNP per Worker
1861–63 to 1881–83	1.8	1.1	0.7	1.9	0.1
1883–87 to 1909–13	3.3	1.6	1.7	1.7	1.6

Sources: The 1861–83 figures are for the fifty European provinces and are from P. R. Gregory, "Economic Growth and Structural Change in Tsarist Russia: A Case of Modern Economic Growth?" *Soviet Studies* vol. 23, no. 1 (January 1972), 422. The 1883–1913 figures are for the Russian empire and are from P. R. Gregory, "Economic Growth and Structural Change in Tsarist Russia and the Soviet Union: A Long-Term Comparison," in S. Rosefielde, ed., *Economic Welfare and the Economics of Soviet Socialism* (Cambridge: Cambridge University Press, 1981).

growth of national income (3.3 percent per annum) was above average when compared to industrialized countries for which we have records and was equaled or surpassed by only four countries.[15]

On a per capita and a per worker basis, the growth of Russian output was average relative to that of the industrialized countries. Russia's above average output growth was largely the consequence of a relatively rapid rate of growth of population and labor force. Thus Russian economic growth was largely **"extensive"** in character, that is, a result of the expansion of inputs rather than expansion of output per unit of input. Less reliable data on the Tsarist capital stock suggests that roughly two-thirds of the growth of Russian output was accounted for by the growth of conventional labor and capital inputs.[16] After the mid-1880s, the Russian empire grew at total, per capita, and per worker rates on a par with those of industrialized countries. Russia's output growth figures do not paint a picture of a collapsing economy, but rather of an economy that was either catching up or holding its own with the most industrialized countries of that era. Although Russia's rate was relatively slow for the entire period after emancipation, this performance is accounted for by the slow growth from the 1860s through the early 1880s.[17]

Structural Change

A major characteristic of modern economic growth is structural change, or shifts away from agriculture and towards industrial and service activities. These sorts of shifts, analyzed in depth in the work of Kuznets, can be used as a benchmark against which to judge structural transformation in Russia.[18] In Table 2.4 (p. 32), we note that the amount of structural change experienced during Russia's industrialization era was about average (or perhaps slightly below) for a country undergoing the initial stages of modern economic growth. The decline in the shares of agriculture and the expansion of industry/construction/transportation suggests that the Russian economy had indeed embarked on a path of modern economic growth.

Investment in Human Capital

Investment in human capital is an important source of modern economic growth. As noted above, labor productivity failed to increase in Russia between emancipation and the 1880s, although thereafter it grew at an average rate relative to the industrialized countries. One possible explanation for this pattern would be increased private and public investment in human capital, especially after 1880. There is very little firm information on Russian literacy rates prior to 1897, but evidence on military recruits from the cities of St. Petersburg and Moscow show that increases in literacy were barely perceptible prior to the early 1880s.[19] From the mid-1880s on, however, the growth of literacy rates accelerated. Between 1884 and 1904, the literacy rates of military recruits more than doubled, from 26 to 56 percent. For the country as a whole, the 1897 illiteracy rate was 72 percent, with urban

Table 2.4

THE RUSSIAN ECONOMY: STRUCTURAL CHANGES 1883–1913
Shares in national product by producing sector (percentages)

	Agriculture	Industry/Construction/ Transport/Communication	Trade and services
1883–87	57.5	23.5	19.0
1909–13	51.0	32.0	17.0

Shares in national product by final use (percentages)

	Personal consumption	Government	Net domestic investment	Net foreign investment
1885–89	83.5	8.1	8.1	0.3
1909–13	79.6	9.7	12.1	−1.5

Source: P. R. Gregory, "Economic Growth and Structural Change in Tsarist Russia and the Soviet Union: A Long-Term Comparison," in S. Rosefielde, ed., *Economic Welfare and the Economics of Soviet Socialism* (Cambridge: Cambridge University Press, 1981).

literacy almost three times rural literacy (Table 2.5). Between 1897 and 1913, further progress was made in the provision of education. A rough estimate places the Russian illiteracy rate in 1913 at approximately 60 percent of the population over ten years old. For comparative purposes, note that in 1900 the comparable illiteracy rate in the United States was 11 percent of the population.

The literacy data suggest that Russia was still a socially backward nation at the turn of the century. This fact could have promoted the use of more capital intensive factor proportions and the use of skilled labor and managers from abroad. However, while the level of achievement in human capital remained low, there was considerable growth after 1880. Kahan has emphasized the rising investment in primary education, the 2650 percent increase in the number of elementary schools and the 3.5 fold increase in primary school enrollment between 1890 and 1914 as a primary source of Russian growth.[20]

Population

Another distinctive feature of modern economic growth is the demographic transition. The dominant trend of the demographic transition is a decline in birthrates, though initially the expansion of income may lead to an increase. During the initial phases of growth, the death rate declines quite rapidly and is the principal factor explaining the initial increase in the rate of population growth. In his analysis of modern economic growth, Kuznets notes that premodern birthrates

Table 2.5

ILLITERACY RATES: RUSSIA (1897 AND 1913); UNITED STATES (1913)
(percent of total population over 10 years of age)

		Urban	Rural	Total
Russia	1897	55*	83*	72
	1913	—	—	60
United States	1900	—	—	11

*percent of the entire population

Source: A. G. Rashin, *Formirovanie rabochego klassa v rossii* [The formation of the working class in Russia] (Moscow: Sotzekisdat), 579–81.

varied substantially among countries, ranging from highs of 55 per 1000 to lows of 31 per 1000.[21] The average premodern death rate was roughly 30 per 1000 in Western Europe and somewhat lower in areas of European settlement in North America and Australia. From these initial levels, both birthrates and death rates declined, the death rate reaching a lower limit of roughly 10 per 1000 in modern times. In Table 2.6 (p. 34) we present basic demographic data for Russia.

Russia began its postemancipation development with a demographic base like that of Western Europe and North America some 75 to 100 years earlier. The Russian birthrates of the early 1860s were exceeded only by the U.S. rates of the period 1790–1800. The Russian death rate in the early 1860s was well above the eighteenth century Western European average of approximately 30 per 1000. The Russian death rate began to decline steadily during the late 1890s but remained high relative to West European standards. The high Russian death rate can be explained by the high rate of infant mortality—27 deaths per 100 during the 1867–71 period and 24 deaths per 100 in 1911.[22] Russia had limited success in reducing infant mortality. The Russian birth rate changed very little in the late 1800s. By 1913 it was still twice the level of the Western European average for the same year. In summary, while Russian birth and death rates began to conform to patterns observed during modern economic growth, the rates were still at premodern levels at the time of the revolution in 1917.

RUSSIA AND THE ROLE OF FOREIGN INVESTMENT

As we will see later in our discussion of the early Soviet era, the issue of capital accumulation is central to modern economic growth. Insofar as savings are required to finance investment, the role of foreign investment could be of major importance in relatively poor countries such as Russia. Although strategies of economic growth

Table 2.6

BASIC DEMOGRAPHIC PATTERNS: RUSSIA, 1861–1913

	Birthrate	Death rate	Rate of natural increase
1861–65	51	37	14
1866–70	50	37	12
1871–75	51	37	14
1876–80	50	36	14
1881–85	51	36	14
1886–90	50	35	16
1891–95	49	36	13
1896–1900	50	32	17
1901–05	48	31	17
1906–10	46	30	16
1910–13	44	27	17

Source: A. G. Rashin, *Naseleniie Rossii za 100 let* [The population of Russia for 100 years] (Moscow: Sotzekidat, 1956), 155.

and development differ, relatively backward countries commonly take advantage of foreign investment during the early stages of development, prior to developing the necessary domestic savings to replace foreign savings. In addition to relying on foreign savings, these countries also rely on imported technology, which they tend to replace with their own as they mature. Some view reliance upon foreign investment as an indicator of the level of development of an economy.

Foreign investment played a substantial role in Russia. The domestic production of capital equipment in Russia was limited. In 1913, engineering products accounted for only 10 and 12 percent of manufacturing net output and labor force respectively. During the same period, the average manufacturing product share of engineering in England, the United States, and Germany was 21 percent.[23] As an industrializing country, Russia needed foreign capital equipment and technology.

In addition to importing technology and equipment from abroad, the Russian economy was also aided by the receipt of foreign savings to finance Russian capital formation along with domestic saving. In fact, Russia was a large debtor country during the period 1880–1913, receiving significant capital inflows from France, England, and Belgium. Foreign capital probably accounted for 40 percent of Russian industrial investment, 15 to 20 percent of Russian total investment, and about 2 percent of Russian output at the end of the Tsarist era.[24] By 1913, Russia was the world's largest debtor, accounting for about 15 percent of world international debt.[25]

How might this experience compare to other debtor countries during their early stages of economic development? In the United States in the mid-1880s, when the country's dependence on foreign capital was at its peak, foreign capital accounted for about 1 percent of U.S. GDP and about 10 percent of U.S. investment. In the case of Japan, foreign capital accounted for 0.2 percent of GDP between 1887 and 1896, rising briefly to a high of 4 percent between 1897 and 1906, after which Japan became a capital exporter.[26]

Tsarist Russia was, therefore, more dependent upon foreign capital in both magnitude and duration than either the United States or Japan during their major periods of dependence. Although Lenin characterized this as a weakness of the Russian economy, the large foreign investments in Russia were a sign of confidence in its potential. Dependence on foreign capital would be a major issue for Bolshevik leaders in the Soviet era.

RUSSIA AS A MARKET ECONOMY

We have described the development of the economy in prerevolutionary Russia without considering its market and commercial institutions. If the basic infrastructure of a market economy was actually in place, market institutions would have provided the basis for a continuation of Russia's economic growth and development in subsequent years. From an ideological perspective, it is important to understand the extent to which the capitalistic institutions had emerged in Russia and were in fact able to create an economic base appropriate for the modernization envisioned in the postrevolutionary era. Although the prerevolutionary period is remote, ending almost 80 years ago, it remains a part of Russia's tradition, just as does the less remote Soviet period.

The framework of modern economic growth is useful for assessing the patterns and trends of the Tsarist economy. Implicit in the notion of modern economic growth, however, is the idea that societies must develop appropriate institutions for economic growth. Was Russia developing the market institutions that accompanied modern economic growth in other countries?

Some historians have argued that the Russian case is in some sense unique. The communal institutions of Russian rural life were unlike those found in market based agriculture. Moreover, the Russian "factories in the field," described by M. Tugan-Baranovsky, differentiated Russian manufacturing from that of Europe.[27] V. I. Lenin described the Russian economy as a dual economy, a blend of backward agriculture and handicraft economy, and a modern (factory) industrial sector. The concept of the dual economy is not limited to Lenin. It is well developed in the contemporary literature on economic development. Although Lenin recognized elements of capitalism in the Russian economy, he viewed custom and tradition as being the guiding mechanisms of resource allocation. However, the most influential purveyor of this point of view was the Russian economist A. V. Chayanov, who argued that the decision-making process in the Russian household was basically different from the sorts of rules guiding decision making in a capitalist farm.[28] The Russian peasant household functioned without hired labor and made its decisions on production, consumption, and leisure in a very different framework from that of a capitalist farm.

A second argument, that the Russian economy was not a market economy, was made by Alexander Gerschenkron. He argued that the Russian state in fact replaced many typical functions of markets to such a degree that the Russian economy was not actually a market economy in the usual sense of the term.[29] He argued that state officials served as entrepreneurs, state orders were pervasive, and the state dictated the directions of industrial development. How might we assess these arguments?

It is now clear that the Russian state was much less pervasive in Russian economic life than Gerschenkron originally thought. State budgetary data do not show significant state budgetary subsidies, which would have formed the backbone of state industrial policy. Tariffs and indirect taxes were levied strictly for revenue purposes and played no role in industrial policy. The state did play an active role in the construction of railroads, though state financing of railroad construction was also used in other industrialized market economies, such as France and Germany.[30] Russia had active commodity markets and was active in world markets. The state did not engage in economic planning, and both product and factor prices were generally set in markets. As we have already emphasized, Russia received substantial foreign capital inflows, a response to traditional signals such as profits sufficient to offset risk. Although industrial trusts and syndicates were created in the early years of the 20th century, their existence does not necessarily imply nonmarket allocation. Rather, Russia might have had some monopolies.

Even Russian agriculture demonstrated the existence of market influences. In spite of the late removal of serfdom, there is evidence of significant peasant mobility, and the completion of an extensive rail network greatly facilitated marketing grain. Moreover, the econometric studies by Soviet historians showed that regional price dispersion fell as transportation costs were lowered, and agricultural marketings and land rents were in fact dictated by "normal" market principles.[31] In fact, turn-of-the-century Russia would be a familiar place to those experienced in modern international business. The hand of the Russian state was heavy. Numerous licenses, permissions, and other papers were necessary; businesses needed powerful government patrons. Bribes changed hands. These practices, common then and now, do not change the fact that basic resource allocation decisions were market driven.

WHAT WOULD HAVE HAPPENED?

We now have the benefit of hindsight to consider what would have happened to Russia if it continued on the market path of economic development that had started in the 1880s. One of Gerschenkron's major insights has proven correct. Countries that get their economic affairs in order with the right institutions and appropriate policies can overcome their relative backwardness. Japan and, more recently, the emerging economies of Southeast Asia provide strong examples of the Gerschenkron phenomenon.

Was Russia in a position to have overcome its relative backwardness had it continued as a market economy? Russian economic growth, in both industry and in agriculture, was impressive in the last thirty years of Tsarist rule. Russia had developed an extensive rail network, integrating its domestic markets and linking them to world markets. The wealth of Russia's raw materials had attracted growing amounts of foreign investment. Russian agriculture was producing well above subsistence, consistently marketing about one-quarter of its output.

The threat of political instability remained a challenge to continued rapid economic development and overcoming relative backwardness. We cannot say what kind of political system would have emerged in Russia had the Bolsheviks not come to power in 1917, but experiences elsewhere have shown that as commercial interests become stronger, there is a natural tendency to move towards the establishment of more solid legal, economic, and political institutions.

As we count down the last few years of the twentieth century, Russia remains a very poor country relative to its neighbors. In fact, Russia today is relatively more backward compared with its immediate neighbors than it was in 1917. With this in mind, it would be hard to develop a scenario in which Russia's relative position today would have been worse with a continuation of the progress towards economic development that it was making on the eve of the socialist revolution.

SUMMARY

The performance of the Russian economy in the prerevolutionary era is important for a variety of reasons. Not only was it a major example of Russia as a market economy, but also it provides us with an understanding of the economic base from which the Soviet era began. These are issues of both practical and ideological importance, important for an understanding of the Soviet era, and ultimately, the base from which transition began in the early 1990s.

The late Tsarist era is typically dated from 1861, the year when serfdom officially ended in Russia. Although the rate of economic growth between 1861 and 1880 was modest, thereafter Russia experienced significant economic growth and important structural change. Although there have been a variety of interpretations of this era, typically it has been viewed as one of "agrarian crisis," in which attempts to create a modern agriculture failed. However, contemporary evidence suggests that judged within the framework of modern economic growth (that is, a statistical profile of structural changes in market economies), Russia did experience significant economic change. Thus, while the Russian economy of 1917 was clearly different from the less developed economies of the 1990s, nevertheless in per capita terms, it clearly lagged.

Terms and Concepts

emancipation   To be freed from control; in the present context, the end of serfdom as an institution that bound individuals to the soil and to the individual who owned the land.

Modern Economic Growth   A widely used framework for statistically analyzing patterns of economic growth (population changes, structural changes, foreign trade patterns); based upon historical patterns observed in a large number of market economies.

relative backwardness   A theory of economic growth and modernization developed by the economic historian Alexander Gerschenkron to explain the pattern of economic growth observed in Russia after 1880; when a country through self-assessment seems to have fallen behind relative to its neighbors and competitors in world markets, the existence of relative backwardness promotes the development of a growth focus.

feudalism   The dominant mechanism for the organization of the rural economy through the end of the eighteenth century in Europe; land was owned by the lord and worked by serfs who were bound to the land.

barshchina   Landlord's land

obrok   Payments made by peasants to landlords in compensation for the use of land.

mir   The dominant organizational arrangement in the Russian countryside, for the communal holding and cultivation of the land and as a mechanism for the organization of rural society and local government.

obshchina   Russian term for the commune, or mir.

Stolypin reforms   Reforms introduced in 1906 and 1910 by P. A. Stolypin intended to allow peasants to change the manner in which land would be used—specifically to allow peasants to own land and to cultivate it in large plots rather than in small, frequently separated strips.

extensive economic growth   Economic growth (the expansion of output) achieved primarily through expansion of the volume of inputs (specifically land, labor and capital); contrasts with *intensive economic growth,* which is the expansion of output achieved primarily through improvement in the quality of the inputs (for example, improvement in the labor force through education or improvement in capital stock through technological change).

Selected Bibliography

Non-Soviet Sources

Antisiferov, A. N. *Russian Agriculture During the War* (New York: Greenwood, 1930).

Blackwell, W., ed. *Russian Economic Development From Peter the Great to Stalin* (New York: New Viewpoints, 1974).

Blum, J. *Lord and Peasant in Russia* (New York: Atheneum, 1965).

Crisp, O. *Studies in the Russian Economy Before 1914* (London and Basingstoke, Macmillan, 1976).

Edmundson, L., and P. Waldron, eds. *Economy and Society in Russia and the Soviet Union, 1860–1930: Essays for Olga Crisp* (London: St. Martin's Press, 1992).

Falkus, M. E. *The Industrialization of Russia, 1700–1914* (London and Basingstoke: Macmillan, 1972).

Gatrell, P. *The Tsarist Economy, 1850–1917* (New York: St. Martin's Press, 1986).

Gerschenkron, A. "Russian Agrarian Policies and Industrialization, 1861–1917," *The Cambridge Economic History of Europe* vol. 6 (Cambridge: Cambridge University Press, 1965), 706–800.

———. "The Early Phases of Industrialization in Russia: Afterthoughts and Counterthoughts," in W. W. Rostow, ed., *The Economics of Takeoff into Sustained Growth* (New York: St. Martin's Press, 1963).

———. "The Rate of Growth in Russia Since 1885," *Journal of Economic History* (Supplement), vol. 7 (1947), 144–74.

Geyer, D., ed. *Wirtschaft und Gesellschaft in Vorrevolutionaren Russland* [Economy and society in prerevolutionary Russia] (Cologne: Kiepenheuer & Witsch, 1975).

Goldsmith, R. "The Economic Growth of Tsarist Russia, 1860–1913," *Economic Development and Cultural Change* vol. 9, no. 3 (April 1961), 441–76.

Gooding, J. *Rulers and Subjects* (New York: St. Martin's Press, 1996).

Gregory, P. R. *Russian National Income, 1885–1913* (Cambridge: Cambridge University Press, 1982).

———. "Russia and Europe: Lessons From the Pre-Command Era," in R. Tilly and P. J. J. Welfens, eds., *European Economic Integration as a Challenge to Industry and Government* (Berlin: Springer, 1996).

Guroff, G., and F. V. Carstensen. *Entrepreneurship in Imperial Russia and the Soviet Union* (Princeton, NJ.: Princeton University Press, 1983).

Hogan, H. *Forging Revolution: Metalworkers and the State in St. Petersburg, 1890–1914* (Bloomington: Indiana University Press, 1993).

Kahan, A. *Russia's Economic History: The Nineteenth Century* (Chicago: University of Chicago Press, 1989).

Kirchner, W. *Die Deutsche Industrie und die Industrialisierung Russlands 1815–1914* (St. Katharinen: Scripta Mercaturae Verlag, 1986).

McCaffray, S. P. *The Politics of Industrialization in Tsarist Russia: The Association of Southern Coal and Steel Producers, 1874–1914* (DeKalb: Northern Illinois University Press, 1996).

McKay, J. P. *Pioneers for Profit: Foreign Entrepreneurship and Russian Industrialization, 1885–1913* (Chicago: University of Chicago Press, 1970).

Mosse, W. E. *An Economic History of Russia, 1856–1914* (New York: St. Martin's Press, 1996).

Munting, R. *The Economic Development of the USSR* (London: Croom Helm, 1982) ch. 1.

Notzold, J. *Wirtschaftspolitische Alternativen der Entwicklung in der Ara Witte und Stolypin* [Economic and political alternatives in the era of Witte and Stolypin] (Berlin: Duncker & Humbolt, 1966).

Owen, T. C. *Capitalism and Politics in Russia: A Social History of the Moscow Merchant* (Cambridge: Cambridge University Press, 1981).

———. *The Corporation Under Russian Law, 1800–1917: A Study in Tsarist Economic Policy* (New York: Cambridge University Press, 1991).

Portal, R. "The Industrialization of Russia," *The Cambridge Economic History of Europe* vol. 6 (Cambridge: Cambridge University Press, 1965), 801–72.

Postan, M. M., and P. Mathias, eds. *The Cambridge Economic History of Europe* vol. 7 (Cambridge: Cambridge University Press, 1978), section on Russia.

Robinson, G. T. *Russia Under the Old Regime* (New York: Macmillan, 1949).

Tugan-Baranovsky, M. I. *The Russian Factory in the 19th Century* translated by A. and C. Levin (Homewood, IL: Irwin, 1970).

Volin, L. *A Century of Russian Agriculture* (Cambridge, MA: Harvard University Press, 1979).

von Laue, T. *Sergei Witte and the Industrialization of Russia* (New York: Columbia University Press, 1963).

White, C. *Russia and America: The Roots of Economic Divergence* (Beckenham, Kent: Croom Helm, 1987).

Soviet Sources

Bovykin, V. I. Formirovanie finansogo kaitala v Rosii [Formation of financial capital in Russia] (Moscow: Nauka, 1984).

Khromov, P. A. Ekonomicheskoe razvitie Rossii [The economic development of Russia] (Moscow: Nauka, 1984).

———. *Ekonomicheskoe razvitie Rossii v 19. i 20. Vekakh* [The economic development of Russia in the nineteenth and twentieth centuries] (Moscow: Gospolitizdat, 1950).

Lenin, V. I. *Development of Capitalism in Russia* (Moscow: Progress, 1977).

Lyaschenko, P. I. *History of the National Economy of Russia to the 1917 Revolution* (New York: Macmillan, 1949).

Mironov, B. N. *Khlerbnye tseny v Rossii za dva stoletiia* [Grain prices in Russia over two centuries] (Leningrad: Nauka, 1985).

Rashin, A. G. *Formirovanie rabochego klassa v Rossii* [The formation of the working class in Russia] (Moscow: Sosteklitizdat, 1958).

———. *Naselenie Rossii 100 let* [The population of Russia over 100 years] (Moscow: Gostatizdat, 1956).

Notes ———————————————————

1. S. Kuznets, *Modern Economic Growth* (New Haven: Yale University Press, 1966).
2. A. Gerschenkron, *Economic Backwardness in Historical Perspective* (Cambridge, MA: Harvard University Press, 1962), ch. 1; W. W. Rostow, *The States of Economic Growth*

(Cambridge: Cambridge University Press, 1965), 67; W. W. Rostow, *The World Economy: History and Prospect* (Austin and London: University of Texas Press, 1978), 426–29; M. E. Falkus, *The Industrialization of Russia, 1700–1914* (London and Basingstoke: McMillan, 1972), 1–25; V. I. Lenin, *The Development of Capitalism in Russia* (Moscow: Progress Publishers, 1977).

3. A. Kahan, "Continuity in Economic Activity and Policy During the Post-Petrine Period in Russia," in W. L. Blackwell, ed., *Russian Economic Development From Peter the Great to Stalin* (New York: New Viewpoints, 1974), 51–70.

4. A. Gerschenkron, "Russian Agrarian Policies and Industrialization, 1861–1917," in *Continuity in History and Other Essays* (Cambridge, MA: Harvard University Press, 1968), 144–47.

5. For case studies, see S. P. McCaffray, *The Politics of Industrialization in Tsarist Russia: The Association of Southern Coal and Steel Producers, 1874–1914* (DeKalb: Northern Illinois University Press, 1996); H. Hogan, *Forging Revolution: Metalworkers and the State in St. Petersburg, 1890–1914* (Bloomington: Indiana University Press, 1993).

6. A. Gerschenkron, "The Early Phases of Industrialization in Russia: Afterthoughts and Counterthoughts," in W. W. Rostow, ed., *The Economics of Takeoff into Sustained Growth* (New York: St. Martins Press, 1963), 152–54; J. P. McKay, *Pioneers for Profit: Foreign Entrepreneurship and Russian Industrialization, 1885–1913* (Chicago: University of Chicago Press, 1970).

7. For a collection of authoritative studies on entrepreneurship in Russia, see G. Guroff and F. V. Carstensen, eds., *Entrepreneurship in Imperial Russia and the Soviet Union* (Princeton, NJ: Princeton University Press, 1983).

8. Arcadius Kahan has examined the pattern of state expenditure during the period of rapid industrialization and found only a very small portion of the Imperial budget devoted to promoting industrialization. Primarily for this reason, Kahan disputes the argument that the state played an important role in Russian industrialization. For details, see A. Kahan, "Government Policies and the Industrialization of Russia," *Journal of Economic History*, vol. 27, no. 4 (December 1967), 460–77.

9. Gerschenkron, *Economic Backwardness*, ch. 1.

10. M. V. Dovnar-Zpol'skii, *Na zare krestianskoi svobody* [At the daybreak of peasant emancipation] (Kiev: 1911), 179.

11. The following discussion is based upon Gerschenkron, "Russian Agrarian Policies," 140–256; and L. Volin, *A Century of Russian Agriculture From Alexander II to Khrushchev* (Cambridge: Harvard University Press, 1970), part 1.

12. Olga Crisp argues that this provision introduced a form of income tax, graduated according to ability to pay within the commune. See O. Crisp, *Studies in the Russian Economy Before 1914* (London and Basingstoke: Macmillan, 1976), essay 3.

13. For important examples of rural poverty in Russia, see for example Y. Yanson, *Opyt statisticheskogo isledovaniia o krestianskikh nadelakh I platezhakh* [Experience of statistical investigations of peasant plots and payments] (St. Petersburg: 1877); A. A. Kornilov, *Krestianskaia reforma* [The peasant reform]; (St. Petersburg: Vaisberg and Gershunina, 1905).

14. Crisp, *Studies in the Russian Economy*, vols. 1 and 3; J. Simms, "The Crisis in Russian Agriculture at the End of the 19th Century," *Slavic Review*, vol. 36, no. 3 (September 1977), 377–98. See also the discussion between J. Sanders and J. Simms in "Once More into the Breach, Dear Friends: A Closer Look at Indirect Tax Receipts and the Condition of the Russian Peasantry, 1881–1899," Slavic Review, vol. 43, no. 4 (Winter 1984), 657–71.

15. P. R. Gregory. "Economic Growth and Structural Change in Tsarist Russia and the Soviet Union: A Long-Term Comparison," in S. Rosefielde, ed., *Economic Welfare and the Economics of Soviet Socialism* (Cambridge: Cambridge University Press, 1981), 25–52.

16. *Ibid.*
17. Goldsmith, "The Rate of Growth in Tsarist Russia," 441–43.
18. These results are reported in Gregory, "Economic Growth and Structural Change in Tsarist Russia and the Soviet Union," 39.
19. Data on Russian investment in schooling are summarized in O. Crisp, "Labor and Industrialization in Russia," *Cambridge Economic History of Europe* vol. 7 (Cambridge: Cambridge University Press, 1978), 387–99; A. Kahan, "Capital Formation During the Period of Early Industrialization in Russia," Ibid., 293–95.
20. Kahan, "Capital Formation During the Period of Early Industrialization in Russia," 307.
21. Kuznets, *Modern Economic Growth*, 40–51.
22. In 1886, the average life span was 29 years for males and 32 years for females, which shows the marked effect that a high rate of infant mortality has on age structure. See A. G. Rashin, *Naseleniie Rossii za 100 let* [The population of Russia over 100 years] (Moscow: Gostatizdat, 1956), 205.
23. P. R. Gregory, *Socialist and Non-Socialist Industrialization Patterns* (New York: Praeger, 1970), 28–29, 34, 171–74.
24. These figures are from B. Bonwetsch, "Das auslandische Kapital in Russland" [Foreign capital in Russia] *Jahrbucher fur die Geschichte Osteuropas* [Yearbook for the History of Eastern Europe] vol. 22, no. 3 (1974), 416–18 and P. R. Gregory, "The Russian Balance of Payments, The Gold Standard, and Monetary Policy," Journal of Economic History, vol. 39, no. 2 (June 1979), 379–99.
25. P. R. Gregory, "Russia and Europe: Lessons From the Pre-Command Era," in R. Tilly and P. J. J. Welfens, eds., *European Economic Integration as a Challenge to Industry and Government* (Berlin: Springer, 1996), 481.
26. Kuznets, *Modern Economic Growth,* 332–34.
27. M. I. Tugan-Baranovsky, *The Russian Factory in the 19th Century,* translated by S. Levin (Homewood, IL: Irwin, 1970).
28. A. V. Chayanov, *The Theory of Peasant Economy,* D. Thorner et al., eds. (Homewood, IL: Irwin, 1966).
29. A. Gerschenkron, *Economic Backwardness in Historical Perspective,* essay 1.
30. These results are summarized from P. R. Gregory, "The Role of the State in Promoting Economic Development: The Russian Case and its General Implications," in R. Sylla and G. Roniolo, eds., *Patterns of European Industrialization* (London: Routledge, 1991), 64–79.
31. B. N. Mironov, *Khlebnye tseny v Rossii za dva stoletiia* [Grain prices in Russia over two hundred years] (Leningrad: Nauka, 1985); I. D. Kovalchenko and L. V. Milov, *Vserossiiski agrarny rynok XVIII–Nachalo XX veka* [The agrarian market of the Russian empire from the eighteenth to the beginning of the twentieth centuries] (Moscow: Nauka, 1974).

CHAPTER 3

War Communism and the New Economic Policy— 1918–1928

I n this chapter, we turn to events following the Bolshevik revolution of 1917. During this period, the Soviet Union operated under two very different economic systems—War Communism (1917–21) and the New Economic Policy (NEP) 1921–28. Although the administrative command economy did not emerge until after 1928, many of the changes implemented by Joseph Stalin during the 1930s and thereafter had roots in the events of the era just after the revolution.

THE REVOLUTION AND ITS AFTERMATH

Two revolutions in 1917 brought Tsarist rule to an end and led to the formation of the Union of Soviet Socialist Republics (**USSR**) and the beginning of the Soviet era. The revolution in March of 1917 overthrew the imperial monarchy and installed a provisional government. The revolution of October 1917, organized by the **Bolshevik** Party led by V. I. Lenin, overthrew the provisional government and dedicated itself to the establishing socialism (a new socialist order as Lenin described it) and ultimately communism.

The Bolshevik's first significant move was the Land Decree of November 8, 1917, which nationalized land and sanctioned its distribution among the peasants. The remaining large estates were broken up into small units. These new ownership arrangements, although already partially in place, would nevertheless have major implications. As proprietors, the peasants would make both production and distribution decisions. For the first time, the peasants, not the large estate owners or the state, would decide output and the portion of output marketed.

After the Bolshevik revolution, there was a revival of the communal **mir,** the institution that had confiscated and redistributed the land of the gentry, to become the principal voice of administrative authority within the village during the early years of Soviet rule.[1] The village assembly settled most questions of interests to peasants, steering a course largely independent of the rural Soviets (the **sel'sovet**), the local and often ineffective administrative unit of the Bolshevik government. Even though the land had been nationalized under the jurisdiction of the mir, this fact did not detract from the peasants' conviction that the land was theirs to farm and manage as they saw fit.[2]

In industry, initially only enterprises of major importance—banking, grain purchasing and storage, transportation, oil, and war industries—were nationalized, marking the beginning of an uneasy truce between the Bolsheviks and the capitalists. Trade unions emerged, and workers' committees, called **workers' soviets,** were formed in privately owned enterprises, although their powers were limited. In a sense, a form of state capitalism was created, in which the state controlled key sectors of the economy.

The uneasy truce between the Bolsheviks and the capitalists did not last long. By the middle of 1918, the Bolshevik forces were locked in a struggle with the White Russian forces which were supported in part by foreign powers. The Germans were in possession of the Ukraine, while the White Russian armies occupied the Urals, Siberia, North Caucasus, and other important regions. The Baltic states and Poland became independent. At one point, the Bolsheviks retained only 10 percent of the coal supplies, 25 percent of the iron foundries, less than 50 percent of the grain area, and less than 10 percent of the sugar beet resources of the former Russian empire.[3] Opponents of Soviet authority occupied three quarters of the territory of the USSR.

Faced with mounting war expenditures and lacking a domestic tax base, the Bolsheviks resorted to printing money. This expansion of the money supply combined with shrinking supplies of consumer goods created hyperinflation. On November 1, 1917, there were 20 billion rubles in circulation. By July 1, 1921, there were 2.5 trillion rubles in circulation. Between 1917 and 1921, prices increased 8000-fold.[4] This hyperinflation led to the near destruction of existing market arrangements. Peasants were reluctant to exchange their produce for money, as were manufacturers and artisans. As a result, barter became widespread, leading to what the Soviets termed "naturalization" (demonetization) of the economy. These events led to the introduction of administrative methods, known as War Communism.

WAR COMMUNISM: 1918–1921[5]

War Communism was a dramatic departure from existing arrangements. Money was virtually eliminated, private trade was abolished, workers were militarized and paid virtually equal wages, and farm output was requisitioned. The critical question about War Communism is this: Were these policies an ideologically-based attempt to move directly towards full communism, or were they measures necessitated by the emergency of civil war?

A widely-held view, postulated by well known British authorities Maurice Dobb and E. H. Carr, has been that civil war forced War Communism on the Soviet leadership, and statements of ideological support were "no more than flights of leftist fancy." In fact, Lenin and Trotsky often referred to War Communism as measures of a "besieged fortress." Other scholars have argued, however, that Lenin introduced War Communism as an essential step towards the creation of a communist economic system, a theory that gains some support in light of efforts to sustain and strengthen War Communism after the end of the civil war.[6]

WAR COMMUNISM—POLICIES

The crux of War Communism was the policy of forcibly requisitioning agricultural surpluses. The police, then called the **Cheka,** and party activists were sent into the countryside to extract grain from the rich and middle peasants. The system of requisitioning (termed the **prodrazverstka**) was initiated on May 9, 1918, through a Commissariat for Food with extraordinary powers to confiscate food products from the rural population. Requisitioning effectively broke the market link between agricultural deliveries and the rewards for those deliveries.[7] Although the state deliveries of industrial goods maintained the link between sales and purchases, the peasants actually received only 12 to 15 percent of prewar supplies of manufactured goods.

The second major policy of War Communism was nationalization. About 37,000 enterprises were nationalized by 1920, roughly half of which were small scale operations not using mechanical power. It is true that there was fear of German takeover of German-owned enterprises and also fear of the backlash of proprietors who had supported the White Russians in the civil war. Nevertheless, the speed, extent, and depth of nationalization appear to be primarily an ideological response, not one based upon the needs of a crisis situation. Since control procedures were lacking, nationalization was also undertaken prematurely. Finally, although there was to be central direction through the national industrial boards and the state budget, in fact central direction was generally lacking.

The third major policy of War Communism was the abolition of private trade, which was viewed as incompatible with centralized requisitioning and allocation. In November of 1918, all private trade was abolished, and the state ostensibly became the sole supplier of consumer goods to the population. Understandably, the black market continued to thrive, tolerated by officials until 1920.[8]

A fourth major policy of War Communism was the change in methods of labor allocation. Semi-military controls were implemented, and the movement of industrial workers restricted. Labor deserters received severe penalties under a decree of November 28, 1919, which placed the employees of state enterprises under military discipline. In large part, the mobilization of labor was managed by Leon Trotsky, the founder of the Red Army. Labor was decreed to be compulsory for all able bodied persons, supervised by a Commission for the Universal Labor Service, which Trotsky created as its head.[9]

Fifth, distribution was changed significantly under War Communism. Under the "class ration" introduced in 1918, wages were based upon type of work. Those in the highest category (those performing heavy work under dangerous conditions) were to receive a ration four times that of the lowest category (those in the free professions and the unemployed). Adhering to this system proved difficult. By 1919, 30 categories of special workers were placed on preferential rations.[10]

Finally, money as a means of exchange was largely eliminated during War Communism. Transactions between city and countryside were largely in kind, and settlements among state enterprises were made largely with bookkeeping entries having little real meaning. In 1920, postal services, gas, electricity, and public transportation were made available free of charge, and it was also decided that foodstuffs provided through the Food Commissariat should also be free of charge.[11]

War Communism—How Effective Was It?

The communist victory in the Russian civil war shows that War Communism enabled the Soviet leadership to win the civil war and sustain its political position. A more fundamental issue, however, is the long-term viability of War Communism as an economic system. Our description of its policies has already revealed its long-run weakness.

First, War Communism's agrarian policy estranged peasants from the Bolshevik leadership and encouraged dysfunctional behavior, such as restricting output and hoarding or concealing surpluses, especially during periods of agricultural shortages.

Second, Soviet industry operated without coordination. While most enterprises had been nationalized, there was no suitable administrative structure to coordinate their activities. The industrial census of 1920 showed over 5000 nationalized enterprises employing only one worker.[12]

No branch of the economy was spared in the ensuing economic collapse. In 1920, industry and transportation were one-fifth of what they had been in 1913. Foreign trade had evaporated. The decline of agriculture was precipitous, although less than industry or transportation. With markets largely eliminated, nationalized Soviet industry functioned without direction, since no administrative mechanism was introduced in their place. Ostensibly, large scale industry was to be coordinated by the Supreme Council of the National Economy **(VSNKh).** It was subdivided into departments **(Glavki),** each of which was to direct a particular industry. Typically, Glavki were grouped into trusts. In addition, the provincial economic councils **(Gubsovnarkhozy)** served as the local organs of the VSNKh to supervise regional industry. These arrangements bordered on chaos. By 1920, there were over 37,000 nationalized enterprises. With totally inadequate information about local enterprises, the Glavki were ineffective in coordinating and directing local activities.[13]

VSNKh, the champion of central control, was under the leadership of Aleksei Rykov. He fought against the "Left Communist" contingent, which favored workers control of factories, and attacked the concept of trade union control of factories, citing Lenin's opposition to worker control and support of rational one-man management. In spite of these efforts, there was limited direction of industry, and while plans were drawn up for some industries, they were not presented as a national plan approved by the government. The first effort at national economic planning in the Soviet Union was the general plan for electrification, called **GOELRO,** completed in December of 1920. Despite these first efforts at planning, industry operated essentially without direction during the period of War Communism. "Shock" **(udarny)** methods were used to attack bottlenecks, but as soon as one problem was eliminated, another would arise.

Finally, the lack of a general system of incentive wages led to problems of labor supply in industry. The legal distribution of consumer goods was controlled by the state, which recognized that wage differentials were necessary to attract workers to particular jobs. The results, however, contradicted the intention. Wage payments were rationed to industrial workers on a fairly equal basis, despite the desire for differentiation. This unintended egalitarianism resulted in an inadequate pool of qualified industrial labor. Instead of being attracted into industry, labor flowed out of the factories during War Communism. The number of townspeople declined from 2.6 million to 1.2 million between 1917 and 1920.[14] Morale was poor, sabotage frequent, and few loyal specialists were available. The data in Table 3.1 (p. 48) summarizes the economic difficulties of War Communism.

By 1920, the crisis of civil war that had given rise to War Communism had ended, and the dangers of continuing the policies of this era were becoming more and more apparent. The still-powerful trade unions were revolting against the centralization of industry and the conscription of labor. The alienated peasant population called for the elimination of the state grain monopoly. In short, the Soviet regime was in danger of falling victim to internal discontent. The final blow was the

Table 3.1

WAR COMMUNISM: PRODUCTION AND TRADE INDEXES, 1913 AND 1920*

Year	Industry	Agriculture	Transportation	Exports	Imports
1913**	100	100	100	100	100
1920	20	64	22	0.1	2.1

*1913 = 100

**The 1913 figures refer to the inter-war territory of the USSR.

Sources: G. W. Nutter, "The Soviet Economy: Retrospect and Prospect," in D. Abshire and R. V. Allen, eds., *Political, Military, and Economic Strategies in the Decade Ahead* (New York: Praeger, 1963), 165; M. Kaser, "A Volume Index of Soviet Foreign Trade," *Soviet Studies,* vol. 20, no. 4 (April 1969), 523–26.

Kronstadt uprising of March 1921, in which the sailors of the Kronstadt naval base revolted in support of the workers of Petrograd. That same month, the Soviet leadership moved quickly to dispel this discontent by replacing War Communism with the New Economic Policy (NEP).

THE NEW ECONOMIC POLICY (NEP): 1921–1928

Lenin described both War Communism and NEP as temporary expedients. He noted that "War Communism was thrust upon us by war and ruin. It was not, nor could it be, a policy that corresponded to the economic tasks of the proletariat. It was a temporary measure."[15] Likewise, NEP was described as transitional, a step backward because of the significant roles of "antisocialist" institutions such as private property, capitalist markets, and private initiative.

The most striking feature of NEP was its attempt to combine market and socialism. Agriculture remained in the hands of the peasant, and industry, with the exception of the "commanding heights," was decentralized. Market links between industry and agriculture and between industry and the consumer replaced state control of production and distribution. Lenin's step backward was only partial. About three-quarters of industrial output remained in the hands of nationalized enterprises, which were to provide general guidance by controlling key sectors, the **commanding heights** of the economy. These sectors included fuel, metallurgy, war industries, transportation, banking, and foreign trade.

The political basis of NEP was the alliance between the Soviet regime and the peasant. This alliance was referred to as the **Smychka.** Requisitioning of agricultural goods was abandoned, and market relationships were reestablished, freeing the peasant to sell surplus agricultural products and to buy industrial products freely. These changes represented a major concession by the Bolshevik Party. While support of the peasant was essential, reestablishing market agriculture created an environment that promoted differentiation among the farm population. The development of a class of middle and wealthy peasants was alien to Marxian thought. It would create a whole class of citizens opposed to the creation of socialism and communism in the Soviet Union.[16]

The Policies of NEP

The cornerstone of the NEP economy was the proportional agricultural tax (called the **prodnalog**), introduced in March of 1921 to replace the War Communism system of requisitions. First paid in kind, and by 1924 in money, it was a single tax based upon a fixed proportion of each peasant's net produce. The prodnalog was differentiated according to income level and by family size. In 1923, for example, the prodnalog differed from 5 percent of annual income on land holdings of less than one-quarter hectare to 17 percent of annual income on land holdings of more than three hectares. The average tax rate on peasant income was below 10 percent. Throughout NEP, the burden of the prodnalog was increasingly shifted to the middle and upper peasants, and it accounted for one-quarter of state revenues during NEP. More recent studies by Western historians conclude that, when all forms are considered, the tax burden during NEP was about the same as in 1913.[17]

Although the prodnalog was a first step towards establishing a market economy, additional steps were necessary. In an effort to stimulate peasant market activity, the state granted the peasants commercial autonomy to sell their output to whomever they wished, be it the state, a cooperative, or a private dealer. In addition, peasants were allowed to lease land and to hire farm laborers, both forbidden under War Communism. With the market link between agriculture and the city reestablished, nine-tenths of all retail trading outlets were private by the end of 1922, and they handled about three-quarters of the value of retail trade turnover. State and cooperative outlets handled the remainder.[18] The private trader, or **Nepman,** was less strongly entrenched in wholesale trade, which remained dominated by state and cooperative organizations. These larger trade companies had the network and distribution infrastructure that gave them an upper hand.

NEP also brought significant changes in the operation of industry. Whether they were state or privately owned, the majority of enterprises were permitted to make their own contracts for the purchase of raw materials and supplies and for the sale of output. State enterprises remained dominant. The industrial census of 1923 showed that private enterprises accounted for only 12.5 percent of employment in "census" establishments.[19] Only two percent of the output of large-scale industry was produced by the private sector in 1924–25.[20]

While much of the large-scale industry remained nationalized during NEP, to a great extent decision making throughout industry was decentralized. Nationalized industries were divided into two categories: The commanding heights of the economy were not separated from the state budget and remained dependent upon centralized supplies of state materials. The remaining nationalized enterprises were granted substantial financial and commercial autonomy from the state budget. These enterprises were permitted to organize into trusts, which became the dominant organizational form. By 1923, the 478 chartered trusts accounted for 75 percent of all workers employed in nationalized industry.[21] The trusts had legal authority to enter into contracts and were only loosely supervised from above, although in some key sectors, VSNKh exercised much stricter control in the form of production and delivery targets.

Although planning authorities provided trusts with "control figures" to guide decision making, NEP was not a planned economy. The limited physical planning was carried out through the Committee of State Orders (representing the various commissariats). It placed orders through the VSNKh, which in turn negotiated the orders with the producer trusts. A major source of control was in fact the people's Commissariat of Finance **(Narkomfin),** which extended its influence through the budget and credit system. Narkomfin's influence was so pervasive during this period that contemporaries spoke of it as a "dictatorship of finance." Planning during the NEP period was carried out by a variety of organizations—VSNKh, the State Planning Committee **(Gosplan)** established in 1921, the commissariats and local authorities. It was not until 1927 that Gosplan established itself as the dominant planning authority.[22]

In the last twenty years of Tsarist rule (Chapter 2), Russian industrial trade organizations organized **trusts** or **syndicates.** Soviet authorities revived them during NEP to facilitate coordination and as a way to achieve scale advantages. By the latter years of NEP, the syndicates accounted for 82 percent of state industry sales in 1927–28 and for all sales of ferrous metals.[23] As was the case in the late Tsarist period, we have no way of gauging the market power of these syndicates. We also do not know the extent of cheating and competition among cartel members.

The use of money was reintroduced with the reopening of the state bank in 1921. Both public and private enterprises were encouraged to deposit their savings in the state bank by removing limitations on private deposits and establishing safeguards to protect deposits from state confiscation. A new, stabilized currency, the **Chervonets,** was issued by the state bank in 1921; the old depreciated ruble (the **Gosznak**) was withdrawn from circulation in the currency reform of 1924. The Chervonets was the last Russian currency until the 1990s to achieve convertibility.

The NEP era also witnessed the attempt to reestablish relatively normal trading relations with the outside world, despite a reluctance to become dependent upon foreign markets.[24] The state trading monopoly focused on importing capitalist technology that could not be produced at home. Foreign concessions were granted, and concessions from abroad were sought. It was hoped that in the scramble for

Russian markets, the capitalist countries would mute their political hostility, which resulted from Lenin's earlier repudiation of Tsarist Russia's foreign debt.

The volume of foreign trade grew rapidly during NEP, from 8 percent of the prewar level in 1921 to 44 percent in 1928.[25] However, unlike the industry's recovery, the volume of foreign trade during NEP remained well below half that of prewar levels, and concessions (of which there were only 59) accounted for less than 1 percent of the output of Soviet industry. As in the 1990s, Soviet trade authorities discovered that foreign trade and foreign capital were not like a tap that could easily be turned on and off. When Lenin repudiated Russia's foreign debt on January 21, 1918, he made it very difficult for the Soviet Union to revive trade with the West less than ten years later.[26]

Economic Recovery During NEP

While the level of economic activity plummeted during War Communism, the reverse was true during the NEP era. In 1928, on the eve of the first five-year plan, both industry and agriculture had surpassed their prewar levels. Although foreign trade was still less than half that of 1913, it had recovered partially from the insignificant volume of trade during War Communism (Table 3.2, p. 52).

Although official Soviet data suggest significant recovery during the NEP era, the reliability of the data has been challenged, even by economists during the Soviet era, who argued that the figures may be too optimistic. However, recovery from the sort of devastation existing during War Communism would not be especially difficult, given the development of a framework suitable for recovery. Whatever the true picture, the NEP recovery was remarkable.

The End of NEP: Performance and Perceptions

Although the NEP economy seemed to reach its peak in 1926 with sustained economic recovery, it was not long before the NEP system was thrown out in favor of a radically different system—the administrative command economy.[27] Why was NEP abandoned at the apparent peak of its success? There are a number of reasons.

First, a great many Communist Party members viewed NEP as a temporary and unwelcome compromise with class enemies. With the state increasing in strength, it was now time to face these enemies.[28] Lenin had taken the one step backward; it was now time to take two steps forward.

Second, the growing strength of the Nepmen and prosperous peasants (termed **kulaks**) was seen as a threat and as a force that was dictating state policies. A classic example of this perceived threat was the scissors crisis of the early 1920s, which is still cited in policy debates in the 1990s. During the 1920s, agriculture had recovered more rapidly than industry, a fact that placed upward pressure on industrial prices relative to agricultural prices. In addition, it was felt that the monopoly power of the trusts was being used to restrict sales and thus raise prices. The relative price

Table 3.2

SOVIET OUTPUT LEVELS—1928 RELATIVE TO 1913

National income		Physical production	
1913 prices	117	grain production	87
1926–27 prices	119	pig iron	79
Industrial production		steel	102
		coal	122
1913 prices	129	cotton cloth	104
1926–27 prices	143–139	freight turnover	104
Agricultural production		electric power	203
		Foreign trade	
1926–27 prices	111		
		exports	38
		imports	49

Sources: A. I. Vainshtein, *Narodny dokhod Rossii I SSSR* [National income of Russia and the USSR] (Moscow: Nauka, 1969), 102; Gosplan SSSR, *Kontrol'nye tsifry narodnogo khoziaistva SSSR na 1928/29 g* [Control figures of the national economy of the USSR for 1928/29] (Moscow: Izd. Planovoe Khoziaistvo, 1929), 68; R. W. Davies, "Soviet Industrial Production, 1928–1937: The Rival Estimates," Centre for Russian and East European Studies Discussion Paper no. 18 (University of Birmingham, 1977), 63; S. G. Wheatcroft, "Grain Production Statistics in the USSR in the 1920s and 1930s," Centre for Russian and East European Studies Discussion Paper no. 13 (University of Birmingham, 1977), 23; S. G. Wheatcroft, "Soviet Agricultural Production, 1913–1940," (Mimeographed, 1979); A. Bergson, *The Real National Income of Soviet Russia Since 1928* (Cambridge, MA: Harvard University Press, 1961), 7; M. Kaser, "A Volume Index of Soviet Foreign Trade," *Soviet Studies,* vol. 20, no. 4 (April 1969), 523–26.

movements took the shape of an open pair of scissors, hence the term "scissors crisis" to describe agriculture's deteriorating terms of trade (Figure 3.1).

Bolshevik leaders feared that agriculture's deteriorating terms of trade would lead to a continuing decline in marketings, therefore threatening the NEP recovery. This posed a dilemma for the leadership—either impose some form of requisitioning, as had been done earlier, or sustain through market means what seemed to be a tenuous armistice between the regime and the peasants. A return to requisitioning would destroy agricultural production as it had during War Communism. But retaining peasant good will by raising agricultural prices would, in fact, place the peasants in control of state policy.

A third major source of dissatisfaction with NEP was the conviction that economic recovery had reached its limits without further significant capital accumulation. The capital stock of heavy industry in 1924 was estimated to be 23 percent below its 1917 peak, primarily because of the destruction of the civil war. Moreover, it was argued that much of the remaining capital stock was outmoded and badly in need of replacement or renewal that could only be brought about with new investment.

Finally, Soviet leaders of the NEP era believed their hands were tied. If they expanded industrial capacity, they feared that in the short run there would be a deficit of industrial goods. Until these long-term investments paid off, any massive investment program would more than likely spark rapid inflation, further turning the terms of trade against agriculture and leading to an agricultural supply crisis.

The End of NEP: A Realistic Posture?

It is still difficult to assess the NEP economy with accuracy. To assess the perceived capital replacement crisis, for example, requires knowing the age structure of the capital stock—a complex measurement issue for which data are unavailable. In any case, if the leadership was truly committed to the creation of a socialist economic system, clearly there would have to be changes for political reasons alone. How capable was the Soviet leadership of assessing the state of the NEP economy?

First, Soviet authorities of the NEP era failed to understand the workings of a market economy. If the authorities set agricultural prices low, then peasants, especially the wealthier peasants, would withhold grain in the expectation of price increases in the future. Such speculative behavior is quite normal in a market setting. In the Soviet Union, it was regarded as sabotage. The Communist leaders interpreted economic behavior as anti-regime political action.

Figure 3.1   The Scissors Crisis

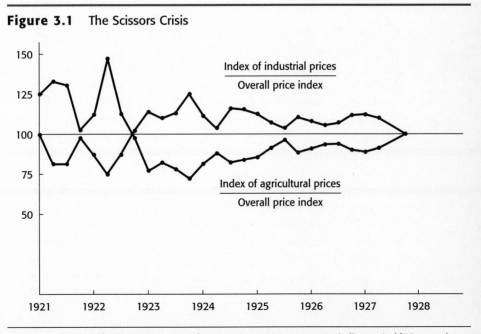

Source: A.L. Vainshtein, *Tseny i tsenoobrazovanie v SSSR v vosstanovitel'ny period* [Prices and price formation in the USSR in the transition period] (Moscow: Nauka, 1972), 158–67.

Second, Soviet authorities failed to appreciate the nature of inflationary pressures in the NEP era. For example, between 1924 and 1927 the money supply grew by 2665 percent. To the extent that price controls were used to control inflation, they would simply lead to distortions in the economy. If the money supply is growing rapidly, trying to hold prices down is like trying to stop a leaking dike with one's thumb.

Third, Soviet authorities failed to appreciate the basic concept of opportunity costs. To the extent that state grain prices were set below peasant opportunity costs of producing grains, it would not be surprising that peasants reduced production and marketings.

Fourth, Soviet authorities seemed to be much more interested in the amount of grain delivered to the state than the total amount of grain provided to the market. The latter was a more critical factor for economic growth and development than the state's own grain collections.

Fifth, market intervention, even by the most sophisticated governments, tends to have unintended consequences. In the early years of the Soviet Union, attempts to intervene in market processes were bound to result in massive unintended consequences.

A striking case of failed state intervention was the scissors crisis mentioned earlier. On the one hand, the state used price controls to bring down industrial prices. At the same time, state authorities also promoted the imports of cheaper foreign industrial products, and credits of the industrial trusts were restricted in an effort to force the sale of excess inventory. VSNKh even began to use quasi-antitrust measures to abolish some syndicates. As a consequence, industrial prices began to fall relative to agricultural prices. Although the closing of the scissors seemed to indicate success of Communist policies, they actually created excess demand for industrial products. A **goods famine** resulted. In the absence of a rationing system, the Nepmen were in a position to reap substantial profits by selling at prices higher than the state prices. Thus the peasants, in spite of the nominal closing of the scissors, lacked the incentive to market their grain surplus because they were the ones paying the higher prices. In fact, there is some evidence to suggest that marketings of grain were falling as the scissors closed.[29]

The side effects of the state's pricing policies eventually destroyed the market economy. Two sets of agricultural and industrial prices existed side by side—lower prices of official state outlets and the higher prices charged by the Nepmen. The Nepmen were quickly viewed as enemies of the state, and steps were taken to eliminate them through controls, taxes, and outright legal restrictions. Similar events took place in agriculture, leading to a "grain procurement crisis." State purchasing agencies began setting grain prices below those offered by private traders. As peasants sold to private buyers or fed grain to their cattle to protest low state prices, a grain procurement crisis was declared.

In a sense, the NEP economy was an economy without direction. The state was increasingly using controls that did not reflect supply and demand, with markets not allowed to function in a normal manner. Moreover, unemployment was viewed as a serious problem, reminding the Soviet leaders of Marx's warnings about market economies and unemployment. There were estimates of rural underemployment reaching 8 to 9 million, while there were over a million unemployed in the cities.

A final source of dissatisfaction with the NEP economy was the issue of security. The fear of imperialist conspiracies, the breaking of diplomatic relations by England in 1927, and Japanese activities in the Far East suggested to the Soviet leadership the need for rapid industrialization to meet the coming military challenge. Indeed, expectations of a war with the capitalist West, including panic purchases by the population, strengthened these views.

The End of NEP: Precedents for the Administrative Command Economy

As we examine the Soviet industrialization debate in the next chapter, it will be evident that the new arrangements of the Stalin era did not arise in a vacuum. The events of War Communism and NEP unquestionably had a profound impact upon the events to follow.

A major issue that would arise in subsequent discussion was the Soviet experience with planning. It was quite clear that if the market was to be eliminated, it must be replaced by some alternative arrangements for resource allocation. As one expert noted, "War Communism cannot be considered a centrally planned economy in any meaningful sense."[30] Even Trotsky argued that under such a system, "Each factory resembled a telephone whose wires had been cut."[31]

A second lesson of this era was the utilization of shock tactics to solve problems in a world of deficient, inadequate information, and imperfect control. To exercise central control, resources were often concentrated in bottleneck areas, a technique that could work in the short run as long as the number of bottlenecks was limited. These techniques were applied consistently, as we will see, during the Soviet plan era. For example, with input supply problems, plan fulfillment would be concentrated in the latter days of the plan period, a technique described as "storming."

A third persistent issue emerging from the 1920s was that of regional versus sectoral direction of economic activity. In the 1920s the conflicts between central and regional authorities (the Glavki, the Sovnarkhozy, and local authorities) revealed an imperfect harmony that persisted throughout the plan era. Moreover, the trusts and syndicates that existed in the 1920s were, in a sense, forerunners of the industrial associations of the plan era. Balancing regional and sectoral interests proved difficult, and with limited exceptions, the sectoral approach typically dominated.

Fourth, Soviet experiences with peasant agriculture in the 1920s had a lasting impact upon the perceptions of the leadership. The state's access to grain was viewed as critical to industrialization. The fear of grain shortages was a major factor leading to the abandonment of individual peasant farming and its replacement with collectivized agriculture after 1929.

Fifth, the failed market interventions of the 1920s left the Soviet leadership with a strongly ingrained mistrust of the market. The trusts used monopoly power to raise prices, the peasants were viewed as withholding their grain, illegal activity was prevalent throughout the economy, and unemployment was rising. The market was viewed as a chaotic mechanism that had to be replaced with planned directed activity in order to achieve state objectives.

A sixth precedent of the 1920s was recognition of the need for appropriate incentives for the allocation of labor. The militarization of labor allocation, attempted during the War Communism period, proved to be ineffective. With the possible exception of the period during World War II, differential incentives were generally used throughout the plan era in an effort to develop necessary human capital and to allocate that capital to appropriate economic activities.

A seventh major precedent was the vision of state control over unions. During the War Communism and NEP periods, strong voices argued in favor of trade union control over enterprises and trade union protection of worker interests. At the same time, there was strong pressure to have state control over unions and "one-man management" in enterprises without union interference. By the end of NEP, the latter voices had won the day, and during the plan era trade unions would remain under tight state control.

SUMMARY

In this chapter, we have examined the periods of War Communism and the New Economic Policy (NEP), which followed the Bolshevik revolution from 1917 to 1928. The War Communism period, from 1917 to 1921, has generally been viewed as a set of emergency measures designed to deal with the civil war and the collapse of the older prerevolutionary order. During this period, there was widespread nationalization, the elimination of money and private market relationships, and the forced requisitioning of grain, all introduced in the absence of significant administrative planning arrangements. Although Bolshevik power was sustained, by 1921 the economy was in serious trouble, and the policies of War Communism were replaced by the NEP era.

The NEP era signaled a return to the market, although the commanding heights of industry remained nationalized and there was significant industrial concentration through trusts and syndicates. Market relations resumed, and the system of forced requisitioning was replaced by a system of state purchases of peasant grain surpluses above that required for subsistence. There was significant economic recovery during the NEP era, and yet NEP was viewed as a temporary expedient. It was a system in large part without direction—markets existed, and yet they were difficult to control—and above all, the problem of accessing grain was, in the view of the Bolshevik leadership, not resolved. In light of these conceptions and the need to establish a major industrial base of security, NEP was abandoned in 1928 to be replaced by a very different economic system.

Terms and Concepts ─────────────

USSR   Union of Soviet Socialist Republics; official name of the Soviet Union after the Bolshevik revolution of 1917; in Russian *CCCP* or transliterated as *SSSR (Soiuznykh Sovietskikh Sotsialticheskikh Respublik).*

Bolshevik   Considered the majority (as opposed to minority or *menshivik*) section of the Russian Social Democratic Labor Party, which was headed by Vladimir Ilich Lenin.

mir   Communal farm organizations carrying over from the prerevolutionary period.

sel'sovet   Rural soviet (council).

worker's soviet   Workers councils in industrial enterprises.

Cheka   Secret police.

prodrazvertstka   Requisitioning system of War Communism.

VSNKh   (Vesenkha) The Supreme Council of the National Economy; in Russian *Vysshi sovet narodnogo khoziaistva.*

Glavki   Main administration.

Gubsovnarkhozy   Regional economic councils.

GOELRO   The State Commission for the Electrification of Russia; in Russian *Gosudarstvennaia komissia po elektrifikatsii Rossii;* also the GOELRO plan, a document for the electrification of Russia and an early example of a plan document.

udarny   Shock method of prioritizing.

Kronstadt   Port city where an uprising of the Soviet fleet took place in 1921.

commanding heights   The important (main) sectors of the economy; specifically industry such as steel, electricity generation, transport, etc.

Smychka   The political alliance between the peasants and the Communist Party.

prodnalog   Proportional agricultural tax introduced during NEP.

Nepman   Private traders in the NEP period of the 1920s.

Narkomfin   The people's commissariat of finance.

Gosplan   The State Planning Commission; in Russian Gosudarstvnnaia planovaia komissia; created in 1921 ultimately to become the main planning body for the Soviet economy.

trusts   Groups of industrial firms making decisions on production, distribution, pricing, etc.; *syndicates*.

Chervonets   Soviet currency introduced during NEP.

Gosznak   Depreciated Russian ruble withdrawn from circulation in 1921.

kulak   A rich peasant in the Marxian schema.

goods famine   Excess demand for goods resulting from state price controls in the 1920s.

Selected Bibliography

Non-Soviet Sources

Betel, W. and J. Notzold. *Deutsch-Sowjetische Wirtschaftsbeziehungen in der Zeit der Weimarer Republik* [German-Soviet economic relations in the time of the Weimar Republic] (Ebenhausen: Wissenschaft und Politik, 1977).

Carr, E. H., and R. W. Davies. *Foundations of a Planned Economy 1926–1929* vol. 1, parts 1 and 2 (London: Macmillan, 1969).

Davies, R. W., ed. *From Tsarism to the New Economic Policy* (London: Macmillan, 1990).

Day, R. *Leon Trotsky and The Politics of Economic Isolation* (Cambridge: Cambridge University Press, 1973).

Dobb, M. *Soviet Economic Development Since 1917* 5e (London: Routledge & Kegan Paul, 1960), chs. 4–9.

Erlich, A. *The Soviet Industrialization Debate, 1924–1928* (Cambridge, MA: Harvard University Press, 1969).

Gregory, Paul R. *Before Command: An Economic History of Russia from Emancipation to the First Five Year Plan* (Princeton, NJ: Princeton University Press, 1994), 5–6.

Harrison, M. "Why Was NEP Abandoned?" in R. C. Stuart, ed., *The Soviet Rural Economy* (Totowa, NJ: Rowman & Allanheld, 1984), 63–78.

Lewin, M. *Russian Peasants and Soviet Power* (London: Allen & Unwin, 1968).

Malle, S. *The Economic Organization of War Communism, 1918–1921* (Cambridge: Cambridge University Press, 1985).

Merl, S. *Der Agrarmarkt und die neue Okonomische Politik* [The agrarian market and the new economic policy] (Munich: Oldenbourg Verlag, 1981).

Nove, A. *An Economic History of the USSR* (London: Penguin, 1969).

Oppenheim, S. "The Supreme Economic Council, 1917–21," *Soviet Studies* vol. 25, no. 1 (July 1973), 3–27.

Reiman, M. *Lenin, Stalin, Gorbachev: Kontinuitat und Bruche in der Sowjetischen Geschichte* [Lenin, Stalin, Gorbachev: Continuity and change in Soviet history] (Hamburg: Junius Verlag, 1987).

Roberts, P. C. *Alienation and the Soviet Economy* (Albuquerque: University of New Mexico Press, 1971).

Szamuely, L. *First Models of the Socialist Economic Systems* (Budapest: Akademiai Kiado, 1974).

Wheatcroft, S. G. "A Revaluation of Soviet Agricultural Production in the 1920s and 1930s," in R. C. Stuart, ed., *The Soviet Rural Economy* (Totowa, NJ: Rowman & Allanheld, 1984), 32–62.

Zaleski, E. *Planning for Economic Growth in the Soviet Union, 1918–1932* (Chapel Hill: University of North Carolina Press, 1971).

Soviet Sources

Avdakov, Y., and V. Borodin. *USSR State Industry During the Transition Period* (Moscow: Progress Publishers, 1977).

Danilov, V. P. *Rural Russia Under the New Regime,* translated and introduced by O. Figes (Bloomington: Indiana University Press, 1988).

Diachenko, V. P. *Istoriia finansov SSSR* [History of finances in the USSR] (Moscow: Nauka, 1978).

Gimpel'son, E. G. *Veliki Oktiabr I stanovlenie sovetskoi sistemy upravleniia narodnym khoiaistvom* [The great October and the creation of the Soviet system of regulation of the national economy] (Moscow: Nauka, 1977).

Vainshtein, A. L. *Narodny dokhod Rossii i SSSR* [National income of Russia and the USSR] (Moscow: Nauka, 1969).

Vinogradov, V. A., et. al., eds., *Istoriia sotsialisticheskoi ekonomiki SSSR* [History of the socialist economy of the USSR] vols. 1–3 (Moscow: Nauka, 1976).

Notes ——————————

1. V. P. Danilov, *Rural Russia Under the New Regime,* translated and introduced by Orlando Figes (Bloomington: Indiana University Press, 1988), ch. 7.
2. M. Lewin, *Russian Peasants and Soviet Power* (London: Allen & Unwin, 1968), 26–28.
3. M. Dobb, *Soviet Economic Development Since 1917* 5e (London: Routledge & Kegan Paul, 1960), 98; V. A. Vinogradov, et al., Istoriia sotsialisticheskoi ekonomiki SSSR [History of the socialist economy of the USSR] vol. 1 (Moscow: Nauka, 1976).
4. L. Szamuely, *First Models of the Socialist Economic Systems* (Budapest: Akademiai Kiado, 1974), 34–35.
5. The discussion of War Communism and NEP are based upon A. Nove, *An Economic History of The USSR* (London: Penguin, 1969), chaps. 3–4; E. Zaleski, *Planning for Economic Growth in the Soviet Union, 1918–1932* (Chapel Hill: University of North Carolina Press, 1917), ch. 2; E. H. Carr and R. W. Davies, *Foundations of a Planned Economy, 1926–1929* vol. 1, part 2 (London: Macmillan, 1969), chs. 33–35.
6. The position that War Communism was adopted for ideological reasons is supported by the Hungarian authority L. Szamuely, *First Models of Socialist Economic Systems,* 7–62. This view was bitterly opposed by Soviet ideology. For an attack on "bourgeois falsifications," see Vinogradov, et al., *Istoriia sotsialisticheskoi ekonomiki SSSR* vol. 1, 251–2. See also the discussion in S. Malle, *The Economic Organization of War Communism, 1918–1921* (Cambridge: Cambridge University Press, 1985), ch. 1.
7. Danilov, *Rural Russia Under the New Regime,* ch. 7.
8. Nove, *An Economic History of the USSR,* 62. Estimates of the period suggest that in the large towns, only 31 percent of all food came through official channels (1919). Szamuely, First Models of the Socialist Economic Systems, 18, supplies similar estimates, showing that most consumption requirements were satisfied in the free (black) market.
9. R. Day, *Leon Trotsky and the Politics of Economic Isolation* (Cambridge: Cambridge University Press), ch. 2.
10. *Ibid.,* 14–17.
11. *Ibid.,* 17–18.

12. Nove, *An Economic History of the USSR,* 70.

13. Dobb, *Soviet Economic Development Since 1917,* 112.

14. Nove, *An Economic History of the USSR,* 66–67.

15. Quoted in Dobb, *Soviet Economic Development Since 1917,* 130. According to P. C. Roberts, *Alienation and the Soviet Economy* (Albuquerque: University of New Mexico Press, 1974), 36–41. This quote does not reflect Lenin's true position during War Communism. Instead, Lenin viewed War Communism as a basically correct movement in the direction of revolutionary socialism, one that he was forced to back away from by the strikes and civil unrest of 1920. Roberts points out the paths Lenin took during this period to justify the abandonment of War Communism on ideological grounds, which would have been unnecessary if War Communism had simply been a temporary wartime measure.

16. A quote from Stalin on this point (from the late 1920s after he adopted his anti-peasant stance): "What is meant by not hindering kulak farming? It means setting the kulak free. And what is meant by setting the kulak free? It means giving him power." I. V. Stalin, *Sochinenia (Collected Works)* vol. 11 (Moscow: 1946–1951), 275, quoted in A. Erlich, *The Soviet Industrialization Debate, 1924–1928* (Cambridge: Harvard University Press, 1960), 172–73.

17. Vinogradov, et al., *Istoriia sotsialisticheskoi ekonomiki SSSR* vol. 2, 37–38; S. Merl, *Der Agrarmarkt und die Neue Okonomische Politik* (Munich: Oldenbourg Verlag, 1981), 303–08.

18. Dobb, *Soviet Economic Development Since 1917,* 143; Merl, *Der Agrarmarkt,* 56.

19. Dobb, *Soviet Economic Development Since 1917,* 135. Census establishments were those employing 16 or more persons and using mechanical power or 30 or more persons but not using mechanical power. G. W. Nutter, *The Growth of Industrial Production in the Soviet Union* (Princeton, NJ: Princeton University Press, 1962), 187–88.

20. Nove, *An Economic History of the USSR,* 104.

21. Dobb, *Soviet Economic Development Since 1917,* 135. See also W. Conyngham, *Industrial Management in the Soviet Union* (Stanford: Hoover Institution Press, 1973), 17–24.

22. Carr and Davies, *Foundations of a Planned Economy,* 787–836.

23. Y. Avdakov and V. Borodin, *USSR State Industry During the Transition* (Moscow: Progress Publishers, 1977), 339.

24. For a discussion of trade policy during the NEP era, see M. R. Dohan, *Soviet Foreign Trade in the NEP Economy and Soviet Industrialization Strategy,* unpublished doctoral dissertation, Massachusetts Institute of Technology, 1969; L. M. Herman, "The Promise of Economic Self-Sufficiency Under Soviet Socialism," in M. Bornstein and D. Fusfeld, *The Soviet Economy: A Book of Readings* 3e (Homewood, IL: Irwin, 1970), 260–90; W. Beitel and J. Notzold, *Deutsch-Sowjetische Wirtschaftsbeziehungen in der Zeit der Weimarer Republik* [German-Soviet economic relations in the time of the Weimar republic] (Ebenhausen: Stiftung Wissenschaft und Politik, 1977).

25. M. Kaser, "A Volume Index of Soviet Foreign Trade," *Soviet Studies* vol. 20, no. 4 (April 1969), 523–26.

26. P. R. Gregory, "Russia and Europe: Lessons from the Pre Command Era," in R. Tilly and P. J. J. Welfens, eds., *European Economic Integration as a Challenge to Industry and Government* (Berlin: Springer, 1996), 480–82.

27. Nove, *An Economic History of the USSR,* 137.

28. *Ibid.,* 138.

29. The marketed share of grain for the Ukraine between 1923 and 1926 was as follows: 1923–24, 26%; 1924–25 15%; 1925–26, 21%.

30. Malle, *The Economic Organization of War Communism,* 318.

31. Quoted in Szamuely, *First Models of the Socialist Economic Systems,* 97.

The Soviet Industrialization Debate: Issues of Growth and Development

In the previous chapter, we examined the economic systems and policies during the decade following the Bolshevik revolution of 1917. By the late 1920s, it was becoming evident that neither War Communism nor NEP served the objectives of the Bolshevik leaders. While NEP would be the only experimentation with market arrangements during the Soviet era, even this limited use of markets would come to a sudden end after 1928. Then Joseph Stalin began pursuing policies of complete nationalization, the collectivization of agriculture, and the implementation of national economic planning to create a set of arrangements that in the 1980s Mikhail Gorbachev termed the administrative command economy.

In this chapter, we focus upon the industrialization debates of the 1920s.[1] While few participants could have predicted how Stalin would behave at the end of the decade, the debates of the 1920s were of major significance, not only for their impact upon the resulting administrative command economy but also for the light they shed upon basic issues of economic growth and development.

ECONOMIC DEVELOPMENT: MODELS AND PERSPECTIVES

When we examined Russian economic growth and development during the late Tsarist era in Chapter 2, we looked primarily at institutional change and its results in terms of structural change and economic growth. In this chapter, we turn to the Soviet debate of the 1920s about the direction of structural change and the rate of economic growth that now, after the Bolshevik revolution, could be better directed by the state. The varying approaches to economic development discussed in this chapter enable us to understand both the Soviet discussions of the 1920s, the paths eventually chosen by Stalin and, most importantly, the results in terms of economic growth and development.

ECONOMIC SYSTEMS AND POLICIES

The pursuit of economic development requires the development of an economic system or set of organizational arrangements that guide resource use. In addition, appropriate policies must be developed and pursued consistent with development objectives.[2] These issues have been central to economic thinking for centuries, and yet there has been considerable disagreement on which types of economic system and which policies should be used. Historically, systems have focused on markets with varying degrees of government intervention.

In the twentieth century there has been a tendency to classify economic systems as market, planned, or mixed systems. There has been a wide array of models or strategies for approaching economic development, and yet many focus on the fundamental sectoral transformation that we observed in the framework of modern economic growth. Thus, much of the literature focuses on some variant of a two-sector model (rural/agricultural and urban/industrial) and how institutions and related policies guide the interaction of these sectors as the urban/industrial sector grows and the rural/agricultural sector shrinks.

Understandably, some economists have focused on a "big push," industry-first strategy, arguing that if the growth of the industrial sector is the ultimate goal, then this is where the emphasis (especially investment) should fall. Others have emphasized the need to develop the source of accumulation, namely the rural/agricultural sector, using this sector as a means to develop the industrial sector. Needless to say, development issues are complex, and related and important areas such as natural resources, trade potential, technological levels, and human capital are all critical elements in the general development equation.

A rather different but important view of economic development originated with **Karl Marx** and his followers.[3] The Marxian view is important in the present context because it provides a conceptual framework for determining sectoral priorities, the central issue in the industrialization debate of the 1920s.

Marx believed that the process of economic development unfolded in stages, beginning with feudalism and proceeding through capitalism, socialism, and ultimately communism. It is important to appreciate that Marx, writing in nineteenth-century England, would have only a limited view of what socialism, let alone communism, would be like. Moreover, he did not cast the discussion within the framework of selecting appropriate institutions (plan or market) and polices but rather viewed development as deterministic, motivated by human betterment and inevitably moving from system to system as the weaknesses of each gradually led to revolutionary change.

The basic contradictions of capitalism, notably the struggle between the worker and the capitalist, would lead to the violent overthrow of the system and its replacement with socialism. While capitalism would be the "engine" for building the industrial base, ultimately the socialist vision of equity, a more egalitarian distribution of income, would prevail. The specifics would differ from case to case, but Marx viewed the process as inevitable, the process of historical materialism. He believed that the transition to socialism would occur in advanced capitalist countries. The economic system would change, shifting towards greater central control over resource allocation and fundamentally different policies of distribution, based largely upon need, although initially there would be inequality.

Marx devoted considerable attention to the conditions necessary to achieve economic growth, specifically to his model of expanded reproduction.[4] Marx divided the economy into two broad sectors, specifically sector I **(producer goods)** and sector II **(consumer goods).** The **labor theory of value** (a term borrowed from David Ricardo) states that the value of output will equal the value of direct and indirect labor inputs plus surplus value (profits). Therefore, the value of each sector's output can be written (subscript 1 refers to sector I and subscript 2 refers to sector II):

$$V_1 = c_1 + v_1 + s_1 \qquad (4.1)$$

$$V_2 = c_2 + v_2 + s_2$$

where: V = value of sector output

c = fixed capital cost, or depreciation

v = variable costs, primarily labor costs

s = surplus value (profits) of each sector

In a stationary (non-growing) economy (what Marx described as simple reproduction[5]), the output of sector I (investment goods) equals the depreciation requirements of both sectors I and II, or in symbols:

$$V_1 = c_1 + c_2 \qquad (4.2)$$

On the other hand, if an economy is to grow (what Marx termed expanded reproduction), the net capital stock must expand. This occurs when the output of sector I (investment goods) exceeds the depreciation and expenses of both sectors I and II, or in symbols:

$$V_1 > c_1 + c_2 \qquad\qquad (4.3)$$

For the economy to be in equilibrium, capital accumulation (saving) must be equal to $V_1 - c_1 - c_2$. Marx assumed that under capitalism, the workers (recipients of v) would ultimately be at the subsistence level and thus would not be a source of capital accumulation. The capitalists, recipients of surplus value (s), would be the source of accumulation, though Marx was not explicit about this process during the early stages of transition, known as *primitive capitalist accumulation*.[6] In the Marxian schema, primitive capitalist accumulation explains how capital comes to be controlled by the capitalist class in the first place, a process that takes place largely through the expropriation of property, not by saving.

Were messages in the Marxian theory relevant to the Soviet experience? First, during transition, distribution should be according to contribution. Second, some sort of planning should replace the anarchy of the market. Third, economic growth can be accelerated by paying attention to the investment goods sector.

The father of the Bolshevik revolution, of course, was **Vladimir Ilich Lenin.** While we think in terms of Marxian economics as a theoretical underpinning for a socialist economic system, the broader aspects of socioeconomic change, in fact, must be based upon an understanding of Marxism-Leninism. Indeed, Lenin made major contributions to Marxian thought.

Marx had predicted that the revolution would occur in advanced capitalist societies. For a variety of reasons, Lenin argued that the revolution would occur in the "weakest link" of the capitalist chain, in this case Russia.[7] Lenin claimed that the backward nature of the Russian economy required a transition period that he termed **state capitalism.**[8] Through nationalization, the state would control major sectors of the economy, using this control to influence the remaining private sector (light industry and agriculture). In the Russian case, Lenin stated, state control would be used to bring the accumulated benefits of capitalism (admired by Marx) to the proletariat.

The failure of the Bolshevik revolution to spark a world revolution presented additional doctrinal difficulties.[9] Was it possible to build "socialism in one country," or would it be necessary to wait for world revolution? **Leon Trotsky** argued that it was necessary to have a **permanent revolution,** since it was in fact not possible to build socialism in Russia without the assistance of other countries. **Nikolai Bukharin,** on the other hand, argued (along with Joseph Stalin) that the resource base of the Soviet Union would permit the building of socialism.

The Industrialization Debate: The Setting

The economic recovery of NEP probably reached its peak in 1926.[10] With limited net investment, it was clear that accumulation was necessary, and yet as we have emphasized, there was a continuing fear of inflationary pressures, the inflationary imbalance dilemma. If inflation was permitted, the terms of trade would shift against the peasant who would become alienated. The basis of NEP, the Smychka, would be jeopardized. At the same time, the alternative of low investment was not attractive, since it would not permit the achievement of long-run economic expansion, a basic goal.

The political context of the debate is also important. After Lenin's death in January of 1924, a bitter factional dispute split the leadership of the Communist Party. The "united opposition" of the left—led by Leon Trotsky, Grigory Zinoviev, and Lev Kamenev—opposed the NEP concessions to the peasants and to private trade and persistently criticized the government's foreign policy. The left argued in favor of super-industrialization and of taking harsh measures against the prosperous peasants.

On the other hand was the party leadership, consisting of a coalition between the Bolshevik "moderates." They included Nikolai Bukharin, the editor of *Pravda* (a recognized Marxist theoretician and popular revolutionary figure); Mikhail Tomsky, the trade union leader; Aleksei Rykov, the head of the government bureaucracy—and Joseph Stalin, the general secretary of the Communist Party. This ruling coalition favored continuing NEP, avoiding a super-industrialization drive, preserving the Smychka, and continuing efforts towards rapprochement with the capitalist world. As we will see later, events of the late 1920s would take a very different course.

The Industrialization Debate: The Alternatives

It should now be evident why the industrialization debate of the 1920s has received so much attention in the literature on the Soviet economy. Clearly, the setting was of interest and importance, major ideological differences were being discussed, and, in the end, the basic issues of economic growth and economic development would surface. The debate began in earnest in 1924, after the death of Lenin. Although the outcome would be clear when NEP was abandoned in 1928, this was not the case during the early and mid-1920s. The focus during this era was fundamentally the choice of an economic system and the strategies of industrialization that might be pursued—imbalanced growth (superindustrialization) or balanced growth that paid attention to both agriculture and industry. We turn to a discussion of the basic approaches.

Unbalanced Growth—Preobrazhensky   E. A. Preobrazhensky, the vocal spokesman of the left wing of the Bolshevik Party, took up where Marxian expanded reproduction left off, arguing that it was necessary to focus on investment goods to support rapid industrialization.[11] Thus he argued against half measures and for a "big push," a position supported by several considerations.

Preobrazhensky argued that inflationary imbalance resulted from the industrial sector's low capacity and from the loss of saving capacity, which was a result of institutional change in agriculture.[12] Before the revolution, the peasants were forced to save in real terms because they had to deliver a substantial portion of their output either to the state or the landlord. This forced saving limited their ability to purchase industrial goods. But after the revolution these requirements ended, and the peasants became accustomed to receiving industrial commodities in return for their agricultural produce. This situation created, according to Preobrazhensky, a "drastic disturbance of the equilibrium between the effective demand of the village and the marketable output of the town." Thus, the peasants' effective demand had increased substantially without a comparable increase in industrial capacity. It was this argument that led Preobrazhensky to strongly support the expansion of net investment in industry. Moreover, he argued that investment should be in industry, not agriculture, even though there might be short-term benefits from investment in agriculture.

Preobrazhensky also argued that limited investment in industry would be self-defeating, noting that Russia was technologically backward and faced a large replacement crisis. Foreign trade, he argued, would be limited due to the hostility of capitalist countries, lack of foreign currency, and a limited exportable surplus.

Preobrazhensky recognized that the benefits of investment in industry would not be sudden. In the meantime, a system of primitive socialist accumulation would be implemented—state trade monopolies would be established and would set prices, purchasing at low prices and selling at higher prices as a source of profit, which would also reduce inflationary pressures.[13] Preobrazhensky also argued that during this period the peasantry could bear the main burden of industrialization through low state purchase prices for agricultural surpluses and high prices of manufactured goods. This strategy would extract forced savings through a reduced peasant standard of living.

Preobrazhensky believed that the peasants had a high saving capacity, but that the state should decide how much would in fact be saved. The state would attempt to equate real savings (voluntary and involuntary) with the output of the capital goods sector (real investment). Thus, the state would in effect transfer resources out of the private sector and into the state sector by imposing "non-equivalent exchanges" between the city and the countryside.[14] Once the state had eliminated the private sector as a viable threat, then the socialized sector would become the source of capital accumulation.

Preobrazhensky recognized that low prices for agricultural produce might cause the peasantry to withdraw from the market. Indeed this was the major criticism voiced by Nikolai Bukharin, an advocate of balanced growth.

Balanced Growth—Bukharin   Nikolai Bukharin was the official spokesman of the right wing of the Bolshevik Party and a potent force in Soviet politics until the Stalin purges of the 1930s.[15] Before NEP, Bukharin's views were closely allied with the left wing of the party, and he even coauthored a standard textbook on communism with Preobrazhensky. The events of NEP, however, changed Bukharin's views.

Whereas Preobrazhensky felt that the victory of socialist ownership over private property had to be engineered by the state through unequal exchanges between city and countryside, Bukharin felt that this outcome would be ensured by the natural superiority of socialist ownership.[16] Thus, nonequivalent exchanges, he argued, would destroy the foundations of economic development. Bukharin argued that state industry would naturally grow more rapidly than the rest of the economy, so its share in the economy would therefore increase. Seeing the superiority of the socialist form, peasants would join producer and consumer cooperatives.

Bukharin argued that the interdependence of the two main sectors, agriculture and industry, required balanced growth. Industry required supplies from agriculture, and agricultural exports would finance the initial purchase of the sophisticated equipment required by industry from abroad. At the same time, peasants relied upon materials from industry that, if not supplied, could result in retaliation.

Bukharin recognized the need for accumulation but argued for balance through a gradual and simultaneous expansion of all sectors. This should create a favorable atmosphere for peasant agriculture, with low prices for industrial goods and high prices for agricultural produce. In this setting, he argued, the peasants would maintain their traditional frugality, creating the savings necessary to finance industry. Bukharin's advice to peasants was to "Get rich," a slogan from which Stalin carefully disassociated himself.

To resolve the incongruence between limited industrial capacity and his call for moderate investment spread evenly among sectors, Bukharin called for a series of measures to utilize capital more fully, especially measures to improve efficiency, for example multiple shifts, completion of construction projects, and more attention to appropriate factor proportions. In the end, Bukharin did admit that his policies would promote only slow progress towards socialism.

STALIN AND THE CONSOLIDATION OF POWER: 1924–1929

In a series of adroit political maneuvers, Stalin consolidated his power within four years of Lenin's death in 1924. First, he allied himself with the right wing of the Bolshevik Party (Bukharin, Tomsky, and Rykov) to purge the left opposition (led by Trotsky) from power, a phase completed by 1927. Then, Stalin turned his attention to the "right deviationist" Bukharanites, who were denounced by the Central Committee of the Communist Party in November of 1928. This occurred just one month after Stalin's adoption of an ambitious draft of the first Five Year Plan, which supported the original left-wing industrialization program.[17]

The first Five Year Plan adopted in 1928 and formally approved in 1929 staggered the imagination of even the superindustrialists. The Soviet capital stock was to double in five years, and even light industry was to expand by 70 percent. This was a radical change from Stalin's earlier position. What had caused the shift?

During the industrialization debate, Stalin was clearly aligned with the Bukharin position, emphasizing the achievements of NEP and ridiculing the left's superindustrialist proposals, which demanded that a "tribute" be paid by the peasants.[18] Although Stalin underscored the advantages of scale in farming, he envisioned a gradual and voluntary move towards collective farming. Then a number of setbacks occurred in 1927. Voluntary grain marketings fell below government targets, and the government suffered serious foreign policy setbacks. The British broke off diplomatic relations, there were troubles in Poland, and Chiang Kai-Shek turned on the Chinese Communists. These events emboldened Trotsky and the left opposition to challenge the leadership. Stalin, allied with the moderates, repulsed this attack and moved towards the adoption of the superindustrialists' program, especially the plan to use coercion to extract grain from the peasants. Increasingly, Stalin called for a superindustrialization drive, reiterated Trotsky's call for a tribute from the peasants, and began to warn of kulak sabotage of grain collections. Encouraged by Stalin's move to the left, former Trotskyites such as Preobrazhensky returned to the Party fold, only to perish later in the Stalinist purges.

The first Five Year Plan was adopted in 1928 amidst a new grain collection crisis.[19] Stalin's answer was a counteroffensive to break the peasant hold on industrialization. In the autumn of 1929, he ordered the wholesale collectivization of agriculture, forcibly establishing collective farms that would be obligated to deliver grain to the state on state-dictated terms. The resulting turmoil would be a major cost for the superindustrialization program.

REHABILITATIONS AND REEVALUATIONS: THE END OF NEP

As we will see in the next chapter, the 1930s was a decade of unbelievable change in the Soviet Union. Stalin's consolidation of power led to a complete end of discussion. Nationalization was completed, agriculture was forcibly collectivized, and national economic planning was established as a mechanism to replace the market guiding of economic activity. Economic growth was rapid, structural change significant, and the loss of life through famine, the brutality of collectivization, and the Stalinist purges great. All of these events would define the decade and would leave us with the inevitable question—was Stalin necessary?

The late Soviet leadership was not willing to dismiss out of hand the accomplishments of the Stalinist model. They emphasized the transformation of industry, although they also spoke more openly about the immense costs of Stalinism and strictly differentiated Stalinism from socialism. The rehabilitation of some major figures of the industrialization debate, such as Bukharin, Tomsky, and Rykov, focused attention on the losing side. This led to an inevitable discussion of Stalin's brutal repression and the possibility of a more gradual transformation.

The official Soviet reevaluation of the industrialization debate credited Bukharin with a better sense of the appropriate pace of transformation, especially his point that resource allocation cannot be permanently based on administrative commands. At the same time, Soviet ideology was not prepared to say that collectivization was a mistake. Rather, Stalin was viewed as pursuing unnecessary extraordinary measures that were costly, extreme, and antidemocratic. However, the modern analysis viewed Bukharin's faith in peasant agriculture as misguided and Stalin's view that private peasant agriculture was incompatible with industrialization as appropriate.

SUMMARY

In this chapter we have focused on the industrialization debate of the 1920s. This debate forms an important part of the overall story of Soviet industrialization as it unfolded in the 1930s. The literature on economic development suggests a variety of alternative mechanisms and policy frameworks that can assist in the industrialization of less developed countries, including the ideological precepts of Marxism-Leninism. Fundamentally, however, Russia was a relatively backward country that had a large agricultural sector and that wished to pursue industrialization at the end of the NEP era, which many believed had exhausted development possibilities.

In this setting, the industrialization debate brought major political figures of the early Soviet era into a major discussion of development alternatives. The focus of these debates was sectoral strategies, especially the nature of accumulation. The variants were balanced growth, or roughly equal emphasis on industry and agriculture, or the big push, superindustrialization approach, which focused on industry. The fundamental underlying issue was the role of the peasants and how the peasant sector could be harnessed to provide accumulation.

Although Stalin initially allied himself with the approach of balance, he subsequently betrayed his political opponents, consolidated power, and adopted the superindustrialist strategy. The results, though with major and long-lasting economic and social costs, became evident in the 1930s. Indeed, as the Soviet era came to an end, the discussion of Stalin and his policies once again surfaced in the Soviet Union.

Terms and Concepts

Karl Marx (1818–1883)   A philosopher and historian who developed a theory of capitalist economic development based upon class struggle and a revolutionary overthrow of capitalism, leading to socialism and ultimately communism.

producer goods   Traditionally, intermediate goods that serve as an input required for the production of some other final good, for example, steel in automobiles; often related to the "A" sector (heavy industry) in the Soviet economy.

consumer goods   Final goods used for consumption.

labor theory of value   Initially developed by David Ricardo and subsequently used by Marx; a theory that suggested that the value of a commodity (and in the long run its price) would be related directly to the amount of labor required for its production.

V. I. Lenin (1870–1924)   Vladimir Ilich Ulyanov; A revolutionary, lawyer, and political activist who played a major role in prerevolutionary activities in Russia and who ultimately became the father of the Soviet state; a major contributor to Marxism-Leninism, especially in areas such as the role of the state, the nature of revolution, and imperialism.

state capitalism   According to Lenin, the stage that follows monopoly capitalism, during which the state, intervening to bring order to the chaos of monopoly capitalists fighting amongst one another, brings order to capitalism.

Leon Trotsky (1879–1940)   A major figure in the Bolshevik Party (after 1917); as a member of the Politburo, Trotsky was a major organizer of the Red Army and ultimately a major challenger to Stalin's power; Trotsky was assassinated by Soviet agents in Mexico in 1940.

permanent revolution   The concept, originating from Marx and developed by Trotsky, suggesting that until the ultimate stage of communism is reached, there will be a continuing series of revolutions, effectively permanent revolution.

Nikolai Bukharin (1888–1938)   An important Marxist theoretician and member of the Politburo; the dominant spokesperson of the right wing of the Bolshevik Party favoring the continuation of NEP; he was eliminated after a show trial in Moscow.

Selected Bibliography

Bukharin, N. *The Politics and Economics of the Transition Period*, K. Tarbuck, ed. (London: Routledge & Kegan Paul, 1979).

Cohen, S. F. *Bukharin and the Bolshevik Revolution* (New York: Knopf, 1973).

Day, R. *Leon Trotsky and the Politics of Economic Isolation* (Cambridge: Cambridge University Press, 1973.

Dobb, M. *Soviet Economic Development Since 1917* 5e (London: Routledge & Kegan Paul, 1960).

Engels, F. *Anti-Duhring* (Moscow: Progress Publishers, 1975).

Erlich, A. "Stalin's Views on Economic Development," in E. Simmons, ed., *Continuity and Change in Russian and Soviet Thought* (Cambridge, MA: Harvard University Press, 1955.

———. *The Soviet Industrialization Debate, 1924–1928* (Cambridge, MA: Harvard University Press, 1960).

Jasny, N. *Soviet Economists of the Twenties: Names to be Remembered* (Cambridge: Cambridge University Press, 1972).

Lenin, V. I. *Imperialism, The Highest State of Capitalism* (Moscow: Progress Publishers, 1970).

Lewin, M. *Russian Peasants and Soviet Power* (London: Allen & Unwin, 1968).

Marx, K. *Critique of the Gotha Program* (Moscow: Progress Publishers, 1971).

Meyer, Alfred G. *Leninism* (New York: Praeger, 1963).

Millar, J. R. "A Note on Primitive Accumulation in Marx and Preobrazhensky," *Soviet Studies* vol. 30, no. 3 (July 1978), 384–93.

Nove, A. "A Note on Trotsky and the 'Left Opposition,' 1929–31," *Soviet Studies* vol. 29, no. 4 (October 1977), 576–89.

——— . *An Economic History of the USSR* (London: Penguin, 1969).

Reiman, M. *Die Geburt des Stalinismus* [The birth of Stalinism] (Frankfurt/Main: EVA, 1979).

Sah, R. K., and J. E. Stiglitz. "The Economics of Price Scissors," *American Economic Review* vol. 74, no. 1 (March 1984), 125–38.

Spulber, N., ed. *Foundations of Soviet Strategy for Economic Growth* (Bloomington: Indiana University Press, 1964).

——— . *Soviet Strategy for Economic Growth* (Bloomington: Indiana University Press, 1964).

Sweezy, P. M. *The Theory of Capitalist Development* (New York: Modern Reader Paperbacks, 1968).

Tucker, R. C., ed. *The Lenin Anthology* (New York: Norton, 1975).

Notes

1. Our discussion of the Soviet industrialization debate draws on the following sources: A. Erlich, *The Soviet Industrialization Debate, 1924–1928* (Cambridge, MA: Harvard University Press, 1960); N. Spulber, *Soviet Strategy for Economic Growth* (Bloomington: Indiana University Press, 1964); N. Spulber, ed., *Foundations for Soviet Strategy of Economic Growth* (Bloomington: Indiana University Press, 1964); A. Erlich, "Stalin's Views on Economic Development," in E. Simmons, ed., *Continuity and Change in Russian and Soviet Thought* (Cambridge, MA: Harvard University Press, 1955), 81–99; M. Lewin, *Russian Peasants and Soviet Power* (London: Allen & Unwin, 1968); S. F. Cohen, *Bukharin and the Bolshevik Revolution* (New York: Knopf, 1973); M. Reiman, *Die Geburt des Stalinismus* [The birth of Stalinism] (Frankfurt/Main: EVA, 1979); A. Nove, "A Note on Trotsky and the 'Left Opposition,' 1929–1931," *Soviet Studies* vol. 29, no. 4 (October 1977), 576–89; J. R. Millar, "A Note on Primitive Accumulation in Marx and Preobrazhensky," *Soviet Studies* vol. 30, no. 3 (July 1978), 384–93; R. Day, "Preobrazhensky and the Theory of the Transition Period," *Soviet Studies* vol. 27, no. 2 (April 1975), 196–219.

2. The Soviet era is a classic example of the pursuit of rapid industrialization using a particular set of organizational arrangements. For a discussion of the development perspective, see for example E. W. Nafziger, *The Economics of Developing Countries* 3e (Englewood Cliffs, NJ: Prentice Hall, 1997); for a systems perspective, see for example P. R. Gregory and R. C. Stuart, *Comparative Economic Systems* 5e (Boston: Houghton Mifflin, 1995).

3. The Marxian view is important here for three major reasons. First, Marxism-Leninism is a different and major view of the manner in which history unfolds through time. Second, whether loyally adhered to or not, it provided the major conceptual underpinning of the

Soviet era. Third, a knowledge of basic Marxian concepts and terms is essential for understanding the Soviet economy.

4. Our discussion is based on P. M. Sweezy, *The Theory of Capitalist Development* (New York: Modern Reader Paperbacks, 1968), chaps. 5 and 10; R. Day, "Preobrazhensky and the Theory of the Transition Period," 196–99; F. Engels, *Anti-Duhring* (Moscow: Progress Publishers, 1975).

5. S. Malle, *The Economic Organization of War Communism, 1918–1921* (Cambridge: Cambridge University Press, 1985), ch. 6, and K. Marx, *Critique of the Gotha Program* (Moscow: Progress Publishers, 1975), 9–21.

6. Sweezy, *The Theory of Capitalist Development*, 75–95 and 162–69.

7. This discussion of primitive capitalist accumulation is based on Millar, "A Note on Primitive Capitalist Accumulation," 384–92.

8. For a discussion of Lenin's revision of Marx in light of the Russian experience, see P. R. Gregory and R. C. Stuart, *Comparative Economic Systems*, ch. 4.

9. In addition to references already cited, see also R. R. Buchanan, "Lenin and Bukharin on the Transition from Capitalism to Socialism: The Meshchersky Controversy, 1918," *Soviet Studies* vol. 28, no. 1 (January 1976), 66–82. For a Soviet viewpoint, see V. I. Bovykin, *Formirovanie finansovogo kapitala v Rossii* [Formation of financial capital in Russia] (Moscow: Nauka, 1984).

10. P. R. Gregory, *Russian National Income, 1885–1913* (Cambridge: Cambridge University Press, 1982), 185–86.

11. For a detailed discussion of this controversy, see R. Day, *Leon Trotsky and the Politics of Isolation* (Cambridge: Cambridge University Press, 1973).

12. The views of Preobrazhensky can be found in his *Novaia ekonomika* [The new economics]. See E. A. Preobrazhensky, *The New Economics*, translated by B. Pierce (Oxford: Oxford University Press, 1964).

13. For further examination of the Preobrazhensky model, see R. K. Sah and J. E. Stiglitz, "The Economics of Price Scissors," *American Economic Review* vol. 74, no. 1 (March 1984), 125–38. In this analysis, the authors conclude that the rate of accumulation can be raised by imposing a price squeeze on peasants, but that it would not be possible to have such a burden borne exclusively by the peasants.

14. Quoted in Erlich, *The Soviet Industrialization Debate*, 56–57.

15. Stalin's solution to the dilemma—collectivization of the peasantry, which eliminated the peasant's freedom to dispose of the surplus—did not occur to Preobrazhensky. Several years after the collectivization decision, Preobrazhensky declared in a speech: "Collectivization—this is the crux of the matter! Did I have this prognosis of the collectivization? I did not." Quoted in Erlich, *The Soviet Industrialization Debate*, 177. Erlich adds to this "He [Preobrazhensky] was careful not to add that neither did Stalin at the time when the industrialization debate was in full swing. And he was wise not to point out that the decision to collectivize hinged not on superior intellectual perspicacity but on the incomparably higher degree of resolve to crush the opponent . . ."

16. Cohen, *Bukharin and the Bolshevik Revolution*.

17. Day, *Leon Trotsky and the Politics of Isolation*, ch. 7.

18. Ibid., 166. It was not until the Stalin purges of the late 1930s that this process was complete. Preobrazhensky, Shanin, and Bukharin all lost their lives during the purges.

19. Scholars have questioned the existence of a grain crisis. We return to this issue in the following chapter as we discuss the collectivization of agriculture.

CHAPTER 5

Creating the Administrative Command Economy: 1928–1940

The administrative command economy of the Soviet Union did not arise out of a vacuum, and yet there were no simple instructions for Soviet leaders to follow. Marxism-Leninism provided an ideological underpinning for reforming capitalism in the socialist mold, and early discussions about balance in the national economy provided a conceptual basis for directing economic activity. Moreover, the events of the 1920s, especially the industrialization debate laid bare the problems to be faced and alternative approaches. Nonetheless, in spite of experimentation with varying forms of rural organization in the 1920s, few were prepared for the speed and the vigor with which Stalin approached the "great experiment" of planned socialism.

The decade after 1928 is, from a development perspective, one of the momentous eras of recent history. Not only did Stalin implement fundamental and far-reaching organizational and policy changes; he did so with tragic brutality, fundamentally altering the nature of the Soviet economy in a very short span of years. Both the mechanisms and results of resource allocation changed fundamentally, creating an economic system that changed remarkably little until its collapse in the late 1980s. The institutions, practices, and policies of the Soviet era would have a major impact upon the process of transition in the 1990s.

In this chapter we examine this decade, especially the nature and the magnitude of the transformation. We begin with a brief examination of the pace of nationalization, followed by a discussion of national economic planning, collectivization, and finally assessment of the results: the major structural transformation of the Soviet economy in the 1930s.

THE TRANSFORMATION OF THE SOVIET ECONOMY: NATIONALIZATION

After the Bolshevik revolution of 1917, the state conducted widespread nationalization. Although this nationalization was not fully sustained during the NEP era of the 1920s, nevertheless the role of the state remained dominant, especially in industry. Clearly, the changes envisioned after 1928 would require a new role for the state, especially in nationalization. New property rights would not only facilitate state control over the means of production but also would insure that the state would be a direct claimant to the output of the economy, thus greatly strengthening the state's role in dictating the directions of resource allocation in the Soviet economy. The pace of nationalization is evident from Table 5.1.

Clearly the private sector was dominant in agriculture through the 1920s. Yet by the mid- to late 1930s, nationalization was virtually complete in all of the major sectors of the economy, including agriculture. Even with some possible misgivings about economic measurement during the 1930s, the message of increasing state control is clear, though how this control would be exercised would remain to be developed in the system of national economic planning.

TRANSFORMATION OF THE SOVIET ECONOMY: NATIONAL ECONOMIC PLANNING

The Organizational Arrangements of Planning

It had become clear from the experiences of War Communism that, if markets are to be subordinated or eliminated, some alternative mechanism for resource allocation must be found.[1] While the concept of **balance** received considerable attention in the 1920s, along with preliminary work on what would later be known as **input-output analysis,** even initial experiments with state-directed economic activity (for example the **GOELRO** Plan), did not provide a clear picture of how economic activity would in fact be planned. Two schools of thought emerged.

The first school, advocated by the **geneticists** (for example, N. D. Kondratiev, V. A. Bazarov, and V. G. Groman), suggested that economic planning should be dictated by consumer demand, which in turn would indicate to planners the directions of economic activity. This was, in a sense, a continuation of NEP and proposed what we now term **indicative planning.**

Table 5.1

SHARE OF THE STATE SECTOR IN THE SOVIET ECONOMY, 1924–1937

	1924	1928	1937
Capital			
Without cattle	58.9	65.7	99.6
Including cattle	35.0	35.1	99.0
In national income	35.0	44.0	99.1
In industrial output	76.3	82.4	99.8
In gross agricultural output	1.5	3.3	98.5
In retail trade	47.3	76.4	100

Source: Goskomstat, *Narodnoe khoziaistvo SSSR za 70 let* [The national economy of the USSR over 70 years] (Moscow: Finansy i statistika, 1987), 42.

The second, or **teleological,** approach, advocated by well-known economists such as S. Strumilin, G. L. Pyatakov, V. V. Kuibyshev, and P. A. Fel'dman, asserted that social engineers should formulate the plan to dictate the directions of economic activity, including industrial production, sectoral investment patterns, and the like. As stated by one teleologist, to accept the direction of the market would mean accepting the "genetic inheritance" of 300 years of tsarism.[2] Clearly this view dominated, and as the decade came to an end, the geneticists came to be accused of counterrevolution and right-wing Menshevism.

Although many agencies dealt with various aspects of planning in the 1920s and thereafter, the agency concerned exclusively and explicitly with planning was **Gosplan,** directed by decree in 1922 to concern itself with "the preparation not only of a long-range plan but also of an operational plan for the current year." Much of the early recognition of Gosplan's importance derived from its annual preparation of preliminary plan targets, or **control figures,** begun in 1925–26. This early experience established the principle that economic policy should be guided on an annual basis, using control figures prepared by Gosplan.

While Gosplan's role in the development of planning arrangements was growing in the late 1920s, it had little to do with the operational details of the economy, which were handled by the VSNKh's planning staff and its sub-departments, the Glavki. Annual plans, including production and financial targets, known as promfinplans, were drawn up on a sector-by-sector basis, with little attention given to the overall result. Gosplan complained that it received the promfinplans too late to coordinate them with the aggregate control figures, complaints that led to an eventual merger of the promfinplans with the overall control figures under Gosplan's direction. By 1926–27, the promfinplan became dependent on the control figures.

During this period the basic machinery for physical planning, the system of **material balances,** was being established. Initially, balances were created for critical industrial commodities: iron and steel in 1925, energy and fuel consumption in 1927, and building materials in 1928.[3] VSNKh and Gosplan coordinated these balances through the promfinplan and control figure system.

The plan era began in 1928 with the First Five Year Plan, at which time the basic principles of Soviet planning emerged.[4] First, Gosplan was to be the central coordinating body to which all other planning bodies were to submit their proposals. Second, the control figures would provide the general direction for the economy. Third, the actual detailed operational plans for enterprises (the promfinplans) were to conform to the control figures. Fourth, materials were to be allocated through the system of balances, which would elaborate the sources and uses of basic industrial materials. Fifth, the long-term planning horizon was set at five years, the average period required for the completion of investment projects.

As one might imagine, the functions of VSNKh became increasingly complex and confused. As a result, Gosplan gained full planning authority in 1932, with the development of the ministerial system. VSNKh was in effect dissolved as a planning agency; its main departments, the Glavki, became ministries with direct power to plan and administer the economic activities of the enterprises under their jurisdiction. VSNKh itself became three separate ministries (Commissariats)—heavy industry, light industry, and woodworking.

Involved in the planning process and making actual distributions of industrial materials, the ministries became the operational links between Gosplan and the enterprises. Gosplan prepared the national economic plan. It was the responsibility of the ministries to execute it.

Central Management Versus Central Planning

From a contemporary theoretical perspective, national economic planning can be viewed as a process for directing economic activity through appropriate organizational arrangements based upon a set of sophisticated plan mechanisms, the latter designed to achieve specified objectives under a variety of resource and other constraints. In fact, planning in the Soviet Union during the early years involved much less.

Gosplan assumed responsibility for drawing up Five Year Plans in 1925, based upon the notion that major construction projects had a five-year gestation period.[5] Typically, two variants were specified, a maximum variant based upon bold assumptions and a more cautious variant based upon more modest assumptions. The maximal variant of the First Five Year Plan (1928–33), which received a great deal of attention, reflected the teleological thinking of Stalin and called for industrialization at a maximum pace. In fact, the plan was so grandiose that subsequent revisions were essential, making the planning process much more erratic than commonly thought (Table 5.2).

Table 5.2

SOVIET PERCENTAGE PLAN FULFILLMENT IN THE 1930s

Objective	First Five Year Plan (1928–32)	Second Five Year Plan (1933–37)
National income		
Official estimate	92	96
Western estimate	70	67
Industrial output		
Official estimate	101	103
Western estimate	60–70	76–93
Producer goods		
Official estimate	128	121
Western estimate	72	97
Consumer goods		
Official estimate	81	85
Western estimate	46	68
Agricultural production		
Official estimate	58	63–67
Western estimate	50–52	66–78
Labor productivity		
Official estimate	65	–
Western estimate	36–42	86
Retail trade		
Western estimate	39	54

Sources: N. Jasny, *Essays on the Soviet Economy* (New York: Praeger, 1962), 266; E. Zaleski, *Stalinist Planning for Economic Growth, 1933–1952* (Chapel Hill: University of North Carolina Press, 1980), 503; A. Nove, *An Economic History of the USSR* (London: Penguin, 1969), 353.

The evidence in Table 5.2 suggests considerable variability in plan fulfillment by sector. Indeed, planning in this era was, in large part, political and ideological. As Eugene Zaleski noted, the Five Year Plan represented "a vision of growth, itself at the service of development strategy."[6] Beyond the details of plan formulation and the development of appropriate organizational arrangements, other elements of planning required increasing attention. For example, centralized price setting, introduced during the early plan era, proved to be a complicated task with significant long-range implications.[7] Price setting was increasingly directed towards achieving state needs rather than reflecting relative scarcities. Money played a decreasing role in the economy, and after a while foreign trade was arranged through a state monopoly that effectively shielded internal prices from world market forces.

Throughout the 1930s, the number of bodies concerned directly or indirectly with price formation expanded significantly. During the same period, there was a measure of consolidation with VSNKh and later with the ministries that became the main price-setting bodies.[8] Financial controls were tightened during this early plan period. Credit operations were centralized in the state bank **(Gosbank),** and commercial credits between enterprises were forbidden. Direct grants from the state budget became the main source of investment finance, as state enterprises were subordinated to the state budgetary system through which both expenditures and revenues had to flow.

Arrangements of the early plan era were chaotic in many dimensions. Clearly the looser controls of the 1920s were replaced by significant and substantial state control over the direction of economic activity. The mechanisms used to control that activity had to be established quickly, without a blueprint. The overriding goal was state direction of economic activity, in some form or another. Therefore, it is inappropriate to compare the result directly to elegant theoretical models of economic planning. But there is much more to be said before we can make a judgment on how well Soviet planning worked.

Planning and the Communist Party

Throughout this book, we focus on the economic rather than the political arrangements of the Soviet Union. This separation is artificial, however, because the Communist Party was a powerful mechanism, influencing all activities, especially economic activities, in the Soviet Union.

The power of the party became evident in the late 1920s and especially the 1930s, when party control over economic activity was solidified. Major economic powers resided in the Politburo under Stalin's direction. The Central Committee of the Party applied direct control to major construction and industrial projects. Stalin immersed himself in directing economic activity, even dealing with minor details. The party cadres department handled nominations for **Nomenklatura** positions to insure that the economy would be administered by "reliable" personnel. Indeed, the Party became and would remain, throughout the Soviet era, the "personnel arm" of the system through its use of the Nomenklatura system.

At all levels, the Party served as a general troubleshooter to handle bottlenecks. Indeed, the Party would play an important role at the enterprise level as well as exercising its critical influence at upper levels in the hierarchy. Finally, a major function of the Party was mass mobilization, to create enthusiasm for fulfilling the plan and building a modern industrial economy. In the 1930s, building enthusiasm was probably largely successful since ordinary people were generally supportive of the idea of building a new socialist society.

THE TRANSFORMATION OF THE SOVIET ECONOMY: COLLECTIVIZATION

The Collectivization Decision[9]

Collectivization involved the forcible establishment of collective farms (the **kolkhoz**) into the Soviet countryside, a process Stalin justified following the events of the grain procurement crisis of 1928.[10] In May of 1928, Stalin put forward data to suggest that 1926–27 grain output was only slightly below the level achieved in 1913, but that the market share of grain had declined substantially.[11] According to Stalin, the gross output of grain declined slightly between 1913 and 1926–27, but the marketed share declined by roughly 50 percent.[12] Even more telling to Stalin was the fact that while grain output and marketings by the kulaks fell sharply (both had declined to less than one-third of prewar levels), output and marketings of the poor and middle peasants had expanded. For Stalin, this provided enough evidence to move against the kulaks, who, in the heat of the collectivization campaign, became any peasant who resisted collectivization.

Did the evidence support the allegations made by Stalin? In Table 5.3 we present data for Soviet agricultural production. It is evident that by 1928, agricultural production had recovered to the 1913 level. In both variants shown in Table 5.3, grain output was still below 1913 levels. However, the production of all other agricultural products (with the exception of sugar) had exceeded 1913 levels. The move against the kulaks was political and ideological, since the bulk of the grain supplies was in the hands of the middle peasants. Indeed, in the turmoil that followed the onset of collectivization, it became necessary to blur the distinction between the kulaks and the middle peasants.

In addition to ideological issues, Jerzy Karcz has pointed out that Stalin's grain information was "...completely misleading and presents an exceedingly distorted picture of the relation between 1913 and 1926–1927 grain marketings."[13] According to Karcz, these data, when appropriately reconstructed as grain balances for these years, shows that gross grain output had, by 1928, all but recovered to prewar levels. This suggests that the problem is the definition of *marketings*. In Stalin's data, gross marketings for 1913 were compared to net marketings for 1926–27.

Another major factor, according to Karcz, was the role of government policy in causing the grain procurement "crisis." Indeed, in the years preceding collectivization, net grain marketings did decline because the state lowered procurement prices, which encouraged peasants to withhold grain and/or shift production capacity to other products.[14] Thus, while grain marketings were declining, the marketing of other products was increasing. The evidence in Table 5.3 (p. 80) does show that the production levels of other farm products recovered more rapidly than grain.

The immediate justification for collectivization may have been based upon inappropriate policies and statistics.[15] Nonetheless, the state viewed the problem as real.

Table 5.3

SOVIET AGRICULTURAL PRODUCTION, 1913–1938*

Year	Gross agricultural production	Grain variants high	** low	Cotton
1913	96	92.7	79	0.5
1924	–	51.4	44	NA
1925	–	72.5	62	0.6
1926	–	76.6	66	0.6
1927	–	71.7	62	0.7
1928	100	73.3	63	0.8
1929	93	71.7	62	0.9
1930	88	78.0	67	1.1
1931	84	68.0	62	1.3
1932	76	68.0	62	1.3
1933	82	74.0	68	1.3
1934	86	75.0	68	1.2
1935	99	80.0	75	1.7
1936	93	66.0	60	2.4
1937	116	100.0	95	2.6
1938	107	76.0	70	2.6

(Continued on facing page)

Despite being a traditional grain exporter, the Soviet Union found itself having to import grain. It was events like this that provided Stalin with the impetus to unleash a campaign to increase state collections (**zagotovki**) through the use of force in the countryside.

The Collectivization Process

It was not until mid-1929 that central control over existing cooperatives was substantially strengthened and the system of grain procurements changed—in short, the beginning of mass collectivization. By the latter part of 1929, the Party organized an all-out drive, largely directed against the kulaks and the middle peasants. The Party sent out 25,000 representatives (police, industrial workers, and Party loyalists) to oversee the process. The speed of collectivization was rapid, as Table 5.4 (p. 82) suggests. Although people maintained the fiction that collectivization was a spontaneous action on the part of the peasantry, resisted only by "kulak saboteurs,"

Sugar	Potatoes	Meat	Milk	Eggs	Livestock
10.8	29.9	4.0	25.1	10.2	87
3.5	35.3	3.3	26.3	NA	–
9.1	38.4	3.7	28.2	9.6	–
6.4	42.8	4.1	30.5	10.5	–
10.4	42.5	4.3	30.6	10.5	–
10.1	45.2	4.9	31.0	10.8	100
6.3	45.1	5.8	29.8	10.1	87
14.0	44.6	4.3	27.0	8.0	65
12.1	40.6	3.9	23.4	6.7	57
6.6	37.2	2.8	20.6	4.4	48
9.0	44.0	2.3	19.2	3.5	51
11.4	44.2	2.0	20.8	4.2	52
16.2	53.8	2.3	21.4	5.8	74
16.8	44.7	3.7	23.5	7.4	76
21.9	58.8	3.0	26.1	8.2	83
16.7	10.5	100	29.0	10.5	100

*All data are million tons, except eggs, which are billion tons, and agricultural production and livestock production, which are constant price indexes (1928 = 100).

**The grain variants are based on differing views regarding the comparability of the pre- and postcollectivization series. The high variant has been adjusted; the low variant has not been adjusted.

Source: S. G. Wheatcroft, "A Reevaluation of Soviet Agricultural Production in the 1920s and 1930s," in R. C. Stuart, ed., *The Soviet Rural Economy* (Totowa, NJ: Roman & Allanheld, 1984), 11, 42–3, 49.

there can be little doubt that it was a policy imposed on an unwilling peasantry by brute force. Officials used vague definitions of what constituted a kulak to arrest and deport peasants who resisted collectivization. The Militia and the secret police (the **GPU**), along with the armed Party faithful, were sent to the countryside to force the peasants into the collective farms. Although Stalin, in a famous speech in March of 1930, warned against excesses, blaming overenthusiastic local Party leaders, the pace of collectivization was rapid and was largely completed by the mid-1930s (Table 5.4). This "dekulakization" drive resulted in the flight, deportation, and execution of millions of peasants. Arrests provided the initial manpower for a vast army of penal labor. According to one estimate, 3.5 million peasants became a part of the

Table 5.4

EXPANSION OF THE COLLECTIVE FARM SECTOR, 1918–1938 (SELECTED YEARS)

Year	Collective farms (1000)	Households in collectives (1000)	Peasant households collectivized (%)
1918	1.6	16.4	0.1
1928	33.3	416.7	1.7
1929	57.0	1,007.7	3.9
1930	85.9	5,998.1	23.6
1931	211.1	12,033.2	52.7
1932	211.1	14,918.7	61.5
1935	245.4	17,334.9	83.2
1938	242.4	18,847.6	93.5

Source: L. Volin, *A Century of Russian Agriculture* (Cambridge, MA: Harvard University Press, 1970), 211.

gulag penal labor force, 3.5 million peasants were resettled, and another 3.5 million died during collectivization.[16]

Throughout collectivization, the Party was a dominant force and was greatly strengthened in 1933, when the political departments *(politotdely)* were established in the **machine tractor stations (the MTS)**.[17] The purpose of the MTS was to supply machinery and equipment to the collectives in return for payment in kind to the state. The stations would play a significant role in the management of the collective farms, along with the collective farm heads, who were largely selected from the ranks of reliable Party members. By the middle of 1930, the Party played a major role in the economic affairs of the countryside, a role as important as that played by the Party in the urban areas. The establishment of Soviet power in agriculture was surely one of Stalin's prized objectives.

The Impact of Collectivization

The most immediate impact of collectivization was a decline in output between 1929 and 1933, evident from the output series presented in Table 5.3 (pp. 80–81). The drop was especially serious in the livestock sector. Although grain output declined in the initial years of collectivization, both gross and net marketings of grain increased between 1929 and 1933, in part due to the sharp decline in the number of cattle for whom fodder would have otherwise been necessary.[18] These factors were important contributors to the famine that peaked in 1932–33.

The loss of lives, both from collectivization per se and from the related famine, especially severe in grain producing regions, was substantial, although the exact

Table 5.5

NUMBERS OF LIVESTOCK IN THE SOVIET UNION, 1928–1935*

Year	All cattle	Cows	Pigs	Sheep	Goats	Horses
1928**	60.1	29.3	22.0	97.3	9.7	32.1
1929	58.2	29.2	19.4	97.4	9.7	32.6
1930	50.6	28.5	14.2	85.5	7.8	31.0
1931	42.5	24.5	11.7	62.5	5.6	27.0
1932	38.3	22.3	10.9	43.8	3.8	21.7
1933	33.5	19.4	9.9	34.0	3.3	17.3
1934	33.5	19.0	11.5	32.9	3.6	15.4
1935	38.9	19.0	17.1	46.4	4.4	14.9

*millions of head

**borders of the Soviet Union as of 1939

Source: E. Strauss, *Soviet Agriculture in Perspective* (London: Allen & Unwin, 1969), 307.

numbers of deaths remain controversial. Destruction of the agricultural capital stock was another immediate outcome of collectivization. In addition to the destruction of buildings, the number of livestock declined sharply (see Table 5.5) as peasants resisted the order to deliver their animals to the newly formed collectives. Finally, the impact of collectivization upon incomes of the farm population was predictable—they fell sharply perhaps to as little as one half of the levels before collectivization (1928).[19]

ASSESSING COLLECTIVIZATION

Even in the post-Soviet era, the collectivization of agriculture remains the most controversial Soviet economic policy promulgated on the eve of the industrialization drive. Collectivization had political goals, namely a means to control the rural population, and economic goals, specifically a mechanism to extract savings from the rural population on terms dictated by the state. Stalin clearly viewed NEP as a transitional system. That status, along with his perceptions of a counterrevolutionary threat and an unreliable (private) supplier of agricultural products, dictated action. Indeed, contemporary analysts often view collectivization as having been implemented inappropriately but as a necessary solution to the problems of NEP agriculture and the need for large scale agriculture.[20]

Although NEP agriculture has been loosely described as private agriculture, Russian peasants had reverted to the repartitional commune after the land decree of 1917. The net result was farms generally smaller than farms before the revolution. Stalin did achieve collectivization's political objective, namely the imposition of Soviet power in the countryside. However, the economic goals of collectivization were not achieved and deserve additional comment.

The literature on economic development has considered the issue of whether collectivization could transform agriculture to support industrialization.[21] Typically, in less developed nations where agriculture is a dominant (if backward) sector, it is called upon to support industrialization. This is a major strand of thinking in the industrialization debates. Thus, as factor proportions change in agriculture (capital replaces labor), labor is freed for use in the growing industrial sector. Also, increasing agricultural productivity through the introduction of modern farming methods provides "agricultural surpluses" to sustain the urban population and to generate export earnings for machinery and equipment imports for all sectors. Did collectivization contribute to Soviet agriculture's ability to support industrial growth?

Collectivization clearly facilitated the shift of vast amounts of manpower from agriculture to industry, though people were "pushed" out of agriculture rather than being "pulled" by a more traditional system of differential incentives. Between 1926 and 1939, the Soviet urban population increased from 26.3 to 56.1 million, a significant portion of which was due to rural-to-urban migration.[22] This fact, along with increasing rates of labor-force participation, resulted in an annual rate of growth of the nonagricultural labor force of 8.7 percent between 1928 and 1937, while the agricultural labor force declined at an annual rate of 2.5 percent during the same period.

The transformation of the Soviet labor force would not have proceeded as quickly without collectivization. Rural dwellers fled the collective farms for the urban areas to escape punishment and deportation and also because of the deteriorating economic conditions in the countryside. A more telling issue is whether such drastic policy shifts were really necessary. In the past, no industrializing economy appears to have had trouble attracting labor from agriculture, so one might well ask why the Soviet Union would have been different.

Did Soviet agriculture provide agricultural surpluses for urban consumption, industrial raw materials, and export? Ironically, the collective farm would seem to have been ideally suited for this function, and yet the issue is one of major controversy. On the kolkhoz, labor was not paid a contractual wage but by the **labor day (trudoden')** system. In effect, collective farmers were paid out of what was left over after compulsory deliveries and other payments. Collective-farm labor was in fact a residual claimant, and the state was a prior claimant through the use of compulsory deliveries at low fixed prices. Grain procurements did increase more rapidly than grain output, from a low of roughly 16 percent of output in 1929 to a high of roughly 43 percent of output in 1938 (see Figure 5.1). The issue of the collective farm's contribution to industrialization is, however, more complicated than just increases in deliveries.

Figure 5.1* Soviet Grain Production and Procurement**

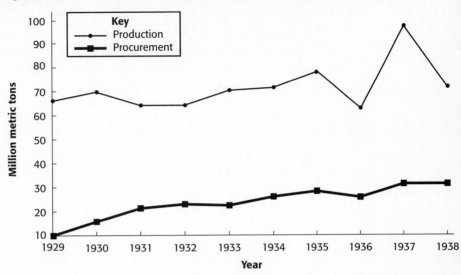

*These data should be interpreted as representing general trends due to important and controversial issues of definition and measurement.

**Grain production is a simple average of the high and low variants presented in Table 5.1.

Source: Grain production data from S. G. Wheatcroft, "A Reevaluation of Soviet Agricultural Production in the 1920s and 1930s," in R. C. Stuart, ed., *The Soviet Rural Economy* (Totowa, NJ: Rowman & Allenheld, 1984), 42–3; procurement data 1929–1932 from R. W. Davies, *The Industrialization of Soviet Russia* (Cambridge, MA: Harvard University Press, 1980), 1, table 8; procurement data for 1932 from J. Karcz, "Khrushchev's Agricultural Policies," in M. Bornstein and D. F. Fusfeld, eds., *The Soviet Economy: A Book of Readings* 3e (Homewood, IL: Irwin, 1970), 44; procurement data for 1933–1938 from E. Zaleski, *Stalinist Planning for Economic Growth, 1932–1952* (Chapel Hill: University of North Carolina Press, 1980), statistical appendix.

Scholars have pointed out that increases in gross marketings could be accounted for simply by the reduced needs of a declining cattle sector. Nevertheless, the sharp decline in living standards during this period and the state success with exporting grain may be important evidence on the issue of extracting surpluses.

Between 1929 and 1931, Soviet imports increased over 60 percent in volume, despite the worsening terms of trade due to collapsing world agricultural markets. During the same period, Soviet exports (by volume) increased by roughly 50 percent, spearheaded by a growing share of agricultural products in Soviet exports. Thus, agricultural exports were used to finance the importation of machinery and ferrous metals. These categories increased from one-third of Soviet imports in 1928 to almost three-quarters by the end of the First Five Year Plan. Clearly, a combination of collectivization and state monopoly in foreign trade put the state in control, even though the costs in terms of living standards and human life were significant. But, was it collectivization that, in effect, provided the surplus from which industrial expansion resulted?

There is a considerable body of research that looks at these issues in a different way. If we apply the traditional argument—that is, that a major reason for collectivization was the extraction of a "surplus"—then the evidence on marketings, along with the organizational arrangements of the kolkhoz and the labor day system of payment, would seem to suggest that a surplus was in fact extracted and was used to finance industrialization. However, there are a variety of definitions of the concept of a "surplus." If one defines surplus as the net difference between product inflows and outflows of agriculture as a sector, collectivization did not change the magnitude of the surplus, even under varying assumptions about critical issues such as prices used for the aggregation of the sectoral flows.[23] In effect, during collectivization the loss of draft animal power required that massive industrial resources be directed towards farm machinery, a contribution back to agriculture. The value of the industrial output sent to agriculture exceeded the value of agricultural surpluses sent to the city. This type of evidence has cast a great deal of doubt upon the economic basis of collectivization.

It is quite clear that NEP agriculture would have had to undergo significant changes to move towards a more modern agriculture. However, collectivization inflicted major costs upon the Soviet people and, indeed, upon the long-term health of Soviet agriculture. Moreover, viewed simply as a cruel but useful device to extract a surplus to finance industrialization, collectivization was not successful. Thus, as is typically the case, the dwellers of both the rural and the urban sectors paid a price for industrialization in terms of significantly reduced standards of living.

THE SOVIET ECONOMY IN THE 1930S

We have now examined the three major changes—nationalization, collectivization, and planning—introduced by Stalin after 1928. These changes defined the administrative command economy and fundamentally changed the nature of resource allocation in the Soviet Union, a fact of fundamental importance in the transition era of the 1990s. These changes were immediate and were fully entrenched by the latter part of the 1930s. Indeed, the outcome of the industrialization debate of the 1920s and the Stalinist response was clear.

How did these major changes affect resource allocation in the Soviet Union? Recall that our examination of the prerevolutionary Russian economy was cast in terms of the basic patterns of industrialization, examined through the framework of modern economic growth. We return to this framework and in Table 5.6 present a picture of the remarkable structural changes in the Soviet economy of the 1930s.

The evidence presented in Table 5.6 illustrates the major structural transformations in the Soviet economy, including structural biases resulting from both

Table 5.6

THE SOVIET ECONOMY IN THE 1930s: STRUCTURAL CHANGES

	1928	1933	1937	1940
A. Changes in Manufacturing				
1. Heavy manufacturing ÷ overall manufacturing				
net product share (1928 prices)	31	51	63	–
labor force share	28	43	–	–
2. Light manufacturing ÷ overall manufacturing				
net product share (1928 prices)	68	47	36	–
labor force share	71	56	–	–
B. Changes in Sectoral Shares				
1. Share in net national product (1937 prices)				
agriculture	49	–	31	29
industry	28	–	45	45
services	23	–	24	26
2. Share in labor force				
agriculture	71	–	–	51
industry	18	–	–	29
services	12	–	–	20
C. GNP by End Use (1937 prices)				
1. Household consumption ÷ GNP	80	–	53	49
annual growth rate (1928–37) (%)			0.8	
2. Communal services ÷ GNP	5	–	11	10
annual growth rate (1928–37) (%)			15.7	
3. Government admin and defense ÷ GNP	3	–	26	21
annual growth rate (1928–37) (%)			15.6	
4. Gross capital investment ÷ GNP	13	–	26	19
annual growth rate (1928–37) (%)			14.4	

Sources: *A:* P. R. Gregory, *Socialist and Non-Socialist Industrialization Patterns* (New York: Praeger, 1970), 28–9, 36; heavy manufacturing is defined according to the International System of Industrial Classification as ISIC 30–38; light manufacturing is defined as ISIC 20–29. *B:* S. Kuznets, "A Comparative Appraisal," in A. Bergson and S. Kuznets, eds., *Economic Trends in the Soviet Union* (Cambridge, MA: Harvard University Press, 1963), 342–60; *C:* A. Bergson, *Real Soviet National Income and Product Since 1928* (Cambridge, MA: Harvard University Press, 1961), 217, 237.

system and policy that would remain evident in the early 1990s. Indeed, these changes became hallmarks of the administrative command economy. Between 1928 and 1940, agriculture's share of net national product and labor force declined from 49 and 71 percent respectively to 29 and 51 percent. At the same time, industry's product and labor force shares increased from 28 and 18 percent respectively to 45 and 29 percent. From a historical perspective, even allowing for problems of measurement, these sorts of changes were unbelievably rapid.

It is also important to note that, as Preobrazhensky had argued earlier, these structural transformations demonstrated the emergence of a major bias in favor of industry, and heavy industry in particular. Between 1928 and 1937, heavy manufacturing's net product share of total manufacturing more than doubled from 31 to 63 percent, while light manufacturing's share fell during the same period from 45 to 29 percent. Again, this sort of bias is extreme by historical standards and would present major problems of privatization of industry during transition in the 1990s.

If structural changes were dramatic, what about the overall performance of the Soviet economy, especially the impact of these dramatic changes upon the consumer? In Table 5.7 we present indicators about these other aspects of 1930s Soviet transformation.

The evidence in Table 5.7 provides further support for our judgments about the major changes during the 1930s. Soviet economic growth between 1928 and 1940 was particularly biased in favor of industry and against agriculture. During the period 1928 to 1937, for example, industrial production grew at an average annual rate of 11 percent, while agricultural production grew at an average annual rate of 1 percent. Changes in the labor force are also striking, with rapid increases in the industrial labor force and declines in the agricultural labor force, an immediate outcome of collectivization and the turmoil in the countryside.

The bias against the consumer is also striking. From Table 5.6 we see that between 1928 and 1937 household consumption scarcely grew at all (an annual rate of just 0.8 percent), and the share of consumption in GNP (measured in 1937 prices) declined markedly from 80 to 53 percent. During the same period, gross capital investment grew at an average annual rate of 14 percent, while the ratio of gross investment to GNP doubled from 13 to 26 percent.

Another interesting piece of evidence on consumer well-being is inflation. Consumer prices increased by 700 percent between 1928 and 1937, and they probably would have risen faster in the absence of rationing. At the same time, average realized farm prices—that is, an average of the very low state procurement prices, the above-quota state delivery prices, and prices on the collective farm market—increased by 539 percent. These facts suggest that the scissors in fact were reopened during the 1930s.

The evidence here also provides important comment on Soviet industrialization policies. Earlier, in our discussion of development strategies, we noted the importance of foreign trade in the Tsarist era, and the use of trade through the strategy of import substitution. From Table 5.7, we note that Soviet foreign trade proportions dropped significantly during the industrialization era. This drop, as we will see later, was caused in part by changes in the terms of trade due to world market conditions in the late 1920s and early 1930s. But the drop is also due to the centralization of

Table 5.7

THE SOVIET ECONOMY IN THE 1930s: PERFORMANCE

	1928	1933	1937	1940
A. Rates of Growth (1928–1937)				
1. GNP (1937 prices) (%)			4.8	
2. Labor force				
nonagriculture (%)			8.7	
agriculture (%)			−2.5	
3. Industrial production (1937 prices) (%)			11.3	
4. Agricultural production (1958 prices) (%)			1.1	
livestock			1.1	
5. Gross industrial capital stock (1937 prices)*	34.8	75.7	119	170
B. Prices				
1. Consumer goods (state and coop stores)**	100	400	700	1,000
2. Averaged realized prices of farm products**	100	–	539	–
C. Foreign Trade Proportions				
1. Exports + imports ÷ GNP (%)	6***	4	1	–

*billion rubles

**1928 = 100

***1929

Sources: *A:* A. Bergson and S. Kuznets, eds., *Economic Trends in the Soviet Union* (Cambridge, MA: Harvard University Press, 1963), 36; *B:* F. D. Holzman, "Inflationary Pressures, 1928–1957: Causes and Cures," *Quarterly Journal of Economics* vol. 74, no. 2 (May 1960), 168–9; *C: Narodnoe khoziaistvo SSSR v 1958 g.* [The national economy of the USSR in 1958] (Moscow: Statistika, 1958), 57.

foreign trade decision making as a state monopoly, a set of systemic arrangements that subsequently proved to be very ineffective. However, it is important to note that while the importance of trade declined as a share of output, Stalin made major changes in the trade mix, importing industrial goods rather than consumer goods, while exporting grain.

In sum, the 1930s was an extraordinary decade. The program of the superindustrialists was implemented in draconian fashion, supplemented by the Stalinist purges, which began in 1934. The economic system was fundamentally changed in ways that would persist, largely unchanged, as the Soviet Union came to an end in 1991. Indeed, as we have emphasized, the changes wrought over so many years would present difficult tasks for transition policymakers of the 1990s.

SUMMARY

The creation of the administrative command economy began in 1928 when Stalin had consolidated his power and began to pursue the superindustrialist strategy. The first major policy change was the nationalization of virtually all private property, a process that was virtually completed by the mid-1930s. Second, the system of central planning was established, begun by the use of the balance method with Gosplan (the state planning agency) developing and implementing annual and five-year balances, or sources and uses, of major industrial commodities. With general directives established by the Communist Party, control figures or preliminary plan targets would be established. At this early stage in the development of planning, the exercise was largely ideological, serving as a device to develop support and enthusiasm for the new era. Third, Stalin began the process of collectivization, in which peasants were forcibly required to join collective farms.

The process of collectivization along with the violence of the Stalinist purges remains controversial. Moreover, as a mechanism to extract product surplus from the countryside to finance the industrialization effort, collectivization may not in fact have changed the net balance of resources shifting from the countryside to the urban industrial sector. However, the immediate impact of these new organizational arrangements and policies was significant. The administrative command economy was put in place, and resource allocation changed fundamentally. The structure of the Soviet economy shifted from agriculture towards industry, especially heavy industry. Resources were moved from consumption to investment, which, along with a state monopoly in foreign trade, facilitated a rapid rate of growth of industrial output at the expense of both urban and rural dwellers. These changes, in spite of many reform attempts, would remain in place for those trying to implement market arrangements after the collapse of the Soviet Union in 1991.

Terms and Concepts

balance   A term associated with early Soviet discussions of planning, specifically relating to the concept of equating supply and demand, for example for inputs in the production process.

input-output analysis   A formal framework for the analysis of the sources and uses of resources in the economy, computed in the aggregate or for sectors or regions of the economy; a useful tool for projecting the impact of changes in a particular variable on other sectors of the economy.

GOELRO   Russian acronym for the State Commission for the Electrification of Russia; developers of the first major economic plan, a document outlining a strategy for the electrification of Russia; viewed by Lenin and others as a cornerstone of industrial development in the Soviet Union during the 1920s.

geneticist A school of thought in the Soviet Union in the 1920s suggesting that planning should be indicative; targets should be developed and implemented, but these targets should be suggestive or non-binding, based upon consumer demand.

indicative planning A school of economic thought that suggests, like the geneticist school but in contemporary times, that planning is useful for influencing economic activity, but that the influence should be derived from market forces. Moreover, the targets so developed, would be a source of information, not to be considered binding.

teleological A school of thought in the Soviet Union in the 1920s suggesting that economic activity should be directed by the development of plan targets, which should be obligatory and binding.

Gosplan Committee with the responsibility to prepare long range plans and yearly preliminary plan targets, or control figures.

control figures Preliminary plan targets, developed by the state planning agency to be disseminated to enterprises and subsequently revised for the purpose of preparing a final plan document.

material balances System by which essential materials such as steel were distributed to enterprises.

Gosbank The state (central) bank of the Soviet Union.

Nomenklatura A list or register of important positions and the personnel who fill those positions, monitored by the Communist Party.

kolkhoz (collective farm) Literally, *collective economy*; a cooperative form of organization in agriculture in which peasants are not paid wages, but rather receive a type of dividend after compulsory deliveries are made to the state.

zagotovki State purchases.

GPU Russian acronym for the political (secret) police.

machine tractor station (MTS) Established in 1933, stations in the countryside for the dissemination of machinery and equipment; also an important mechanism for the supervision of the rural economy, especially by the Communist Party through the political departments of the MTS.

labor day (trudoden') Literally, the distribution of a residual; the mechanism used for the payment of peasants on collective farms until the mid-1960s; a measure of work time, termed a *labor day*, the value of which would be determined at the end of the year by dividing residual product (total output minus compulsory state deliveries) by the total number of labor days earned in the collective. Then, each member having accumulated labor days for tasks completed would know (in money and product) the value of his or her labor days.

Selected Bibliography

Avdakov, Y., and V. Borodin. *USSR State Industry During the Transition Period* (Moscow: Progress Publishers, 1975).

Carr, E. H., and R. W. Davies. *Foundations of the Planned Economy, 1926–1929* vol. 1, parts 1 and 2 (London: Macmillan, 1969).

Davies, R. W. *The Industrialization of Soviet Russia*, 1, 2 (Cambridge, MA: Harvard University Press, 1980).

Dobb, M. *Soviet Economic Development Since 1917* 5e (London: Rouledge & Kegan Paul, 1960).

Dunmore, T. *The Stalinist Command Economy* (New York: St. Martins Press, 1980).

Erlich, A. *The Soviet Industrialization Debate, 1924–1928* (Cambridge, MA: Harvard University Press, 1960).

Harrison, M. *Soviet Planning in Peace and War, 1938–1945* (Cambridge: Cambridge University Press, 1985).

Hunter, H., and J. M. Szyrmer, *Faulty Foundations: Soviet Economic Policies, 1928–1940* (Princeton, NJ: Princeton University Press, 1992).

Jasny, N. *Soviet Industrialization, 1928–1952* (Chicago: University of Chicago Press, 1961).

———— . *The Socialized Agriculture of the USSR* (Stanford: Food Research Institute, 1949).

Karcz, J. F. "From Stalin to Brezhnev: Soviet Agricultural Policy in Historical Perspective," in J. R. Millar, ed., *The Soviet Rural Community* (Urbana: University of Illinois Press, 1971), 36–70.

———— . "Thoughts on the Grain Problem," *Soviet Studies* vol. 18, no. 4 (April 1967), 399–434.

Lewin, M. *Russian Peasants and Soviet Power* (London: Allen & Unwin, 1968).

———— . "The Immediate Background of Collectivization," *Soviet Studies* vol. 17, no. 2 (October 1965), 183–97.

Linz, S. J., ed. *The Impact of World War II on the Soviet Union* (Totowa, NJ: Rowman & Allanheld, 1985).

Millar, J. R. "Financing the Soviet Effort in World War II," *Soviet Studies* vol. 32, no. 1 (January 1980).

Nove, A. *An Economic History of the USSR* (London: Penguin, 1969).

———— . *Economic Rationality and Soviet Politics* (New York: Praeger, 1964).

Smolinski, L. "Planning Without Theory, 1917–1967," *Survey* vol. 64 (July 1968).

———— . "Soviet Planning: How it Really Began," *Survey* vol. 64 (April 1968).

Spulber, N., ed. *Foundations for Soviet Strategy of Economic Growth* (Bloomington: Indiana University Press, 1964).

———— . *Soviet Strategy for Economic Growth* (Bloomington: Indiana University Press, 1964).

Vinogradov, V. A., et al., eds. *Istoriia sotsialisticheskoi ekonomiki SSSR* [History of the socialist economy of the USSR] 1–5 (Moscow: Nauka, 1976).

Volin, L. *A Century of Russian Agriculture* (Cambridge, MA: Harvard University Press, 1970).

Voznesensky, N. A. *Soviet Economy During the Second World War*, translated from the Russian edition (New York: International Publishers, 1949).

Zaleski, E. *Planning for Economic Growth in the Soviet Union, 1918–1932* (Chapel Hill: University of North Carolina Press, 1971).

———— . *Stalinist Planning for Economic Growth, 1933–1952* (Chapel Hill: University of North Carolina Press, 1980).

Notes ————————————————————————

1. Our discussion of planning debates in the 1920s is based upon E. H. Carr and R. W. Davies, *Foundations of a Planned Economy, 1926–1929* 1, 2 (London: Macmillan, 1969); N. Spulber, *Soviet Strategy for Economic Growth* (Bloomington: Indiana University Press, 1964).
2. Statement of P. Vaisburg in *Planovoe khoziaistvo* [The planned economy], cited in Carr and Davies, *Foundations of a Planned Economy*, 818.
3. Carr and Davies, *Foundations of a Planned Economy*, 830–31; see also Z. K. Zvezdin, *Ot Goelro k planu pervoi piatiletki* [From Goelro the first five year plan] (Moscow: Nauka, 1979).
4. This discussion is based upon Carr and Davies, *Foundations of a Planned Economy*; A. Nove, *An Economic History of the USSR* (London: Penguin, 1969); M. Dobb, *Soviet Economic Development Since 1917* (London: Routledge & Kegan Paul, 1960); E. Zaleski, *Planning for Economic Growth in the Soviet Union, 1918–1932* (Chapel Hill: University of North Carolina Press, 1971); Y. Avdakov and V. Borodin, *USSR State Industry During the Transition Period* (Moscow: Progress Publishers, 1977); W. Conyngham, *Industrial Management in the USSR* (Stanford: Hoover Institution Press, 1973).
5. Zaleski, *Planning for Economic Growth*, 29–73.
6. In this section we rely on Zaleski, *Planning for Economic Growth*, and Nove, *An Economic History of the USSR*.
7. Our treatment of price setting is based upon R. Hutchings, "The Origin of the Soviet Industrial Price System," *Soviet Studies* vol. 13, no. 1 (July 1961), 1–22.
8. E. Zaleski, *Stalinist Planning for Economic Growth, 1933–1952* (Chapel Hill: University of North Carolina Press, 1980), 483.
9. In this section, we rely upon J. F. Karcz, "From Stalin to Brezhnev: Soviet Agricultural Policy in Historical Perspective," in J. R. Millar, *The Soviet Rural Community* (Urbana: University of Illinois Press, 1971), 36–70; J. F. Karcz, "Thoughts on the Grain Problem," *Soviet Studies* vol. 18, no. 4 (April 1967), 399–434; M. Lewin, *Russian Peasants and Soviet Power* (London: Allen & Unwin, 1968); J. R. Millar and C. R. Guntzel, "The Economics and Politics of Mass Collectivization Reconsidered: A Review Article," *Explorations in Economic History* vol. 8, no. 1 (Fall 1970), 103–16; A. Nove, "The Decision to Collectivize," in W. A. Douglas Jackson, ed., *Agrarian Policies and Problems in Communist and Non Communist Countries* (Seattle: University of Washington Press, 1971), 69–97; E. Strauss, *Soviet Agriculture in Perspective* (London: Allen & Unwin, 1969), chaps. 5–6; L. Volin, *A Century of Russian Agriculture* (Cambridge, MA: Harvard University Press, 1970), chaps. 10–11; R. W. Davies, "A Note on Grain Statistics," *Soviet Studies* vol. 21, no. 3 (January 1970), 314–29; S. G. Wheatcroft, "The Reliability of Russian Prewar Grain Output Statistics," *Soviet Studies* vol. 26, no. 2 (April 1974), 157–80; A. Vyas, "Primary Accumulation in the USSR Revisited," *Cambridge Journal of Economics* vol. 3 (1979), 119–30; R. W. Davies, *The Industrialization of Soviet Russia*, 1, 2 (Cambridge, MA: Harvard University Press, 1980).
10. Millar and Guntzel, "The Economics and Politics of Mass Collectivization," 112.
11. For a discussion of output series, see S. G. Wheatcroft, "A Reevaluation of Soviet Agricultural Production in the 1920s and 1930s," in R. C. Stuart, ed., *The Soviet Rural Economy* (Totowa, NJ: Rowan Allanheld, 1984), 32–62; R. W. Davies, Mark Harrison, and

S. G. Wheatcroft, eds., *The Economic Transformation of the Soviet Union* (Cambridge: Cambridge University Press, 1994), ch. 6.

12. For details of Stalin's argument and related data see Karcz, "Thoughts on the Grain Problem," 399–402.

13. Karcz, "Thoughts on the Grain Problem," 403.

14. Gross marketings include sales to other peasants within the village while net marketings include only sales outside agriculture.

15. Karcz's analysis of grain marketings and agricultural performance during the late 1920s has been disputed by R. W. Davies. Thus we cannot know for sure whether Stalin's analysis of the agricultural "crisis" was erroneous. For example, Davies estimates that the 1926–27 net grain marketings were slightly more than half of prewar marketings—a figure close to Stalin's. See Davies, "A Note on Grain Statistics," 328, and also S. G. Wheatcroft, "A Reevaluation of Soviet Agricultural Production in the 1920s and 1930s."

16. S. Swianiewicz, *Forced Labor and Economic Development* (London: Oxford University Press), 123.

17. For a detailed account of the history and functions of the Machine Tractor Stations, see R. F. Miller, *One Hundred Thousand Tractors* (Cambridge, MA: Harvard University Press, 1970).

18. Karcz, "From Stalin to Brezhnev," 42.

19. For estimates, see N. Jasny, *The Socialized Agriculture of the USSR* (Stanford: Food Research Institute, 1949), and N. Jasny, *Essays on the Soviet Economy* (New York: Praeger, 1962), 107.

20. For a discussion of this issue, see Frederic Pryor, "The Plantation Economy as an Economic System," *Journal of Comparative Economics* vol. 6, no. 3 (September 1982), 301–7.

21. There is a large literature devoted to these issues. For a summary, see for example E. Wayne Nafziger, *The Economics of Developing Countries* 3e (Englewood Cliffs, NJ: Prentice Hall, 1997), ch. 7.

22. W. Eason, "Labor Force," in A. Bergson and S. Kuznets, eds., *Economic Trends in the Soviet Union* (Cambridge: Harvard University Press, 1963), 72–3.

23. There is a large volume of literature on this subject. For a summary of the evidence and appropriate references, see J. R. Millar, "Mass Collectivization and the Contribution of Soviet Agriculture to the First Five Year Plan: A Review Article," *Slavic Review* vol. 33, no. 4 (December 1974), 750–66; J. R. Millar, "Soviet Rapid Development and the Agricultural Surplus Hypothesis," *Soviet Studies* vol. 22, no. 1 (July 1970). The original data can be found in A. A. Barsov, *Balans stoimostnykh obmenov mezhdu gorodom I derevnei* [Balance of the value of the exchange between the city and the country] (Moskva: Nauka, 1969). See also M. Ellman, "Did The Agricultural Surplus Provide the Resources for the Increase in Investment in the USSR During the First Five Year Plan?" *Economic Journal* vol. 85, no. 4 (December, 1975); A. Vyas, "Primary Accumulation in the USSR Revisited," *Cambridge Journal of Economics* vol. 3, no. 3 (1979), 119–30; J. R. Millar, "Views on the Economics of Soviet Collectivization of Agriculture: The State of the Revisionist Debate," in R. C. Stuart, ed., *The Soviet Rural Economy*, 109–17; David Morrison, "A Critical Examination of A. A. Barsov's Empirical Work on the Balance of Value Exchanges Between the Town and the Country," *Soviet Studies* vol. 34, no. 4 (October 1982), 570–84; H. Hunter, "Soviet Collectivization With and Without Collectivization," *Slavic Review* vol. 47, no. 2 (Summer 1988), 210–11; H. Hunter and J. M. Szyrmer, *Faulty Foundations: Soviet Economic Policies, 1928–1940* (Princeton: Princeton University Press, 1992).

PART TWO

How the Administrative Command Economy Operated: Theory and Practice

CHAPTER 6

Planning in Theory and Practice

In Chapter 4 we concluded that the new organizational arrangements and policies of the 1930s fundamentally changed the allocation of resources in the Soviet Union. In this chapter, we examine the administrative command economy under which the Soviet Union operated from the early 1930s to its demise in 1991. Understanding the administrative command economy is important for several reasons. First, the Soviet experience was the first attempt to use economic planning on a comprehensive, nationwide scale. Second, we must establish why the Soviet Union and its command economy came to an end. Did it fail because of human error, inappropriate policy choices, or for more fundamental systemic reasons? Third, we must determine the impact of the Soviet economy's working arrangements upon the creation of a market economy during the transition era.

Modern economies allocate resources via relatively decentralized market arrangements. Although the Soviet economy was by no means an example of a pure planned economy, nevertheless the plan, not markets, was the dominant mechanism of resource allocation. The plan incorporated the basic decisions for resource use—production and distribution.

PLANNING AND THE SOVIET ECONOMIC SYSTEM

An economic system is a set of organizational arrangements established for the purpose of allocating resources in a particular setting.[1] An organization is a group of individuals interacting in a systematic fashion that is governed by a set of established rules. The rules and the structures derived from these rules form a hierarchy (Figure 6.1). Notice that at this stage our characterization of an economic system as an organization is general—it could be a small, simple organization such as a small enterprise, or it could be a complex national economy.[2] Indeed, in the Soviet case, the organizational arrangements were among the most complex, especially the arrangements among the different organizational layers.

While plan arrangements differ from one application to another, all share basic similarities. A plan is a document that specifies economic objectives and explains how they will be achieved. Planning is the process through which a plan is developed, after which comes implementation. Once implemented, plan fulfillment is monitored so that future plan variants can be changed and improved. The planning process, like the functioning of markets, takes place within a set of organizational arrangements or structures. In this sense, the planned economy represents a classic example of the principal-agent problem arising within a familiar hierarchical organizational framework. That is, in a plan, principals specify objectives (targets), which are to be carried out by enterprise managers (agents), who are influenced by appro-

Figure 6.1   The Soviet Organizational Hierarchy

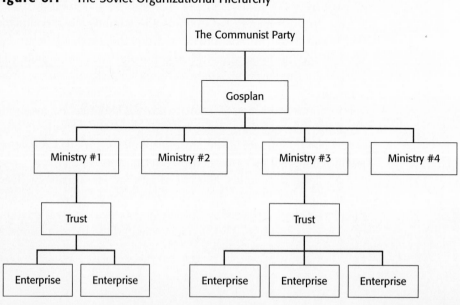

priate incentive arrangements. For the planned economy to work well, agents must be properly motivated to work in the interest of the objectives set by the principal. In this chapter, we examine the organizational arrangements of the Soviet economy, and the nature of the planning process—i.e., the principals who formulate the plan. In the next chapter, we will examine plan execution by agents, specifically enterprise management in the Soviet planned economy.

The Soviet Economic Bureaucracy[3]

The Soviet administrative command economy can be characterized as a set of organizational arrangements with complex interrelationships among principals and agents. At the apex of the administrative command economy was the Politburo of the Communist Party of the USSR. It determined the general direction of the economy via **control figures** (preliminary plan targets), major investment projects (capacity creation), and general economic policies. Below the Politburo was a vast economic bureaucracy charged with executing and monitoring economic policy.

The Soviet economic bureaucracy included the economic departments of the Communist Party and the vast state bureaucracy. The latter included the state planning apparatus, the industrial ministries, the trusts (which were intermediate between the ministries and the enterprises), and finally, the state enterprises. While Figure 6.1 captures the essence of the hierarchical structure, Figure 6.2 (p. 100) provides a more realistic picture of actual relationships among the various subunits. The nature of these subunits deserves additional attention.

The Communist Party

The Communist Party of the Soviet Union (**CPSU**) was the dominant ruling force in the Soviet Union. Throughout the period of its existence, the CPSU dealt with a myriad of issues relating to propaganda, media control, foreign policy, and the like. It also played the central role in the economic sphere, from determining general policy directives to controlling personnel appointments and monitoring activities from top to bottom. At the highest level of the economic bureaucracy, the Department of Planning and Finance Organs (**Otdel planovykh i finansovykh organov**) of the Central Committee of the CPSU was responsible for issuing instructions to the highest state planning organs, in order to direct and coordinate overall plan activity. In the central committee were industrial departments responsible for monitoring specific branches. Moreover, these Party industrial branches paralleled the industrial departments of the planning organs and the ministries.

The CPSU exercised control from Moscow, but it did much more. Regional and local Party organs—the **oblast** (province) Party committees (**obkoms**), the city Party committees (**gorkoms**), and the regional Party committees (**raikoms**)—were also involved heavily in economic affairs. For example, the first secretary of the Party in an oblast oversaw the economic affairs of that province and was responsi-

Figure 6.2   Relationships Within the Soviet Bureaucracy

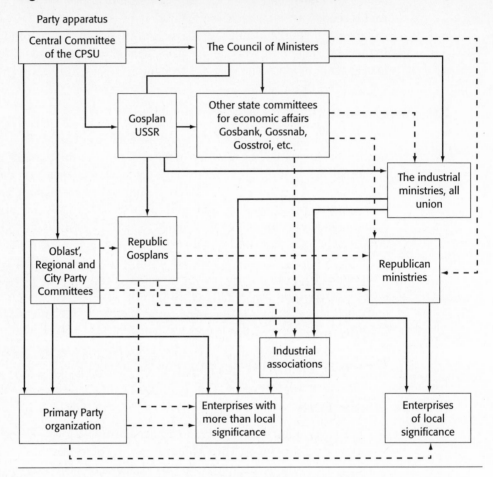

ble for outcomes. In a city, for example Moscow, the first secretary of the gorkom had general oversight responsibilities for city affairs, especially for the affairs of enterprises located within the city.

As we will see, the industrial enterprise not only influenced the development of plan targets but also was responsible for carrying out those targets. Within each enterprise was a primary Party organization (PPO), which, in large enterprises, was headed by a full-time Party professional. Although the power of the Party representative in the enterprise was limited, the presence of the Party served as a source of information and propaganda, creating a climate appropriate for plan fulfillment. The Party was responsible, through the Nomenklatura system, for the selection of important and reliable personnel.

The State Bureaucracy

While the CPSU concerned itself with developing policies, monitoring plan fulfillment, and placing personnel necessary to achieve Party goals, the state bureaucracy was charged directly with the task of achieving Party objectives. Although there was an elected government (the Supreme Soviet), the USSR Council of Ministers conducted the business of government and constituted the government bureaucracy of the Soviet Union. Moreover, each of the fifteen union republics had its own state apparatus, which paralleled that of the USSR as a whole.

The Council of Ministers was composed of industrial ministers, chairmen of various state committees, and chairmen of agencies with ministerial status. The chairman of the Council of Ministers occupied the most powerful position in the state apparatus, in effect the position of prime minister. At various stages of Soviet history, the head of the Party and the head of state was the same person, but this was not always the case.

Of the more than twenty state committees, the most important were **Gosplan** (the state planning committee), **Gosbank** (the state bank), Gossnab (the state committee for material technical supply), Gosstroi, (the state committee for construction), Gostsen (the state committee for price setting), Minfin (the ministry of finance), and TsSU (the central statistical administration). Although nominally responsible to the USSR Council of Ministers, Gosplan was by far the most important agency in the state bureaucracy. Gosplan was subdivided into industrial departments, such as coal, ferrous metals, machine building, and the like. It also had summary departments such as finance, dealing with issues that crossed functional boundaries.

Ministries, Industrial Associations, and Enterprises

Ministries performed key roles in the Soviet organizational structure, supervising enterprises that fell within their domain. Thus the ministry of ferrous metallurgy supervised those enterprises producing ferrous metals and was responsible for the actual operation of the economy. Ministries were a critical conduit for information flowing up and down in the system between planners and operational enterprises. In the formulation of the plan, the ministries were responsible for the disaggregation of the control figures (preliminary plan targets) relevant to their particular enterprises. Ministries also were responsible for allocating supplies to their enterprises, an especially critical task in the Soviet setting, where producer goods markets did not exist. In Soviet jargon, the ministries were "fund holders" **(fondoderzhateli)**. The orderly allocation of inputs was a critical function in the Soviet setting, as we will see when we discuss plan fulfillment in Chapter 7.

Ministries were divided into main administrations **(Glavki),** which were responsible for different functions within the ministry. The ministry of construction materials, for example, was broken down into a number of main administrations, each of which handled different types of construction materials. The routine business of the ministry was handled by its collegium, which was staffed by the minister, deputy ministers, heads of the main administrations, and directors of major enterprises. The minister was held responsible for the "final results" of the ministry, although the deputy minister was often saddled with blame for failures. The collegium could advise, but the minister made the final decisions.

With the exception of a brief experiment with regional planning during the Khrushchev era in the 1950s, Soviet planning was done on a sectoral or product basis rather than on a regional basis. However, this simple distinction hides a complex reality. Ministries were of three general types. All-union ministries managed enterprises under their jurisdiction directly from Moscow. These relatively centralized ministries tended to be the most important, dealing with sectors such as defense, machine building, communications, and the like.

The second type of ministry was the union-republican ministry, whose enterprises were subordinated both to Moscow and to the republic. Sectors organized in this fashion tended to be those where actual production activity was concentrated regionally in one or more republics. Examples would be agriculture and coal production. The third type of ministry was the republican ministry, which managed enterprises at the republic level.

The basic production unit of the Soviet economy in industry was the enterprise **(predpriiatiie);** in agriculture the basic units were the state farm **(sovkhoz)** and collective farm **(kolkhoz).** Enterprises in the industrial sector of the Soviet economy were supposed to run on an independent accounting system **(khozraschet),** under which they would cover costs with revenues and hopefully make a "normal" profit. However, these enterprises were *budget financed* in the sense that profits flowed into the state budget, shortfalls were covered by subsidies, and investment finance was provided from the budget. In this sense, as we will see in the next chapter, the concept of profit in a Soviet enterprise was very different from profit in a firm operating in a market economy. Enterprises were headed by a professional manager (a director) aided by a staff of engineers, accountants, design personnel, and economists. State farms were headed by directors, while collective farms had (in theory) elected presidents. While the enterprise was subordinated to the relevant ministry and industrial association, enterprises in fact enjoyed considerable autonomy, as will be discussed in the next chapter.

Planning: Theory Versus Soviet Practice[5]

Planning is a process through which a plan is developed and implemented, to guide the allocation of available resources towards the achievement of specified objectives. In theory, developing a plan is not especially difficult. It can be thought of simply as an exercise in maximization under constraints, for which mathematical tools are readily available. The literature on planning provides a wide variety of approaches. Among them, however, there is considerable uniformity, although as we move into the real world, understanding planning and plan variants becomes much more difficult. In reality, national economic planning is a complex task, burdened by the sheer magnitude of a large national economy and inadequate information for decision making.

In theory, planning involves using knowledge about the economy's capacity, as determined by production technology and resource constraints, to develop a set of output targets that relate to that capacity. Obviously, targets must be feasible in the sense that they can be met, but, more important, the targets should be optimal—that is, by some criterion, they should be the best of all feasible plan variants. Aggregate planning models typically use an iterative (sequential) process. Planners communicate with managers (usually through intermediate authorities—in the Soviet case, the ministries), to discover capacity, so that the "best" targets can be specified. Once specified, targets are disseminated through the hierarchy, and the plan becomes operational. At this point, implementation begins, largely the responsibility of enterprise managers (see Chapter 7). Over time, feedback facilitates the correction of plan errors.

A conceptually similar but somewhat different approach is provided by input-output analysis, a technique developed by Wassily Leontief from work done in the Soviet Union during the 1920s.[5] The input-output approach looks at the economy as a web of interconnected sectors, some providing outputs, others using these outputs as inputs. Input-output planning makes sure that when a sector needs an input, another sector is providing it as an output, for example, steel used in the production of automobiles. This approach, and its similarity to Soviet practice, can best be understood by examining a simple balance of the sources and uses of commodities in a hypothetical economy. In Table 6.1 we present a simple algebraic example of balance to examine supply and demand (sources and uses).

Table 6.1

ALGEBRAIC EXPRESSION OF A BALANCE

Sources			Distribution				
X_1	$+ V_1$	$+ M_1$	$= X_{11}$	$+ X_{12}$	$+ \ldots +$	$X_{1,2000}$	$+ Y_1$
X_2	$+ V_2$	$+ M_2$	$= X_{21}$	$+ X_{22}$	$+ \ldots +$	$X_{2,2000}$	$+ Y_2$
.	.	.	.	.			.
X_{2000}	$+ V_{2000}$	$+ M_{2000}$	$= X_{2000,1}$	$+ X_{2000,2}$	$+ \ldots +$	$X_{2000,2000}$	$+ Y_{2000}$

Key: Balance of sources and uses: Planned supply of S is the sum of planned output (the control figure) denoted as X_1; available stocks are V_1 and planned imports M_1. The total demand for the first commodity (D_1) is the sum of its interindustry demands ($X_{11}, X_{12}, X_{13} \ldots X_{1,2000}$), and its final demand is denoted as Y_1.

In this example, a balance is achieved when the supply of each commodity equals the demand for that commodity. On the supply side, aggregate supply (S_i) consists of three sources, namely production (X_i), available inventory (V_i), and imports (M_i). On the demand side, the aggregate demand (D_i) consists of intermediate demand (X_i) and final demand (Y_i).

A numerical example of an input-output balance is provided in Table 6.2, where sources (output, inventory, and imports) are equated to uses (intermediate demand and final demand). A balance exists when demand and supply are equated. Although these examples of balance are simple, they provide us with insights into both the theoretical planning problem and reality of the Soviet planning system.

Why is the creation of a balance of the sort demonstrated in Table 6.2 useful for understanding the planning problem? First, although the numerical example is simple, consisting of only four sectors, it is possible in reality to develop a table that incorporates a great deal of disaggregation, with input-output information for a large number of sectors. Second, this approach is, in effect, a snapshot of the national accounts of an economy. As such, it provides us with sectoral source and use relationships, a production function, if you will, that is a useful tool for understanding structural relationships in the economy. Third, if we think of an algebraic table of sources and uses, achieving balance becomes an exercise in solving a system of equations. Therefore, if a number of technical considerations are met, we have a practical tool for finding balance, and, most importantly, for quickly computing the impact of changes on the basic balance. Conceptually, one can use this approach to develop a number of plan variants, from which the "best" variant can be chosen. How does this methodology relate to Soviet reality?

SOVIET MATERIAL BALANCES

In practice, Soviet planning proceeded from the establishment of a series of balances. In the Soviet economy, although there were a potentially very large number of balances (for example sources and uses of material inputs), in Soviet practice, planning survived through a number of important simplifications. First, as we will see shortly, central planning by Gosplan was limited to a relatively small number of commodities. It was argued that major directions could be effectively controlled by planning key commodities at the center. Second, while production relationships (production functions) are in fact complex, Soviet planners could make important simplifying assumptions, such as linear relationships that did not change with scale of output. Third, the planning process did not begin afresh each year; rather the plan in year t represented some upward adjustment of the plan from period $t-1$. While these limiting assumptions might well have created suboptimal plans, they nevertheless made Soviet planning feasible.

With the simplifications noted above, the supply and demand for commodities in the Soviet economy were brought into balance by administrative procedures. It

Table 6.2

A SAMPLE BALANCE OF MATERIALS

	Sources			Intermediate inputs required by			Final use		
	output	stocks	imports	coal	steel	machinery	consumption	exports	imports
Coal (tons)	1,000	10	0	10	500	50	50	100	210
Steel (tons)	2,000	0	20	200	400	1,000	300	100	20
Machinery	100	5	5	20	40	10	20	10	10
Consumer Goods	400	10	20	0	0	0	100	100	230

Demonstration of a balance: sources of coal = 1010; uses of coal 1010, etc.

was Gosplan's task, with the assistance of the ministries and the state supply committee, to achieve this result. Even then, industrial supply and distribution plans compiled by Gosplan totaled 70 volumes of almost 12,000 pages dealing with over 30,000 commodities.[6] The following is a simplified version of the Soviet balancing procedure:

1. The Party establishes its priorities for the forthcoming plan period. Output targets (generally expressed as target rates of growth) are established for key commodities and sectors.
2. Output targets are disseminated through the state apparatus to Gosplan, which has gathered data on plan fulfillment. Gosplan prepares control figures, or preliminary plan targets, for 200 to 300 product groups. Input requirements are also estimated. The ministries are informed of their material "limits." The planning departments of the ministries then aid Gosplan to develop a full set of control figures along with input requirements, a process involving bargaining between the ministries and their superiors.
3. The ministries disseminate control figures to the enterprises, disaggregated into specific tasks. The ministry receives its control targets, which are then disaggregated by branches within the ministry, until each enterprise receives its own control figures. At this stage, the ministry's planning office prepares a list of tentative input requirements, based on the ministry's control figures, for internal use by each enterprise.
4. Through the planning hierarchy, information begins to flow up from the enterprise through its respective ministry to Gosplan. The enterprise relates input requirements to its superior, which in turn are aggregated. At each stage, requested inputs are compared to estimated input needs. If a ministry proposes higher material input requirements than those estimated

by Gosplan, the ministers must "defend" their needs to Gosplan. In a similar fashion, enterprise demands must be justified at the ministerial level.

5. After the bargaining process has been completed, the consistency of the control figures must be checked. An equilibrium is achieved when the planned supplies of each commodity are equal to the material inputs requirements and final uses. If demand exceeds supply, demand must be reduced, supply increased, or a combination of the two. Notice that an effort to increase supply in one sector could lead to imbalances elsewhere. Soviet preference was for cutting demand, especially in low priority ("buffer") sectors, a fact apparent in the plan fulfillment data we examine in Chapter 7.

6. After a balance is achieved, the final version of the plan is presented for approval, after which the finalized targets will be sent down through the hierarchy to the individual enterprises. This final form of the plan, known as the **techpromfinplan,** establishes enterprise output targets as well as input allocations, supply plans, delivery plans, financial flows, wage bills, and many other targets.

While the outline above provides us with a picture of Soviet planning in practice, we will see in Chapter 7 that plan fulfillment and subsequent adjustment were major components of the planning story. But, beyond commodity balances, there were other major components in the planning process, especially investment, the issue of money and credit, and consumer balances.

Capacity Creation: Investment in the Soviet Economy[7]

Investment is a critical component of any economy. Not only does investment influence economic growth in a major way, but also it directly influences where resources will be allocated, that is, which sectors and/or regions will grow or not grow. In market economies, such decisions are largely governed by a cost-benefit framework in which projected benefits from investment projects are compared to estimated costs. Investment costs and benefits must be converted to present values using interest rates from financial markets. In the planned Soviet economy, there were no financial markets. Such decisions were made by planners and enterprise managers.

To meet the expansion of output called for by both current and future plans, enterprise capacity must be increased. Output plans are based upon past performance plus projected capacity increases. Thus output plans determine investment plans. In the Soviet case, the investment plan was formulated by Gosplan, the ministries, and various state committees, after which it was submitted to the Council of Ministers for approval. Once approved, the various R & D organizations, Gosplan, and the ministries supervised its implementation by the project-making organizations.

Just as the material balance plan had its financial counterpart, so too did the investment plan. To finance various projects, the Ministry of Finance provided a portion of the funds derived directly from the state budget, to which all enterprises were connected. The financial institution directly in charge of disbursement was the Investment Bank (Stroibank), with Gosbank providing funds for general repairs. The financial counterpart of the investment plan was used to identify deviations from the investment plan, in much the same manner as it was used to monitor other enterprise functions. If there were an overcommitment of investment resources, financial authorities would provide insufficient financial resources to complete the project on schedule. This practice tended to bring investment supplies and demands into balance but built costly delays into underfinanced investment projects. And there was a tendency to overcommit investment resources, due in part to the ministries' desire to get as many projects started as early as possible so as to establish a priority claim on investment.

Although investment decisions in the Soviet economy were made on administrative grounds rather than through market forces, nevertheless planners still required some choice mechanism for the allocation of scarce investment resources. What mechanisms were used?

Investment Choice

Investment choice in the Soviet Union was complicated by a variety of factors. First, throughout much of the Soviet era, there was no interest rate and hence no recognition of the time discount factor. In market economies, investment projects that promise to yield large returns in the distant future are ranked against projects yielding smaller but quicker returns by computing the present discounted value of each project, using the interest rate as a common discount factor. A high interest rate discourages long-term projects with delayed returns.

Second, as we look at price formation in the Soviet economy, we will see that industrial prices, like most prices, were administratively set with little relation to relative scarcities. The lack of reliable messages from an administered price system tends to make planners rely upon other signals. Thus, planners in the Soviet Union often looked to savings of material inputs and projected increases in labor productivity to evaluate investment projects.

Third, from an ideological perspective, interest was not a legitimate cost. Thus interest rates throughout much of the Soviet era were very low, designed simply to capture the administrative costs of providing the funds, not to serve as a scarcity price. To the extent that investment funds were provided as interest-free grants from the state budget, enterprises regarded these funds as a free factor of production to be used as long as the marginal product was greater than zero. While depreciation was recognized as a cost of capital, obsolescence was not, the latter being viewed as a residual from capitalist market economies.

Investment Rules

Soviet planners paid a great deal of attention to the development of investment rules, changing them frequently. Typically, they simply mimicked the rate-of-return calculations used in market economies. Most rules were oriented towards selecting among competing projects (all of which yielded the same increase in output) on the basis of cost savings. One common formulation called for selecting that investment project whose operating and imputed capital costs were the lowest:

$$C_i + E_n K_i = \text{minimum}$$

where: Ci = the current expenditures of the ith variant
            Ki = the cost of the investment project
            En = the uniform normative coefficient of effectiveness of
                capital investment could or could not be the same for
                all branches

Such formulas allowed planners to select from among investment projects the one that had the lowest cost. The project's capital cost was calculated by imputing a capital charge, using an interest-like coefficient.

How much impact did these sorts of calculations have? The answer is probably minimal. In the Soviet economy, the notion that the center should decide upon investment projects dominated.

MONEY AND CREDIT IN THE ADMINISTRATIVE COMMAND ECONOMY

Thus far we have examined the planning arrangements that, in theory, could be carried out in physical units. What is the function of money in a planned economy? In some respects, money could play roles similar to those in a market economy, namely as a store of value, as a medium of exchange, and as a unit of account. There is, however, a fundamental difference. In market economies, money variables influence real variables through a variety of channels, such as interest rates, unanticipated inflation, and changes in relative prices. In the administrative command economy, there is little or no connection between money phenomena and real phenomena; in this sense, money is neutral in terms of economic activity.

Janos Kornai has argued that in the administrative command economy, money acts as a soft budget constraint.[8] Thus financial outcomes, such as profits or credits, do not affect real variables, such as output and employment. If an enterprise fails to cover its costs, automatic subsidies prop it up, making the concept of profits meaningless in this system. Profits do not have an impact upon economic activity, and real capital allocation is decided by administrative decree, not by the availability of credits.

As well as physical input and output indicators, the Soviet enterprise plan included a pervasive financial plan. It consisted of a wage bill, planned cost reductions, and credit plans, along with many other targets. Thus financial targets were the monetary counterparts of enterprise input and output targets.

Managers regarded the fulfillment of financial plans (such as cost reduction, wage bills, and credit plans) as less important than output plans. But financial plans enhanced the system called *ruble control* (see Chapter 7), through which planners were able to exercise control over enterprises. Deviations from a financial plan were an important signal of deviations from the physical plan. Since all interfirm transactions were handled by the state bank, the monetary counterpart of a physical transaction could be closely monitored.

One dysfunctional aspect of this system was the fact that managers were motivated to seek sources of supply that did not require bank clearing, thus circumventing formal controls. Moreover, to the extent that successful firms were not held accountable, financial controls tended to become mainly a system for monitoring deviations from plan.

BANKING AND THE CREDIT SYSTEM[9]

In market economies, credit balances are achieved mainly through interest rates. In the Soviet administrative command economy, planners were responsible for credit balances, with the state bank supplying credit in accordance with the credit requirements planned by the Ministry of Finance. Like other macrobalances, the credit balance was achieved administratively. A macrobalance was achieved in credit markets when the aggregate demand for credit was equalized to the aggregate supply of credit.

Banking services were provided by Gosbank. This bank combined the services of a central bank and a commercial bank, but owing to the absence of money and capital markets, Gosbank did not perform some traditional banking functions (open market operations, commercial paper transactions, and the like). It did perform four major functions: to make short-term loans for working capital, to oversee enterprise plan fulfillment, to monitor payments to the population as a center for all accounts and, finally, to create money. Thus, enterprises held their accounts with a local branch of Gosbank, upon which they were dependent for short-term credit to finance inventories and for working capital. Receipts were normally deposited with the bank, and cash for wage payments was drawn at the discretion of the bank. In addition, profits remained in special accounts in the bank.

Gosbank was the sole provider of short-term credit, with interfirm lending strictly prohibited. Indeed, with the exception of small payments, all interfirm transactions were handled by and supervised through Gosbank. In these respects, Gosbank was in a unique position to monitor enterprise activities, as the single clearing agent and the sole source of short-term credit. In drawing up short-term credit plans and in controlling enterprise accounts, Gosbank played a largely passive role, providing the credit necessary to implement the physical plan. In making short-term loans, Gosbank granted credit for specific targeted purposes. For example, if a particular transaction was called for in the input plan, the enterprise was automatically granted credit for this purpose. All interfirm transactions were cleared by Gosbank, which required evidence such as a lading bill for each transaction. Even if an enterprise built up excess balances with Gosbank, this liquidity did not represent a command over producer goods unless specifically called for in the plan.

In sum, Gosbank had little influence over the physical flows of production but rather served as a monitoring mechanism. Moreover, the credit balance was achieved by administrative means. The demand for credit was a byproduct of physical planning; the supply was a response by Gosbank to the administrative decisions of planners.

THE MONEY SUPPLY

In any economy, market or administrative command, the demand for money must be balanced with the supply of money. Gosbank, in conjunction with the Ministry of Finance, formally controlled the supply of money. While the role of a central bank in a market is well understood, much less is known about the role of Gosbank and the Soviet money supply. In the Soviet Union, the narrow money supply consisted of cash and currency outside the banking system. Gosbank created new money by authorizing enterprises to pay wages even though they had inadequate cash reserves. Branches of Gosbank in the republics would have sufficient cash funds to meet wage payments if cash inflows into the banks (primarily through consumer goods purchases in the region) equaled the requirements of the wage bill. In the case of a shortfall, fresh cash would be released into the economy if permission could be gained from Moscow. Shortfalls in consumer goods sales could result in an expansion of the money supply, since enterprise wage bills had to be met.

Another source of monetary expansion was budget deficits. If government expenditures exceed government revenues and the difference is not offset by household saving, new cash must be released into the economy to pay those working on state budget accounts. In a market economy, a budget deficit can lead to an expansion of the money supply when the central bank monetizes the debt. In the Soviet case, the same result would be realized through the release of cash funds. In fact, during the last decade of Soviet power, the Soviet state budget had deficits that probably contributed to monetary expansion.

While planners controlled the supply of money, the population determined the demand for money, using it primarily for transaction purposes. In a market economy, cash balances in the hands of the population can be used to purchase goods and services, but in the Soviet case, goods and services were often not available in sufficient quantities and qualities. Planners viewed the accumulation of cash reserves in response to consumer goods shortages (described as **monetary overhang**) as an inflationary threat to macroeconomic stability, especially in the latter years of the Soviet era.

CONSUMER GOODS BALANCE: THE HOUSEHOLD

Thus far we have emphasized planning and financial controls from the perspective of the enterprise and the production of producer goods. Planners must also be concerned with consumer goods, specifically microbalances for the supplies and demands for individual items, and, on the macroeconomic level, with a macrobalance of all consumer goods and services. Although there was an effort to emphasize public consumption over private consumption in the Soviet Union, nevertheless households earned incomes that they could use for the purchase of consumer goods or for savings. If households were unable to convert incomes to goods, a variety of incentive problems could arise. For example, in the event of excess demand for consumer goods, one would expect households to react by working less and/or accumulating savings. From the planners' viewpoint, it was necessary to balance the output of consumer goods and services with the flow of income to the population. A simple macroeconomic balance can be illustrated as follows:

$$PQ = WL + 0 - T - R$$

where P = the prevailing price level
Q = the real output of consumer goods
W = the average annual wage rate
L = the average annual employment
0 = earnings other than wage earnings (interest or private sector)
T = tax payments on income
R = personal savings

In this relationship, personal disposable income can be represented by $WL + 0 - T$, which, when personal savings are subtracted, represents the demand for consumer goods. Note that a macrobalance does not mean that each consumer market is in equilibrium; rather it means that the aggregate supply of consumer goods equals the aggregate demand at established prices.

Planners must ensure the compatibility of the output of consumer goods at established prices with employment levels and wage rates. The smaller the output of consumer goods and the larger the number employed and the higher the wage rate, the more likely it is that aggregate demand will exceed available supply at established prices. This problem arose if there was an imbalance between the planned production of producer goods and consumer goods.

Assume that the output plan calls for enterprises to produce Q_1 units of consumer goods and Q_2 units of producer goods. Through the use of input-output coefficients, the planners determine that L_1 units of labor are required to produce Q_1 and L_2 units of labor are required to produce Q_2. Employment levels are targeted accordingly, and the workers are paid the prevailing wage rate (W_1 and W_2) in the consumer and producer goods sectors respectively. In this setting, an annual wage income of $W_1L_1 + W_2L_2$ is created.

The demand for goods and services is represented by income that is not taxed or saved. With personal taxes denoted by T and personal savings by R, the money demand for consumer goods is:

$$D = W_1L_1 + W_2L_2 + 0 - T - R$$

where 0 denotes the earnings from non-wage sources, for example interest or private sector activity. The total supply of consumer goods at established prices (S) at level (P_1) is the total value of all consumer goods and services:

$$S = P_1 Q_1$$

The task of Soviet planners was to strike a balance between demand and supply. We will return to this issue when we examine the performance of the Soviet economy.

Soviet planners fought a constant battle for the consumer goods balance throughout the Soviet era. In the early years, wages were rising and priorities were shifting from consumer to producer goods. The result was both open and repressed inflation. After World War II, Soviet planners kept wages under better control, and they were actually able to increase the output of consumer goods. By the end of the Soviet era, however, Soviet planners were plagued by what they perceived as a substantial and growing monetary overhang.

THE STATE BUDGET

We have emphasized that the state budget played an important role in the administrative command economy.[10] Indeed, major allocation decisions were reflected in the annual budget, which determined the allocation of total output among private consumption, public consumption, investment, defense, and administration. The USSR's annual budget was a consolidated budget, meaning that it encompassed the budgets of all administrative levels—the all-union budget, the budgets of republics, and local budgets, including those of cities. In this sense, the USSR's budget was much more comprehensive than that of the United States, the latter including only federal revenues and expenditures.

As one might expect, a much larger share of Soviet GNP flowed through the Soviet budget than in the case of the United States. For example, since 1929, roughly 10 to 30 percent of American GNP has been channeled through government budgets (including state and local government budgets). In the Soviet Union, the cumulative average for the postwar period was about 45 percent. The relatively greater importance of the state budget in the USSR derived from two facts: Most investment was financed directly from the state budget, and communal consumption (public health, education, and welfare) represented a larger share of total consumption.

The budget of the USSR directed resources into consumption, investment, defense, and administration in the following manner: The state collected revenues from sales taxes (specifically the turnover tax), deductions from enterprise profits, direct taxes on the population, and social insurance contributions (see Table 6.3). These revenues were then directed through the budget levels to finance investment in the form of grants (the "national economy" category), communal consumption ("social and cultural undertakings"), and defense and administration.

In the 1980s, although Soviet officials claimed that the budget was balanced, deficits were between 2 and 8 percent of GNP.[11] Indeed, in 1988 the Minister of

Table 6.3

THE BUDGET OF THE USSR

	1931	1934	1937	1940	1950	1960	1970	1978	1984	1988
Receipts: Percent of Total										
Turnover tax	46	64	69	59	56	41	32	32	30	24
Deductions from profits	8	5	9	12	10	24	35	30	30	37
Social insurance	9	10	6	5	5	5	5	5	7	8
Taxes on the population	4	7	4	5	9	7	8	8	8	9
Other revenue	33	14	12	19	20	23	20	25	25	22
Expenditures: Percent of Total										
National economy	64	56	41	33	38	47	48	54	56	53
Social/cultural undertakings	14	15	24	24	28	34	36	34	33	33
Defense	5	9	17	33	20	13	12	7	5	4
Administration and justice	4	4	4	4	3	2	1	1	1	1
Other expenditures	13	16	14	6	11	4	3	4	5	5

*As will be explained later, official defense data grossly understate actual expenditure.

Sources: *Narodnoe khoziaistvo SSSR v 1970 g* [The national economy of the USSR in 1970] (Moscow: Statistika, 1971), 731; *The Soviet Financial System* (Columbus: Bureau of Business Research of Ohio State University, 1951), 84–87; *Narodnoe khoziaistvo SSSR v 1978 g* [The national economy of the USSR in 1978] (Moscow: Statistika, 1979), 534; *SSSR v tsifrakh v 1984 g* [The USSR in figures in 1984] (Moscow: Finansy i Statistika, 1985), 50–51; CIA, *Sharply Higher Budget Deficits Threaten Perestroika* (Washington, DC: CIA, 1988), 18.

Finance acknowledged large deficits, which would greatly complicate the search for fiscal stability in the transition era of the 1990s. Budget deficits in the 1980s were due to both falling revenues and increasing expenditures. Declining economic growth meant a reduction of revenues from profits, while falling oil prices reduced revenues from foreign trade, and subsidies cut into turnover tax collections. More than half of this deficit was financed by monetary creation, with serious long-run inflationary implications.

THE ADMINISTRATIVE COMMAND ECONOMY: DID IT WORK?

In Chapter 10 we will provide an overall assessment of the Soviet economic system in terms of widely accepted performance criteria. Now, after examining the process of plan formulation, we should be in a position to consider the strengths and weaknesses of Soviet planning. Recall that in our discussion of the principal/agent problem we noted that when individuals pursue self-interest in the pursuit of objectives, two broad classes of difficulty emerge. The first set of problems, typically identified as *technical/administrative,* refer broadly to problems of individual limitations (bounded rationality) and inadequate or inappropriate information. The second set of problems, broadly identified as *agency/managerial,* relate largely to incentive compatibility issues. In the present context, the latter really relate most closely to the plan implementation issues discussed in Chapter 7, while the former relate to issues discussed in this chapter, specifically information problems.

Practical experience with the administrative command systems suggests that information problems were in fact serious. Moreover, the number of simplifications required to make planning work in the real world enhanced these problems. For example, aggregation limited the number of sectors to be dealt with, but at the same time, it made the plan directives much less meaningful. Assumptions about constant coefficients did violence to reality, especially in sectors of the economy experiencing significant technological change. Judged from the perspective of the post-plan era, it would seem that the inability to adjust and the inflexibility in the planning process was severe. Outputs were engineering decisions having little to do with economic reality and needs. Investment changed capacity, and technological change altered the way things would be done, most of which was not reflected in plan variants.

SUMMARY

In this chapter we have examined the nature of planning in the Soviet administrative command economy. Fundamentally, the Soviet economic system can be modeled as a hierarchy, with principals (planners) instructing enterprises (agents) through intermediate agents (ministries) to fulfill plan targets. In addition to the state structure, the Communist Party was an active participant in both the formulation and dissemination of national objectives and in the development of a local climate to facilitate the achievement of these objectives.

In theory, plan formulation is quite elegant, being the development of a set of objectives or targets consistent with the available capacity of the economy. In practice, however, such a system has great information requirements, such that the usual outcome is a simplification of tasks, which leads to a feasible, if nonoptimal, outcome. In the Soviet case, plan targets were often simply adjustments from previous targets for highly aggregated sectors of the economy based upon strong simplified assumptions about the technology of production.

Although the literature on planning focuses largely on plan targets and how they are formulated, Soviet reality focused on a series of balances in both physical and money terms. Thus while money had little impact upon the real economy, money balances were nevertheless important, integrating the banking structure with the state budget and the planning arrangements. In a sense, the financial side of the Soviet economy was used largely as a monitoring device for assessing plan and other target fulfillment, especially at lower levels of the hierarchy.

As we judge the positive and negative features of this planning system, emphasis is understandably placed upon the massive information requirements.

Terms and Concepts

control figures Preliminary plan targets.

CPSU The Communist Party of the Soviet Union.

Otdel planovykh I finansovykh organov Department of Planning and Finance Organs of the Central Committee of the CPSU.

oblast Province; the geographical unit below the republic level.

obkom Party committee of the province (oblast).

gorkom Party committee of the city (gorod).

raikom Party committee of the region (raion).

Gosplan The state planning committee.

Gosbank The state (central) bank.

fondoderzhateli Literally, "fund holders."

glavk Main administration.

predpriiatiie Enterprise; basic production unit in industry.

sovkhoz State farm.

kolkhoz   Collective farm.

khozraschet   An independent accounting system that was supposed to be used in enterprises in the industrial sector.

techpromfinplan   Literally, the technical-industrial-financial plan; the final form of the state plan setting directives to be fulfilled by enterprise.

monetary overhang   The accumulation of cash reserves in response to consumer goods shortages.

Selected Bibliography

Political Institutions and Control of the Economy

Conyngham, W. *The Modernization of Soviet Industrial Management* (Cambridge: Cambridge University Press, 1982).

Gregory, P. R. *Restructuring the Soviet Economic Bureaucracy* (Cambridge: Cambridge University Press, 1989).

Hough, J. F., and M. Fainsod. *How the Soviet Union Is Governed* (Cambridge, MA: Harvard University Press, 1979).

Nove, A. *The Soviet Economic System* (London: Allen & Unwin, 1977).

Shapiro, L. *The Government and Politics of the Soviet Union* (Essex: Hutchison Publishing Group, 1978).

Supply and Output Planning

Bergson, A. *The Economics of Soviet Planning* (New Haven: Yale University Press, 1964).

Bernard, P. *Planning in the Soviet Union* (Oxford: Pergamon Press, 1966).

Bor, M. *Aims and Methods of Soviet Planning* (New York: International Publishers, 1967).

Davies, R. W. "Planning a Mature Economy," *Economics of Planning* vol. 6, no. 2 (1966), 138–53.

———. "Soviet Planning for Rapid Industrialization," *Economics of Planning* vol. 6, no. 1 (1966), 53–67.

Dyker, D. *The Future of the Soviet Economic Planning System* (Beckenham-Kent: Croom Helm, 1984).

Ellman, M. "The Consistency of Soviet Plans," *Scottish Journal of Political Economy* vol. 16, no. 1 (February 1969), 50–74.

———. *Socialist Planning* (Cambridge: Cambridge University Press, 1979).

Kushnirsky, F. *Soviet Economic Planning, 1965–1980* (Boulder: Westview Press, 1980).

Levine, H. "The Centralized Planning of Supply in Soviet Industry," in U.S. Government, Joint Economic Committee, *Comparisons of the United States and Soviet Economies* (Washington, DC: U.S. Government Printing Office, 1959).

Manove, M. "A Model of Soviet-Type Planning" *American Economic Review* vol. 61, no. 3, part 1 (June 1971), 390–406.

Marczewski, J. *Crisis in Socialist Planning, Eastern Europe and the USSR* (New York: Praeger, 1974).

Montias, J. M. "Planning with Material Balances in Soviet-Type Economies," *American* vol. 49, no. 5 (December 1959), 963–85.

Rutland, P. *The Myth of the Plan* (LaSalle, IL: Open Court, 1985).

Schroeder, G. E. "Recent Developments in Soviet Planning and Managerial Incentives," in U.S. Congress, Joint Economic Committee, *Soviet Economic Prospects for the Seventies* (Washington, DC: U.S. Government Printing Office, 1973), 11–38.

——— . "The 'Reform' of the Soviet Supply System" *Soviet Studies* vol. 24, no. 1 (July 1972), 97–119.

——— . "Soviet Economic 'Reform' Decrees: More Steps on the Treadmill," in U.S. Congress, Joint Economic Committee, *Soviet Economy in the 1980s* vol. 1 (Washington, DC: U.S. Government Printing Office, 1982), 312–40.

Wilhelm, J. "The Soviet Union Has an Administered, not a Planned Economy," *Soviet Studies* vol. 37, no. 1 (January 1985), 118–30.

Zaleski, E. *Stalinist Planning for Economic Growth* (Chapel Hill: University of North Carolina Press, 1980).

Investment

Abouchar, A. "The New Soviet Standard Methodology for Investment Allocation," *Soviet Studies* vol. 24, no. 3 (January 1973).

——— . "The Time Factor and Soviet Investment Methodology," *Soviet Studies* vol. 37, no. 3 (July 1985), 417–27.

——— . "Western Project-Investment Theory and Soviet Investment Rules," *Journal of Comparative Economics* vol. 9, no. 4 (December 1985), 345–62.

Bergson, A. *The Economics of Soviet Planning* (New Haven: Yale University Press, 1964).

Durgin, F. A. "The Soviet 1969 Standard Methodology for Investment Allocation Versus 'Universally Correct' Methods," *ACES Bulletin* vol. 19, no. 2 (Summer 1977), 29–54.

Dyker, D. A. *The Process of Investment in the Soviet Union* (New York: Cambridge University Press, 1981).

——— . *The Future of the Soviet Economic Planning System* (London: Croom Helm, 1985).

Giffen, J. "The Allocation of Investment in the Soviet Union: Criteria for the Efficiency of Investment," *Soviet Studies* vol. 32, no. 4 (October 1981), 593–609.

Goldberg, P. "Consistency in Soviet Investment Rules," *Journal of Comparative Economics* vol. 12, no. 2 (June 1988), 244–47.

Grossman, G. "Scarce Capital and Soviet Doctrine," *Quarterly Journal of Economics* vol. 67, no. 3 (August 1953), 311–43.

Harmstone, R. C. "A Note on Soviet Fixed Asset Replacement in the 1970s and 1980s," *Soviet Studies* vol. 38, no. 3 (July 1986), 416–29.

——— . "Background to Gorbachev's Investment Strategy," *Comparative Economic Studies* vol. 30, no. 4 (Winter 1988), 58–91.

Kohn, M. J., and R. E. Leggett. "A Look at Soviet Capital Retirement Statistics: Unraveling Some Mysteries," *Comparative Economic Studies* vol. 28, no. 2 (1986), 29–31.

——— . "Soviet Investment Policy: The Key to Gorbachev's Program for Revitalizing the Soviet Economy," in U.S. Congress, Joint Economic Committee, *Gorbachev's Economic Plans* vol. 1 (Washington, DC: U.S. Government Printing Office, 1987), 236–56.

Rumer, B. *Investment and Reindustrialization of the Soviet Economy* (Boulder, CO: Westview Press, 1984).

———. "Some Investment Patterns Engendered by the Renovation of Soviet Industry," *Soviet Studies* vol. 36, no. 2 (April 1984), 257–66.

Financial Planning

Diachenko, V. P. *Istoriia finansov SSSR* [History of finances in the USSR] (Moscow: Nauka, 1978).

Central Intelligence Agency. *USSR: Sharply Higher Deficits Threaten Perestroika* (Washington, DC: CIA, September 1988).

Garvy, G. *Money, Financial Flows, and Credit in the USSR* (Cambridge, MA: Ballinger, 1977).

Grossman, G. "A Note on Inflation," in U.S. Congress, Joint Economic Committee, *Soviet Economy in the 1980s* (Washington, DC: U.S. Government Printing Office, 1982), 267–86.

Holzman, F. D. "Financing Soviet Economic Development," in M. Abramovitz, ed., *Capital Formation and Economic Growth* (Princeton, NJ: Princeton University Press, 1955), 229–87.

———. "Soviet Inflationary Pressures, 1928–1957: Causes and Cures," *Quarterly Journal of Economics* vol. 74, no. 2 (May 1960), 167–88.

———. *Soviet Taxation: The Fiscal and Monetary Problems of a Planned Economy* (Cambridge, MA: Harvard University Press, 1955).

Hutchings, R. *The Soviet Budget* (Albany: State University of New York Press, 1983).

Laulan, M. Y., ed. *Banking, Money and Credit in the Soviet Union and Eastern Europe* (Brussels: NATO Directorate of Economic Affairs, 1975).

Pryor, F. L. *Public Expenditures in Communist and Capitalist Nations* (Homewood, IL: Irwin, 1968).

Zwass, A. *Money, Banking, and Credit in the Soviet Union and Eastern Europe* (White Plains, NY: M. E. Sharpe, 1979).

Notes

1. For an approach cast in terms of the economic system (organizational arrangements), see for example P. R. Gregory and R. C. Stuart, *Comparative Economic Systems* 5e (Boston: Houghton Mifflin, 1995).
2. For an introduction to the problems of asymmetric information, see for example H. Varian, *Microeconomic Theory* 3e (New York: Norton, 1992), ch. 25.
3. This section is based upon F. Kushnirsky, *Soviet Economic Planning, 1965–1980* (Boulder, CO: Westview Press, 1982); A. Nove, *The Soviet Economic System* (London: Allen & Unwin, 1977), chaps. 1–4; W. J. Conyngham, *Industrial Management in the Soviet Union* (Stanford: Hoover Institution Press, 1975); W. Conyngham, *The Modernization of Soviet Industrial Management* (Cambridge: Cambridge University Press, 1982); A. C. Gorlin, "The Soviet Economic Associations," *Soviet Studies* vol. 26, no. 1 (January 1974), 3–27; G. Grossman, "The Party as Manager and Entrepreneur," in G. Guroff and F. Carstensen, eds., *Entrepreneurship in Russia and the Soviet Union* (Princeton, NJ: Princeton University Press, 1983), 284–305; P. R. Gregory, *Restructuring the Soviet Economic Bureaucracy*

(Cambridge: Cambridge University Press, 1989); P. R. Gregory, "The Stalinist Command Economy," in J. Prybla, ed., *Privatizing and Marketizing Socialism,* The Annals of the American Academy of Political and Social Sciences (January 1990), 18–25.

4. The literature on planning is large. See for example J. Bennett, *The Economic Theory of Central Planning* (Cambridge, MA: Blackwell, 1989); M. Bornstein, ed., *Economic Planning, East and West* (Cambridge, MA: Ballinger, 1975); R. A. Bowles and D. K. Whynes, *Macroeconomic Planning* (London: Unwin Hyman, 1979); P. Chander and A. Pavikh, "Theory and Practice of Decentralized Planning Procedures," *Journal of Economic Surveys* vol. 4 (1990), 19–58; G. M. Heal, *Theory of Economic Planning* (New York: American Elsevier, 1973); Z. Kenessey, *The Process of Economic Planning* (New York: Columbia University Press, 1978); D. Lavoie, *National Economic Planning: What Is Left?* (Cambridge, MA: Ballinger, 1985); A. Qayum, *Techniques of National Economic Planning* (Bloomington: Indiana University Press, 1975); G. Sirkin, *The Visible Hand: The Fundamentals of Economic Planning* (New York: McGraw-Hill, 1968); N. Spulber and I. Horowitz, *Quantitative Economic Policy and Planning* (New York: Norton, 1976).

5. There is a large literature on input-output analysis. See for example H. B. Chenery and P. B. Clark, *Interindustry Economics* (New York: Wiley, 1959); W. W. Leontief, *Input-Output Economics* (New York: Oxford University Press, 1966); M. P. Todaro, *Development Planning: Models and Methods* (Nairobi: Oxford University Press, 1971); V. Treml, "Input-Output Analysis and Soviet Planning," in J. Hardt, et al., eds., *Mathematics and Computers in Soviet Planning* (New Haven: Yale University Press, 1967); E. W. Nafziger, *The Economics of Developing Countries* 3e (Englewood Cliffs, NJ: Prentice Hall, 1997), ch. 19.

6. The most important industrial materials such as steel, cement, machinery, and the like were known as *funded commodities.* Gosplan was in charge of drawing up output and distribution plans for funded commodities, specifically approved by the USSR Council of Ministers. The number of funded commodities varied. For example, between 1928 and 1980, Gosplan developed annual balances for between 277 and 2390 separately funded product groups. In the mid-1980s, Gosplan prepared some 2000 balances. In addition to funded commodities, output and distribution plans were also drawn up for two other groups of commodities. *Planned commodities* were those industrial products planned jointly and distributed by Gosplan, Gossnab (the state committee for material technical supply), and the All-Union Main Supply and Sales Administration. Twenty-five thousand or more commodities were planned in this category. Finally, *decentrally planned commodities* were planned and distributed by the territorial administrations of Gossnab and by the ministries, without the explicit approval of higher organs. Over 50,000 commodities were planned in this category. There were also "non-planned" commodities, largely for internal use. In the 1970s, there were 26,000 commodities in this category.

7. There is a large literature on investment choice in the Soviet Union. We rely upon Bergson, *The Economics of Soviet Planning,* ch. 11; G. Grossman, "Scarce Capital and Soviet Doctrine," *Quarterly Journal of Economics* vol. 67, no. 3 (August, 1953); A. Zauberman, *Aspects of Planometrics* (New Haven: Yale University Press, 1967); A. Abouchar, "The New Soviet Standard Methodology for Capital Allocation," *Soviet Studies* vol. 24, no. 3 (January 1973), 402–10; J. S. Berliner, *The Innovation Decision in Soviet Industry* (New Haven: Yale University Press, 1976); S. H. Cohn, "Deficiencies in Soviet Investment Policies and the Technological Imperative," in U.S. Congress, Joint Economic Committee, *Soviet Economy in a New Perspective* (Washington, DC: U.S. Government Printing Office, 1979), 447–59; S. H. Cohn, "Soviet Replacement Investment: A Rising Policy Imperative," in U.S. Congress, Joint Economic Committee, *Soviet Economy in a Time of Change,* 230–45; M. Ellman, Socialist Planning (Cambridge: Cambridge University Press, 1979); D. A. Dyker, *The Process of Investment in the Soviet Union* (New York: Cambridge University Press, 1981); J. Giffen, "The Allocation of Investment in the Soviet

Union: Criteria for Efficiency of Investment," *Soviet Studies* vol. 32, no. 4 (October 1981), 593–609; R. E. Leggett, "Soviet Investment Policy in the 11th Five Year Plan," in U.S. Congress, Joint Economic Committee, *Soviet Economy in the 1980s: Problems and Prospects* part 1, 129–52; S. H. Cohn, "Sources of Low Productivity in Soviet Capital Investment," in *Soviet Economy in the 1980s*, 1969–94; R. E. Leggett, "Soviet Investment Policy: The Key to Gorbachev's Program for Revitalizing the Soviet Economy," in U.S. Congress, Joint Economic Committee, *Gorbachev's Economic Plans* vol. 1 (Washington, DC: U.S. Government Printing Office, 1987), 236–56; D. Dyker, *The Future of the Soviet Economic Planning System* (London: Croom Helm, 1985); P. Goldberg, "Consistency in Soviet Investment Rules," *Journal of Comparative Economics* vol. 12, no. 2 (June 1988), 244–47; A. Abouchar, "Western Project-Investment Theory and Soviet Investment Rules," *Journal of Comparative Economics* vol. 9, no. 4 (December 1985), 345–62; A. Abouchar, "The Time Factor and Soviet Investment Methodology," *Soviet Studies* vol. 37, no. 3 (July 1985), 417–27; R. C. Harmstoner, "Background to Gorbachev's Investment Strategy," *Comparative Economic Studies* vol. 30, no. 4 (Winter 1988), 58–91; B. Rumer, *Investment and Reindustrialization of the Soviet Economy* (Boulder: Westview Press, 1984).

8. J. Kornai, *The Economics of Shortage* (New York: North Holland, 1980).

9. Our discussion of banking arrangements is based upon G. Garvy, *Money, Financial Flows, and Credit in the Soviet Union* (Cambridge, MA: Ballinger, 1977); A. Zwass, *Money, Banking, and Credit in the Soviet Union and Eastern Europe* (White Plains, NY: M. E. Sharpe, 1979); Z. V. Atlas, *Sotsialisticheskaia denezhnaia sistema* [The socialist monetary system] (Moscow: Finansy, 1969).

10. M. V. Condoide, *The Soviet Financial System* (Columbus: Bureau of Business Research of Ohio State University, 1951); A. Nove, *The Soviet Economic System,* ch. 9; R. Hutchings, *The Soviet Budget* (Albany: State University of New York Press, 1983); I. Birman, *Secret Incomes of the Soviet State Budget* (Boston: Martinus Nighoff, 1981).

11. CIA, *USSR: Sharply Higher Budget Deficits Threaten Perestroika* (Washington, DC: CIA, 1988).

CHAPTER 7

The Administrative Command Economy: Management, Labor, and Pricing

In Chapter 6 we examined how the Soviet economy was organized and how it was planned. Our focus was on the formulation of the national economic plan. In this chapter we turn to plan execution—specifically, the role of managers in carrying out the plan and the forces influencing managerial actions. While managers in Western firms seek to achieve a variety of objectives (such as expansion of market shares, corporate growth, and profit maximization), managers in the Soviet Union were primarily responsible for plan fulfillment and specifically for the achievement of gross output targets. The Soviet managerial milieu was quite different from that found in the typical Western enterprise.

THE SOVIET ENTERPRISE[1]

The basic unit of industrial production in the Soviet Union was the enterprise **(predpriiatie).** The enterprise was headed by a manager (director) and a professional management staff. This staff generally consisted of a deputy director, a chief engineer, a chief accountant, a chief economist, and a chief technologist. Enterprises received plan directives from the relevant superior agency, the main administration of a ministry, an industrial association, or in rare cases directly from

Gosplan. Managers were expected to fulfill these directives, and incentive arrangements were established by their superiors to motivate compliance.

In the enterprise, the principle of one-person management (**edinonachalie**) prevailed, a system favored by Lenin many years earlier. The concept of one-person management meant that the manager was responsible for carrying out plan directives, and the staff within the enterprise was subordinated to the manager.

The Soviet Enterprise: Asymmetric Information[2]

As we noted in Chapter 6, the Soviet organizational hierarchy can be understood and analyzed within the framework of contemporary organization theory, specifically the principal/agent problem. In the Soviet case, the planning process resulted in a set of targets that enterprise managers were to meet. While managerial rewards (incentive arrangements) were related to plan fulfillment, many constraints (random breakdowns, supply uncertainties, party pressure) limited managerial action.

Two broad classes of problems confront an enterprise manager pursuing self-interest by maximizing some utility function. First, due to **bounded rationality,** the manager must face **technical/administrative problems.** For example, managers must deal with skill limitations, outdated equipment, uncertain supplies, or limited ability to access information required for rational (goal-oriented) behavior. All managers must address these sorts of problems, not just those in the Soviet setting. Second, there are a variety of **agency/managerial problems** that involve **information asymmetries.** There is asymmetric information when the manager (the agent) possesses more local information than the principal (the ministry or Gosplan). Information asymmetry gives the manager the opportunity to engage in opportunistic behavior.

These problems can be addressed in three major ways. First, management literature emphasizes the possibility of changes in organizational arrangements, for example the **span of control.** An example of a reduced span of control would be to reduce the number of industrial enterprises supervised by a particular ministry. This was a central issue in the Soviet Union, especially with regard to the appropriate organization of a ministry. In the Soviet case, organizational change was frequently implemented to attempt to resolve information problems.

A second approach focuses on improving the nature and availability of information. The Soviets simplified the planning task greatly by aggregation, a form of simplification that in fact produced serious information problems. Planners found that it was simpler to plan the output of one type of steel rather than twenty specific types. However, if different types of steel are needed for automobiles, pipelines, tool-making, and the like, aggregation does not provide "enough" information. To increase the availability of useful information, Soviet planners attempted to computerize the planning process, to facilitate disaggregation, and to speed up information flows, but with limited success.

Finally, the most substantive approach for solving agency problems is adjustment of incentive arrangements, to create **incentive compatibility.** If the objectives of Soviet enterprise managers could be fully harmonized with the objectives of the principal, information asymmetries would be less of a problem because agents would not take advantage of their superior local information. In effect, the agent would always act in the best interest of the principal.

PLANNING AND THE ENTERPRISE MANAGER

Soviet industry was governed by a long-term plan, a five-year plan broken down into sub-plans, (by product and by time period), each comprising a variety of targets. Although there was much discussion of the five-year plans, in fact the real operational plans of the Soviet economy were its annual plans and quarterly plans. The five-year plans were a vision of the future with little or no operational significance. Specifically, the enterprise plan (techpromfinplan) included output levels (in physical and value terms), the required output assortment, labor and other input requirements, productivity indices, profit norms, and credit and wage bill plans.

The most important element of the plan was production. The value of output was specified, along with a commodity assortment and a delivery schedule. As we noted in Chapter 6, targets were based upon some estimate of enterprise capacity (typically past performance plus some increment for capacity expansion), expected resource utilization, and estimated productivity increases. The development of the final plan from estimated control figures involved a degree of bargaining between the lower and the upper levels of the hierarchy.

The existence of comprehensive enterprise plans seems to imply that Soviet managers had very limited decision-making flexibility. Such was not the case. Planners could not specify all details. Managers were required to translate plan targets into daily enterprise tasks. Indeed, managers participated in the bargaining for input and output targets. The manager was faced with the need to achieve multiple targets (output, cost reduction, innovation, timely delivery) while facing multiple constraints. Only a perfect plan and full information would insure that all targets were compatible. In fact, managers had to choose between those targets that could be fulfilled and those that could not.

Enterprise managers made decisions based upon priorities. If all targets could not be simultaneously achieved, which should be sacrificed?[3] Such tradeoffs are more transparent in market economies, where scarcity-based prices provide managers with the necessary information about their alternatives. Despite the planned nature of the Soviet economy, Soviet managers still faced tradeoffs like their Western counterparts.

For Western managers, profit maximization is the single most important criterion of enterprise success. This was not the case for Soviet managers. While profits were always a part of the formal Soviet accounting arrangements, profit maximization was not a primary enterprise goal. Indeed, given the nature of Soviet pricing, which we examine later, profits did not send signals regarding managerial performance. The major target in Soviet enterprises was fulfilling gross output and subsequent refinements of the gross output concept.

THE SUCCESS INDICATOR PROBLEM[4]

The choice of gross output as the major indicator of enterprise performance created a variety of managerial problems. For planners, it was difficult to define output with precision, whether in physical or value terms. If output was measured in terms of weight, such as industrial castings, managers ignored the dimensions and created a product much heavier than necessary, thereby wasting material inputs. If size was the indicator, such as meters of cloth, managers favored production of a single large size, largely ignoring product mix or assortment.

A second major managerial problem arose from the setting of targets. As we noted in Chapter 7, plan targets were, in part, based upon information provided by the managers themselves in the process of bargaining over control figures. Managers knew their bonuses were based upon the fulfillment and overfulfillment of plan targets. They also knew that when a plan was overfulfilled, planners had a tendency to increase ("ratchet up") output targets. (This behavior came to be known as the **ratchet effect**.[5]) As a result, managers had an incentive to understate capacity, to receive an "easy" target, and then to overfulfill only by a small margin. In that way, targets in subsequent years would not be increased.

So, quantity targets provided Soviet managers with an incentive to conceal information about enterprise capacity, and the ratchet effect gave them an incentive to produce below actual capacity. This manifested itself in two ways. For example, suppose a bonus system provided no payment for 99 percent plan fulfillment but significant rewards for 100 to 105 percent fulfillment. First, managers would have a strong incentive to manipulate their superior information to gain an "easy" target. That would assure a bonus. Second, since rewards began at 100 percent, managers would not want to overfulfill much above that level. Otherwise, the next set of targets would be increased. This is an example of incentive compatibility.

Achieving Incentive Compatibility: Soviet Managerial Rewards

Managerial rewards were the basic arrangements that Soviet planners used to direct Soviet managers towards plan fulfillment. While Soviet managers received base pay, bonuses constituted a major portion of earnings along with a number of nonmonetary perquisites of the managerial position.[6]

Although fulfilling output targets was the fundamental priority for Soviet enterprise managers, they faced a myriad of other targets whose priorities changed over time. Both official and unofficial information helped managers place appropriate weights on the differing and sometimes contradictory objectives. The formal reward structure directed them to fulfill output targets, and less formal means reinforced managerial understanding that targets such as gross output took priority over, say, product assortment. Lack of managerial attention to product mix helps us understand the peculiarities of the Soviet marketplace, in which there was an abundance of one product, and severe shortages of others.

The managerial reward system in the Soviet Union differed from typical market-type arrangements. First, in market economies, bonuses are important and are generally paid for both long- and short-run achievements, judged by such general indicators as profitability, expansion of market share, or a rising stock price.[7] In the Soviet case, bonuses tended to be paid for achieving specific short-run tasks, for example producing square meters of cloth equal to or greater than some planned target. This milieu tended to emphasize short-run gains at the expense of the long-run health of the enterprise and to create dysfunctional behavior.

Second, in market economies, while bonuses assume a variety of forms, it is not unusual to have a bonus system that pays considerable attention to tax implications. Stock distribution is a case in point. Since income taxes on managerial incomes in the Soviet Union were minimal, Soviet incentive schemes were not affected by tax considerations.

Third, bonus arrangements in market economies are often tied to seemingly quite vague goals, for example long-run profitability, or the creation of merger and/or acquisition opportunities. In the Soviet case, bonuses were paid for the achievement of well-defined objectives, a system that contributed to serious agency/managerial problems noted above.

Fourth, while money bonuses were important in the Soviet case, one should not underestimate the importance of nonmonetary incentives, both negative and positive. On the negative side, nonfulfillment of assigned targets always carried with it the threat of removal from the managerial position, though in fact managerial turnover in the Soviet Union declined significantly after the tumultuous years of the 1930s.[8] On the positive side, successful managers were rewarded with privileges such as a summer home (dacha), an automobile, or health care in a restricted clinic, all rare in the Soviet Union. These nonmonetary bonuses were significant in an economy where such benefits could not be purchased.

The Soviet Managerial Environment: External Organizations

Enterprise managers in the Soviet Union were important people. They were, after all, the front line of plan fulfillment. The rewards for managerial success could be great. At the same time, the Soviet manager operated within a framework of considerable stress. While plan fulfillment could bring rewards, many forces were quite capable of limiting these rewards.

Regional bodies and ministerial organizations were significant players, interested in forcing "their" enterprises to do better. The ministry practices of holding back supply allotments (**reserving**) and planning enterprise targets to exceed the aggregate ministry target were part of external pressure on managers. Indeed, some have used the complex adversary-protector relationship between an enterprise and its ministry to suggest that the Soviet system was more a managed than a planned economy, in the sense that ministries could manipulate their various enterprises. In actual practice, the plan targets tended to be firmer the higher up one moved in the administrative hierarchy. Individual enterprise plans tended to be changed frequently, while ministry plans were reasonably firm. In effect, the ministry could shuffle plan fulfillment among its enterprises, giving enterprises the impression that plans really did not count, whereas the ministry in fact was attempting to fill a relatively firm plan.

In addition to the ministry, regional and local Party officials continually interfered with enterprise activities. Local and regional Party officials were judged on the basis of the performance of local and regional enterprises. The activities of Party officials could be negative or positive as far as enterprises were concerned. The local Party could assist enterprises in dealings with the ministries and other upper level state organizations. When local or regional enterprises lacked materials or cash, Party officials could help. On the other hand, local Party officials could hurt by monitoring local enterprises for superior organizations and even by initiating measures to remove local managers. The interaction among enterprise managers and their superiors was like a large strategy game, with managers engaging in strategic behavior and their superiors attempting to restrain them through rules, incentives, and external controls. One should not overstate the flexibility of Soviet managers. Enterprises could "fool" their superiors only at the margin.[9] All players worked within the framework of the plan, which effectively limited the leeway of all participants.

Finally, the state could exercise indirect control over enterprises through the system of ruble control, mentioned in Chapter 6. **Ruble control** was potentially a powerful mechanism of control in the administrative command economy. Although monetary targets per se were much less important in the Soviet nonmarket economy, they did provide a powerful means of monitoring plan fulfillment. When enterprises were given physical targets, for example the hiring of 2500 workers, a wage fund was specified to limit wage expenditures to paying 2500 workers, thereby effectively monitoring the amount of labor utilized. Overspending of the wage fund would indicate that the manager was trying to utilize too much labor.

INPUTS AND THE SOVIET ENTERPRISE MANAGER

Soviet managers pursued targets, the achievement of which determined managerial rewards. All targets were pursued within a framework of significant constraints. A major one that enterprise managers faced was the availability of inputs.[10] In Chapter 6 we discussed the material technical supply system and the creation of capacity through investment; here we discuss the problem of obtaining intermediate materials and labor.

Intermediate Materials: Kornai's Inherent Shortages

In Chapter 6 we discussed the planning of material-technical supplies through the material balance system. In theory, materials were allocated to the ministries, then by the ministries to the enterprises by administrative means. Let's consider the actual implementation of the supply plan and how Soviet managers could affect the distribution of materials.

Since Soviet enterprises were not judged on the basis of the "bottom line" (profits), reducing materials costs or finding better ways to combine resources was not especially important. Enterprises could ignore the bottom line because they were subject to what Janos Kornai termed the **soft budget constraint.** Enterprises operating under a soft budget constraint knew that if they failed to cover costs, they would be bailed out by subsidies or transfers from other enterprises.

Kornai also discussed the issue of inherent shortages. Materials were allocated to enterprises through ministries called "fund holders." Along with the output plan that we have discussed, each enterprise received a plan for material-technical supply. In theory, the material-technical supply plan was to determine the enterprise's use of intermediate inputs. In fact, the material-technical supply plan was only the first step.

Soviet enterprise managers knew that the material-technical supply plan was full of uncertainties. Would an enterprise actually receive what was scheduled for delivery according to the plan? If the answer was affirmative, when could delivery be expected? Supply uncertainty meant that Soviet enterprise managers spent a great deal of their time dealing with supply problems—cajoling reluctant suppliers, swapping materials with other enterprises on an informal basis, and using informal "connections" to obtain supplies through alternative sources. The true test of a good Soviet enterprise manager was his ability to understand priorities and to arrange the delivery of needed material inputs in the face of persistent uncertainty.

Kornai's inherent shortage explains continuing to rely on supply planning instead of obtaining material supplies through a wholesale market. With soft budget constraints, wholesale markets would not work because enterprise managers would constantly over-order materials, no matter what the price. Constraining costs was not a priority for the enterprise manager, while the uncertainties surrounding material supplies could threaten plan fulfillment and potential bonuses.

Labor Planning

In the administrative command economy, superior authorities largely determined the enterprise's labor requirements as an integral part of the planning process. The enterprise plan contained not only input and output targets, but also specific plans for labor inputs.[11] Staffing arrangements were quite detailed, specifying the enterprise wage bill, the distribution of the enterprise labor force by wage class, average wages, planned increases in labor productivity, and so on. While the enterprise manager could exercise discretion, enterprise staffing was basically a decision made by planners. The basic task facing planners was establishing labor balances between the demands for labor and the supplies of labor in various branches and regions.

Labor supply in the Soviet Union was ultimately decided by the household, although the system put considerable pressure on household members to participate in the labor force.[12] The Soviet household was not, like enterprises, directly within the purview of planners. Although planners could directly allocate materials, finance, and investment goods to enterprises, they could not do the same for labor. Accordingly, like households elsewhere, the Soviet household faced a labor/leisure tradeoff (including occupational choice), although with some constraints peculiar to the Soviet setting.

Although planners knew that household members could themselves decide where to work and in what branch and occupation, planners could still compile labor balances of labor demand and labor supply. The labor supply estimates of Soviet planners were based upon age-based participation rates that allowed for male/female, rural/urban, and other differences. After Gosplan estimated the available supply of labor, demand requirements had to be estimated before a labor balance could be achieved. Labor demands could be estimated using an **input-output coefficient** in much the same way as was done for material inputs. Specifically, once output plans were known, labor demands could be specified using established norms. If the output plan called for the production of 10 million tons of steel, planners could look at past experience to determine how much labor was required to produce this amount. Labor productivity projections added another dimension to the estimation process, because productivity improvements meant that the same amount of output could be produced with less labor.

As was true for material inputs, enterprises tended to overstate their labor needs while upper level organizations tried to reduce enterprise demands in an effort to bring demand and supply into equilibrium. Once plan authorities drew up the balance of labor resources, another problem arose. How were they to bring the appropriate amount of labor into the various enterprises, or to use the planning terminology, how are they to "guarantee the labor requirements of the national economy"?[13]

Wages in the Soviet Economy

Labor allocation in the Soviet Union was a complex process that combined administration, force, material and moral incentives, and a comprehensive system of training and educational advancement. Throughout this process, household decision-making flexibility was constrained to differing degrees and in different ways. While there was great emphasis on educational planning, labor authorities used formal organized recruitment, an internal passport system, and closed cities to supplement the use of wage and income differentials to shift labor from one region or sector to another.[14]

Soviet labor planning recognized the allocative function of wages, arguing that equality, poverty, and related issues should be addressed by other means.[15] Ideologically, wage differentials were justified by the socialist principle of "equal pay for equal work" and by Lenin's admonition against "equality mongering."

How were wages set? In each industrial branch, base rates specified the absolute ruble wage of the lowest paid occupation.[16] Then, a schedule was established for each branch, giving the wages of higher paid occupations as percentages of the lowest grade rate. By altering the base rate, planners could influence the labor supply to a particular branch. During the early years of industrialization, high average wages in priority sectors were used to attract labor out of agriculture and light industry and into heavy industry. In the postwar era, a positive correlation existed between the average wage of a branch and its importance in the national economy.

Wage differentials were also used to encourage education. In the 1930s, Stalin established schedules that favored skilled workers to encourage the then untrained workers to acquire more training. Soviet industrial wage differentials in the 1930s were even greater than those in the United States.[17] With the growing level of education, the extreme differentials of the 1930s were reduced after World War II. Two other factors contributed to the leveling of differentials. Minimum wage levels were increased dramatically, and the percentage of workers making low wages declined markedly.[18]

In addition to differentials by sector and education, wages were differentiated by region to encourage mobility into rapidly growing areas such as Siberia, Kazakhstan, and Central Asia. Regional differentials were computed by means of a uniform system of coefficients, which were multiplied by the standard wage rates to yield regionally differentiated wages. For example, the coefficients used to compute wages in the far north ranged from 1.5 to 1.7. That is, wages in these regions were 50 to 70 percent higher than the standard rates paid for performing the same basic tasks in European Russia.[19]

Higher rates were also paid for dangerous work or work performed under arduous conditions. For example, underground mining occupations received higher wages than similar occupations above ground. In the chemicals industry, work performed under especially hot, heavy, and unhealthy conditions received higher pay.[20]

In addition to the base system described above, workers were also eligible for a variety of bonus payments. They were usually paid for the overfulfillment of plan norms or for special working conditions. In the 1930s, planners relied heavily on piece-rates to encourage laborers to work hard. At that time, most industrial workers were on some kind of piece-rate system, though after World War II, this proportion declined. In the 1960s and 1970s, the Soviets tried a number of experiments with bonuses based on profitability, quality improvements, or growth of labor productivity, but they failed to become widespread.

ADMINISTRATIVE CONTROLS OVER LABOR[21]

Education and the Labor Force

In the Soviet system, central controls over education had a major influence on labor supply. The Soviet Ministry of Education was charged with developing a long-term plan for supplying the national economy with required skills and general educational attainment consistent with national economic objectives. The completion of secondary education (through eighth grade after 1973) in general education schools was compulsory.[22] Beyond this level, the Soviet Union had a network of specialized educational institutions, under differing jurisdictions, devoted to specialized training. The rapid expansion of the Soviet educational establishment demonstrated its priority.

Soviet education reflected the official view that education must serve the needs of the economy within a Marxist-Leninist framework. Accordingly, there was little evidence of what in the West would be described as "liberal arts." Soviet education was devoted to the development of the new Soviet person, above all with Communist morality and beliefs and, in addition, skills useful to the Soviet economy. Soviet education emphasized science, engineering, and technical specialties. Entry to the humanities was restricted. In fact, admission into the humanities and the language programs was regarded as a privilege for a select few. The system relied heavily upon specialized secondary schools that provided professional vocational training to medical assistants, draftspersons, skilled mechanics, engineers, and the like.

Attempts were made, from Gosplan down through the local districts, to plan labor requirements, and on this basis to provide the educational capacity necessary to meet these planned needs. Unlike the West, where students are free to select majors, the administrative command system placed students into career tracks according to long-term planning goals.

Graduates of higher education were required to complete two years of work assignment at a specified location.[23] Similar types of assignments were used to place more highly skilled graduates to offset labor shortages in areas such as Siberia.

Organized Recruitment[24]

Another mechanism for the administrative control of labor was organized recruitment, used to a greater degree during the early years of the administrative command experience. During the 1930s, the All-Union Resettlement Committee and the Administration for Organized Recruitment (**Orgnabor**) transferred labor from rural to urban areas by recruiting labor for factories from state and collective farms. Some 3 million persons were transferred from village to city through Orgnabor contracts. After World War II, Orgnabor was used to transfer workers among industrial enterprises and among regions. By the late 1950s, Orgnabor was used for recruiting labor for the vast construction projects and new industries located in the East and North.

Party organizations were also used throughout the Soviet period for the recruitment of labor for specific purposes. For example, it was not uncommon for youths to spend time helping with the agricultural harvests, organized by the Communist Party Youth Organization (**Komsomol**).

Legal Controls

The competitive bidding for industrial workers, many of whom were untrained peasants from the countryside, created what was perceived as excessive job turnover in the 1930s.[25] This forced the state to adopt additional extra-market controls over labor mobility. During the 1930s, absenteeism was subject to severe penalties, such as eviction from factory housing and loss of social benefits. In addition, "closed shops" were used to reward reliable workers, and enterprise controls over housing were used as a lever to promote labor stability. Between 1938 and the end of World War II, controls became more severe. Labor books, in which a person's work record was recorded, were issued to all employed persons. Internal passports were used to control movement of the population, and permission was required to change jobs. Failure to comply was a criminal offense.

Labor controls were especially severe during World War II. In addition to mobilizing specialists, lengthening the work day, and criminalizing absenteeism, labor reserve schools were established. Labor laws during this period were severe and resulted in numerous instances of prosecution and imprisonment. In the early 1950s, most of these regulations fell into disuse and in the mid-1950s were finally repealed. Nonetheless the problem of "rolling stones," or workers who changed jobs too frequently, remained a matter of concern. The state introduced a number of incentives to encourage workers to remain on their jobs and thus decrease excessive job turnover after the relaxation of administrative controls in the 1950s and thereafter.[26]

Penal Labor[27]

The most glaring deviation from the principle of a labor market was the creation of a large penal labor force, starting with forced collectivization in 1929. The number of prisoners in Soviet concentration camps, the **Gulag** population, cannot be known with precision. However, a variety of sources all point to the existence of a large number of forced laborers. The Gulag population reached 1 to 2 million persons during the collectivization drive of the early 1930s. The numbers increased when the Stalin purges began in 1934. Estimates of the size of the forced labor camps in 1939 vary from 2 to 11 million. The camp population reached its peak during World War II and immediately thereafter. Figures for the period 1945–50 range from 4 to 15 million. Ex-prisoners of war, resettled minorities, citizens of occupied territories, and many other groups were incarcerated during and after the war years. Although the gulags were officially abolished by Nikita Khrushchev in 1956, numbers of the Gulag population remained in the 2-to-4 million range as late as 1959. The proportion of the Soviet labor force in concentration camps was probably 5 percent in the 1930s, increasing to 10 percent during the war years.[28]

The legal foundation for mass political internment was provided by Article 56 of the 1926 Soviet criminal code, which declared actions directed toward weakening state power a crime against the Soviet state. Falling under this classification were a wide variety of offenses, including sabotage, propaganda, conscious failure to carry out one's duties, subversion, and suspicion of espionage. While the Soviet state did seek to derive economic benefit from this system, its costs were immense.[29]

Nomenklatura Controls

In Chapter 6, we noted that the Party used the nomenklatura system to control personnel appointments and placements throughout the economy. Under these arrangements, the most important positions were filled from a list of candidates maintained by the cadre departments of the Communist Party. Other key appointments fell under the nomenklatura of state agencies. This appointment system decided all important administrative positions and gave the Party control over skill requirements and loyalty. Another means of control over loyalty was more direct. Virtually all farm heads and enterprise directors were members of the Communist Party.

LOCAL VS. CENTRALIZED LABOR MARKETS

Our discussion of Soviet labor allocation has emphasized the role of the center. Labor planners set wage rates, directed the educational system to create specialists, conducted organized recruitment campaigns, controlled key appointments, and even used prison labor as the ultimate form of centralized labor control.

The reality of everyday Soviet labor allocation was somewhat different. Throughout the Soviet period, labor was allocated by a mix of central directives and local initiative. At the local level, local Party officials directed labor to different factories or farms, sometimes convincing reluctant enterprise directors to take on additional young workers. Enterprise managers operated with a great deal of leeway, even within the centralized system of wages and bonuses. If centrally established wages were not high enough to attract the necessary number of specialists for an enterprise, the manager could easily reclassify workers into higher skill categories, create extra wage pools through manipulations of the employment roster, and offer hidden bonuses. This local flexibility gave the Soviet system an ability to respond to varying local conditions. While the enterprise manager could manipulate plan targets, he could also achieve flexibility by manipulating the labor allocation process.

prise efficiency, nor did the presence or absence of profits have much operational significance for enterprises.

During the early years of Soviet planning, the prices of industrial products were purposely kept low, with many enterprises operating under state subsidies. However, since enterprises were state owned and financed, profitability was not a significant indicator, and entry and exit from an industry was an administrative, not a market-regulated, function. In rare cases, for example in extractive industries, where there were significant locational cost variations across producers, "accounting prices" were used. In these cases, producers received differentiated prices based upon cost differences, while purchasers paid the same price. Low-cost producers were in effect paying a differential rent to the state.

Also in rare cases, pricing authorities adjusted the prices of close substitutes for differences in "use values." Examples were in oil and coal, and in ferrous and non-ferrous metals. The "use values" of fuel oil and nonferrous metals were perceived to be higher than those of coal and ferrous metals, respectively; therefore, prices in excess of branch average cost were set for fuel oil and nonferrous metals (the difference between average branch costs and wholesale prices being a turnover tax).

The treatment of "new" products and of those sold in Western markets was problematic.[31] If Marx's labor theory of value were followed, "new" products produced by a new technology that results in labor savings should be priced relatively low. Enterprise directors, who risked introducing labor-saving technology, would be paid lower prices instead of earning higher profits. In effect, the profits of innovative enterprises would be passed on to users in the form of price reductions. Such an approach did not encourage the introduction of new technology, and pricing authorities sought ways to exempt "new" products from the labor theory formula. One source of progress in market economies is technological advances, which lower production costs and raise profits. In the Soviet economy, this incentive to innovate was removed by the use of the standard pricing formula.

Differentials between domestic wholesale prices and world market prices were also troublesome. In the case of imports from the West, the planners sold equipment purchased in world markets at a high price and to the domestic enterprise often at a low price. In the case of exports (oil for example), the product sold in world markets at a price much higher than the price paid to the domestic producing enterprise. When domestic and world prices differ substantially, false signals are sent out to domestic consumers and producers. Domestic producers of oil, for example, considered oil's value to be the (low) domestic price rather than its "true" value, the world price.

Soviet authorities sought to set industrial wholesale prices equal to average branch costs, subject to the exceptions noted above. Adherence to these formulas meant that prices should be changed whenever costs changed. Indeed, throughout most of the Soviet period, labor costs were rising. A major problem was the sheer complexity of the task of changing thousands of prices. In fact, Soviet pricing authorities thought in terms of "price reform" rather than in terms of gradual

Experts on the Soviet administrative command economy believe that th labor market, despite the array of administrative controls, came relatively market allocation process. The main proof of this proposition was the Soviet citizens had a fair degree of freedom of occupational choice, if no It was argued, therefore, that the Soviet labor market would be the easie form to full market arrangements in transition.

PRICES AND THE PLANNING SYSTEM[30]

In a market economy, prices are formed by the interplay of dema Demand depends on marginal utility for consumer goods and on th ductivity of inputs. Supply depends upon the marginal cost of p competitive conditions. Prices in the Soviet Union were determi administrative decree, using accounting formulae, rather tha demand. Price setting functions were shared by the Price Burea Ministry of Trade, the Ministry of Finance, the State Con (Goskomtsen), the Republican Councils of Ministers, and vario We examine five different types of prices: industrial wholesale agricultural prices, collective farm market prices, and finally, pr underground economy.

Industrial Wholesale Prices

In the Soviet system, wholesale prices were administrat cost of production. The **factory wholesale price** was the prise sold to the state wholesale trade network. The **indus** the price charged to buyers by wholesale trading establis were based on average branch cost plus a small markup f prise costs, Soviet accounting practice included wage pa ate materials, depreciation, insurance, and paym Depreciation did not include charges for obsolescenc wear and tear. Throughout most of the Soviet perio charges were not part of production costs because en capital or land.

The average branch cost formula meant that e would often have different costs. Therefore, lo "planned profits," and high-cost producers would in cost producers enjoyed some advantage, such as reflected in cost differences. Lower cost was not management. The ministry simply subsidized hi of low-cost producers. Under this pricing formu changes in prices. The pattern was for industrial prices to remain unchanged for long periods of time (sometimes a decade or more) and then for virtually all prices to be adjusted in a general price reform. As costs increased over time, subsidies were required for a higher proportion of enterprises until the next price reform.[32]

Retail Prices

Retail prices were also set administratively, although the general goal was to clear the market, a goal that was only met on occasion. Soviet authorities needed a market distribution of consumer goods to preserve incentives to work. If retail prices were set generally too low, queues would serve as a rationing device, and there would be no incentive for workers to strive for higher wages and bonuses.

The retail price was simply the industry wholesale price plus a retail trade margin plus a **turnover tax.** The turnover tax was included directly in the retail price, so the consumer had little idea of its existence or magnitude. The size of the turnover tax could vary considerably from one item to the next and was a function of the industry wholesale price and the supply-demand conditions in the market. In Figure 7.1, for example, if the wholesale price was OP and the equilibrium (clearing) price OP', the turnover tax would be PP' or less if the price were set below the clearing level. Thus the turnover tax was price determined, not price determining. The turnover tax would rise if the demand increased or if the wholesale price fell.

Figure 7.1 The Soviet Turnover Tax

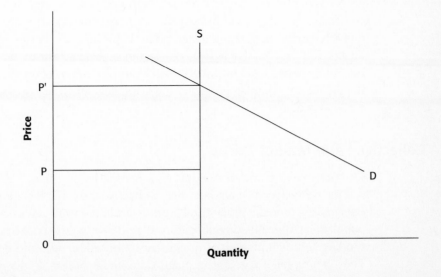

If the industry wholesale price were above the clearing price OP', then a subsidy was required. Subsidies were widespread during the last decades of the Soviet era. At that time, state prices for farm products were increased, but prices of food products to consumers were not, resulting in very large subsidies that severely burdened the Soviet budget.

Agricultural Procurement Prices

The collectivization campaign of the 1930s established the collective farm as the dominant organizational form in the Soviet countryside. As time passed, emphasis shifted from the collective farm to the state farm, and, through agro-industrial integration, many of the differences between state and collective farms had disappeared by the 1970s. These different organizational forms resulted in differing channels through which agricultural products were marketed. For much of the Soviet period, the state used two-level procurement prices for state purchases of agricultural products from collective farms. For compulsory deliveries, a low fixed price was established; while for deliveries above basic targets, an above-quota higher price would be paid. Until the 1950s, there was no cost accounting on collective farms. Subsequent studies revealed that for much of the Soviet period, production costs were substantially above even the higher, above-quota prices.

At the same time, state farms operated under a system essentially the same as that used in industry. They sold to the state at industrial wholesale prices that equaled average branch cost plus a profit margin. That meant the financial arrangements for state farms were similar to those for industrial enterprises, but collective farm financial arrangements were not—to their detriment. As we will see later, there were considerable modifications of agricultural pricing arrangements, although the basic arrangements were sustained through the end of the Soviet period. The major change in pricing that began in the late 1950s recognized that low delivery prices had harmed agricultural productivity. Soviet pricing authorities abandoned the idea that agriculture should subsidize industry. In fact, by the end of the Soviet period, agriculture was heavily subsidized, insofar as average branch costs in agriculture generally exceeded the artificially low retail prices the state charged for food products.

Collective Farm Market Prices

The most significant example of a market-based price in the Soviet economy was the collective farm market price. Collective farm markets, prevalent throughout the country, brought agricultural produce from the rural private sector to the urban population. After meeting obligatory state delivery targets, farmers could sell their produce in urban markets at prices that more or less reflected demand and supply. They were generally higher than state food prices, a phenomenon partially explained by quality differentials and partly by the state policy of keeping state prices at artificially low levels. However, as one of the few examples of a market in an otherwise administered economy, collective farm market prices were of interest as an indicator of repressed inflation. Repressed inflation was considered to be most severe when the gap between collective farm market prices and prices for similar products in state stores widened.

Second Economy Prices

The second, or underground, economy in the Soviet Union was a phenomenon that received significantly increased attention through the 1970s and 1980s. A common feature of the administrative command economy, second economy activities were defined by two conditions: (1) the activity was conducted for private gain, and (2) the activity knowingly contravened existing law. In the Soviet case, a wide variety of second economy activities arose for a number of reasons. The second economy was concentrated in the service sector, for understandable reasons. Apart from the generally limited availability (and poor quality) of services in the Soviet Union, Marxian principles prohibited one person from hiring another. Thus the need for a tutor, for example, would lead to second economy activity. In many cases, the second economy was intertwined with the state economy, for example an enterprise might make an illegal sale of output to raise cash for other purposes. In many cases, bribery and corruption were involved—buying influence and favors that only state and party officials could provide.

By their basic nature, prices in the second economy were market-determined prices, though the specific price setting conditions varied considerably from one case to another. However, unlike collective farm market prices, the state officially ignored the second economy, while tolerating its existence. We must use partial information to discover its size and operational characteristics. The second economy and its impact will be discussed in the next chapter.

PLANNING AND PRICES IN THE SOVIET UNION

Thus far we have examined the operational features of the Soviet price system and have looked at examples. But a more fundamental set of issues remains to be examined—what role did prices play in the Soviet administrative command economy?

In a market economy, relative prices reflect relative scarcities and thus facilitate the rational use of resources. Put another way, scarcity prices are formed by the interaction of demand and supply and should reflect relative scarcities. Decisions on what to produce, how to produce, what to consume, and what to set aside for future consumption are all influenced by relative prices. In effect, relative prices are signals about what is becoming more scarce and what is becoming more abundant.

As we noted in Chapter 6, balance planning in the Soviet Union was carried out both in physical terms (units) and in value terms (physical units multiplied by prices). Insofar as most Soviet prices were administered, these prices typically did not reflect relative scarcities. For this reason, neither planners nor managers could use Soviet prices as guides to relative scarcities.

Prices and Resource Allocation

The Soviet administrative command economy was operated with little attention to and assistance from relative prices. Most planning decisions were made in physical terms, such as how much steel to produce or how many engineers to hire. The administrative achievement of balances was viewed as superior to the achievement of balances through equilibrium prices. Given this philosophy, it should not be a surprise that Soviet prices were ill-suited as signals for resource allocation. They were never intended to serve as mechanisms for guiding such decisions.

Even if Soviet planners had wished to use prices for allocating resources, these prices were not suited for the task. Wholesale prices were based upon average branch cost that throughout most of the Soviet period did not include charges for capital or land. The administrative complexity of changing thousands of prices (price reform) was so great that most of the time, established prices did not even reflect average branch costs. Moreover, the basic average cost formula meant that prices were determined by averaging the costs of low-cost and high-cost producers. As such, Soviet prices did not reflect the cost of the last unit produced and thus could not be used to determine how to allocate resources at the margin.

Some prices in the Soviet Union did play an allocative role. Soviet administrators saw that it made little sense to allocate consumer goods administratively, so in this sector planners used relative prices. Likewise, relative wages were used to allocate labor. Thus relative consumer goods prices and relative wages came as close to a "market" price as possible in the administrative command economy.

Recall, however, that Soviet pricing broke the link between consumer goods prices and wholesale prices. In Figure 7.1 (p. 135), we saw that the signal between a market-based price and the industry price was broken by the turnover tax. If, in Figure 7.1, demand had increased (indicating a greater willingness to purchase), this would have resulted in higher retail prices, a higher turnover tax, but no increase in the wholesale price. The wholesale price was determined strictly by cost. If demand had increased and costs had fallen, the gap between the retail price and the wholesale price would have grown, and producers would receive the false signal that the good had declined in importance, despite increased demand.

One of the most important functions of prices in a market economy is to determine which producers survive and which fail. In market economies, enterprises whose average cost exceeds their selling price will eventually go out of business. In the Soviet administrative command economy, prices did not fulfill this function. Given the failure to include in prices a charge for capital or land, it is entirely possible that low-cost producers had low costs because they were not being charged for their capital or locational advantages. High-cost producers whose costs were above the wholesale price (and who would go out of business in a market economy) may have been run more efficiently than low-cost enterprises; they simply lacked capital or locational advantages. Enterprise losses and profits did not indicate who should survive and who should fail. It would have been incorrect for planners to make decisions on bankruptcies or expansions on the basis of enterprise profits.

Prices and Control

In hierarchical organizations such as the administrative command economy, prices provide critical elements of information. In any hierarchy, principal/agent problem(s) can be addressed by degrees of decentralization of authority and responsibility. Thus a principal could either instruct an agent to function in terms of quantitative (physical) directives or to follow market forces (information signals) and maximize profits. Under a set of carefully specified conditions, the outcomes could be much the same, but in reality, the outcomes would likely be very different. Thus it matters whether physical targets or value categories are used, and in the Soviet case, where administered prices did not reflect relative scarcities, it mattered to a great degree.

In fact, Soviet enterprises were often judged in value rather than physical terms. It was simply too difficult to express all targets in physical terms. Thus output would be measured in ruble amounts, along with additional (if less important) targets such as cost reduction. In this setting, whether it be profits, the value of output, or some other price-related indicator, Soviet pricing arrangements must have introduced considerable distortions into both plan formulation and plan execution.

Prices and Measurement

We have noted that plan formulation and execution can, conceptually, be done in either physical or value terms. In reality, people use prices to measure the results of economic activity. An understanding of economic activity typically requires aggregation of dissimilar products, and aggregation requires valuation. Without prices, one cannot determine at what rate the economy is growing or whether the capital/output ratio is falling, all important variables in the planning process. For example, if Party directives at the highest level dictate a rate of growth for heavy industry, one must use prices to add up the outputs and compute rates of growth for the various branches.

Both control and measurement functions are more easily carried out when prices do not change. But from an allocative point of view, stable prices is not a desirable characteristic, since underlying cost characteristics change over time, and stable prices no longer reflect current cost relationships. In the Soviet case, prices were generally not changed for two basic reasons: First, the informational requirements for such changes were massive, and second, changing prices significantly complicated the planners' tasks.

The best known problem of prices and measurement in the Soviet case is the issue of measuring Soviet economic growth, an issue central to understanding the Soviet economic record. As we examine this issue in Chapter 11, we will note that in the 1930s, sharp structural changes that were not reflected in prices created serious measurement problems.

Prices and Income Distribution

In a market economy, prices play a critical role in determining the distribution of income. However, in an administrative command economy, prices played an important role in determining the distribution of income. For ideological reasons, Soviet authorities believed that public goods should replace private goods and that the distribution of income should be much more even than would typically be the case in a market economy. Accordingly, price setting reflected these beliefs. For example, housing rents were held very low and kept stable over time in spite of continuing excess demand for housing. User charges, for example for electricity, were virtually nonexistent. Charges for medical care, education, and the like were modest, rationing being done by non-price means where necessary. Automobiles, on the other hand, were prohibitively expensive and available only after many years of waiting for those who did not occupy privileged positions.

Thus pricing was an important mechanism for influencing the distribution of real income. While there was some leveling of wage incomes, the use of wage differentials for incentive purposes seemed to dominate as a policy for wage setting. Wage leveling was not used on the grounds that this would weaken the incentive system.

PRICES AND MARKET REFORMS

By the end of the Soviet era, the price system had developed certain characteristics that would have an impact upon the transition era. Soviet consumer prices, particularly the prices of food products and energy, had been kept artificially low to achieve the goals of income distribution. Although the costs of producing these goods had risen, their prices to end consumers had not. This discrepancy meant that if administered pricing was to end, there would have to be substantial upward adjustment in end-user prices.

The administered nature of Soviet prices meant that producers and consumers were not linked by markets. Most materials and capital goods were supplied administratively through the material technical supply system, not through wholesale markets. Any move from administered to market pricing would therefore require the creation of missing market institutions, specifically wholesale markets.

With capital allocated administratively and its finance provided by the state budget, another institution missing at the end of the Soviet era was capital markets. These institutions would have to be developed to put a price on credit and to equate the supply of and demand for credit.

The administrative command economy lacked market institutions and thus developed a set of prices that could not be used for allocative purposes. Given the tendency to set prices low relative to the real costs of production, one would expect that any move towards market pricing would result in a substantial upsurge in retail prices. As we shall see, when the Soviet administrative command economy was abandoned in late 1991, the first effect was substantial inflation.

SUMMARY

In this chapter we have examined plan execution, specifically the managerial function in combining inputs to fulfill output targets. The managerial function in the Soviet Union was a classic example of the principal/agent problem and asymmetric information. With some influence from managers, plan targets were formulated and enterprise managers were expected to fulfill them. But, the managerial milieu gave the enterprise directors considerable flexibility, a lack of decision-making tools, and information with which to work—but with significant rewards for success. In this setting, it is not surprising that managers would attempt to limit constraints and pursue success whenever possible.

One of the important constraints facing management was guaranteed input supplies. While the allocation of inputs was, like other plan elements, based upon the balance concept, labor inputs were influenced by relative wages. In turn, relative wages were influenced by education as in other economies. At the same time, labor allocation was also influenced by a variety of administrative controls varying from obligatory placement after education through the penal labor system prominent in the Stalin era.

An important issue in both plan formulation and plan execution is that of prices and valuation. In both aspects of planning, physical targets and value categories were used—tons of steel and rubles of steel output. At the same time, the managerial information arrangements and reward structures paid rather more attention to target fulfillment (in physical or value terms) than traditional indicators such as profits, the latter largely meaningless in the Soviet case.

The problem of value categories derived largely from Soviet price-setting procedures. With interesting exceptions, such as the collective farm markets, Soviet prices were administered using a cost-based formula plus selected markups, including the turnover tax at the retail level. These arrangements resulted in prices that were generally quite stable over time but that bore very little relation to relative scarcities.

Judged by traditional indicators, Soviet prices were useful for control and income distribution functions but were relatively unimportant and in fact were dysfunctional for allocative functions. Based upon our discussion of money and prices, it is evident that financial variables were of limited importance in the Soviet economy and where used may have resulted in allocative distortions.

Terms and Concepts ───────────

predpriiatie   The enterprise, or basic unit of industrial production, in the former Soviet Union.

edinonachalie   One-man management; the manager of an enterprise is ultimately responsible for the operations of the enterprise.

bounded rationality   Individual limitations, such as lack of skills, outdated equipment, uncertain suppliers, or limited access to required information.

technical/administrative problems   Problems arising from bounded rationality.

agency/managerial problems   Problems arising from information asymmetry.

asymmetric information   A situation where two parties to a contract (for example a planner and an enterprise director) have different information that affects the behavior of the contracting parties.

span of control   A concept in organization theory/management that refers to the number of subunits that a manager or supervisor is able to control effectively.

incentive compatibility   A system of incentives that harmonizes the behavior of an agent with the desired objective of the principal such that the objective is achieved.

ratchet effect   A problem common to piece work arrangements or plan setting and fulfillment; agent argues for an "easy" target to overfulfill and receives a bonus; principal views overfulfillment as evidence of greater capacity and raises the target for the next period.

reserving   Holding back supply allotments as a safety factor.

ruble control   A method of control used to monitor enterprises in the Soviet Union; specifically, targets (for example the hiring of labor in man-hours) would have a ruble counterpart in a state bank account, the balance of which could be monitored.

soft budget constraint   A concept enunciated by Janos Kornai about enterprise behavior in planned socialist economic systems, noting that such enterprises do not pay attention to cost containment.

input-output coefficient   The relation between the amount of input required to produce a unit of output; for example, if 25 units of labor are needed to produce 50 units of steel, then the coefficient for labor is .5.

Orgnabor   Soviet acronym for the organization concerned with the organized recruitment of labor for various projects, regions, and the like.

Komsomol   Communist Party Youth Organization.

Gulag   Soviet concentration camps, which served as penal labor pools.

factory wholesale price   The price at which a Soviet enterprise would sell an item to the wholesale trade network; composed of average branch cost (typically without a charge for land or capital but including wage payments, cost of intermediate materials, depreciation, insurance payments, and overhead) and a small profit markup.

industry wholesale price   The price at which an item is sold to buyers outside the industry. Based upon the factory wholesale price plus additional markups, such as transportation.

turnover tax   A tax added to the industry wholesale price at the retail level in the Soviet Union, the magnitude of the tax determined by the difference between the level of the price (and a retail trade margin) and equilibrium of supply and demand.

Selected Bibliography

The Enterprise: Theory

Conn, D. "Effort, Efficiency, and Incentives in Organizations," *Journal of Comparative Economics* vol. 6 (September 1982), 223–34.

Farrell, J. "Information and the Coase Theorem," *Journal of Economic Perspectives* vol. 1 (Fall 1987), 113–29.

Grossman, S., and O. Hart. "The Costs and Benefits of Ownership: A Theory of Vertical and Lateral Integration," *Journal of Political Economy* vol. 94 (August 1986), 691–719.

Kumar Sah, R., and J. E. Stiglitz. "The Architecture of Economic Systems: Hierarchies and Polyarchies," *American Economic Review* vol. 76 (September 1986), 716–27.

Laffont, J., and E. Maskin. "The Theory of Incentives: An Overview," in W. Hildebrand, ed., *Advances in Economic Theory* (Cambridge: Cambridge University Press, 1982).

Pratt, J., and R. Zeckhauser, eds. *Principals and Agents: The Structure of Business* (Cambridge, MA: Harvard Business School, 1985).

Putterman, L., and G. Skillman. "The Incentive Effects of Monitoring Under Alternate Compensation Schemes," *International Journal of Industrial Organization* 6 (March 1988), 109–20.

Sappington, D. E. M. "Incentives in Principal-Agent Relationships," *Journal of Economic Perspectives* vol. 5 (Spring 1991), 45–66.

Simon, H. A. "Organization and Markets," *Journal of Economic Perspectives* vol. 5 (Spring 1991), 25–44.

Stiglitz, J. E. "Symposium on Organization and Economics," *Journal of Economic Perspectives* vol. 5 (Spring 1991), 15–24.

————. *Whither Socialism?* (Cambridge, MA: MIT Press, 1994).

Williamson, O., ed. *Organization Theory: From Chester Barnard to the Present and Beyond* (Oxford: Oxford University Press, 1990).

Enterprise Management

Berliner, J. S. *Factory and Manager in the USSR* (Cambridge, MA: Harvard University Press, 1957).

————. *The Innovation Decision in Soviet Industry* (Cambridge, MA: MIT Press, 1976).

————. "Managerial Incentives and Decision-Making: A Comparison of the United States and the Soviet Union," in M. Bornstein and D. Fusfeld, eds., *The Soviet Economy* 3e (Homewood, IL: Irwin, 1970), 165–95.

Bornstein, M. "Improving the Soviet Economic Mechanism," *Soviet Studies* vol. 37, no. 1 (January 1985), 1–30.

Conyngham, W. J. *The Modernization of Soviet Industrial Management* (New York: Cambridge University Press, 1982).

Freris, A. *The Soviet Industrial Enterprise* (New York: St. Martins Press, 1984).

Granick, D. *Management of the Industrial Firm in the USSR* (New York: Columbia University Press, 1954).

————. *Managerial Comparisons of Four Developed Countries: France, Britain, United States and Russia* (Cambridge, MA: MIT Press, 1972).

————. *The Red Executive* (Garden City, NY: Doubleday, 1960).

————. *Soviet Metal Fabricating and Economic Development* (Madison: University of Wisconsin Press, 1967).

Guroff, G., and F. V. Carstensen, eds. *Entrepreneurship in Imperial Russia and the Soviet Union* (Princeton, NJ: Princeton University Press, 1982).

Hanson, P. "Success Indicators Revisited: The July 1979 Decree on Planning and Management," *Soviet Studies* vol. 25, no. 1 (January 1983), 1–13.

Kroll, H. "The Role of Contracts in the Soviet Economy," *Soviet Studies* vol. 40, no. 3 (July 1988), 349–66.

Linz, S. J. "Management's Response to Tautness in Soviet Planning: Evidence from the Soviet Interview Project," *Comparative Economic Studies* vol. 30, no. 1 (Spring 1988), 65–103.

Nove, A. *Economic Rationality and Soviet Politics* (New York: Praeger, 1964).

Richman, B. M. *Management Development and Education in the Soviet Union* (East Lansing: Michigan State University Press, 1967).

————. *Soviet Industrial Management* (Englewood Cliffs, NJ: Prentice Hall, 1965).

Labor

Adam, J. *Employment Policies in the Soviet Union and Eastern Europe* 2 rev. ed. (London: Macmillan, 1987).

Arnot, B. *Controlling Soviet Labour* (London: Macmillan, 1988).

Bergson, A. *The Economics of Soviet Planning* (New Haven: Yale University Press, 1964).

———. *The Structure of Soviet Wages* (Cambridge, MA: Harvard University Press, 1944).

McCauley, M. *Labor Disputes in Soviet Russia 1957–1965* (Oxford: Oxford University Press, 1969).

Rapawy, S. "Labor Force and Employment in the USSR," in U.S. Congress, Joint Economic Committee, *Gorbachev's Economic Plans* vol. 1 (Washington, DC: U.S. Government Printing Office, 1987), 187–212.

Ruble, B. A. *Soviet Trade Unions* (New York: Cambridge University Press, 1981).

Slider, D. "Reforming the Workplace: The 1983 Soviet Law on Labour Collectives," *Soviet Studies* vol. 37, no. 2 (1985), 173–83.

Yanowitch, M. *Work in the Soviet Union* (New York: M. E. Sharpe, 1985).

The Price System

Aouchar, A., ed. *The Socialist Price Mechanism* (Durham, NC: Duke University Press, 1977).

Becker, A. "The Price Level of Soviet Machinery in the 1960s," *Soviet Studies* vol. 26, no. 3 (July 1974), 363–80.

Bergson, A. *The Economics of Soviet Planning* (New Haven: Yale University Press, 1964).

Bornstein, M. "The Administration of the Soviet Price System," Soviet Studies vol. 30, no. 4 (October 1978), 466–90.

———. "The 1963 Soviet Industrial Price Revision," *Soviet Studies* vol. 15, no. 1 (July 1963), 43–52.

———. "The Soviet Debate on Agricultural Prices and Procurement Reforms," *Soviet Studies* vol. 21, no. 1 (July 1969), 1–20.

———. "Soviet Price Policy in the 1970s," in U.S. Congress, Joint Economic Committee, *Soviet Economy in a New Perspective* (Washington, DC: U.S. Government Printing Office, 1976), 17–66.

———. "The Soviet Price Reform Discussion," *Quarterly Journal of Economics* vol. 78, no. 1 (February 1964), 15–48.

———. "Soviet Price Theory and Policy," in M. Bornstein and D. Fusfeld, eds. *The Soviet Economy: A Book of Readings* 3e (Homewood, IL: Irwin, 1970), 106–37.

———. "The Soviet Industrial Price Revision," in G. Fink, ed. *Socialist Economy and Economic Policy: Essays in Honor of Friedrich Levcik* (New York: Springer Verlag, 1985).

———. "Soviet Price Policies," *Soviet Economy* vol. 3, no. 2 (1987), 96–134.

Campbell, R. W. "Marx, Kantorovich and Novozhilov: Stoimost' Versus Reality," *Slavic Review* vol. 20, no. 3 (October 1961), 402–18.

Hanson, P. *The Consumer Sector in the Soviet Economy* (Evanston, IL: Northwestern University Press, 1968).

Hutchings, R. "The Origins of the Soviet Industrial Price System," *Soviet Studies* vol. 13, no. 1 (July 1961), 1–22.

Nove, A. *The Soviet Economic System* (London: Allen & Unwin, 1977).

Pickersgill, J. "Soviet Household Saving's Behavior," *Review of Economics and Statistics* vol. 58, no. 2 (May 1976), 139–47.

Schroeder, G. E. "The 1966–67 Soviet Industrial Price Reform: A Study in Complications," *Soviet Studies* vol. 20, no. 4 (April 1969), 462–77.

Steiner, J. E. "Disguised Inflation in the Soviet Union," *Journal of Comparative Economics* vol. 6, no. 3 (September 1982), 278–87.

Notes

1. There is a large literature devoted to Soviet enterprise management. Our discussion is based upon: J. S. Berliner, *Factory and Manager in the USSR* (Cambridge, MA: Harvard University Press, 1957); D. Granick, *Management of the Industrial Firm in the USSR* (New York: Columbia University Press, 1964); B. M. Richman, *Soviet Industrial Management* (Englewood Cliffs, NJ: Prentice Hall, 1965); D. Granick, *Managerial Comparisons of Four Developed Countries: France, Great Britain, United States, and Russia* (Cambridge, MA: MIT Press, 1972); D. Granick, *Soviet Metal Fabricating and Economic Development* (Madison: University of Wisconsin Press, 1967); J. S. Berliner, *The Innovation Decision in Soviet Industry* (Cambridge, MA: MIT Press, 1976); G. Guroff and F. V. Carstensen, eds., *Entrepreneurship in Imperial Russia and the Soviet Union* (Princeton, NJ: Princeton University Press, 1983); W. J. Conyngham, *The Modernization of Soviet Industrial Management* (New York: Cambridge University Press, 1982); J. C. Thompson and R. F. Vidmer, *Administrative Science and Politics in the USSR and the United States* (New York: Praeger, 1983); H. Bherer, *Management Sovietique* (Paris: Presses de la Fondation Nationale des Sciences Politiques, 1982); S. J. Linz, "Management's Response to Tautness in Soviet Planning: Evidence from the Soviet Interview Project," *Comparative Economic Studies* vol. 30, no. 1 (Spring 1988), 65–103; A. Freris, *The Soviet Industrial Enterprise* (New York: St. Martin's Press, 1984).

2. There is a large and diverse literature on information and organization issues. For an introduction, see for example Hal Varian, *Microeconomic Theory* 3e (New York: Norton, 1992), ch. 25. For a useful discussion of the relevance of information/organization literature in the comparative context, see A. Ben-Ner, J. M. Montias, and E. Neuberger, "Basic Issues in Organizations: A Comparative Perspective," *Journal of Comparative Economics* vol. 17 (1993), 207–42.

3. H. Kuromiya, "Edinonachalie and the Soviet Industrial Manager, 1928–1937," *Soviet Studies* vol. 36, no. 2 (April 1984), 185–204.

4. The phrase *success indicators* is a traditional reference to a wide array of problems relating to the assessment of managerial performance in the Soviet setting. See, for example, A. Nove, "The Problem of Success Indicators in Soviet Industry," in *Economic Rationality and Soviet Politics* (New York: Praeger, 1964), 83–98; for a different view, see P. Hanson, "Success Indicators Revisited: The 1979 Soviet Decree on Planning and Management," *Soviet Studies* vol. 25, no. 1 (January 1983), 1–13; M. Bornstein, "Improving the Soviet Economic Mechanism," *Soviet Studies* vol. 37, no. 1 (January 1985), 1–30.

5. See for example M. Weitzman, "The 'Ratchet Principle' and Performance Incentives," *The Bell Journal of Economics* vol. 11, no. 1 (Spring 1980), 302–08; M. L. Weitzman, "The New Soviet Incentive Model," The Bell Journal of Economics vol. 7, no. 1 (Spring 1976), 251–57; J. A. Yunker, "A Dynamic Optimization Model of the Soviet Enterprise," *Economics of Planning* 13, 1–2 (1973), 33–51.

6. During the 1950s, bonus and incentive payments accounted for roughly 40 percent of average industrial incomes, a figure which dropped to around 30 percent by the late 1970s.

7. For comparisons, see Granick, *Managerial Comparisons of Four Developed Countries*, ch. 9.

8. While turnover of upper level managerial personnel decreased, stagnation may have increased. On this see W. J. Conyngham, *The Modernization of Soviet Industrial Management* (New York: Cambridge University Press, 1982) and also Granick, *Managerial Comparisons of Four Developed Countries*.

9. S. J. Linz, "Managerial Autonomy in Soviet Industrial Firms," *Soviet Studies* vol. 40, no. 2 (April 1988), 175–95.

10. For a discussion of problems imposed by the supply system, see G. E. Schroeder, "The 'Reform' of the Supply System in Soviet Industry," *Soviet Studies* vol. 24, no. 1 (July 1972), 105–07; G. E. Schroeder, "The Soviet Economy on a Treadmill of 'Reforms,'" in U.S. Congress, Joint Economic Committee, *Soviet Economy in a Time of Change* vol. 1 (Washington, DC: U.S. Government Printing Office, 1979), 323–24; G. E. Schroeder, "Soviet Economic 'Reform' Decrees: More Steps on the Treadmill," in U.S. Congress, Joint Economic Committee, *Soviet Economy in the 1980s: Problems and Prospects* part 1 (Washington, DC: U.S. Government Printing Office, 1982), 65–88.

11. Discussion of the planning of labor by Gosplan can be found in *Metodicheskie ukazaniia i razrabotke gosudarstvennykh planov ekonomicheskogo i sotsialnogo razvitiia SSSR* [Methods for elaborating the state plan for the economic and social development of the USSR] (Moscow: Ekonomika, 1980), ch. 6; Y. Dubrovsky, *Planning of Manpower in the Soviet Union* translated from the Russian (Moscow: Progress Publishers, 1975). For discussion of these issues in the Western literature, see for example, Rapawy, "Labor Constraints in the Five Year Plan," in U.S. Congress, Joint Economic Committee, *Soviet Economic Prospects for the Seventies* (Washington, DC: U.S. Government Printing Office, 1973), 485–507; M. Feshbach and S. Rapawy, "Soviet Population and Manpower Trends and Policies," in U.S. Congress, Joint Economic Committee, *Soviet Economy in a New Perspective* (Washington, DC: U.S. Government Printing Office, 1976), 113–54; S. Rapawy, "Labor Force and Employment in the USSR.," in U.S. Congress, Joint Economic Committee, *Gorbachev's Economic Plans* vol. 1 (Washington, DC: U.S. Government Printing Office, 1987), 187–212.

12. G. Ofer and A. Vinokur, *The Soviet Household Under the Old Regime* (New York: Cambridge University Press, 1987).

13. Efimov, et al., *Ekonomicheskoe planirovanie*, 171.

14. For a discussion of the passport system, see V. Zaslavsky and Y. Luryi, "The Passport System in the USSR and Changes in Soviet Society," *Soviet Union* vol. 6, no. 2 (1979), 137–53.

15. See A. McCauley, *Economic Welfare in the Soviet Union* (Madison: University of Wisconsin Press, 1979), 174–86.

16. For a discussion of Soviet wage setting arrangements, see L. J. Kirsch, *Soviet Wages: Changes in Structure and Administration Since 1956* (Cambridge, MA: MIT Press, 1972); J. G. Chapman, "Soviet Wages Under Socialism," in A. Abouchar, ed., *The Socialist Price Mechanism* (Durham, NC: Duke University Press, 1977), 246–81; McCauley, *Economic Welfare in the Soviet Union*, ch. 8; B. M. Sukharevsky, "Zarabotnaia plata i material'naia zainteresovannost'," [The wage and material incentives] in A. P. Volkov, et al., eds., *Trud I zarobotnaia plata v SSSR* [Labor and wages in the USSR] (Moscow, 1968).

17. A. Bergson, *The Structure of Soviet Wages* (Cambridge, MA: Harvard University Press, 1944), ch. 8, and Sukharevsky, "Zarabotnaia plata," 291.

18. McCauley, *Economic Welfare in the Soviet Union*, 201; Kirsch, *Soviet Wages*, ch. 4; M. Yanowitch, "The Soviet Income Revolution," *Slavic Review* vol. 22, no. 4 (December 1963),

reprinted in M. Bornstein and D. Fusfeld, eds., *The Soviet Economy* 2e (Homewood, IL: Irwin, 1966), 228–41; Sukharevsky, "Zarabotnaia plata," 196; Vestnik statistiki [Herald of Statistics] vol. 6 (1983), 61–62.

19. Chapman, "Labor Mobility," 23.

20. Sukharevsky, "Zarabotnaia plata," 292; Kirsch, *Soviet Wages,* Table 6-1, 125.

21. For a discussion of Soviet education see M. Matthews, *Education in the Soviet Union: Policies and Institutions Since Stalin* (Boston: Allen & Unwin, 1982); R. B. Dobson, "Education and Opportunity," in J. Pankhurst and M. P. Sacks, eds., *Contemporary Soviet Society: Sociological Perspectives* (New York: Praeger, 1980); R. B. Dobson, "Soviet Education: Problems and Policies in the Urban Context," in H. W. Morton and R. C. Stuart, eds., *The Contemporary Soviet City* (Armonk: M. E. Sharpe, 1984), 156–79; CIA, *USSR Trends and Prospects in Educational Attainment, 1959–79* (Washington, DC: CIA, 1979).

22. Dobson, "Soviet Education," 156.

23. For a discussion of changes in these requirements, see Goodman and Schleifer, "The Soviet Labor Market in the 1980s," 336–39.

24. For a discussion of controls, see E. Nash, "Recent Changes in Labor Controls in the Soviet Union," in U.S. Congress, Joint Economic Committee, *New Directions in the Soviet Economy,* part 3 (Washington, DC: U.S. Government Printing Office, 1966), 849–71; Goodman and Schleifer, "The Soviet Labor Market in the 1980s" B. Arnot, *Controlling Soviet Labour* (London: Macmillan, 1988).

25. For a detailed discussion of labor controls from the mid-1930s through the mid-1950s, see A. Nove, *An Economic History of the USSR* (London: Penguin, 1969), 195–98; 260–63.

26. D. Granick, *Job Rights in the Soviet Union: Their Consequences* (New York: Cambridge University Press, 1987). In 1956, criminal liability for leaving a job without permission and for absenteeism were abandoned and social benefits were raised. Turnover rates in the 1980s were similar to those in the United States.

27. This discussion is based on the following sources: S. Rosefielde, "How Reliable are Available Estimates of Forced Concentration Camp Labor in the Soviet Union ?" *Soviet Studies* vol. 32. no. 4 (October 1981); D. Dallin and B. Nicolevsky, *Forced Labor in Soviet Russia* (New Haven: Yale University Press, 1947); N. Jasny, "Labor and Output in Soviet Concentration Camps," *Journal of Political Economy* vol. 59, no. 5 (October 1951), 405–19; A. Solzhenitsyn, *The Gulag Archipelago,* (New York: Harper, 1973); S. Swianiewicz, *Forced Labor and Economic Development* (London: Oxford University Press, 1965); S. Rosefielde, "An Assessment of the Sources and Uses of Gulag Forced Labor," *Soviet Studies* vol. 32, no. 1 (January 1981), 51–87; S. G. Wheatcroft, "On Assessing the Size of Concentration Camp Forced Labor in the Soviet Union, 1929–56," *Soviet Studies* vol. 32, no. 2 (April 1981), 265–95; R. Conquest, "Forced Labor Statistics: Some Comments," *Soviet Studies* vol. 34, no. 3 (July 1982), 434–39; S. G. Wheatcroft, "Towards a Thorough Analysis of Soviet Forced Labour Statistics," *Soviet Studies* vol. 35 (April 1983), 223–37; J. Barber, "The Development of Soviet Labour and Employment Policy, 1930–41," in D. Lane, ed., *Labour and Employment in the USSR,* 50–65.

28. For summary estimates, see S. Rosefielde, "How Reliable are Available Estimates ?" Tables 1 and 4; and Wheatcroft, "On Assessing the Size of Forced Concentration Camp Labour," 267–68.

29. S. Rosefielde, "Excess Mortality in the Soviet Union: A Reconsideration of the Costs of Forced Industrialization 1929–1949," *Soviet Studies* vol. 35, no. 3 (July 1983), 385–409; B. Anderson and B. Silver, "Demographic Analysis and Population Catastrophes in the USSR," *Slavic Review* vol. 44, no. 3 (Fall 1985), 517–36.

30. For a discussion of Soviet prices, see M. Bornstein, "Soviet Price Theory and Policy," in M. Bornstein and D. Fusfeld, eds., *The Soviet Economy: A Book of Readings* 3e (Homewood, IL: Irwin, 1970), 106–37; P. Hanson, *The Consumer Sector in the Soviet Economy* (Evanston, IL: Northwestern University Press, 1968), ch. 8; M. Bornstein, "The Soviet Price Reform Discussion," *Quarterly Journal of Economics* vol. 78, no. 1 (February 1964), 15–48; A. Bergson, *The Economics of Soviet Planning* (New Haven: Yale University Press, 1964), ch. 8; M. Bornstein, "The Soviet Debate on Agricultural Prices and Procurement Reforms," *Soviet Studies* vol. 21, no. 1 (July 1969), 1–20; M. Bornstein, "The Administration of the Soviet Price System," *Soviet Studies* vol. 30, no. 4 (October 1978), 466–90; M. Bornstein, "Soviet Price Policy in the 1970s," in U.S. Congress, Joint Economic Committee, *Soviet Economy in a New Perspective* (Washington, DC: U.S. Government Printing Office, 1976), 17–66; M. Bornstein, "The Soviet Industrial Price Revision," in G. Fink, ed., *Socialist Economy and Economic Policy: Essays in Honor of Friedrich Levcik,* (New York: Springer Verlag, 1985); M. Bornstein, "Soviet Price Policies," *Soviet Economy* vol. 3, no. 2 (1987), 96–134.

31. The problem of pricing "new" products is discussed in J. S. Berliner, *The Innovation Decision in Soviet Industry* (Cambridge, MA: MIT Press, 1976); M. Bornstein, "The Administration of the Soviet Price System," and V. G. Treml, "Foreign Trade and the Soviet Economy: Changing Parameters and Interrelationships," in E. Neuberger and L. Tyson, eds., *The Impact of International Disturbances on the Soviet Union and Eastern Europe* (New York: Pergamon, 1980).

32. Wholesale prices remained roughly constant between 1929 and 1936, such that by 1936, due to rapidly increasing wage costs, subsidies were the rule. Major price increases in 1936 and again in 1949 attempted to eliminate subsidies. Again, after a reform in 1955, prices remain virtually unchanged until 1966–67, and thereafter until a major price reform in 1982. Official Soviet wholesale price indices revealed very little inflation. Western recomputations also failed to show significant inflation. See A. Bergson and L. Turgeon, "Basic Industrial Prices in the USSR, 1928–1950," (Santa Monica: Rand, 1955); for a discussion of the 1982 reform, see M. Bornstein, "The Soviet Industrial Price Revision"; for Western computations of industrial prices, see A. Becker, "The Price Level of Soviet Machinery in the 1960s," *Soviet Studies* vol. 26, no. 3 (July 1974), 363–80, and J. E. Steiner, *Inflation in Soviet Industry and Machine Building and Metalworking* (Washington, DC: CIA, 1978).

CHAPTER 8

Beyond the Enterprise: Households, the Second Economy, and the Rural Sector

THE HOUSEHOLD

In any economic system, there are three main economic agents: enterprises, the state, and households. Thus far we have examined state economic activity and the functioning of Soviet enterprises in great detail, referring to households only as suppliers of labor. This treatment does not imply that households were of less importance in the Soviet system but rather reflects the simple fact that during the Soviet era official secrecy and the absence of even minimal data made it very difficult to study the Soviet household. It was, however, an important player in the Soviet economy.

Conceptually, one might argue that the household in the Soviet Union would behave like one in a different economic system. Thus, household members would provide labor services to enterprises and other organizations, in the Soviet case through the planning process examined earlier. Moreover, households could either spend their income or save it, under the usual assumption of maximizing utility under constraints. In fact, Soviet household behavior was more complex.

We have already discussed matters of labor supply to the national economy.[1] While specific incentives, social pressure, and for some, conscription (for example after education or in the military) all influenced labor force participation, for the most part the tradeoff between work and leisure was made within the household. The Soviet labor force was formally defined by age, that is, 16–55 years for women and 16–59 years for men. **Labor force participation** rates were high in the Soviet Union, especially for women, where numerous incentives (for example provision of child care facilities) encouraged participation. The issue of women in the Soviet labor force deserves additional attention.

Women in the Soviet Labor Force

The traditional view of women in the Soviet labor forced was based in part on the argument that given the fact that women appeared to enjoy high participation rates, even in key fields such as medicine, allocative inefficiency from discrimination was largely avoided. Indeed the overall participation rate for both men and women was very high, approximately 88 percent.

However, as more empirical evidence on Soviet labor allocation became available, a different picture emerged. As in the West, women tended to predominate in sectors with relatively low pay. Moreover, within low paying sectors, women occupied fewer technical and higher-paying positions than men. Moreover, although Soviet women enjoyed a high rate of participation in the labor force and access to higher education, the typical Soviet woman bore a rather large burden of household work, in part due to the nature of the household and the distribution of work among household members, but also due to the absence of time-saving household appliances.

Recent empirical evidence suggests that there were in fact significant male-female differentials. Earnings functions estimated on Soviet data have generally indicated a male-female gap roughly similar to that found in the United States, when similar explanatory factors such as education and experience are considered.[2] In an early study on male-female differentials in the Soviet Union, Gur Ofer and Aaron Vinokur found an hourly male-female wage ratio of .70, not dissimilar to that found elsewhere. Indeed, they conclude that ". . . by and large both the levels of the pay differential by sex and the main explanatory factors are similar to those in the developed Western economies."[3] Indeed, in a subsequent study of the Soviet household, the authors conclude ". . . that Soviet women do react and respond to changes in the economic environment along similar lines to women elsewhere."[4] They note, however, that while other authors have found differing results (in particular a negative relation between education and participation), the relation between the high level of female participation observed in the Soviet Union and the usual economic and demographic variables remains.[5]

The Soviet Household: Work Patterns and Outcomes

There is no theory of the socialist household. As noted above, the household was one of the less accessible parts of the Soviet economy. Moreover, with limited published data on the Soviet household, it proved very difficult to answer even basic questions about Soviet household behavior, questions that can be readily answered in Western market economies. It is important, however, to examine aggregate patterns that can be observed with reasonable accuracy.

Population dynamics in the Soviet Union differed from those of other countries at similar levels of economic development. In particular, the **demographic transition** took place over a much shorter span of years in the Soviet Union than occurred elsewhere.[6] During the Soviet era, we observe a significant decline in birth rates and death rates, such that the rate of growth of the population resembled that of a country at a much higher level of economic development. In addition, there were important regional differentials—relatively high rates of population growth in the South, and relatively low rates of population growth in the North.[7]

Although we have observed that controls were important for the regional distribution of the Soviet population, the use of controls declined after World War II. Instead, regional wage differentials were used to attract labor to areas such as Siberia, where Soviet leaders sought to promote economic development under very harsh conditions.[8] At the same time, there was major growth of the urban sector of the Soviet Union, resulting in part from the creation of new cities, the expansion of existing cities, and an ongoing migration from rural areas. Migration from rural areas was influenced by many factors, including rural-urban wage differentials and the relative attractiveness of Soviet urban areas relative to the backward conditions of the rural sector.[9]

We have also emphasized the importance the Soviet Union placed upon education. Although the bias was in favor of scientific and technical education (as opposed the social sciences and humanities), the stock of human capital increased significantly during the Soviet era.[10] This increase, for which there was reward, was a major factor contributing to increased household earnings.

While the 1897 census showed 78 percent of the over 15-year-old population to be illiterate, this rate had dropped to 56 percent in 1926 and 20 percent by 1939. After World War II, the Soviet Union had one of the world's most literate populations, particularly for a country not at a high level of affluence.

The Soviet system focused on the development of scientific manpower through the system of higher education institutions under the jurisdiction of the Academy of Sciences and various ministries.[11] The expansion of human capital was impressive. For example, in 1914–15, 127,000 students were enrolled in establishments of higher education. By 1940–41, this number reached 812,000 and by the 1980s was over 5 millions. Comparing the Soviet Union and the United States is instructive. In the early 1980s, the number of scientists employed in the United States was about 75 percent of those employed in the Soviet Union. Indeed, while the two countries were roughly even in terms of the number of degrees granted in the physical and life sciences, the Soviet Union placed a much greater emphasis on engineering.

Despite the slower rate of growth of population after 1917, the Soviets were able to expand their total labor force at a rate of 2.5 percent between 1928 and 1937. This was high by international standards and represented an expansion of the industrial labor force, a continuing shrinkage of the agricultural labor force, and the massive drawing of women into the work force.[12]

The expansion of the Soviet labor force was in part explained by a number of policies that contributed to high rates of participation. First, low wages in agriculture contributed to the shift of labor from agriculture to industry. Second, both moral and legal incentives encouraged participation. These pressures, set in place in the 1930s, were expanded through the 1940s but thereafter were used less. Labor was shifted into high priority sectors and branches partially through wage incentives but also through other methods such as closed-shop privileges.

As we have emphasized, the increase in the Soviet labor force was largely explained by increases in participation rates, not increases in the population. However, household decision making also plays a role in the size of the labor pool. After the 1960s, there was a significant decline in the rate of growth of the population.[13] Death rates continued to decline, but birth rates also declined. Fewer women were in their child-bearing years, and those women were choosing to have fewer children.[14] Then, after a long decline through the 1970s, crude death rates increased in the 1980s, rising from 7.1 per 1000 in 1960 to 10.3 per 1000 in 1980. Several factors contributed to this change: aging of the population, rising infant mortality, and rising death rates for males aged 20–44. Specific death rates increased for most segments of the prime-aged population, although the death rate for males was higher than that for females. The net result of these factors was a sharp slowdown in the net increase of the labor force between the 1960s and 1980s.

So, although Soviet public policies concerning labor achieved significant increases in the labor supply during the 1930s, demographic trends during the mature phase of the administrative command economy pointed to growing weaknesses in the system and its policies. Sharply declining birth rates and rising death rates in European Russia and the Baltics pointed to long-term growth problems. These trends, in addition to major regional differentials, would all become issues of fundamental importance in the transition era.

Efficiency and the Use of Human Capital

Although there was a significant increase in the stock of human capital in the Soviet Union, the effective use of that capital is a different issue. Conceptually, planners with appropriate information ought to be able to place the labor force in its most productive activity. Throughout the Soviet era, **full-employment policies** were followed with unemployment being officially "liquidated" in 1930. Studies of the Soviet labor market in the 1960s and 1970s suggested very low levels of unemployment.[15]

The Soviet Union was an economy characterized by what David Granick termed a **"job right constraint,"** an issue we examine in some depth in Chapter 10. Throughout the Soviet era, there was growing concern with the issue of labor turnover. While effective and necessary as a means to allocate labor most productively, the effective guarantee of employment may have in fact resulted in excessive turnover and resulting efficiency losses. Adjustments considered basic in a market economy, for example the closing of outmoded plants or the layoff of unneeded workers, could not take place in the Soviet Union. Although there was experimentation with alternative labor force arrangements in the 1960s and thereafter, fundamentally the job right concept was sustained through the Soviet era.[16]

For both men and women, labor force participation rates in the Soviet Union were high and did not change significantly over time. Income was derived almost exclusively from wages in the absence of returns for capital and land.[17] However, in addition to household incomes from official sources, a significant component of household income derived from the informal or second economy, an issue we discuss below.

While there was a major thrust in the Soviet Union to expand the importance of **"social income"** as a portion of total income (reported to be roughly 15 percent of total income), the impact of this component is difficult to measure. It arose largely through in-kind services or services provided for payment where user charges were heavily subsidized. In nominal terms household incomes grew steadily in the Soviet era, largely the result of scheduled increases in state set wages, though the level and change in the level of real incomes is a much more complex issue. There were substantial differences in household incomes across Soviet republics, though wage and income differentials measured in other dimensions were less significant. Although traditional measures of wage and income inequality **(the Gini coefficient)** were difficult to establish during most of the Soviet era, more recent evidence suggests that there were important wage and income differentials, that the magnitude of these differentials differed by region (republic), and that the inequality most probably grew over time. In spite of the difficulties of data collection and analysis pertaining to income distribution, the available evidence deserves attention. In Table 8.1 we present a summary of early results (McCauley and Ofer-Vinokur) with comparisons to Western countries made by Abram Bergson.[18]

During the 1950s and 1960s, there was a marked reduction in industrial wage differentials, a factor that probably reduced income differentials. However, the evidence in Table 8.1 (p. 156) suggests that the Soviet distribution of income was not very different from similar distributions in a number of industrialized countries. For example, the 1972–74 Soviet distribution looked very much like the Swedish and Norwegian after-tax distributions.

To what extent can this earlier evidence be confirmed by more recent evidence? First, in the 1980s new data pertaining to both wage and income distribution became available. Although these data contain many of the problems already discussed (omission of some groups, open-ended categories at the upper and lower ends of the distributions, and absence of second-economy earnings), they nevertheless provide new insights. In Table 8.2 (p. 157) we present and an analysis developed by Michael Alexeev and Clifford Gaddy, who conclude that "Wage inequality in the Soviet Union as a whole has remained relatively stable since 1969, with a slight

Table 8.1

DISTRIBUTION OF INCOME, SOVIET UNION AND WESTERN COUNTRIES, HOUSEHOLDS BY PER CAPITA HOUSEHOLD INCOME

	Income Share of			
	Lowest 10%	**Lowest 20%**	**Highest 20%**	**Highest 10%**
USSR, nonfarm households, before tax (1967)*	4.4	10.4	33.8	19.9
USSR, urban households, after tax (1972–74)**	3.4	8.7	38.5	24.1
Selected countries; all households				
Australia (1966–67)				
Before tax	3.5	8.3	41.0	25.6
After tax	3.5	8.3	40.9	25.5
Norway (1970)				
Before tax	3.5	8.2	39.0	23.5
After tax	4.7	10.5	35.6	22.4
United Kingdom (1973)				
Before tax	3.5	8.3	39.9	23.9
After tax	4.2	9.7	38.3	22.7
France (1970)				
Before tax	2.0	5.8	47.2	31.8
After tax	1.9	5.8	47.1	31.2
Canada (1969)				
Before tax	2.2	6.2	43.6	27.8
After tax	2.8	7.2	41.3	25.7
United States (1972)				
Before tax	1.8	5.5	44.4	28.6
After tax	2.3	6.5	42.5	26.8
Sweden (1972)				
After tax	3.5	9.3	35.2	20.5

*McCauley

**Ofer-Vinokur

Note: The posttax figures (except for Sweden) are calculated from the posttax/pretax ratios for total household income (Bergson, p. 1072).

Source: A. Bergson, "Income Inequality Under Soviet Socialism," *Journal of Economic Literature* vol. 22, no. 3 (September 1984), 1070, 1072. Bergson uses the work of McCauley, Ofer-Vinokur, and A. Sawyer in his comparisons.

increase in inequality in the 1980s."[19] Second, if one examines recent trends in the distribution of income (excluding illegal income) for the entire country, there appears to be essentially no change in inequality during the first half of the 1980s, a pattern rather different from that observed for wages.

Table 8.2

DISTRIBUTION OF SOVIET WORKERS AND EMPLOYEES, 1956–86
By Wage and Salary Level (%)

Rubles earned per month	March 1956	April 1968	March 1972	April 1976	March 1981	April 1986
Under 80	71.0	32.7	23.6	15.2	6.4	4.9
80–100	13.2	21.3	18.5	14.6	13.6	11.3
100–120	6.6	15.1	14.7	13.2	12.3	10.3
120–140	3.6	10.7	12.1	12.9	12.5	11.0
140–160	2.0	7.3	9.5	11.6	11.7	11.4
160–200	1.9	7.4	11.9	16.2	19.2	18.4
200–250	1.2	3.1	5.6	9.0	12.5	15.3
250–300	–	1.3	2.1	3.8	5.6	7.7
Over 300	0.4	1.1	2.0	3.4	6.2	9.6

Source: M. V. Alexeev and C. G. Gaddy, "Trends in Wage and Income Distribution Under Gorbachev: Analysis of New Soviet Data," *Berkeley-Duke Occasional Papers on the Second Economy in the USSR* (Bala Cynwyd, PA: WEFA Group, 1991).

Third, a major feature of recent evidence is coverage of the former republics. Alexeev and Gaddy compute Gini coefficients for the republics and conclude that "both wage and income inequality are clearly greater in the Soviet South than in the North."[20] Moreover, while inequality increased in every republic in the 1980s, the extent of increase was greater in the South than in the North, probably due to the greater extent of second-economy activity in the South. These facts will be important for the transition era in the South.

Would the inclusion of second-economy income changes these findings? Alexeev and Gaddy conclude that "when we take into consideration the additional factor of the second economy, a factor largely ignored in official income statistics, we corroborate our original finding that the Soviet South displays greater income inequality than the North and that inequality in the Soviet Union has grown during the Gorbachev period."[21]

These latter findings are confirmed in a recent study by Anthony Atkinson and John Micklewright.[22] In addition to a reexamination of the earlier McCauley and Ofer-Vinokur evidence, Atkinson and Micklewright examine the Family Budget Survey data and conclude that after 1980 there was an apparent widening of income inequality. They note that for the USSR as a whole, between 1980 and 1989, the Gini coefficient increased from 24.5 to 28.4, ranging from a low of 23.4 in Belarus to a high of 32.7 in Azerbaidzhan.[23]

Although the distribution of income in the Soviet Union was compressed, two additional issues deserve mention. First, along with the serious measurement problems we have emphasized, we know little about incomes at the upper levels, especially about the extent of in-kind benefits. At the other end of the income spectrum, there is more evidence.

Poverty in the Soviet Union

Poverty is a difficult concept to define and to estimate. There were special problems in the Soviet Union. In the Soviet case, the "minimum material satisfaction budget" (the MMS budget) was described as containing the "volume and structure of necessaries of life required for the reproduction of labor power among unskilled workers." A study of poverty in the Soviet Union done by Alastair McCauley in the late 1970s provides these estimates for 1967: 42 million non-agricultural employees and their dependents, 5-to-10 million state farm families, and 32 million families on collective farms had incomes at or below the MMS level.[24] These figures add up to an astonishing 79 million (roughly one-third of the Soviet population at that time) below the minimum MMS budget. It may be that the MMS budget was a liberal estimate of requirements, but even with a much more conservative definition (one-half of the MMS level) there were roughly 25 million Soviet citizens (approximately 10 percent of the Soviet population) below the poverty level in 1967.

Although additional studies have been reported by Mervyn Matthews, all researchers emphasize the difficulties of assessment.[25] According to a recent study by Atkinson and Micklewright on income distribution, the official (Goskomstat) figures indicated that in 1989 there were 40 million persons who were poor (approximately 14 percent of the population).[26] The authors emphasize that major difficulties of measurement complicate the interpretation of these numbers. Moreover, they point out that aspects of the safety net, for example low pensions, are important in understanding the poverty issue. Finally, they emphasize that there are major regional differentials. For example, the five republics of Central Asia, which accounted for 17 percent of the Soviet population in 1989, accounted for just over half of those in poverty under the Goskomstat definition.

The Soviet Union had a minimum wage set at 60 rubles per month in the late 1960s, raised to 70 rubles in the 1970s. Although poverty levels are difficult to measure and especially difficult to compare across countries, Gur Ofer and Aaron Vinokur, based upon émigré data, concluded that in the 1970s, roughly 16 percent of households were in poverty, judged by the official Soviet definitions.[27] However, while those in serious need accounted for a larger percentage of families, the share of households in poverty declined between the 1960s and the 1980s. For the most part, Soviet households in poverty were those not participating actively in the economy, though there was also poverty among active participants.

Consumption in the Soviet Union

How well an economy meets the material needs of its population with a given productive capacity is an important measure of the performance of the system. However, measuring levels of consumer well-being and comparing these levels to those in other countries is difficult. Quite apart from the usual problems of data availability, pricing problems in aggregation, accounting for cultural and historical differences and the like, even selecting an appropriate yardstick can be problematic.

In Table 8.3 we present summary evidence, analyzed by Abram Bergson, comparing consumption in the Soviet Union to that in other countries. According to this evidence, Soviet per capita consumption in 1985 was just 28.6 percent of the level in the United States and well below that in other countries. This estimate represents a downward adjustment of earlier estimates made by Gertrude Schroeder and Imogene Edwards.[28]

Most would agree that even allowing for quite significant measurement errors, levels of consumption in the USSR were low compared to what one might expect after a long period of economic growth. Moreover, the annual rate of growth of consumption decreased from 3.8 percent in the period 1961–70 to 0.7 percent in the period 1981–85 immediately prior to the Gorbachev era.[29]

There are two fundamental reasons why we might observe low levels of consumption in the Soviet Union. First, it is possible that the output simply did not exist in the first place. Second, even if the output did exist, it may not have been direct-

Table 8.3

CONSUMPTION IN A COMPARATIVE PERSPECTIVE: 1985*

Country	Per Capita Consumption
USA	100.0
USSR	28.6
France	68.1
Japan	65.7
Italy	64.6
Austria	59.0
Spain	46.1
Portugal	32.3
Turkey	30.0

*USA = 100

Source: Abram Bergson, "The USSR Before the Fall: How Poor and Why?" *Journal of Economic Literature* vol. 5, no. 4 (Fall 1991).

ed towards meeting consumer needs. In the past, analysts generally thought that the per capita output of the Soviet economy was roughly 50 percent that of the United States. In recent years, that figure has been adjusted downwards. For example, the study by Abram Bergson cited earlier suggests that in 1985, GDP per capita in the Soviet Union was roughly 36 percent of that in the United States.[30]

It is also worth noting that most studies comparing the Soviet Union and the United States have observed the existence of a consumption gap, that is, comparative consumption much lower than comparative output. At the same time, there were important differences in the structure of consumption. For example, apart from quality differentials, the Soviet Union placed a great deal of emphasis on education and health care. For example, while there were important dietary differences between the two countries, daily caloric intake was similar.

Another example of significant differences was that of consumer durables. While comparison of caloric intake would produce one sort of judgment, a comparison of automobiles per 1000 population would produce a very different result. Although we tend to assume that increases in output—especially per capita output—lead to increases in consumer well-being, such is not always the case. For example, in a recent study, Gene Hsin Chang argues that during the early years, the Soviet Union may have been a case of **immiserizing economic growth.**[31]

THE SECOND ECONOMY

Thus far we have treated the administrative command economy as a system guiding resource allocation largely through instructions flowing from one decision making unit to another in a hierarchical organization. Although we have emphasized the important differences between planning and managing, nevertheless, our picture thus far represents much of the formality of the Soviet system. In fact, a significant and growing volume of economic activity in the Soviet economy was carried out in what was termed the **second economy,** economic activity that was important to the Soviet household. What was the second economy?

Although definitions vary somewhat, second economy was generally characterized as fulfilling two basic tests: (1) the activity conducted must be for private gain, and (2) the activity must knowingly contravene existing law.[32] So judged, it was not difficult to find second economy activity in the Soviet Union, though precise measurement of its volume and its impact upon the economy in terms of resource use, incentives, and the like were matters of much greater complexity. For example, a physician might treat a patient for a fee outside traditional medical channels, or a salesperson might set aside special merchandise (for example, merchandise in short supply) for a customer and receive a bribe in return, either in money or in kind.

Although examples of second economy activity were more apparent in the consumer sector, due to Soviet biases against providing consumer goods and especially consumer services, nevertheless second economy activity also flourished in the producer goods sector and in the administrative structure of the economy. For example, in an enterprise, a manager could divert production into the second economy to raise needed cash or to engage in barter trade. It was not unusual for production organizations, for example in construction, to perform activities for private gain on the side (na leva), outside the plan. While private gain motivates second or underground economic activity in any economic system, tax considerations are more important in Western economies, while shortages or ideological constraints were more important in the planned socialist economies. For example, if household services such as cleaning, repair, or tutoring of school children were desired, they would have to be acquired largely in the second economy.

How important was the second economy in the Soviet Union? Unfortunately, given the illegal nature of second economy, measurement was always very difficult although most observers would argue that it was important (especially in sectors such as services) and was growing over time due to the inability of the Soviet system to meet consumer needs. It was widely argued that some 80 percent of the fur market and some 25 percent of fish sales were private. The Ofer-Vinokur study of the Soviet household concludes, "The urban private sector is a significant element in the household economy on both the income and the expenditure sides. About 10 percent, perhaps 12 percent of total income is derived privately, and about 18 percent of all consumption expenditure are conducted between private individuals."[33]

Thus far we have examined the Soviet household largely from a microeconomic perspective. In part, this perspective reflects out interest in the decision making within the household about important issues such as labor force participation. But it also reflects a perception that, from a macroeconomic point of view, the planners were able to control the critical variables in the economy such as consumption, investment, and the like.

Beginning in the early 1970s, there was a growing perception that planners' controls were not adequate, given the growing evidence of **disequilibrium** in the economy. Specifically, it was argued that with fixed prices, the continuing use of money incentives for the household, and the absence of adequate supplies of consumer goods, there would be growing excess demand or disequilibrium in consumer goods markets. While the immediate impact of this situation might simply be longer queues, there were more fundamental effects. In effect, households would be forced to change their behavior, either increasing savings and/or reducing labor force participation and effort, due to the disincentive effect. What evidence is available?

This issue, of major importance in the later years of the Soviet era, in effect disappeared during transition, when the release of prices in 1992 resulted in sudden and sharp increases in most retail prices. However, during the 1980s the concern was with the phenomenon of **monetary overhang,** in effect the alleged existence of large sums of idle rubles in the hands of the population and no goods and services available for purchase.

The concept of disequilibrium and its measurement in the real world are complex. Although one might look directly at savings rates to consider levels and rates and how they might differ from savings patterns in market economies, this approach did not produce substantive results.[34] However, while more sophisticated general equilibrium modeling of the economy seemed to demonstrate the existence of feed-back effects on labor force participation, sectoral studies that examined selected aspects of consumer goods markets suggested more complex relationships between shortages of consumer goods, second economy markets, and household behavior.[35] Many studies based on macroeconomic data failed to find conclusively that disequilibrium affected saving, labor force, and monetary behavior; however, microeconomic evidence from émigré surveys seem to support this proposition.

AGRICULTURE IN THE SOVIET ECONOMY

We have emphasized that agriculture plays a critical role in the process of economic development, supplying food products to the population, inputs for industry, and releasing labor for the urban industrial sector. Moreover, in the Soviet case, Stalin's developmental strategies in the 1930s relied heavily upon agriculture as a sector and upon a variety of organizational arrangements peculiar to the Soviet economic system. At the same time, we know that agriculture was a central and controversial issue in the Soviet Union, yet one that would be all but forgotten in the transition era. Why was Soviet agriculture controversial?

There are three major reasons for this controversy. First, the organizational arrangements and policy initiatives employed in Soviet agriculture were, on many grounds, quite different from typical Western perspectives. Heavy reliance was placed on socialized agriculture with major state involvement. Second, in the era after World War II, agriculture was a continuing focus of Soviet leaders, especially Nikita Khrushchev in the 1950s, with frequent attempts at reform. Indeed, when Khrushchev was dismissed in the early 1960s, he would be described as a "hair-brained schemer," primarily because of his many attempts to improve the performance of Soviet agriculture. Finally, in spite of these changes, agricultural performance in the Soviet Union was a perennial problem, such that the Soviet Union shifted from being a major grain exporter to being a major grain importer.

Organizational Arrangements

As noted earlier, Soviet agriculture utilized three major organizational arrangements, specifically the state farm (sovkhoz), the collective farm (kolkhoz) and the private sector, the latter associated with state and collective farms and sometimes with industrial enterprises. These organizational arrangements, summarized in Table 8.4 (pp. 164–65), were very different and would be altered significantly throughout the Soviet era.

The state farm was a "factory in the fields" in the sense that it was, like an industrial enterprise, budget financed with a state-appointed director. Workers on state farms were state employees and received wages determined much as wages in industry. The internal workings of the state farm were similar to that of an enterprise. The state farm was part of the planning structure, and financial arrangements, including investment, were part of the budgetary system. Moreover, the distribution of output occurred through state distribution channels also in much the same fashion as for an industrial firm.

The Soviet collective farm was quite different. In theory, the kolkhoz was a cooperative, and its members were peasants, not workers.[36] While the kolkhoz was also part of the general agricultural planning arrangements, significant differences existed. First, while the head of the kolkhoz was supposed to be elected, in fact this was an important nomenklatura position over which local Party influence was great. Second, prior to the mid-1960s the method of payment was the labor day (trudoden') system, which differed fundamentally from a wage payment system.

Tasks on the kolkhoz were assigned a certain number of labor days. Peasants who completed these assigned tasks would accumulate labor days. At the end of the year, the value of each labor day (and hence the earnings of each peasant) would be determined by dividing net farm output (gross output minus deliveries to the state) by the number of labor days. This reward system was the subject of considerable controversy. The rating of tasks was totally arbitrary. Moreover, from an incentive point of view, the peasant had little or no idea about the magnitude of reward (or its form—in kind or in money) at the time a task was performed.

Finally, in addition to the state and collective farms, families (mainly on state and collective farms) were entitled to the use of a subsidiary plot of land, usually about one half acre in size.[37] The family might sell the output from these plots to the state, distribute it locally, or sell it in the collective farm markets. Although these plots accounted for a very small portion of land inputs to agriculture, much less was known about other inputs, especially labor and capital. However, for the production of many products, especially fruits, vegetables, and the like, the private sector was a major, though declining, contributor. For example in 1965, the private sector produced 40 percent of meat, though this number declined to 19 percent by the 1980s. Fully 67 percent of egg production was private in the 1960s, though this figure would be cut in half to roughly 30 percent in the 1980s.[38]

Policy Perspectives

The agricultural sector was a matter of major policy concern and controversy throughout the Soviet era, for several reasons. First, as we have emphasized, the organizational arrangements used in the Soviet Union were different and often controversial. Second, due to these differences and Soviet natural conditions, output fluctuations were of major importance, especially in critical products such as

Table 8.4

THE ORGANIZATIONAL ARRANGEMENTS OF SOVIET AGRICULTURE

	1928	1932	1940	1953
Number of collective farms (in thousands)	33.3	211.7	236.9	97.0
Sown area of collective farms as a portion of total sown area (%)	1.2	70.5[a]	78.3	83.9
Size of collective farms (acres per farm)	237	2,218	3,530	10,374
Number of state farms	1,407	4,337	4,159	4,857
Sown area of state farms as a portion of total sown area (%)	1.5[b]	NA	7.7	9.6
Size of state farms (acres per farm)	—	—	30,134	32,357
Number of interfarm enterprises and organizations	—	—	—	—
Sown area of the private sector as a portion of total sown area (%)[c]	97.3	NA	13.0	4.4

[a]Based upon aggregate sown area for 1933.   **(Continued on facing page)**

[b]Includes state farms and other state agricultural enterprises.

[c]The private sector consists of three parts: (1) private plots of collective farm members; (2) private plots of workers in industry and other state organizations; (3) the private peasant economy. The last was of minimal importance after the 1930s.

[d]1975

Sources: Selected volumes of *Narodnoe khoziaistvo SSSR* [The national economy of the USSR]; *Sel'skoe khoziaistvo SSSR* [Agriculture of the USSR]; and *SSSR v tsifrakh* [The USSR in figures].

grains.[39] Third, in spite of the focus placed on agriculture, the availability of food products, both on a year-to-year basis and seasonally, was very uneven. Fourth, and possibly most important, the shift of resources from agriculture to non-agriculture, typical in the development experience, was not accompanied by adequate productivity growth in the Soviet case. The results were a growing reliance on imports to satisfy domestic needs and a large and growing subsidy to the agricultural sector. For these reasons, Soviet agriculture was typically viewed with concern.

Although in broad perspective the organizational arrangements and policies in Soviet agriculture seemed to be largely unchanged in the era after World War II, this was really not the case. There were a number of very basic changes, none of

(SELECTED INDICATORS)

1957	1960	1965	1970	1978	1983	1988
78.2	44.9	36.9	33.6	26.7	25.0	27.3
68.4	60.6	50.2	47.9	44.2	43.75	43.80
—	16,302	15,067	15,067	16,549	16,055	22,130
5,905	7,375	11,681	14,994	20,500	22,313	23,300
25.7	33.1	42.6	44.4	51.2	53.35	53.46
60,021	64,714	60,762	51,376	43,472	41,002	NA
—	—	3,354	4,580	8,907	9,897	6,748
3.8	3.3	3.2	3.2	3.0[d]	2.89	2.72

which seemed to improve performance. First, there were ongoing organizational changes. For example, beginning in the 1940s, there was a continuing program of amalgamation, especially in the collective farm sector, decreasing the numbers of farms from roughly 240,000 in the early 1940s to some 30,000 in the late 1980s. At the same time, there was a growing reliance on state farms, the result of both amalgamation and the conversion of weak collective farms to state farms. Finally, beginning in the 1960s, farms were integrated with processing and distribution facilities in a process termed agro-industrial integration. Both vertical and horizontal integration were major thrusts of organizational change in Soviet agriculture in the years prior to the collapse of the Soviet Union.

Second, the agricultural sector was subjected to persistent organizational change above the farm level at both the raion and the oblast levels, as well as to changes in the administrative and planning arrangements. Like other reform programs in the Soviet Union, these changes seemed to have little effect upon Soviet agricultural performance.

Third, beginning under Khrushchev in the 1950s, there was a major thrust to improve agricultural performance. In addition to raising rural incomes vis-a-vis urban incomes, there were substantial increases in inputs to agriculture, including investment and purchased inputs such as chemical fertilizers.

Performance

Probably no sector of the Soviet economy was more controversial than the agricultural sector, in part because of the perception (and in large part reality) that the farm system was a continuing headache for Soviet leaders. As an economy grows, typically the agricultural sector shrinks (in relative terms) but output grows due to productivity improvement which arises from factor substitution (typically capital replaces labor as the latter migrates to the urban sector). In the Soviet case, the broad patterns of change are instructive.

During the 1950s, Nikita Khrushchev implemented a variety of significant changes in the agricultural sector. Broadly speaking, there was significant expansion of both land area and purchased inputs, while the size of the rural labor force shrunk. During the early postwar years, the decline in the rate of growth of factor productivity was offset by increases in non-labor inputs (basically a pattern of extensive economic growth). However, beginning roughly in the 1960s, there came an end to the expansion of land input, which the continued expansion of purchased inputs was insufficient to offset. The net result of these forces was a lengthy period of major year-to-year fluctuations in grain output around a trend that was insufficient to meet domestic grain needs. The result was a sharp growing reliance on imports. For example, between 1961 and 1965, the average annual output of grain was just over 130 million metric tons. For the period 1981–84, the comparable figure was 175 million metric tons, and still the Soviet Union was a net importer of over 30 million metric tons of grain annually in the early 1980s.

At the same time, efforts were made to increase rural productivity. In addition to the expansion of purchased inputs such as chemical fertilizers, Soviet leaders paid special attention to incentives, raising purchase prices to increase rural incomes. For example, between 1960 and 1978, while sown area increased from just over 203 million hectares (one hectare = 2.417 acres) to just over 218 million hectares, capital investment increased from 6.5 billion to 31.2 billion rubles (measured in comparable prices). This raised agriculture's share in total investment from approximately 20 percent in 1960 to 27 percent in the late 1970s. For the same periods, electricity use increased from 3.5 million kilowatt hours per 100 hectares of land to 32.4 million kilowatt hours, while mineral fertilizers (tons of effective nutrient per 100 hectares of land) increased from 0.9 to 6.2. In spite of these major increases in inputs, productivity declined, the result being a steady increase in farm costs. With a state reluctant to increase the retail prices of farm products, the result was a large and growing subsidy, a major problem for the Soviet state budget.[40]

The productivity record in Soviet agriculture was always a matter of concern. Consider for example the evidence presented in Table 8.5. Even allowing for a margin of measurement error, we observe a significant and continuing decline in the average annual rate of growth of output. At the same time, while there was an effort to sustain the growth of inputs, the average annual rate of growth of inputs nevertheless also declined, though at a slower pace than was the case for output.

Table 8.5

FACTOR PRODUCTIVITY IN SOVIET AGRICULTURE, 1951–79*

	1951–60	1961–*70	1971–79	1951–79
Output	4.8	3.0	1.8	3.4
Inputs	2.7	2.1	1.6	2.1
Factor Productivity	2.1	1.0	0.2	1.2

*average annual rate of growth

Source: D.B. Diamond, L.W. Bettis, and R.E. Ramsson, "Agricultural Production," in A. Bergson and H.S. Levine, eds., *The Soviet Economy Towards the Year 2000* (Winchester, MA: Allen & Unwin, 1983), 146.

The net result was a decline in the average annual rate of growth of factor productivity from a respectable 2.1 percent in the 1950s to a very poor 0.2 percent in the 1970s.

The productivity dilemma emphasized above is confirmed by a more recent study of agricultural productivity in centrally planned economies by Lui-Fai Wong and Vernon Ruttan.[41] Wong and Ruttan indicate that for the Soviet Union during the period 1950 to 1980, both labor productivity and land productivity increased, while total factor productivity declined persistently. Moreover, their examination of the contribution of technological change indicates that it was negative, meaning that output gains were made with input gains, the source of continuing cost increases and resultant state subsidies.[42]

In light of the persistent problems associated with agriculture during the Soviet era and the apparently evident problems of lack of specialization, pricing, and incentives, it is perhaps ironic that relatively little attention would be paid to rural reform during the Gorbachev era. Although there was attention given to changing land use policies, varying from new arrangements for organizing labor to leasing, agriculture in fact was placed on the back burner, where it has remained during transition.

SUMMARY

In this chapter we examined a variety of economic issues related to the Soviet household. As a source of labor in the Soviet economy, we emphasized the observed high rates of labor force participation for both men and women in a setting where the demographic transition was accelerated compared to trends observed in other industrializing economies.

Although Soviet full-employment policies undoubtedly contributed to a misallocation of labor resources, nevertheless wages and social consumption funds were the major components of household income. While studies of income distribution suggested outcomes in the Soviet Union much like those in a number of industrialized countries, nevertheless there were significant differentials within the Soviet Union (especially North to South) and evidence of growing inequality in the 1980s. While estimates of poverty in the Soviet Union indicated differences depending upon measurement assumptions, nevertheless the available evidence suggests that poverty was a serious problem, though its incidence was decreasing over time.

To the extent that the household functioned beyond the immediate purview of planners, we noted the importance of the underground, or second, economy as a part of household income and expenditure. Moreover, there is some evidence that plan control weakened after the late 1960s as signs of disequilibrium began to emerge. Though difficult to measure, it was often argued that there was persistent excess demand for consumer goods, and in the 1980s, monetary overhang, or excess purchasing power vis-a-vis available consumer goods and services.

Finally, our examination of the Soviet rural economy indicated that under very different organizational arrangements and policies, Soviet agriculture was a matter of continuing controversy. In spite of a continuing increase of inputs to the agricultural sector, the rate of growth of total factor productivity declined throughout the postwar era, which resulted in rising costs, a large and growing subsidy, and growing net imports of grain to meet Soviet domestic needs. It is evident that the agricultural transformation that normally accompanies the process of industrialization was incomplete in the Soviet case, an issue that would be troublesome in the transition era.

Terms and Concepts

labor force participation   The ratio of those in the labor force (in the Soviet Union, males 16–59 and females 16–55) to the total population.

demographic transition   The relationship between birth rates, death rates and the resulting rate of growth of the population over the course of economic growth and economic development.

full-employment policies   In the Soviet Union, the concept that under Soviet (socialist) policies and institutions, unemployment would be eliminated.

job right constraint   The argument, made by David Granick for the Soviet Union, that an element of the Soviet planners' objective function was a requirement that full employment prevail, implying changes in labor allocation arrangements, for example the absence of dismissal, overstaffing and the like.

social income   An important element of income in the Soviet Union, defined as state provided (subsidized) benefits such as education, medical care, old age benefits and inexpensive public services such as transportation.

Gini coefficient   A measure of income inequality ranging from one hundred (absolute inequality) to zero (absolute equality); defined as the ratio of the area between a line of perfect equality and the lorenz curve, and the area between lines of perfect equality and perfect inequality.

immiserizing economic growth   A case where, in a large country, there is positive economic growth but a reduction in the standard of living.

second economy   A term applied to economic activity in the Soviet Union beyond the control of the administrative command economy and normally in violation of Soviet law—private trade, the sale of services, etc.

disequilibrium   The concept that in the planned socialist economic systems, markets (for example the supply of and demand for consumer goods) might not be in equilibrium and would not be subject to the equilibrating forces normally found in a market economy.

monetary overhang   The concept that purchasing power in the economy exceeds, possibly by a substantial degree, the value of available goods and services. An issue discussed with increasing fervor in the Soviet Union in the late 1970s and 1980s.

Selected Bibliography

The Household

Alexeev, Michael V., and Clifford D. Gaddy. "Trends in Wage and Income Distribution Under Gorbachev," *Berkeley-Duke Occasional Papers on the Second Economy in the USSR* (Bala Cynwyd: WEFA, 1991).

Bergson, A. "Income Inequality Under Soviet Socialism," *Journal of Economic Literature* vol. 22, no. 3 (September 1984), 1052–99.

Chapman, J. G. "Earnings Distribution in the USSR, 1968–1976," *Soviet Studies* vol. 25, no. 3 (July 1983), 410–13.

———— . "Income Distribution and Social Justice in the Soviet Union," *Comparative Economic Studies* vol. 31, no. 1 (Spring 1989), 14–45.

CIA. *USSR: Estimates of Personal Incomes and Savings* (Washington, DC: CIA, 1989).

Ellman, M. "A Note on the Distribution of Earnings in the USSR Under Brezhnev," *Slavic Review* vol. 39, no. 4 (December 1987), 669–71.

Granick, D. *Job Rights in the Soviet Union: Their Consequences* (New York: Cambridge University Press, 1987).

Gregory, P. R., and I. L. Collier, Jr. "Unemployment in the Soviet Union: Evidence from the Soviet Interview Project," *American Economic Review* vol. 78, no. 4 (September 1988), 613–32.

McCauley, A. *Economic Welfare in the Soviet Union* (Madison: University of Wisconsin Press, 1979).

Matthews, M. *Privilege in the Soviet Union: A Study of Elite Life-Styles Under Communism* (London: Allen & Unwin, 1978).

Millar, J., ed. *Politics, Work, and Daily Life in the USSR* (New York: Cambridge University Press, 1987).

Ofer, G., and A. Vinokur. *The Soviet Household Under the Old Regime* (New York: Cambridge University Press, 1992).

——— . "Earnings Differentials by Sex in the Soviet Union: A First Look," in S. Rosenfielde, ed., *Economic Welfare and the Economics of Socialism: Essays in Honor of Abram Bergson* (Cambridge: Cambridge University Press, 1981), 127–62.

Yanowitch, M. *Social and Economic Inequality in the USSR* (White Plains, NY: M. E. Sharpe, 1977).

Women in the Soviet Economy

Anderson, B. A. "The Life Course of Soviet Women Born 1905–1960," in J. R. Millar, ed., *Politics, Work, and Daily Life in the USSR* (New York: Cambridge University Press, 1987).

Bartol, R. A. "Women in Professional and Managerial Positions: The United States and the Soviet Union," *Industrial and Labor Relations Review* vol. 28, no. 4 (July 1975).

Berliner, J. "Education, Labor Force Participation, and Fertility in the USSR," *Journal of Comparative Economics* vol. 7. no. 2 (June 1983).

Dodge, N. T. *Women in the Soviet Economy* (Baltimore: Johns Hopkins Press, 1966).

Gregory, P. R. "Fertility and Labor Force Participation in the Soviet Union and Eastern Europe," *Review of Economics and Statistics* vol. 64, no. 1 (February 1983).

Kuniansky, A. "Soviet Fertility, Labor Force Participation, and Marital Instability," *Journal of Comparative Economics* vol. 7 (June 1983).

McCauley, A. *Women's Work and Wages in the Soviet Union* (London: Allen & Unwin, 1981).

Moroney, J. R. "Do Women Earn Less Under Capitalism?" *Economic Journal* vol. 89, no. 355 (September 1979).

Moskoff, W. *Labor and Leisure in the Soviet Union* (New York: St. Martins Press, 1984).

——— . *Women in Soviet Society: Equality, Development and Social Change* (Berkeley: University of California Press, 1978).

Ofer, G. and A. Vinokur. "Earnings Differentials by Sex in the Soviet Union: A First Look," in S. Rosenfielde, ed., *Economic Welfare and the Economics of Soviet Socialism* (New York: Cambridge University Press, 1981).

Sacks, M. P. *Women's Work in Russia: Continuity in the Midst of Change* (New York: Praeger, 1976).

——— . *Work and Equality in Soviet Society* vol. 38, no. 4 (December 1979).

Warshofsky-Lapidus, G. *Women, Work and Family in the Soviet Union* (Armonk: M. E. Sharpe, 1982).

Income and Income Distribution

Alexeev, M. V., and C. G. Gaddy. "Trends in Wage and Income Distribution Under Gorbachev," *Berkeley-Duke Occasional Papers on the Second Economy in the USSR* (Bala Cynwyd: WEFA, 1991).

Atkinson, A. B., and J. Micklewright. *Economic Transformation in Eastern Europe and the Distribution of Income* (Cambridge: Cambridge University Press, 1992).

Bergson, A. "Income Inequality Under Soviet Socialism," *Journal of Economic Literature* vol. 22, no. 3 (September 1984).

———. "The USSR Before the Fall: How Poor and Why?" *Journal of Economic Perspectives* vol. 5, no. 4 (Fall 1991).

Chapman, J. G. "Earnings Distribution in the USSR, 1968–1976," *Soviet Studies* vol. 25, no. 4 (July 1983).

———. *Economic Welfare in the Soviet Union* (Madison: University of Wisconsin Press, 1979).

Ofer, G. and A. Vinokur. "Earnings Differentials by Sex in the Soviet Union: A First Look," in S. Rosenfielde, ed., *Economic Welfare and the Economics of Soviet Socialism* (New York: Cambridge University Press, 1981).

———. *The Soviet Household Under the Old Regime* (New York: Cambridge University Press, 1992).

Wiles, P. J. D. *Distribution of Income East and West* (Amsterdam: North-Holland, 1974).

Yanowitch, M. *Social and Economic Inequality in the USSR* (White Plains, NY: M. E. Sharpe, 1977).

The Soviet Second Economy

Ericson, R. E. "The 'Second Economy' and Resource Allocation Under Central Planning," *Journal of Comparative Economics* vol. 8, no. 1 (March 1984), 1–24.

———. "An Allocative Role of the Second Economy," in P. Desai, ed., *Marxism, Central Planning and the Soviet Economy* (Cambridge: MIT Press, 1983), 110–32.

Feldbrugge, F. J. M. "Government and the Shadow Economy in the Soviet Union," *Soviet Studies* vol. 36, no. 4 (October 1984), 528–43.

Grossman, G. "The Second Economy in the Soviet Union and Eastern Europe: A Bibliography," (Durham, NC: The Berkeley-Duke Occasional Papers on the Second Economy of the USSR, July 1990).

———. "The 'Second Economy' of the USSR," *Problems of Communism* vol. 26 (September-October 1977), 25–40).

———. "Notes on the Illegal Private Economy and Corruption," in U.S. Congress, Joint Committee, *Soviet Economy in a Time of Change* vol. 1. (Washington DC: U.S. Government Printing Office, 1979), 834–55.

Katsenelinboigen, A. "Coloured Markets in the Soviet Union," *Soviet Studies* vol. 29 (January 1977), 62–85.

O'Hern, D. "The Consumer Second Economy: Size and Effects," *Soviet Studies* vol. 32, no. 32 (April 1980).

Rumer, B. "The 'Second' Agriculture in the USSR," *Soviet Studies* vol. 32 (April 1980).

Schroeder, G. E., and R. Greenslade. "On the Measurement of the Second Economy in the USSR," *ACES Bulletin* vol. 21, no. 1 (Spring 1979), 3–22.

Simes, D. "The Soviet Parallel Market," *Survey* vol. 21 (Summer 1975), 42–45.

———. "The Soviet Parallel Market," *Economic Aspects of Life in the USSR* (NATO: Directorate of Economic Affairs, 1975), 91–100.

The Soviet Rural Economy

Boyd, M. L. *Performance & System Choice: East European Agricultural Development* (Boulder, CO: Westview, 1991).

Gray, K. R., ed. *Soviet Agriculture: Comparative Perspectives* (Ames: Iowa State University Press, 1990).

Johnson, D. G., and K. M. Brooks. *Prospects for Soviet Agriculture in the 1980s* (Bloomington: Indiana University Press, 1983).

Liefert, W., M. R. B. Koopman, and E. C. Cook. "Agricultural Reform in the Former USSR," *Comparative Economic Studies* vol. 35, no. 4 (Winter 1993).

Millar, J. R., ed. *The Soviet Rural Community* (Urbana: University of Illinois Press, 1971).

OECD. *The Soviet Agro-Food System and Agricultural Trade: Prospects for Reform* (Paris: OECD, 1992).

Stuart, R. C., ed. *The Soviet Rural Economy* (Totowa, NJ: Rowman & Allanheld, 1984).

——— . *The Collective Farm in Soviet Agriculture* (Lexington, MA: D. C. Heath, 1972).

Volin, L. *A Century of Russian Agriculture* (Cambridge, MA: Harvard University Press, 1970).

Wadekin, K. E. *Agrarian Policies in Communist Europe* (The Hague: Martinus Nijhoff, 1982).

Notes

1. There is a large body of literature pertaining to labor force issues in the Soviet Union. See for example W. E. Eason, "Labor Force," in A. Bergson and S. Kuznets, eds., *Economic Trends in the Soviet Union* (Cambridge, MA: Harvard University Press, 1963), 53–56; J. Adam, *Employment Policies in the Soviet Union and Eastern Europe* 2 r/e (London: Macmillan, 1987); M. McCauley, *Labor Disputes in Soviet Russia 1957–1965* (Oxford: Oxford University Press, 1969); B. A. Ruble, *Soviet Trade Unions* (New York: Cambridge University Press, 1981); D. Slider, "Reforming the Workplace: The 1983 Soviet Law on Labour Collectives," *Soviet Studies* vol. 37, no. 2 (1985); M. Yanowitch, *Work in the Soviet Union* (New York: M. E. Sharpe, 1985).
2. G. Ofer and A. Vinokur, "Earnings Differentials by Sex in the Soviet Union: A First Look," in S. Rosenfielde, ed., *Economic Welfare and the Economics of Socialism: Essays in Honor of Abram Bergson* (Cambridge: Cambridge University Press, 1981).
3. Ofer and Vinokur, "Earnings Differentials by Sex in the Soviet Union: A First Look," 154.
4. G. Ofer and A. Vinokur, *The Soviet Household Under the Old Regime* (New York: Cambridge University Press, 1992), 310.
5. G. Ofer and A. Vinokur, *The Soviet Household Under the Old Regime*, 310–17; see also the findings reported in P. R. Gregory, "Fertility and Labor Force Participation in the Soviet Union and Eastern Europe," *Review of Economics and Statistics* vol. 64, no. 1 (February 1983);
A. Kuniansky, "Soviet Fertility, Labor Force Participation, and Marital Instability," Journal of Comparative Economics vol. 7 (June 1983); J. Berliner, "Education, Labor Force Participation, and Fertility in the USSR," *Journal of Comparative Economics* vol. 7. no. 2 (June 1983); A. McCauley, *Women's Work and Wages in the Soviet Union* (London: Allen & Unwin, 1981); G. Warshofsky-Lapidus, *Women, Work and Family in the Soviet Union* (Armonk: M. E. Sharpe, 1978).
6. P. R. Gregory, "Fertility and Labor Force Participation in the Soviet Union and Eastern Europe"; see also P. R. Gregory, "Soviet Theories of Economic Demography: A Survey," *Journal of Comparative Economics* vol. 7 (June, 1983).

7. See for example M. Feshbach, "Trends in the Soviet Muslim Population—Demographic Aspects," in U.S. Congress, Joint Economic Committee, *Soviet Economy in the 1980s: Problems and Prospects* (Washington DC: U.S. Government Printing Office, 1982); M. Feshbach, "Prospects for Out-Migration from Central Asia and Kazakhstan in the Next Decade," in U.S. Congress, Joint Economic Committee, *Soviet Economy in a Time of Change* vol. 1 (Washington, DC: U.S. Government Printing Office, 1979); S. E. Wimbush and D. Ponomarett, *Alternatives for Mobilizing Central Asian Labor: Out-Migration and Regional Development* (Santa Monaco: Rand Corporation, 1979).

8. For a discussion of the role of controls after World War II, see E. Nash, "Recent Changes in Labor Controls in the Soviet Union," in U.S. Congress, Joint Economic Committee, *New Directions in the Soviet Economy* (Washington, DC: U.S. Government Printing Office, 1966).

9. For a specific discussion of rural-to-urban migration, see R. C. Stuart and P. R. Gregory, "A Model of Soviet Rural-Urban Migration," *Economic Development and Cultural Change*, vol. 26, no. 1 (October 1977); for a general discussion of urban issues, see for example James H. Bater, *The Soviet City* (Beverly Hills: 1980); H. W. Morton and R. C. Stuart, *The Contemporary Soviet City* (Armonk: M. E. Sharpe, 1984).

10. For a discussion of education, see for example M. Matthews, *Education in the Soviet Union: Policies and Institutions Since Stalin* (Winchester MA, 1982); S. Jacoby, Inside Soviet Schools (New York: 1983); J. Dunstan, *Paths to Excellence and the Soviet School* (Windsor, England: 1978); R. B. Dobson, "Soviet Education: Problems and Policies in the Urban Context," in Morton and Stuart, *The Contemporary Soviet City*, 156–79; for a discussion of science education, see C. Ailes and F. Rushing, *A Summary Report on the Educational Systems of the United States and the Soviet Union*, SRI International (March 1980); S. Kassell and C. Campbell, *The Soviet Academy of Science and Technological Development* (Santa Monica: Rand Corporation); J. J. Tomiak, ed., *Soviet Education in the 1980s* (New York: St. Martins Press, 1983); J. R. Thomas and U. Kruse-Vaucienne, eds., *Soviet Science and Technology* (Washington, DC: George Washington University Press, 1977); E. Zaleski, et al., *Science Policy in the USSR* (Paris: OECD, 1969).

11. For evidence on the early years, see N. DeWitt, "Education and Development of Human Resources: Soviet and American Effort," in U.S. Congress, Joint Economic Committee, *Dimensions of Soviet Economic Power* (Washington, DC: U.S. Government Printing Office, 1952).

12. R. Moorsteen and R. Powell, *The Soviet Capital Stock, 1928–1962* (Homewood, IL: Irwin, 1966).

13. W. W. Kingkade, "Demographic Trends in the Soviet Union," in U.S. Congress, Joint Economic Committee, *Gorbachev's Economic Plans* vol. 1. (Washington, DC: U.S. Government Printing Office, 1987).

14. For a discussion of these issues, see M. Feshbach, "Issues in Soviet Health Problems," in U.S. Congress, Joint Economic Committee, *Soviet Economy in the 1980s: Problems and Prospects* part 2, 203–27; C. Davis, "The Economics of the Soviet Health System," in *Soviet Economy in the 1980s: Problems and Prospects*, 22864; B. A. Anderson and B. D. Silver, "Infant Mortality in the Soviet Union: Regional Differences and Measurement Issues, *Population and Development Review* vol. 12 (December 1986); E. Jones and F. W. Grupp, "Infant Mortality Trends in the Soviet Union," *Population and Development Review* vol. 9 (June 1983); C. Davis and M. Feshbach, *Rising Infant Mortality in the U.S.S.R. in the 1970s* (Washington, DC: U.S. Bureau of the Census, 1980).

15. P. D. J. Wiles, "A Note on Soviet Unemployment in U.S. Definitions," *Soviet Studies* vol. 23, no. 2 (April 1972); P. R. Gregory and I. L. Collier, Jr., "Unemployment in the Soviet Union: Evidence from the Soviet Interview Project," *American Economic Review* vol. 78, no. 4 (September 1988).

16. For a discussion of reform attempts in labor markets in the 1960s, see P. Rutland, "The Shchekino Method and the Struggle to Raise Labor Productivity in Soviet Industry," *Soviet Studies* vol. 26, no. 3 (July 1984).

17. An important exception was the social consumption funds. For a discussion of the sources of household income and especially the social consumption funds, see Ofer and Vinokur, *The Soviet Household Under the Old Regime*, chs. 2 and 5.

18. A. Bergson, "Income Inequality Under Soviet Socialism," *Journal of Economic Literature* vol. 22, no. 3 (September 1984).

19. M. V. Alexeev and C. G. Gaddy. "Trends in Wage and Income Distribution Under Gorbachev," *Berkeley-Duke Occasional Papers on the Second Economy in the USSR* (Bala Cynwyd: WEFA, 1991).

20. *Ibid.*

21. *Ibid.*

22. A. B. Atkinson and J. Micklewright, *Economic Transformation in Eastern Europe and the Distribution of Income* (Cambridge: Cambridge University Press, 1992).

23. *Ibid.*, Table U13.

24. A. McCauley, *Economic Welfare in the Soviet Union* (Madison: University of Wisconsin Press, 1979), 18.

25. M. Matthews, *Privilege in the Soviet Union: A Study of Elite Life-Styles Under Communism* (London: Allen & Unwin, 1978).

26. A. B. Atkinson and J. Micklewright, *Economic Transformation in Eastern Europe and the Distribution of Income*, ch. 8.

27. G. Ofer and A. Vinokur, *The Soviet Household Under the Old Regime*, ch. 6.

28. G. E. Schroeder and I. Edwards, *Consumption in the USSR: An International Comparison* (Washington DC: U.S. Government Printing Office, 1981). See also I. Birman, *Personal Consumption in the USSR and the USA* (New York: St. Martins Press, 1989).

29. CIA, *Handbook of Economic Statistics 1991* (Washington DC: CIA, 1991).

30. A. Bergson, "The USSR Before the Fall: How Poor and Why?" *Journal of Economic Perspectives* vol. 5, no. 4 (Fall 1991) Table 4.

31. G. H. Chang, "Immiserizing Growth in Centrally Planned Economies," *Journal of Comparative Economics* vol. 15, no. 4 (December 1991).

32. There is a large literature on second economy issues. See for example A. Katsenelinboigen, "Coloured Markets in the Soviet Union," *Soviet Studies* vol. 29, no. 1 (January 1977); D. K. Simes, "The Soviet Parallel Market," *Economic Aspects of Life in the USSR* (Brussels: NATO, 1975); G. Grossman, "The 'Second Economy' of the USSR," *Problems of Communism* vol. 26 (September-October 1977), 25–40); G. Grossman, "Notes on the Illegal Private Economy and Corruption," in U.S. Congress, Joint Committee, *Soviet Economy in a Time of Change* vol. 1; V. G. Treml, "Production and Consumption of Alcoholic Beverages in the USSR: A Statistical Study," *Journal of Studies on Alcohol* vol. 36 (March 1975); G. E. Schroeder and R. Greenslade. "On the Measurement of the Second Economy in the USSR," *ACES Bulletin* vol. 21, no. 1 (Spring 1979), 3–22; D. O'Hern, "The Consumer Second Economy: Size and Effects," *Soviet Studies* vol. 32, no. 32 (April 1980); F. J. M. Feldbrugge, "Government and the Shadow Economy in the Soviet Union," Soviet Studies vol. 36, no. 4 (October 1984); B. Rumer, "The 'Second' Agriculture in the USSR," *Soviet Studies* vol. 33, no. 4 (October 1981); R. E. Ericson, "The 'Second Economy' and Resource Allocation Under Central Planning," *Journal of Comparative Economics* vol. 8, no. 1 (March 1984); R. E. Ericson, "An Allocative Role of the Second Economy," in P. Desai, ed., *Marxism, Central Planning and the Soviet Economy* (Cambridge, MA: MIT Press, 1983), 110–32; G. Ofer and A. Vinokur, *Family Budget Survey of Soviet Immigrants in the Soviet Union* (Jerusalem: Soviet and East European

Research Center, 1977); G. Ofer and A. Vinokur, *Family Budget Survey of Soviet Immigrants in the Soviet Union* (Santa Monica: Rand, 1980).

33. G. Ofer and A. Vinokur. *The Soviet Household Under the Old Regime,* 100.

34. See for example J. Pickersgill, "Soviet Inflation: Causes and Consequences," *Soviet Union* vol. 4, no. 2 (1977); J. Pickersgill, "Soviet Household Saving Behavior," *Review of Economics and Statistics* vol. 58, no. 2 (May 1976); G. Ofer and J. Pickersgill, "Soviet Household Saving: A Cross-Section Study of Soviet Emigrant Families," *Quarterly Journal of Economics* vol. 95, no. 3 (August 1980); I. Birman, *Secret Incomes of the Soviet State Budget* (The Hague: Nijhoff, 1981); I. Birman, "The Budget Gap, Excess Money and Reform," *Communist Economies* vo. 2, no. 1 (1990); I. Birman and R. A. Clarke, "Inflation and Money Supply in the Soviet Economy," *Soviet Studies* vol. 37, no. 4 (October, 1985); G. Peebles, "Choosing Hypotheses in Comparative Economic Studies: Lessons from a Current Case Study," *Comparative Economic Studies,* vol. 34, no. 1 (Spring 1992).

35. See for example D. H. Howard, "The Disequilibrium Model in a Controlled Economy: An Empirical Test of the Barro-Grossman Model," *American Economic Review* vol. 65, no. 5 (December 1976); see also C. Davis and W. Charemza, eds., *Models of Disequilibrium and Shortage in Centrally Planned Economies* (London: Chapman and Hall, 1989).

36. The organizational arrangements of the collective farm are described in R. C. Stuart, *The Collective Farm in Soviet Agriculture* (Lexington, MA: D. C. Heath, 1972).

37. K. E. Wadekin, *Agrarian Policies in Communist Europe* (Berkeley: University of California Press, 1973); A. Lane, "U.S.S.R.: Private Agriculture on Center Stage," in U.S. Congress, Joint Economic Committee, *Soviet Economy in the 1980s: Problems and Prospects,* part 2.

38. These data are from various issues of *Narodnoe khoziaistvo SSSR* [The national economy of the USSR].

39. The impact of hostile natural conditions in Soviet agricultural performance was always an issue of controversy. See D. G. Johnson and K. M. Brooks, *Prospects for Soviet Agriculture in the 1980s* (Bloomington: Indiana University Press, 1983).

40. For a discussion of subsidies, see V. G. Treml, "Subsidies in Soviet Agriculture: Record and Prospects," in U.S. Congress, Joint Economic Committee, *Soviet Economy in the 1980s: Problems and Prospects.*

41. L. Wong and V. Ruttan, "A Comparative Analysis of Agricultural Productivity Trends in Centrally Planned Economies," in Kenneth R. Gray, ed., *Soviet Agriculture: Comparative Perspectives* (Ames: Iowa State University Press, 1990).

42. L. Wong and V. Ruttan, "A Comparative Analysis of Agricultural Productivity Trends in Centrally Planned Economies," Table 2.6.

CHAPTER 9

Foreign Trade in the Administrative Command Economy

T he Soviet foreign trade system and accompanying policies were very different from those typically found in market economies. Foreign trade was conducted through the planning system and state trading organizations. Although there were efforts to change this system during perestroika (Chapter 12), fundamentally the Soviet Union remained economically isolated from world market influences. It was not until the beginning of transition that these arrangements would be dismantled and new organizations and policies put in their place. As we will emphasize when we examine the institutions of transition in Chapter 14, the legacy of the old order had a significant impact on the new era. Here, we examine how the administrative command economy conducted foreign trade.

TRADE IN THE ADMINISTRATIVE COMMAND ECONOMY[1]

In the administrative command economy, foreign trade was managed by a state monopoly. The organization responsible for foreign trade was the **Ministry of Foreign Trade,** subordinate to Gosplan and the Council of Ministers (Figure 9.1, p. 178). The organizations that did the actual buying and selling were the **Foreign**

Figure 9.1   The Organization of Soviet Foreign Trade

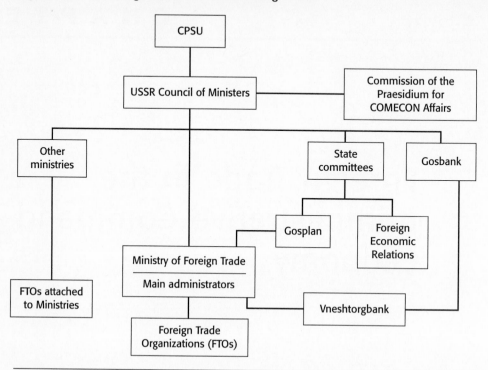

Sources: Compiled from B. P. Gruzinov, *The USSR's Management of Foreign Trade* (White Plains, NY: M. E. Sharpe, 1979), 26, 75, 79; E. A. Hewett, "Most-Favored Nation Treatment in Trade Under Central Planning," *Slavic Review*, vol. 37, no. 1 (March 1978), 28; P. K. Cook, "The Political Setting," in Joint Economic Committee, *Soviet Economy in a Time of Change* (Washington, DC: U.S. Government Printing Office, 1979), vol. 1, no. 2, face p. 50.

Trade Organizations (FTOs). These organizations, generally organized by product, were subordinated to the Ministry of Foreign Trade and were financially independent. The FTOs might handle imports, exports, or both. In some cases, special FTOs deal with a special product area or region. For example, trade in the United States was handled by Amtorg, the American Trading Corporation. In addition to conducting trade, the FTOs were also responsible for technical and financial services. Their revenue was calculated as a percentage of turnover (imports plus exports).

The financial arrangements for foreign trade were handled by the **Bank for Foreign Trade (Vneshekonbank)**.[2] Though traditionally under the supervision of the state bank (Gosbank), the foreign trade bank functioned in close cooperation with the main foreign exchange administration. In addition to a large number of correspondent banks in foreign countries, Vneshekonbank also operated through Soviet-owned banks abroad, for example, the Moscow Nardony Bank of London.

The Planning of Foreign Trade

Like other sectors of the Soviet economy, foreign trade was an integral part of the material balance planning system.[3] Planners generally sought to avoid heavy reliance upon imports and exports, though both could be balancing items in the plan. Trade objectives were expressed in three plans: (1) an import-export plan; (2) a plan for support materials and services for foreign projects; (3) a balance of payments plan. These plans were separated according to region. For example, in the case of the trade patterns with countries of the Socialist trade bloc, the **Council for Mutual Economic Assistance,** or COMECON, had the goal of integrating trade plans with the general plans for each country, though, as we shall see, the effectiveness of these arrangements was limited.

The foreign trade plans contained detailed targets. The import-export plan indicated the regional distribution of imports and exports, the tasks of each organization involved (the ministries and the FTOs), and the schedule of deliveries. The balance of payments plan was developed by the Ministry of Foreign Trade in conjunction with the Ministry of Finance. It showed both payments and receipts (on a current and on a credit basis) for various categories of goods and services distinguished by currency type, specifically in convertible currencies and in transferable rubles. The **transferable (valuta) ruble** was used as an accounting tool and had little relation to internal ruble prices. In addition to the balance of payments plan, a capital plan prepared by the Ministry of Finance, Gosplan, and Vneshekonbank summarized claims and credits on an annual basis.

The integration of foreign trade planning with the national economic plan was incomplete. There was no comprehensive plan to translate foreign trade flows into domestic prices. Because the trade plans were expressed in foreign trade rubles, relationships to domestic prices were unclear.

The FTO was a mechanism connecting the internal producer or consumer with the external world while placing this connection fully under state control. The FTO would purchase authorized export items from the domestic producer at internal ruble prices and sell the items in foreign markets at agreed-upon (typically world-market) prices. Among the COMECON countries, the trade would take place in transferable rubles. On the import side, an FTO would purchase an item at an agreed-upon price in the external market, but the domestic user paid the internal ruble price for the imported item. The financial aspects of these transactions were the responsibility of various financial organs involved with foreign trade along with the Ministry of Foreign Trade. If the imported item was sold at a domestic price that was higher than that paid by the FTO, a surplus would enter the state budget. In the late 1970s, surplus earnings accounted for some 10 percent of state revenues.[4]

Trade Policies

It was often argued that the Soviet Union followed a deliberate policy of "trade aversion." This argument was based upon the fact that the volume of Soviet foreign trade as a ratio to the volume of Soviet domestic output was relatively small when compared to such ratios in market economies at roughly comparable levels of economic development.[5] Although a variety of factors (such as resource endowments) could explain such differentials, the Soviet case was significant for a variety of reasons.

First, Marxist-Leninist ideology rejected traditional Western arguments regarding the potential benefits of international trade, in particular the notion of comparative advantage. This attitude was not peculiar since most Western "economic laws" were rejected as not applicable to the new Soviet (socialist) setting. In particular, Western markets were viewed as subject to chaotic fluctuations capable of jeopardizing the Soviet economic achievement.

A second major factor in trade aversion was the Soviet perception of a "hostile capitalist encirclement." Political events tended to reinforce the view that Western countries were hostile to the Soviet regime and would engage in restrictions, embargoes, and the like.

A third major factor was the Soviet desire to isolate itself from what it viewed as the negative features of the world market economy. In particular, it was argued that such evils as inflation and unemployment could be avoided if the usual transmission mechanisms were interrupted.

Fourth, quite apart from Soviet policies with regard to foreign trade, one could argue that the organizational arrangements of trade would effectively limit trade, isolating domestic producers and consumers from their counterparts in the world arena. The isolation of Soviet domestic producers from world markets, for example, made it very difficult for them to have knowledge of foreign markets, and thus compete effectively in them.

Finally, it is important to note that the events of the early plan era must have had a strong impact upon trade policies. During the Great Depression, the terms of trade turned against the Soviet Union as the prices of Soviet exports declined to a greater degree than the prices of Soviet imports.[6] It is not surprising, therefore, that during the early 1930s, the volume of Soviet foreign trade relative to Soviet output declined sharply. Beyond these considerations, however, a number of other factors, especially the financial aspects of trade, were important in the Soviet case.

Internal Barriers to Foreign Trade

As we have emphasized, Soviet access to foreign markets was limited by their inability to understand and compete effectively in these markets.[7] But, to the extent that exports were limited, foreign exchange earnings were also limited, thus restricting imports.[8] As we noted while discussing the Tsarist era, countries normally undergo changes in the commodity composition of trade during the process of economic development. Thus during the early stages of development, countries export what they have—in the Soviet case raw materials and semi-manufactured goods—and import what they do not have—namely machinery and equipment, especially technology-based equipment. Such was the case in the Soviet Union, a resource-rich country (see Table 9.1, pp. 182–83). But, there were other complications.

The Soviet ruble was a nonconvertible currency, that is, a currency not traded in world currency markets and thus not acceptable (or available to) world trading partners. Ruble inconvertibility along with arbitrary price setting mechanisms meant that prices used in foreign trade transactions (valuta rubles) bore no relation to relative scarcities, either in the domestic or the world economy. These arrangements had several critical consequences.

First, there was no common scale with which to assess the potential advantages or disadvantages of a trade decision. Put another way, it was impossible to decide whether or not trade would be advantageous and would lead to gains for the Soviet economy. This fact meant that potential gains from specialization would be ignored. For example, even if there were substantial gains to be made from trading Bulgarian consumer goods for Soviet machines, it would be impossible to observe these gains under Soviet pricing and costing arrangements. Thus a clear reason for expanding foreign trade—gains made from specialization—was largely absent in the Soviet case.

Second, in the absence of an acceptable currency and a means to make rational trade decisions, much Soviet trade was conducted in the form of bilateral or barter agreements. Such a process was excessively cumbersome and slow, limiting trade and necessitating a balancing in world market prices.

Soviet authorities sought to offset these difficulties by developing **Foreign Trade Efficiency Indices (FTEI)** for evaluating both imports and exports on a rational basis.[9] These rules were used among the COMECON countries in the 1960s in an attempt to provide rules for calculating the ratios of domestic to foreign costs of potential import and export items.

Third, the difficulty of devising appropriate financial arrangements to handle trade deficits was another major internal impediment to the growth of Soviet foreign trade. Since a nonconvertible currency cannot be used in the payment for goods and services, trade with each partner must be balanced. If trade is not balanced, the payment must be made in the form of a convertible currency, gold, or through arranged credits. In contrast, if the United States were to buy more goods and services from Canada than Canada bought from the United States, Canada would be willing to hold U.S. dollars. Canada could then use the money to make subsequent purchases from the United States or other countries (when the dollars were converted at the prevailing exchange rates). Or, Canada could use them to purchase U.S. equities. In this arrangement, an imbalance of trade between the two countries would be financed automatically.

Such an imbalance was not possible between the Soviet Union and Poland. Rubles were of no use to Poland and thus were unacceptable as payment for Polish

Table 9.1

THE PATTERN OF SOVIET TRADE

(a) The Commodity Composition of Soviet Exports (percentages of total exports)

	1950	1955	1960	1965	1970	1975	1977	1982	1986
Machinery	11.8	17.5	20.5	20.0	21.3	18.5	18.7	12.9	15.0
Fuels and energy	3.9	9.6	16.2	17.2	15.6	31.4	35.0	52.1	47.3
Metal ores, minerals	12.3	18.6	21.6	23.2	21.5	17.0	13.1	5.5	8.4
Chemicals, fertilizer, rubber	4.0	2.7	2.9	2.8	3.5	3.5	2.8	2.5	3.5
Construction products	0.2	0.5	0.3	0.5	0.6	0.6	0.5	0.1	—
Forest products, paper	3.0	5.0	5.5	7.2	6.5	5.7	5.0	2.4	3.4
Fibers	11.2	10.1	6.4	5.1	3.4	3.0	3.2	2.8	1.4
Agricultural raw materials	3.8	1.9	2.0	1.3	1.0	0.5	0.5	1.7	—
Grain and oilseed	12.9	8.6	8.6	3.4	3.3	1.6	1.1		
Sugar	0.9	0.7	0.5	0.6	0.8	0.07	0.05		
Other foodstuffs	3.3	2.5	3.8	4.3	4.1	2.0	1.4		
Cloth, clothing, shoes	2.2	1.5	1.2	0.8	0.7	0.5	0.4	22.0	21.0
Small consumer durables	0.2	0.2	0.8	0.7	0.9	1.1	0.9		
Other consumer manufacturing	2.4	1.4	0.8	0.8	1.1	1.5	1.4		
Unclassified	27.7	19.0	8.8	11.8	15.5	12.9	15.7		

Sources: Computed from M. R. Dohan, "Export Specialization and Import Dependence in the Soviet Economy, 1970–77," in U.S. Congress, Joint Economic Committee, *Soviet Economy in a Time of Change* vol. 2 (Washington, DC: U.S. Government Printing Office, 1979), 38071; *Vneshnaia torgovlia SSSR v 1982 g* [Foreign trade of the USSR in 1982], 18; and Goskomstat, *Narodnoe khoziaistvo SSSR za 70 let* [The national economy of the USSR over 70 years] (Moscow: Finansy i Statistika, 1987), 647.

goods. The tendency, therefore, was to pursue a balance between the Soviet Union and each of its trading partners, whereas rational trading patterns would call for imbalances vis-a-vis individual trading partners. Barter trade restricted the volume of trade.

THE PROBLEMS OF ECONOMIC INTEGRATION

Since World War II, there has been a major expansion of world trade, in part as a result of the reduction of tariff barriers, the creation of common markets and trade zones, and the general reduction of non-tariff barriers. We have already noted that the Soviet Union attempted to promote economic integration with Eastern Europe through the creation of COMECON in 1949.[10] These arrangements were intended to integrate the planned socialist systems of Eastern Europe with the Soviet Union

(b) The Commodity Composition of Soviet Imports (percentages of total imports)

	1950	1955	1960	1965	1970	1975	1977	1982	1986
Machinery	21.5	30.2	29.7	33.4	35.1	33.2	37.5	34.4	40.7
Fuels and energy	11.5	8.1	4.2	2.5	2.0	3.9	3.6	4.6	4.6
Metal ores, minerals	15.1	16.6	17.0	10.0	10.7	12.5	10.2	9.9	8.3
Chemicals, fertilizer, rubber	6.9	3.4	6.0	6.2	5.7	4.7	4.4	4.4	5.1
Construction products	1.4	0.6	0.8	0.7	0.4	0.3	0.4	NA	NA
Forest products, paper	3.9	3.0	1.8	1.9	2.2	2.1	1.8	1.5	1.3
Fibers	7.8	5.4	6.4	4.4	4.8	2.4	2.7	1.5	1.3
Agricultural raw materials	0.4	2.2	2.2	1.0	2.0	1.4	1.7	1.6	—
Grain and oilseed	1.0	0.8	1.0	5.0	1.1	7.4	3.4 ⎫		
Sugar	3.1	2.8	2.3	3.8	3.4	5.9	6.1 ⎬		
Other foodstuffs	11.9	16.3	9.7	12.0	11.1	9.1	10.2 ⎭		
Cloth, clothing, shoes	5.6	3.8	13.8	9.3	12.3	8.9	8.6 ⎫	43.6	39.0
Small consumer durables	0.07	0.2	0.5	0.2	0.3	0.1	1.4 ⎪		
Other consumer manufacturing	1.7	0.8	3.0	4.7	5.7	3.9	4.2 ⎬		
Unclassified	6.5	5.5	1.5	5.0	3.0	4.0	5.0 ⎭		

through the specialization of trade and production among member countries. Trade with COMECON members accounted for more than 50 percent of Soviet foreign trade throughout the postwar era (see Table 9.2, p. 184). However, for a variety of reasons, only a limited degree of integration occurred.[11]

First, in spite of the economic and political pressures for integration, the countries of Eastern Europe focused on developing their own economies, including heavy industry and a degree of industrial diversification.[12] Eastern European countries were basically unwilling to specialize to any degree, fearing loss of economic independence. Moreover, the COMECON arrangements lacked any supranational authority over members, a direction opposed by the members who retained veto power.

Second, although there was a measure of coordination, there was no integration of planning. Only preliminary steps were taken to develop common yardsticks (such as common costs), and no convertible currency existed. Fundamentally, even with similar planning and pricing mechanisms among bloc members, the barriers to trade discussed above still existed, and trade tended to be conducted on a bilateral basis, as was the case with market economies.[13]

Table 9.2

SOVIET FOREIGN TRADE TURNOVER: GEOGRAPHIC DISTRIBUTION
(percentages)

	1946	1950	1953	1956	1959	1962	1965	1970	1975	1982	1988
1. Socialist countries*	54.5	81.1	83.2	75.7	75.3	70.2	68.8	65.2	56.3	54.3	65.3
CMEA	40.6	57.4	59.3	49.6	52.0	57.5	58.0	55.6	51.7	49.1	59.7
2. Capitalist countries	45.5	18.9	16.8	24.3	24.7	29.8	31.2	34.7	43.6	45.7	34.7
Industrial	38.4	15.1	14.5	16.8	15.9	18.1	19.3	21.2	31.2	31.6	23.4
LDCs	7.1	3.8	2.3	7.5	8.8	11.7	11.9	13.5	12.4	14.1	11.3

*Includes China, Cuba, Vietnam, North Korea, Yugoslavia

Sources: Compiled from official Soviet foreign trade handbooks. *Vneshnaia torgovlia SSSR* [Foreign trade of the USSR] and *Statisticheski ezhegodnik Stran chlenov S.E.V.* [Statistical yearbook of the member countries of S.E.V.] *Narodnoe khoziaistvo SSSR* [The national economy of the USSR], selected years.

To attempt movement towards a multilateral system, the **Bank for International Cooperation** was created in 1964. Trade was conducted in transferable rubles, a nonconvertible currency. Trade in hard currencies was very limited, as was the degree of multilateral clearing.[14] As a result, there tended to be shortages of "hard goods" (goods in deficit and wanted by everybody) and surpluses of "soft goods" (goods in excess supply and wanted by nobody). When a bilateral deficit occurred, it was typically resolved by adjusting future targets or through shipments of soft goods.

Trade in the bloc was determined with little or no reference to the usual tools of costs and benefits. Throughout the planned socialist economies, internal prices bore little or no relation to relative scarcities or world market prices and thus proved useless for making foreign trade decisions. In the absence of appropriate prices, the usual approach was to determine what the commodity would have cost in world markets. The ambiguity led to an ongoing controversy over who did or did not benefit from bloc trade.[15]

TRADE WITH THE WEST

Soviet trade with capitalist countries increased significantly after World War II, from roughly 19 percent in 1950 to 35 percent in 1988 (see Table 9.2). However, a declining trend for the share of Soviet trade with socialist countries came to an end in the early 1980s. Trends in the 1970s and 1980s were influenced by major changes in world oil markets, caution on hard-currency debt, and an unwillingness on the part of the Soviet Union to become dependent on technology imports. By the mid-1980s, the Soviet Union had a trade volume in hard currency of roughly 50 billion dollars.[16] The bulk of this trade was with developed capitalist countries, specifically West Germany, France, Italy, and Japan.

In the 1980s, Soviet hard currency exports were dominated by oil and oil-related products, natural gas, and military hardware. Of lesser importance were machinery and equipment, and chemicals. On the import side, agricultural products accounted for roughly one-third of hard currency imports, while machinery and equipment, chemicals, metals, and fuels accounted for the remainder. Soviet trade with Western industrialized countries focused on the growing Soviet demand for industrial technology and grain and on a Soviet drive to expand exports to pay for these imports.

Soviet trade with LDCs expanded from very low levels in the 1950s and varied from 11 to 14 percent of total Soviet foreign trade to around 11 percent in the 1980s. Asia was the dominant region and India the dominant country. Africa was of secondary importance, with Latin America in third position. The Middle East was important in the sense that the Soviet Union imported oil from OPEC for reexport. Argentina was an important trading partner primarily for agricultural products. The Soviet Union exported fuels and machinery to LDCs with primary products and food products as the dominant imports.

BALANCE OF PAYMENTS ISSUES: THE WEST

On a formal level, administrative command economies did not suffer from balance of payments problems. Both imports and exports were planned by the state trade monopoly, and the foreign trade plan included a plan to balance international payments. If the projected receipts of foreign (convertible) currencies were to fall short of requirements, projected imports could be reduced (or exports expanded) to achieve a trade balance. In the case of intra-bloc trade, there were typically no balance of payments problems due to bilateral balancing. Balance of payments problems concerned the supply of and demand for convertible currencies.

On a more substantive level, a balance of payments problem was related to the fact that (in the absence of credits) purchases from the West were limited to the amount of sales to the West. As noted above, unlike Western countries, the administrative command economies could not pay for Western imports with their own currencies. At the same time, the East bloc countries had difficulties competing in Western markets due to problems of quality and the inability to meet service requirements that these markets demanded. The burgeoning Eastern demand for technology basically meant that less had to be purchased than would have been desired, exports serving as an effective constraint.

A trend towards normalization of East-West trade patterns beginning in the 1970s served to ease (but not solve) the balance of payments problem. West

European countries were willing to grant credits, guaranteed by governments, to gain access to the Eastern European markets. Moreover, increases in the prices of raw materials raised the Soviet Union's earnings of convertible currencies in the 1970s and early 1980s.[17] Between 1975 and 1980, hard currency debt in Eastern Europe grew by a factor of almost three. Both Western recessions and détente contributed to this growing debt. However, much of this lending failed to yield hard currency returns, resulting in subsequent debt service problems; moreover, recessions in the late 1970s and early 1980s restricted international lending. As a result of these changes, East European hard currency debt increased by only 4 percent between 1980 and 1985.[18]

Why did the East European economies experience marketing difficulties? A large part of the problem, especially with regard to manufactured goods, has been explained by the organizational arrangements of foreign trade, which limited the contact between the producer and the Western consumer.[19] In addition, enterprises were reluctant to produce for export, just as they were reluctant to produce spare parts. The governments of Eastern Europe also argued that Western governments tended to discriminate against exports from socialist countries, an argument often made to explain the existence of hard currency problems.[20]

Soviet Foreign Debt

The growth of Soviet imports from the industrialized West was concentrated in two broad areas—industrial goods and services to support the technological needs of the Soviet economy, and agricultural goods (largely grain and fertilizer) to offset harvest reverses and to stimulate the growth of agricultural productivity. Although Soviet hard currency imports grew sharply in the 1970s, the dollar volume of these imports peaked in the early 1980s and declined thereafter through the mid-1980s. With a leveling and thereafter a shrinkage of hard currency exports through the mid-1980s, the Soviet gross debt (that is, outstanding debt denominated in hard currency but not including Soviet hard currency assets in Western banks) grew significantly. The gross debt of $12.5 billion in 1975 grew to $22 billion in the early 1980s, to $38 billion by the mid-1980s, and finally to $47.8 billion in 1989.[21]

The burden of Soviet hard currency debt can be measured in two ways. A common measure of debt burden is the debt-service ratio: the ratio of hard currency debt payments (interest and principal payments) to total hard currency earnings. Judged by this indicator, the Soviet hard currency debt position was not of major concern in the early 1980s. The pattern of the debt service ratio is of interest, however. From a low of just over 10 percent in the mid-1970s, the Soviet debt service ratio grew to 25 percent in the mid-1980s, declining somewhat thereafter to 23 percent in 1989.

A second measure of debt burden is the ratio of gross hard currency debt to hard currency earnings. This ratio was 73 percent in 1980 and increased to 115 percent by 1985. The increase in Soviet hard currency debt during the 1980s was the result of a slackening of hard currency export earnings (in part because of weak oil prices) and a resulting expansion of Soviet borrowing, largely through commercial debt. When the Soviet Union collapsed, the debt burden became unmanageable, as oil exports fell and central control over currency earnings dissipated. The Soviet Union found itself unable to service its external debt.

DIRECT FOREIGN INVESTMENT

International trade is composed of the flows of goods and services and, in addition, flows of capital. In most market economies, foreign capital has been used at one time to finance industrialization, as was clearly the case in Tsarist Russia. However, such was not the case in the administrative command economy. The only capital that the Soviet economy succeeded in attracting was bank loans, often guaranteed by a foreign government. Direct foreign investment, so important in market economies, was lacking.

Although attempts were made to introduce changes during perestroika (Chapter 12), the absence of equity rights for foreigners made direct foreign investment impossible. Moreover, the few significant Soviet East-West ventures that were in effect prior to the breakup of the Soviet Union required innovative, high risk solutions to the problem of equity. In some cases, complicated counter trade arrangements were used. In other cases, Western partners were granted shares in production. Although there were some successful ventures, on balance there was a striking absence of these sorts of arrangements in the administrative command economy.

The inability of the Soviet Union to attract foreign capital must be considered a major weakness of the administrative command economy. Indeed, the fact that such capital was unavailable placed a major burden on the domestic economy and the Soviet people.

SUMMARY

In contemporary times, globalization has facilitated the emergence of most nations into the process of international specialization and trade. Both organizational arrangements and foreign trade policies in the administrative command economy were fundamentally different from those typically found in market economies.

As with other components of the economy, foreign trade was integrated into the process of national economic planning, controlled centrally through the Ministry of Foreign Trade, related financial institutions such as the Bank for Foreign Trade (Vneshekonbank), and finally the Foreign Trade Organizations (FTOs), which connected internal producers and consumers to world markets.

Soviet foreign trade was planned in terms of imports and exports, support services, and the balance of payments. As with other plans, these plans were developed at an aggregate level and broken down for individual FTOs. However, while FTOs were financially independent, the nature of Soviet foreign trade arrangements and policies dictated very different outcomes from those in market economies.

In the absence of a convertible currency and prices meaningful for making trade decisions, much confusion surrounded the determination of Soviet trade flows. With the rejection of Western laws such as comparative prices and in the absence of meaningful prices, it was difficult to make rational trade decisions. The volume of Soviet foreign trade was low, relative to what one might expect in a market economy. The arrangements and lack of a convertible currency dictated bilateral trade agreements, where balance was essential. These barriers to foreign trade meant that the Soviet Union could not benefit from foreign trade, as had been the case in open economies.

The patterns of Soviet trade were rather typical of a less developed economy. Exports were basic materials or semi-fabricated products or energy (especially oil). At the same time, imports were largely technology-based, with the exception of grain imports necessitated by lagging agricultural productivity.

Although the country composition of Soviet foreign trade changed over time, the socialist countries accounted for a major share. However, efforts to integrate these economies with that of the Soviet Union through the Council of Mutual Economic Assistance (COMECON) largely failed, so trade was mostly conducted on a bilateral basis.

From a formal point of view, the Soviet Union did not have balance of payments problems, since exports were required to pay for imports. However, with increasing East-West cooperation, the Soviet Union was able to accumulate debt denominated in hard currencies, a problem which became acute by the end of the Soviet era.

Unlike market economies undergoing economic development, the lack of equity rights in the Soviet Union meant that there was virtually no direct foreign investment, except through some special joint venture projects. Although changes were made during perestroika, it was not until the collapse of the administrative command economy that fundamental changes took place.

Terms and Concepts

Ministry of Foreign Trade   The ministry in the USSR concerned with all facets of foreign trade: imports, exports, and balance of payments issues.

Foreign Trade Organizations (FTOs)   Soviet foreign trade organizations that connect Soviet domestic buyers and sellers with the external world; usually organized by product and functioning on a self-sustaining (khozraschet) basis.

Bank for Foreign Trade (Vneshekonbank)   The Soviet bank (formerly called the Vneshtorgbank) concerned with all financial aspects of Soviet foreign trade.

Council for Mutual Economic Assistance   (also known as COMECON, CMEA, and SEV) A trade bloc of the planned socialist countries for the purpose of conducting trade and integrating these economies.

transferable ruble (valuta ruble)   The unit of currency used for trade among the socialist countries.

Foreign Trade Efficiency Indices (FTEI)   Indices used for calculating the ratios of foreign costs of potential import and export items.

Bank for International Cooperation   A bank established by the Soviet Union in 1964 to handle trading issues among the COMECON countries.

Selected Bibliography

Adler-Karlsson, G. *Western Economic Warfare: 1947–1967* (New York: Humanities Press, 1968).

Bach, Q. V. S. *Soviet Economic Assistance to the Less Developed Countries: A Statistical Analysis* (New York: Oxford University Press, 1988).

Boltho, A. *Foreign Trade Criteria in Socialist Economies* (Cambridge: Cambridge University Press, 1971).

Brada, J. C., ed. *Quantitative and Analytical Studies in East-West Economic Relations* (Bloomington: Indiana University Press, 1976).

Brown, A. A., and E. Neuberger, eds. *International Trade and Central Planning* (Berkeley: University of California Press, 1968).

Campbell, R., and P. Marer, eds. *East-West Trade and Technology Transfer* (Bloomington, IN: International Development Research Center, 1964).

Carvounis, C. C., and B. Z. Carvounis. *U.S. Commercial Opportunities in the Soviet Union* (New York: Quorum Books, 1989).

Dohan, M. R. "Soviet Foreign Trade in the NEP Economy and Soviet Industrialization" (unpublished doctoral dissertation, Massachusetts Institute of Technology, 1969).

Fallenbuchl, Z., and C. H. McMillan, eds. *Partners in East-West Economic Relations: The Determinants of Choice* (London: Pergamon Press, 1980).

Fogarty, C., and K. Tritle. "Moscow's Economic Aid Programs in Less-Developed Countries: A Perspective on the 1980's," in U.S. Congress, Joint Economic Committee, Gorbachev's *Economic Plans* vol. 2 (Washington, DC: U.S. Government Printing Office, 1987), 532–41.

Gardner, H. S. *Soviet Foreign Trade: The Decision Process* (Boston: Kluwer-Nihoff, 1983).

Goldman, M. E. *Soviet Foreign Aid* (New York: Praeger, 1967).

Grossman, G. "U.S.-Soviet Trade and Economic Relations: Problems and Prospects, *ACES Bulletin* vol. 15, no. 1 (Spring 1973).

Gruzinov, V. P. *The USSR's Management of Foreign Trade* (White Plains, NY: M. E. Sharpe, 1979).

Hanson, P. *Trade and Technology Transfer in Soviet-Western Relations* (New York: Columbia University Press, 1981).

Hewett, E. A. *Foreign Trade Prices in the Council for Mutual Economic Assistance* (Cambridge: Cambridge University Press, 1974).

——— . "Most-Favored Nation Treatment in Trade Under Central Planning," *Slavic Review* vol. 37, no. 1 (March 1978), 25–39.

Holzman, F. D. "East-West Trade and Investment Policy Issues," in *United States International Economic Policy in an Interdependent World* (Washington, DC: U.S. Government Printing Office, 1971).

——— . "Foreign Trade," in A. Bergson and S. Kuznets, eds., *Economic Trends in the Soviet Union* (Cambridge, MA: Harvard University Press, 1963).

——— . "Foreign Trade Behavior of Centrally Planned Economies," in H. Rosovsky, ed., *Industrialization in Two Systems: Essays in Honor of Alexander Gerschenkron* (New York: Wiley, 1966).

——— . *Foreign Trade Under Central Planning* (Cambridge, MA: Harvard University Press, 1974).

——— . *International Trade Under Communism* (New York: Basic Books, 1976).

——— . "The Significance of Soviet Subsidies to Eastern Europe," *Comparative Economic Studies* vol. 28, no. 1 (Spring 1986).

Kaser, M. *COMECON: Integration Problems of Planned Economies* 2e (London: Oxford University Press, 1967).

Lavigne, M. "Soviet Trade with LDC's," in U.S. Congress, Joint Economic Committee, *Gorbachev's Economic Plans* vol. 2 (Washington, DC: U.S. Government Printing Office, 1987).

Malish, A., Jr. *United States–East European Trade: Considerations Involved in Granting Most-Favored-Nation Treatment to the Countries of Eastern Europe* (Washington, DC: United States Tariff Commission, Staff Research Studies 4, 1972).

Marer, P. *Soviet–East European Trade (1946–1969): Statistical Compendium and Guide* (Bloomington: Indiana University Press, 1972).

Marrese, M., and J. Vanous. *Soviet Subsidization of Trade with Eastern Europe: A Soviet Perspective* (Berkeley: University of California Institute for International Studies, 1983).

McIntyre, J. F. "Soviet Efforts to Revamp the Foreign Trade Sector," in U.S. Congress, Joint Economic Committee, *Gorbachev's Economic Plans* vol. 2 (Washington, DC: U.S. Government Printing Office, 1987).

——— . "The USSR's Hard Currency and Payments Position," in U.S. Congress, Joint Economic Committee, *Gorbachev's Economic Plans* vol. 2 (Washington, DC: U.S. Government Printing Office, 1987).

McMillan, C. H. *Changing Perspectives in East-West Commerce* (Lexington, MA: Heath, 1974).

——— . *Multinationals from the Second World: Growth of Foreign Investments by Soviet and East European State Enterprises* (London: Macmillan, 1987).

Montias, J. M. *Economic Development in Communist Romania* (Cambridge, MA: MIT Press, 1967).

Parrott, B., ed. *Trade, Technology and Soviet-American Relations* (Bloomington: Indiana University Press, 1985).

Pryor, F. L. *The Communist Foreign Trade System* (Cambridge, MA: MIT Press, 1963).

Quigley, J. *The Soviet Foreign Trade Monopoly: Institutions and Laws* (Columbia: Ohio State University Press, 1974).

Smith, G. A. *Soviet Foreign Trade: Organization, Operations, and Policy, 1918–1930* (New York: Praeger, 1973).

Sutton, A. C. *Western Technology and Soviet Economic Development 1917 to 1930* (Stanford: Hoover Institution, 1968).

——— . *Western Technology and Soviet Economic Development 1930 to 1945* (Stanford: Hoover Institution, 1971).

——— . *Western Technology and Soviet Economic Development 1945 to 1965* (Stanford: Hoover Institution, 1973).

Treml, V. G. "Foreign Trade and Soviet Economy: Changing Parameters and Interrelationships," in E. Neuberger and L. Tyson, ed., *Transmission and Response: The Impact of International Disturbances on the Soviet Union and Eastern Europe* (New York: Pergamon Press, 1980).

U. S. Congress, Joint Economic Committee, "Foreign Economic Activities," *Soviet Economy in a New Perspective* part 3 (Washington, DC: U.S. Government Printing Office, 1979).

——— . "Foreign Economic Activities," in *Soviet Economy in a Time of Change* vol. 2, part 4 (Washington, DC: U.S. Government Printing Office, 1979).

——— . "Foreign Economic Relations," in *East-European Economies Post-Helsinki* part 3 (Washington, DC: U.S. Government Printing Office, 1977).

——— . "Foreign Economy," in *Soviet Economic Prospects for the Seventies* part 7 (Washington, DC: U.S. Government Printing Office, 1973).

——— . *Soviet Economy in the 1980's: Problems and Prospects* (Washington, DC: U.S. Government Printing Office, 1982).

van Brabant, J. M. *East-European Cooperation: The Role of Money and Finance* (New York: Praeger, 1977).

Weiss, H. W. "U.S.-Soviet Trade Trends," in U.S. Congress, Joint Economic Committee, *Gorbachev's Economic Plans* vol. 2 (Washington, DC: U.S. Government Printing Office, 1987).

Wilczynski, J. *The Economics and Politics of East-West Trade* (New York: Praeger, 1969).

Wiles, P. J. D. *Communist International Economics* (Oxford: Blackwell, 1968).

Wolf, T. *East-West Trade Policy* (Lexington, MA: Heath, 1973).

——— . "Estimating 'Foregone Gains' in Soviet–East European Trade: A Methodological Note," *Comparative Economic Studies* vol. 27, no. 3 (Fall 1985).

Notes

1. There is a large literature devoted to trade in the administrative command economy. See for example F. D. Holzman, *International Trade Under Communism* (New York: Basic Books, 1976); A. A. Brown, "Towards a Theory of Centrally Planned Foreign Trade," in A. A. Brown and E. Neuberger, eds., *International Trade and Central Planning* (Berkeley: University of California Press, 1968); for a survey of the literature, see F. D. Holzman, *Foreign Trade Under Central Planning* (Cambridge, MA: Harvard University Press, 1974); for details of organizational arrangements, see V. P. Gruzinov, *The USSR's Management of Foreign Trade* (White Plains, NY: M. E. Sharpe, 1979); S. Bozek, "The U.S.S.R.: Intensifying the

Development of Its Foreign Trade Structure," in U.S. Congress, Joint Economic Committee, *Soviet Economy in a Time of Change* (Washington, DC: U.S. Government Printing Office, 1983); U.S. Congress, Joint Economic Committee, *Gorbachev's Economic Plans* vol. 2 (Washington, DC: U.S. Government Printing Office, 1987).

2. For a discussion of financial arrangements, see G. Garvy, *Money, Financial Flows, and Credit in the Soviet Union* (Cambridge, MA: Ballinger, 1977).

3. This discussion is based on L. J. Brainard, "Soviet Foreign Trade Planning," in U.S. Congress, Joint Economic Committee, *Soviet Economy in a New Perspective* (Washington, DC: U.S. Government Printing Office, 1976), 695–708; V. G. Treml, "Foreign Trade and Soviet Economy: Changing Parameters and Interrelationships," in E. Neuberger and L. Tyson, ed., *Transmission and Response: The Impact of International Disturbances on the Soviet Union and Eastern Europe* (New York: Pergamon Press, 1980); H. Levibe, "The Effects of Soviet Foreign Trade on Planning Practices," in A. A. Brown and E. Neuberger, eds., *International Trade and Central Planning*, 225–27; *Metodicheskie ukazaniia k razrabotke gosudarstvennykh planov ekonomischeskogo i sotsial'nogo razvitiia SSSR* [Methodological directives to working out the state plan of economic and social development of the USSR] (Moscow: Ekonomika, 1980), ch. 25.

4. See Treml, "Foreign Trade." This surplus is the consequence of overvalued exchange rates used to translate valuta ruble prices into domestic prices and the rise in world process of Soviet raw material exports.

5. See for example P. R. Gregory, *Socialist and Nonsocialist Industrialization Patterns* (New York: Praeger, 1970); F. L. Pryor, *The Communist Foreign Trade System* (Cambridge, MA: MIT Press, 1963), ch. 1. According to Treml, "Foreign Trade," the Soviets abandoned their policy of "trade aversion in the 1970s with a trade share in national income of 21 percent. However, there was always much dispute over this issue caused in large part because of the difficulty of translating Soviet trade data in valuta rubles into domestic prices."

6. For discussion see M. R. Dohan, "Soviet Foreign Trade in the NEP Economy and Soviet Industrialization" (unpublished doctoral dissertation, Massachusetts Institute of Technology, 1969).

7. P. G. Ericson, "Soviet Efforts to Increase Exports of Manufactured Products in the West," in U.S. Congress, Joint Economic Committee, *Soviet Economy in a New Perspective,* 709–27; H. H. Kravailis, et al., "Soviet Exports to the Industrialized West: Performance and Prospects," in U.S. Congress, Joint Economic Committee, *Soviet Economy in a Time of Change* vol. 2, 414–62.

8. F. D. Holzman, "Some Theories of the Hard Currency Shortages of Centrally Planned Economies," in U.S. Congress, Joint Economic Committee, *Soviet Economy in a Time of Change* vol. 2, 297–316.

9. For a discussion of the FTEI, see L. Brainard, "Soviet Foreign Trade Planning," 701–07; C. H. McMillan, "Some Recent Developments in Soviet Foreign Trade Theory," *Canadian Slavonic Papers* vol. 12, no. 3 (Fall 1970); A. Boltho, *Foreign Trade Criteria in Socialist Economies* (Cambridge: Cambridge University Press, 1971). Typically, FTEI were calculated separately for potential exports and imports.

$$i.e. \quad = \quad \frac{(Z_i X_{i.eq})}{Vi}$$

X_{ie} = the index of import effectiveness of the product
V_i = the foreign exchange cost of one unit of the product
Z_i = the domestic cost of producing one unit of the product
$X_{i.eq}$ = the ratio of foreign exchange receipts from the country in question from exported goods to the domestic cost of producing the goods

The import effectiveness index is easy to understand except for *Xi.eq*, which plays the role of a crude exchange rate. The Z values represent the internal ruble prices of imported items, and the V values represent foreign prices expressed in transfer (valuta) rubles. They were determined administratively and would vary for each of the USSR's trading partners. The problem is translating these foreign prices into domestic prices—a role played by exchange rates in market economies. For this purpose, a form of opportunity cost measure is calculated for each trading partner. For the import index, this is the average domestic cost of producing goods domestically to earn the foreign exchange necessary to import the item from the particular country. It is calculated by taking the foreign exchange earnings from Soviet exports to that country and dividing by the domestic cost of producing these goods for export.

The general principle underlying FTEI formulas was that foreign trade prices should be translated into domestic prices by calculating the amount of domestic production required to earn the foreign exchange (valuta rubles) needed to purchase the foreign item (in the case of the FTEI, for imports). These formulas bore only a distant resemblance to the relative cost comparisons typically made in market economies. To be an accurate index of the opportunity cost of production versus foreign production, internal prices must reflect domestic relative scarcities, and the implicit exchange rates used in the indexes must indicate the relative purchasing power of the foreign exchange accounting units. These conditions were not met.

10. The members of COMECON were Bulgaria, Cuba (after 1972), Czechoslovakia, German Democratic Republic, Hungary, Poland, Romania, Mongolia, and the Soviet Union. For a discussion of bloc trade, see M. Kaser, *COMECON: Integration Problems of Planned Economies* 2e (London: Oxford University Press, 1967); F. L. Pryor, *The Communist Foreign Trade System;* J. M. van Brabant, *East-European Cooperation: The Role of Money and Finance* (New York: Praeger, 1977); E. A. Hewett, *Foreign Trade Princes in the Council for Mutual Economic Assistance* (Cambridge: Cambridge University Press, 1974).

11. For a discussion of the degree of integration of the COMECON countries, see Pelzman, "Trade Creation and Trade Diversion in Eastern Europe: A Comment," *ACES Bulletin* vol. 19, no. 1 (Spring 1977).

12. For a discussion of an important case, see J. M. Montias, *Economic Development in Communist Romania* (Cambridge, MA: MIT Press, 1967), ch. 4; J. M. Montias, "Socialist Industrialization and Trade in Machinery Products," in A. A. Brown and E. Neuberger, eds., *International Trade and Central Planning.*

13. See M. Bornstein, "East-West Economic Relations and Soviet–East European Economic Relations," in U.S. Congress, Joint Economic Committee, *Soviet Economy in a Time of Change* vol. 1, 281–311; A. Smith, "The Council for Mutual Economic Assistance in 1977: New Economic Power, New Political Perspectives, and Some Old and New Problems," in U.S. Congress, Joint Economic Committee, *East European Economies Post-Helsinki* (Washington, DC: U.S. Government Printing Office, 1977); M. Lavigne, "The Soviet Union in COMECON," *Soviet Studies* vol. 35, no. 2 (April 1983).

14. For details see van Brabant, East European Cooperation, ch. 3–4; M. Kohn and N. Lang, "The Intra-CMEA Foreign Trade System: Major Price Changes, Little Reform," in U.S. Congress, Joint Economic Committee, *East European Economies Post-Helsinki,* 137.

15. M. Marrese, and J. Vanous. *Soviet Subsidization of Trade with Eastern Europe: A Soviet Perspective* (Berkeley: University of California Institute for International Studies, 1983); J. Brada, "Soviet Perspective of Eastern Europe: The Primacy of Economics over Politics," *Journal of Comparative Economics* vol. 9, no. 1 (March 1985); F. D. Holzman, "The Significance of Soviet Subsidies to Eastern Europe," *Comparative Economic Studies* vol. 28, no. 1 (Spring 1986). Michael Marrese and Jan Vanous claimed that at times the USSR

deliberately subsidized Eastern Europe by selling Soviet raw materials at low prices to gain political leverage. On the other hand, Josef Brada finds that Soviet export pricing to Eastern Europe was the neutral result of relative resource endowments. More recently, Franklyn Holzman, a long-term analyst of Soviet foreign trade, suggested that Soviet transfers to Eastern Europe may be explained by the fact that ". . . has many of the characteristics of a highly autarkic customs union."

Prior to 1975, COMECON prices were fixed over the life of long-term national plans. According to pricing formula agreed upon in Bucharest in 1958, the world market prices of 1957 were applied to intra-bloc transactions until 1965. For the planning period 1966–70 , average 1961–76 world market prices were used, and then average world market prices for the period 1966–70 were used for the period 1971–75. The explosion of energy and other raw materials prices in the 1970s caused the USSR to change this pricing formula, as the former USSR remained the dominant energy supplier to Eastern Europe. In 1975, COMECON adopted a new "sliding pricing formula" whereby average word market prices of the preceding five years would be used. Thus rising energy prices were gradually passed on to COMECON partners. Also, provision was made to pay for Soviet energy deliveries about targeted levels in hard currencies at prevailing world market prices. These changes led to a substantial improvement of the Soviet Union's terms of trade with Eastern Europe during the energy crisis of the 1970s.

16. See J. F. McIntyre, "The USSR's Hard Currency and Payments Position," in U.S. Congress, Joint Economic Committee, *Gorbachev's Economic Plans* vol. 2, 474–88.

17. J. Vanous, "Soviet and Eastern European Foreign Trader in the 1970s: A Quantitative Assessment," in U.S. Congress, Joint Economic Committee, *East European Economic Assessment,* part 2 (Washington, DC: U.S. Government Printing Office, 1981); A. Lang and H. Kravalis, "An Analysis of Recent and Potential Soviet and East European Exports to Fifteen Industrialized Western Countries," in U.S. Congress, Joint Economic Committee, *East European Economies Post-Helsinki,* 1074–75.

18. CIA, *Handbook of Economic Statistics 1990* (Washington, DC: CIA, 1990), 48.

19. For a case study of manufactured exports see P. Ericson, "Soviet Efforts to Increase Exports of Manufactured Products to the West," in U.S. Congress, Joint Economic Committee, *Soviet Economy in a New Perspective,* 709–26.

20. R. Campbell and J. Hardt, "The US-Soviet Agreement on Trade: Three Interpretations," *Aces Bulletin* vol. 15 (Spring 1973), 108–13; see also "Commercial Relations" (Contributions by Jurew, Bresnick, and Prejelj) in U.S. Congress, Joint Economic Committee, *East European Economic Assessment,* part 2, 635–84.

21. McIntyre, "The USSR's Hard Currency Trade and Payments Position," 482.

PART THREE

Performance and Decline: The End of the Soviet Era

CHAPTER 10

Soviet Economic Performance: A Theoretical Appraisal

The previous four chapters described how the Soviet administrative command economy worked. This chapter looks at how well we would expect the Soviet administrative command economy to work.

The performance of an economy, or an economic system for that matter, cannot be judged in absolutes. We must always consider economic performance in relative terms. In the case of the Soviet administrative command economy, we must evaluate it relative to its alternative—the market economy. Market economies have a number of weaknesses, which have been discussed at great length in the theoretical literature: potential monopoly problems, information problems, macroeconomic instability. Moreover, as we compare different systems, we must be careful either to compare the model of one economic system against the model of another or to compare the realities of different systems. It would be inappropriate, for example, to examine the weaknesses of planned socialist systems judged against the ideal of a perfect competitive market economy.

Cast in these terms, how do we assemble a set of expectations about the administrative command economy? The most appropriate framework would seem to be a simple picture of the nature of a planned socialist economic system cast in terms of its socialist character, and the use of national economic planning as the dominant mechanism for resource allocation.[1]

In this chapter, we consider the potential strengths and weaknesses of the Soviet administrative command economy, judged in terms of theoretical expectations, criticisms of those expectations over time and evidence from the operation of this system in the real world. In Chapter 11, we turn to the empirical issue of how well the Soviet administrative command economy actually worked compared to its alternative, the market economy.

THE PLANNED SOCIALIST ECONOMY: MODELS AND PERSPECTIVES

While the socialist idea is one of long standing, much less attention has been paid to the formal modeling of the planned socialist economy, that is, in terms comparable to the general equilibrium models of the competitive market economy. Typically, however, the literature characterizes the planned socialist system in two major dimensions: first, its socialist character, and second, its use of planning as a mechanism for decision making about resource allocation. This twofold characterization enables us to identify the features of a planned socialist economic system, leading to an understanding of operational dimensions. Indeed, centrally planned socialism can be characterized in four dimensions: (1) **property rights** are predominantly held by the state, (2) information mechanisms for decision making are primarily through a **planning** mechanism, (3) decision making is substantially **centralized** at high levels of the organizational hierarchy, and (4) **incentives** are mixed, with substantial reliance on moral as opposed to material incentives. Why might such a set of arrangements be appealing from a socialist perspective?

First, with property rights held by the state, it is the state that has control over the use of resources, that is, how the resources will be used and the benefits that accrue from use.[2] Thus in the typical configuration of centrally planned socialism, resources can be directed to building heavy industry, for example, rather than producing consumer goods. Not only can the state decide what to produce, it can decide what share of production will be devoted to saving as opposed to consumption; hence, the fundamental issue of economic growth is influenced directly by behavior of the state and its agents.

Second, and possibly more controversial, the use of a plan for directing resource allocation is seen as avoiding (as it has been frequently described in the socialist literature) the "anarchy" of the market. Under limiting conditions about the simplicity of production relationships, principals can formulate output and other objectives, instructing agents to fulfill the objectives. In this sense, it is often noted that **planners' preferences** supplant **consumer preferences,** significantly altering the output mix of the economy.

Third, centralized decision making has always been appealing in socialist models. As noted, at least in theory, major directives about resource allocation can be developed at the center, which has an all-encompassing vision of the economy and its path through time. Monitoring, it is argued, can be direct and effective, insuring the achievement of state objectives.

Fourth, since socialism envisions a much more egalitarian distribution of income, relying on the state to determine payments to labor provides a powerful mechanism for such an outcome, constrained only by issues of **incentive compatibility.** Moreover, even if there is a charge for capital and land, typically those sums go to the state as owners, fundamentally changing the nature of the social contract under socialism. Private economic activity is replaced with public economic activity, and individuals increasingly rely upon public goods rather than private goods for their well being.

While there are many variants of the above characteristics, fundamentally the socialist idea envisions social control of the production process critical for directing the nature of production, the distribution of goods and services, and the expansion of production over time.[3] It is a vision which differs fundamentally from the market capitalist economic system, driven by consumer demand. How has vision been received over time?

THE AUSTRIAN CRITIQUE OF SOCIALISM

Already in the 1920s, well before Stalin had made the choice of the administrative command economy, two Austrian economists, Ludwig von Mises and subsequent Nobel Laureate Freiderich Hayek, launched their telling critique of the administrative command economy.[4] They argued the administrative command socialist economy would have a number of inherent weaknesses that would threaten not only its economic efficiency but also its ability to survive. Although the issues raised by Mises and Hayek can now be analyzed using the contemporary tools of information economics, nevertheless the historical perspective is instructive, since it was a major component of the Western discussion of socialism, sometimes termed the "socialist controversy."

Information Problems

Specifically, Hayek and Mises focused on the information problems of an administrative command economy run by a **Central Planning Board (CPB).**[5] In order to plan the economy with any degree of success, the CPB would have to gather massive amounts of information, which would have to be processed and kept up to date. Since a modern economy produces millions of distinct goods and services and consists of millions of households and, at a minimum, hundreds of thousands of enterprises, the information problems facing the CPB would well exceed its capacity to handle information.

Even if the CPB let a market mechanism produce and distribute consumer goods, this still left the CPB with the task of gathering information on millions of producer goods and capital goods to be produced by hundreds of thousands of enterprises. Economies are dynamic, with changing technology and changing consumer tastes. Therefore, the task of information gathering would never end. Even if the

CPB could gather sufficient information to plan an administrative command economy at a particular point in time, it would have to start all over again whenever tastes and technology changed, which they are bound to do in a dynamic economy.

Although Hayek and Mises wrote their socialist critique before the days of the powerful computer, we believe that they would have concluded that even in the computer age the information task facing the CPB would still be too large. Indeed, cast in the contemporary language of organization theory and information, we have already emphasized the critical and difficult information issues in the hierarchical economic system. While we know much more about these issues at the end of the twentieth century, nevertheless, they are not new. Information issues are fundamental to understanding differences across economic systems. Based upon contemporary theorizing, and the analysis of **principal-agent relationships,** what expectations might we have about information issues in the administrative command economy?

In earlier chapters, we cast the Soviet system in terms of the economics of agency. Specifically, a principal-agent structure exists where a principal (in this case the state planning apparatus) issues instructions to agents (enterprises and other organizations). This structure functions well when agents cannot engage in **rent-seeking** (opportunistic) **behavior.** Smooth functioning is generally the case under three conditions.[6] First, agents must not have information that is unknown to the principal. Second, the principal must have full knowledge such that efficient outcomes can be chosen and outcomes will be certain. Third, there must be no risk for agents. Given the importance of prices as purveyors of information, let us consider these requirements in the Soviet administrative command economy, under a system which placed limited reliance on prices as purveyors of information.

Prices and Information

Hayek and Mises both wrote admiringly of the ability of market economies to generate valuable information very efficiently. A market economy spontaneously generates enormous amounts of information required by producers and consumers, but this information does not overwhelm participants in a market economy like it would overwhelm the CPB in a socialist economy. Through market forces, a market economy automatically generates information in the form of millions of consumer and producer prices, hundreds of thousands of wages and rents. And the market economy does this continually, not just once. Market prices, wages, and rents change regularly when market conditions change and are the fundamental information upon which resource allocation decisions will be made.

In a market economy, participants do not have to know all this information to make rational decisions. Each participant simply specializes in that information that he or she requires. The automobile manufacturer needs simply to know the prices of automobiles consumers are prepared to pay, the prices of materials required to produce cars, and the prices of the factors of production used in automobile manufacturing, along with engineering and marketing skills. The car manufacturer does not need to know the motivations of consumers or of automobile workers; the only required information is price information produced automatically by the market.

Hayek and Mises concluded that lacking market allocation, the socialist administrative command economy could not generate this type of information on relative prices, relative wages, and relative factor costs. Only markets can produce such relative price information. Although it might be theoretically possible for the CPB to calculate relative prices through mathematical calculations or through market simulations, such indirect procedures would not work in practice.[7]

Hayek and Mises characterized the socialist administrative command economy as lacking the most vital information required to operate the economy—information on what is cheap and what is expensive. Without knowing relative prices, even the best-intentioned enterprise managers or central planners could not make rational economic decisions. Managers would not know what inputs to choose; they would not know how to make proper capital investment decisions; and they could not weigh economic costs at the margin. Consumers would not even know what is cheap and what is expensive.

Chapter 7 discussed the role of prices in the Soviet administrative command economy. It showed that Mises and Hayek, writing before the true creation of the administrative command economy, showed tremendous insight into the limitations of pricing in the administrative command economy. As Chapter 7 demonstrated, with the possible exception of some consumer goods, black market goods, and wage rates, Soviet prices were basically accounting prices calculated from formulae that did not consider relative scarcities. Moreover, the process of setting prices was so complicated that prices rarely changed when underlying cost conditions changed. Price changes did not take place as they do in a market economy; rather they took place after years of accounting work. Soviet planners did not speak of price changes; they spoke instead of general price reform—pervasive changes in prices that took place every five or ten years.

Stuck with cost-based accounting prices that were frequently out of date, Soviet prices had relatively little information value. Managers and planners did not look at relative prices to make decisions. If they had, their decisions would have been wrong anyway. Soviet prices did not provide information on relative scarcities. In the administrative command economy, retail and wholesale prices of consumer goods did not send out reliable signals. Recall from Chapter 7 that retail prices were often set to clear the market; that is, retail prices tended to reflect demand. Producers, on the other hand, were paid the factory wholesale price, which was exclusively determined by accounting costs. If the demand for product X increased, there was indeed a tendency for the retail price to increase. In market economies, increased demand encourages producers to produce more due to the higher relative price. In the administrative command economy, the producer would get no signal of the increase in demand because, unless costs changed, the price that the producer received was unaffected.

Although the reality of the typical market economy usually includes **administered prices,** state regulation, price fixing, and some degree of non-competitive markets, nevertheless markets tend to provide reasonable signals and thus serve as effective information carriers for resource allocation decisions. The administrative command economy was different in several dimensions.

Even though directives, by design, replaced prices as sources of information in the administrative command economy, this arrangement could violate efficiency considerations. First, a persistent problem was the fact that agents (for example enterprises) possessed substantial amounts and types of information unavailable to planners. In large part, this turned out to be a function of the sheer size and complexity of the economy, an issue noted earlier by Mises and Hayek. Under these conditions, one might expect a reduction of **technical efficiency.**[8]

Second, the system violated the assumption that planners had full information, either about alternatives available to them or the outcomes of possible alternative actions. Although planners were aware of the possibility of major adjustments in resource allocation, for example, the building of a major dam, much less was known about the costs and benefits of likely outcomes, given the frailty of the existing price structure and the lack of effective alternative information mechanisms. Under these conditions, one might expect a reduction of both technical efficiency and **allocative efficiency.**

Third, there is no question that in the administrative command economy, agents were not **risk-neutral.**[9] Managers in the administrative command economy could engage in opportunistic behavior, substantially complicating the principal-agent relationship and leading to outcomes that were perverse, from the perspective of the planner. This theme dominates the literature on enterprise management, what we earlier termed the "success indicator" problem. Cast in this perspective, we would expect both technical and allocative inefficiency.

In any principal-agent relationship, conceptually, the details of the relationship will be specified in a contract. If information conditions are not violated, the specification and execution of such a contract may be relatively straightforward.[10] Suppose that some or all of these conditions are violated, leading to rent-seeking behavior by agents. In this case, the nature of contractual arrangements becomes more complicated.

Property Rights, Motivation, and Principal-Agent Relationships

In the administrative command economy, all property, or, at a minimum, the "means of production" (to use Marx's term), belongs to the state. Although citizens and managers might be paid some kind of social bonus based upon the earnings of the means of production under their control and disposition, this does not change the fact that property belongs to the state. As Soviet citizens would later say, "Property belongs to everyone and hence to no one."

With no clear property owners, Hayek and Mises argued that even enterprise managers with good intentions would not be motivated to make rational economic decisions. Their principals in the CPB, perhaps, could instruct them to maximize profits, but without a system of rational prices to guide them, profit maximization would not prompt them to make correct decisions. They might be given general instructions like "operate the enterprise in the public interest," but such instructions are operatively meaningless. Given the output orientation of the administrative command economy, the manager would be told, more often than not, how much to produce, and would be judged according to production. But even these instructions lacked the information content necessary to have transparency in the planner-manager relationship.

Lacking a clear incentive to maximize profits for owners and given the lack of a rational price system, managers had little incentive to seek out least-cost combinations of resources. Enterprise managers, operating on the basis of vague instructions such as "operate in the public interest" or on specific instructions such as "produce a certain level of output," would not be constrained to limit their demands for inputs. There would be little or no reward for limiting resource demand.

Chapter 7 discussed the immense problems encountered by the Soviet administrative command economy in trying to develop a rational (incentive compatible) incentive system for managers and for ministry officials. The fruitless search for a panacea-type economic reform (discussed in Chapter 12) would be simply an exercise in experimentation, with one managerial incentive scheme being tried and abandoned after another. In fact, since planners could not observe enterprise behavior, substantial reliance was placed upon assessing managerial behavior in terms of performance, plan fulfillment, and the like.

The source of the perennial managerial problem in the Soviet administrative command economy was that because the system was administrative in nature, it paid little attention to prices focusing managerial attention on physical production targets. Rewards were given for fulfilling production targets, and managers were penalized for failing to fulfill them. Production targets, however, do not cover as much territory as profit maximization in a market economy, because profit maximization requires that managers consider not only marginal revenues but also marginal costs. By focusing on output targets, Soviet managers were relieved of the responsibility of cost minimization, satisfying consumer demand, or creating and implementing new technologies. The latter problem was magnified since enterprise managers looked to planners for instructions, not to consumers.

In the Soviet system, penalties for plan failure had to be severe. As non-owners, managers could not be persuaded to fulfill targets for other reasons. Because penalties for failure were severe, managers had an incentive to lobby for "easy" targets, which they could do if they successfully concealed capacity from their superiors. Thus, Soviet enterprise managers had a built-in incentive to report false information to their superiors. Not only did the administrative command economy lack informative relative prices; it had within itself a built-in incentive to report false information. Under these conditions, it is not surprising that **agency problems** were persistent.[11]

Economic Growth and the Socialist System

We have emphasized that advocates of the socialist economic system have argued that it may well be superior to the market-based capitalist economy with regard to economic growth. This superiority is based upon two considerations. First, the state substitutes its **time preference** for that of individuals, enabling a higher level rate of savings than would be attained in a decentralized market economy. Second, the state controls the sectoral expansion of the economy, thus allocating resources to those sectors that will contribute most to economic growth.[12] What expectations might we have for economic growth in the administrative-command economy?

Hayek and Mises argued that the weaknesses of the socialist administrative command economy would be so pervasive that its viability was subject to a strong question mark. At a minimum, the socialist administrative command economy would not perform well compared to its market alternative, which had several centuries of history by the time Mises and Hayek began writing. The market alternative would be superior in terms of information generation, rationality of economic decision making, and managerial motivation.

One interpretation of Mises and Hayek is that they concluded that the administrative command economy could not survive. Given that conclusion, it would make little sense to debate the superiority of market versus administrative command economies because the latter would not survive. An alternate interpretation of Mises and Hayek is that the administrative command economy could survive; it would simply be highly inefficient relative to its market alternative. However we interpret this historical perspective, economic growth was viewed as inadequate to improve consumer well-being and to sustain the economic system over time.

The matter of efficiency is critical to understanding the issue of viability. Although we discuss efficiency outcomes in detail in Chapter 11, it is worth emphasizing that Soviet leaders viewed efficiency from an interesting perspective. It was frequently argued, for example during the 1930s, that the socialist system was superior on two major grounds. First, allocative efficiency was superior because central planners could focus resources on high growth sectors. Second, technical efficiency was superior because, as we noted earlier, in reality the production process was viewed as simple (contrary to the market perception of important and difficult tradeoffs among resources in the production process). Thus, while mistakes might be made, the socialist system would generate rapid economic growth.

Throughout the history of the Soviet economic system, Western economists generally agreed with this claim but have added that this growth was achieved in a relatively inefficient manner, with large and potentially serious incentive costs paid for by consumers. In addition, while it was generally argued that high rates of economic growth could not be sustained for a variety of reasons, supporters of socialism generally did not view slowdown as threatening the viability of the economic system. In the next chapter, we examine the empirical evidence on the relative performance of the administrative command economy.

Socialism as Shortage Economy: Kornai

The Hungarian economist, Janos Kornai, had an alternate view of administrative command socialism.[13] According to Kornai, the administrative command economy would inevitably be an economy of shortage. The pervasiveness of shortage in the administrative command economy was well established as an empirical fact by the time Kornai began to write: It was clear that producer goods, intermediate materials, and even labor were shortage goods. Managers wanted more cement, steel, gasoline, plastics, and so on than were available. Consumers wanted more television sets, VCRs, meat, and so on than were available. Everyone wanted more than was available. Kornai sought to explain why.

Prior to Kornai, the popular explanation for pervasive shortages was planning errors. Planners simply were not good at matching supplies and demands. If they could only plan better, it was thought, shortages would disappear. Kornai cited a more fundamental source of shortage—the **soft budget constraint.** In the administrative command economy, enterprises exist to produce outputs, not to make a profit. Prices are based on arbitrary accounting formulae, which make accounting profits also arbitrary. Therefore, if and when administrative pricing adjustments lag behind changes in costs, whole industries make planned losses.

In such a system, not only will enterprises not pay much attention to costs or to the bottom line of profits, but also their superiors will not allow them to fail because their production is needed for plan fulfillment. Market economies work differently. Enterprises in market economies face a **hard budget constraint:** If they cannot cover their costs, they will fail either immediately or eventually. Enterprises in the administrative command economy face a soft budget constraint: If they do not cover their costs, they will be subsidized either within the ministry or through subsidies from the state budget.

Soft-budget enterprises see no reason to constrain their demand for resources. More is always better because it gives them a better chance to meet their output targets. But if everyone wants more, and no one is penalized for taking more, the demand for materials and resources will far exceed any conceivable supply. Even if planners planned the economy perfectly, there would still be general shortages because of the natural tendency of enterprises to over-demand.

What are the adverse consequences to an economy of inherent shortage? With shortage everywhere, planners are confronted with the difficult task of interpreting signals. All enterprises claim that they are desperately short of a particular material.

Some truly need the material; others need it only marginally; all give the appearance of needing the material in the worst way. Clearly, an economy must have a means of prioritizing to insure that resources go to their best and highest use. The Soviet administrative command economy did have methods of prioritizing—based on the importance of the branch, location, relevance to defense industries, or Party connections. By definition, a good Soviet manager knew how to get materials that all other enterprises also wanted at the same time. Therefore, the principal risk of a shortage economy is that priorities cannot be effectively established. Inefficient distribution is characterized by random distribution of resources or even by perverse distribution, in which resources go to their lowest and least valuable use. If either happens, the efficiency of the economy would suffer.

Raymond Powell argued that, in practice, the Soviet administrative command economy was able to see through conflicting claims for resources to determine their best and highest use.[14] According to Powell, there was a logic to the Soviet system. Even though prices did not provide information on priorities, Soviet administrators did have access to non-price indicators of scarcity. Ministry officials were able to judge, on the basis of how urgent telephone calls appeared to be, or through the frequency of complaints, where materials really needed to go. Local party or state officials could intervene, either perfunctorily or vehemently. In short, Powell argued that planners would know how to interpret the signals correctly.

Through this informal non-price information system, Soviet planners were able to make the system work. Powell did not argue, with his thesis, that the Soviet administrative command economy did a good job prioritizing; he simply argued that it worked well enough to make the system "work."

Economic Growth and Technological Change

Thus far we have discussed economic growth in a very limited frame of reference, focusing specifically on predictions based upon socialist theory. There is much more to economic growth than issues of sectoral allocation of resources at particular points of time.

An economy can be judged on the basis of how well it utilizes existing resources with existing technology. If an economy is getting the maximum output out of its available resources and technology, it is said to be statistically efficient. The next chapter will explain that **static efficiency** means that an economy is operating on the frontier of its production possibilities. But the growth of an economy depends both on its static efficiency and on its ability to introduce new technologies. With greater static efficiency, an economy produces the maximum output from its available resources and hence achieves a higher volume of savings, *ceteris paribus*.

The ability of an economy to introduce new technologies obviously affects its economic growth. With technological change, the economy's production possibilities frontier expands because the economy is able to produce more output from the same amount of inputs. The concepts of static and dynamic efficiency are illustrated in Figure 10.1. The capacity of the economy is given by the frontier *aa*. If the economy is actually operating at point *A* (inside *aa*), it is inefficient. If, on the other hand, it is operating at point *B* (on the frontier *aa*) it is operating at full capacity. If the economy increases its capacity through economic growth, then the capacity of the economy would be represented by a new production possibilities frontier, namely *bb*.

In market economies, the incentive to introduce technological advances is fostered by the need to remain competitive, by the advantages of cost reductions achieved through new technologies, and through the ability of new products and new technologies to generate market growth. In fact, the economic growth of market economies appears to have been defined by waves of technological advances, sometimes rapid and sometimes slow.

Were there similar motivations and incentives to introduce new technologies in the administrative command economy? Technological change was not an issue of major focus in early theorizing about socialist economic systems. Indeed, the socialist perception of production is one of constant factor proportions in which input-output relationships are readily knowable at a point in time and unchanging through time.[15] Moreover, it was generally argued in the Soviet Union that with great emphasis on scientific research and a system in which there would be no corporate secrecy, new ideas would be developed and disseminated without difficulty. How do these ideas relate to the reality of the administrative command economy?

Joseph Berliner studied this matter in depth and concluded that the Soviet administrative command economy inherently erected a number of barriers to technological advances.[16] Soviet enterprise managers and planners were rewarded for

Figure 10.1 Production Possibilities and Economic Growth

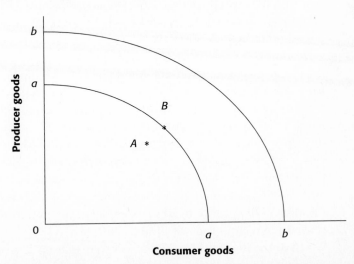

expanding physical production targets, for producing some percent more output. New technologies introduced new products and required new sources of supply, both of which made the life of the enterprise manager more difficult. If production down-time were associated with the switch to new products and new technologies, the enterprise manager was penalized for failing to increase production.

New technologies brought many risks and few rewards for the Soviet enterprise manager. Moreover, information on new technologies was largely in the purview of the enterprise manager, not the planner. Superior technology failed to bring about rewards in terms of higher product prices. If an enterprise introduced a new technology that created a new product but lowered the cost of production, the new product was priced low by existing pricing formulas. Although the Soviet administrative command economy attempted to introduce price increases for "new" products, this incentive was easily abused—enterprise managers made very minimal changes in existing products, then claimed the "new product" pricing incentives. As a result, the administrative command economy found it difficult to reward managers properly for introducing new products.

Another obstacle to new technologies was that they greatly complicated the process of planning. New technologies required the introduction of new material balances, new supply relationships, new prices, and other new procedures. Planning officials worked best in an environment of little change. A static planning environment can be created when technological change is limited. Surprisingly, even those participants who should be most supportive of new technology—ministry and planning commission officials—were not necessarily supportive, because new technology complicated the planning task.

It is worth observing that if systemic problems inhibit the diffusion of new technologies, the source of these new technologies really does not matter. Thus whether new technologies are developed at home or imported from abroad, domestic systemic barriers will limit their effectiveness. This fact presents us with an irony in light of significant Western concerns about Soviet importation and use of new technologies during the era of the cold war.

A different perspective is presented by Marshall Goldman, who has argued that the productivity gains from imported technology is much lower than that achieved from indigenous technological change.[17] Put differently, this means that if a country is to sustain or advance its economic position among world economies, it must not rely heavily upon borrowing new technology from abroad. Studies of the Soviet technology gap conclude that the Soviet Union began its economic development with a large technology gap, which either grew larger or, at best, remained the same throughout the Soviet period.[18] Sectoral studies showed that "there is no evidence of a substantial diminution of the technological gap between the Soviet Union and the West in the past 15 to 20 years, either at the prototype/commercial application stages or in the diffusion of advanced technology."[19]

Soviet technological achievements were uneven. There were areas (for example metallurgy and welding) where Soviet methods were advanced. In other critical areas (computers, for example), the reverse was true. In the 1980s, it was estimated that the Soviet Union lagged behind the United States in the development of computers by 9–15 years (mainframes), 4–10 years (microcomputers) and 8–10 years (macrocircuits).[20]

The Soviet Union relied heavily upon imports to sustain and to improve its level of technology. While such a posture might be quite rational as a country pursues economic growth and economic development, in the Soviet case, there were problems. Growing complementarities among technologies make it difficult to jump from behind and sustain a lead simply by importing them.[21] Also, implementation was a major problem in the Soviet Union. Evidence suggested that lead times between the granting of a patent and its practical implementation were generally longer in the Soviet Union than in Western industrialized nations.

The Soviet experience, therefore, deviated dramatically from that of some market economies also having technology gaps relative to the most advanced industrialized economies. These economies, such as the Four Tigers of Southeast Asia, Spain, Portugal, and Italy, grew more rapidly throughout the postwar era largely because of their ability to imitate more advanced technology.

BUREAUCRATIC DECISION MAKING

We are all familiar with bureaucratic decision-making processes. The Soviet administrative command economy was the example par excellence of bureaucratic decision making, for bureaucratic decision making applied to the entire economy.[22]

In the case of private decision making in a private market economy, the decision makers, be they the owners or the agents of the owners, are willing to make risky decisions because of the risk-reward tradeoff. If they make a risky decision and it turns out to be correct, they will personally benefit in the form of greater profits, more valuable stock options, or profit-related bonuses. If they approve a risky decision that turns out to be wrong, they will personally suffer through lower profits, less valuable stock options, or loss of their jobs. Private enterprise managers must weigh the costs and benefits of risk, and they are prepared to assume risk as long as the marginal benefits exceed the cost. The risk-reward tradeoff is structured by the incentive system, which can be calibrated to encourage or discourage risk-taking.

The administrators of an administrative command economy have a different attitude towards risk. If a risky decision is taken and the decision proves to be the correct one, those who made the decision stand to benefit very little. They are not the owners; they can be awarded some kind of bonuses, but they will likely not compensate managers enough to balance out the chance that the risky decision may be the wrong one. If a risky decision turns out to be wrong, then the enterprise or ministry loses as a consequence, and those who made the decision will be penalized. The Soviet asymmetry between risk and reward, therefore, discourages risk-taking in an administrative command economy. In fact, there is ample evidence to suggest that the administrators of the administrative command economy were strong risk avoiders, since risk-taking offered few or no personal benefits. In the Soviet system whenever risky decisions needed to be made, they were made by committee or by a complicated signing-off process (called the visa process), in which every possible affected party needed to sign off on the decision. With so many approvals required, decision making was slowed or even impossible.

The Soviet administrative command system reinforced risk aversion through a well-developed system of blame allocation. Whenever a decision or an action led to unfavorable results, the system insisted on having a sacrificial lamb to take the blame. The blame typically shifted down the hierarchy as much as possible, but if the mistake was a serious one, even the top official could not avoid being sacrificed.

The lack of balance between risks and rewards, combined with the sacrificial lamb process, forced Soviet administrators to form protective groups to spread risk, limit the flow of information to superiors, and to short circuit external monitoring. These protective groups might consist of local enterprise managers and local Party and state officials, the latter presumably responsible to the center for accurate information.[23] In fact, the formation of local self-protection groups has been cited as the origin of corruption and mafia forces that became dominant after the collapse of the administrative command economy.[24]

PROBLEMS OF INVESTMENT CHOICE

The choices of new technology and of new investment are interrelated. Above, we discussed the problems of technological choice. Here we discuss the problem of rational investment decision making.

In market economies, there are pressures on enterprises to make "rational" investment decisions, and market-generated information assists in the selection of investment projects. Corporations must raise investment finance at the cost of dilution of ownership (if the investment project is financed by the sale of new shares) or at the cost of interest and principal payments (if the investment is financed by debt). In either case, the corporation knows the cost of the investment project and will automatically select only those investment projects that yield reasonable rates of return. The corporation can make appropriate comparisons of incomes and costs over time because interest rates allow cumulated costs and benefits to be reduced to the common denominator of present discounted value.

The Soviet enterprises or ministries did not know the cost of investment finance. Throughout most of the Soviet era, investment finance was provided to the ministry/enterprise free of charge. During the latter decades of the Soviet period, there was an interest charge for capital, but it was nominal, and Soviet enterprises faced few incentives to minimize production costs, including capital charges. The true benefits of investment projects were not quantifiable either. Benefits were typically measured in terms of operating-cost reductions or increases in enterprise capacity, but most often investment projects were chosen automatically to meet the production increases called for in the output plan, without consideration of cost/benefit calculations.

In market economies, there is a tendency to equalize rates of return on capital investments. If higher rates of return can be earned in industry X than in industry Y, there will be a tendency to shift capital from Y to X as the owners of capital seek out the highest rate of return. In the Soviet administrative command economy, with its administrative allocation of investment, there was no pressure to equalize rates of return. If the plan required a 10% increase in sector A, that is where capital went, even if the rate of return would have been higher in B. As a result, the economy is producing below its production potential. With quite different rates of return in different branches and in different enterprises, more output would have been produced in the long run by a redistribution of capital among enterprises and branches.[25]

CONSUMER WELFARE AND QUANTITY CONSTRAINTS

We have emphasized that the planned socialist economy was not designed to operate on the basis of consumer sovereignty. The basic decisions of what to produce, how to produce, and for whom to produce were made by the planners and the political authority, not by consumers voting in the market place. Such was the case in the Soviet administrative command economy.

Although the Soviet state tolerated an unofficial black market, it did not account for a major share of consumer purchases except in a small number of markets (see Chapter 8). Most of the consumer budget was met by production from the state sector, which operated according to the rules previously described. Although pricing authorities sought to set consumer prices to clear the market, many significant consumer markets were characterized by excess demand. Soviet enterprises simply did not produce enough dairy products, quality clothing and footwear, apartments, and automobiles to satisfy market demand at prevailing prices.

Soviet officials could have responded to the excess demand for specific products by allowing prices to rise to their equilibrium levels, but they chose not to do so for reasons of income distribution and propaganda. Instead of allowing all prices to rise to market clearing levels, Soviet authorities used **quantity constraints**—in other words, they used quantitative restrictions (such as ration coupons), requiring people to stand in line to obtain products, or distributing through special privilege arrangements that determined who got the most desired products.

Quantity constraints have a number of negative economic effects that reduce the economy's efficiency of resource use. In Figure 10.2 (p. 210) we use indifference curves to show that when consumers' freedom of choice is restricted by quantity constraints (they are allowed to consume only a restricted amount of product X), their consumer welfare declines as compared to unrestricted choice. That is, if

Soviet consumers had been allowed unrestricted choice of consumer goods (and market prices had been allowed to adjust to equilibrium in all cases), Soviet consumers would have achieved a higher level of welfare with the same amount of production and resources.[26]

In Figure 10.2, with unrestricted choice and existing tastes and prices, the consumer would maximize utility at point A on indifference curve b. However, if a quantity constraint of oq was placed on good X, then under the existing prices and preferences, the consumer would maximize utility at point B on indifference curve a. In this particular case, the consumers' level of satisfaction would be reduced, and less of good X and slightly more of good Y would be consumed. The specific outcome would depend, of course, on the specific conditions.

Quantity constraints have other negative effects on the economy. When consumers' choices are restricted, their earned income becomes less meaningful. Why should they work hard if their ability to buy goods depends not on their income but on their willingness to stand in line? Accordingly, the stronger the quantity constraints, the weaker the willingness to work. Quantity constraints may also affect the willingness to save.[27] In fact, there is empirical evidence to suggest that quantity constraints did indeed cause Soviet workers to work less and to save less.

So, empirical analysis shows that quantity constraints do indeed negatively affect household behavior in economies like the Soviet administrative command economy. However, these studies do not conclude that the effect is overwhelming. Such analysis may be misleading. It may be that the effect was substantial and was a prime contributing force behind the move to perestroika and transition.

Figure 10.2   Consumer Preferences and Quantity Constraints

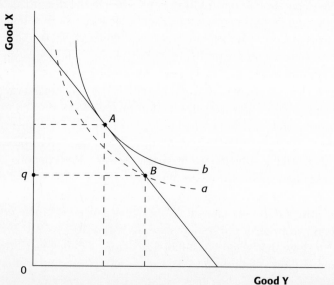

If an economy cannot satisfy its consumers, dissatisfaction is inevitable. For years Soviet consumers were promised a better life. In the 1930s, this promise was accepted because everyone understood that the Soviet Union began as a relatively poor economy. Overnight change would not come without sacrifice. In the late 1930s and 1940s, everyone understood that a better life cannot come during a major world war. But, as the Soviet economy experienced decades of development after World War II and consumer satisfaction continued unabated, consumer dissatisfaction must have boiled over in a way that the Soviet leadership could not ignore.

While models of socialist economic systems might suggest less attention, at least initially, to consumer goods, there is no prediction in socialism that suggests abandoning consumer well-being. In fact, quite the opposite is true. However, if consumer goods are to be sacrificed for the initial achievement of high rates of economic growth, the time must come in the evolution of socialism when this initial sacrifice comes to an end. Soviet consumers did not believe this was happening. Moreover, a fundamental tenet of socialism is the replacement of private consumption by public or social consumption. While this replacement took place to some degree in the Soviet Union—for example public transportation replacing private means, to a large extent—it remains to discover whether the incentive effects of these public goods were in fact adequate to motivate workers to expand production.

Job Rights and Performance Expectations

In Chapter 8 we examined the household and labor force participation. However, an alternative to the disequilibrium model discussed above is the **Job Rights Overfull Employment (JROE)** hypothesis suggested by David Granick.[28]

As we emphasized, the Soviet labor market relied more on market allocation than other markets. Generally, Soviet workers had freedom of choice of occupations, and supplies and demands were roughly equated by relative earnings. However, while market-type mechanisms may have been in use, the allocation of labor differed in many ways from that in market capitalist economies. Soviet workers were rarely dismissed, enjoying considerable protection in their jobs. Moreover, where separations occurred, they were usually initiated by the worker, not the enterprise. Granick sought to explain these stylized facts through the JROE approach.

It had usually been argued that the stylized facts of the Soviet labor market could be explained by persistent excess demand and regional imbalances rather than being the result of deliberate policy. Thus enterprises overdemanded labor just as they overdemanded other inputs in a soft budget setting. In the JROE model, Granick noted that while enterprises had a virtually unlimited desire to add to their labor force, they did face a wage fund constraint. But, the wage fund was fungible since it did not make sense for the center to specify detailed staffing patterns for enterprises. Faced with a hard but fungible wage fund, enterprise managers needed to allocate the wage fund in a rational manner.

Granick's main proof of the hardness of the wage constraint was the careful planning of nominal earnings per employee. If Soviet enterprises had truly had an unconstrained ability to demand labor, central planners could not have controlled inflation as successfully as they did. Granick argues that Soviet workers had job rights not because of widespread excess demand for labor, but rather because job rights were part of the leadership's objectives. Job rights and overfull employment were system goals. Moreover, job rights and overfull employment limited the ability of the center to engage in regional differentiation—thus general overfull employment guaranteed overfull employment across regions. More controversial was Granick's claim that workers were not only protected by job security, they were also protected from "unwanted idleness." Not only did workers have guaranteed jobs, but managers also had to insure that workers did not stand idle for extended periods.

What are the implications of job rights? Granick speculated that the Soviet leadership may have viewed full employment as a moral outcome or as an implicit contract with labor. Also, since in the ideology of socialism, unemployment was to be eliminated, its existence, even "necessary" unemployment for adjustment purposes, would be viewed with embarrassment, notwithstanding efficiency implications.

However, JROE had serious costs. The rigidity of the demand side of the Soviet occupational structure partially explains the ineffective use of fixed capital investment. Further, JROE forced over-investment in human capital. Granick contends that the social return to higher education was negative in the Soviet Union (after adjustment for foregone earnings during education). Basically, there was over-investment in human capital because educated persons were more flexible in their choice of occupations. Since the Soviet occupational structure could not be changed from the demand side, Soviet authorities had to create a large pool of occupation-changers, which authorities did by creating too many highly educated persons. Granick also argued that JROE was a factor limiting the willingness of Soviet authorities to decentralize price setting arrangements. This, it was argued, would lead to "unwanted idleness" at the enterprise level. Moreover, the absence of labor market discipline could lead to additional problems, especially reduction of effort on the job.

Economists are ambivalent about the issue of job rights. Granick argued that there were excessive costs to job rights in the Soviet case. Yet in the analysis of other systems, it has been argued that job rights can improve economic efficiency. For example, the lifetime contracts of Japanese workers have been cited as a reason for success of the Japanese economy.[29]

SUMMARY

In this chapter, we consider performance predictions for the administrative command economy based upon its basic features as a planned socialist economy. These predictions are cast in terms of predictions made throughout the past fifty years and contemporary agency analysis of the arrangements of the Soviet economic system.

The planned socialist economic system can be characterized in terms of property rights (held by the state), the mechanism used for decision making about resource allocation (the central plan), the level of decision making (centralized), and finally the nature of incentive arrangements (material and moral incentives).

As we have emphasized in earlier chapters, agency relationships are useful in analyzing the administrative command economy. Indeed, we predicted efficiency problems based upon inadequate information at the planning level, information at the enterprise level unknown to planners, and finally, a setting in which rent-seeking by managers was likely. These characteristics, examined by Mises and Hayek, can be discussed using contemporary information economics. While we conclude that these problems introduced a bias against efficiency, viability of the administrative command economy remains a matter of long-term economic growth.

While incentive arrangements may partially offset these problems, we note that the administrative command economy lacks the signals necessary for the rational allocation of investment resources, thus achieving short-term economic growth at the expense of consumer well-being, a long-term incentive problem. Moreover, the inability of the administrative command economy to develop and effectively diffuse new technologies limited its ability to benefit from technological change, a limitation that is fundamentally systemic in character.

Although there are a variety of historical attempts to model the planned socialist economic system, much of the reality of the contemporary administrative command economy is incorporated in the model of the shortage economy constructed by Janos Kornai. This model attempts to capture reality by suggesting that the existence of a soft as opposed to a hard budget constraint leads to persistent excess demand for inputs. Persistent and pervasive shortages create a system in which barter exchanges tend to supplant more traditional money-commodity relationships.

Finally, we have observed that both the disequilibrium and the job rights models explicitly consider the importance of non-price resource allocation in the Soviet economy, though with varying efficiency predictions.

Terms and Concepts

property rights   Claims that a person or persons has over an asset or bundle of assets, permitting control of its use, disposition, and the gain or benefit derived from it.

planning   A process for bringing resources together to achieve desired objectives, typically in a hierarchical organization where principals (planners) instruct enterprise managers (agents).

centralization   The placement of information necessary for decision making at high levels of an organizational hierarchy, where both the authority and the responsibility for making decision rest.

incentives   Rewards (which can be material or moral) designed to induce desired behavior from participants; for example, rewards paid to an enterprise manager for the achievement of planners' objectives.

planners' preferences   Generally in the planned socialist economy; planners determine output decisions instead of consumers.

consumer sovereignty   Generally in a market economy; output decisions are strongly influenced by the consumer through the marketplace.

incentive compatibility   Incentive arrangements that harmonize agent behavior with desired principal's outcomes.

Central Planning Board (CPB)   A genetic expression associated with the Polish economist Oskar Lange and his model of market socialism; a board that oversees decisions about resource allocation in a socialist economy.

principal-agent structure   An organization whose participants can be characterized as a principal (who issues instructions about desired outcomes) and an agent (who is responsible for carrying out the principal's instructions).

rent-seeking behavior   Usually associated with an agent; the pursuit of self-interest; typically, opportunistic behavior that can arise where there are incomplete contracts.

administered prices   Prices generally set not by the forces of supply and demand, but by adherence to a predetermined formula, such as average cost plus some markup.

technical efficiency   Least-cost production of a given output.

allocative efficiency   Allocation of resources to, for example, various sectors of the economy such that the benefits exceed the costs by the greatest amount when compared to allocation to an alternative sector.

risk neutrality   The willingness to accept a probabilistic outcome; for example, a risk-neutral person considers the following outcomes are equal: (1) a sure payment of $1000 or (2) a risky payment of $2000 but with a known probability of occurring of .5.

agency problems   Problems that arise out of agency relationships; for example moral hazard, where an agent may conceal information and alter behavior after entering into a contract; or adverse selection, where an agent can benefit vis-a-vis the principal by hiding information.

time preference   The discount factor applied when comparing expected future gains to present gains; socialists argue that in market economies, future gains are downgraded and hence there is a tendency to emphasize present consumption (present gains) over savings (which promote future gains).

soft budget constraint   From the work of Janos Kornai, the notion that enterprises in planned socialist systems typically do not experience a hard budget constraint, leading to excess demand for inputs and the existence of persistent shortages.

hard budget constraint   Budget constraints in which a company's profits must cover its costs in order for the company to succeed.

static efficiency   Efficiency (output per unit of input) at a point in time, generally characterized by how close an economy is operating to its production possibilities frontier.

quantity constraints   Limitations expressed in quantity rather than value terms; for example a rationing system that limits a person to two loaves of bread a week.

Job Rights Overfull Employment (JROE)   A model proposed by David Granick to explain aspects of Soviet labor market behavior; specifically, systemic excess demands of enterprises for labor, which result in part from maintaining the right to a job as part of the central planners' objectives.

Selected Bibliography

The Planned Socialist Economic System

Amann, R., and J. Cooper, eds. *Industrial Innovation in the Soviet Union* (New Haven: Yale University Press, 1982).

Amann, R., J. Cooper, and R. W. Davies. *The Technological Level of Soviet Industry* (New Haven: Yale University Press, 1977).

Berliner, J. *The Innovation Decision in Soviet Industry* (Cambridge, MA: MIT Press, 1976).

Dobb, M. *Welfare Economics and the Economics of Socialism* (Cambridge: Cambridge University Press, 1969).

Goldman, M. I. *Gorbachev's Challenge: Economic Reform in the Age of High Technology* (New York: Norton, 1987).

Gregory, P. R. *Reforming the Soviet Economic Bureaucracy* (New York: Cambridge University Press, 1990).

Gregory, P. R., and R. C. Stuart. *Comparative Economic Systems* 5e (Boston: Houghton Mifflin, 1995).

Kornai, J. *The Socialist Economy: The Political Economy of Communism* (Princeton, NJ: Princeton University Press, 1992).

Parrott, B. *Politics and Technology in the Soviet Union* (Cambridge, MA: MIT Press, 1982).

Stiglitz, J. E. *Whither Socialism?* (Cambridge, MA: MIT Press, 1994).

Agency Relationships

Ben-Ner, A., J. M. Montias, and E. Neuberger. "Basic Issues in Organizations: A Comparative Perspective," *Journal of Comparative Economics* vol. 17 (1933), 207–42.

Besanko, D., D. Dranove, and M. Shanley. *Economics of Strategy* (New York: Wiley, 1996).

Grossman, S., and O. Hart. "The Costs and Benefits of Ownership: A Theory of Vertical and Lateral Integration" *Journal of Political Economy* vol. 94 (August 1986), 691–719.

Milgrom, P. "Employment Contracts, Influence Activities and Efficient Organizational Design," *Journal of Political Economy* vol. 96 (February 1988), 42–60.

Milgrom, P. and J. Roberts. *Economics, Organization and Management* (Englewood Cliffs, NJ: Prentice-Hall, 1992).

Pratt, J. and Richard Zeckhauser, eds. *Principals and Agents: The Structure of Business* (Cambridge, MA: Harvard Business School, 1985).

Putterman, L. "Ownership and the Nature of the Firm," *Journal of Comparative Economics* vol. 17 (1993), 243–63.

Ross, S. "The Economic Theory of Agency: The Principal's Problem," *American Economic Review* vol. 63 (1973), 134–9.

Sappington, D. E. M. "Incentives in Principal-Agent Relationships," *Journal of Economic Perspectives* vol. 5 (Spring 1991), 45–66.

Varian, H. *Microeconomic Theory* 3e (New York: Norton, 1992).

Williamson, O., ed. *Organization Theory: From Chester Barnard to the Present and Beyond* (Oxford: Oxford University Press, 1990).

Notes

1. Although there are a variety of socialist variants, for example those using market arrangements for allocative purposes, we limit ourselves to the model most appropriate for understanding the Soviet case, specifically the planned socialist economic system.

2. The issue of property rights is much more complex than presented here. In fact, even in the Soviet case, where the state exercised substantial control, it was not dominant in all cases.

3. For a discussion of the planned socialist model, see for example P. R. Gregory and R. C. Stuart, *Comparative Economic Systems* 5e (Boston: Houghton Mifflin, 1995). For a general discussion of the socialist idea, see for example T. Bottomore, *The Socialist Economy: Theory and Practice* (New York: Harvester Wheatsheaf, 1990).

4. For a discussion, see A. Bergson, "Socialist Economics," in A. Bergson, *Essays in Normative Economics* (Cambridge, MA: Harvard University Press, 1966); L. von Mises, "Die Wirtschaftschnung in Sozialistischein Gemeinwison," *Archiv fur Sozialwissenschaffen* (April 1920); F. A. Hayek, ed., Collectivist Economic Planning 6e (London: Routledge & Kegan Paul, 1963).

5. The specific concept of a central planning board (CPB) is typically associated with the model of market socialism developed by Oskar Lange. See B. Lippincott, ed., *On the Economic Theory of Socialism* (New York: McGraw-Hill, 1964).

6. There is a large and growing literature on agency. For an excellent discussion with references to key sources, see D. Besanko, D. Dranove, and M. Shanley, *Economics of Strategy* (New York: Wiley, 1966), part 4.

7. The use of mathematical solutions to the socialist pricing problem was first explored by Enrico Barone, "The Ministry of Production in the Collectivist State," in Hayek, ed., *Collectivist Economic Planning*, 245–90. The use of market simulation to generate prices was discussed by Oskar Lange in M. M. Lippincott, ed., *On the Economic Theory of Socialism*.

8. Conceptually, the advent of computers ought to offset some of the information noted here, facilitating storage and dissemination. Although Soviet leaders devoted considerable effort to the development of a nationwide computer network, most observers would probably argue that the system gained little benefit from this effort.

9. A risk-neutral agent, say an enterprise manager in the administrative command economy, would be indifferent between a guaranteed payment of say, $1000 for just meeting the plan directives and a payment of $2000 for a specified over-fulfillment of the plan directives achievable with a probability of .5. In fact, the managerial milieu was much more complicated.

10. This would be termed a "first-best efficient contract." See Besanko, Dranove, and Shanley, *Economics of Strategy,* 616–17.

11. Earlier we noted that there is no single, simple model of the administrative command economy comparable to that of the perfectly competitive market economy. Indeed, in the latter case, where requirements are violated, there are second-best alternatives. However, insofar as we can characterize the administrative command economy within the framework of an agency model, second-best contracts may be considered. See Besanko, Dranove, and Shanley, *Economics of Strategy,* ch. 16.

12. Even in variants of centrally planned socialism, for example the Lange model, state control of investment is seen as a major advantage of the socialist economic system.

13. Kornai has written extensively on the socialist economy. For a recent major work with citations to his earlier works, see J. Kornai, *The Socialist System: The Political Economy of Communism* (Princeton, NJ: Princeton University Press, 1992). See also J. Kornai, *The Economics of Shortage* (New York: North-Holland, 1980); "Resource Constrained Versus Demand Constrained Systems," *Econometrica* vol. 47 (July 1979); *Anti-Equilibrium: On Economic Systems Theory and the Tasks of Research* (Amsterdam: North-Holland, 1971); *Rush Versus Harmonic Growth* (Amsterdam: North-Holland, 1972); *Overcentralization in Economic Administration* (London: Oxford University Press, 1959); *Growth, Shortage and Efficiency: A Macrodynamic Model of the Socialist Economy* (Berkeley: University of California Press, 1983).

14. R. P. Powell, "Plan Execution and the Workability of Soviet Planning," *Journal of Comparative Economics* vol. 1, no. 1 (March 1977), 69–73.

15. For a classic discussion of this point, see M. Dobb, *Welfare Economics and the Economics of Socialism* (Cambridge: Cambridge University Press, 1969).

16. The classic work is J. Berliner, *The Innovation Decision in Soviet Industry* (Cambridge, MA: MIT Press, 1976). For additional discussion see J. Berliner, "Prospects for Technological Progress," in U.S. Congress, Joint Economic Committee, *Soviet Economy in a New Perspective* (Washington, DC: U.S. Government Printing Office, 1976); A. Amann, J. Cooper, and R. W. Davies. *The Technological Level of Soviet Industry* (New Haven: Yale University Press, 1977); J. R. Thomas and U. Kruse-Vaucienne, eds., *Soviet Science and Technology* (Washington, DC: George Washington University, 1977); E. Zaleski, et al., *Science Policy in the USSR* (Paris: OECD, 1969); J. Martens and J. P. Young, "Soviet Implementation of Domestic Inventions: First Results," in U.S. Congress, Joint Economic Committee, *Soviet Economy in a Time of Change* (Washington, DC: U.S. Government Printing Office, 1979); J. Grant, " Soviet Machine Tools: Lagging Technology and Rising Inputs," in U.S. Congress, Joint Economic Committee, *Soviet Economy in a Time of Change;* P. Hanson, "International Technology Transfer from the West to the USSR," in U.S. Congress, Joint Economic Committee, *Soviet Economy in a New Perspective;* R. Amann and J. Cooper, eds., *Industrial Innovation in the Soviet Union* (New Haven: Yale University Press, 1982); B. Parrott, *Politics and Technology in Soviet Union* (Cambridge, MA: MIT Press, 1982).

17. For a discussion of this issue, see M. I. Goldman, *Gorbachev's Challenge: Economic Reform in the Age of High Technology* (New York: Norton, 1987), ch. 5.

18. There is a large literature on technological change in the Soviet Union. See for example R. Amann, J. Cooper, and R. W. Davies. *The Technological Level of Soviet Industry;* R. Amann and J. Cooper, eds., *Industrial Innovation in the Soviet Union;* B. Parrott, *Politics and Technology in Soviet Union.*

19. These basic conclusions, from the late 1970s, are from R. Amann, J. Cooper, and R. W. Davies, eds., *The Technological Level of Soviet Industry.*

20. S. E. Goodman, "The Prospective Impacts of Computing: Selected Economic-Industrial-Strategic Issues," in U.S. Congress, Joint Economic Committee, *Gorbachev's Economic*

Plans (Washington, DC: U.S. Government Printing Office, 1987); CIA, *The Economy in 1988: Gorbachev Changes Course* (Washington, DC: CIA, 1988); M. I. Goldman, *Gorbachev's Challenge* (New York: Norton, 1987).

21. M. I. Goldman, *Gorbachev's Challenge.*

22. For a discussion of these issues, see P. R. Gregory, *Reforming the Soviet Economic Bureaucracy* (New York: Cambridge University Press, 1990).

23. See P. R. Gregory, *Reforming the Soviet Economic Bureaucracy.*

24. M. Olson, "The Devolution of Power in Post-Communist Societies," in Robert Skidelsky, ed., *Russia's Stormy Path to Reform* (London: Social Market Foundation, 1995), 942.

25. J. Thornton, "Differential Capital Charges and Resource Allocation in Soviet Industry," *Journal of Political Economy* vol. 79 (May-June 1971); P. Desai and R. Martin, "Efficiency Losses from Resource Misallocation in Soviet Industry," *Quarterly Journal of Economics* vol. 98 (August 1983). A summary of studies can be found in P. Murrell, "Can Neoclassical Economics Underpin the Reform of Centrally Planned Economies?" *Journal of Economic Perspectives* vol. 5 (Fall 1991); see also A. Bergson, *The Economics of Soviet Planning* (New Haven: Yale University Press, 1964); D. A. Dyker, *The Process of Investment in the Soviet Union* (New York: Cambridge University Press, 1981); M. J. Kohn and R. E. Leggett, "Soviet Investment Policy: The Key to Gorbachev's Program for Revitalizing the Soviet Economy," in U.S. Congress, Joint Economic Committee, *Gorbachev's Economic Plans;* and B. Rumer, *Investment and Reindustrialization of the Soviet Economy* (Boulder, CO: Westview Press, 1984).

26. I. Collier, "Effective Purchasing Power in a Quantity Constrained Economy: An Estimate for the German Democratic Republic," *Review of Economics and Statistics* vol. 68, no. 1 (February 1986), 24–32; I. Collier, "The Measurement and Interpretation of Real Consumption and Purchasing Power Parity for a Quantity Constrained Economy: The Case of East and West Germany," *Econometrica* vol. 62, no. 1 (January 1993), 1–28; R. D. Portes, "The Theory and Measurement of Macroeconomic Disequilibrium in Centrally Planned Economies," in C. Davis and W. Chramza, eds., *Models and Disequilibrium and Shortage in Centrally Planned Economies* (New York: Chapman and Hall, 1989); R. D. Portes and D. Winter, "The Demand for Money and Consumption Goods in Centrally Planned Economies," *Review of Economics and Statistics* vol. 60 (February 1978); R. E. Quandt and S. Yeo, "Tests of the Chronic Shortage Hypothesis: The Case of Poland," *Review of Economics and Statistics* vol. 60 (February 1988).

27. P. J. Neary and K. W. S. Roberts, "The Theory of Household Behavior Under Rationing," *European Economic Review* vol. 13 (March 1980); M. Mokhtari and P. Gregory, "Backward Bends, Quantity Constraints, and Soviet Labor Supply: Evidence from the Soviet Interview Project," *International Economic Review* vol. 34, no. 1 (1993).

28. D. Granick, *Job Rights in the Soviet Union: Their Consequences* (New York: Cambridge University Press, 1987).

29. R. Freeman and J. Medoff, "The Two Faces of Unionism," *Public Interest,* vol. 57 (Fall 1979), 73–80.

CHAPTER 11

The Administrative Command Economy: Economic Growth

The ultimate test for any economic system is its ability to grow and to provide increases in the standard of living. This was no less true for the Soviet Union, a country that placed great emphasis on **economic growth.** And yet in the end, after significant rates of economic growth in its early years, it would be a steadily declining rate of growth of output that would become a hallmark of the Soviet decline through the 1980s. In Chapter 10, we examined a wide range of reasons why the Soviet administrative command economy might be expected to have economic difficulties. We turn now to the evidence.

In this chapter, we examine the Soviet record of economic performance, and in particular, the record of economic growth. We cover the period from the first Five Year Plan to the mid-1980s. The story is complex, and yet the message of decline is clear. We begin with an examination of measurement problems, after which we examine the empirical evidence. Finally, we examine the major forces that underlie and help explain the Soviet growth record.

ECONOMIC GROWTH IN THE SOVIET UNION

Background Issues

Performance comparisons across differing economies and economic systems are fraught with difficulties. From the outset, it is necessary to select the criteria by which an assessment can be made.[1] For our examination of Soviet economic performance we focus on the rate of growth of output and of productivity, keeping in mind we might use other indicators, which might produce different conclusions. For example, while economic growth is a key factor influencing levels of well-being of the population, clearly other indicators, such as income distribution, shed light on other aspects of performance. We must bear in mind that different indicators may tell different stories, which means that we have no single, clearly unambiguous indicator from which to judge which economy has better performance.

Second, as we examine Soviet economic performance, we must bear in mind the importance of the former USSR as a world power and as a prototype of the planned socialist economic system. For these reasons, we have tended to compare the Soviet record against performance trends in major industrialized market economies. Comparing the former Soviet Union against countries such as the United States, Germany, and Japan is a tough standard. However, such comparisons are traditionally made, largely due to the USSR's status as a superpower and its often stated intention to overtake the West in economic power.

Third, the time period we select for comparison can affect the outcome. If we compare, for example, Soviet and American economic growth during the 1930s, we get a quite different answer than if we looked at the 1970s and 1980s. In this chapter, we focus on long-run performance, though even when looking at the big picture, we must make some judgments. What years should be included for our examination of the USSR? Should we include only "normal" years (whatever this may mean), and omit the years of World War II and the Stalinist purges? "Comparable" time periods are generally quite arbitrary. If we wish to contrast Soviet and U.S. economic growth, should we select different time periods, when both countries were at the same "stage of development"?

Fourth, in addition to measurement problems, there are a variety of well-known and perhaps insoluble technical problems, all of which complicate international comparisons. There are different ways to measure growth of output and productivity, and each approach can affect the outcomes. To facilitate an understanding of the Soviet performance record, we need to discuss several basic measurement issues.

Economic Growth—Measurement

Measuring Soviet economic growth was a subject of major importance during the Soviet era. Soviet authorities heralded the country's rapid economic growth as a major indicator of the superiority of the Soviet system. Western governments, on the other hand, devoted considerable resources to recalculating Soviet economic growth. The proper measurement of economic growth requires agreement on problems of definition, aggregation, and a common unit of measure.

Definition   Economic growth refers to rates of change in aggregate output, usually Gross National Product (GNP) or Gross Domestic Product (GDP). In normal Western accounting practices, GDP is measured on the income or the product side of the national accounts, the latter being the weighted sum of the value added by sectors in the economy. Market prices from a base year are the weights used to aggregate physical output series over a period of time. The annual rate of change in GDP can be measured through time by way of changes in the GDP series in constant prices of the base year.

In the Soviet Union, the equivalent concept of output in Marxian terms was **Net Material Product (NMP).** NMP differed from GDP in many ways, some of which could be adjusted to convert NMP into GDP. NMP was generally not computed on a value added basis, and thus suffered from an unknown degree of double counting. Steel used by an automobile factory could be counted twice rather than once, as in Western accounting practice. In addition, ideological biases would affect what would be included. Thus the services of a medical doctor related to material production (in an industrial enterprise) would be included, while the doctor's services for private patients would not be included. In general, services were viewed as "unproductive" in the Marxian schema.[2]

Aggregation   Any composite measure of output requires the use of prices for aggregation purposes. In a market economy, relative prices reflect relative scarcities in the economy, and hence prices (with adjustment for taxes and other distortions) are reliable measures of the relative importance (weight) of different outputs added together to capture total output. Soviet prices suffered from a number of deficiencies, discussed in Chapter 7. For much of the Soviet era, capital charges were not used. Depreciation for obsolescence and depletion were both considered alien to the Soviet setting. If price omitted scarce resource inputs, they would provide inaccurate guides to aggregating outputs. Soviet prices were cost-based, often bearing little or no relation to relative scarcities and thus having an unknown meaning when used for purposes of aggregating the output of different sectors in the economy.

Another problem with Soviet prices was their rigidity. Given the complexity of changing prices in the Soviet setting, prices tended to be fixed over long periods of time, especially prior to the 1950s. Accordingly, throughout much of the Soviet period, prices did not even reflect costs of production as measured by Soviet concepts.

The choice of price weights can affect the calculated growth rate. According to the index number relativity effect, if one measures the long-run rate of economic growth using fixed prices (as weights) from an early year, the resulting growth estimate will be higher than if later-year prices were used. The index number relativity effect derives from the work of Alexander Gerschenkron and the measurement of Soviet industrial growth.[3]

Index number relativity, while affecting growth measurement generally, affects the measurement of Soviet economic growth in an especially strong manner. There is a negative correlation between the growth of sector outputs and sector prices in rapidly growing economies. In sectors that experienced rapid growth during industrialization—for example machinery, electricity, and transportation—economies of scale are significant. As these sectors expand, their production costs fall relative to slow-growing or declining sectors. Thus if the growth of output is measured using preindustrialization price weights, fast-growing sectors receive relatively much larger weights than would be the case using prices of a later period. In the Soviet case, the pioneering work of Abram Bergson demonstrated this effect for the economy as a whole. He found that the rate of growth of real Soviet GNP between 1928 and 1937 was 11.9 percent using preindustrialization (1928) price weights, and 5.5 percent using postindustrialization (1937) price weights.[4] While both rates of economic growth are rapid, a 12 percent annual rate of growth would be considered exceedingly high, while a 5.5 percent growth rate would be considered rapid.

Conversion   The total output of an economy is measured using domestic prices. GDP in the United States is measured in U.S. dollars, while Soviet output was measured in Soviet rubles. Apart from the issues of price formation, growth rate comparisons can be made using each country's own domestic prices. We simply look at changes in the ruble size of aggregate Soviet output over time and compare these to changes in the dollar size of U.S. output.

If our interest is the size of Soviet GDP or GDP per capita relative to the United States, it would be necessary to convert ruble output to a "comparable" dollar value, using some sort of conversion. In international comparisons, conversion to a common currency, such as United States dollars, is made through market exchange rates or calculated purchasing power exchange rates. As we emphasized in Chapter 9, the Soviet Union used arbitrary exchange rates such that exchange rate conversions would be impossible. To overcome these problems, various calculations of the purchasing power of rubles were undertaken. These calculations required computation of what Soviet products would have sold for (cost to produce) in the United States. Such estimates are speculative.

Economic Growth—Results

In light of the many difficulties enumerated above, how can we derive satisfactory conclusions about Soviet economic growth? We provide a variety of different estimates, appreciating the fact that there is no single "correct" estimate, but rather a series of estimates that, in total, help us understand general issues of magnitude and ranges. We try to use estimates measured with postindustrialization prices to avoid serious problems of index number relativity. Moreover, we use Soviet series that have been recomputed to make them more comparable to Western GDP definitions.

In Table 11.1, we provide summary estimates of the growth of Tsarist GNP (1885–1913) and the growth of Soviet real GNP during the plan era (1928–84). In this table, we use the estimates developed by Abram Bergson, updated by Central Intelligence Agency (CIA) estimates.[5]

What conclusions can be drawn about Soviet economic growth from the evidence in Table 11.1? First, as we would expect from the discussion above, the Soviet official estimates using "early" year weights and excluding services produce much higher results than Western estimates. Second, it is also evident, as we would expect, that the differences between the two sets of estimates become less important over time insofar as both series switch to late-year prices for later periods. Third, it is evident that whichever estimates we choose, Soviet rates of economic growth slowed considerably over time.

Table 11.1

ECONOMIC GROWTH IN THE USSR
(annual rates of economic growth)

USSR	American Estimates	Official Soviet Estimates
1885–1913	3.3[c]	——
1928–40	5.4[a]	14.6[d]
1950–60	6.0[c]	10.1
1960–70	5.1[c]	7.0
1970–80	3.7[c]	5.3
1980–84	2.0[c]	3.2
1984–88	——	3.5
1928–84	4.3[b]	8.8
1928–84 effective years	4.8[b]	9.7
1950–84	4.4[c]	7.6

[a]1950 prices

[b]Combined index: 1950 prices 1928–50; 1970 prices thereafter

[c]1970 weights

[d]1926–27 prices

[e]1913 prices

Sources: A. Bergson, *The Real National Income of Soviet Russia Since 1928* (Cambridge, MA: Harvard University Press, 1961), 210; H. Block, "Soviet Economic Performance in a Global Context," in U.S. Congress, Joint Economic Committee, *Soviet Economy in a Time of Change* vol. 1(Washington, DC: U.S. Government Printing Office, 1979), 135; P. Gregory, *Russian National Income, 1885–1913* (Cambridge: Cambridge University Press, 1982), table 1; A. L. Vainshtein, *Narodny dokhod Rossii i SSSR* [The national income of Russia and the USSR] (Moscow: Statistika, 1969), 119; *Narodnoe khoziaistvo SSSR v 1978 g* [The national economy of the USSR in 1978] (Moscow: Statistika, 1979), 31–33; CIA, *Handbook of Economic Statistics 1984* (Washington, DC: CIA, 1984), 22; *Dostizheniia sovestskoi vlasti za 40 let v tsifrakh* [The accomplishments of the Soviet regime over forty years in numbers] (Moscow: Gostatizdat, 1957), 327.

Rates of economic growth mean little in isolation. Soviet rates of growth must be compared to those in other countries. Allowing for appropriate corrections, are Soviet rates of economic growth high when compared to other countries? We begin with Soviet-American comparisons.

To make a Soviet-American comparison, we examine comparable historical series for the United States presented in Table 11.2. A comparison of the evidence in Tables 11.1 and 11.2 suggests that Soviet growth after 1928 was more rapid than American growth during the same period. For example, the average annual rate of growth of the Soviet Union between 1928 and 1984 was 4.3 percent, whereas the rate of economic growth for the United States between 1929 and 1984 was 3.1 percent. The performance comparison is more favorable to the Soviet case if one looks at the "effective" years, that is, eliminating the effects of World War II.[6]

The Soviet rate of growth during the postwar period (1950–84) of 4.4 percent exceeded the comparable American rate of 3.4 percent for the same period. However, American rates of economic growth during the U.S. industrial revolution were closer to the Soviet rates of the early plan era. The most striking difference between U.S. and Soviet long-term growth is the long-term decline in the Soviet growth versus the relative stability of U.S. growth rates. The first three decades of Soviet growth were rapid. Thereafter, each decade saw slower and slower growth. As we will point out in the next chapter, the decision to attempt reform and ultimately to abandon the administrative command economy was motivated by this disturbing decline.

Table 11.2

ECONOMIC GROWTH IN THE USA

	1860 prices	1929 prices	1958 and 1972 prices
1834–43 to 1879–88	4.4	—	—
1879–88 to 1899–1908	3.7	3.8	—
1899–1908 to 1929	—	3.4	—
1929–50	—	—	2.5
1950–60	—	—	3.3
1960–70	—	—	3.9
1970–84	—	—	3.0
1929–84	—	—	3.1
1950–84	—	—	3.4

Sources: *The Economic Report of the President* (selected years); R. Gallman, "Gross National Product in the United States, 1834–1909," *Output, Employment and Productivity in the United States After 1800* (New York: National Bureau of Economic Research, 1966), 26.

Economic Growth: Contemporary Judgments

Our earlier comparisons were cast largely in historical perspective. As the Soviet Union began to collapse, allowing open criticism, Soviet and Russian scholars began to make their own unofficial calculations of postwar Soviet growth. As we examine contemporary alternative estimates, it is important to reemphasize the limitations of growth measurement and the comparisons that we are able to make. In Figure 11.1 we present alternative assessments of the Soviet record of economic growth (official Soviet estimates, estimates by other Soviet economists, and CIA estimates) for sub-periods of the post–World War II era. What conclusions can we derive from these estimates?

First, apart from quite substantial differences across the series, the significant downward trend is evident in all estimates. Although more recent estimates present a picture of sharper decline than earlier estimates, they do not differ fundamentally from them. The unofficial Soviet/Russian estimates do help to explain the sense of emergency that the Soviet leadership felt in the 1980s. In fact, the unofficial estimates show Soviet growth as threatening to disappear completely in the 1980s.

Second, although we might expect more recent estimates to be based upon better information after the demise of the Soviet Union, the basic measurement issues remain: All estimates ultimately depend on the accuracy of Soviet physical output

Figure 11.1   Soviet Economic Growth

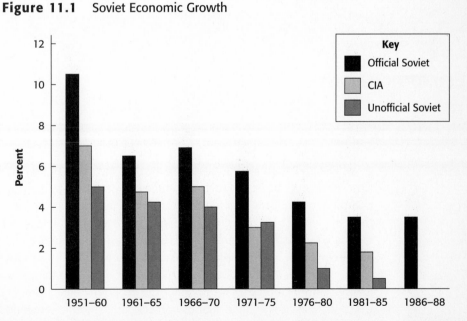

Sources: CIA, *Revisiting Soviet Economic Performance Under Glasnost: Implications for CIA Estimates* (Washington, DC: CIA, 1988); CIA, *Handbook of Economic Statistics* (Washington, DC: CIA, various years).

series. The unofficial Soviet/Russian recalculations argue that managerial incentive schemes forced managers and administrative personnel to overstate output growth. The magnitude of such biases, however, remains a guess.

The issue of product quality is also a source of distortion. If a product is useless, we must seriously question whether it should be included in aggregate output at any price, let alone the ruble price. In recent estimates, there has been more willingness to drop "useless" products, while official Soviet estimates include such products, either at their ruble price or their ruble cost.

The unofficial estimates focus on the issue of unknown (hidden) inflation. Although we have already discussed the issue of pricing and its impact on aggregate output series, the use of constant ruble prices for growth measurement may conceal serious amounts of hidden inflation.[7] If there is inadequate adjustment for inflation, then growth rates computed from ruble aggregates will overstate real rates of economic growth. Although Western specialists had suspected hidden inflation for years, they were unable to capture it using traditional statistical measures. Contemporary Soviet/Russian scholars have been willing to make ad hoc adjustments for hidden inflation.

Although the issue of Soviet economic growth is one of complexity and remaining uncertainty, many would argue that even with future revisions, Soviet growth will probably be viewed as relatively "good" in the early plan years but decline steadily and significantly thereafter. Indeed, such a pattern is quite consistent with the Soviet growth model—specifically, sharp expansion of inputs but limited attention to productivity and technological change. Put another way, we need to understand the Soviet growth model, to which we now turn our attention.

ECONOMIC GROWTH

The Sources

Economic growth is a complex issue, but the Soviet approach to economic growth can be unraveled. Economic growth is the result of two intertwined forces—the expansion of inputs (land, labor, and capital) and the better use of those inputs as a result of technological change and/or the improved quality of the inputs. Although there are a myriad of measurement issues, we usually think in terms of two concepts: **extensive growth,** in which growth is the result of expansion of inputs, and **intensive growth,** in which growth is the result of improved use of available inputs.

It is obviously preferable to be more efficient rather than less efficient. But the issue is more complex. If we examine the economic development of the industrialized countries, it is evident that the process of economic growth and accompanying economic development involves a transition from extensive growth to intensive growth. In a poor country during the early stages of modernization, the task is to bring idle and/or underutilized resources into the production process. But, as economic growth proceeds, the task becomes better use of inputs and/or qualitative improvements in the inputs, because limitations on the growth of inputs serve as a binding constraint. Put another way, we know that long-run growth must come from efficiency improvements because inputs cannot continue to expand indefinitely at a rapid pace.

Measuring the effectiveness of resource utilization is complex. It can be described in terms of a production possibilities frontier (see Figure 11.2, p. 233). Over time, **dynamic efficiency** is measured by the rate of growth of output per unit of combined inputs. Dynamic efficiency improves when the production possibilities frontier shifts outwards (towards the north-east) without a corresponding increase in factor inputs. In effect, dynamic efficiency means that the economy is producing more from the same inputs. At any point in time, we think in terms of how close we are to the current production possibilities frontier, or the concept of **static efficiency.** An economy that does not operate on its production possibilities frontier is wasting resources.

It is difficult to measure either efficiency concept with precision. However, we can measure dynamic efficiency as the difference between the rate of growth of inputs and the rate of growth of output. For example, if input grows at 2 percent and outputs grow at 5 percent, then we argue that the difference of 3 percent results not from expansion of inputs, but better use of inputs and/or qualitative improvements in the inputs, what we term *dynamic efficiency*. This empirical concept, which we term **total factor productivity,** is only an indirect link to dynamic efficiency. Not only is it difficult to measure inputs, but we are also generally limited to including traditional inputs, excluding, for example, nonquantifiable inputs such as improved management. We have no direct measure of static efficiency. All we can observe is what an economy is producing from its inputs. We cannot directly measure what it is capable of producing at maximum efficiency.

The Evidence: Dynamic Efficiency

Although measurement issues are complex, we can in fact examine empirical evidence on output and input patterns and derive useful conclusions concerning factor productivity. We proceed as follows: First, we examine long-term international comparisons, after which we turn to trends since World War II. Next, we turn to the issue of the sources of the Soviet productivity decline.

In Table 11.3 (p. 230), we relate several measures of rates of growth of factor productivity in the Soviet Union, the United States, and selected other countries for long-run periods.

Examining the trends in Table 11.3 it is evident that the Soviet Union, when compared to other countries, experienced a more rapid growth of both labor and capital. Columns 2 and 3 show that labor and capital grew much more rapidly than in other countries—inputs grew, at a minimum, three times faster than in other

Table 11.3

INPUTS AND PRODUCTIVITY: USSR, USA, AND SELECTED COUNTRIES: LONG-TERM

	(1) Output	(2) Labor, employment	(3) Fixed capital	(4) Combined inputs	(5) Output per unit of combined input (1–4)	(6) Labor productivity (1–2)	(7) Capital productivity (1–3)
USSR (GNP) 1928–66	5.5	2.2	7.4	3.5	2.0	3.3	−1.9
United States (GNP) 1929–69	3.3	0.8	2.0	1.1	2.2	2.5	1.3
UK (GDP) 1925/29–63	1.9	0.8	1.8	1.1	0.8	1.1	0.1
France (GDP) 1913–66	2.3	−0.5	2.0	0.2	2.2	2.8	0.3
Canada (GDP) 1926–56	3.9	0.8	2.9	1.2	2.7	3.1	1.0
Norway (GDP) 1899–56	2.8	0.3	2.5	0.7	2.1	2.5	0.3

Sources: R. Moorsteen and R. Powell, *The Soviet Capital Stock* (Homewood, IL: Irwin, 1966), 38, 166, 315, 361–62, 365; A. Becker, R. Moorsteen, and R. Powell, *Soviet Capital Stock: Revisions and Extensions, 1961–1967* (New Haven: Economic Growth Center, 1968), 11, 25, 26; Kuznets, *Economic Growth of Nations*, 74; E. Denison, *Accounting for United States Economic Growth, 1929–1969* (Washington, DC: Brookings Institution, 1974), 54, 186; B. J. Wattenberg, ed., *The Statistical History of the United States from Colonial Times to the Present* (New York: Basic Books, 1976), 257–58.

countries. Soviet output, however, while growing more rapidly than in other countries, did not grow three times as fast. If the Soviet economy had experienced no productivity growth, output and inputs would have expanded at the same rate of 3.5 percent. In actuality, Soviet output expanded at a rate of 5.5 percent, for a 2.0 percent growth rate of total factor productivity. If we divide column 1 by column 4, it is evident that in the USSR, roughly 65 percent of the long-run growth was accounted for by the expansion of inputs, whereas in other countries (the United Kingdom is an exception), a much smaller portion of growth can be attributed to input expansion. In the U.S., for example, about one-quarter of output growth can be explained by input growth.

Turning to the rate of growth of output per unit of combined input (column 5), the long-term Soviet rate of 2.0 percent was somewhat below or roughly equivalent to the long-term productivity growth rates of other countries. Given likely statistical errors, the Soviet rates of growth of total factor productivity are quite comparable to those of other countries, except the United Kingdom.

The rate of growth of Soviet labor productivity (column 6) was slightly above most other countries, and well above the rate of the United Kingdom. On the other hand, Soviet capital productivity (column 7) was −1.9 percent, indicating a rising capital/output ratio. Of the countries surveyed here, none except the Soviet Union experienced a negative rate of growth of capital productivity. We shall return to the issue of negative capital productivity below. For now, we recall the lack of Western-style investment criteria throughout the Soviet era as a possible source of negative capital productivity.

The long-run trends examined in Table 11.3 indicate that Soviet dynamic efficiency, measured indirectly by the rate of growth of combined inputs, was neither exceptionally large nor exceptionally small when compared to long-term trends in the United States and other industrialized countries. But, the relatively low proportion of Soviet output growth explained by productivity growth means that Soviet economic growth was of the "high cost" extensive variety.

While these patterns are important, they measure a relatively small sample of countries over a relatively long span of years, which gives rise to a variety of measurement complications. In Table 11.4 (p. 232), we provide similar estimates, but for a larger sample of countries for the era since World War II.

The evidence in Table 11.4 for the postwar period also confirms Soviet input growth was rapid by international standards, but not unique. Canada (which experienced rapid labor force growth), West Germany (rapid growth of both labor and capital), and Japan (rapid growth of both labor and capital), matched the Soviet postwar growth of combined inputs. It is notable, however, that in the case of West Germany (1950–62) and Japan (1953–70), the payoff to rapid input growth (in terms of output growth) was much higher than in the Soviet Union.

While the growth of Soviet labor productivity in the early postwar period was rapid, it was matched by a number of countries. By the 1980s, Soviet labor productivity growth was, if anything, relatively low—about the same as the U.S., which was experiencing a low rate of labor productivity growth at the time. Also, after 1960 the Soviet Union recorded a dismal record of declining capital productivity, decreasing by 3.5 percent or more each year. Only Japan, in the period 1970–80, came close to matching this record.

Table 11.4 reveals another disconcerting fact about Soviet economic growth during the postwar period: Soviet economic growth continued its extensive pattern, despite the declining growth rates of labor and capital inputs. By the early 1980s, labor was growing at 0.5 percent per annum and capital at 5.8 percent, down from 1.2 percent and 9.4 percent respectively in the 1950s. The declining rate of growth of inputs meant that Soviet economic growth had little prospect of recovering without introducing fundamental changes in the economic system.

The Evidence: Static Efficiency

Static efficiency is the efficiency of an economy at a point of time and is defined intuitively by Abram Bergson as "the degree to which, equity apart, the community is, in fact, able to exploit the opportunities that are open."[8] Static efficiency, therefore, depends upon the state of technological knowledge and the effectiveness with which it is used. Dynamic efficiency relates to the movement outward of the

Table 11.4

INPUTS AND PRODUCTIVITY: USSR, USA, AND SELECTED COUNTRIES: SHORT-TERM

	(1) Output	(2) Labor, employment	(3) Fixed capital	(4) Combined inputs	(5) Output per unit of combined input (1–4)	(6) Labor productivity (1–2)	(7) Capital productivity (1–3)
USSR							
1950–60	5.8	1.2	9.4	4.1	1.7	4.8	1.7
1960–81	4.1	1.4	7.6	3.3	0.8	2.7	−3.5
1983–87	2.0	0.5	5.8	2.7	−0.7	1.5	−3.8
United States							
1948–60	3.2	1.4	3.2	2.0	1.2	1.7	0.0
1960–81	3.5	2.0	3.6	2.6	0.9	1.4	−0.1
Canada							
1960–80	4.6	2.9	4.9	3.6	1.0	1.7	−0.3
Belgium							
1950–62	3.2	0.6	2.3	1.2	2.0	2.6	0.9
Denmark							
1950–62	3.5	0.9	5.1	2.4	1.1	2.6	−1.6
France							
1950–62	4.9	0.1	4.2	1.5	3.4	4.8	0.7
1960–80	4.8	0.8	5.0	2.3	2.3	3.6	−0.4
West Germany							
1950–62	7.3	2.0	6.9	3.5	3.8	5.3	0.9
1960–80	3.8	0.0	4.8	1.7	2.1	3.8	−1.0
Italy							
1950–62	6.0	0.6	3.5	1.6	4.4	5.4	2.5
Netherlands							
1950–62	4.7	1.1	4.7	3.1	1.6	3.6	0.0
Norway							
1950–62	3.5	0.2	4.2	1.6	1.9	3.3	−0.7
1960–80	4.7	0.5	4.1	1.7	3.1	4.1	0.6
United Kingdom							
1950–62	2.3	0.7	3.4	1.7	0.5	1.6	−1.1
1960–80	2.3	0.4	3.4	1.5	0.8	1.9	−1.1
Japan							
1952–70	10.0	1.7	9.8	4.5	5.5	8.3	0.2
1970–80	5.0	0.9	8.4	3.5	1.5	4.1	−3.4
Greece							
1960–80	6.1	0.0	6.2	2.2	3.9	6.1	−0.1

Sources: *Handbook of Economic Statistics* (various years); U.S. Department of Labor, *Trends in Multifactor Productivity 1948–81* (Washington, DC: U.S. Department of Labor, 1983), 22; E. Denison, *Why Growth Rates Differ* (Washington, DC: Brookings Institution, 1967), 42, 190, and ch. 21; E. Denison, *Accounting for United States Economic Growth, 1929–1969* (Washington, DC: Brookings Institution, 1974), 32, 58; E. Denison and W. Chung, *How Japan's Economy Grew So Fast* (Washington, DC: Brookings Institution, 1976), 19, 31; OECD, *Flows and Stocks of Fixed Capital, 1955–1980* (Paris: OECD, 1983), 1–39; *World Tables* (1980), country tables and Table 5.

production possibility frontier over time, while static efficiency refers to how closely one operates to the frontier at a point of time. Although the relationship is complex, static efficiency is necessary but not sufficient to achieve dynamic efficiency.

The measurement of static efficiency in different systems at differing levels of economic development is difficult. Consider, for example, the evidence in Figure 11.2. Suppose one country is at a higher level of economic development (frontier *aa*) than that of another country (frontier *bb*). If we define the PPF as a combined unit of conventional resources, both countries may be operating at maximum static efficiency (points *A* and *B*), even though *A*'s measured productivity is higher due to its superior economic institutions, greater scientific and technical knowledge, and better management. In such a case, both countries are operating at full potential.

We can only measure static efficiency imperfectly. We cannot directly observe the location of a country's PPF. All we can observe is its actual output (the points *A* and *B* in Figure 11.2) and the magnitude of those inputs that can be quantified (such as dollars of capital or hours of labor). In other words, unfortunately, we can only examine the magnitude of output that is derived from a unit of "combined" inputs. When we make such comparisons across countries at a point of time, in effect we are assuming that the underlying production conditions are identical when, in fact, there are likely to be many differences, such as quality, scale, and the like. There are, however, other serious measurement problems when comparing Soviet static efficiency with that of other countries.

To compute the relative magnitudes (as opposed to rates of growth) of output per unit, both inputs and outputs must be measured in a common unit, such as U.S.

Figure 11.2 Economic Development, Static Efficiency, and the PPF

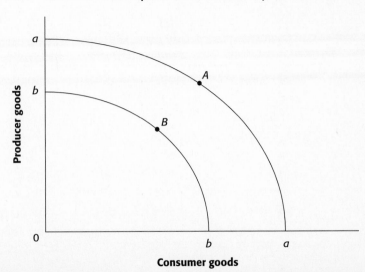

dollars. Thus as we aggregate output and inputs, valuation problems discussed earlier will surface, once again distorting our computations. We must value Soviet GDP and Soviet capital stock in dollars.

In productivity comparisons, whether we are interested in static or dynamic efficiency, there is an additional problem for the aggregation of inputs in the Soviet case. In market economies, aggregation is done by using prices. Thus on the input side, the labor input is weighted by the wage rate, land is weighted by the land rental charge, and so on. While in market economies these price weights may depart from theoretical ideals for a variety of reasons, in the Soviet case there was no charge for capital or land and hence no price weight for aggregation. In practice, synthetic factor shares (shares based on market economic experience) have been used to aggregate Soviet input series.[9]

Table 11.5 summarizes contemporary evidence on Soviet static efficiency from the year 1975. This study, done by Abram Bergson, uses a Cobb-Douglas production function to relate output per worker to capital per worker and land per worker (relative to the United States). The year 1975 is appropriate because it captures the USSR's relative position at a time when its administrative command economy had reached a mature stage. Table 11.5 shows that Soviet per capita GDP was 60 percent of the United States, despite the fact that Soviet labor inputs per capita were 25 percent greater, capital per capita inputs three-quarters, and farm land per capita were equal to that of that of the United States. Column 2 shows that Soviet output per worker (labor productivity) was 47 percent of the United States and well below Spain.

Table 11.5

GDP PER CAPITA AND FACTOR INPUTS PER CAPITA, 1975
(UNITED STATES = 100)

Country	(1) GDP per capita	(2) GDP per worker	(3) Employment per capita	(4) Capital per capita	(5) Farm land per capita
United States	100.0	100.0	100.0	100.0	100.0
France	89.5	90.7	99.1	83.0	40.1
West Germany	88.3	94.1	100.6	107.3	14.8
United Kingdom	73.5	68.6	109.4	77.2	14.5
Italy	60.7	71.0	87.4	61.6	24.9
Japan	75.5	56.9	115.0	95.2	5.4
Soviet Union	60.2	47.4	125.2	73.2	103.5
Spain	62.0	56.0	96.3	47.7	67.0

Source: A. Bergson, "Comparative Productivity: The USSR, Eastern Europe, and the West," *American Economic Review* vol. 11, no. 3 (June 1987). 347.

Labor productivity, however, depends on the availability of capital per worker. Bergson uses dummy variables to isolate the effect of the Soviet system from differences in capital and land. He finds that the difference in output per worker between the Soviet and Western industrialized economies varied from a 32 to 41 percent deficit relative to the market economies, the specific amount depending upon measurement assumptions. What this study suggests is that, given the Soviet economy's factor endowment, its mature labor productivity was 32 to 41 percent below what it should have been.

In a subsequent study, Bergson examined evidence on GDP per worker for 1985.[10] He found that GDP per worker in the Soviet Union in 1985 was 36.7 percent of that in the United States, while France was 81.4 percent, Italy 81 percent, and Spain 73.7 percent of the United States. Thus the Soviet economy had lost ground in terms of labor productivity between 1975 and 1985.

We have already noted that evidence on static efficiency is important yet difficult to interpret. Is static efficiency related to the level of economic development? It has been argued, for example, that the Soviets may have sacrificed static efficiency to achieve political objectives. In the end, however, lower static efficiency means a higher cost for growth in the sense of foregone consumption.

Figure 11.3   Factor Productivity in the USSR

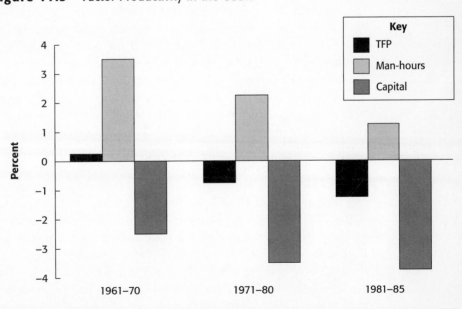

Note: *Gross National Product* is defined as nonagricultural, nonservice GNP, based on 1982 ruble indexes at factor cost.

Source: CIA, *Handbook of Economic Statistics, 1991* (Washington, DC: CIA, 1991), Tables 35–36.

ECONOMIC GROWTH: EVIDENCE AND EXPLANATIONS

Thus far we have characterized Soviet economic growth in terms of the rate of growth of output and its slowdown and the rate of growth of inputs. From the evidence presented in Figure 11.3 (p. 235), it is quite evident that factor productivity declined significantly in the postwar era, up through the end of the Soviet era. Specifically, while labor productivity remained positive, it declined. Capital productivity was negative throughout and increased in magnitude. In a recent reexamination of Soviet economic growth, William Easterly and Stanley Fischer conclude that "Soviet growth from 1960 to 1989 was the worst in the world after we control for investment and human capital; the relative performance worsens over time."[11] The authors also state that with a constant rate of growth of total factor productivity, the declining growth experience can be accounted for by a declining marginal product of capital. Finally, the authors conclude that market economies also relied upon extensive growth but that in the Soviet case ". . . a low elasticity of substitution between capital and labor implied especially acute diminishing returns to capital compared with the case of market economies.[12]

What explains deterioration in factor productivity performance? One explanation is that a number of interrelated factors adversely affected the Soviet economy: the economy had become too complex, labor discipline declined, and the Soviet population was simply exhausted. Another explanation is poor **elasticity of substitution**—or the difficulty of capital-labor substitution. Let's look first at the theory, then the evidence. If capital and labor inputs are growing at markedly different rates (as was the case in the Soviet Union, with its rapid growth of capital), the rate of growth of output would not be affected if one input can readily be substituted for another. In Figure 11.4 we examine the two possible extreme cases.

Notice that in Panel A, the isoquant (equal production line) is negatively sloped and flat, representing an elasticity of substitution of unity, or perfect substitutability of the two inputs. In Panel B, on the other hand, there is no substitutability at all (the elasticity of substitution is zero). This case is described as "corner solution," since there is only one mix of capital and labor. Even if more labor is used, for example labor increases from L0 to L1, more input cannot be produced as long as K remains fixed. Recall also from earlier discussions of planning theory and practice and from the assumptions underlying the socialist economy, that theorists believed that factor proportions were fixed and were constant through time. While this assumption may violate reality, it greatly facilitated computing a plan. Assuming that coefficients were stable was typical in planned socialist economic systems.[13] What is the evidence on the elasticity of substitution in the Soviet economy?

In an early study, Martin Weitzman argued that the Soviet growth problem did involve the elasticity of substitution of capital for labor.[14] However, subsequent work by others raised doubts. A study by Erik Bairam suggested that the elasticity of substitution of capital for labor in the Soviet Union was close to unity, implying that capital-labor substitution problems were not major.[15] Bairam argued that in the

Figure 11.4   Capital-Labor Substitution

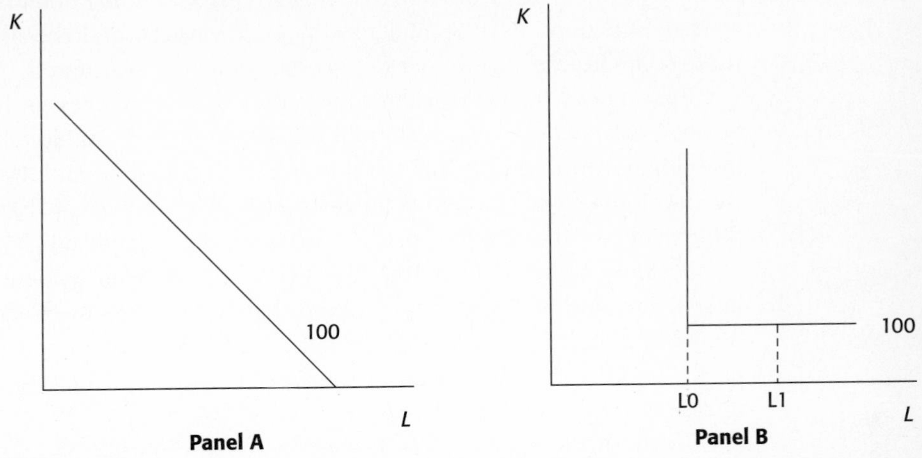

Panel A

Panel B

aggregate, there were constant or decreasing returns to scale in Soviet industry. This evidence seemed to confirm results of Padma Desai, who argued that it was not a low elasticity of substitution that explained the Soviet growth slowdown, but rather a declining rate of growth of the unexplained productivity residual.[16]

In another study of Soviet economic growth, Easterly and Fischer note that the extensive growth pattern in the Soviet Union was in fact not that unusual compared to some market economies.[17] In fact, Japan and the emerging economies of Southeast Asia have substituted capital for labor without difficulties. However, the authors argue that in the Soviet case, there was indeed a low elasticity of substitution of capital for labor resulting in ". . . acute diminishing returns to capital . . ."[18] The fact that rapidly growing industrialized countries did not experience this suggests that factors specific to the administrative command economy were to blame.

ECONOMIC GROWTH AND THE ISSUE OF TECHNOLOGY

It is quite usual for an economy to expand output through the expansion of inputs in its earlier stages of growth and development. It is equally likely, however, that as development proceeds, efficiency improvements will replace input expansion as a source of economic growth. Probably the most striking conclusion from our analysis of Soviet economic growth is the fact that this replacement never occurred. How might this outcome be explained?

An issue critical to understanding the Soviet experience and its demise is, broadly, technological change. However, measuring technological change is difficult in any system, let alone the Soviet system. While industry studies could provide a partial picture, it is also necessary to appreciate the fact that appropriate technology varies significantly from one case to another, depending upon factors such as the level of economic development, factor endowments, and the like. Having noted these complications, a number of generalizations are warranted.

First, Soviet technological achievements were very uneven. In some areas the Soviet Union could produce state of the art results, for example in metallurgy and in welding. At the same time, the Soviet Union lagged behind the United States in the development of computers by 9–15 years (mainframes), 4–10 years (microcomputers) and 8–10 years (macrocircuits). These were significant gaps in critical areas.

Second, studies done in the late 1970s indicated no tendency for this gap to lessen. The authors of one study noted that "there is no evidence of a substantial diminution of the technological gap between the Soviet Union and the West in the past 15 to 20 years, either at the prototype/commercial application stages or in the diffusion of advanced technology."

Third, the Soviet Union relied heavily upon imports to sustain and improve its technological level. While this strategy may be effective and useful, it has been pointed out, for example by Marshall Goldman, that growing complementarities among technologies may make it difficult to jump from behind and to sustain a lead simply by importing new technologies.

Fourth, implementing technological change was a major problem in the Soviet Union. In a major study of this issue, discussed in the previous chapter, Joseph Berliner argued that most of the reasons for the lack of diffusion of new ideas in the Soviet Union were systemic. Indeed, we have examined these issues—rigidities of the planning system, information problems, complications with incentive arrangements, and the like. Put simply, a major shortcoming of the Soviet system was its rigid inability to implement change at the lowest levels of the hierarchy. It is perhaps ironic that in an attempt to save the Soviet economic system in the late 1980s, Mikhail Gorbachev placed great emphasis upon the need for productivity improvement.

SUMMARY

In this chapter we examine the empirical record of Soviet economic growth. For a variety of measurement issues, this record is difficult, though not impossible, to evaluate. Soviet output data was compiled using the concept of Net Material Product, or the measurement of aggregate output based upon Marxian definitions, excluding capital charges, depreciation, and the like. Aggregation used Soviet cost-based prices (typically fixed base-year prices, which overestimated rates of growth), with conversion to dollar values based on various ruble-dollar exchange rate estimates.

While long-term rates of economic growth would be judged as good by international standards, other countries, such as Japan and Germany, matched or exceeded Soviet rates. Most importantly, a variety of contemporary growth estimates reveal a significant and continuing decline in the years since World War II.

Contemporary studies of Soviet economic growth generally rely upon production function estimates relating outputs to inputs, the latter aggregated using synthetic factor shares in the absence of prices for capital and land in the Soviet setting. While these studies reveal a variety of subtle differences, the Soviet record reveals extensive growth (matched by some Western countries) with a reasonable record of total factor productivity but sharply declining capital productivity and an inability to substitute between capital and labor.

Terms and Concepts

economic growth   Expansion of output over time, usually measured in aggregate or per capita terms.

Net Material Product (NMP)   The Soviet concept of aggregate output based in Marxian definitions and differing from GDP and GNP in important ways, such as the absence of capital charges, obsolescence, and "non-productive" economic activity, and often including double counting rather than value added.

extensive growth   Generally defined as output achieved by the expansion of inputs.

intensive growth   Generally defined as growth achieved through productivity improvements generated from such sources as qualitative improvements in inputs or better ways of doing things (organizational change).

dynamic efficiency   Efficiency gains (output per unit of input) through time, often approximated by observed rats of economic growth through time; movement of the production possibilities frontier to the north-east.

static efficiency   Efficiency (output per unit of input) measured at a point of time; usually how close the economy operates to its production possibilities frontier.

total factor productivity   An indirect link to dynamic efficiency; output per unit of combined inputs measured through time.

elasticity of substitution   The ease with which one factor (say, capital) can be substituted for another (say, labor); specifically the slope of an isoquant relating labor to capital; easy substitution implies a relatively "flat" isoquant, while substitution would be impossible with an isoquant that illustrates a "corner" solution.

Selected Bibliography

Bergson, A. "East-West Comparisons and Comparative Economic Systems: A Reply," *Soviet Studies* vol. 23, no. 1 (October 1971), 282–95.

——— . *The Economics of Soviet Planning* (New Haven: Yale University Press, 1964), ch. 14.

——— . "National Income," in A. Bergson and S. Kuznets, eds., *Economic Trends in the Soviet Union* (Cambridge, MA: Harvard University Press, 1963), 1–37.

Campbell, R., et al. "Methodological Problems Comparing the US and USSR Economies," in U.S. Congress, Joint Economic Committee, *Soviet Economic Prospects for the Seventies* (Washington, DC: U.S. Government Printing Office, 1973), 122–46.

Easterly, W., and S. Fischer. "The Soviet Economic Decline," *The World Bank Economic Review* vol. 9, no. 3 (September 1955), 341–71.

Eckstein, A., ed. *Comparison of Economic Systems* (Berkeley: University of California Press, 1971).

Edwards, I., M. Hughes, and J. Noren. "U.S. and U.S.S.R.: Comparisons of GNP," in U.S. Congress, Joint Economic Committee, *Soviet Economy in a Time of Change* vol. 1 (Washington, DC: U.S. Government Printing Office, 1979), 369–401.

Hanson, "East-West Comparisons and Comparative Economic Systems," *Soviet Studies* vol. 22, no. 3 (January 1971).

Kurtzweg, L. "Trends in Soviet Gross National Product," in U.S. Congress, Joint Economic Committee, *Gorbachev's Economic Plans* vol. 2 (Washington, DC: U.S. Government Printing Office, 1987), 126–65.

Marer, P. *Dollar GNPs of the Soviet Union and Eastern Europe* (Baltimore, MD: Johns Hopkins Press, 1985).

Prell, M. A. "The Role of the Service Sector in Soviet GNP and Productivity Estimates," *Journal of Comparative Economics* vol. 13, no. 3 (September, 1989), 383–405.

Treml, V. G., and D. Gallik. *Soviet Studies on Ruble/Dollar Parity Rations,* U.S. Department of Commerce, Foreign Economic Reports, vol. 4 (November 1973).

Treml, V. G., and J. P. Hardt, eds. *Soviet Economic Statistics* (Durham: University of North Carolina Press, 1972).

U.S. Congress, Joint Economic Committee. *Measures of Soviet Economic Growth and Development 1950–1980* (Washington, DC: U.S. Government Printing Office, 1982).

Wilber, C. K. "Economic Development, Central Planning, and Allocative Efficiency," *Yearbook of East-European Economics* (Munich: Gunter Olzog Verlag, 1971), 221–46.

Soviet Economic Growth

Becker, A. *Soviet National Income, 1958–1964* (Berkeley: University of California Press, 1969).

Bergson, A. *Productivity and the Social System: The USSR and the West* (Cambridge, MA: Harvard University Press, 1978).

——— . *The Real National Income of Soviet Russia Since 1928* (Cambridge, MA: Harvard University Press, 1978).

Block, H. "Soviet Economic Performance in a Global Context," in U.S. Congress, Joint Economic Committee, *Soviet Economy in a Time of Change* vol. 1, 110–40.

Bornstein, M. "A Comparison of Soviet and United States Industrial Product," in M. Bornstein and D. Fusfeld, eds., *The Soviet Economy* (Homewood, IL: Irwin, 1962).

Cohn, S. *Economic Development in the Soviet Union* (Lexington, MA: D. C. Heath, 1969).

PART FOUR

Transition: Russia and the Independent States

CHAPTER 12

The Administrative Command Economy: Change

Thus far we have focused on the working arrangements of the administrative command economy but have paid no attention to change. The story of change in the Soviet economy is ironic in the sense that change had two major components, both ending in failure. First, economic reform, or attempts to modify the existing economic system and related economic policies, was a persistent theme during the post–World War II era. Beginning in the 1950s, numerous and varied reform programs were announced, yet if one judges the success of reform by improvements in economic performance, all attempts failed.

Second, the final and most significant reform was perestroika, introduced by Mikhail Gorbachev after he became General Secretary of the Communist Party in March of 1985. While the advent of perestroika generated a great deal of interest in the late 1980s, we now think of it as the final attempt to reform the Soviet economic system, an attempt which led to its ultimate collapse in 1990. What was the nature of economic reform in the Soviet Union and why did it fail?

TAXONOMY OF ECONOMIC REFORM

There is a large literature devoted to the subject of reform in administrative command economies.[1] The writings examine change within existing systemic arrangements, as opposed to the contemporary literature on change, which is typically cast within the framework of **transition,** or the replacement of the administrative command system by market arrangements. Understanding change in the command systems is a matter of importance because many now argue that these systems in fact failed because they lacked dynamism.

Throughout the post–World War II era, there were many attempts to change systemic arrangements in the Soviet Union. There is no simple classification of these changes, yet they did exhibit common characteristics that we may use for purposes of classification. First, the hierarchical structure of the Soviet economy was subjected to numerous changes, which we denote as **organizational change.** Second, there were numerous attempts to improve the system of national economic planning, changes which we denote broadly as **planning reform.** Finally, a major focus of reform we denote as **decentralization.** The concept of decentralization is complex. In the context of reform, we think of it as the devolution of decision-making authority and responsibility from higher to lower levels in the organizational hierarchy. Devolution frequently took place as changes in the dissemination and use of information, though it also included changes in the decision rules operative at particular levels of the hierarchy.

Organizational Reform

In Chapter 6 we examined the organizational arrangements of the administrative command economy, concluding that they represented a classic example of a hierarchical organizational framework, appropriately analyzed within the principal-agent framework. There was a persistent struggle between center and periphery in the administrative command economy. When economic performance did not achieve central objectives, there was a tendency to place blame on various levels in the hierarchy. For example, in the 1950s, Khrushchev argued that the intermediate levels, specifically the ministries, had too much authority. In a major reform, which would be reversed after his departure in the early 1960s, Khrushchev attempted to introduce regional economic councils (**sovnarkhozy**) to shift from a sectoral to a regional focus.

Throughout the Soviet era, agriculture went through ongoing organizational change. No level escaped attention. At the highest level, the organizational arrangements were frequently changed, while at the farm level, amalgamation of individual farms and their integration into the agro-industrial complexes changed the organizational arrangements of agriculture fundamentally.

Organizational change in the Soviet economy was controversial. Even in sectors where changes were in fact implemented, such as agriculture, most observers remained skeptical about the potential benefits. Organizational change was generally conceived at the center, with negligible performance benefits.

Improvement of Planning

We have already emphasized that while theoretical models of national economic planning can be sophisticated and attractive, real world information and incentive requirements are complex and frequently unattainable. Centralizing decision making in the Soviet Union unquestionably facilitated the attainment of selected Party and state objectives, yet the cost was great. Soviet planning arrangements of the 1930s may have been crude and simplistic, but over time improvements were made and arrangements grew more sophisticated. However, the system's information requirements increased dramatically, and many of the simplifications which seemed to make planning "work" carried major costs. Technological change dictated the need to change coefficients, while aggregation became less feasible as the product range increased. Ironically, while Soviet authorities pursued the concept of a computerized information system, in practice such a system was never realized.

Decentralization

Much of the discussion of economic reform was cast within the framework of decentralizing decision making. Although it was difficult to characterize reform programs with decision, decentralizing decision making typically involved either what was termed *administrative decentralization* (greater authority at enterprise levels but controlled by administrative rules set by the center), or *economic decentralization* (greater authority at the enterprise level not directly controlled by upper level authorities).[2]

Typically, much of Soviet economic reform was of the administrative sort. For example, managerial guidelines would be changed, an approach often characterized as changing the "economic levers." One such guideline was profit. While profit was a meaningful guideline for managerial success in a market context, it was never clear what meaning profit might have in the Soviet context. Nevertheless, reform was a continuing theme in the Soviet context.

Soviet Economic Reform: A Survey

Although we tend to characterize economic reform in the administrative command economy as an attempt to modify and to improve its working arrangements, it was actually much more, including a substantial political component. Indeed as far back as the NEP era, economic reform was cast in terms of fundamental changes after the end of War Communism and focused on the commanding heights for general directions. "Experts" at the enterprise level made the daily production decisions.

In terms of perfecting the model of national economic planning, the 1920s were productive, yet under Stalin, as we have seen, politics held sway over economics. During the 1920s there was important theorizing about the nature of planning in socialist economic systems. At the time, talented economists and statisticians worked on the concept of **national balances,** a major example being the well-known 1923–24 balance of the national economy, prepared by the Central Statistics Board under the direction of P. I. Popov. [3] These early efforts were the intellectual precursors of **input-output analysis** developed later in the United States by Wassily Leontief. The theorizing of this era was the foundation for fundamental mathematical modeling of the planned economy, a path that Stalin rejected.

During the Stalin era, brutal repression of economic science brought an end to the search for rational administrative planning procedures. The system was declared to be infallible; mistakes could only be the result of errant individuals or outright acts of sabotage. Stalin declared that the "law of value" or supply and demand was inoperative in the socialist economy, to be replaced by the planning principle. Concepts developed by bourgeois economists were declared to be irrelevant, if not dangerous. Anti-market bias was dominant; the "chaos" of the market was to be replaced by the "rationality" of the plan, the latter developed by engineers.[4]

In the 1930s, the approach was not to simulate the market, but to replace it. Concepts such as equilibrium and balanced growth were dangerous and were to be replaced largely by ad hoc responses.[5] Two major attempts to initiate high-level reform (in 1933 and again in 1947) led to the execution of the ill-fated reformers.[6]

The death of Stalin in 1953 and the emergence thereafter of Nikita Khrushchev introduced a new political era in the Soviet Union. Khrushchev was willing to experiment with organizational change and did so in both industry and agriculture. Moreover, there was a resurgence of interest in mathematical models of national economic planning. Prominent Soviet economists such as Nobel Laureate L. V. Kantorovich, V. V. Novozhilov, and V. S. Nemchinov argued that it was possible to use resources more effectively—without losing central control—if attention was paid to rational planning methods.[7] The work of these economists was recognized both at home and abroad. Economic reform once again become a topic for discussion in economics journals.

The Khrushchev era signaled significant changes in thinking about the Soviet economy, yet it was not until the emergence of an article entitled "Plan, Profits, and Bonuses" by a then-obscure economist, Evsei Liberman, of Kharkov University, that the external world paid attention to the reform issue.[8] This article, published in Pravda in 1962, discussed the issue of how central planners could guide managers in the management of their enterprises.

The Liberman Proposals

Liberman's reform proposals received attention well out of proportion to their importance largely because they placed a new emphasis on profit, a concept considered alien in the Soviet setting. However, Liberman was quite clear in pointing out that central planning would be fully maintained and that profits would serve as a basis for managerial rewards only after targets for quantity and assortment were met. If these targets were not met, enterprises would be "deprived of the right to bonuses." Profits would be one of many criteria for the guidance of enterprise activity.[9]

Specifically, Liberman proposed that bonus payments (after the fulfillment of the planned output target) should be an increasing function of the rate of profit (profit/capital ratio), which would encourage expanding profits and reducing capital usage. Profitability norms established for each industry would serve as the basis for evaluating managerial performance. To encourage managers to set ambitious targets for themselves, rewards would be higher for successful fulfillment, or perhaps even under-fulfillment, of an ambitious profitability plan than for overfulfillment of an easy target.

The Liberman proposals argued for simplification that focused on quantity, assortment of output, and delivery. The enterprise would be responsible for planning materials needs, labor, and technology. Under Liberman's new arrangements, managers would have a vested interest in cost reduction and thus would seek out ways to lower costs rather than to build up excess stocks.

On the crucial issue of centralization versus decentralization, Liberman remained ambiguous. All of the instruments of central planning, including material technical supply, were to remain in place. Liberman did not spell out how this system would be compatible with enterprises planning their own material inputs, except to suggest that "with reasonable confidence" the two could prove compatible. Liberman's conservative posture on supply was in stark contrast to "marketeers" such as Nemchinov and Birman, who advocated free trade in producer goods.[10] Liberman also equivocated on the crucial issue of prices, although he did suggest that existing Soviet prices would give unfair profitability advantages to some producers while discriminating against others. He believed that if his reforms were implemented, managers would press for more rational prices.[11]

During the early 1960s, there was considerable discussion of the Liberman concepts, and some experimentation with them. However, it was the light industry experiments and the Kosygin reforms of 1965 that took center stage. The Central Committee sanctioned the light industry experiment in 1964.[12] Attempting to resolve the long-standing problem of connecting producer and user in the administrative command economy, this experiment focused on two enterprises, the Bolshevichka in Moscow and the Maiak in Gorky. Both enterprises were allowed to receive their production orders directly from a select group of retail outlets, rather than being assigned quantitative production targets. Unsold stock, or returned output, was to be deducted from fulfillment of output targets. Consumer demand was to become a motivating force, with bonuses (set between 40 and 50 percent) dependent upon fulfillment of delivery and profit plans, not output plans.[13] This experiment was considered to be successful and was expanded. By 1965, the light industry experiment was extended to 25 percent of garment factories, 28 percent of footwear factories, 18 percent of textile mills, and 30 percent of the leather factories.

The Kosygin Reforms of 1965

Although reform was a persistent theme in the Soviet economy, a series of specific reform attempts tended to dominate the discussion. Following the Liberman reforms of the late 1950s and early 1960s, the single most important reform program was the Kosygin reform, named after the then–prime minister, Alexei Kosygin. The thrust of the Kosygin reform was first to reduce the number of enterprise plan targets, and, most important, to replace gross output with "realized output," or sales. In addition, the number of targets for labor (previously four) was reduced to a single wage fund indicator. Managers faced eight specific targets:

1. Value of goods to be sold
2. Main assortment
3. Wage fund
4. Amount of profit and level of profitability
5. Payments to and allocations from the state budget
6. Volume of investment and exploitation of fixed assets
7. Assignments for the introduction of new technology
8. Material and technical supplies

The Kosygin program also included several changes in financial planning. An interest charge on fixed and working capital was introduced at a rate of 6 percent. In addition, Gosbank was given an expanded role, to provide investment funds at differentiated rates, and the importance of the state budget in investment finance was reduced. Emphasis was also placed on self-financing through the use of a production development fund. This would reduce the role of the state budget subsidies. Automatic subsidies to loss-making enterprises were to end. The Kosygin reform program was important both for its immediate context and for the process of implementation, which emerged through the 1970s.

The Economic Levers: Profits and Incentives

We have emphasized that a major focus of reform in the administrative command economy was the changing of decision-making arrangements within the enterprise, an approach that is not readily classified either as centralization or decentralization. In the Kosygin program, profit was to be given increased attention, with prices revised to allow enterprises to be profitable under normal conditions. Profits were to be a source of funds for decentralized investment (a 20 percent share of decentralized investment was envisioned) and for the payment of bonuses. Investment funds were to be channeled through two funds—the production development fund and the fund for social welfare and housing (to build factory-owned housing)—while bonus funds would be channeled through a new material incentive fund. These three funds were to replace the old enterprise fund and were designed to enhance the role of profits and increase the freedom for managerial decision making within the enterprise.

In addition to changes in the role of profits, complex new rules were introduced for the use of the incentive fund.[14] However, this fund was to be at the disposal of the enterprise, and was designed to provide incentive payments beyond those traditionally envisioned in the wage fund. In the end, it was evident that sales would remain the dominant success indicator. However, a variety of regulations circumscribed the degree of flexibility the enterprise had over the use of profit.

Organizational Change

Another common feature of change in the administrative command economy was organizational change. While changes in the "economic levers" seemed to indicate that enterprise managers had increased decision-making authority, the economic bureaucracy was in fact recentralized under the Kosygin program. Power was returned to the ministries, and the regional economic councils (the Sovnarkhozy) established by Khrushchev in 1957 were abolished. Decision-making authority was shifted away from the regional level to the national level.

In addition, there were a variety of organizational changes in economic planning and management.[15] Key functions were centralized in three new and powerful state committees: the **State Committee for Material Technical Supply** (Gossnab), the **State Committee for Prices** (Gostsen), and the **State Committee for Science and Technology** (Gostekhnika). Industrial enterprises were to be combined into organizations called *production associations,* and research enterprises and institutes were to be grouped into organizations called *science production organizations.* The rationale for these new organizations was achievement of economies of scale, reduction of bureaucracy, and improvement of the planning process. Gossnab had the primary responsibility for the allocation of producer goods, and the ministerial supply organizations that had dominated the rationing of funded goods largely disappeared. Gossnab was to apply itself to the creation of a wholesale trade system based upon direct contracts between suppliers and users.

Improving the Planning System

A third major strand in reform was improvements in the planning arrangements. Under the Kosygin program, there was to be a renewed emphasis on long-term plans. The scientific basis of planning was to be improved through greater use of computers and new planning techniques such as mathematical programming. In addition, enterprises were encouraged to propose counterplans, plans more difficult than those demanded by the ministries. The concept of counterplanning derived directly from the theoretical literature on planning, where counterplans were a mechanism that encouraged enterprises to reveal knowledge about their production capacity to planners. Instead of being penalized by more difficult future targets, enterprises proposing more difficult counterplans were to be rewarded with bonuses. Emphasis on long-term planning, it was argued, would encourage enterprises to engage in serious counterplanning.

Rejection: Lessons from the Administrative Command Reform Experience

The Kosygin reforms of 1965 provide us with a valuable case study of how the administrative command economy in fact rejected change. Formally, the reform was to be implemented in two stages. During the first, or "extensive," phase (between 1965 and 1970), nonagricultural enterprises would be gradually converted to the new system. Thereafter, the second, or "intensive," phase would begin, during which the true potential of the reform would be achieved.[16] In terms of the original format, by 1968 all industrial enterprises would be converted to the new system, with the remainder of the economy to be converted by the end of 1970. Change in agriculture was to take place at a slower pace.

Although there was evidence of increased managerial spontaneity during the late 1960s, in 1971 came a series of changes that substantially modified the original intent of the reform. For example, the ministry, based upon limits set by Gosplan, was allowed to set the size of enterprise funds by fixing planned incentive fund targets. The size of the various enterprise funds came to depend on enterprise performance vis-a-vis plan indicators such as profitability, output, and labor productivity targets. Three additional targets were introduced—the plan for key products in physical units, the plan for consumer goods, and the plans for changes in product quality and new products. Furthermore, the size of the enterprise fund was tied to the tautness of the enterprise plan: the higher the output, profitability, and labor productivity targets, the larger the potential incentive funds. These restrictions on enterprise funds restored to the ministries the authority to determine the conditions under which the incentive funds were accumulated and disbursed. For failing to meet ministry targets, enterprises could be punished by fund reductions.

Strict controls over enterprise funds were introduced. New regulations limited the growth of managerial bonuses. Average wages were not allowed to increase faster than labor productivity, and new regulations reduced bonus differentials among branches. Significantly, managerial bonuses were tied to the fulfillment of sales and profitability plans *plus* the fulfillment of the physical assortment plan. The ministries were allowed to add additional conditions if they desired. The ministry could deny bonuses if delivery plans were not met.

The manager's discretion over the production development fund (for investment) was circumscribed. Under the modified rules, the ministry set the proportion of enterprise profits allocated to this fund, in accordance with bank credits planned for decentralized investments. As a result, the incentive effects of the enterprise development fund were nullified. Under these decrees, the difference between centralized and decentralized investment lost its meaning. At the same time, while managers were encouraged to invest on a decentralized basis, they were unable to purchase investment goods through the material technical supply network. Supply problems persisted in spite of efforts to apply fines for nondelivery and to develop "free sales."[17]

The envisioned expansion of the banking system as a supplier of credit did not materialize. Credits, though available, remained a minor source of finance. Bank financing of state centralized investment accounted for only 2.3 percent of all investment in 1973. In fact, due to the absence of a mechanism for decentralized investment, enterprises were unable to spend production development and housing funds and, therefore, had a surplus working capital.

Proposed changes in planning failed to materialize. Throughout the period, the annual plan remained dominant, in spite of an effort to make the five-year plan the operative plan. In 1977, only 13,000 enterprises prepared counterplans. By 1981, only 6.6 percent of industrial enterprises prepared counterplans. Moreover, enterprise directors prepared cosmetic counterplans that did not change the substance of planning.[18] The ratchet effect was a continuing fear for enterprise managers.

Many proposed organizational changes simply did not materialize.[19] During the early years of the reform, production associations were not formed, requiring an additional decree in April of 1973. In fact, when the associations did form, they often meant little more than changing names on doors in Moscow; supervisory powers remained in the hands of the main administrations of the ministries. The bureaucracy increased by 60 percent between 1966 and 1977.[20] The ministries continued to be the center of economic power, dictating the incentive arrangements of enterprises and industrial associations and controlling investment. Gossnab was supposed to replace the ministerial supply organs, but by the late 1970s Gossnab handled only one half of the value of rationed goods. The market for producer goods failed to emerge, and the traditional system of material supplies and balances continued to function.

Finally and perhaps most significant, the number of enterprise targets expanded. New targets were reinstated in the 1970s: labor productivity, gross output, consumer goods assignments in heavy industry, quality targets, materials and fuel economy targets, delivery obligations, new product guidelines, and the size of basic incentive funds.

Most observers agreed that by the mid-1970s, the Kosygin reforms that began with great fanfare in 1965 were effectively dead. Nevertheless, the Soviet Union remained on a treadmill of reforms, continuing experiments begun in the 1960s.[21] In the 1970s the emphasis seemed to be upon better planning rather than decentralized decision making. One Western student of the reform wrote in 1973 that "... after seven years of reform, economic methods or 'levers' have been effectively converted into administrative 'levers' ... as a consequence, centralized planning and administration are even more entrenched ..."[22] Did the apparent failure of the

Kosygin reform mean a change in reform strategies? The answer is no. Although continuing reform took place with less fanfare—that is, until the final reform of perestroika—nevertheless the late 1970s and early 1980s witnessed continuing attempts to change the working arrangements of the administrative command economy. One of the last reform attempts was the 1979 decree "On Improving Planning."

Improving Planning: The Decree of July 1979

In July of 1979 came a decree entitled "On Improving and Strengthening the Economic Mechanism's Influence on Raising the Effectiveness of Production and the Quality of Work." [23] Generally abbreviated as **PIEM,** or Program to Improve the Economic Mechanism, this decree was not a systematic attempt to change the economic system. In a major study of PIEM, Morris Bornstein described it "as an attempt within the framework of 'traditional' ('Soviet type') socialist centrally planned economy to improve economic performance through changes in the arrangements for the choice of output, the allocation of resources to produce it, and the distribution of personal income."[24] The aim of the PIEM program was ". . . to increase output; to reduce cost, and particularly the use of materials and fuels; to improve quality through the introduction of new products; to secure the timely delivery of output according to the contracted product mix and to cut production time and costs." These objectives were to be pursued through "a variety of measures affecting planning, performance indicators, incentives, and finance."[25]

Planning was to be improved in five general areas. First, enterprise capacity was to be more accurately known through a "passport" system, which involved systematic, regular information-gathering about production capacity in each production unit.

Second, the norming process was to be improved and was to replace "directive indicators," in order to simplify the planning process and account for differing local conditions. Instead of telling an enterprise how much labor it could use for a particular task, a ministry would set a predetermined norm for the particular application, and enterprise performance would be judged by the achievement of this norm.

Third, enterprises were encouraged to operate under taut plans, as measured by indicators such as the percentage use of capacity. Rewards could be provided for adopting counterplans requiring more than official plans.

Fourth, long-term planning was once again emphasized, but with focus on the coordination of the one-year, five-year, and regional plans. The emphasis was on firm plans that would not be subject to ongoing change.

Finally, the material supply system was to be improved largely through the expanded use of contracting. Enterprises were encouraged to establish supply contracts with user enterprises that could fulfill contract terms.

A crucial part of the PIEM decree was related to performance indicators. The decree addressed three traditional problem areas, namely, the overutilization of material inputs, inattention to product quality, and neglect of product mix. Using gross output as an enterprise success indicator had led to overutilization of inputs. Under the new system, labor productivity was to be a key indicator, measured as net output per worker through norms established by planning authorities. The basic idea of normed net output was to calculate enterprise value added (net output) by subtracting planned costs from gross output. An enterprise that overused material inputs or substituted expensive inputs would be penalized because it used only normed costs. Costs in excess of planned costs would not enter into the value of output.[26]

The PIEM decree emphasized quality by making it a basic indicator of enterprise performance related to bonus payments. A commission was established to categorize products by their level of quality. Enterprises were to be rewarded according to the percentage of better quality products in their output mix. The assortment problem was attacked by trying to improve plan specification of assortment and tying rewards to the completion of delivery contracts. Output specifications were to be more detailed so that deviations from plan could be spotted more readily.

PIEM also included changes in bonus arrangements. Although enterprise performance remained the main source of bonuses, the rules for forming and disbursing bonus payments became more complex. Labor productivity and product quality indicators were to be more important. The PIEM was an important program, and yet with other reform ventures, it did not make major changes in the working arrangements of the administrative command economy. Moreover, basic problems, for example the nature of price formation, remained unresolved.

From our discussion of reform in the post–World War II era, hindsight shows that, judged by almost any set of criteria, economic reform in the Soviet Union failed. Most important, while these reform programs were being formulated and implementation being attempted, the Soviet economy continued to decline (Chapter 11). Cast against this long period of failed reform, it is perhaps not surprising that the last major attempt to reform the Soviet system, perestroika, begun by Mikhail Gorbachev in 1985, would differ in a number of dimensions from earlier attempts.

PERESTROIKA: THE FINAL SOVIET REFORM

It is convenient to examine perestroika, the final years of the Soviet economic system, in four phases.[27] Phase I we characterize as the introduction of perestroika, the early years from 1985 into 1986, when Mikhail Gorbachev spoke about the vision of perestroika (long on rhetoric, short on specifics).

During the second phase, from the latter part of 1986 through the early part of 1988, perestroika began to take shape as a flow of legislation gave it content. If one could criticize Gorbachev for lack of specifics in the early phase of perestroika, one could not say the same for the second phase.

The third phase of perestroika, from 1988 into 1989, was to be a period of implementation. Although it is difficult to judge why perestroika ultimately failed, it was during this period of implementation that the problems of reform in the administrative command economy surfaced once again.

Finally, in phase IV, through the end of 1989, it was evident that perestroika lacked both the totality and the sequencing necessary to seriously implement change. The traditional system was collapsing, but nothing was taking its place. In a real sense, partial reform was failing. For many who analyze the Soviet system, perestroika remains a critical period, during which change seemed to be essential, yet unreachable.

Perestroika: The Early Years

At the Twenty-Seventh Part Conference in February of 1986, Mikhail Gorbachev called for **radical reform** (radikal'naia reforma).[28] It was clear he was proposing major changes in what he termed the "administrative command system," to reverse the long period of **stagnation** (period zastoia) of the Brezhnev era. This was a period of new slogans, which would be heard and echoed both at home and abroad.

Perestroikia literally meant *restructuring*, a major attempt to reverse the declining fortunes of the Soviet economy, specifically through technological change. If perestroika focused upon the economy, much attention was given to the political side, characterized as glasnost, or openness. Glasnost was a very broad concept, envisioning the opening of Soviet society through daily discussion, the media, literature, and the conduct of daily life. Gorbachev envisioned an opening of Soviet society through **democratization** (demokratizatsiia) of daily political life. While this concept would applied to the citizen in daily life, it was also to apply to the worker in the enterprise decision-making process.

The opening of Soviet society was to lead to an **acceleration** (uskorenie) of economic activity. Even in the initial absence of a formal reform program, these were exciting new themes. Above all, economic change was to be linked to social change, though, as we shall see, as economic reform began to unfold through the legislative process, perestroika repeated many of the failed programs and processes of the past.

Economic reform was linked to social reform for a variety of basic reasons. First, Gorbachev concluded that the **"human factor"** contributed significantly to the stagnation of the Brezhnev era.[29] Thus, any reform program that failed to come to grips with motivational factors stood little chance of success. In political terms, if workers had an increasing voice in enterprise and in political affairs, they would be less likely to be alienated from the Soviet economic system.

Second, if ordinary Soviet citizens were to support perestroika, they must have a better understanding of both the costs and the potential benefits of economic reform. Moreover, candor might lessen the voices of opposition, especially those in the upper level of the Communist Party, traditional sources of opposition to economic reform.[30]

Third, by giving ordinary citizens more say in their daily lives, democratizing Soviet life would make them more willing to bear the costs of restructuring. Democratization was widely viewed as a way to increase morale in the workplace, to bring forth the long-discussed but ever absent "hidden reserves."

Fourth, both glasnost and democratization were seen as mechanisms to enhance the standing of the Soviet Union in the world community. Key features of perestroika, especially generating technological change to modernize the Soviet economy, required the support and participation of the industrialized nations. The role of the external world was very important in perestroika.

Could perestroika succeed? While Gorbachev was viewed as a serious reformer, the alternatives were few and a number of conditions had to be met if reform were to succeed. Bureaucratic resistance had been a major obstacle to reform in the past, an obstacle that would have to be overcome if reform was to succeed in the 1980s. Moreover, Gorbachev had learned that piecemeal reforms would fail. Change had to be comprehensive and integrated, and it had to be cast in a manner that would generate support at all levels, especially among enterprise managers, who would ultimately be responsible for implementing much of the change.

Although the early period of perestroika was short on specifics, general patterns of change emerged. Enterprises were to have greater control over their affairs, and **petty tutelage** from above (opeka) was to be reduced.[31] Enterprises were to take charge of their own affairs, and upper level bodies (such as ministries) were to be responsible for long-term change, technological change, and the like.

The Content of Perestroika: The Legislative Onslaught

The content of perestroika was contained in a variety of major decrees introduced in late 1985 and thereafter in 1986 and 1987. In addition to the specific legislation, there was significant organizational change. Late in 1985 the Machine Building Bureau was established to coordinate the activities of all of the machine-building ministries. In early 1986 the Fuel and Energy Bureau was created. In late 1985, agricultural ministries were consolidated to form a "super ministry" (Gosagroprom), with reduced central staffs and expanded regional activities.[32] Similar reorganization of construction ministries took place in August of 1986, and in September of that year, the Foreign Economic Commission was created, an important signal of change in the foreign sector. This latter change gave a limited number of enterprises the right to engage directly in foreign trade, a major change in Soviet policies. As time passed, this right was granted to increasing numbers of enterprises, leading to increasing chaos in foreign trade dealings.

The Enterprise Under Perestroika

Probably the single most influential piece of legislation was the **Law of the State Enterprise (LSE),** enacted in mid-1987.[33] As with previous reforms, LSE envisioned a reduction in interference in enterprise affairs. Upper level officials were to be concerned with long-term issues such as investment and technological change, while firms were given increased freedom to enter into contracts with other enterprises without approval of their superiors. Plan targets were to be replaced by **state orders** (zakazy), which the centralized supply system would control. This was seen as an important change in the role of the state, though state orders declined as a share of enterprise output as perestroika proceeded.

Ministries and planners were to influence enterprise actions, not through directives but through indirect instruments such as rules, norms, and laws. Local units of the Communist Party were to eliminate their tutelage of local enterprises, eliminate local redistribution of materials, and end the practice of requiring local enterprises to perform civic tasks.

Since "direct links" was to replace much of the administrative supply system, there would be new emphasis on contract enforcement through legal channels. Central authorities would determine if their supply plan (plan postavok) had been fulfilled, including issues of assortment, timeliness, and the like.

A new state committee, Gospriemka, was established to monitor quality. This agency was fully independent of enterprises and thus in a position to act on issues of product quality. These new regulations seemed to reduce the extent of control over enterprise activities; at the same time, enterprises were being asked to take greater responsibility for their actions.

Enterprise Accountability Under Perestroika

Under perestroika, enterprises were to be responsible for their "final results." Each enterprise was to be self-financing in the long run, meeting wage payments and other obligations with enterprise revenues. Investment requirements were to be met with retained earnings and/or bank credits, while bonus payments were to be made from enterprise profits. The implication was that enterprises would be placed on full **economic accounting** (pol'ny khozraschet).[34] With an end to automatic subsidies, this level of accountability implied that unprofitable enterprises would eventually go out of business. While this system was not new, there seemed to be a new seriousness of intent.

Under the new arrangements, enterprises were to operate on the basis of self-management (samoupravlenie). Managers would be elected and would work with a council selected from among the workers. This was a major component of democratization.[35]

The new arrangements for enterprises were designed to induce economically rational behavior. Enterprises unable to produce quality products wanted by customers would be unable to survive. Workers would exercise a new measure of influence, and a hard budget constraint would be substituted for the soft budget constraint of the past. To influence appropriate behavior, there were strong financial incentives for both managers and for workers.

Beyond the Enterprise: Cooperatives, Property Rights, and Agriculture

The Law on Private Economic Activity, passed in late 1986, allowed individuals to engage in a wide range of economic activities heretofore deemed (at least officially) to be illegal.[36] For example, private activity in taxicab services, dry cleaning, restaurants, and repair services would be legal, although these activities were to be carried out by able-bodied individuals on a part-time basis (in addition to holding a main job in the state sector) or by students, housewives, and others, who were permitted to work on a full-time basis. This activity would be licensed and an appropriate license fee charged.

State employees were also permitted to form cooperatives for the production of consumer goods. After paying income taxes to the state, after-tax income would be distributed among members as a form of profit sharing. Cooperatives would be free to contract for materials and services and would set their own prices. The major restriction was that these cooperatives were not envisioned as full-time activity, and, in addition, there were severe restrictions on the cooperative's ability to hire labor. This legislation brought some second economy activity to the surface and provided improved consumer goods.

The extension of private economic activity to agriculture was very limited. Gorbachev envisioned retention of the state and collective farms, though he did argue in favor of long-term leasing arrangements. For observers of the early Gorbachev era, it seemed striking that so little attention would be paid to agriculture, especially to the limited processing, storage, and distribution facilities.

The Technology Issue

Gorbachev's major industrial policy was that of modernization, to raise the technological level of Soviet industry to those in the United States and Western Europe by the end of the 1990s. Such changes would require the extensive retooling of production facilities, in addition to overcoming the traditional reasons for failed reforms in the Soviet Union. To achieve this rapid modernization, Gorbachev emphasized the need to improve the quality of the capital stock, not simply making additions to existing capital stock.

How would Soviet industry be modernized quickly? First, Gorbachev envisioned opening up the Soviet economy to foreign influence, for example through sanctioning joint ventures with Western firms to attract new capital and managerial skills. Second, industrial policy would emphasize sectoral priorities, accelerated retirement of old equipment, and emphasis on quality. Although Gorbachev did resort to outmoded methods (for example the creation of super-organizations to centralize research and development work), he also emphasized limits on new construction and promoted the modernization of existing facilities.

Foreign Trade: Opening the Soviet Economy

In a series of legislative acts beginning in 1986, the foreign trade arrangements of the Soviet Union were to undergo significant change.[37] The monopoly of the Ministry of Foreign Trade was to be relaxed with ministries and enterprises increasingly able to enter directly into foreign trade arrangements, accumulating hard currency for their own use. In 1986, the State Committee for Foreign Economic Relations was created to coordinate foreign trade under the new decentralized arrangements.

A further major change in trading arrangements was the introduction of joint ventures. Beginning in 1987, new Soviet legislation encouraged joint ventures between Soviet firms and Western firms. In the initial phases, legislation was quite restrictive with regard to key issues such as equity arrangements and repatriation of profits. However, relaxation was quick, though it proved very difficult to attract foreign capital.

Beyond changes in the organizational arrangements and the policies of Soviet foreign trade, the Soviet Union also moved towards full partnership in the international community. Steps were taken to obtain Soviet membership in GATT, the World Bank, and the International Monetary Fund. Discussions were begun with regard to ruble convertibility.

Price Reform Under Perestroika

Much of the emphasis of perestroika was the development of new enterprise rules and a new framework in which these rules would operate. Lack of serious price reform had been a key reason for the failure of earlier reform attempts and had to be taken seriously if perestroika were to succeed. The initial decrees proposed only modest changes to be introduced over a relatively long span of years.

Initially, the intent was to create an industrial wholesale price system in which only a few nationally important items had centrally set prices. Most remaining wholesale prices were to emerge from contract negotiations between buyers and sellers operating in a framework of rules established by central authorities. Prices on a number of products (presumably those of lowest national importance) were to be set freely (independent of existing rules), according to contracts and/or market conditions.

Retail prices were also to be reformed. An initial goal was to remove subsidies, which would lead to significant adjustments in relative prices and increases in prices. However, in the face of the usual political difficulties of price reform, formulas for change were modest.

PERESTROIKA: IMPLEMENTATION AND DECLINE

As the final phase of the Soviet experience, the era of perestroika remains of interest to observers of the Soviet system. It was the last major attempt to reform the economic system, and yet it was much more, including political and social reform and a final attempt to unleash the "hidden reserves." As with previous reforms, it was difficult to judge implementation. Consider, for example, the switch from state plans to state orders (zakazy). What was the difference? As perestroika unfolded, it soon became evident that if there had ever been a consistent and comprehensive reform program, it was not being implemented. Moreover, if performance was reasonable in the mid-1980s, the performance declines of the late 1980s were traumatic. By the late-1980s, it became clear that the traditional arrangements of the Soviet system were collapsing, but nothing was being put in their place. For several basic reasons, the last reform was failing.

First, perestroika was clearly much less than a comprehensive reform program. There were major internal problems and inconsistencies. Consider the enterprise law, a major component of perestroika. It maintained a delicate and probably impossible balance between central control and local initiative. Enterprises were to respond to prices, but the center would maintain control through rules. Judged against previous reform, one could have little faith in either component. Soviet prices remained irrational and irrelevant for decision-making purposes. Little attention was paid to changing property rights, a fundamental component of any new system of price formation.

A second major problem of perestroika was that of timing and complementarity. For example, if enterprises are to have contractual dealings with one another, there must be a legal system. However, the legal system was largely absent and there was no agreement about whether it should be developed before interenterprise arrangements were changed. Issues of timing clearly became the basis for arguing that even if change were to occur, there would have to be a period of declining economic achievement.[38]

A third major problem with perestroika was the matter of input selection. If enterprises were to be freed from the rigid rules under which inputs had traditionally been allocated and used, a replacement system must be put in place. In the absence of fundamental change, specifically the creation of wholesale markets, it is not surprising that enterprises continued to pursue old ways. In a sense, Gorbachev was seeking to impose change on an existing system.

Fourth, bureaucratic resistance had always been a major problem for those who attempted to reform the Soviet economic system.[39] Such resistance was often described in Soviet and Western literature as motivated solely by a fear of loss of prestige and authority. But bureaucrats resist change for a number of more basic reasons. Ministerial officials would resist decentralizing decision making to the enterprise level as long as the officials retained responsibility for enterprise achievement under the traditional rules of the game. The ministries applied their own levers, not necessarily because they enjoyed such actions, but because they led to goal achievement and rewards under existing rules. The role of bureaucrats and the ministries was basically unresolved under perestroika.

A fifth major problem during perestroika was uncertainty. This problem faces the players in any economic system; nonetheless, in a market setting, with reasonable stability of objectives, rules, and the decision-making environment, players can act in a rational manner. In the Soviet setting, change was dominant, and the players were entering an environment in which they had little or no experience.

Finally, if perestroika was to improve the Soviet economy's performance, it did not do so. The year 1989 was in fact pivotal. Performance problems led to emergency measures to deal with the emerging crisis—administrative controls were reintroduced, financial discipline was tightened, consumer goods price ceilings were introduced, and wage increases were controlled.

Although performance improved during the early years of perestroika, by 1989 the turnaround in the growth of output and factor productivity was clearly evident (see Figure 12.1). Moreover, while personal money income grew rapidly throughout the period, real consumption grew at a much slower pace. By 1989 the average annual rate of growth of repressed inflation was thought to be over 5 percent. The Soviet budget deficit increased rapidly from roughly 4 percent of GNP in 1985 to over 10 percent in 1989. In 1984, gross hard currency debt of the Soviet Union was estimated to be about U.S. $22 billion, a figure that would double by 1989. The

Figure 12.1   Perestroika: Aggregate Economic Performance

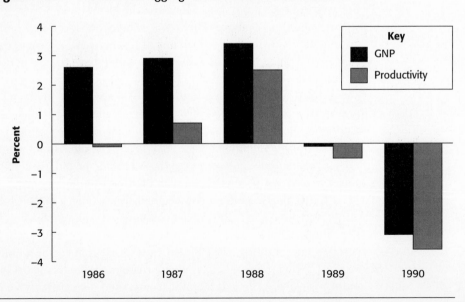

Source: CIA, *Handbook of Economic Statistics, 1991* (Washington,DC: 1991).

value of the ruble against the dollar fell rapidly. The increase in currency in 1985 was 4.1 billion rubles, while in 1990, the increase was 28 billion rubles.[40]

During 1989, a new Economic Reform Commission was created, later to be headed by Leonid Abalkin. The goal of this commission was legislation focused on market economic reforms. After some delay, the work of Abalkin and subsequent revisions by prime minister Nikolai Ryzhkov led Gorbachev to endorse a set of proposals that would, within a specified time frame, comprehensively shift the administrative command economy towards markets. The plan that received the most attention was the Shatalin 500 day plan, a plan developed in 1990 by a team of advisors to Gorbachev and Russian president Boris Yeltsin. This plan, subsequently modified, became known as the "Presidential Plan" to take effect in November of 1990.

The shift from economic reform to transition was fundamental. The discussion moved quickly from how planning could be made to work to strategies to develop a market economy—the microeconomic basis through the creation of private property rights and the macroeconomic basis through the creation of financial markets and a new role for money and the state budget. The imminent collapse of the Soviet Union would fundamentally change the course of events.

SUMMARY

The working arrangements of the Soviet economy were subjected to considerable change over time, and yet economic reform failed insofar as it did nothing to improve the performance of the economy. Reform, or change, generally focused on the organizational arrangements, the nature of planning, and levels of decision making in the system.

During the postwar era, attention focused both on several major reform attempts and on a continuing series of lesser reforms. While Khrushchev experimented with change in a variety of ways in the 1950s (for example the attempt to introduce regional planning through the sovnarkhozy), the major reform program of the era was that suggested by economist Evsei Liberman in the late 1950s and early 1960s. This program, focusing on enterprise management, was replaced by the Kosygin program in 1965, a major attempt to change the "economic levers" through which enterprise behavior would be manipulated.

On balance, these programs had little impact on the economy. They failed to address fundamentals such as price reform, and bureaucratic resistance was a major factor in their failure. Finally, in 1979, along with a continuing series of lesser reform attempts and experiments, the Program to Improve the Economic Mechanism (PIEM) was introduced, focusing on a broadly similar set of issues, namely enterprise guidance.

The final attempt to change the Soviet system came with the leadership of Mikhail Gorbachev in 1985. Although perestroika was ultimately rejected by the

Soviet system, the Gorbachev era commanded a great deal of attention as it focused on important changes in the management of the economy, the functioning of foreign trade, and the opening of political participation combined with the human factor. After a period of rhetoric, a series of major legislative decrees outlined the content of perestroika. However, while there were temporary performance improvements, a partial reform of the Soviet system proved to be impossible, turning the discussion to transition—replacing the plan with the market.

Terms and Concepts

transition   The replacement of one economic system by another, for example the replacement of planned (socialist) systems by market arrangements.

organizational change   Changes in the structure of the organizational hierarchy of an economic system; for example, the number and arrangement of subunits or changes in the supervisory (span of control) dimensions.

planning reform   Attempts to improve the system of balance planning, including changes in plan formulation, information requirements, dissemination of plan targets, and the like.

decentralization   Generally characterized as the devolution of decision-making authority and responsibility in a hierarchical organization; for example, shifting decision making from the ministry to the enterprise level.

sovnarkhoz   Regional economic council, established by Nikita Khrushchev as part of more general economic reform in the 1950s; the concept reduced the amount of control centered in the (sectoral) ministries and expanded it on a regional basis.

national balances   Developed in the 1920s; broadly concerned with bringing the supply of and demand for individual products and products in the aggregate into equality.

input-output analysis   A framework based upon national accounts for understanding and analyzing the sources and uses of inputs and outputs in a national economy; a formalization of the balance concept.

State Committee for Material Technical Supply   The state committee concerned with material technical supply or the distribution of inputs to enterprises, a critical state function in the absence of markets.

State Committee for Prices   The state committee with price-setting responsibilities.

State Committee for Science and Technology   The state committee concerned with issues inherent in science and technology, especially research and development and the dissemination of new ideas in the economy.

PIEM   The Program to Improve Economic Management, introduced in the summer of 1979 and designed broadly to improve the Soviet planning system within traditional guidelines.

radical reform   A concept popularized during the Gorbachev era; delineated and defined Gorbachev's program of economic reform as much more fundamental and more serious than the myriad of earlier reform programs.

stagnation   An expression (the period of stagnation) frequently used during the Gorbachev era to describe the serious slowdown of rates of economic growth that occurred during the late-Brezhnev era of the 1970s.

democratization   During the Gorbachev era, the stated goal of opening Soviet society to a greater degree, largely through citizen participation in the political process.

acceleration   Increasing the pace of economic activity, specifically the rate of economic growth.

human factor   An often ill-defined notion that Soviet citizens in fact were capable of using their "hidden reserves" of energy and talent if only the appropriate system of incentives could be found; exploiting the human factor was viewed as critical for the successful implementation of perestroika.

petty tutelage   System in which ministries have control over the functioning of enterprises, especially interference in day-to-day activities.

Law of State Enterprise (LSE)   A centerpiece of new legislation during perestroika (1987); designed to make fundamental changes in the operation of Soviet enterprises, especially the manner in which state enterprises interacted with their superiors.

state orders   A critical component of the Law on the State Enterprise; plan directives were to be replaced with state orders to enterprises; if implemented, such a change implied the state could purchase at least cost, providing a new element of cost pressure on enterprises.

economic accounting   The Soviet concept (khozraschet) of economic accounting; broadly, the concept that revenues should cover costs.

Selected Bibliography

Economic Reform

Balinky, A., et al. *Planning and the Market in the USSR: The 1960s* (New Brunswick, NJ: Rutgers University Press, 1967).

Berliner, J. *The Innovation Decision in Soviet Industry* (Cambridge, MA: MIT Press, 1976).

———. "Planning and Management," in A. Bergson and J. Levine, eds., *The Soviet Economy: Towards the Year 2000* (London: Allen & Unwin, 1983).

Bornstein, M. "Improving the Soviet Economic Mechanism," *Soviet Studies* vol. 37, no. 1 (January 1985), 1–30.

Bush, K. "The Implementation of Soviet Economic Reform," *Osteuropa Wirtschaft* vols. 2 and 3 (1970).

CIA. *Organization and Management in the Soviet Economy: The Ceaseless Search for Panaceas* (Washington, DC: 1977).

Cohen, S. F. "The Friends and Foes of Change: Reformism and Conservatism in the Soviet Union," *Slavic Review* vol. 38, no. 2 (June 1979).

Dyker, D. A. "Decentralization and the Command Principle: Some Lessons from Soviet Experience," *Journal of Comparative Economics* vol. 5, no. 2 (June 1981).

Fdeoryenko, N., et al. *Soviet Economic Reform: Progress and Problems,* trans. from the Russian (Moscow: Progress Publishers, 1972).

Feiwel, G. R. *The Soviet Quest for Economic Efficiency* (New York: Praeger, 1972).

Felker, J. L. *Soviet Economic Controversies* (Cambridge, MA: MIT Press, 1972).

Gorlin, A. C. "Industrialization Reorganization: The Associations," in U.S. Congress, Joint Economic Committee, *Soviet Economy in a New Perspective* (Washington, DC: U.S. Government Printing Office, 1976).

Hanson, P. "Success Indicators Revisited: The July 1979 Decree on Planning and Management," *Soviet Studies* vol. 25, no. 1 (January 1983), 1–13.

Katsenelinboigen, A. *Studies in Soviet Economic Planning* (White Plains, NY: M. E. Sharpe, 1978).

Keizer, W. *The Soviet Quest for Economic Rationality* (Rotterdam: Rotterdam University Press, 1971).

Kosygin, A. "On Improving Management in Industry, Perfecting Planning, and Enhancing Economic Incentives in Industrial Production," in M. Bornstein and D. Fusfeld, eds., *The Soviet Economy: A Book of Readings* 3e (Homewood, IL: Irwin, 1970).

Lieberman, E. G. *Economic Methods and the Effectiveness of Production* (White Plains, NY: M. E. Sharpe, 1978).

Linz, S. J. "Managerial Autonomy in Soviet Firms," *Soviet Studies* vol. 4, no. 2 (April 1988).

Litwack, John M. "Ratcheting and Economic Reforms in the USSR." *Journal of Comparative Economics* vol. 14, no. 2 (June 1990).

———. "Coordination, Incentives and the Ratchet Effect," *Journal of Comparative Economics* vol. 14, no. 2 (June 1990).

Nove, A. *The Soviet Economic System* (London: Allen & Unwin, 1977).

Qian, Y. "Equity, Efficiency, and Incentives in a Large Economy," *Journal of Comparative Economics* vol. 16. no. 1 (March 1992).

Rutland, P. "The Shchekino Method and the Struggle to Raise Labour Productivity in Soviet Industry," *Soviet Studies* vol. 36, no. 3 (July 1984).

Ryavec, K. W. "Soviet Industrial Managers: Challenge and Response, 1965–1970," *Canadian Slavic Studies* vol. 3 (Summer 1972).

———. "Soviet Industrial Managers, their Superiors and the Economic Reform: A Study of an Attempt at Planned Behavioral Change," *Soviet Studies* vol. 21, no. 2 (October 1969).

Schroeder, G. E. "The 1966–67 Industrial Price Reform: A Study in Contradictions," *Soviet Studies* vol. 20, no. 4 (April 1969).

——— . "Recent Developments in Soviet Planning and Managerial Incentives," in U.S. Congress, Joint Economic Committee, *Soviet Economic Prospects for the Seventies* (Washington, DC: U.S. Government Printing Office, 1973), 11–38.

——— . "The 'Reform' of the Soviet Supply System" *Soviet Studies* vol. 24, no. 1 (July 1972), 97–119.

——— . "Soviet Economic 'Reform' Decrees: More Steps on the Treadmill," in U.S. Congress, Joint Economic Committee, *Soviet Economy in the 1980s* vol. 1 (Washington, DC: U.S. Government Printing Office, 1982), 312–40.

——— . "The Soviet Economy on a Treadmill of 'Reforms'" in U.S. Congress, Joint Economic Committee, *Soviet Economy in a Time of Change* vol. 1 (Washington, DC: U.S. Government Printing Office, 1979).

Sharpe, M. E., ed. *Planning, Profit and Incentives in the USSR* vol. 1 and 2 (White Plains, NY: International Arts and Sciences Press, 1966).

Smolinski, L., ed. *L. V. Kantorovich: Essays on Optimal Planning* (White Plains, NY: International Arts and Sciences Press, 1976).

Zaleski, E. *Planning Reforms in the Soviet Union 1962–1966* (Chapel Hill: University of North Carolina Press, 1967).

Zauberman, A. "Liberman's Rules of the Game for Soviet Industry," *Slavic Review* vol. 22, no. 4 (December 1963).

——— . *The Mathematical Revolution in Soviet Planning* (Oxford: Oxford University Press, 1975.

Perestroika

Works by Soviet Authors

Aganbegian, A. *The Economic Challenge of Perestroika* (Bloomington: Indiana University Press, 1988).

——— . *Inside Perestroika* (New York: Harper Collins, 1990).

Aganbegian, A., and T. Timofeyev. *The New Stage of Perestroika* (Boulder, CO: Westview Press, 1988).

Gorbachev, M. *Perestroika: New Thinking for our Country and the World* (New York: Harper & Row, 1987).

Shemelyev, N., and V. Popov. *The Turning Point: Revitalizing the Soviet Economy,* trans. by M. A. Berdy (New York: Doubleday, 1989).

Early Works on Perestroika

Aslund, A. "Gorbachev's Economic Advisors," *Soviet Economy* vol. 3, no. 3 (July-September, 1987).

Dyker, D. A., ed. *The Soviet Economy Under Gorbachev: The Prospects for Reform* (London, Croom Helm, 1987).

Goldman, M. I. *Gorbachev's Challenge: Economic Reform in the Age of High Technology* (New York: Norton, 1987).

"Gorbachev's Economic Reform: A Soviet Economy Roundtable," *Soviet Economy* (January-March, 1986).

Hanson, P. "The Shape of Gorbachev's Economic Reform," *Soviet Economy* vol. 2, no. 4 (January-March, 1986).

Harmstone, R. C. "Background to Gorbachev's Investment Strategy," *Comparative Economic Studies* vol. 30, no. 4 (Winter 1988), 58–91.

Hewett, E. A. *Reforming the Soviet Economy* (Washington, DC: Brookings Institution, 1988).

Juviler, P., and H. Kimura, eds. *Gorbachev's Reforms: U.S. and Japanese Assessments* (New York: Aldine de Gruyter, 1988).

Kulikov, V., et al., eds. *The USSR: Acceleration of Socio-Economic Development* (Moscow: USSR Academy of Sciences, 1987).

Linz, S. J., ed. "A Symposium of Reorganization and Reform in the Soviet Economy," *Comparative Economic Studies* vol. 29, no. 4 (Winter 1987).

Linz, S. J., and M. Moskoff, eds. *Reorganization and Reform in the Soviet Economy* (Armonk: M. E. Sharpe, 1988).

McCauley, M., ed. *The Soviet Union Under Gorbachev* (New York: St. Martins Press, 1987).

Medvedev, Z. *Gorbachev* (Oxford: Blackwell, 1986).

NATO. *The Soviet Economy After Brezhnev* (Brussels: NATO, 1984).

Ruble, B. A. "Realities of Gorbachev's Economic Program," *Problems of Communism* vol. 35, no. 3 (May-June 1986).

Schroeder, G. E. "Anatomy of Gorbachev's Economic Reform," *Soviet Economy* vol. 3, no. 3 (July-September 1987).

U. S. Congress, Joint Economic Committee. *Gorbachev's Economic Plans* (Washington, DC: U. S. Government Printing Office, 1987).

Weickhardt, G. W. "Gorbachev's Record on Economic Reform," *Soviet Union* vol. 12, no. 3 (1985).

Zaslavskaya, T. "The Novosibirsk Report," *Survey* vol. 28, no. 1 (1984).

Statistics: New Interpretations Under Perestroika

Boretsky, M. "The Tenability of CIA Estimates of Soviet Economic Growth," *Journal of Comparative Economics* vol. 11, no. 4 (December 1987).

Brada, J. C., and R. L. Groves. "The Slowdown in Soviet Defense Expenditures," *Southern Economic Journal* vol. 54, no. 4 (April 1988).

——— . "CIA's Queries About Boretsky's Criticism of the Estimates of Soviet Economic Growth," *Journal of Comparative Economic Economics* vol. 14, no. 2 (June 1990).

CIA. *The Impact of Gorbachev's Policies on Soviet Economic Statistics* (Washington, DC: CIA, 1988).

——— . *Measuring Soviet GNP: Problems and Solutions* (Washington, DC: CIA, 1990).

——— . *Revisiting Soviet Economic Performance Under Glasnost: Implications for CIA Estimates* (Washington, DC: CIA, 1988).

Pitzer, J. S. "The Tenability of the CIA Estimates of Soviet Economic Growth: A Comment," *Journal of Comparative Economics* vol. 14, no. 2 (June 1990).

Steinberg, D. *The Soviet Economy, 1970–1990: A Statistical Analysis* (San Francisco: International Trade Press, 1990).

Agriculture Under Perestroika

Cook, E. C. "Soviet Food Markets: Will the Situation Improve Under Gorbachev?" *Comparative Economic Studies* vol. 29, no. 1 (Spring 1987).

Gray, K. R., ed. *Soviet Agriculture: Comparative Perspectives* (Ames: Iowa State University Press, 1990).

Moskoff, W., ed. *Perestroika in the Countryside: Agricultural Reform in the Gorbachev Era* (Armonk: M. E. Sharpe, 1990).

Wegren, S. K. "Dilemmas of Agrarian Reform in the Soviet Union," *Soviet Studies* vol. 44, no. 1 (1992).

Foreign Trade Under Perestroika

Aslund, A. "The New Soviet Policy Towards International Organizations," *The World Today* vol. 44, no. 6 (February, 1988).

Collins, S. M., and D. Rodrik. *Eastern Europe and the Soviet Union in the World Economy* (Washington, DC: Institute for International Economics, 1991).

Geron, L. *Soviet Foreign Economic Policy Under Perestroika* (London: Pinter Publishers, 1990).

Hewett, E. A. "The Foreign Economic Factor in Perestroika," *The Harriman Forum* vol. 1, no. 8 (August 1988).

Hewett, E. A., and C. D. Gaddy. *Open for Business: Russia's Return to the Global Economy* (Washington, DC: Brookings Institution, 1992).

Holzman, F. D. "Moving Toward Ruble Convertibility," *Comparative Economic Studies* vol. 33, no. 3 (Fall 1991).

General Works on Perestroika

Aslund, A. *Gorbachev's Struggle for Economic Reform,* rev. ed. (London: Pinter Publishers, 1991).

——— . The Making of Economic Policy in 1989 and 1990," *Soviet Economy* vol. 6, no. 1 (1990).

CIA. *Gorbachev's Modernization Program: A Status Report* (Washington, DC: CIA, 1987).

——— . *Beyond Perestroika: The Soviet Economy in Crisis* (Washington, DC: 1991.)

——— . *The Soviet Economy in 1988: Gorbachev Changes Course* (Washington, DC: CIA, 1989).

——— . *Gorbachev's Economic Program: Problems Emerge* (Washington, DC: CIA, 1988).

Dyker, D. A. *The Future of the Soviet Economic Planning System* (London: Croom Helm, 1985).

Ellman, M., and V. Kontorovich, eds. *The Disintegration of the Soviet Economic System* (London: Routledge, 1992)

Ericson, R. E. *The Soviet Union, 1979–1990* (San Francisco: ICS Press, 1992).

Goldman, M. E. *What Went Wrong with Perestroika* (New York: Norton, 1992).

Gregory, P. R. *Restructuring the Soviet Economic Bureaucracy* (Cambridge: Cambridge University Press, 1989).

———— . "The Soviet Bureaucracy and Perestroika," *Comparative Economic Studies* vol. 31, no. 1 (Spring 1989).

Hanson, P. "Property Rights in the New Phase of Reforms," *Soviet Economy,* no. 6, no. 2 (1990).

Hewett, E. A. "The New Soviet Plan," *Foreign Affairs* vol. 69, no. 5 (Winter 1990/91).

Hewett, E. A., and V. H. Winston, eds. *Milestones in Glasnost and Perestroyka* (Washington, DC: Brookings Institution, 1991).

IMF. *The Economy of the USSR: Summary and Recommendations* (Washington, DC: IMF, et al., 1990).

Moskoff, W. *Hard Times: Impoverishment and Protest in the Perestroika Years* (Armonk: M. E. Sharpe, 1993).

NATO. *Soviet Economic Reform: Implementation Underway* (Brussels: NATO, 1989).

———— . *The Soviet Economy Under Gorbachev* (Brussels: NATO, 1991).

Noren, J. H. "The Soviet Economic Crisis: Another Perspective," *Soviet Economy* vol. 6, no. 1 (1990).

Ofer, G. "Budget Deficit, Market Disequilibrium and Soviet Economic Reforms," *Soviet Economy* vol. 5, no. 2 (1989).

Peck, M. J., and T. J. Richardson, eds. *What Is to Be Done: Proposals for the Transition to the Market* (New Haven: Yale University Press, 1991).

Standing, G., ed. *The New Soviet Labour Market: In Search of Flexibility* (Geneva, IL.: ILO, 1991).

Szamuely, L. *First Models of the Socialist Economic Systems* (Budapest: Akademiai Kiado, 1974).

"Symposium on Economic Transition in the Soviet Union and Eastern Europe," *Journal of Economic Perspectives* vol. 5, no. 4 (Fall 1991).

Tedstron, J. E., ed. *Socialism, Perestroika, and the Dilemmas of Soviet Economic Reform* (Boulder, CO: Westview, 1990).

Weickhardt, G. G. "The Soviet Military-Industrial Complex and Economic Reform," *Soviet Economy* vol. 2, no. 3 (July-September 1986).

Wilczynski, J., ed. *The Gorbachev Encyclopedia* (Salt Lake City, UT: Charles Schlacks, Jr., 1993).

Notes

1. There is a great deal of literature dealing with economic reform in the Soviet Union. Useful sources are A. Bergson, *Planning and the Market in the USSR: The 1960s* (New Brunswick: Rutgers University Press, 1967), 43–64; G. E. Schroeder, "The 'Reform' of the Supply System in Soviet Industry," *Soviet Studies* vol. 24, no. 1 (July 1972), 97–119; G. E. Schroeder, "The Soviet Economy on a Treadmill of Reforms," in U.S. Congress, Joint Economic Committee, *Soviet Economy in the 1980s: Problems and Prospects* part 1 (Washington, DC: U.S. Government Printing Office, 1982), 66–88; S. F. Cohen, "The Friends and Foes of Change: Reformism and Conservatism in the Soviet Union," *Slavic Review* vol. 38, no. 2 (June 1979).

2. See M. Bornstein, "Economic Reform in Eastern Europe," in U.S. Congress, Joint Economic Committee, *East European Economies Post-Helsinki* (Washington, DC: U.S.

Government Printing Office, 1977); R. G. Lynch, "Centralization and Decentralization Redefined," *Journal of Comparative Economics* vol. 13, no. 1 (March 1989).

3. See comments by V. S. Nemchinov in his *The Use of Mathematics in Economics* (Cambridge, MA: MIT Press, 1964); for a translation of original balance of 1923–24, see N. Spulber, ed., *Foundations of Soviet Strategy for Economic Growth* (Bloomington: Indiana University Press, 1964); see also "The Origins of Soviet Mathematical Economics," in H. Raupach, ed., *Yearbook of East-European Economics* vol. 2 (Munich: Gunter Olzog Verlag, 1971).

4. See E. H. Carr and R. W. Davies, *Foundations of a Planned Economy, 1926–1929* (London: Macmillan, 1969).

5. Spulber, ed., *Foundations of Soviet Strategy for Economic Growth*, ch. 2; B. Grossman, "Scarce Capital and Soviet Doctrine," *Quarterly Journal of Economics* vol. 67, no. 3 (August 1953); R. Dunayevskaya, "The Origins of Soviet Mathematical Economics."

6. Cohen, "The Friends and Foes of Change."

7. For a review of these contributions, see R. W. Campbell, "Marx, Kantorovich and Novozhilov: Stoimost' Versus Reality," *Slavic Review* vol. 20, no. 3 (October 1961); M. Ellman, *Proposals for an Optimally Functioning Economic System* (Cambridge: Cambridge University Press, 1971); A. Zauberman, *The Mathematical Revolution in Soviet Planning* (Oxford: Oxford University Press, 1975); A. Katsenelinboigen, *Studies in Soviet Economic Planning* (White Plains, NY: M. E. Sharpe, 1978); L. Smolinski, ed. *L. V. Kantorovich: Essays on Optimal Planning* (White Plains, NY: International Arts and Sciences Press, 1976).

8. For the original article and related discussion, see M. E. Sharpe, ed., *Planning, Profit and Incentives in the USSR* vol. 1 and 2 (White Plains, NY: International Arts and Sciences Press, 1966).

9. E. G. Liberman, in M. Bornstein and D. Fusfeld, eds., *The Soviet Economy: A Book of Readings* 3e (Homewood, IL: Irwin, 1970); see also E. G. Liberman, *Economic Methods and Effectiveness of Production* (White Plains, NY: International Arts and Sciences Press, 1971).

10. A. Nove, *The Soviet Economic System* (London: Allen & Unwin, 1977), 309–10.

11. M. Kaser, "Kosygin, Liberman, and the Pace of Soviet Industrial Reform," in G. R. Fiewel, ed., *New Currents in Soviet-Type Economies: A Reader* (Scranton, PA: International Textbook, 1968).

12. See Goldman, "Economic Growth and Institutional Change,"; Kaser, "Kosygin, Liberman"; E. Zaleski, *Planning Reforms in the Soviet Union, 1962–1966* (Chapel Hill: University of North Carolina Press, 1967).

13. M. Goldman, "Economic Growth and Institutional Change," in P. Juviler and H. Morton, eds., *Soviet Policy Making: Studies of Communism in Transition* (New York: Praeger, 1967); M. Goldman, "Economic Growth and Institutional Change," and G. Feiwel, *The Soviet Quest for Economic Efficiency* (New York: Praeger, 1972).

14. K. Bush, "The Implementation of Soviet Economic Reform," *Osteuropa Wirtschaft* vols. 2 and 3 (1970).

15. For a discussion of organizational changes, see Kushnirsky, *Soviet Economic Planning*, and CIA, *Organization and Management in the Soviet Economy: The Ceaseless Search for Panaceas* (Washington, DC: 1977).

16. G. E. Schroeder, "Recent Developments in Soviet Planning and Managerial Incentives," in U.S. Congress, Joint Economic Committee, *Soviet Economic Prospects for the Seventies* (Washington, DC: U.S. Government Printing Office, 1973).

17. Goldman, "Economic Growth and Institutional Change," 323; Schroeder, "Recent Developments in Soviet Planning," 107–11; on the material supply problem and its relation

to decentralized investment, see for example D. Allakhverdian, "O finasovykh problemakh khoziaistvennykh reformy," [About the financial problems of economic reform], *Voprosy ekonomiki* [Problems of economics] vol. 11 (1970).

18. S. J. Linz, "Managerial Autonomy in Soviet Firms," *Soviet Studies* vol. 40, no. 2 (April 1988).

19. This discussion is based upon M. Bornstein, "Improving the Soviet Economic Mechanism," *Soviet Studies* vol. 37, no. 1 (January 1985); Schroeder, "Soviet Economic 'Reform' Decrees"; Schroeder, "The Soviet Economy on a Treadmill of 'Reforms'"; Schroeder, "Post-Khrushchev Reforms and Public Financial Goals," in Z. M. Fallenbuchl, ed., *Economic Development in the Soviet Union and Eastern Europe* (New York: Praeger, 1976); CIA, *Organization and Management in the Soviet Economy;* A. C. Gorlin, "Industrial Reorganization: The Associations," In U.S. Congress, Joint Economic Committee, *Soviet Economy in a New Perspective* (Washington, DC: U.S. Government Printing Office, 1976); Kushnirsky, *Soviet Economic Planning.*

20. Schroeder, "The Soviet Economy on a Treadmill of 'Reforms,'" 314.

21. For a discussion of the Shchekino experiment, see P. Rutland, "The Shchekino Method and the Struggle to Raise Labour Productivity in Soviet Industry," *Soviet Studies* vol. 36, no. 3 (July 1984); B. Arnot, "Soviet Labour Productivity and the Failure of the Shchekino Experiment," Critique vol. 1, no. 5 (1981); and B. Arnot, *Controlling Soviet Labour* (London: Macmillan, 1988).

22. P. K. Cook, "The Political Setting," in U.S. Congress, Joint Economic Committee, *Soviet Economic Prospects for the Seventies* (Washington, DC: U.S. Government Printing Office, 1973).

23. This discussion is based upon Bornstein, "Improving the Soviet Economic Mechanism"; Schroeder, "Soviet Economic 'Reform' Decrees"; P. Hanson, "Success Indicators Revisited: The 1979 Soviet Decree on Planning and Management," *Soviet Studies* vol. 35, no. 1 (January 1983); N. Nimitz, "Reform and Technological Innovation in the 11th Five Year Plan," in S. Bialer and T. Gustafson, eds., *Russia at the Crossroads* (London: Allen & Unwin, 1982.

24. M. Bornstein, "Improving the Soviet Economic Mechanism," *Soviet Studies* vol. 37, no. 1 (January 1982), 2.

25. *Ibid.,* 23.

26. Schroeder, "Soviet Economic 'Reform' Decrees," 82.

27. See for example the treatment in A. F. Dowlah, *Soviet Political Economy in Transition: From Lenin to Gorbachev* (Westport: Greenwood Press, 1992).

28. For an excellent discussion of the early years of perestroika and the background, see E. A. Hewett, *Reforming the Soviet Economy* (Washington, DC: Brookings Institution, 1988).

29. See E. Teague, "Gorbachev's 'Human Factor' Policies," in U.S. Congress, Joint Economic Committee, *Gorbachev's Economic Plans* vol. 1 (Washington, DC: U.S. Government Printing Office, 1987).

30. For a discussion of bureaucratic resistance, see P. R. Gregory, "The Soviet Bureaucracy and Perestroika," *Comparative Economic Studies* vol. 31, no. 1 (Spring 1989); P. R. Gregory, *Restructuring the Soviet Bureaucracy* (New York: Cambridge University Press, 1990).

31. Changes in enterprise relations with superiors was a major theme of the Gorbachev era and would be a focus on the Enterprise Law. See R. E. Ericson, "The New Enterprise Law," *Harriman Forum* vol. 1 (February 1988).

32. For a discussion of changes in agriculture, see J. Butterfield, "Devolution of Decision Making and Organizational Change in Soviet Agriculture," *Comparative Economic Studies* vol. 32, no. 2 (Summer 1988).

33. Ericson, "The New Enterprise Law."

34. Although the concept of economic accountability was one of long standing in Soviet practice, adherence was limited. Moreover, it was generally interpreted to mean a mechanical balance between revenues and expenditures, a meaningless concept given the nature of Soviet prices. During the Gorbachev era, the implication seemed to be that enterprise accountability would be taken seriously, and if this were the case, loss-making enterprises might eventually be liquidated. This latter interpretation was fundamentally different from earlier thought and practice.

35. Gorbachev called for increased worker participation in the selection of enterprise managers.

36. For a discussion of ownership arrangements in different sectors, see K. Plokker, "The Development of Cooperative and Individual Labour Activity in the Soviet Union," *Soviet Studies* vol. 2 (July 1990); K. Brooks, "Lease Contracting in Soviet Agriculture in 1989," *Comparative Economic Studies* vol. 32, no. 2 (Summer 1990); Nicoletta Amodio, "Forms of Ownership in the USSR," *Most* vol. 1, no. 1 (1991).

37. Under perestroika, there were to be important changes in the organizational arrangements and the policies pertaining to foreign trade. See A. Aslund, "The New Soviet Policies Towards International Organizations," World Today vol. 44, no. 6 (February 1988); F. D. Holzman, "Moving Towards Ruble Convertibility," *Comparative Economic Studies* vol. 33, no. 3 (Fall 1991); C. M. McMillan, "Strategy or Tactics? Recent Initiatives in Soviet Foreign Economic Policy," in NATO, *Soviet Economic Reforms*, 157–84.

38. For a discussion of early plan targets and their relationship to those developed under perestroika, see R. C. Stuart, "Soviet Plan Targets and Achievements: The Part Programmes," *Communist Economies* vol. 2, no. 3 (1990).

39. See P. R. Gregory, "The Impact of Perestroika on the Soviet Planned Economy: Results of a Survey of Moscow Officials," *Soviet Studies* vol. 42, no. 5 (1991).

40. See A. Aslund, *Gorbachev's Struggles for Economic Reform* rev. ed. (London: Pinter Publishers, 1991).

CHAPTER 13

The Theory of Transition

In Chapter 12 we examined the many attempts to change the Soviet economy through economic reform. Indeed, we emphasized two fundamental issues, namely that change was important for any economic system in the global setting of the late twentieth century and that economic reform in the Soviet Union failed. Thus, for a variety of economic and noneconomic reasons, the Soviet Union as a political and economic entity collapsed and was replaced by Russia and fourteen other newly independent states.

The era following the collapse of the Soviet Union and other planned socialist economic systems is one of **transition.** Transition involves the replacement of one economic system by another, in this case, the replacement of the administrative command economy by the market. Although our focus in this book is Russia and the former Soviet republics, the process of transition is much more widespread. Moreover, while we knew little about transition at the end of the 1980s, now as we approach the end of the 1990s, we can look back on a significant body of evidence, which has fundamentally changed the way we look at transition. In this chapter, we examine the general issues of transition, and in the next chapter, we examine the specifics of the Russian case.

TRANSITION: THE BASICS

The process of transition has unfolded largely absent any significant theoretical underpinning. Thus, during the 1990s there has been a burgeoning literature based upon real-world experience and observed fundamental differences from one transition setting to another. In this sense, conceptions about transition have evolved over time, with considerable variation, depending upon the cases being studied. During the early discussions of transition, economists placed considerable emphasis upon issues of speed and sequencing, with an initial apparent dichotomy between the so-called "big bang," or rapid, approach and the "gradualist," or slower, approach. With subsequent experience, this dichotomy has come to be viewed as simplistic, though the underlying issues of sequencing remain important.[1]

Beyond the initial discussion of the speed and sequencing of transition, the components of transition were typically classified in four major dimensions. First, the **microeconomics of transition** focused on creating markets and market price signals through privatization. Second, the **macroeconomics of transition** centered on creating a money-financial system, specifically a financial infrastructure, and developing a new role for the state, through the budgetary process and appropriate monetary and fiscal policies to guide macroeconomic performance. Third, major emphasis has been placed upon **international trade** and finance, specifically new trading arrangements and policies, and most important, movement towards a convertible currency. Finally, a matter of importance is the **safety net,** or the infrastructure and policies for the provision of medical services, unemployment benefits, pensions, and the like. Clearly these four components of the transition process are closely intertwined; yet they provide convenient points of departure for understanding the issues at hand. We begin with general issues of transition, turning thereafter to a discussion of the basic components.

TRANSITION: THE BEGINNINGS

It should now be evident to the reader that at the time of collapse, almost every major dimension of the economy of the Soviet Union was fundamentally different from the dimensions of a market economy, even one at a similar level of economic development. Most important, the mechanisms of resource allocation and the policies implemented over many years established an economic structure fundamentally different than would have existed under market arrangements. Indeed, the failure of economic reform in the planned socialist systems left those systems fundamentally unchanged from their beginnings. How, then, should transition proceed?

Two major forces affect the nature of transition: the **initial conditions** and the **transition policies** developed and implemented during the transition process itself.[2] Both are interrelated and have an impact upon both the speed with which the transition can proceed and the sequence of transition components. The appropriate pace of transition varies from case to case, depending upon a number of factors.

First, there is a political argument for moving quickly. While the political vacuum at the end of the planned socialist era provided an opportunity for change, if change is not implemented quickly, the seemingly inevitable downturn in the economy can result in discontent and resulting retrenchment.

Second, the matter of initial conditions is fundamental. For example, in the case of a small, relatively open economy that has already achieved a medium or better level of economic development, the issue of initial stabilization may not be of major importance. On the other hand, for a large, relatively closed economy, where only limited economic development has taken place, the initial downslide may be severe, necessitating policies to stabilize the economy as steps towards transition are taken.

Third, while we know that the planned socialist economies were distorted relative to possible market patterns, the nature and degree of this distortion (or, put differently, the nature of initial conditions) matters. Consider, for instance, a microeconomic example. Where there has been little, if any, private activity and ownership claims from earlier generations must be arbitrated, privatization may be slow. The result will be a sharp decline in real output. On the other hand, where the industrial structure is less biased against the light industrial and service sectors, privatization may be accomplished quickly, with limited impact upon the level of output.

The purpose of privatization, as we will see, is the creation of private ownership and thus markets in which prices are formed by the forces of supply and demand. The prices will be used for the allocation of resources. At the same time, since one of the initial conditions is the distortion of prices from the plan era, the speed with which prices are released becomes an important policy issue. From the point of view of expectations, it makes sense to release prices quickly, and yet, in the absence of market institutions and especially the absence of appropriate macroeconomic mechanisms and policies for stabilization, the potential for inflation may be far too great.

In part, the issues raised here pertain to **sequencing.** For example, if the price-setting function of the state is to be eliminated, does it make sense simply to release prices to be determined by market forces, when in fact those market forces do not exist? In fact, the issue of sequencing is more complex because it is seldom a matter of existence or nonexistence. In fact, in transition economies, the state may well sustain control over the prices in certain sectors, for example energy, while releasing prices in other sectors to market forces. Nonetheless, in the released sectors, market conditions may or may not exist, and even if they do, they may be far from competitive.[3]

Both the speed and the sequencing of transition are also tied closely to a much more fundamental and complex issue, namely the nature of change. Thus far, we have treated change as a relatively mechanical issue: One selects appropriate policies and implements them on a time spectrum determined by such issues as the nature of initial conditions in the transition setting. However, the paradigm of **evolutionary economics** provides a different perspective.[4] The advocates of this paradigm suggest that contemporary neoclassical microeconomic theory does not provide an adequate underpinning for understanding change.

Specifically, while neoclassical economic theory postulates that change emerges from the behavior of rational agents who maximize known objectives with available information, resulting in the achievement of equilibria through time, the evolutionary approach presents a different picture. The evolutionary approach suggests that institutions emerge only slowly and sequentially in a path-dependent world from the behavior of agents with limited knowledge and foresight. In this world, the emergence of new institutions is a slow and sequential process.

In a sense, understanding change does not require choosing a paradigm. Unquestionably, there are cases where the end point of transition is known, and a particular change can be formulated and implemented without a long evolutionary process. However, we now know from real-world transition experience that the path of transition differs fundamentally from one case to another, and for reasons that can be observed, such as severe distortions as initial conditions. Also, quite apart from the strategy of transition appropriate in a particular setting, little attention has been paid to the end of transition.

The concept of transition implies the movement from one position to another. The position to which the economic system is moving cannot be characterized simply by observing the formality of a new set of institutions or policies. The economy must undergo **restructuring.** With restructuring, when transition comes to an end, new institutions and policies are in place, they are functioning, and most important, they are influencing resource allocation, so the process and the outcomes no longer resemble those of the planned socialist era.[5] Such an outcome is far more difficult to characterize than, for example, simply changing the shareholding arrangements of an industrial enterprise.

THE MICROECONOMICS OF TRANSITION: PRIVATIZATION

In Chapter 10 we emphasized that state (or, more generally, public) ownership is a cornerstone of socialism and a systemic characteristic that allowed the state to control and direct resource use through central planning. The cornerstone of the capitalist economy is markets based upon private ownership, creating supply and demand and resultant prices that serve as the fundamental mechanism for decision making about resource allocation. It is not surprising, therefore, that **privatization** holds center stage in contemporary transition economies.[6]

How will privatization be achieved? Although the process of privatization has differed considerably from case to case in the transition economies of the 1990s, the process and the issues involved have a decisive commonality, illustrated in Figure 13.1. The process of privatization can be characterized in terms of a typical, though by no means unique, sequence. First, while there are sectors and cases where privatization can be "spontaneous," most planned socialist systems are characterized by a large, overly capital-intensive industrial sector. In such cases, the first step is the creation of an agency (typically a state agency) that oversees the process of privatization.

Second, it is essential that the legislative process develop legislation appropriate to the privatization process. For the Russian case, this legislation (discussed in Chapter 14) specified the nature of the privation process—which sectors would be priorities, the nature of changing equity arrangements, and the disbursement of these new shares.

Third, the state agency is responsible for identifying state properties that will be privatized. This process involves the implementation of a basic privatization policy (that is, which sectors will be privatized and which will not) and the specific identification of properties that will be privatized.

Fourth, the property fund must "prepare" the properties for privatization. Based upon existing legislation and the specific nature of the property in question, the share structure is identified and prepared for distribution.

Fifth, the shares must be distributed. It is this process that has received the most attention in the literature on privatization. There are a variety of approaches, all of which have advantages and disadvantages. The process of privatization depends largely on the nature of the assets being privatized. For example, in some cases privatization took place through **restitution,** though this process has tended to be localized, limited in volume, and not of serious import for the entire privatization process.

In addition to restitution, there has been a significant amount of what is usually termed **small scale privatization.** This refers largely to the privatization of small businesses, especially those in sectors such as retail trade. While generally important, this component of the privatization process is difficult to track, largely because it is frequently accomplished under local auspices through various means (direct sale, auction, and vouchers) and includes both privatized existing businesses and those started from scratch.

Figure 13.1   Privatization: The Sequence

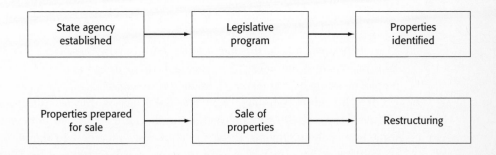

The most observed form of privatization is **mass privatization,** or programs that attempt to change equity arrangements on a large scale over a short period of time, directed especially at the major enterprises. The process of mass privatization can be accomplished in a variety of ways, though outcomes tend to differ considerably from case to case. We examine both the approaches and the outcomes.

State enterprises can be sold in several ways. First, after completion of corporatization, shares can be sold either to the public, through auctions, and/or through negotiated arrangements. A second general approach is what is usually termed **insider privatization,** or sale of shares to participants in the organizations (workers and managers), according to established guidelines. To appreciate the nature of these alternatives, we need to examine the difficulties associated with the general privatization process.

First, even where legislation provides for establishing a corporate share structure, the issue of **valuation** is difficult in most transition cases.[7] The traditional methods used in market economies, such as accounting measurement, present value calculations of expected future profits, or stock valuations, are all generally unavailable. Moreover, the matter of stock ownership and transfer lacks transparency, a feature that only emerges as capital markets are developed. For this reason, it is difficult for potential investors to assess the costs and benefits of any particular investment project.

Second, in order to sell enterprises, potential investors must have access to investment capital. In the absence of domestic capital markets during the initial years of transition, transition economies frequently turn to foreign sources, which may or may not be available. Moreover, selling domestic enterprises to foreigners raises the usual issues associated with direct foreign investment, especially important at a time when political leaders are looking for domestic support for the transition process.

Third, the absence of domestic investment funds, institutions necessary for channeling such funds into the purchase of equities, and traditional equity considerations has led to the use of **voucher privatization.** A number of transition economies have used variants of the voucher process. We examine the details of the Russian voucher privatization program in Chapter 14; however, the general pattern is as follows.[8] Vouchers are issued at a given face value to the population. These vouchers can be transferred into enterprise equity (or sold in secondary markets) in a variety of ways, such as through mutual funds (where these exist), bidding in direct sales or auctions, and most likely, through the purchases of shares at the place of employment—what we termed "insider privatization."

It is difficult to generalize about these alternatives. In various transition settings, all have been used to varying degrees, and all are subject to criticisms of various sorts, especially judgments about the equity of outcomes. In the absence of well-established and transparent capital markets, is it possible that equities are in fact accumulated by a small number of influential and (now) wealthy individuals? In this sense, while there has been a great deal of privatization in the transition economies, including Russia, the ultimate result has yet to be determined.

But is privatization the end of the story? As we noted above, while privatization is fundamental to transition, privatization is, in a sense, just the beginning. After ownership arrangements are changed, it is necessary to undergo restructuring. As we have described privatization, it is a redistribution of equity rights from the state to individuals. The fundamental objective is to change the way that decisions are made, so that the allocation of resources will no longer change as directed by a plan but by the forces of supply and demand. These forces are themselves only beginning to emerge.

The empirical evidence on restructuring is mixed. Recall that privatization, driven by considerations of both equity and efficiency, is a widespread phenomenon in recent years, by no means limited to transition economies. Available evidence shows that in cases that have been identified in Western market economies, privatization has led to efficiency gains. In transition cases, however, while privatization has been successful (in the general sense of transferring ownership to the non-state sector), the equity and efficiency outcomes are much less clear. Why is this so?

Most microeconomic analyses of privatized enterprises in transition economies, especially in the Russian case, conclude that restructuring has been a long and difficult process and will continue to be so. First, to the extent that state funds still find their way into enterprises, especially in sectors such as heavy industry and defense, hard budget constraints have not replaced soft budget constraints. Second, although formal ownership arrangements have changed, it is not clear that new coalitions have emerged to influence decision making. Third, in the absence of capital, enterprises are generally strapped for funds, necessitating a return to the old ways of barter. Fourth, in the absence of a flexible and meaningful price system, information signals in the transitions setting have limited use. What does all of this mean? While the privatization phase of transition is definitely being implemented, there is still much formalization, after which more serious economic consequences could follow as hard budget constraints are implemented.

THE MACROECONOMICS OF TRANSITION: MONETARY AND FISCAL ARRANGEMENTS

One of the most difficult issues of transition is the immediate onset of macroeconomic imbalance.[9] In almost all transition economies, two fundamental issues require immediate attention. First, these are systems without a traditional (market-type) set of macroeconomic institutions and policies. Second, with the collapse of the old order, the immediacy of macroeconomic imbalances—for example budget deficits, unemployment, and inflation—is apparent. What should be done in these circumstances?

Creating macroeconomic institutions and policies is inevitably one of the most difficult elements of transition, largely because these institutions and related policies were absent in earlier planned socialist economic systems. Moreover, in such systems the concept of influencing economic outcomes through indirect policy mechanisms was alien to decision makers.

Identifying the macroeconomic concepts of transition presents a difficult task. Where does one start? By definition, the macroeconomy is a circular flow in which, during transition, all of the components and associated policies must be created. Thus, early on, when prices are released, serious inflation creates the need for guidance through monetary and fiscal mechanisms that do not exist. While microeconomic arguments suggest that prices should be released, the macroeconomic economy is not ready. What should be done?

During the early stages, the state's role is less than clear. However, the demands for government services, for example safety net requirements, seldom shrink. Moreover, the economy is only slowly emerging from a scenario in which most, if not all, work for the state. While demands are sustained, revenues shrink quickly as the economy collapses, and, in the absence of a tax system, the state no longer has direct access to enterprise revenues.

Under these circumstances, the state must seek alternative sources of revenues, but these are not available. Financial markets are in their infancy, foreign support may or may not be available, and a central bank is yet to be established. Thus, deficits seem inevitable, and inflation is fueled by the printing of money to monetize the government deficits.

While the state's role is critical, a major early step is the creation of a central bank and an appropriate commercial banking structure. The specifics of the banking system in the Russian case will be examined in detail in the next chapter. While both the appropriate organizational arrangements and infrastructure must be created, the economy must gradually move from the administrative command model to a model based upon market relationships. Enterprises must be shifted to hard budget constraints, and the financing of enterprise activity must be through emerging financial markets based upon interest rates and commercial relations.

International Trade During Transition

International trade policies during transition are defined and difficult.[10] First, as we emphasized earlier in this book, the arrangements and policies of foreign trade in the administrative command economy were very different from those typically found in market economies. That necessitates major changes. Second, even under administrative command arrangements, the role of foreign trade differed significantly among the planned socialist economic systems. So, we would expect transition arrangements and policies to differ.

Two major components are associated with foreign trade and transition. First, the old arrangements must be abolished, and the necessary policies and infrastructure must be created for the creation and expansion of foreign trade on a decentralized basis. As we will see when we examine the Russian case in detail, this is a difficult task for an economy under central controls for fifty years. Second, it is necessary to create the financial underpinnings required to conduct foreign trade, most notably, the conditions requisite for establishing a convertible currency. While the initial emphasis in transition economies seemed to be on the need for external assistance, events proved·that domestic reform must take place to establish a competitive position in the global economy.

For economic systems that have been substantially isolated from real-world market forces, establishing an appropriate valuation of currency is a complex task. While initial valuation is difficult, it is then necessary to establish a regime to sustain the exchange rate, implying appropriate support for intervention that is inevitably necessary.

TRANSITION AND THE SAFETY NET

Throughout this book we have emphasized the fundamental differences between the administrative command economy and the market economy. One of the most important differences was a fundamental attempt to change the social contract, reflecting one of the fundamental differences between planned socialism and market capitalism. Indeed, throughout the Soviet era, there was a continuing attempt to reduce the importance of purchased social services, which were instead provided as part of the social wage.

As the economy of the Soviet Union collapsed, it is important to bear in mind that however we may judge the "benefits package" that was available—that is, on grounds of equity and efficiency—it was nevertheless fundamental to the system. Indeed, whether it pertained to child care, grade school education, higher education, medical care, or retirement benefits, the state was the major, if not the only, actor. How would these requirements be handled during transition? Although there is no simple answer to this question, a variety of issues must be addressed.[11]

First, it is quite clear that during transition the social contract will change fundamentally and the package of benefits will shrink. This shrinkage reflects both difficulties with the package believed to exist under the old order and the inability of the new order to provide the necessary financial underpinning.

Second, it is also evident that the nature of the demands on the system will change. For example, while retirement, medical, and related requirements remain, it is also evident that a new set of demands—specifically unemployment and related benefits—will emerge. How will these demands be met under transition?

During transition it is essential to focus on three basic aspects of the safety net. First, needs must be identified. For example, requirements of the aging population must be established, along with required medical services. Second, it is essential to develop the infrastructure necessary to deliver services. To some degree, existing institutions may serve, though the decision-making arrangements of the old era must be changed to focus on efficiency. Third, and most difficult, new sources of funding must be established. Meeting these conditions is difficult, especially in a system where the basic requirements for good health—for example a clean environment, healthy foods and dietary habits, and a lifestyle conducive to good health—may be absent.

SUMMARY

In this chapter we have summarized the basic issues in the process of transition, that is, the replacement of the administrative command economy with market arrangements. It is important to appreciate the fact that transition has been fundamentally "learning by doing" since, prior to the present transition era, there was little theory and even less experience. No literature on transition existed prior to the collapse of the planned socialist economic systems in the late 1980s.

Our examination of transition has proceeded in two dimensions. First, there are important general issues of transition strategy, specifically the issues of the speed and the sequencing of transition. While simplistic early alternatives such as the "big bang" and "gradualism" emerged, the contemporary analysis sees these issues as much more complex, differing from one case to another.

Analysis of the transition usually incorporates four major components. First, the microeconomics of transition includes the creation of markets through the process of privatization. In the case of transition economies, mass privatization involves the development of appropriate legislation, preparation of properties, sale, and finally restructuring. While changes in ownership have generally been rapid, the process of restructuring, or fundamental changes in decision-making arrangements in enterprises, has been much slower.

Second, the macroeconomics of transition involves the creation of the institutions and policies of the macroeconomy—financial institutions (first and foremost banking institutions and capital markets) and a state budgetary structure that can perform the usual functions of providing public goods and implementing monetary and fiscal policies.

Third, transition involves creating new arrangements for the conduct of international trade. In addition to developing an appropriate infrastructure for the decentralized conduct of trade through market mechanisms, the establishment of a convertible currency is fundamental.

Finally, transition economies must develop new institutions and polices to support the safety net. During the planned socialist era, participants became accustomed to "free" services such as medical care, education, and pensions. Although the transition era introduces new demands, for example unemployment benefits, the basic issue is the creation of new market arrangements to provide access to the basic needs of the population.

Terms and Concepts

transition   The replacement of one economic system by another; in the 1990s, the replacement of the centrally planned socialist economic system (the administrative command economy) by the market economy.

microeconomics of transition   The creation of markets and market institutions and the forces of supply and demand through the privatization of formerly state-owned assets.

macroeconomics of transition   The creation of the macroeconomic institutions of a market economy, especially banking and financial institutions and appropriate new roles for the state through the state budget and related monetary and fiscal policies.

international trade   The creation of market-type institutions and policies for the exercise of international trade, including appropriate financial mechanisms for a convertible currency.

safety net   The policies pertaining to social support services, such as pension systems, medical support arrangements, unemployment insurance, etc.

initial conditions   Refers to the state of the economy; for example, microeconomic features such as industrial structure, and macroeconomic conditions such as the presence or absence of inflationary pressures at the beginning of the transition process.

transition policies   The policy measures developed to guide the transition process.

sequencing   The timing of transition policies, especially their implementation and coordination through time.

evolutionary economics   A body of economic thought that views changes in an economic system as taking place in a path-dependent, sequential, and iterative fashion incapable of being implemented in a direct and non-time-dependent manner.

restructuring   An amalgam of changes that take place after and in response to privatization in an enterprise; generally, changes in the decision-making procedures leading to enterprise restructuring; changes in input and output mixes and the like.

privatization   Shifting enterprise ownership from public to private hands.

restitution   The return of property rights to former claimants; in the case of planned socialist systems, the return of property rights to those from whom they were (usually) confiscated at the time of the socialist takeover.

small scale privatization   The privatization of small businesses, often in sectors such as retail trade, consumer services, and the like.

mass privatization   The pattern of general privatization that has taken place in the former Soviet Union and Eastern Europe, as opposed to selective privatization in market economies often pursued to achieve efficiency gains.

insider privatization   Privatization in which the equity rights are distributed to those involved directly in the organization—for example the workers, employees, and managers of an existing industrial enterprise.

valuation   The process of establishing a value and hence a price for an enterprise or other organization that is to be privatized through public sale; in a market economy, typically a present value calculation, an accounting calculation, or a calculation based upon outstanding valuation of share capital.

voucher privatization   Privatization that takes place through the issuance of vouchers with a given face value, which can then be exchanged for shares of the newly corporatized enterprise or organization.

Selected Bibliography

Transition: General Issues

Blanchard, O. J., K. A. Froot, and J. D. Sachs, eds. *The Transition in Eastern Europe* vols. 1 & 2 (Chicago: University of Chicago Press, 1994).

Clague, C., and G. C. Rausser, eds. *The Emergence of Market Economies in Eastern Europe* (Cambridge, MA: Blackwell Publishers, 1992).

Dallago, B., and L. Mittone. *Economic Institutions, Markets and Competition* (Cheltenham: Edward Elgar, 1996).

Dewatripont, M., and G. Roland. "Transition as a Process of Large-Scale Institutional Change," *Economics of Transition* vol. 4, no. 1 (1996), 1–30.

Hausner, J., B. Jessop, and K. Nielsen. *Strategic Choice and Path-Dependency in Post-Socialism* (Cheltenham: Edward Elgar, 1995).

Islam, S., and M. Mandelbaum, eds. *Making Markets: Economic Transformation in Eastern Europe and the Post-Soviet States* (New York: Council on Foreign Relations, 1993).

Lazear, E. P., ed. *Economic Transition in Eastern Europe and Russia* (Stanford: Hoover Institution Press, 1995).

"Symposium on Economic Transition in the Soviet Union and Eastern Europe," *Journal of Economic Perspectives* vol. 5, no. 4 (Fall 1991).

Winiecki, J. *Post-Soviet-Type Economies in Transition* (Brookfield, VT: Avebury, 1993).

Microeconomic Issues: Privatization

General References

Allen, J. W., et al. *The Private Sector in State Service Delivery: Examples of Innovative Practices* (Washington, DC: Urban Institute, 1989).

Aoki, M., and H. Kim. *Corporate Governance in Transitional Economies* (Washington, DC: World Bank, 1995).

Baumol, W. J. "On the Perils of Privatization," *Eastern Economic Journal* vol. 19 (Fall 1993), 419–40.

Bos, D. *Privatization: A Theoretical Treatment* (Cambridge, MA: Blackwell, 1992).

Boycko, M., A. Shleifer and R. W. Vishny, "A Theory of Privatisation, "*Economic Journal* vol. 106 (March 1996), 309–19.

Bradford, R. "Privatization of Natural Monopoly Public Enterprises: The Regulation Issue" *Review of Industrial Organization* vol. 10, no. 3 (June 1995), 249–67.

Donahue, J. D. *The Privatization Decision* (New York: Basic Books, 1989).

Estrin, S., and R. Stone. "A Taxonomy of Mass Privatization," *Transition* vol. 7, no. 11–12 (November-December 1996).

Goodman, J. B., and G. W. Loveman. "Does Privatization Serve the Public Interest?" *Harvard Business Review* (November-December 1992), 26–38.

Jones, L. P., T. Tandon, and I. Vogelsgang. *Selling Public Enterprises: A Cost-Benefit Methodology* (Cambridge, MA: MIT Press, 1990).

Kay, J. A., and D. J. Thompson, "Privatization: A Policy in Search of a Rationale," *Economic Journal* vol. 96 (March 1986), 18–32.

McLinden, M. *Privatization and Capital Market Development: Strategies to Promote Economic Growth* (Westport, CT: Praeger, 1996).

Morgan, P., ed. *Privatization and the Welfare State: Implications for Consensus and the Welfare* (Brookfield, VT: Aldershot, 1995).

Nellis, J. "So Far So Good? A Privatization Update," *Transition* vol. 7, nos. 11–12 (November-December 1996).

OECD. *Methods of Privatising Large Enterprises* (Paris: OECD, 1993).

———— . *Valuation and Privatisation* (Paris: OECD, 1993).

Pack, J. R. "Privatization of Public-Sector Services in Theory and Practice," *Journal of Policy Analysis and Management* vol. 6 (1987), 523–40.

Pannier, D., ed. *Corporate Governance of Public Enterprises in Transitional Economies* (Washington, DC: World Bank, 1996).

Pendleton, A., and J. Winterton, eds. *Public Enterprise in Transition* (London and New York: Routledge, 1993).

Ramanad Lam, V. V., ed. *Privatization and Equity* (New York: Routledge, 1995).

Savas, E. S. *Privatization: The Key to Better Government* (Chatam, NJ: Chatam House, 1987).

Seibert, H., ed. *Privatization: A Symposium in Honor of Herbert Giersch* (Tubingen: Institut fur Weltwirtschaft an der Universitat Kiel, 1992).

Shirley, M., and J. Nellis. *Public Enterprise Reform: The Lessons of Experience* (Washington, DC: World Bank, 1991).

Suleiman, E. E., and J. Waterbury, *The Political Economy of Public Sector Reform and Privatization* (Boulder, CO: Westview Press, 1990).

Vickers, J., and G. Yarrow. *Privatization: An Economic Analysis* (Cambridge, MA: MIT Press, 1988).

Wolf, Jr., C. *Markets or Governments: Choosing Between Imperfect Alternatives* (Cambridge, MA: MIT Press, 1988).

Regional Literature

Bos, D. "Privatization in Europe: A Comparison of Approaches," *Oxford Review of Economic Policy* vol. 9, no. 1 (1993), 95–110.

Boycko, M., A. Schleifer, and R. Vishny. *Privatizing Russia* (Cambridge, MA: MIT Press, 1995).

Buck, T., I. Filatotchev, and M. Wright. "Employee Buyouts and the Transformation of Russian Industry," *Comparative Economic Studies* vol. 36 (Summer 1994), 1–16.

Carlin, W., and C. Mayer. "The Truhandanstalt: Privatization by State and Market," in O. J. Blanchard, K. A. Froot, and J. D. Sachs, *The Transition in Eastern Europe,* vol. 2 (Chicago: University of Chicago Press, 1994), 189–207.

Eliasson, G. "The Micro Frustrations of Privatizing Eastern Europe," working paper (Stockholm: Industrial Institute for Economic and Social Research, 1992).

Ernst, M., M. Alexeev, and P. Marer. *Transforming the Core* (Boulder, CO: Westview Press, 1996).

Estrin, S. "Privatization in Central and Eastern Europe: What Lessons Can Be Learnt for Western Experience," *Annals of Public and Cooperative Economy* vol. 62, no. 2 (April-June 1991), 159–82.

Estrin, S., and X. Richet. "Industrial Restructuring and Microeconomic Adjustment in Poland: A Cross Sectoral Approach," *Comparative Economic Studies,* vol. 35, no. 4 (Winter 1993), 1–19.

Frydman, R., and A. Rapaczynski, eds. *Privatization in Eastern Europe: Is the State Withering Away?* (New York: Oxford University Press, 1994).

Hachette, D., and R. Luders, *Privatization in Chile* (San Francisco: ICS Press, 1993).

Liberman, I. W., et al., eds. *Mass Privatization in Central and Eastern Europe and the Former Soviet Union: A Comparative Analysis* (Washington, DC: World Bank, 1995).

Leeds, E. M. "Voucher Privatization in Czechoslovakia," *Comparative Economic Studies* vol. 35, no. 3 (Fall 1993), 19–38.

Nelson, L. D., and I. Y. Kuzes. "Evaluating the Russian Voucher Privatization Program," *Comparative Economic Studies* vol. 36 (Spring 1994), 55–68.

Richardson, J., ed. *Privatisation and Deregulation in Canada and Britain* (Brookfield, VT: Aldershot, 1990).

Slider, D. "Privatization in Russia's Regions," *Post Soviet Affairs* vol. 10, no. 4 (October-December 1994), 367–96.

Wissel, R. H. "Privatization in the United States" *Business Economics* vol. 30, no. 4 (October 1995), 45–50.

Less Developed Countries

Cook, P., and C. Kirkpatrick, eds. *Privatisation in Less Developed Countries* (New York: St. Martins Press, 1988).

Hanke, S. H., ed. *Privatization and Development* (San Francisco: Institute for Contemporary Studies, 1987).

Ott, A. F., and K. Hartley, eds. *Privatization and Economic Efficiency: A Comparative Analysis of Developed and Developing Countries* (Brookfield, VT: Elgar, 1991).

Prager, J. "Is Privatization a Panacea for LDC's? Market Failure Versus Public Sector Failure," *Journal of Developing Areas* vol. 26 (April 1992), 301–22.

Roth, G. *The Private Provision of Public Services in Developing Countries* (Oxford: Oxford University Press, 1987).

The Results of Privatization

Bishop, M., J. Kay, and C. Mayer, eds. *Privatization and Economic Performance* (New York: Oxford University Press, 1994).

Galal, A., L. Jones, P. Tandon, and I. Vogelsgang, *Welfare Consequences of Selling Public Enterprises: An Empirical Analysis* (New York: Oxford University Press, 1994).

Linz, S. J. "Russian Firms in Transition: Champions, Challengers, and Chaff." *Comparative Economic Studies* (forthcoming).

Kikeri, S., J. Nellis, and M. Shirley. *Privatization: The Lessons of Experience* (Washington, DC: World Bank, 1992),

Megginson, W. C., R. C. Nash, and M. van Randenborgh. "The Financial and Operating Performance of Newly Privatized Firms: An International Empirical Analysis," *Journal of Finance* vol. 49 (June 1994), 403–52.

OECD. *Mass Privatisation: An Initial Assessment* (Paris: OECD, 1995).

Macroeconomic Issues

Bird, R., et al. *Decentralization of the Socialist State: Intergovernmental Finance in Transition Economies* (Aldershot, England: Avebury, 1996).

Hanke, S. H., L. Jonung, and K. Shuler. *Russian Currency and Finance: A Currency Board Approach to Reform* (New York: Routledge, 1993).

Herr, H., ed. *Macroeconomic Problems of Transformation: Stabilization Policies and Restructuring* (Aldershot, England: Edward Elgar, 1994).

McKinnon, R. I. "Financial Control in the Transition from Classical Socialism to a Market Economy," *Journal of Economic Perspectives* vol. 5 (Fall 1991), 107–22.

——— . *The Order of Economic Liberalization: Financial Control in the Transition to a Market Economy* (Baltimore: Johns Hopkins Press, 1991).

Mitchell, J. "Managerial Discipline, Productivity, and Bankruptcy in Capitalist and Socialist Economies," *Comparative Economic Studies* vol. 32 (Fall 1990), 93–137. OECD. *Transformation of the Banking System: Portfolio Restructuring, Privatisation, and the Payment System* (Paris: OECD, 1993).

World Bank. *Russia: The Banking System During Transition* (Washington, DC: World Bank, 1993).

International Trade

Artisien-Maksimento, P., and Y. Adjubei, eds. *Foreign Investment in Russia and Other Successor States* (New York: St. Martins Press, 1996).

OECD. *Barriers to Trade with the Economies in Transition* (Paris: OECD, 1994).

——— . *Trade Policy and the Transition Process* (Paris: OECD, 1996).

Wang, Z. K. "Integrating Transition Economies Into the Global Economy." *Finance and Development* vol. 33, no. 3 (September 1996), 21–23.

The Safety Net

Barr, N. "People in Transition: Reforming Education and Health Care," *Finance and Development* vol. 33, no. 3 (September 1996), 24–27.

————. ed. *Labor Markets and Social Policy in Central and Eastern Europe: The Transition and Beyond* (New York: Oxford University Press, 1996).

Chu, K., and S. Gupta. "Protecting the Poor: Social Safety Nets During Transition," *Finance and Development* vol. 30 (June 1993), 24–27.

Davis, C. M. "The Health Sector in the Soviet Union and Russian Economies: From Reform to Fragmentation to Transition," in U. S. Congress, Joint Economic Committee, *The Former Soviet Union in Transition* vol. 2 (Washington, DC: U.S. Government Printing Office, 1993), 852–72.

Kopits, G. "Reforming Social Security Systems," *Finance and Development* vol. 30, no. 2 (June 1993), 21–23.

Millar, J. R., and S. L. Wolchik, eds. *The Social Legacy of Communism* (New York: Cambridge University Press, 1994).

OECD. *The Changing Social Benefits in Russian Enterprises* (Paris: OECD, 1996).

————. *Unemployment in Transition Economies: Transient or Persistent?* (Paris: OECD, 1994).

Schieber, G. "International Report: Health Care Financing Reform in Russia and Ukraine," *Health Affairs,* supplement, (1993), 294–99.

World Bank. *Social Indicators of Development* (Washington, DC: World Bank, 1996).

Notes ───────────────────────────

1. See for example H. W. Hoen, "Shock versus Gradualism" in "Central Europe Reconsidered," *Comparative Economic Studies* vol. 38, no. 1 (Spring 1996); P. Murrell, "Evolutionary and Radical Approaches to Economic Reform," *Economics of Planning* vol. 25, no. 1 (1992); J. Brada, "The Transformation from Communism to Capitalism: How Far? How Fast?" *Post-Soviet Affairs* vol. 9, no. 2 (1993); P. Hare and T. Revesz, "Hungary's Transition to the Market: The Case Against a Big-Bang," *Economic Policy* vol. 14 (1992); H. W. Hoen, "Theoretically Underpinning Transition to the Market: An Austrian View," *Economic Systems* vol. 19, no. 1 (1995); J. van Brabant, "Lessons from the Wholesale Transformations in the East," *Comparative Economic Studies* vol. 35, no. 4 (1993); H. Van Ees and H. Garretsen, "The Theoretical Foundations of the Reforms in Eastern Europe: Big Bang versus Gradualism and the Limitations of Neo-Classical Theory," *Economic Systems* vol. 18, no. 1 (1994).
2. In addition to sources cited in note 1, see also S. Fischer and A. Gelb, "The Process of Socialist Economic Transformation," *Journal of Economic Perspectives* vol. 5, no. 4 (Fall 1991); M. Ernst, M. Alexeev, and P. Marer, *Transforming the Core* (Boulder, CO: Westview Press, 1996), ch. 1–2; World Bank, *World Development Report 1996* (Washington, DC: World Bank, 1996); N. Funke, "Timing and Sequencing of Reforms: Competing Views and the Role of Credibility," *Kyklos,* 3 (1993).
3. P. Murrell and Y. Wang, "When Privatization Should Be Delayed: The Effects of Communist Legacies on Organizational and Institutional Reforms," *Journal of Comparative Economics* vol. 17 (1993).
4. There is a large literature on this subject. See for example P. Murrell, "Evolution in Economics and in the Economic Reform of the Centrally Planned Economies," in C.

Clague and G. C. Rausser, eds., *The Emergence of Market Economies in Eastern Europe* (Cambridge, MA: Blackwell, 1992), 35–53; P. Murrell and M. Olson, "The Devolution of Centrally Planned Economies," *Journal of Comparative Economics* vol. 15 (1991).

5. S. J. Linz, "Russian Firms in Transition: Champions, Challengers and Chaff," typescript, Michigan State University, 1996; see also A. S. Bim, D. C. Jones, and T. E. Weisskopf, "Hybrid Forms of Enterprise Organization in the Former USSR and the Russian Federation," *Comparative Economic Studies* vol. 35, no. 1 (Spring 1993); T. Buck, I. Filatotchev and Y. van Frausum, "The Process and Impact of Privatization in Russia and Ukraine," *Comparative Economic Studies* vol. 38, nos. 2/3 (Summer-Fall 1996); T. Buck, I. Filatotchev and M. Wright, "Employee Buy-Outs and the Transformation of Russian Industry," *Comparative Economic Studies* vol. 36 (1994); G. Krueger, "Transition Strategies of Former State-Owned Enterprises in Russia," *Comparative Economic Studies* vol. 37, no. 4 (Winter 1995).

6. There is a large and growing literature on privatization world wide. Sources cited at the end of this chapter isolate early studies on strategies in socialist and non-socialist cases, initial outcomes, and longer-term progress on restructuring.

7. OECD, *Valuation and Privatization* (Paris: OECD, 1993).

8. L. D. Nelson and I. Y. Kuzes, "Evaluating the Russian Voucher Privatization Program," *Comparative Economic Studies* vol. 36 (Spring 1994).

9. For an early discussion, see R. McKinnon, "Financial Control in the Transition From Classical Socialism to a Market Economy," *Journal of Economic Perspectives* vol. 5, no. 4 (Fall 1991); O. J. Blanchard, K. A. Froot, and J. D. Sachs, eds., *The Transition in Eastern Europe* vols. 1–2 (Chicago: University of Chicago Press, 1994); H. Herr, ed., *Macroeconomic Problems of Transformation: Stabilization Policies and Restructuring* (Aldershot, England: Elgar, 1994); E. P. Lazear, ed., *Economic Transition in Eastern Europe and Russia* (Stanford, CA: Hoover Institution, 1995).

10. See for example OECD, *Trade Policy and the Transition Process* (Paris: OECD, 1996); OECD, *Barriers to Trade With the Economies in Transition* (Paris: OECD, 1994); A. Smith, *Russia and the World Economy: Problems of Integration* (New York: Routledge, 1993); A. Hillman, "The Transition from the CMEA System of International Trade," in M. Keren and G. Ofer, eds., *Trials of Transition: Economic Reform in the Former Communist Bloc* (Boulder, CO: Westview Press, 1994); for an analysis of initial problems of trade liberalization in Russia, see D. Tarr, "The Terms of Trade Effect of Moving to World Prices on Countries of the Former Soviet Union," *Journal of Comparative Economics* vol. 18, no. 1 (February 1994).

11. N. Barr, "People in Transition: Reforming Education and Health Care," *Finance and Development* vol. 33, no. 3 (September 1996); G. Kopits, "Reforming Social Security Systems," *Finance and Development* vol. 30, no. 2 (June 1993); J. R. Millar, and S. L. Wolchik, eds., *The Social Legacy of Communism* (New York: Cambridge University Press, 1994); G. Schieber, "International Report: Health Care Financing Reform in Russia and Ukraine," *Health Affairs,* Supplement, (1993); OECD, *The Changing Social Benefits in Russian Enterprises* (Paris: OECD, 1996); C. M. Davis, "The Health Sector in the Soviet Union and Russian Economies: From Reform to Fragmentation to Transition," in U.S. Congress, Joint Economic Committee, *The Former Soviet Union in Transition* vol. 2 (Washington, DC: U.S. Government Printing Office, 1993); V. A. Pestoff, ed., *Reforming Social Services in Eastern Europe—An Eleven Nation Overview* (Cracow: Cracow Academy of Economics and Friedrich Ebert Stiftung, 1995); L. T. Orlowski, "Social Safety Nets in Central Europe: Preparation for Accession to the European Union?" *Comparative Economic Studies* vol. 37, no. 2 (Summer 1995).

CHAPTER 14

Creating the Institutions of a Russian Market Economy

Soviet leaders created the institutions of an administrative command economy in the 1930s. In the 1990s, Russia was faced with a quite different task—the creation of institutions for a market economy. The Soviet administrative command economy was not formed overnight. Likewise, a market economy cannot be established overnight from the ashes of the disintegrated command economy.

There are many different kinds of economic systems in the world today. All are different for historical, geographical, and cultural reasons. The nature of different systems depends upon when a particular economy began its economic development and the initial conditions from which it started. Russia's initial conditions have already been explained. In the Soviet period, resources were allocated by administrative orders and commands; the Communist Party determined economic priorities and monitored plan fulfillment. Balances were attempted by administrative methods rather than by equilibrium prices. All property was owned by the state. The legal system was designed to suit the needs of an administrative command economy. Administrative decrees served in place of voluntary contracts between buyers and sellers. Money and credit played a secondary role to physical allocation decisions. There were no financial markets and no markets for buying and selling property.

When Russia decided in late 1991 to embark upon transition, it implicitly made the decision that it had to create a new institutional framework suited for a market economy. There were few or no guideposts for creating institutions for a transition economy like Russia. Insofar as Russia's initial "Soviet" conditions were unique, the format for creating Russia's new institutions could not be extracted from a cookbook or set of established rules. Markets in the West evolved over centuries, not years.

In the Soviet administrative command economy, the state owned virtually all property—for example equipment, structures, inventories, and automobiles. As participants in the system would say, "Property is owned by everyone and hence by no one." It would be difficult to conceive of a market economy that did not allow and encourage private ownership fundamental to the rational allocation of resources; therefore, a key task of the Russian transition was to create a legal framework for private ownership, that is, to create private property rights. Once the right to private property had been created, it would then be necessary to distribute the existing property that society decided to place in private hands among its members, to go through the process of privatization. Privatization would be only one task of transition. Markets had to be created; laws had to be passed; new taxation and fiscal systems had to be put in place.[1]

Transition from Soviet to Russian Government[2]

Chapter 6 dealt with the governmental structure of the Soviet administrative economy. The Soviet economy was administered by the Communist Party of the USSR and by a state apparatus. Although there was a nominally elected government (the Supreme Soviet), the actual affairs of state were managed by the Party, at the top of which was the Politburo. The USSR Council of Ministers managed the state bureaucracy of ministries and state committees.

The USSR consisted of fifteen republics. The Russian Federation was the largest Soviet republic, accounting for over 60 percent of Soviet GDP and over half of the Soviet population. Russians also dominated the Soviet military, the Communist Party, and the KGB. In the late 1980s, the USSR began to weaken, caused partly by the republics' growing demands for independence and by Gorbachev's perestroika reforms, which undermined the communist system. In August 1991, anti-reform hardliners attempted a military coup in protest against "radical" reform and a weakening of the Communist Party. The coup's failure marked the downfall of communist power. The republics declared independence, and the Communist Party was suspended. By the end of 1991, the Soviet Union was disbanded.

Political Events

With the collapse of the Soviet Union, the politically unstable Russian Federation became an independent country. Boris Yeltsin had been elected President of Russia in June 1991, prior to the coup, in the first free presidential election in Russia. No longer fettered by Soviet politics, the Yeltsin government launched strong economic reforms and macroeconomic stabilization policies.[3] The new Russian Constitution approved by referendum in December 1993 replaced the "Brezhnev" Constitution adopted in 1978, even though between 1986 and 1991 Gorbachev had amended it more than one hundred times. Radical reform policies were opposed by conservatives, represented by the Congress of People's Deputies and the Supreme Soviet, the majority of which represented the old Soviet nomenklatura. Much of Russia's political instability arose from the dispute over whether the president of Russia or the legislature held ultimate constitutional power. In December 1992, the Russian legislature succeeded in forcing out Egor Gaidar, the acting prime minister and architect of reform, and replaced him with the more conservative Viktor Chernomyrdin. In April 1993, President Yeltsin held a referendum to confirm the electorate's confidence in his government. The results showed strong support for Mr. Yeltsin and his reforms.

The open conflict between the president and the legislature continued. In September 1993, President Yeltsin dissolved the Congress of People's Deputies and the Supreme Soviet. Yeltsin's opponents refused to comply and, on October 3, 1993, led an armed insurrection, which failed after Yeltsin ordered the military to shell the parliament building in Moscow.

After the failed legislative coup, Russia held elections for the newly created State Duma, which resulted in surprising gains for Communist deputies and for the right wing party, led by nationalist Vladimir Zhirinovsky. Presidential elections were held in June 1996. After a close election in which no party won a plurality, Boris Yeltsin managed a rather comfortable run-off victory against the Communist Party candidate, Gennady Zyuganov.[4]

The Presidency

The "Yeltsin" Constitution approved in December of 1993 granted considerable powers to the Russian president, strengthening the position significantly at the expense of the parliament. The Russian president is elected by direct universal suffrage for a four-year term but cannot serve more than two terms consecutively. (Yeltsin was elected in June 1991 but was allowed to carry out his first term, which ended in June 1996, prior to a second term in July of 1996.) The president appoints the prime minister and the cabinet, as well as the chairman of the National Bank and senior figures in the judiciary. The Duma must ratify these appointments, but it if rejects the president's choice three times, the president can dissolve the Duma and call new elections. The president can also rule by decree.

The Legislature

The 1993 Russian constitution changed the legislature to create a **Federation Council** (with two representatives from each of Russia's 89 regional units, including ethnic republics and other regional units) and a more powerful **State Duma** (with 450 representatives). These two groups form the upper and lower houses respectively of the bicameral Federal Assembly of the Russian Federation. The first Federal Assembly met for two years (until the elections of December 1995) and subsequently will meet for four-year periods. The Federal Council represents the interests of Russia's 89 republics and regions within the legislature. Deputies in the Council are predominantly high-ranking officials from the regions, including local prime ministers and major industrialists. The Federation Council provides some checks to the president's power through its jurisdiction over relations between Moscow and the regions. It must approve major economic and military policies and has jurisdiction over the army.

The State Duma is also protected from presidential abuse. During the first year following elections, the president cannot dissolve the Duma after a vote of no-confidence, nor can it be dissolved during a state of emergency or if the president is being impeached. Within the State Duma, half of the deputies are elected by proportional representation from Party lists, with a 5 percent national threshold required for parliamentary representation. The remaining 225 deputies are elected from single-member constituencies on a "first-past-the-post" system.

Of the 21 political parties who submitted applications to contest the December 1995 elections, only 13 were allowed to participate. The most notable exclusions were the National Salvation Front, Workers' Russia, and Russian Unity, all opponents of Yeltsin. Of the 13 parties running, only eight passed the 5 percent threshold set for the 225 seats elected according to Party lists. Three other parties secured representation through first-past-the-post constituency seats, which were also contested by "independents." Only three of the parties contending in the December 1995 elections (the LDP, the Communists, and the Agrarian Party) were strongly opposed to Yeltsin's reforms.

The Cabinet

The Cabinet of Ministers of the Russian Federation has nine members: the prime minister, two first deputy prime ministers, and six deputy prime ministers. There are 27 ministers, one for each of the 26 ministries and one minister without portfolio. They are charged with managing particular industries, such as fuel and energy, or with running government institutions, such as the Central Bank or Ministry of Finance. Deputy prime ministers are charged with specific tasks, such as economic reform or privatization. A large and growing bureaucracy is associated with the Office of the Russian Presidency. In fact, by some counts the Russian State bureaucracy was larger in 1997 than it was during the Soviet period.

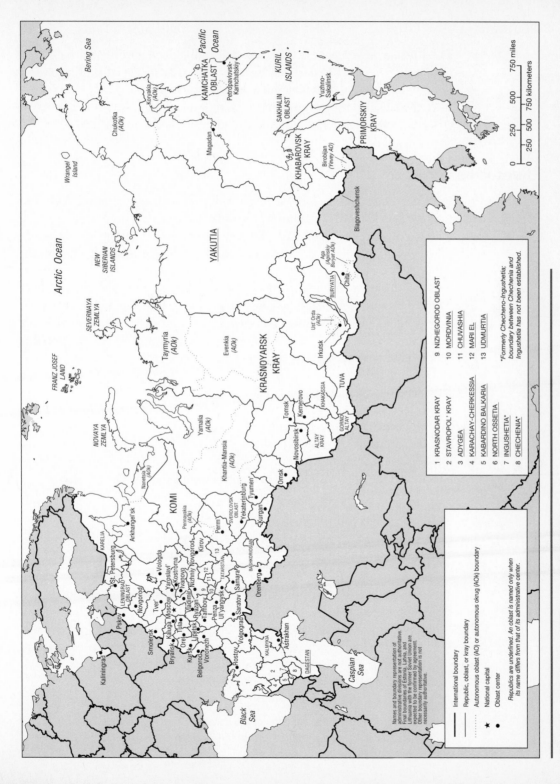

Figure 14.1 Russia's Administrative Divisions

Federalism

The Russian government consists not only of a federal government but also of state and local governments, each having an executive branch headed by a governor or mayor and an elected legislative branch. The distribution of power between the central, regional, and local governments is being worked out, with a number of conflicts over jurisdiction, such as overtaxation, authority, and privatization.

Unresolved Issues

Russian government decision making is still confused, even after the reelection of President Yeltsin in July of 1996, for a number of reasons:

First, confusion persists over the distribution of political authority between the federal, regional, and local governments, as power-sharing arrangements remain unresolved.

Second, transition has divided Russian voters into opposing and warring blocs. The Duma has been dominated by conservative forces (the Communist Party and its allies), while the executive branch is comprised of pro-reform or moderate officials appointed by the president. The same divisions characterize state and local levels, with persistent friction between the legislative and judicial branches. The different views of the legislature and the executive have made it difficult to pass legislation and have required the president to rule by presidential decree.

Third, there has been a gap between legislation and its enforcement and execution. The power of the judicial branch has remained weak.

Fourth, acceptable rules of behavior for Russian officials have not been formulated. Russian officials appear not to be bound by conflict of interest rules, bribery is rampant, and the public is justifiably skeptical about public ethics.

ECONOMIC LAWS: THE CONSTITUTION AND OTHER BASIC LEGISLATION[5]

The 1993 **Russian Constitution** is the highest law of the land, superceding all other laws or regulations in the case of conflicts. The document sets the legal framework for the Russian market economy. Particularly, the Constitution addresses issues of private property, directly addressing the right of citizens to own private property and to use that property to engage freely in economic activity as noted in the following passages:

Article 8
1. In the Russian Federation, the unity of the economic territory, the free exchange of goods, service and financial resources, and freedom of economic activity are guaranteed.

2. In the Russian Federation, private, state, municipal and other forms of property are recognized and protected to the same degree.

Article 9

1. Land and other natural resources can be held as private, state, or municipal property.

Article 35

1. The right of private property is protected by law.

2. Every citizen has the right to own property and to use and distribute and dispose of this property either individually or with other persons.

3. No one can be deprived of their property except according to a decision of the court.

4. The right of inheritance is guaranteed.

Article 36

1. Citizens or groups of citizens have the right to private ownership of land.

2. Private owners of land and natural resources can freely use them except in the case of environmental damage or the disruption of the legal interests of others.

Article 37

1. Labor is free. Everyone has the right to freely use one's own labor and to choose the type of activity and profession.

2. Slavery is prohibited.[6]

These same rights and others relating to the freedom to engage freely in economic activity are also provided by the **Civil Code** *(Grazhdansky Kodeks)* passed on October 21, 1994.[7] The Civil Code defines juridical persons and sets their rights equal to those of private persons, specifies procedures for the registration of companies, for their liquidation, and for bankruptcy. It also establishes the rights and legal forms of partnerships, corporations, and cooperatives. Also spelled out are the legal foundations for corporations (closed or open), how they are formed, charter capital, the emission of shares, and their reorganization or liquidation. The Civil Code establishes the ruble as the sole legal currency and provides the right of citizens to hold foreign currency. The Civil Code establishes procedures for collateral, bank guarantees, protection of legal contracts, and provides for intellectual property rights. A number of more specialized laws address particular industries or particular types of business activities, such as the Law on Underground Resources, banking legislation, securities laws, licensing regulations, taxation laws, laws on foreign investment, and so on.

The general framework legislation of the Russian Federation formally establishes the legal environment for a market economy in Russia. The legislative framework, however, is only part of the process of creating legal institutions. Each separate piece of legislation usually requires a whole series of regulations (or, as the Russians say, "normative acts") that supply the specifics for the general legislation.

In addition to gaining passage of legislation, the major challenge to Russia has been enforcing laws and legal guarantees. A legal system must be established to enforce the law and to insure compliance. Government agencies and officials must obey the law, and, if they do not, they must be brought into compliance. Tax authorities must faithfully execute laws on taxation, and so on. In practice, the problem in Russia has been not the legislation itself but carrying out this legislation. Specifically, Russian citizens, both private and juridical, have lacked access to a strong court system that can enforce compliance and to a government that itself obeys the law.

PRIVATIZATION[8]

The Russian Constitution sets private property on an equal footing with other forms of property. At the start of the Russian transition, virtually all property was in the hands of the state. Methods and procedures, therefore, had to be created to transfer resources designated by the state for private ownership into private hands through the process of privatization.

In October of 1992, the Russian government, under the direction of the **State Property Committee** (*Goskomimushchestvo,* headed by Anatoly Chubias), began Russia's mass privatization program, the largest privatization program ever attempted.[9] In its first stage, called the **voucher privatization** check phase, voucher or privatization checks were distributed to every one of the 148 million Russian men, women, and children. These vouchers could be used to buy shares of the 15,000 medium and large Russian companies that were the first to be privatized. Owners of vouchers could invest their vouchers directly in companies, in one of the many voucher investment funds for diversification and professional management, or could sell them in the secondary market that had developed.

Vouchers could be invested in companies that were placed on the privatization list—companies that had been transferred and incorporated to the state property fund. Local and regional enterprises were transferred to the **Federal Property Fund.** Enterprises judged to be of national significance or of military importance were initially exempted from privatization.

Enterprises that had been transferred into property funds were obligated to transform themselves in 1992 into open joint stock companies, whereafter they could be privatized according to three privatization alternatives. In most cases, employees and managers of enterprises were given the opportunity to acquire ownership shares, often at preferential prices in "closed subscriptions." In some cases, employees had the right to acquire 5–10 percent of shares through an employee shareholding fund that had been accumulated out of past enterprise profits. Medium and large scale open-type companies were required to offer at least 29 percent of their shares to the general public by way of voucher auction, although in many cases this rule was not observed. Voucher privatization was completed in June 1994. Although significant shares of privatized companies had passed into private hands, in most cases the government either maintained majority interest or retained "golden shares," which allowed the government to veto significant majority share-holder action.[10]

The second stage of privatization was governed by the State Privatization Program, "On the Fundamental Provisions of the State Privatization Program for State and Municipal Enterprises in the Russian Federation After July 1, 1994." Under it, the remaining shares of enterprises to be transformed into open joint stock companies were sold through investment tenders, cash auctions, or specialized auctions (tenders) for the sale of shares. An **investment tender** involved the purchase of a defined percentage of shares through sealed bids. The winning investor had to pay a fee to the property fund and then to pay the bid amount of investment directly to the company. A **commercial tender** was one in which the winner was required to fulfill certain conditions (such as develop a particular oil field), with the winning bid being that which most closely satisfied the requirement of the tender and offered the highest price.

Privatization Results

The pace of privatization is shown in Tables 14.1 and 14.2 (pp. 302–03), which show that more than 100,000 enterprises were privatized between October 1992 and July 1994. Between July 1994 and February 1996, another 20,000 enterprises were privatized, signaling a slowing pace of privatization as most of Russia's industrial enterprises were already in private hands.[11] Table 14.2 shows that, although about 20 percent of the shares of companies were offered during the voucher auction, typically about half of those shares were actually redeemed.

By late 1994 or early 1995, the ownership structure of the Russian economy had shifted from government to "nongovernment" ownership. Beginning with virtual full-government ownership in 1989, the shares of nongovernment ownership of capital took a huge leap in 1993 to 47.2 percent. By 1995 the figure rose to 65 percent of total capital. The share of private ownership of the housing stock increased from less than 10 percent to about 40 percent by late 1994 (Table 14.3, p. 304). The shares of labor force working in nongovernmental enterprises went from less than 10 percent in 1985 to almost 50 percent by 1995 (Table 14.4, p. 305). Although the Russian privatization process can be criticized, in particular for permitting insiders to grab property, it resulted in a massive change in property rights within a period of approximately two years.

The change in property rights had a substantial effect upon how Russians earned incomes and upon how that income was distributed. Figure 14.2 (p. 306) shows that by 1995, Russian citizens were earning almost half of their income not through wages and salaries but through earnings from entrepreneurial activity—dividends, profits, and other forms of private earnings. This share is distorted by the

Table 14.1

NUMBER OF ENTERPRISES PRIVATIZED BY ACTIVITY

	1/1/93	1/1/94	7/1/94	Percent privatized by 7/94
Light industry	776	1,112	1,431	5.2
Food industry	1,558	2,972	3,208	4.2
Construction	2,344	5,253	6,132	11.0
Construction materials	806	1,385	1,474	2.0
Agriculture	1,560	3,938	4,389	3.0
Automobile and repair	1,010	3,220	4,294	3.8
Retail trade	18,803	30,638	33,511	NA
Wholesale trade	573	1,339	1,727	28.8
Public catering	4,487	8,061	9,367	5.4
Consumer services	10,982	17,198	18,457	12.3
Unfinished construction sites	651	1,503	1,776	NA
Other	4,715	12,195	18,030	36.6
Total	48,295	88,814	103,796	NA

Source: International Monetary Fund, *Rossia v tsifrakh 1995,* 131.

way Russian income statistics are gathered, but even allowing for distortions, the change in property rights turned Russia into a nation of entrepreneurs.[12]

Figure 14.3 (p. 307) shows that the shift from state to nonstate property has also resulted in a massive redistribution of income in the direction of greater inequality. Whereas in the Soviet period the distribution of household income was characterized by considerable income equality, by the mid-1990s, the Russian distribution of income had become much more unequal—so much so that the Russian income distribution now resembles that of the United States.

Corporate Control

Corporate control defines who controls an enterprise and who reaps the rewards from its successes. In Western corporations, corporate control is exercised by the board of directors and by the company's management. The Russian privatization program set the stage for a massive battle over corporate control. Formerly, corporate control was exercised by ministry officials, planning committee officials, and state enterprise managers. With the announcement of the voucher program, corporate control over Russian enterprises became an open question.

At the start of the privatization program, a number of vested interests wished to either retain or acquire corporate control over potentially profitable enterprises in line to be privatized. These vested interests included the current state managers and

Table 14.2

VOUCHER AUCTIONS AS OF JUNE 24, 1994

Sector	Number of companies	Average charter capital (million rubles)	Average block of shares (%)	Percent of total shares redeemed
Machinery and equipment	1,661	69	20.8	11.4
Metallurgy	382	273	22.1	11.1
Chemicals	1,281	72	20.0	10.5
Oil and gas exploration	22	3,945	15.5	9.1
Oil refining	58	1,575	10.3	8.9
Electricity	65	1,807	12.1	8.1
Postal service and communications	49	129	21.8	5.8
Transportation machinery building	163	316	29.2	5.0
Food industry	899	21	21.8	4.7
Construction	2,041	17	22.3	3.2
Timber	841	27	22.1	3.0

Source: *Kommersant Weekly* no. 25 (1994).

their staffs, ministry officials who had been responsible for the state enterprise, the workers of the enterprise, local and regional officials, local and regional residents, and the general public.[13]

In order to execute the difficult process of privatization in a politically charged climate (where privatization officials could be accused of giving away companies too cheaply or could be charged with corruption), it would not be possible to carry out privatization without the consent and approval of strong vested interests. As a result, one can understand the course of Russian privatization, which gave existing vested interests preferential treatment in the acquisition of corporate control. In the end, insiders gained control of 74 percent of privatized enterprises. (Of the remaining enterprises, 24 percent were controlled by minority insider shares and 2 percent were restructured.) To quote an analyst of this "control" phase of privatization: "In order to implement the program, government reformers were forced to co-opt the support of people who could push for privatization at a regional and individual company level. The initial privatization phase therefore put the majority of industrial companies into the hands of a relatively narrow group of interests, namely enterprise managers and their close associates."[14]

During the battle for corporate control, insiders were able to control the flow of shares through a variety of means. First, the rules of privatization often gave insiders preferential treatment by setting aside significant shares for management at preferential prices. They were also allowed to purchase blocs of shares through company funds. And they were able to use more sinister methods of control. They protected themselves from outside purchasers by retaining control of shareholder registries, timing stock sales inconveniently, canceling airline flights to the headquarters city, arbitrarily dropping shareholders from registers, and issuing new shares to dilute the holdings of outside shareholders. Perhaps the most significant means of insuring insider control was to effectively eliminate foreign purchasers for the most desired Russian companies. Auctions and tenders were also limited to a few bidders, who often colluded among themselves. Most experts agree that by 1995 the first phase of the battle for corporate control had ended and that existing vested interests had purchased the most profitable companies.

As we emphasized in Chapter 13, privatization pertains initially to formal changes in ownership arrangements, or equity rights. Ultimately, however, the reason for changing these rights is the anticipation that they will be exercised in ways that will change resource allocation. This principle is the essence of restructuring, especially in economic sectors in which there is limited entry/exit action, for example heavy industry. Thus after equity rights have been changed, we expect new coalitions to emerge, changing both organizational arrangements and decision-making arrangements. Do we observe these sorts of changes?

Unfortunately, evidence on restructuring is much more complex than simply examining shareholding arrangements. In the Russian case, however, in spite of employee buyouts as a dominant mechanism for privatization, there is initial evidence that corporate governance can change. There has been a shift in the nature of managerial training and recruitment in favor of individuals with marketing and financial skill, long absent in the old order. Moreover, there has been a trend towards growing transparency for corporate operations (for example a recent decree to require stock registers to be held apart from the corporate entity), and a voice for employees. In the end, privatization will succeed only if corporate governance changes.

Table 14.3

PRIVATIZATION OF RUSSIAN HOUSING (CUMULATIVE TOTALS)

	1989	1990	1991	1992	1993	1994
Percent of privatized housing	0.03	0.13	0.17	8.17	26.17	35.17
Units (millions)	0.01	0.05	0.18	2.8	8.6	11.0

Sources: *Sotsial' naia sfera*, p. 26; DIW, *Die Wirtschlaftslage Russland* Report 5, Parts 1 and 2 (November 1994; December 1995); *Devolvoi Mir* (December 1, 1994); M. Bornstein, "Russia's Mass Privatization Programme," *Communist Economies and Economic Transformation* vol. 6, no. 4 (1994); *Rossia v Tsifrakh* (1995), 135.

FROM ADMINISTRATIVE CONTROL TO ECONOMIC FREEDOM

As noted above, the Constitution of the Russian Federation gives its citizens considerable freedom in the conduct of their economic affairs—freedom of contract, freedom from government intervention, freedom of location. These freedoms are in marked contrast to the Soviet period, where economic actions were directed by a rigid administrative decision process.

Throughout much of the transition, economic decision making has been a mix of private and government actions. Until April of 1995, the Russian Central Bank allocated credits in much the same fashion as under Soviet rule, using dedicated, or "directed," credits for purposes specified by the Ministry of Finance. Freedom to buy and sell raw materials was restricted by continued state controls of prices and by the issuing of licenses, such as licenses for oil exports. The state budget continued to play a strong role in the distribution of subsidies to industrial enterprises and farms. State officials were particularly influential in controlling the allocation of property through the process of privatization.

With the passage of time, more and more economic activities have gained freedom from government control. Most prices are now set by market forces; credits are allocated increasingly through credit markets; the central bank provides credits generally to the banking system and does not allocate credit for designated purposes. These changes have been gradual and scarcely perceptible, but in the long run, they prepare the way for a market economy in Russia. State controls remain in a number of significant areas. For example, the Russian state still dictates the amount of state-owned oil that passes through Russia's congested oil pipeline system.[15]

Table 14.4

DISTRIBUTION OF RUSSIAN LABOR FORCE (TYPE OF ENTERPRISE)

Type of Enterprise	1985	1990	1994
State	91.1	82.6	44.7
Private	8.9	12.5	33.0
Communal	0.0	0.8	0.7
Joint venture	0.0	0.1	0.4
Mixed	0.0	4.0	21.2

Sources: *Sotsial' naia sfera*, p. 26; DIW, *Die Wirtschlaftslage Russland* Report 5, Parts 1 and 2 (November 1994; December 1995); *Devolvoi Mir* (December 1, 1994); M. Bornstein, "Russia's Mass Privatization Programme," *Communist Economies and Economic Transformation* vol. 6, no. 4 (1994); *Rossia v Tsifrakh* (1995), 135.

Figure 14.2   Shares of Personal Income: Russia 1990 to 1995

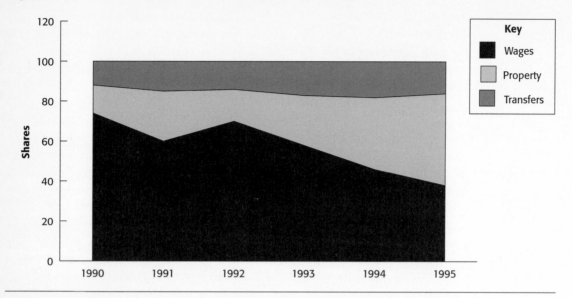

Source: *Sotsial' naia sfera Rossii* (1995), 36.

COMPLEX MARKETS

Although the administrative command economy had a number of markets that operated according to supply and demand (see Chapters 6 and 7), such as labor, second-economy markets, and many retail markets, there were other markets— wholesale products, capital, and land markets—that were entirely administrative in nature.

When an economy converts from administrative command to market allocation, some markets form easily, virtually simultaneously. Examples would be most consumer markets and markets for personal services. They do not require government supervision or extensive rules; they tend to be competitive and easy to enter. Other markets are much more difficult to organize. They require a more complex set of rules developed either by tradition or government regulations. These markets may require extensive supervision and rule-making, and they may be monopolistic. They may require the flow of considerable information, such as in financial markets, and information requirements may need to be regulated.

Subsequent chapters address the issue of how complex markets either were created or are in the process of being created in Russia. Capital markets that could encourage and transmit savings to borrowers through financial intermediaries were entirely lacking in the administrative command model. Markets for foreign exchange were also not present in the Soviet model. Since the private corporation did not exist, securities markets have had to be developed. These markets are more

Figure 14.3 Income Distribution: Russia and the U.S.

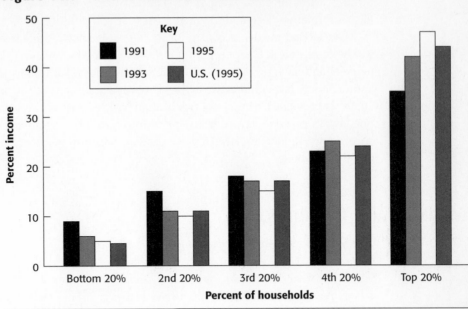

Sources: *Ekonomika Rossii v 1995 g,* 67; *Sotsial'naia sfera Rossii (1995),* 36.

complicated than retail markets or markets for personal services. The creation of capital markets is discussed in Chapter 16, the market for foreign exchange in Chapter 17. In each case, we shall study the arrangements used to bring buyers and sellers together and to disseminate information.

The Soviet economy was characterized by monopoly producers. Planners found it easier to plan an economy that consisted of a small number (or even one) supplier. Accordingly, when the Soviet economy began to transform itself into a market economy, care had to be given to avoid serious monopoly problems. Table 14.5 (p. 309) provides information about the concentration of specific Russian markets as of the mid-1990s.

The Russian state has chosen to deal with monopoly problems—such as a monopoly gas company or a monopoly supplier of submersible pumps—by two means. On the legislative front, the Russian Duma passed an anti-monopoly law, "On Competition and Limitation of Monopoly Activities," on June 14, 1995.[16] This law, which is similar in nature and content to U.S. antitrust laws, establishes the **Federal Anti-Monopoly Commission** to police the antimonopoly law. It applies to the entire territory of the Russian Federation, not simply to interstate commerce. It outlaws abuses of monopoly power by dominant firms, and it prohibits agreements among producers to limit competition. Surprisingly, it also restricts the powers of federal, state, and local governments to engage in acts (such as restrictive licensing or control of entry) that limit competition. It forbids government officials from occupying responsible positions in potentially monopolistic industries or from owning shares in these companies. The law also forbids the deliberate spread of false information designed to create losses for competitors.

The second means of control of monopoly is allowing relatively free trade. As will be discussed in Chapter 17, imports have indeed grown as a share of consumer markets and have provided considerable competition for domestic producers. The antimonopoly law is indicative of the Russian situation as of the second half of the 1990s. It provides for strict control of monopoly actions and is a strong anticorruption law. In practice, however, the provisions have not been obeyed by the Russian government and its officials. However, as the transition progresses, we would expect more compliance.

MARKETS AND CORRUPTION

The Soviet administrative command economy was noted for nonmarket distribution of resources. Loyal workers and Party officials received privileges such as free vacations, chauffeur-driven cars, or better medical care, either as a consequence of their official positions or of their ability to pay bribes to officials who controlled access to these resources.

The collapse of the Soviet Union, the Communist Party, and internal security forces brought with it a collapse of discipline. It also created opportunities for personal enrichment to individuals with connections, former ties with the state bureaucracy, access to Party cash, and outright criminal groups. This enrichment has taken many forms: Government officials have used control over licenses (for example export licenses, licenses to buy government bonds, licenses to export oil) to obtain bribes or hidden income. Threats of violence and actual violence have prevented entry into otherwise competitive businesses. Many bankers have been assassinated for failure to deliver financial information to criminal groups. Profiteers have bought price-controlled products at low prices to be resold at higher prices in other markets.

Mancur Olson has described why the Soviet administrative command economy spawned "Crony Capitalism," **"Mafia Capitalism,"** or "Wild Capitalism" (diki kaptalizm), as the Russians call it. In the administrative command economy, local officials had to form into cohesive groups to survive the constant pressure for plan fulfillment and limited resources. These cohesive groups formed the basis for the later government Mafias, industrial "structures," or outright criminal groups that became powerful during the early years of transition.[17]

Andrei Schliefer and Robert Vishny describe another source of Crony Capitalism in the transition phase.[18] They argue that in the transition there is pressure from commercial structures to preserve price controls, often under the guise of protecting low-income families. Price controls create two types of profit opportunities: One is the opportunity to buy low and sell high for immediate profit. The

Table 14.5

RUSSIAN OLIGOPOLISTIC MARKETS: 1993

	Number of enterprises	Percent of Market
Magnetic tapes	2	100
Road construction grinders	3	100
Steel turbines	3	100
Calcium soda	3	92
Tires for agricultural equipment	4	82

Sources: V. Capelik, "Should Monopoly Be Regulated in Russia?" *Communist Economies and Economic Transformation* vol. 6, no. 1 (1994), 19–32; *Ekonomika i zhizn 6*, (1994), 7; *Osnovnye pokazaleteli raboty promyshlennosti za janviar-juin 1994*, Moscow.

other profit opportunity is that a price-controlled business can restrict its output to the point that buyers are willing to pay a price higher than the controlled price. Since the controlled price must be registered as the official transaction price, the seller collects the difference between the market price and the official price as a bribe or hidden payment. Another advantage of the hidden payment is that it escapes notice and taxation and can be transferred abroad or into cash. (See the explanation in Figure 14.4, p. 310). Schleifer and Vishny, therefore, identify a potentially powerful vested interest against full market reform. Complete market allocation would deprive managers and state officials of under-the-table income.

FISCAL SYSTEM AND FISCAL POLICY[19]

The Russian transition economy must make the transition from a Soviet-style fiscal system to one compatible with a market economy. Chapter 6 showed that the Soviet system relied primarily on indirect sales taxes (turnover taxes), which were differentiated by product, and on profits taxes of enterprises for its revenues. The income tax was a minor source of revenue for the Soviet state.

Taxes

Market economies rely primarily on sales taxes (such as value added taxes) and on payroll taxes and personal income taxes to collect revenues. Profits taxes on enterprises have played a minor role primarily because taxes on enterprise profits will be double-taxed as a part of personal income. Although industrialized market economies collect other types of taxes, they tend to be relatively minor.

The Russian tax system evolved during the 1990s. Figure 14.5 shows that the major sources of revenue continued to be profits taxes and sales taxes. However, the unusual feature of the Russian tax system has been the continued importance of special taxes, like export taxes or transportation taxes, which play relatively minor roles in the West. In the Russian system, payroll taxes and personal income taxes have not been significant. In fact, income taxes as a percentage of personal income in Russia are only 7 percent, which shows the minimal tax burden on personal incomes.[20]

Why has Russia adopted such a tax system as opposed to the greater taxation of personal income and payroll taxes? The main factor has been the state's inability to identify and measure personal taxable income. Record keeping on wages and income has been very poor, and enterprises have found ways to conceal payments to workers and employees. Since payroll taxes are usually levied as a percentage of wages and salaries, concealing income reduces the state's ability to collect.

In effect, the Russian tax system represents a pragmatic approach to collecting sorely needed tax revenues during a period of a declining tax base. State tax collections have been severely damaged by the decline in economic output, by the fact that much economic output is underground and out of the reach of the taxing authority, by the ability of influential enterprises to bargain down their tax obligations, and by the general decline in tax discipline. Taxes on enterprises, which are supposed to be on net income, are often levied on gross sales. The most visible enterprises, especially those that sell to international markets, are often targeted, on

Figure 14.4   Corruption

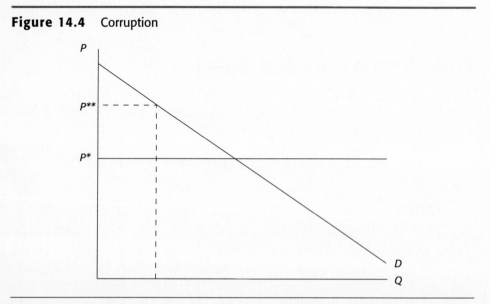

Note: In cases where the state sets a price at *P** with the firm facing a demand curve given by *D*, there will be strong motivation to restrict quantity and to raise price. For example, if the price is raised to *P*** the revenue difference between *P** and *P*** can be kept unofficial, eluding taxation and other reporting requirements.

the grounds that they can afford to pay. As Figure 14.6 (p. 312) shows, the Russian state collects a relatively small share of GDP in taxes as compared to the European industrialized market economies. However, Russian government revenues (as a percent of GDP) are similar to the lower-tax-burden industrialized countries such as the United States and Japan. Russia's very small per capita income dictates a very low level of per capita government revenues (Figure 14.7, p. 313). Figure 14.8 (p. 314) demonstrates that the relative size of the Russian government has declined, as measured both by revenues and expenditures during the transition. The non-government share of the economy has increased as tax collections have fallen faster than GDP.

State tax collections are also plagued by disputes over taxing authority between federal, state, and local governments. These disputes deprive the federal government of tax revenues, which state and local collectors can more readily collect, being closer to the source. However, the distribution of tax collections between the federal, state, and local levels appears to be similar to that in industrialized capitalist countries.

Although Russian taxation is severely criticized for its anti-efficiency nature (sometimes taxing nearly 100 percent of enterprise net profits), it is caught in a vise between the need for tax revenues in a period of declining tax base and massive tax evasion.

Figure 14.5   Structure of Russian Taxes, 1995 (compared to industrialized economies)

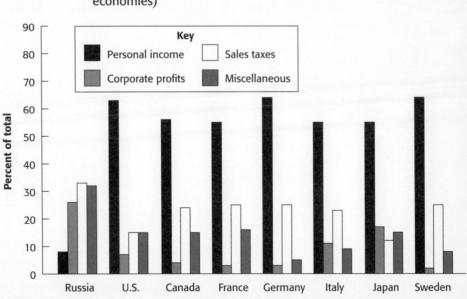

Sources: *Statistical Abstract of the United States 1995*, 860; DIW (March 1996), 22.

Figure 14.6   Government Revenues as percent of GDP (Russia and other countries)

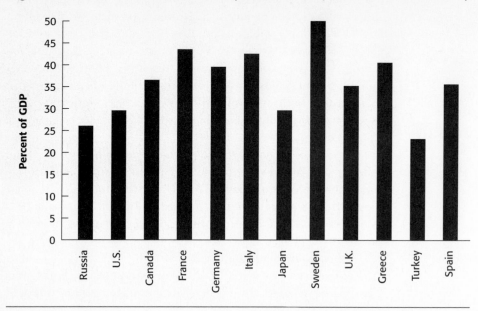

Sources: *Statistical Abstract of the United States 1995; PlanEcon* (selected issues); DIW (March 1996), 22.

Government Expenditures

In the Soviet administrative command economy, the consolidated state budget accounted for a larger share of economic activity than in the industrialized West. One major item that was not present in the West was the financing of most investment directly out of the state budget. In the West, such financing came primarily through private capital markets. The state budget also had to pay for a massive military establishment and for a large scientific and educational establishment. Also, throughout the transition the state budget had to provide massive subsidies to keep loss-making enterprises and whole industries in business.

Because of all these special circumstances, the Russian budget entered the transition period with a declining tax base, deteriorating tax discipline, and heavy obligations to pay military, education, science, and business subsidies. The state budget was subject to strong political pressures because the recipients of state payments represented powerful voting blocs, such as agriculture and the military.

Budget Deficits

Figure 14.8 (p. 314) shows consolidated budget deficits of the Russian state for the period 1992 to 1996. The deficit (as a percent of GDP) can be read as the ver-

Figure 14.7   Government Revenues per Capita (Russia and other countries)

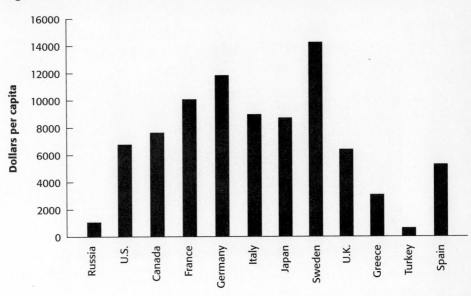

Source: *Statistical Abstract of the United States 1995.* Russian figures from *PlanEcon* and DIW (March 1996), 22.

tical distance between expenditures and revenues for each year. As is evident, the budget deficit has soared in nominal terms and fluctuated as a percentage of GDP, peaking at 10 percent in 1994. The state deficit has been the subject of intense negotiation with international lending organizations such as the IMF, which use deficit as a benchmark for granting international credits. It should be noted that Figure 14.8 understates the actual deficit because the Russian finance ministry does not include interest payments. If such payments were included, the Russian state deficit would more than double.[21]

Prior to 1995, budget deficits were financed either by the issuance of new currency or by the issue of credit by the Russian Central Bank. Rubles were printed in ever-larger denominations to allow the state to pay its bills. Later, the budget deficit was financed by having the Central Bank of Russia (CBR) purchase the major portion of the debt. In April of 1995, new procedures were passed (to be discussed in the chapter on credit markets) that prohibited the CBR from financing the state deficit. Instead, the Ministry of Finance and Treasury would have to finance the debt by selling bonds to the public and to foreigners. These treasury bills are called GKOs (or *gosudarstvennye kratkosrochnye obiazonnosti*), and their rates are shown in Table 14.6 (p. 316).

The main advantage of GKO sales is that they allow for deficit finance that does not result in an increase in the money supply and in credit to the economy, so the

Figure 14.8   Revenues, Expenditures, Deficits (Russian Consolidated Budget)

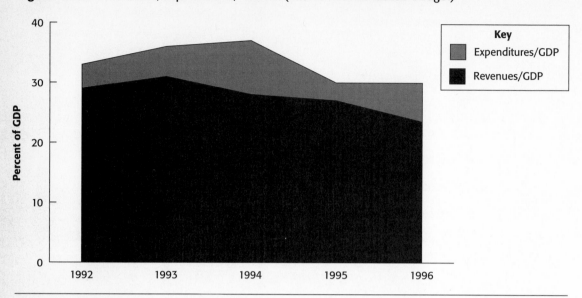

Source: Compiled by authors.

strategy is not inflationary. The disadvantage is that GKO sales crowd out private credit demands and leave fewer funds for industrial investment.

Modernization of the Russian Tax Code

As Figure 14.5 (p. 311) pointed out, Russia's system of taxation differs significantly from those of the industrialized market economies. In particular, Russia relies primarily on special taxes and sales and profits taxes as opposed to income and payroll taxes. Figure 14.9 shows that income taxes have remained a relatively small share of the total from 1992 to 1996 and that "other taxes" have made up an increasing share of the total. Throughout the period, Russian taxes have declined somewhat as a percentage of GDP.

During 1996, the Russian government worked on a new tax code that was supposed to be approved by the Duma and operational by 1997. The goal is a new, modernized tax code, making Russian taxes stable and transparent and also regulating relationships between the federal, regional, and local taxation. The new tax code is supposed to abolish taxes of a nonmarket character (such as the tax on "excess" wages) and will introduce new taxes, such as a unified social tax and various property taxes. The code is also supposed to reduce the number of taxes from 150 to 30 and will curtail special tax breaks for specific enterprises.

As of early 1997, the new tax code was still in preparation.[22] Delays in passage of the reformed tax code reflect the common difficulty of reconciling differences between the government and parliament and also dealing with vested interests that favor the status quo. It is now expected that the new code will not be effective until around the turn of the century.

Russian Federalism

In the Soviet period, there was extreme centralization of the USSR budget, although budget positions existed for republican, regional, and local governments. With the creation of the Russian Federation, a new equilibrium between the federal government and state and local governments had to be reached. Figure 14.10 shows that taxation authority had become fairly evenly split by the mid-1990s, with the federal government accounting for half of revenues.

MONETARY POLICY

In the administrative command economy, the money supply was controlled administratively (Chapter 7). One of the most important features of an efficient market economy is its use of money exchange. Money exchange is used in place of barter transactions whenever there is reasonable trust in the nation's currency. Trust is lost if inflation is excessive or if there is hyperinflation, which destroys money's function as a store of value and which diverts economic activity from productive activity to

Figure 14.9   Structure of Russian Revenues (Russian Consolidated Budget)

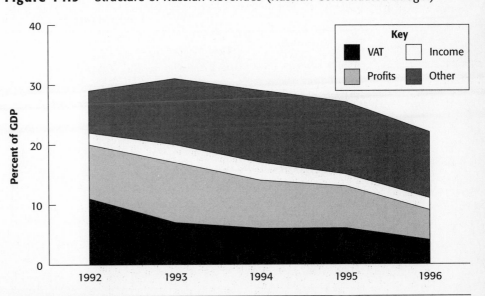

Source: Compiled by authors.

hedging against inflation. Since most money in a market economy is bank money rather than currency, the Russian transition required a conversion from administrative control of the money supply to control exercised by the central bank.

Banking Legislation, 1990–1992[23]

In the Soviet period, steps began to create a two-tiered banking system, consisting of a central bank and commercial banks. In 1986, the central banking function became the responsibility of the State Bank of the Soviet Union (Gosbank) and financing clients became the responsibility of five specialized sectoral banks. In 1987 Gosbank changed its name to the Central Bank of the Soviet Union (CB of the USSR). A decree of July 13, 1990 changed the name from Russian Office of the Central Bank of the USSR to the State Bank of the Russian Federation, answering directly to the Supreme Council of the Russian Federation. The offices of the CB of the USSR and the special banks were declared the property of the Russian Federation, to be transformed into joint stock companies or cooperatives.

The July 1990 decree effectively converted the CB of the USSR into an umbrella organization for the central banks of the countries that later joined the Commonwealth of Independent States (CIS). After the formation of the CIS, the Russian State Bank still had to face conflict because the other Soviet republics were unwilling to submit to the Russian State Bank the right to issue rubles and to stay

Table 14.6

GKO RATES

	6 month rate	Annualized rate
December 1993	8.5	102.0
March 1994	9.4	112.8
May 1994	7.3	87.6
September 1994	6.4	76.8
December 1994	12.6	151.2
January 1995	15.7	188.4
March 1995	10.6	127.2
May 1995	7.5	90.0
August 1995	8.7	104.4
December 1995	7.1	85.2
January 1996	5.7	68.4
March 1996	6.3	75.6
April 1996	10.7	128.4

Source: *Russian Economic Trends* vol. 5, no. 1 (1996), 146.

with the ruble zone. In November 1991, the **Central Bank of Russia** (CBR) formally took over the responsibilities of the CB of the USSR, which had continued to exist until the collapse of the Soviet Union in December 1991. This led to the eventual emergence of independent banking structures in Russia and the other republics of the CIS.

In October of 1991, the Bank of Foreign Economic Affairs (VEB) assumed the responsibility of servicing the debts of the Soviet Union. Following the formal dissolution of the Soviet Union in December of 1991, the VEB was moved from Gosbank's jurisdiction to the CBR and continued operating as a commercial bank. In July 1992, Russia assumed the foreign debt of the Soviet Union, and the VEB acted as agent in its settlement.

During the first four years of transition, the **Law on the Central Bank of the RSFSR** (approved in 1990), the **Law on Banks and Banking Activity in the RSFSR,** and **Statutes of the CBR** (both implemented in 1991 and amended in 1991 and 1992) governed banking in the Russian Federation. They assigned a number of tasks to the CBR, such as granting licenses banks, controlling and inspecting banks, regulating the money supply, refinancing banks, carrying out monetary and foreign exchange policy, and stabilizing the ruble. The CBR was made accountable to the Supreme Soviet of the RSFSR. It was entitled to issue money but was prohibited from printing money to cover the federal budget deficit.

The 1990–92 banking legislation called for a two-tiered banking system, with the Central Bank supervising all commercial banks and credit institutions. The CBR was declared independent of the government and was to function as the banks' bank

Figure 14.10 Russian Fiscal Federalism: Shares of Federal Versus Local Revenues

Source: Compiled by authors.

and as lender of last resort. This banking legislation implied that the CBR was obligated to finance the federal government's budget deficits. This obligation hindered the CBR from maintaining macroeconomic stability. During this early transition period, most commercial bank credit consisted of "directed" credits from the government to industries, agriculture and, to some extent, to the banking sector itself. Easy access to financing directly from the CBR, together with its position as a distributor of financing, made commercial banking one of the most profitable businesses in Russia.

The 1990–92 legislation gave the CBR flexibility to introduce further legislation and to determine operating rules for commercial banks. This CBR practice of management through instructions reversed the formal hierarchy set out in Russian legislation: CBR instructions became more important than parliamentary laws or presidential, governmental, or local government decrees.

In the Russian case, the regime based on a large number of instructions issued by the CBR and by governmental or presidential decrees created considerable confusion. Neither the commercial banks nor their clients could be sure about the legality of their operations. Ambiguous and occasionally controversial rules encouraged the tendency to take advantage of legislative inadequacies and slowed down day-to-day banking operations due to time wasted in trying to verify their legality.

The commercial banking legislation of 1990–92 created the foundations for modern banking in Russia, despite its many weaknesses and ambiguities. It defined a new two-tiered banking structure in Russia; it set out the permissible banking operations, the conditions of licensing and recalling licenses, the commercial banks' obligations and rights vis-a-vis the CBR, and the relations between the commercial banks and their clients. It provided rules on banking secrets, relating to bank-client relations. With certain exceptions, all information on a bank's accounts and its clients' accounts and related operations were declared secret, although this rule was not often changed.

The commercial banking legislation defined the concept of a commercial bank and its tasks; the legislation also provided procedures for opening and closing a bank and gave liquidity and solvency criteria. The banks were free to set their own commissions and interest rates on borrowing and lending, provided, however, that they were within the limits of the monetary and credit policy of the CBR. Cartels were forbidden. All banks could accept deposits.

New Banking Legislation, 1995

The Russian parliament approved the new **Federal Law of the CBR** on April 12, 1995. Unlike the preceding legislation, the new federal law very clearly defined the Central Bank's objectives: to defend the stability of the ruble and the Russian banking system, in conformity with the task allotted to it in the Russian Constitution. According to the 1995 CBR legislation, the CBR is an economically independent juridical person. Its capital and assets are owned by the Russian

Federation. The Russian State is not, however, responsible for the debts of the CBR. Neither is the CBR responsible for the government's debt. The CBR alone finances its expenditure and is not responsible for the liabilities of commercial banks.

The 1995 CBR legislation stipulated that the Central Bank has no right to grant credits to the government to cover budgetary deficits. This represented a significant reversal of earlier legislation that more-or-less obligated the CBR to finance the government deficit. Hence, it opened the door for conducting independent monetary and credit policies. The importance of this feature in reducing excessive money supply will be discussed in the next section.

The 1995 CBR legislation placed the CBR under the control of the Duma. By December of each year, the CBR is required to submit general consolidated guidelines on monetary and credit policy to the Duma, after they have first been presented to the president and the government.

The Duma nominates the chairperson of the CBR for a period of four years, based on the proposal of the President of the Russian Federation and the members of the board. Twice a year, the chairman of the CBR reports to the Duma on the bank's activities. The Duma can request the presence of representatives of the CBR. The CBR's annual report and auditors' report have to be confirmed by the Duma.

The 1995 CBR legislation represented a modernization of Russian banking legislation. The CBR's monetary instruments now included interest rate policy, reserve requirements, open market operations, refinancing of banks, foreign exchange control and regulation of money aggregates, and quantitative regulations. After 1995, the CBR began to control the money supply much like central banks in the industrialized market economies.

A key question concerning any country's banking system is the degree of the central bank's independence. The 1995 CBR legislation

> leaves the idea of an independent central bank, as defined in the Russian constitution, somewhat ambiguous and, in any case, subject to the way it will be observed in practice. Experience shows that the personalities of the leaders and the power relations between the institutions concerned are of greater significance in day-to-day operations than the formal legislative framework. In the case of weak State Duma and a strong government, the CBR may be expected to act more like a governmental bank. On the other hand, even if an independent central bank were subordinated to a strong parliament, the former would still be expected to cooperate and compromise with governmental policies.[24]

Macroeconomic Stability, Deficits, and Money Supply

Monetary and fiscal policies have been closely intertwined throughout the Russian transition. The creation of macroeconomic stability in Russia has required a coordination of monetary and fiscal policy, as well as developing methods to finance Russian budget deficits in a noninflationary manner.

As noted above, from 1991 to 1995, banking legislation of Russia seemed to imply that the Central Bank of Russia was obligated to finance budget deficits of the Russian federal government. This financing was done via Central Bank credits both to the Russian Ministry of Finance and to commercial banks. In effect, when federal deficits were financed in this fashion, federal deficits caused expansions of the money supply.

Figures 14.11 and 14.12 show the relationship between federal deficits, monetary growth, and inflation for the period 1991 to 1996. It shows that throughout the period, inflation rates have been strongly positively correlated with the growth of the money supply, albeit with a lag. During the early transition period, when money was growing rapidly, inflation was also rapid. During the later transition period, when monetary growth was slower, inflation also slowed down. The positive, lagged correlation between Russian monetary growth and inflation has been studied and demonstrated in numerous authoritative studies.[25] The correlation between the growth of the federal deficit and the money supply is complicated, but since 1995, they appear uncorrelated.

Although in the early years various Russian economic administrators, including chairpersons of the Central Bank of Russia, had to be convinced of the positive correlation between monetary growth and inflation (preferring instead to blame monopoly and structural factors for inflation), eventually even the most skeptical critics became convinced that inflation was caused by excessive monetary growth.

Under the prodding of the International Monetary Fund and under domestic pressure to create a sound currency, the new central banking rules of April 1995

Figure 14.11   Growth of Russian CPI and M2 (monthly growth rate)

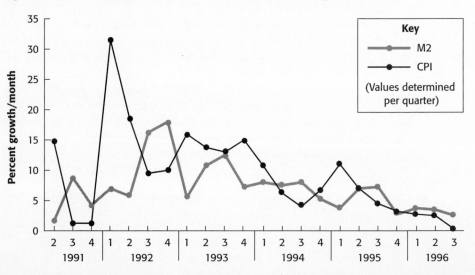

Source: Compiled by authors.

made the CBR more independent of the Russian government and freed the CBR from the obligation to monetize the Russian government debt. Instead of financing the federal deficit via credit expansion, the federal deficit had to be financed in credit markets through the sale of government treasury bills (called GKOs). The deficits of regional and local governments also have been increasingly financed in credit markets.[26] The Russian government has also been under pressure from the IMF to limit federal deficits, thereby attacking the inflation problem from both sides—by creating mechanisms to reduce monetary expansion and to reduce government deficits as a potential source of monetary and credit expansion.

As Figure 14.11 showed, the CBR has succeeded in reducing the growth of the money supply from its peak growth rates in 1992 and 1993. Since then, the rate of inflation has been contracting, so that by 1996, the inflation rates fell to less than 1.5 percent per month.

SUMMARY

Russia began its transition to a market economy in January of 1992, when most prices were freed from state price controls. At that time, Russia lacked virtually all institutions of a market economy, except for a flourishing underground economy and a quasi-market in labor. By early 1996, Russia had made considerable progress

Figure 14.12　Federal Deficit and M2 (monthly growth rate)

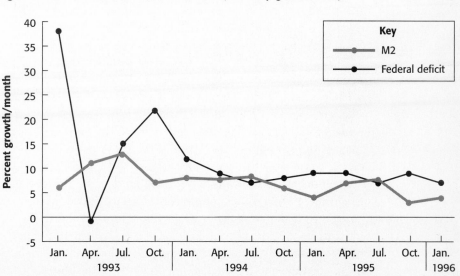

Source: Compiled by authors.

towards creating the institutions for a market economy. A two-tiered banking system was created that was actually able to limit the growth of the money supply and of credit, despite the considerable pressure for credit expansion. Although the privatization process was deeply flawed, it nevertheless resulted in a vast shift of property rights away from the state sector and towards the private and corporate sectors. Virtually overnight, Russia went from being a society characterized by an equal distribution of income to one with a highly unequal income distribution. Virtually overnight, Russia went from being an economy in which all earnings were derived from wages and salaries to one in which some half of all earnings were earned from entrepreneurial activity.

Faced with the daunting prospect of declining tax revenues and stiff revenue obligations, Russia did not make much progress during the first few years of transition towards developing a modern fiscal system based upon income and payroll taxation and value added taxes. Russian fiscal authorities simply had to scramble to gather tax revenues from all conceivable sources, ignoring the disincentives that resulted from the often-excessive tax rates.

Russia did achieve a degree of macroeconomic stability by the mid-1990s. Inflation rates had fallen from more than 10 percent per month to less than 1.5 percent per month. Prices and the money supply were growing at about the same rate as inflationary expectations subsided. Federal deficits were being financed through the sale of government securities in the open market, a noninflationary means of deficit finance albeit at the cost of financial resources available for the private sector.

The Russian exchange rate (to be discussed in a later chapter) had also achieved some degree of stability by the mid-1990s. Although the ruble continued to depreciate against major currencies, its decline was steady and remained within ranges desired by financial authorities. In fact, the ruble exchange rate was appreciating in real terms (the fall in its nominal value did not keep pace with Russia's higher relative rate of inflation) because of the growing attractiveness of Russian securities and Russia's strong positive balance of trade.

The Russian system of government installed during the transition resembles many industrialized Western economies. It consists of two houses—a more powerful lower house, the Duma, and a less powerful upper house (the Federation Council)—an executive and judicial branch. The powers of the judicial branch remain to be tested. The unusual feature of the current Russian system of government is the strength of the office of the president due to the length of the presidential term and the president's ability to call for new elections, to make key appointments, and to rule by presidential decree. The executive branch runs the government of the Russian republic, which is headed by a prime minister nominated by the president and approved by the Duma.

Russia's major institutional weakness remained political uncertainty, even though much political uncertainty was dispelled with the reelection of Boris Yeltsin in July of 1996 and the decline in popularity of the Russian Communist Party. The major source of political uncertainty remained the division of Russian government between a more reform-minded president and cabinet and a more conservative legislature.

Terms and Concepts

Federation Council   The upper house of the Federal Assembly of the Russian Federation, consisting of two deputies elected from each of the Russian republics and regions.

State Duma   The lower house of the Federal Assembly of the Russian Federation.

Russian Constitution   The highest law of Russia, approved in December 1993.

Civil Code   Defines juridical persons and provides the fundamental law defining various forms of ownership.

State Property Committee   Formed in October 1992; the committee in charge of state property.

voucher privatization   Privatization taking place through the distribution of vouchers to the population; vouchers have a face value and can be used to purchase shares.

Federal Property Fund   The fund that holds properties (federal as opposed to local) that are readied for distribution (through vouchers) or direct sale to the population.

investment tender   Purchase of a defined percentage of shares through sealed bids; the winning investor had to pay a fee to the property fund and then to pay the bid amount of investment directly to the company.

commercial tender   The winner was required to fulfill certain conditions (such as develop a particular oil field), with the winning bid being that which most closely satisfied the requirement of the tender and offered the highest price.

restructuring   Changes in the organizational arrangements and decision making procedures that take place in an organization after privatization.

Federal Anti-Monopoly Commission   A commission created to enforce the anti-monopoly law (June 1995) designed to limit the abuses of monopoly power throughout the Russian Federation.

Mafia Capitalism   One of several terms (also Crony Capitalism and Wild Capitalism) used to describe the powerful and cohesive groups who came to exercise substantial control of organizations during privatization through inside information and connections developed in the Soviet era.

Central Bank of Russia   The Central Bank of Russia emerged through legislation in the period 1990–92; it functioned as an independent central bank, a banker's bank, and the lender of last resort in the Russian Federation.

Selected Bibliography

Bim, A. S., D. C. Jones, and T. Weisskopf. "Hybrid Forms of Enterprise Organization in the Former USSR and the Russian Federation," *Comparative Economic Studies* vol. 35, no. 1 (Spring 1993), 1–38.

Bird, R., et al., eds. *Decentralization of the Socialist State: Intergovernmental Finance in Transition Economies* (Aldershot, England: Avebury, 1996).

Blasi, J. R., M. Kroumova, and D. Krise. *Kremlin Capitalism* (Ithaca, NY: Cornell University Press, 1997).

Bornstein, M. "Russia's Mass Privatization Programme," *Communist Economics and Economic Transformation* vol. 6, no. 4 (1994), 419–57.

Boycko, M., A. Schliefer, and R. Vishny. *Privatizing Russia* (Cambridge, MA: MIT Press, 1995).

Buck, T., I. Filatotchev, and M. Wright. "Employee Buyouts and the Transformation of Russian Industry," *Comparative Economic Studies* vol. 36 (Summer 1994), 1–16.

Buck, T., I. Filatotchev, and M. Wright., and Y. von Frausum. "The Process and Impact of Privatization in Russia and Ukraine," *Comparative Economic Studies* vol. 39, no. 2/3 (Summer-Fall 1996), 47–69.

Ernst, M., M. Alexeev, and P. Marer. *Transforming the Core* (Boulder, CO: Westview Press, 1996).

Friedgut, T., and J. Hahn, eds. *Local Power and Post-Soviet Politics* (Armonk: M. E. Sharpe, 1994).

"If You Can't Beat Them," *Russian Petroleum Investor* (December 1996/January 1997), 8–11.

Hahn, J. W., ed. *Democratization in Russia* (Armonk: M. E. Sharpe, 1996).

Hoffman, E. P. "Challenges to Viable Constitutionalism in Post-Soviet Russia," *The Harriman Review* vol. 7, nos. 10–12 (November 1994), 19–56.

Hoggarth, G. "Monetary Policy in Russia," in J. Rantava, ed., *Russia's Financial Markets and the Banking Sector in Transition* (Helsinki: Bank of Finland, 1995).

Hough, J. "The Russian Election of 1993: Public Attitudes Towards Economic Reform and Decentralization," *Post-Soviet Affairs* vol. 10, no. 1 (January-March 1994), 1–37.

Komnsitutsia Rossiski Federatsii, 12.12.1993, reprinted in *Universal'ny iuridicheski spravochnik predprinimatelia* (Moscow: Tikhimorova, 1996), 22–25.

Korhonen, I. "An Error Correction Model for Russian Inflation," *Review of Economies in Transition* vol. 4 (1996), 53–62.

Krueger, G. "Transition Strategies of Former State-Owned Enterprises in Russia," *Comparative Economic Studies* vol. 37, no. 4 (Winter 1995), 89–110.

Laurila, J. "Russian Banking Legislation and Supervision," in J. Rantava, ed., *Russia's Financial Markets and the Banking Sector in Transition* (Helsinki: Bank of Finland, 1995).

Le Hoverou, P., and M. Rutkowski. "Federal Transfers in Russia: Their Impact on Regional Revenues and Incomes," *Comparative Economic Studies* vol. 38, no. 2/3 (Summer/Fall 1996), 21–44.

Linz, S. J. "Russian Firms in Transition: Champions, Challengers, and Chaff," forthcoming, *Comparative Economic Studies* (Summer 1997).

Morgan Stanley. "Russian Equity Market: Not If, but When," Investment Research, U.K. and Europe (February 2, 1996), 4.

Natsional'nye scheta Rossi v 1989–1994 gg (Moscow: Goskomstat Rossii, 1997), 61.

Noren, J. H. "The Russian Economic Reform: Progress and Prospects," *Soviet Economy* vol. 8, no. 1 (1992), 3–31.

O konkurentsii I ogranichenii monopoliticheskoi deiatel'nosti, 14.06.95 FZ, No. 88-F3.

Olson, M. "The Devolution of Power in Post-Communist Societies," in R. Skidelsky, ed., *Russia's Stormy Path to Reform* (London: The Social Market Foundation, 1995), 9–42.

Prospectus: Templeton Russia Fund, Inc. (June 15, 1995).

"Run for the Border," *Russian Petroleum Investor* (December 1996/January 1997), 24–29.

Russian Economic Trends 1996 vol. 5, no. 1.

Schliefer, A., and M. Boycko. "Next Step in Privatization: Six Major Challenges," in I. Libermann and J. Willis, eds., *Enterprise and Efficient Markets* (World Bank: Washington, DC: 1994).

Schliefer, A., and R. Vishney. "Politicians and Firms," *Quarterly Journal of Economics* vol. 109, no. 4 (1994).

——— . "Corruption," *Quarterly Journal of Economics* vol. 108, no. 3 (1993).

Shlapentokh, V. "Privatization Debates in Russia: 1989–1992," *Comparative Economic Studies* vol. 35, no. 2 (Summer 1993), 19–32.

Slider, D. "Privatization in the United States," *Business Economics* vol. 30, no. 4 (October 1995), 45–50.

Smith, G. B. *Reforming the Russian Legal System* (New York: Cambridge University Press, 1996).

Sutela, P. "But . . . Does Mr. Coase Go To Russia?" *Review of Economics in Transition* no. 4 (1995), 47–55.

——— . "Insider Privatization in Russia: Speculation in Systematic Change," *Europe-Asia Studies* vol. 35, no. 3 (June 1996).

White, S., A. Pravda, and Z. Gitelman, eds. *Developments in Russian and Post-Soviet Politics* (Durham, NC: Duke University Press, 1994).

World Bank. *Fiscal Management in Russia* (Washington, DC: World Bank, 1996).

——— . *Russian Federation: Toward Medium-Term Viability* (Washington, DC: World Bank, 1996).

Zyuganov, G. *My Russia* ed. V. Medish (Armonk: M. E. Sharpe, 1997).

Notes

1. During the final days of the Soviet era and the early days of transition, the issue of property rights was debated actively. However, as transition proceeded, it quickly became evident that mass privatization would be pursued. For a discussion, see V. Shlapentoky, "Privatization Debates in Russia: 1989–1992," *Comparative Economic Studies* vol. 35, no. 2 (Summer 1993), 19–32. See also A. S. Bim, D. C. Jones, and T. Weisskopf, "Hybrid Forms

of Enterprise Organization in the Former USSR and the Russian Federation," *Comparative Economic Studies* vol. 35, no. 1 (Spring 1993), 1–38.

2. J. W. Hahn, ed., *Democratization in Russia* (Armonk: M. E. Sharpe, 1996).

3. These new policies emerged from the 50-day plans (1990 and 1991). For a discussion, see J. H. Noren, "The Russian Economic Reform: Progress and Prospects," *Soviet Economy* vol. 8, no. 1 (1992), 3–41.

4. G. A. Zyuganov, *My Russia,* ed. Vadim Medish (Armonk: M. E. Sharpe, 1997).

5. For a discussion of legal fundamentals, see G. B. Smith, *Reforming the Russian Legal System* (New York: Cambridge University Press, 1996).

6. Komnstitutsia Rossiski Federatsii, 12.12.1993 reprinted in *Universal'ny iuridicheski sprav-ochnik predprinimatelia* (Moscow: Tikhimorova, 1996), 22–25.

7. Op cit., 25–146.

8. M. Boycko, A. Schleifer, and R. Vishny, *Privatizing Russia* (Cambridge: MIT Press, 1995); T. Buck, I. Filatotchev, and M. Wright, "Employee Buyouts and the Transformation of Russian Industry," *Comparative Economic Studies* vol. 36 (Summer 1994), 1–16; M. Ernst, M. Alexeev, and P. Marer, *Transforming the Core* (Boulder, CO: Westview Press, 1996); D. Slider, "Privatization in the United States," *Business Economics* vol. 30, no. 4 (October 1995), 45–50; S. J. Linz, "Russian Firms in Transition: Champions, Challengers, and Chaff," forthcoming, *Comparative Economic Studies* (Summer 1997); G. Krueger, "Transition Strategies of Former State-Owned Enterprises in Russia," *Comparative Economic Studies* vol. 37, no. 4 (Winter 1995) 89–110; T. Buck, I. Filatotchev, M. Wright, and Y. von Frausum, "The Process and Impact of Privatization in Russia and Ukraine," *Comparative Economic Studies* vol. 38, no. 2/3 (Summer-Fall 1996), 47–69.

9. See M. Bornstein, "Russia's Mass Privatization Programme," *Communist Economics and Economic Transformation* vol. 6, no. 4 (1994), 419–57; A. Schleifer and M. Boycko, "Next Step in Privatization: Six Major Challenges," in I. Liebermann and J. Willis, eds., Russia: *Creating Private Enterprise and Efficient Markets* (Washington, DC: World Bank, 1994). For a detailed legal description of the Russian privatization program, see *Prospectus: Templeton Russia Fund, Inc.* (June 15, 1995), Appendix B.

10. For a discussion of "golden shares," see "If You Can't Beat Them," *Russia Petroleum Investor* (December 1996/January 1997), 8–11.

11. *Russian Economic Trends 1996,* vol. 5, no. 1, 103–06.

12. For a discussion of the measurement of entrepreneurial income, see *Russian Economic Trends 1996,* vol. 5, no. 1, 65.

13. P. Sutela, "But . . . Does Mr. Coase Go To Russia?" *Review of Economics in Transition* no. 4 (1995), 47–55; P. Sutela, "Insider Privatization in Russia: Speculation in Systematic Change," *Europe-Asia Studies* vol. 35, no. 3 (June 1996).

14. Morgan Stanley, "Russian Equity Market: Not If, but When," *Investment Research, U.K. and Europe* (February 2, 1996), 4.

15. "Run for the Border," *Russian Petroleum Investor* (December 1996/January 1997), 24–29.

16. O konkurentsii I ogranichenii monopoliticheskoi deiatel'nosti, 14.06.95 FZ, No.88-F3.

17. M. Olson, "The Devolution of Power in Post-Communist Societies," in R. Skidelsky, ed., *Russia's Stormy Path to Reform* (London: Social Market Foundation, 1995), 9–42.

18. A. Schliefer and R. Vishny, "Politicians and Firms," *Quarterly Journal of Economics* vol. 109, no. 4 (1994); Schliefer and Vishny, "Corruption," *Quarterly Journal of Economics* vol. 108, no. 3 (1993).

19. Richard Bird et al., eds., *Decentralization of the Socialist State: Intergovernmental Finance in Transition Economies* (Aldershot, England: Avebury, 1996); P. Le Hoverou and M. Rutkowski, "Federal Transfers in Russia: Their Impact on Regional Revenues and Incomes," *Comparative Economic Studies* vol. 38, nos. 2/3 (Summer/Fall 1996), 21–44;

World Bank, *Fiscal Management in Russia* (Washington, DC: World Bank, 1996); World Bank, *Russian Federation: Toward Medium-Term Viability* (Washington, DC: World Bank, 1996).

20. *Natsional'nye scheta Rossi v 1989–1994 gg.* (Moscow: Goskomstat Rossii, 1997), 61.
21. *Russian Economic Trends 1996* vol. 5, no. 2, 12.
22. *Russian Economic Trends 1996*, vol. 5, no. 1, 10.
23. This section is based on J. Laurila, "Russian Banking Legislation and Supervision," in J. Rantava, ed., *Russia's Financial Markets and the Banking Sector in Transition* (Helsinki: Bank of Finland, 1995).
24. J. Laurila, op. cit., 92.
25. G. Hoggarth, "Monetary Policy in Russia," in J. Rantava, ed., *Russia's Financial Markets;* I. Korhonen, "An Error Correction Model for Russian Inflation," *Review of Economies in Transition* vol. 4, 1996, 53–62.
26. *Russian Economic Trends 1996*, vol. 5, no. 2, 27–28.

CHAPTER 15

Russian Economic Performance During the Transition

THE TURNPIKE ANALOGY

In the 1960s, some theorists of economic growth used the analogy of a turnpike to consider the best path to sustained economic growth. They argued that a developing economy might need to slow its growth deliberately in order to get its house in order before it could achieve sustained and rapid growth.[1] This "turnpike theorem" was originally applied to developing countries that must first alter the structure of production before embarking upon a trajectory of balanced long-term growth.

The **turnpike analogy** can be applied to the Russian transition because it is necessary first to develop new institutions and policies and to wreck old institutions and policies before creating conditions for sustained long-term economic growth. And it may well be that Russia may have to spend some years wandering along a confusing network of cross streets, looking for the on-ramp to the turnpike. There will be starts and stops and many instances of traveling in the wrong direction. In economic terms, the period of searching for the turnpike's on-ramp will be characterized by negative growth. The longer it takes to establish the conditions for sustained growth, the deeper the drop in output.

The challenge of the transition in Russia and in other transition countries is to develop the institutions and policies for sustained economic growth within as brief a period of time as possible in order to reverse the economic decline of the Soviet period. The performance of the Soviet economy was discussed in earlier chapters in two contexts: Chapter 11 studied the performance of the Soviet administrative command economy in a long-run context. Chapter 12 discussed why faltering Soviet economic performance after 1960 compelled the Soviet leadership to opt for "radical" reform, or perestroika. These earlier chapters concluded that the Soviet administrative command economy grew at relatively rapid rates during the early period, but, after the 1960s, experienced declining rates of growth of both output and productivity. The choice of perestroika was dictated by the bitter conclusion that the administrative command economy simply could not make the transformation from extensive to intensive growth. With declining growth of factor inputs, the only way to raise economic performance was to unleash the "hidden reserves" of productivity improvement promised by a generation of Soviet economic reformers.

Our earlier discussion of the performance of the administrative command economy also focused on measurement problems. The administrative command economy deliberately did not use relative prices to allocate resources—prices did not reflect opportunity costs, nor did they reflect relative values to consumers. Accordingly, we calculated the GDP of the administrative command economy in terms of resource (or factor) costs. Even if planners chose to produce goods and services that offered little or no value to consumers, those goods were nevertheless valued in terms of their factor costs.

The economic performance of the Soviet administrative command economy was not measured exclusively in terms of output and productivity growth. Other factors such as economic stability (the stability of prices, wages, and employment, and the distribution of income) were also used. Chapter 10 showed that the Soviet economy was a job rights economy that ensured employment, albeit at substantial costs of lost productivity and labor discipline. Soviet financial planners restrained the rate of inflation by strictly controlling the money supply, limiting wage increases to productivity increases, and at times accepting hidden inflation over overt inflation. The Soviet distribution of income was more equal than in those industrialized market economies (such as the United States and Canada) that do not extensively redistribute income as in the welfare states of Scandinavia, France, and Germany.

The growth of the Russian economy during the transition years will not reveal much about its long-term growth potential after it completes its transition. We currently have too little information to form such a judgment. Instead, we can only study the transition years to gauge the costs of transition, as reflected in the loss of output associated with the move from command to market, and study the structural shifts that occur during this process. If the cost of transition proves to be too great, forces will be unleashed that either slow its progress or cause a movement back towards the administrative command system.

MEASUREMENT OF RUSSIAN TRANSITION PERFORMANCE

When Russia made the decision in late 1991 to abandon the administrative command economy and to move to a market economy, the country also decided to adopt the economic measurement methods of the rest of the world. In August of 1991, the Presidential Decree on Maintenance of Economic Basis of the Russian Federation Independence was issued, calling for the creation of statistical accounts that would meet international standards by January 1993.[2] Russia's State Statistical Committee **(Goskomstat)** was directed to abandon the **Material Product System** (MPS) of national accounts used in Soviet times in favor of the **System of National Accounts** (SNA) used by the rest of the world.

Converting from MPS to SNA

Soviet national accounting practices were developed to aid economic officials in planning the production, distribution, and use of material products. Soviet planners and national-income accountants neglected "nonproductive spheres," such as personal services, that were not directly related to production. Moreover, planners focused on gross production, not on net production or value added, in that they planned gross rather than net outputs.

The MPS system had major drawbacks. It was not comparable with the SNA statistics used by other countries and recognized by international organizations. MPS did not allow the simultaneous measurement of the economy's total output by sector of origin, final expenditures, and sum of factor incomes; MPS omitted a number of economic activities that created income and required expenditure. Therefore, final output did not equal factor income. In the SNA system, the value of all final goods and services equals the aggregated value added of each of the economy's sectors, which equals the sum total of factor income of all the economy's factors of production. These alternate SNA balances, which are all conceptually equal, allow analysts to view the economy from three separate angles: output, use of output, and generation of income.

Goskomstat's acceptance of the SNA methodology in 1991 does not automatically mean that Russian statistical calculations since that time have been comparable to Western national accounts. In fact, the Russian conversion from the MPS to the SNA system has taken place under the extremely difficult circumstance of the Russian transition.

Measurement Problems

With the assistance from experienced statistical experts from the World Bank, Russian statistical authorities have had to resolve the following measurement problems: First, as Russia makes the transition from state to private enterprises, it must register and measure the economic performance of smaller private enterprises, which represent a growing share of the economy. The change from registered state enterprise to unregistered, small private enterprises has been rapid. Prior to 1994, only industrial enterprises employing more than 50 workers (plus joint ventures) were reported. Small enterprises were either left out entirely or were covered by crude guesses by statistical authorities. In 1992, according to Goskomstat statistics, large enterprises accounted for 94 percent, and in 1993, they accounted for 92 percent, of industrial output.[3] An even greater problem than the statistical capturing of new enterprises is that of the "shadow economy" (*tenevaia ekonomika*). This "second economy" existed during the Soviet period (Chapter 8), and it has continued to prosper during the transition. According to expert estimates of Russian statistical authorities, the shadow economy accounts for about 20 percent of GDP, and it includes both criminal activities (narcotics, contraband, and prostitution) and businesses that could be converted into normal activities under a more normalized economic system.[4]

Second, one of the most significant sources of the Russian government's tax revenues is from taxes on enterprises, either on their profits or their gross revenues. In fact, Russian corporations must provide statistical reports, not to inform shareholders about the company's performance, but to satisfy the reporting requirement of Russian tax authorities. As a World Bank joint report concludes: "The most probable source of downward bias in output is underreporting by the industrial enterprises due to tax evasion. The magnitude of underreporting is very difficult to assess and to quantify directly."[5]

Underreporting takes place in two forms: First, established and registered companies have an incentive to underreport their revenues and to overstate their costs in order to reduce their profits taxes. Second, newly-formed enterprises or established enterprises can escape taxation by remaining unregistered. Although Russian tax and statistical authorities have attempted to limit registration avoidance by linking the opening of bank accounts to statistical registration, a large number of companies still escape registration. Russian authorities are attempting to correct the problem of underregistration by conducting surveys of small enterprises.

Third, a market economy requires more types of businesses than an administrative command economy. Entirely new activities have emerged—for example accounting, advertising, financial services, real estate, and personal services—none of which existed earlier. Newly-formed companies performing entirely new services escape detection more readily. For example, the number of reporting units producing paid services to households actually decreased significantly from 137,000 in 1991 to 116,000 in 1994, despite the fact that this was obviously one of the fastest-growing Russian sectors.[6]

Fourth, the ultimate value of reported data depends upon the validity of the underlying enterprise accounting system. If the resulting statistical aggregates are to be comparable, Russian enterprise accounting must observe the same standards as Western accounting practices. Although there have been significant changes in accounting away from Soviet practices, Russian accounting still reflects the vestiges of them.[7] Specifically, there is no allowance for deducting certain production costs; depreciation rates are strictly prescribed by the government, based upon periodic revaluations of fixed assets; the absence of inflation accounting creates artificial inventory profits; and there are no provisions for dealing with bad debts, which have accumulated to alarming proportions during the Russian transition.[8] These differences in accounting tend to overstate enterprise profits and enterprise value added.

Fifth, as we learned in studying the performance of the Soviet economy in the 1930s, it is more difficult to measure the performance of an economy that is undergoing rapid change. In the 1930s the Soviet economy transformed itself from a backward agrarian economy into an industrial economy. The process of transformation caused vast shifts in the structure of output and employment and significant changes in relative prices. In the Russian transition we have a rapidly moving economy that is leaving behind the employment, output, and relative price structures of the administrative command economy and moving towards a new economic structure with different employment, output structures, and relative prices.

Sixth, Russia suffered very high rates of inflation during the first three years of transformation. Rapid inflation complicates the calculation of real output and provides additional incentives to underreport output and overstate costs.[9]

Structural Change and Growth Measurement

Figure 15.1 (p. 334) shows the dramatic changes that occurred between 1990 and 1995 in Russia's industrial structure. It also shows Russia's industrial structure becoming more "Westernized," e.g. moving towards that of the United States. Between 1990 and 1995 alone, there were substantial increases in the shares of trade, financial services, and personal services—all of which are in greater demand in a market economy—and significant declines in the shares of agriculture and industry, reflecting the decline of production units unsuited to a market environment.

The move from administered to market prices can affect the measurement of Russian economic growth. As more prices are set freely by supply and demand, and as export and import products are priced at world market prices (net of export and import taxes), the outputs of Russian businesses can be better aggregated in terms of meaningful prices that do not simply measure the costs of resources.

Changes in relative prices can affect the measurement of Russian growth in different directions. Presumably, Soviet prices did not measure consumer welfare. With price liberalization, therefore, the relative prices should rise the most for products whose prices were most suppressed by the system and, at the same time, are products that are in the greatest demand. We expect the relative prices of Russian products that are demanded in a market setting to rise more than products more suited to an administrative command economy. Therefore, the supply of Russian products that command value in a market setting would be expected to grow the

Figure 15.1   Structure of Russia's GDP, 1990 and 1995

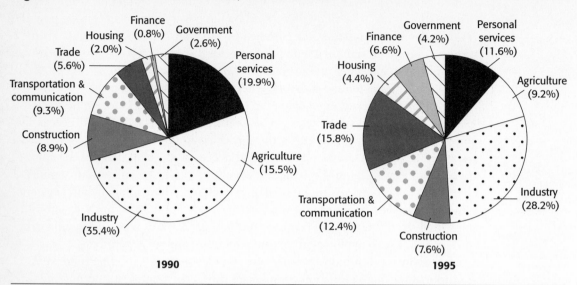

1990

1995

Source: World Bank, *Russian Federation: Report on the National Accounts,* Tables 2-2A and 2-2B.

most (or fall the least) because their demand is increasing in relative terms. *If there is a positive correlation between prices and quantities, we would get a higher rate of growth if market prices (say from 1996) are used instead of administered prices of, say, 1990.*

However, differential supply-side effects or monopoly pricing could affect prices in the opposite direction. If Russian monopoly producers act as monopolists and restrict output to raise prices, this would effect an inverse relationship between prices and quantities. If the change in relative prices is motivated by reductions in supply associated with differential supply disruptions, higher relative prices would be due to supply-side shocks. *Lower relative supplies would bring forth higher relative prices for the monopolist, thereby yielding an inverse relationship between prices and quantities, if supply effects dominate.*

The scatter diagram in Figure 15.2 correlates the average annual growth rates of prices and real outputs for 13 branches of the Russia economy. It shows a weak but positive relationship between the growth of output (or the relative decline in output) and prices. This weak positive relationship suggests two things about the sources of growth during the Russian transition: First, it suggests that differential rates of growth (or declines in output, as is true in most cases) have been caused principally by relative changes in demand, rather than by relative changes in supply. Second, the weakness of the correlation suggests that the disruption of output caused sector supply curves to shift to the left, the effects of which weakened the positive correlation between outputs and prices. The weak positive correlation in

Figure 15.2 Branch Output Growth vs. Inflation in 13 Sectors (1991–95)

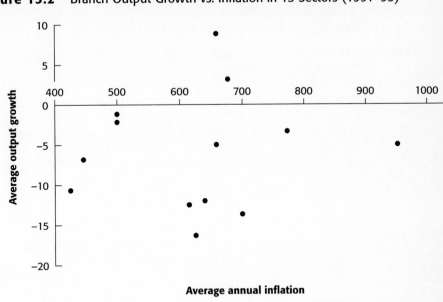

Source: World Bank, *Russian Federation: Report on the National Accounts,* Tables 2-2A and 2-2B.

Figure 15.2 shows that the shifts in demand away from command branches in favor of market branches appeared to outweigh the supply-side shocks.

The weak positive correlation also suggests that the growth of the Russian economy will be only slightly higher if measured in prices from the early transition. If prices are drawn from the late transition, the fastest-growing sectors (or, more realistically, those that are declining the least) will also have the highest relative prices.

Table 15.1 (p. 336) makes this point via an extreme calculation. It computes the growth of Russian industry using 1991 prices and world market prices. Table 15.2 (p. 337) shows the differential growth rates of industrial branches from 1990 to 1995. World market prices are very forward looking because they suggest the eventual direction of Russian prices. As Table 15.1 shows, the rate of growth of Russian industry is basically the same, whether calculated in 1991 prices or world market prices, although world market prices yield a slightly smaller decline.

RUSSIAN ECONOMIC GROWTH DURING THE TRANSITION

Although there have been substantial changes in the structure of the Russian economy, it appears that the relative price changes associated with these structural shifts do not materially affect measurement of economic growth. Instead, we have to look

Table 15.1

INDUSTRIAL GROWTH IN RUSSIA
(percentage figured in terms of 1990 prices)

	1990	1991	1992	1993	1994	1995
Russian prices	+0.2	−6.25	−14.0	−12.0	−25.0	−7.5
World prices	−1.0	−7.0	−13.5	−14.75	−22.5	−4.0

Sources: W. Schrettl and U. Weissenburger, "Russland: Fortsetzung des Niedergangs oder Bginn eines Aufschwungs?" *Vierteljahrshefte zur Wirtschaftsforschung* vol. 65 (1995), 35; C. Buckley, "The Russian Oil and Gas Industry," Morgan Stanley, *Europe: Russia* (February 2, 1996), 41.

at other sources of bias—in particular at the biases associated with concealed data, underlying accounting methods, new enterprises, and the underground economy—if we want to ferret out major differences.

Alternate Estimates

There are several competing estimates of Russian economic growth during the transition. They differ because of difficulties and ambiguities of measurement. Because most experts believe the most reliable data are for industrial outputs, the alternative GDP estimates all make use of the sector-of-origin approach—an approach which is criticized in the following section.

Table 15.3 (p. 338) shows the various estimates of Russian growth from 1990 to the present, starting with the official calculation of Goskomstat and including the suggested revisions of a joint team of World Bank and Goskomstat experts, independent adjustments made by scholars supported by the International Monetary Fund and a Japanese scholar. For reference purposes, also included in Figure 15.3 are two major historical economic cataclysms; namely, the United States depression from 1929 to 1934 and the effect of World War II on Soviet real GDP.[10]

The official Goskomstat figures make some adjustment for underreporting, tax evasion, and the other distortions discussed above, but, according to international expert analysis, Goskomstat probably overstated the decline. The Goskomstat figure shows the Russian economy in 1995 producing slightly more than half of what it produced six years earlier, on the eve of the transition. The alternate estimates show a lesser decline, with the Russian economy in 1996 producing slightly less than 70 percent of its 1990 level. It appears that Russian statistical authorities have accepted the joint World Bank/Goskomstat estimates, which are now cited in official publications.[11] The smallest drop in output (25 percent) is calculated by a Japanese scholar, M. Kuboniwa, who adjusts Russian industrial output using econometric estimates based on electricity output.[12] No matter which estimate one uses, the

Table 15.2

THE GROWTH OF RUSSIAN INDUSTRY BY BRANCH
(annual rates of growth)

	1990	1991	1992	1993	1994	1995
Electricity	2.0	0.3	−4.7	−5.3	−8.8	−4.0
Fuels	−3.3	−6.0	−7.0	−15.0	−11.0	−2.0
Metallurgy	−2.2	−7.8	−20.5	−16.7	−15.4	7.8
Chemicals	−2.2	−6.3	−21.7	−21.5	−28.9	12.0
Machinery	1.1	−10.0	−14.9	−15.6	−38.1	−6.0
Paper	−1.2	−9.0	−14.6	−18.7	−31.2	−7.0
Construction materials	−0.9	−2.4	−20.4	−17.6	−28.9	−6.0
Light industry	−0.1	−9.0	−30.0	−23.4	−47.3	−33.0
Food products	0.4	−9.5	−16.4	−9.2	−21.9	−9.0
Total	−0.1	−8.0	−18.0	−16.2	−20.9	−3.0

Source: DIW, *Wochenbericht,* 51-52195, 898.

decline in Russian output was cataclysmic, far exceeding the drop in U.S. output during the Great Depression and the drop in Soviet output during the first three years of World War II.[13]

Is the Decline Overstated?

A number of specialists have argued that the decline in Russian output is still overstated by the estimates in Table 15.3. Gavrilenkov and Koen provide the most comprehensive arguments in favor of overstatement.[14] We have already discussed the problem of underreporting, which will affect sectors that are expanding most rapidly: the new market-oriented businesses. In support of this proposition, Gavrilenkov and Koen note that 50 percent of bank credits and 60 percent of bank accounts are held by "other" businesses, which are very difficult to identify.[15]

There is another source of discrepancy. The figures and tables cited above take as their 1990 starting point the production base inherited from the Soviet period, and that base is likely to be overstated due to the tendency of Soviet managers and ministry officials towards overreporting. Once into the Russian transition period, incentives reversed from over- to underreporting, as registered enterprises sought to minimize their taxes and qualify for subsidies and cheap credits.

Goskomstat and its international advisors have concluded that the most reliable data for the Russian economy are to be found on the output (sector of origin) side. Sector of origin estimates use physical output series, which are easier to measure during periods of rapid inflation. International teams concluded that measuring

Table 15.3

ALTERNATE ESTIMATES, OUTPUT DECLINE
Russia, 1990 to 1996

	1991	1992	1993	1994	1995	1996
Official	87	70	61	52	49	47
Japanese	97	88	83	75	73	—
World Bank	95	81.5	74	64	61	59
IMF	94	82	74	67	—	—
United States 1929–33	91(30)	77(31)	76(32)	80(33)	—	—
Soviet Union 1940–43	98(41)	82(42)	86(43)	—	—	—

Source: Evgeny Gavrilenkov and Vincent Koen, "How Large Was the Output Collapse in Russia? Alternative Estimates and Welfare Implications," *IMF Working Paper, No. 94/154* (December 1994); World Bank, *Russian Federation: Report on the National Accounts* 116–17.

end-use consumption and investment or factor incomes provides less reliable measures of Russian GDP. Even if consumption and income figures are less reliable than sector of origin estimates, they can still be used for consistency checks.

There are a number of inconsistencies between sector of origin and end-use figures. Although output statistics show the *production* of consumer goods declining at rapid rates, figures on consumption show the *consumption* of the same goods to be either rising or falling at slow rates.[16] Goskomstat figures show that ownership of selected consumer durables generally increased since 1990 (Table 15.4). Although imports can account for divergences between production and consumption, that does not seem to explain this situation.

Other experts argue that any Russian aggregated series is so distorted that it is better to use some simple physical indicators, such as transportation deliveries or electricity production to measure the Russian output decline. For example, if electricity production is used, the Russian decline would be substantially less.[17]

Yet other experts argue that we should measure Russian performance not by sector outputs but by consumer welfare. The most comprehensive measures of consumer welfare are real per capita consumption and income, which have not declined as much as physical output measures such as industrial production. They show that real per capita income plunged to about half of the 1991 level during the process of price liberalization in January of 1992, but it has been increasing since then, reaching about 90 percent of the starting level by 1995.[18]

Although a portion of the phenomenon of consumption recovering much faster than production could be explained by imports and by the decline in other parts of the economy (such as investment or government spending) the situation still suggests that private real income has definitely not collapsed as much as measured

Table 15.4

RUSSIA: OWNERSHIP OF SELECTED CONSUMER DURABLES
(units per 100 households)

	1990	1993
TV sets	111	115
Radios	99	103
Recorders	59	62
Refrigerators	95	95
Washing machines	78	80
Vacuum cleaners	52	53
Cars	19	23
Motorcycles	22	23
Cameras	35	37

Source: Goskomstat of the Russian Federation (1995), cited in Gavrilenkov and Koen, 117.

production. Since total factor income must equal total final output, this discrepancy suggests possible underreporting of measured production.

A final complexity about the measurement of Russia's decline is the issue of improving product choice and quality. A major weakness of the administrative command economy was its inability to produce high quality goods and market them efficiently. Russian consumers now have a wide choice of goods and services without waiting in lines. Earlier studies show that consumers in an administrative command economy were willing to sacrifice 10–15 percent of their income for the privilege of greater freedom of choice and not standing in line.[19] Russian consumers now have that choice.

Comparisons with Transition Successes

The experiences of other transition economies show that a decline in output is inevitable when transition commences. The collapse of the administrative command system, the disruption of traditional supply relationships both at home and abroad, the change in relative prices, the general confusion and chaos—all result in declining output. Although Soviet officials, including Gorbachev, initially felt that it would be possible to transverse the transition without serious economic declines, this did not prove to be the case when the actual transition began. That the first phase of transition was accompanied by economic declines is not surprising. The institutions of a market economy cannot be established overnight; the actors must learn how to play in a market economy; new markets must be discovered and old ones phased out. Property rights must be established. Price liberalization must work its way through domestic markets. The institutions of monetary and fiscal policy must be established.

A number of countries began transition before, at the same time, or after Russia. The countries of Central Europe—Poland, Czech Republic, and Hungary—began serious transition in the late 1980s, so their experience provides a longer frame of reference. The countries of the former Soviet Union (FSU) began their transitions at about the same time as Russia, with varying degrees of success. We have a number of success stories and an even greater number of failures. Let's begin by comparing Russia with the transition success stories.

Table 15.5 compares Russia with Poland, the Czech Republic, and Hungary, the three transition success stories. As this information indicates, the typical pattern of a successful transition begins with an inevitable drop in output. The drop appears to occur whether the country uses a strategy of **shock therapy** or **gradualism**. As will be pointed out below, the best indicator of shock therapy versus gradualism is inflation—whether monetary and fiscal policies are adopted that cause inflation to decel-

Table 15.5

RUSSIA VERSUS TRANSITION SUCCESSES
(annual inflation rates)

	1988		1989		1990		1991	
	Inflation rate (annual)	GDP growth rates	Inflation rate (annual)	GDP growth rates	Inflation rate (annual)	GDP growth rates	Inflation rate (annual)	GDP growth rates
Russia	1.5	1.5	4.5	2.5	11.5	−2.0	122.9	−9.0
Poland	60.0	4.1	252.0	0.2	585.0	−11.6	70.0	−7.6
Hungary	16.5	0.4	17.0	0.7	29.0	−3.5	35.0	−11.5
Czech Republic	0.2	2.5	2.3	1.4	11.0	0.4	57.0	−14.2

	1992		1993		1994		1995	
	Inflation rate (annual)	GDP growth rates	Inflation rate (annual)	GDP growth rates	Inflation rate (annual)	GDP growth rates	Inflation rate (annual)	GDP growth rates
Russia	1,700.0	−19.0	919.0	−12.0	257.0	−15.0	125.0	−2.7
Poland	43.0	1.0	35.0	4.0	30.0	4.0	25.0	3.0
Hungary	23.0	−4.4	22.0	−1.6	19.0	−1.6	17.0	2.0
Czech Republic	11.0	−7.1	21.0	−1.0	11.0	−1.0	10.0	5.0

Sources: PlanEcon, *Review and Outlook for the Former Soviet Republics* (selected issues); PlanEcon, *Review and Outlook for Eastern Europe* (selected issues).

erate soon after the initial upward adjustment in prices occurs. In Table 15.5, Russia experienced a more severe and prolonged upsurge in inflation than the transition successes. In those cases where shock therapy is used, the deceleration in inflation occurs relatively soon; in gradualist countries, the deceleration is delayed.

Successful transition is associated with declining output for two to three years followed by positive, then accelerating growth. This pattern appears to apply to Poland, the Czech Republic, Hungary, and the Baltic States. In the case of gradualist countries (such as Ukraine, most of Central Asia, and a number of Central European countries), decelerated inflation is delayed or does not come at all. But even in gradualist countries, real output eventually stops falling, although after a much longer decline (three years or more). In the countries undergoing successful transition, the cessation of the decline in output appears to be caused by positive forces, such as the inflow of foreign or domestic investment, completion of privatization, or macroeconomic stabilization. In the less successful cases, the decline in output ceases simply because there appear to be natural limits below which real output cannot fall.

Figure 15.3 summarizes the output decline of countries in the Former Soviet Union and in parts of Central Europe that are undergoing economic transition. This

Figure 15.3   Output Decline During the Transition (1989–95)

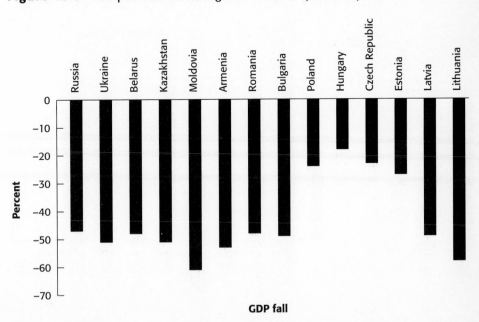

Sources: PlanEcon, *Review and Outlook for the Former Soviet Republics* (selected issues); PlanEcon, *Review and Outlook for Eastern Europe* (selected issues).

figure shows that the Russian experience is by no means unusual. Although substantial, Russia's output decline (using the official statistics and assuming that the other countries are calculated in much the same way), was, if anything, slightly less traumatic than in other countries. Only three countries—Poland, Hungary, and the Czech Republic—were able to avoid substantial losses in output during the early years of transition. The "successful" transition countries of the Baltic States—Estonia and Latvia—underwent substantial drops in output. Most were like Russia in the sense that they went five or more years without regaining positive economic growth.

Shock Therapy Versus Gradualism

As Chapter 13 indicated, transition countries can choose between shock therapy and gradualism. Although shock therapy and gradualism can be characterized by a number of factors—macroeconomic stabilization, speed of privatization, and price liberalization, adoption of a convertible currency—the speed with which inflation is tamed is perhaps the best single indicator of shock therapy versus gradualism.

Figure 15.4 shows the average rate of inflation during the first six years of transition for the same countries whose output declines are shown in Figure 15.3. By

Figure 15.4   Average Inflation During the Transition (1989–95)

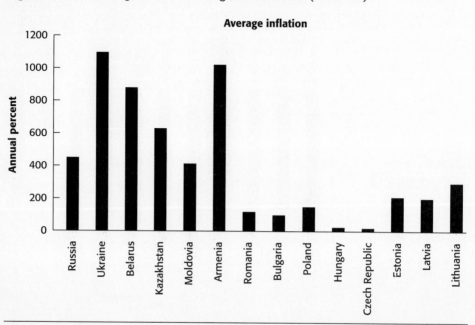

Sources: PlanEcon, *Review and Outlook for the Former Soviet Republics* (selected issues); Plan Econ, *Review and Outlook for Eastern Europe* (selected issues).

comparing the two figures, it becomes clear that those countries that experienced smaller output declines also experienced lower inflation. The negative relationship exists, but it is not overwhelming: The scatter diagram in Figure 15.5 reveals a negatively-sloped but generally weak relationship. Countries such as Poland, Hungary, the Czech Republic, Latvia, and Estonia, all of which undertook more strict shock therapy, regained positive economic growth earlier than those that opted for gradualism.

What is the link between inflation control and economic growth? The standard textbook answer is that rapid inflation diverts attention from productive investment, causes the most skilled business managers to engage in speculation as opposed to productive investment, causes the economy to revert to barter, and so on. With high and rising inflationary expectations, nominal interest rates soar, credit markets evaporate, and enterprises are unable to raise capital through debt markets. The efficiency of money transactions is lost. The country's exchange rate fluctuates and depreciates. For a number of reasons, it is difficult for a country to grow under the threat of hyperinflation.

Russia, along with other countries undergoing transition, debated the sources of high inflation. Obviously, the initial jump in inflation was inevitable since it was associated with the one-time upward adjustment of prices associated with price liberalization. There is no strong reason, however, why this one-time adjustment should be transformed into ongoing and accelerating inflation. Although a number of Russian

Figure 15.5   GDP Decline vs. Inflation (transition economies, 1989–95)

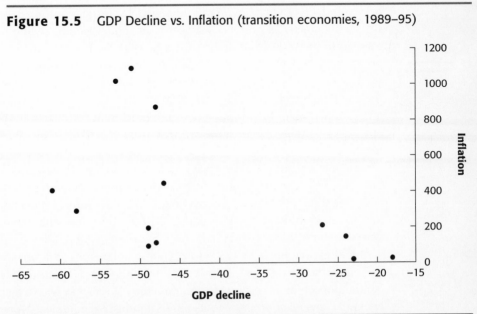

Sources: PlanEcon, *Review and Outlook for the Former Soviet Republics* (selected issues); PlanEcon, *Review and Outlook for Eastern Europe* (selected issues).

economists made structural arguments for inflation—such as inflation being caused by the monopoly power of suppliers—this argument is not credible. The exercise of monopoly power should lead to one-shot inflation, not continuing inflation.

Figure 15.5 also shows the interplay between the inflation rate and economic growth for the transition economies. It shows that positive growth (or a slowing of the decline in output) was typically associated with a deceleration of inflation. True, tight money made credit tighter and investment funds more difficult to obtain, but creating a more stable investment climate also created greater interest in equity investment. The decline in interest rates associated with the drop in inflationary expectations also resulted in lower interest rates, which made investment projects based upon borrowed funds more credible.

The Russian experience seems to be different from the experiences of successful transition economies insofar as the recovery of real GDP growth has lagged well behind the deceleration of inflation. Why has the return to positive economic growth been so delayed in Russia?

Dissecting Russia's Output Decline

If we compare Russia's recovery prospects with those of the other transition economies, we can enumerate factors that favor an early recovery as well as factors that delay recovery. On the positive side, we should note that Russia is a resource-rich country, freed by the collapse of the Soviet Union and its Eastern European empire from delivering its raw material riches to allied countries at subsidized prices. In fact, as Chapter 17 will demonstrate, throughout much of the transition, Russia maintained a positive balance on current account, selling more goods and services to the rest of the world than it bought. Such sales, largely at world market prices, have brought immense wealth to those who control Russia's raw materials, both private and public. A second positive feature (perhaps unexpected) has been the fact that Russia completed its privatization process in a surprisingly timely fashion. Completion of privatization does not mean that privatization was done fairly or efficiently. It does mean, however, that property rights issues have been largely decided.

On the negative side, because Russia is a large and diverse country with diverse interests, it has found it difficult to unite behind a consistent transition strategy. Although it adopted a new constitution, it has had difficulty passing laws, given the long-standing friction between parliament and the president. Russia has vacillated between shock therapy and gradualism, between easy credits for failing enterprises and tight money, between going tough on tax collections and providing tax relief for economic incentives. As a former world military power that devoted an unprecedented portion of its resources to the military, Russia has had to face an exceedingly tough conversion process for its military-industrial complex. Moreover, it has had to face the extensive criminalization of its society by mafia gangs and corrupt economic officials.

Figure 15.6 dissects Russia's decline in output by examining the changing structure of final demand. It shows that the collapse in output was largely a collapse in investment rather than of private or public consumption or of exports and imports. In fact, Figure 15.6 attests to the considerable strength of private consumption and of exports and imports. The latter achieved positive growth despite the enormous restructuring of trade away from the former Soviet empire and towards the West.

If Russia had been able to sustain its investment spending, it could have largely avoided the collapse in output. The collapse in investment spending is discussed in Chapter 16, on the Russian capital market. For now, we should note that the collapse in investment was a consequence both of deficient investment demand and of domestic production constraints. On the demand side, Russia had to make the difficult transition from budget finance to private investment finance. With the collapse in tax discipline and the numerous demands on the state budget, investment finance was no longer automatically forthcoming from the national budget. At the same time, a private capital market had yet to be developed. Even if a private market for capital had indeed existed, the uncertainty surrounding the future of the Russian economy would have dissuaded potential investors in capital projects, who could earn higher rates of return through trading and through speculative investment.

Figure 15.6 Russian GDP: Components of Final Demand (annual growth rates)

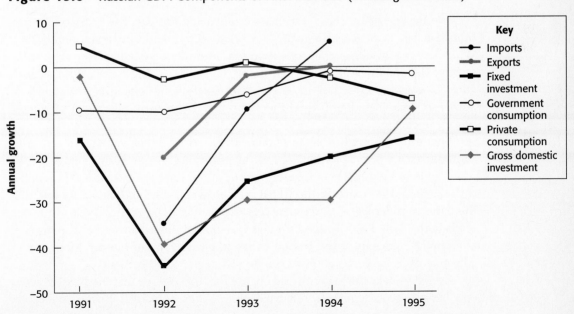

Source: PlanEcon, *Review and Outlook for the Former Soviet Republics* (selected issues).

On the supply side, the Russian capital goods industry had been distributed throughout the former Soviet Union, and its supply links had been in many cases disrupted. More importantly, Russian capital goods may not have been of sufficient quality to compete in a market environment. Without considerable investment in new technology and products, Russian capital goods would not be in demand. An added factor that discouraged investment was the surprisingly high relative price of investment goods in Russia. According to studies of the purchasing power of the ruble, as of 1993, Russian capital goods were more than twice as expensive as consumer goods.[20]

The negative growth rates of capital productivity at the end of the Soviet period attest to the overaccumulation of capital in the Russian economy and to the low quality of Russian capital goods. The steepest production declines were for locomotives, freight cars, bulldozers, cranes, tractors, machine tools, and electric motors. As is noted by two experts from the IMF, "That such equipment virtually ceased to be produced should not be lamented as an output "loss," rather, it should be interpreted as a sign that market forces were beginning to operate."[21]

RUSSIA'S RELATIVE POSITION

Russia's Decline During the Transition

The decline in Russian GDP that accompanied the first five years of Russian transition has made Russia's relative position in the world economy deteriorate. While the industrialized countries experienced positive growth during the 1990s, most of the countries of the former Soviet Union, including Russia itself, experienced negative growth. For some countries (such as the emerging economies of Southeast Asia, including China) the 1980s and 1990s were periods of extremely rapid growth.

Figure 15.7 shows Russia's position in 1989 and 1993 relative to other countries as measured by per capita income. All measures are in purchasing power parity, which reflects the relative purchasing power of the various currencies. If we begin with Russia in 1989 (we take the USSR average as reflective of Russia), we find that there was considerable disagreement on Russia's relative position in 1989. Estimates made in the early 1990s by the CIA and Goskomstat placed Soviet per capita GDP at around 65 percent of the United States (the first Russian figure). More recent adjustments by Goskomstat lower the Russian figure to 40 percent.[22]

Even if we take the lower Russian figure for 1989, we see that the Russian economy has suffered a significant relative decline. Whereas in 1989, Russia's per capita income was in the neighborhood of Spain, Greece, and Portugal, by 1993, Russia was well below Turkey and Mexico.

Figure 15.7 Russian Per Capita GDP, 1989 and 1993 (as a percent of U.S.)

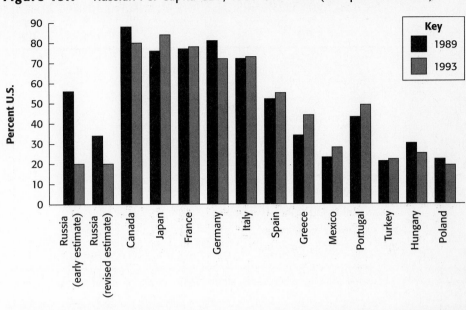

Sources: Goskomstat, *Mezhdunarodnye sopostavleniia VNP za 1993 god* (Moscow: Goskomstat, 1996), 72; *Handbook of International Economic Statistics 1992*, 28, 59; *Statistical Abstract of the United States* (International Statistics).

Inferred Growth Rates

Above, we noted that one potential problem in assessing Russian growth during the transition is that the Soviet period base may be overstated. We can test for overstatement and for implicit growth rates by comparing 1989 Russian GDP with 1993 Russian GDP, both as a percent of the U.S.[23] If we take the higher 1989 estimate, then Russia fell from 42 percent to 12 percent of the United States. If we take the lower 1989 figure, Russian GDP fell from 26 to 12 percent of the United States between 1989 and 1993. After adjusting for U.S. growth, we find that the implicit decline in Russian GDP is as follows: If we take the lower 1989 figure, Russian 1993 GDP was 50 percent of 1989. If we take the higher 1989 figure, Russian 1993 GDP was only 30 percent of 1989. For this reason, we can conclude that even the lower 1989 figure was overstated. None of the available estimates provide output declines sufficiently large to have deteriorated Russia's relative position by that much.

Russian Productivity

Russian statistical authorities have done extensive work on revaluing the Russian stock of capital assets, as well as the above work on Russian relative GDP

Table 15.6

PRODUCTIVITY COMPARISONS*, RUSSIA AND THE UNITED STATES, 1993

	(US = 100)
Russian/US GDP	12
Russian/US capital[1]	16
Russian/US capital[2]	27
Russian/US labor force	56
Capital productivity[1]	74
Capital productivity[2]	43
Labor productivity	21
Total productivity[1]	37
Total productivity[2]	23
Russian/US earnings[a]	4
Russian/US earnings[b]	16

*Capital and labor productivity averaged using weights of .3 and .7 respectively.

Key: [1]Converts Russian capital stock into dollars using the PPP rate for capital investment.

[2]Converts Russian capital stock into dollars using the average PPP exchange rate.

[a]Converts ruble wages into dollars using market exchange rate.

[b]Converts ruble wages into dollars using PPP exchange rate.

Sources: *Natsional'nye scheta Rossii v 1989–1994 gg,* 69; *Mezhdunarodnye Sopostovaleniia VNP za 1993 g,* 45, 66–67, 72; *Sotsial'naia sfera Rossii 1995,* 42; U.S. figures from *Statistical Abstract of the United States.*

(conducted in conjunction with international statistical authorities). From this capital data and from information on the size of the Russian labor force, we can make rough calculations of factor productivity of the Russian economy as of the end of 1993, after two years of transition.

The results of these productivity calculations are shown in Table 15.6. In 1993, Russian real GDP was 12 percent of the United States, but its capital stock was between 16 and 27 percent, depending upon how we convert Russian capital into dollars.[26] The Russian labor force in 1993 was 56 percent of the United States. Although it would be more accurate to adjust the relative labor force figures for quality differences, we simply take the relative physical labor force figures.

Table 15.3 shows that in 1993 Russian labor was one-fifth as productive as U.S. labor, that Russian capital was between one-fourth and one-half as productive as U.S. capital, and the total factor productivity in Russia was between one-fifth and one-third of the United States. These productivity calculations should be taken as most approximate. They rely on shaky calculations of the Russian capital stock, which has to be frequently revalued to adjust for inflation and depreciation. We have already noted above the potential measurement errors with respect to Russian output.

Nevertheless, if Table 15.6 is to be believed, the Russian economy employs its resources at levels that would produce between one-fifth and one-third of U.S. output (if Russian capital and labor resources equaled those of the United States). This result is consistent with the calculation of Russia's per capita GDP at around one-fifth of the United States.

Table 15.6 also speaks to the relative level of Russian wages. Converted into dollars at the official exchange rate (which would be the rate that foreigners would actually have to pay for Russian labor), the Russian wage rate equaled 4 percent of the United States in 1993, or 20 percent of its relative productivity. If we convert Russian wages into dollars using purchasing power parity (PPP) exchange rates, then Russian wages equaled 16 percent of the United States in 1993, a rate roughly equal to its relative productivity. Thus, as of 1993, Russian labor was priced (in terms of market exchange rates) well below its productivity, proving that Russian labor has been a relatively cheap resource throughout the transition.

SUMMARY

We now have more than half a decade's worth of experience with transition. Russia is only one case of a former administrative command economy going through transition, although it is the most important. Much hinges on the outcome of Russia's transition.

The evidence presented in this chapter makes a persuasive case that Russian recovery is inevitable as long as reasonable political stability is achieved. We have seen that the consumer and export sectors have shown vitality, that real per capita incomes and real consumption have most likely been rising, and that we have probably overstated the Russian decline. It is quite possible that the Russian economy, if measured properly, has been growing for a year or two.

The factors that have dragged down the Russian recovery cannot be resolved overnight. If they were easy to solve, they would have been resolved already. Investment will not recover until the institutional, legal, and tax environment of Russia is conducive to investment. Chapter 17 will show that, in fact, there appear to be ready sources of finance if the investment climate were better. The conversion of obsolete heavy industry and conversion of the defense establishment require time. Heavy industry and the military-industrial complex represent important lobbying groups in Russia, and there is not enough political will or power to cut them loose to sink or swim in a market environment.

Terms and Concepts ————————————

turnpike analogy   The argument that a country may need to make short-term adjustments to its growth path in order to achieve long-term sustained economic growth.

Goskomstat   Russia's statistical committee.

Material Product System (MPS)   The system of national accounting used in the Soviet Union, a system of accounting which differed in many respects from practices standard in Western countries.

System of National Accounts   The standard for national income and product evaluation used throughout the world, defining the value of final goods and services as the sum of value added by each sector of an economy; this sum equals the aggregate of incomes earned by the factors of production.

shock therapy   A strategy of conducting the transition from plan to market at a rapid pace, for example privatization, creation of markets, release of prices, change in tax systems, etc.

gradualism   A strategy of conducting the transition from plan to market on a gradual basis, for example the gradual emergence of new ownership arrangements rather than the sudden disbursement of property through immediate direct sale or voucher arrangements.

Selected Bibliography

Aslund, A. "Russia's Success Story," *Foreign Affairs* vol. 75, no. 5 (1994).

Biznes v Rossii: universal'ny juridicheski spravochnik predprinimatelia [Business in Russia: Universal legal handbook for participants] (Moscow: Tikhimorova, 1996).

Dimitrieva, O. *Regional Development: The USSR and After* (New York: St. Martins Press, 1996).

Dobozi, I., and G. Pohl. "Real Output Decline in Transition Economies: Forget GDP, Try Power Consumption Data!", *Transition*, vol. 8, 1–2.

Fischer, S., R. Sahay, and C. A. Vegh. "Stabilization and Growth in Transition Economies: The Early Experience," *Journal of Economic Perspectives* vol. 10, no. 2 (Spring 1996).

Gavrilenkov, E., and V. Koen, "How Large Was the Output Collapse in Russia? Alternative Estimates and Welfare Implications," IMF Working paper 94/154 (December 1994).

Goskomstat. *Rossii v tsifrakh 1995* [Russia in figures in 1995] (Moscow: Goskomstat Rossii, 1995)

———— . *Natsional'nye scheta Rossii v 1989–1994 g* [The national accounts of Russia, 1989–1994] (Moscow: Goskomstat, 1995).

———— . *Mezhdunarodnye sopostavleniia valovogo vnutrennogo produkta za 1993 god* [International comparisons of gross domestic product for 1993] (Moscow: Goskomstat, 1996).

Kuboniwa, M. "Russian Output Drop in Early Transition and its Macroeconomic Implications," Hitotsubashi University, Institute of Economic Research, D96–11, (November 1996).

Morgan Stanley. "The Russian Oil and Gas Industry," *Investment Research UK and Europe: Russia* (February 2, 1996).

World Bank. *Russian Federation: Report on the National Accounts* (Washington, DC: World Bank, 1995).

——— . *The World Development Report 1996* (Washington, DC: World Bank, 1996).

——— . *Statistical Handbook 1995: States of the Former USSR* (Washington, DC: World Bank, 1996).

Notes

1. R. Dorfman, P. Samuelson, and R. Solow, *Linear Programming and Economic Analysis* (New York: McGraw Hill, 1958), 331.
2. This discussion of Russian statistical practices is based upon World Bank and Government of the Russian Federation, *Russian Federation: Report on the National Accounts* (October 1995).
3. World Bank, op. cit., 40.
4. This calculation of the size of the shadow economy is from Goskomstat, *Rossiia v tsifrakh 1995* (Moscow: Goskomstat Rossii, 1995), 19.
5. World Bank, op. cit., 41.
6. World Bank, op. cit., 47.
7. For relevant Russian accounting rules, see Order of the Ministry of Finance of the Russian Federation, no. 170 of December 26, 1994; Chart of Accounts of Financial and Economic Activities of Enterprises, Ministry of Finance of the USSR, no. 56, November 1, 1991 (with Amendments of December 28, 1994 and July 28, 1995). Also see *Biznes v Rossii Universal'ny juridicheski spravochnik predpinimatelia* (Moscow: Tikhimorova, 1996), Part V.
8. J. Smith, "Tax and Accounting in Russian Companies," Morgan Stanley, *Investment Research UK and Europe: Russia* (February 2, 1996), 26–29.
9. M. Kuboniwa, "Russian Output Drop in Early Transition and its Macroeconomic Implications," Institute of Economic Research, Hitotsubashi University, D96-11 (November 1996).
10. E. Gavrilenkov and V. Koen, "How Large Was the Output Collapse in Russia? Alternative Estimates and Welfare Implications," *IMF Working Paper*, no. 94/154 (December 1994); World Bank, *Russian Federation: Report on the National Accounts*, 116–117.
11. See Goskomstat, *Natsional'nye scheta Rossii v 1989–1994 g* (Moscow: Goskomstat, 1995), 5.
12. M. Kuboniwa, op. cit., Table 8.
13. Gavrilenkov and Koen suggest these statistics as benchmarks for the Russian decline in the 1990s.
14. Gavrilenkov and Koen, 106–07.
15. Gavrilenkov and Koen, 110.
16. For example, production of meat products in 1994 was between 30 and 50 percent less than in 1991, but consumption was shown to be only 7 percent less. Milk product production was shown to be about 50 percent less in 1994 than in 1991, but milk product consumption was only 14 percent less. Goskomstat has revised its average annual growth rate of real retail sales for the 1991 to 1994 period from –11 percent per annum to –0.5 percent per annum. Gavrilenkov and Koen, 109, 111.
17. I. Dobozi and G. Pohl, "Real Output Decline in Transition Economies: Forget GDP, Try Power Consumption Data!" *Transition*, vol. 8, no. 1–2; A. Aslund, "Russia's Success Story," *Foreign Affairs*, vol. 75, no. 5 (1994), 58–70.

18. Gavrilenkov and Koen, 116.

19. I. Collier, "Effective Purchasing Power in a Quantity Constrained Economy: An Estimate for the German Democratic Republic," *Review of Economics and Statistics,* vol. 68, no. 1 (February 1986), 24–32.

20. Goskomstat, *Mezhdunarodnye Sopostavleniia valovogo vnutrennogo produkta za 1993 god* (Moscow: Goskomstat, 1996), 46.

21. Gavrilenkov and Koen, 113–14.

22. S. Rosefielde and R. Pfouts, "Value Imputed: Adjusted Factor Cost and the Overstatement of Soviet Economic Performance," a paper presented at the American Association for Slavic Studies Meeting, Boston, MA (November 1996). As this paper points out, originally there was agreement between the CIA and Goskomstat about Russia's relative per capita income at about 65 percent of the U.S. Goskomstat then revised its figure down to 40 percent.

23. The 1989 Soviet figures are converted into Russian figures by multiplying by Russia's share of Soviet GDP (65 percent).

24. The Russian capital stock figures are from Goskomstat, *Natsional'nye scheta Rossii v 1989–1994 gg* (Moscow: Goskomstat Rossii, 1995), 69. The 1993 capital stock figures are for the book value of Russia's capital stock after a revaluation conducted in January of 1994. The purchasing power parity (PPP) exchange rates are from Goskomstat, *Mezhdunarodnye sopostavlenia valovogo vnutrennogo produkta za 1993 g* (Moscow: Goskomstat Rossii, 1996), 45, 72. The PPP exchange rate for capital investments in 1993 was 1.7 times the average PPP. Variant (1) in the table uses the specific PPP for capital investments. Variant (2) uses the average Russian PPP conversion rate.

Russian Capital Markets

FROM BUDGET FINANCE TO PRIVATE CAPITAL MARKETS

Under the Soviet administrative command economy, almost all enterprises were owned by the state. They received their investment capital from the state budget. If a firm were profitable, its profits were largely paid into the state budget to finance reinvestment or investment in other, less profitable firms. Ministries reallocated profits from profitable enterprises to those that required subsidies. Enterprise managers were state employees. Although they were rewarded according to bonus schemes, they had little or no incentive to maximize profits or to work in other ways to increase the value of the enterprise. The Soviet enterprise's **working capital** was provided through a credit plan worked out by the industrial ministry (the finance ministry) and the monopoly state bank. This credit plan was part of the enterprise operating plan and provided cash for enterprise employee payments and credit for purchases from other enterprises. Investment capital was provided from the state budget and managed by specialized banks such as the Industrial Construction Bank. Although Soviet enterprises operated on the basis of an accounting system, they knew that they would remain in business thanks to subsidies from the state budget or reallocations within the ministry.

The breakdown of the Soviet administrative command economy meant that new methods of meeting the need for operating capital and investment capital had to be developed. With the declining economy, collapse of taxpayer discipline, and the growing disputes between the federal and local governments over tax collections, the federal budget no longer had the resources to finance the investment needs of the entire economy. As the transition began, instead of serving as a source of national savings, the federal budget became a drain on national savings as its expenditures exceeded its revenues.

In any economy, the supply of savings for investment finance (I) must come from the following sources:

$$I = S + (T - G) + (M - X)$$

where S denotes private saving either of individuals or of businesses,

$T - G$ denotes the government surplus (if T exceeds G) or deficit
   (if G exceeds T)

$M - X$ denotes foreign saving, which equals the excess of imports of
   goods and services over exports of goods and services.

If a country is running a current account deficit (M greater than X), its capital account is positive, and it is receiving net savings from the rest of the world in the form of stock purchases, purchases of private or public bonds, purchases of real estate, and bank deposits by foreigners. If it is running a current account surplus, it is supplying savings to the rest of the world in the form of acquiring assets in other countries. Russia's current and capital accounts with the rest of the world are discussed in Chapter 17.

Each category of saving depends on a range of factors. Private saving depends on interest rates, income, and taxes. Government surpluses or deficits depend on political processes and the state of the economy. The supply of foreign saving depends on relative rates of return and political stability, among other things.

In the Soviet period, savings to finance investment were supplied primarily through the state budget's "expenditures for the national economy." Some enterprise investment was financed through enterprise depreciation and profit reinvestment accounts, which had been deposited into investment banks, but these accounts were strictly controlled, and the central planning authorities governed investment closely. Soviet households did indeed accumulate private savings, primarily in the form of cash or deposits in the state savings bank system, which represented a source of private savings. In sum, although there were sources of investment finance in addition to the state budget "surplus," virtually all investment funds were under the strict control of the planners, even if they had been generated within the enterprise or household.

CREATING A RUSSIAN CAPITAL MARKET

In market economies, investment finance and working capital are generated by private capital markets. Although governments can and do finance a portion of a nation's capital investments, the primary source of investment finance is private capital markets. In fact, in most industrialized market economies, the state now is a competitor with businesses for the limited supply of investment finance since the majority of governments are now running deficits.

When Russia began its transition in December of 1991, it had no private capital market, and its traditional "state" capital market was collapsing with its rising state deficit. A major task of transition, therefore, was the timely creation of a private capital market that mobilized the private saving of individuals, businesses, and foreigners to meet its investment requirements. The creation of a Russian capital market has not been an easy challenge. It has required the formation of appropriate institutions for channeling domestic and foreign saving into productive investment through **financial intermediation** and, more difficult, it has required an investment climate that promotes the demand for productive investment.

As we examined the sharp decline of the Russian economy from 1989 to the present (Chapter 15), it was evident that the disintegration of investment spending was the major source of the collapse of the Russian economy. The implosion of investment spending was not unexpected, given the sudden disappearance of the state capital market before a private capital market had been created in its place.

The steps to creating a viable private capital market in Russia involve not only the creation of appropriate institutions for saving and for financial intermediation between savers and investors, but also the creation of a base for private domestic saving and for attracting foreign saving. The financial system affects both the supply of savings and the efficient use of saving.[1] Russia, or any other country, would wish to use its limited savings effectively. The effective use of savings is normally accomplished through financial intermediation, where organizations like banks, which specialize in making loans to credit-worthy customers, mobilize the savings of private households, who have no specialized knowledge in making loans. The effective use of savings also requires investment (merchant) banks and underwriters, who are able to arrange the sale of new shares of stock to savers. If a country's savings go into the hoarding of foreign exchange, real estate, holding excessive inventories, or capital flight, even a high-saving country can have a low rate of real capital formation. For stock markets and credit markets to function well, there must be well-established procedures and institutions to bring savers and investors together.

Private Saving in Russia

Private saving takes place when households spend less than their disposable income and when businesses accumulate after-tax profits (which are either reinvested in their own companies or invested elsewhere) or set aside funds in deprecation accounts. Households save for a variety of reasons: for retirement, for major purchases, or to meet unexpected emergencies. Businesses save primarily, although not entirely, for the purpose of raising investment funds inside the company, without having to rely on third parties.[2]

Both household and business saving depend upon institutional arrangements, such as the existence of vehicles for saving (such as stock and bond markets or secure banks), tax rules concerning saving (tax laws that encourage saving), or state pension plans. Saving also depends upon the state of the economy (are incomes rising? what is the degree of uncertainty? is the currency secure?).

Economic theory suggests that household saving is a function of household after-tax income, which determines the base from which private savings can be accumulated. However, factors other than after-tax household income affect consumption; different households with the same income have different saving rates, and different countries have quite different savings rates after adjustment for income level.

Russian household savings are a key to the formation of a viable Russian capital market in the sense that they are the primary source of net savings for the capital market. Table 16.1 (p. 358) shows the behavior of Russian household savings in the 1990s as compared to the late administrative command era. The table makes clear that Russian household savings have increased as a percentage of household income from the late Soviet era through the mid-1990s. In the mid-1980s, Russian households saved about 5 percent of their income. By the mid-1990s, Russian households were saving almost 30 percent of their income.[3] In fact, Russian household savings in the 1990s constituted a higher percentage of household income than in most affluent market economies. At first blush, the increase in the Russian household saving rate is unexpected in view of the decline in Russian real GDP that occurred between 1989 and the present.

A number of reasons can be cited to explain the relatively high Russian rate of personal saving in the 1990s, during the most difficult period of transition:

1. In real terms, the runaway inflation that occurred between 1992 and 1994 wiped out most of household saving accumulated during the Soviet period. Russian households, in effect, had to start their savings programs from scratch. The high rate of saving could therefore be a response to the need to replenish the assets that inflation had destroyed.
2. Personal savings tend to increase during periods of uncertainty. Families protect themselves from uncertainty by saving more. The early transition years were a period of extreme uncertainty concerning the future. One source of uncertainty remained the Russian political system, with the threat of a communist resurgence in the presidential elections of 1996 and thereafter the precarious health of President Boris Yeltsin.
3. With the collapse of the state budget and rising inflation, state pension programs ceased to provide income security for retirement, disabilities, and

old age. Also the collapse of the Soviet system of free medicine provided another reason for Russian households to save for emergencies.

4. Individuals who began acquiring ownership shares in newly privatized businesses or starting up their own small businesses remained uncertain about their ownership rights and privileges. With secure property rights, business owners are prepared to reinvest the company's profits back into the company. With uncertain property rights, such as the threat of renationalization, business owners prefer to funnel enterprise profits to their own incomes, particularly with poor tax discipline and financial control, and save in their own accounts. This converts business savings into private savings.

5. In the absence of management ownership and control, business managers are prepared to ignore business profits and divert enterprise income to their own pockets, thereby secretly raising their own incomes.

6. During the Soviet period, Russian households were not allowed to own significant assets, such as apartments or land. As Russia moved towards a market economy, households were now entitled to buy homes, apartments, and land. The ability to buy significant assets creates an incentive to save.

7. The tax burden on Russian households actually fell as the tax system collapsed. Lower taxes on income encourage saving.

8. The official statistics may overstate savings, which is calculated as the difference between after-tax income and consumption. Official statistics may include unpaid wages as income, which, if not eventually paid, would overstate saving.[4]

Table 16.1 (p. 358) breaks down the savings of Russian households into their various components. By the mid-1990s, less than one-third of household saving was in the form of savings account deposits and stock purchases. More than two-thirds of household saving was in the form of foreign currency hoarding or increases in holdings of domestic currency. The household saving figure does not include another form of saving which is common in a high-inflation economy, namely, purchases of consumer durables as an inflation hedge. Russian household survey data from late 1994 and early 1995 shows that Russian households spent 12 percent of their purchases on consumer durables like automobiles and housing.[5] Therefore, if we include consumer durable purchases in saving, the 1994 saving rate would be just about 40 percent.

The composition of Russian household savings points to a weakness of the Russian financial system. As of late 1995, it had not succeeded in attracting household savings either for direct investments in Russian companies (purchases of stock) or for use by Russian financial intermediaries. The overwhelming portion of investment went into "unproductive uses," such as foreign currency hoarding, domestic currency hoarding, or purchases of consumer durables.

Why was such a small percentage of household savings directed into financial intermediaries, such as commercial banks, during this period? As was discussed in

Chapter 14, Russia's commercial banking institutions were in the process of development, and Russia experienced a number of banking crises, which frightened away potential depositors. The only deposits currently insured by the Russian federal government are deposits in the state-owned **Sberbank (Saving Bank),** which accounts for more than 60 percent of household savings in depository institutions. In addition, having lost most of their savings from the Soviet era to inflation, households were wary about traditional instruments of saving, such as savings accounts in domestic currency. Although the Russian Duma passed a law in May of 1995 to compensate savers who had lost their savings through inflation, Russian households still have not been compensated, nor is it clear how such a law would be applied.[6] To attract depositors, banks must offer nominal interest rates in excess of anticipated inflation; that is, they must offer positive real interest rates. Figure 16.1 shows that both commercial bank and savings bank (Sberbank) deposit rates were below the inflation rate for much of the period 1992 through 1995.

Let us consider the amount of savings that Russian households were generating in the mid-1990s. According to official statistics, the Russian household sector saved 105 trillion Russian rubles in 1994. At the official exchange rate of 2204 rubles to the dollar, this translates into 48 billion U.S. dollars. At the exchange rate that reflects the purchasing power of the ruble (950 rubles = $1), saving would have amounted to $110 billion.[7] This amount of potential domestic saving, compared with current injections of foreign investment (Chapter 17), is substantial.

So, Russian households are potentially able to supply considerable sums of savings for investment finance—amounts well in excess of any anticipated foreign investments. Moreover, private savings should rise as the Russian economy recovers and grows. The basic problem has been that household savings have been directed into nonproductive uses. Of the 48 to 102 billion dollars of *annual* household savings, less than one-third went into bank deposits for financial intermediation or into direct stock purchases.

Table 16.1

RUSSIAN HOUSEHOLD SAVINGS RATES (PERCENT OF HOUSEHOLD INCOME)

	1985	1990	1991	1992	1993	1994
Goods and services	82.7	75.3	62.3	72.9	68.9	64.5
Savings deposits and stocks	12.3	12.0	8.3	8.2	7.6	6.8
Taxes and fees	5.0	13.0	29.0	19.0	24.0	29.0
Foreign currency	4.0	8.0	20.0	5.0	6.0	7.0
Saving rate	0.0	0.0	0.0	1.0	8.0	18.0
Increase in money	1.0	5.0	10.0	14.0	9.0	5.0

Source: Goskomstat, *Natsional'nye schete Rossii v 1989–1994 gg* (Moscow: 1955), 61.

RUSSIAN DEBT MARKETS

Savings can be used either to purchase ownership interests (equity) in businesses or to supply credit for the long-term and short-term credit needs of the economy. Household, business, and foreign saving constitute the loanable funds or credit in any economy. Loanable funds do not go only into productive investments. They can also be used to purchase consumer durables, land, precious metals, working capital for speculation, and so on. Where these savings go depends on customs, equity alternatives, **debt-market** institutions, and rates of return expected in these various activities.

In industrialized market economies, significant amounts of investment in plant, equipment, and inventories are financed through credit or debt. Rarely is credit supplied directly from the ultimate saver to the ultimate borrower. Instead, debt capital is typically provided through financial intermediaries such as banks or insurance companies. For Russia to have a developed debt market, it must create the institutions that attract savings and reliably link savers and business borrowers.

In the Soviet administrative command economy, the distinction between debt and equity financing was blurred. Investment finance was provided through an

Figure 16.1 Russia: Monthly Real Interest Rates 1992–97 (percent)

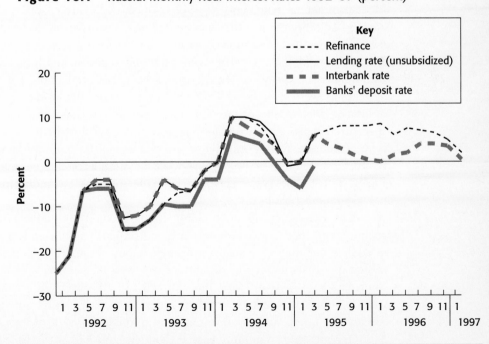

Source: *Russian Economic Trends,* quarterly and monthly updates.

investment plan administered by the Ministry of Finance, the State Bank (Gosbank), and specialized investment banks. Some funds allocated for investment were indeed indirectly supplied by the enterprises themselves through deposits of profits in investment accounts or through profits taxes, but the bulk of investment finance was provided by the state budget. Once enterprises received investment funds, they were not obligated to repay these "loans"; rather, for most of the Soviet period, did not even have to pay interest. With the collapse of the Soviet administrative command economy, the monopoly supply of credit collapsed. Russia was faced with the task of creating a market system of financial intermediation. Since insurance companies have been slow to emerge, the major potential source of financial intermediation has been private commercial banking.

The Russian Banking System

Market economies have a two-tier banking system in which a central bank (the top tier) supervises commercial banks and thrift institutions (the bottom tier) and controls the money supply. The commercial banks and thrift institutions then deal with personal and business customers. It is the bottom tier that conducts financial intermediation between lenders and borrowers.

As Russia entered its transition period, it began to form a "market" banking system, which consisted of commercial banks and savings banks and the **Central Bank of Russia** (CBR) which was the regulatory and supervisory body for private banks. Most commercial banks are privately owned with the exception of the Russian Saving Bank (Sberbank), which is state owned. As discussed in Chapter 14, under laws passed in the Soviet period in 1987, then by the Russian parliament in 1991 and amended in 1995, the Central Bank of Russia registers and monitors commercial banks and issues licenses. During the early years of transition, a large number of new banks were chartered. The first commercial banks were created either by industries (such as the "Automobile Bank") or were successors to various Soviet-era specialized banks (Promstroibank, Agroprombank, Zhilsotsbank). In addition to carryovers from the Soviet era, a large number of new commercial banks were created. At the beginning of 1996, there were 2578 domestic and commercial banks in Russia, 532 of which were carryovers from the Soviet period and 2046 of which were new commercial banks.[8]

Many Russian banks of the early 1990s, created under the relaxed licensing requirements, had limited capital, engaged primarily in currency speculation, and made few commercial loans. Accordingly, many commercial banks began to fail, raising questions about the stability of the Russian banking system. On "Bloody Thursday" in August of 1995, the entire Russian banking system was threatened when commercial banks refused to honor transfer requests among themselves. Thereafter, the CBR raised reserve requirements (to 30 percent on demand deposits), increased minimum capital requirements, and began to withdraw licenses from poorly managed and inadequately capitalized banks.[9] Despite stricter regulations, many Russian commercial banks remained on shaky ground as late as 1997.

As poorly managed and inadequately capitalized commercial banks failed, the Russian banking industry became more concentrated, with a few large banks coming to dominate the market, such as Menatep, the Imperial Bank, Oneximbank, and Stolichny Bank Sberezhenii. The state-owned savings bank Sberbank continued to account for over 70 percent of household deposits.[10]

The initial source of capital for Russian commercial banks was either of industrial origin, such as from energy or minerals, from former Soviet banks, or from mysterious sources (rumors of Communist Party money or mafia sources). The shares of these banks are tightly held, usually by the founding institution. Foreign investors must obtain permission from the CBR to purchase bank shares. The privatization of the Russian commercial banking system was rapid. As of 1996, only three large banks were still owned by the state.

The two-tiered Russian banking system initially retained some characteristics of the administrative command economy, which have been gradually eliminated, as detailed in Chapter 14. Prior to 1995, the CBR granted **directed credits** to the commercial banking system. These credits were earmarked by the Russian government for specific enterprises or for specific regions. Rather than allowing commercial banks to decide to whom credit would be granted, this decision was made at the central level. Another administrative command feature was that the CBR was allowed (expected) to directly finance the federal government deficit. If the federal government ran a deficit, either direct additional cash would be printed or the CBR would supply credits to the Ministry of Finance.

On April 12, 1995, the Russian Duma approved the Federal Law of the Central Bank of Russia.[11] The new banking law made the CBR an independent juridical person, not responsible for the federal government's debt or for the liabilities of commercial banks. In particular, the new banking law made the CBR responsible for the domestic stability of the Russian ruble and for the stability of the Russian ruble exchange rate. The April 1995 law appeared to remove the last vestiges of Soviet tradition.

Under the new banking law, the CBR was prohibited from granting credits to the federal government to cover budget deficits. Rather, such deficits had to be financed in private credit markets. Moreover, the CBR was prohibited from granting directed credits, a carryover from the administrative command economy. Instead, the CBR was to supervise the banking system and to increase or reduce credit to the banking system generally, not to specific banks for specific directed purposes.

The CBR's monetary policy was discussed in Chapter 14. The banking legislation of April 1995 made it possible for the CBR to conduct an independent monetary policy and was important for the structure of the Russian banking system.

Despite improvements, the Russian two-tiered banking system has a number of problems that hinder its ability to effectively intermediate between savers and industrial borrowers:

First, many Russian banks were often formed from funds from specific industries, like automobiles, textiles, or communal housing. Contrary to the common banking practice of risk diversification, industry banks are directed to provide credit for specific industries or for specific regions. This concentration has led to a high percentage of bad loans, which threaten the stability of industry banks. In industrialized market economies, banks direct their credit to the most credit-worthy customers and naturally diversify their loan portfolio to protect shareholders.

Second, Russian banks have yet to gain the confidence of depositors, who have seen their savings eaten away by inflation or failures of their own banks. Russian commercial banking is in the process of development; banking legislation is just being enacted. Accordingly, many households still prefer to place their savings in instruments other than bank deposits, such as foreign exchange or consumer durables.

Third, the Russian banking system is still not well integrated regionally. Because of difficulties in transmitting funds from one bank to another or from one region to another, the Russian banking system is divided into a number of regional markets that offer various deposit rates and various degrees of stability.[12]

Fourth, since Russian banks are unsure of their depositor base (will deposits perhaps be withdrawn?), they are willing only to lend short-term. Most Russian bank loans are for maturities well below one year. Although some banks have begun making loans for more than one year, such loans were still relatively rare in 1996.[13] Short-term lending policies work to the disadvantage of Russian enterprises who need to borrow for investment. Most investment projects are long-term and therefore require long-term loans, but Russian commercial banks restrict themselves to short-term loans.

The lack of development of Russia's commercial banking is seen in its lack of financial depth. **Financial depth** is measured by the ratio of financial assets (currency in circulation, demand deposits, and time deposits) to GDP.[14] Whereas the measure of the financial depth of industrialized market economies, such as the UK or the United States, is one or more (the total of financial assets roughly equals one year's production or more), in Russia in 1995 the ratio of financial assets to GDP was less than 20 percent. Russia's lack of financial depth shows the limited amount of financial intermediation in the Russian economy; it also shows the preference of savers for real estate, cash dollars, and consumer durables.

Other Credit Markets

In the industrialized West, commercial banks and credit institutions supply credit by intermediating between private household savers and commercial borrowers. Credits are granted on commercial terms for the purpose of enabling credit-worthy firms to finance ordinary operations or to expand operations. In transition Russia, enterprise credit has typically been granted not on the basis of intermediated savings from households but from non-banking sources. (Household savings remain largely in the savings banks, not commercial banks, if they are deposited in banks at all.) Often, the purpose of these credits has not been to provide for the normal credit needs of enterprises but to keep inherently insolvent businesses in operation.

In transition Russia, credit has been generated in numerous forms, although most credit comes through the banking system (see Figure 16.2). Between 1992 and 1994, enterprises received credit in the form of government grants of freshly printed cash (which entered the state budget in the form of subsidy grants). Thereafter, the government provided credit to failing enterprises through its sale of high-yield treasury bills called **GKOs** (*gosudarstevennye kratkosrochnye obligatsii*). The practice has been to funnel high-yield GKOs through various pocket banks that offer yields high enough to attract deposits into that bank. For example, GKO rates in the GKO auction of May 1996 were 189 percent per annum. Only a limited number of banks were initially allowed to participate in the auction of GKOs. Foreign purchasers of GKOs were strictly limited until late 1996. Government proceeds from GKO auctions were used, in addition to other things, to grant credit to enterprises.[15]

A most unusual form of credit in the Russian transition economy is "forced" credit from one enterprise to another. Because insolvent enterprises are unable to pay their bills, pressure is brought to bear on suppliers, in particular energy suppliers, to continue to supply enterprises unable to pay in return for IOUs. These inter-enterprise arrears expand the credit base of the economy, independently of the banking system.

Figure 16.3 (p. 364) shows the relative magnitudes of payment arrears in the Russian economy at the end of 1994. Slightly over 20 percent of all arrears were overdue tax payments; the remaining arrears were overdue payments to suppliers.

Figure 16.2   The Russian Credit Market—January 1, 1995 (billions of rubles)

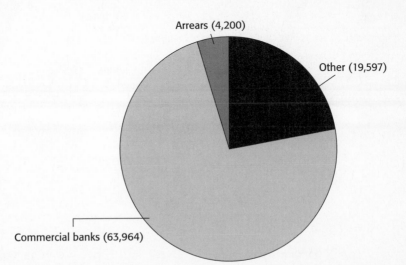

Arrears (4,200)

Other (19,597)

Commercial banks (63,964)

Source: Goskomstat, *Rossiia v tsifrakh 1995*, 174–75.

As of May 1996, the overdue debts of Russian enterprises accounted for 92 percent of Russian GDP. Russian enterprises cash (liquidity) between January 1994 and June 1995 fell from about one-half of overdue debts to about 20 percent of arrears.[16]

Figure 16.3 does not capture all arrears in the Russian economy. One of the largest debtors was government itself. In fact, some statistics show that state debts to enterprises—for electricity, transportation, and supplies, especially the debts of the Russian military and state-owned agricultural enterprises—may be greater than the tax arrears of enterprises.[17] The figures also do not capture fully the overdue debts of enterprises located in the former Soviet Union, for example the massive payment arrears of Ukrainian enterprises for Russian energy shipments.

We can offer a number of explanations for the growing arrears problem in the Russian transition economy. First, in an inflationary environment, there is a tendency for all participants to attempt to delay payment and accelerate receipts. Even if unintentional, delays would still be substantial because of the slowness of bank clearing operations and the problems of transmitting money from one region to another. Second, as noted above, the arrears issue is complicated by the fact that a given enterprise may be both a creditor and a debtor. For example, the Russian state is both a creditor in terms of overdue tax collections and a debtor via its failure to

Figure 16.3   Overdue Enterprise Debts, December 1994 (billions of rubles)

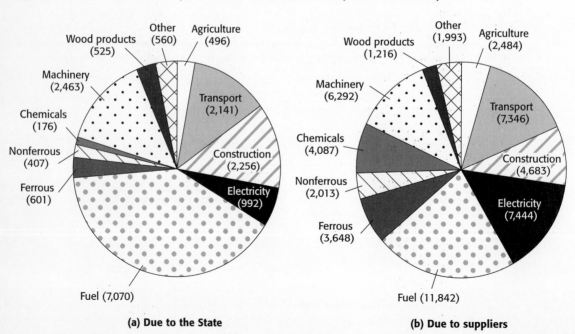

(a) Due to the State

(b) Due to suppliers

Source: I. Hirvensalo, "Payments Arrears and Russian Reforms," in Rautava, 178, 184; *Russian Economic Trends 1996*, 43.

pay for military purchases. The Russian state is not represented by one single body. Therefore, enterprises that owe taxes but are due payments from the Russian military cannot simply net out the two.

Third, in a rapidly changing economy that has had high inflation rates, there are often disputes between the parties concerning the size of debts and receivables. Statistics show large differences between the sum of overdue receivables and overdue debts; in theory they should be equal.

Fourth, and most important, in a carryover from the administrative command period, many enterprises remain subject to a soft budget constraint. Enterprises, particularly those that employ large numbers, perceive that they will not be allowed to fail when they do not pay arrears. Instead, enterprises wait for bailouts in the form of new state credits. (These bailouts have become more difficult to obtain as time passes.) Enterprises also use their political clout to insure continued deliveries from their suppliers even though their arrears are increasing. Other debtors, such as Gazprom, the state-owned natural gas company, count on their political clout to avoid being forced to pay their tax arrears. Moreover, a company like Gazprom can point to its uncollected debts as a reason for not paying taxes due from its own customers, including the Russian military.

The substantial arrears of Russian enterprises affect the CBR's ability to control money and credit in the Russian economy. The CBR may wish to pursue a tight credit policy exactly at the time when interenterprise "credit" is growing through rising arrears. Figure 16.4 shows the relative share of arrears in the total supply of credit.

Russian enterprises face not only payment arrears with respect to materials. They also have payment arrears with respect to unpaid wages. Although unpaid wages account for about 6 percent of total payment arrears, they account for nearly 20 percent of wages and salaries.[18] For the economy as a whole, wage arrears equaled 1.4 months of pay. Arrears varied from a low of 1.2 months in industry to more than 2 months in agriculture.[19]

Wage payment arrears are explained by the same lack of liquidity that accounts for nonpayments for materials and taxes. Wage arrears appear also to be explained by the fact that many employers have more workers on the payroll than can be justified by the current level of business. Unpaid wages, therefore, have not led to strikes, since workers fear for their jobs. In effect, employers use unpaid wages as an informal mechanism to reduce wages in a slack labor market.[20]

Debt Securities Markets

Banks are not the only source of credit. In industrialized market economies, enterprises and government sell **debt securities** to savers, be they individuals, companies, or government entities. To date, Russian companies have not been able to sell substantial amounts of notes and bonds to the public, either at home or abroad. The main reasons for the failure have been the high rate of inflation, which makes the public reluctant to buy fixed income securities; the lack of information on risks (most Western debt securities have clear debt ratings); and, simply, the general lack of savings available for financial investments.

Although Russian enterprises have not been successful in selling debt securities, the Russian government has been able to sell its debt both at home and increasingly to foreign buyers. As early as 1993, Russia sold $8 billion of dollar-denominated debt through the Ministry of Finance, along with 240 billion rubles in treasury bills. This market has continued to develop with the emergence of the GKO market. GKO stands for State Short-Term Debt (*gosudarstvennye kratkosrochnye obligatsii*), and the notes are like U.S. Treasury Bills, which are discounted notes that pay a face value on maturity (say after 6 months). The Russian Ministry of Finance began issuing increasing amounts of GKOs when CBR rules were changed to prevent the CBR from automatically financing the state deficit. Remember, at that time rules were also put in place to prevent the Russian government simply from financing the deficit by printing money.

After mid-1995, the Russian federal deficit was financed primarily through the auctioning of GKOs to selected banks, who could then resell them to their customers. Figure 16.4 shows the interest rates paid on GKOs since their inception. The sale of GKOs played a major role in dampening Russian inflation because Russia's state deficit was no longer financed by expansion of the money supply. However, the cost of relying so heavily on GKO debt finance has been that GKOs have basically crowded private companies out of the debt market. Buyers of Russian debt prefer buying from the Russian government, whose credit risks are better understood, than from private companies, whose credit ratings are not known.

Thus the GKO market provides a classic case of "crowding out," namely, the crowding out by public debt finance of private debt financing opportunities.

RUSSIAN EQUITY MARKETS

In the administrative command economy, there was no **equity market** in which savers could purchase ownership interests in Russian companies—the public could not buy shares in state-owned companies. The Russian privatization process, begun in October of 1992, created the foundations of a Russian equity market. With more than 60 percent of the economy now in private hands (due to the rapidity of the privatization program), an equity market has developed that now allows Russian households, businesses, banks, and foreign entities to buy ownership shares in Russian companies.

Russian Stock Markets as Emerging Markets

In the past two decades, a number of new stock (equity) markets have come onto the world scene in Southeast Asia, Latin America, China, and India. All attract

Figure 16.4 Annualized 6-Month GKO Rates

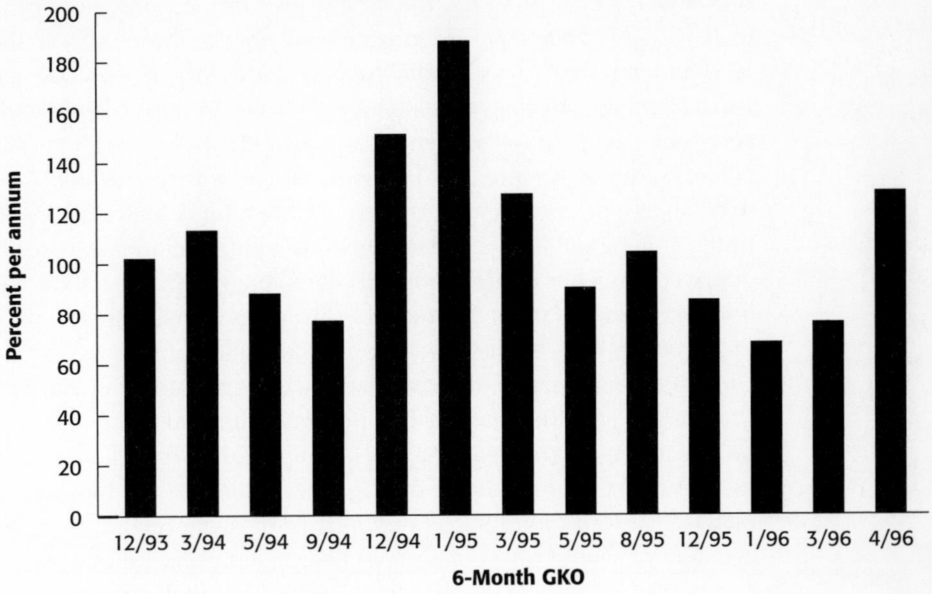

Source: *Russian Economic Trends* (selected issues).

investors because the underlying economies are growing rapidly, stocks in the more developed markets may be overpriced, and these stock markets offer opportunities for higher returns than mature markets.

The emerging equity market of Russia holds some natural attractions for domestic and foreign investors because the country is geographically the largest country in the world, it has a key geographic location between the East and West, and it has ample natural energy resources—more than one-third of the world's known gas reserves and 10 percent of world oil reserves—which can be developed relatively cheaply. Russia is a significant producer of gold and diamonds and is one of the last frontiers of unexploited timber reserves. Russia has a domestic market of 150 million consumers and is completing one of the world's largest privatization programs, which has shifted the labor force from state to private employment and almost overnight has created a new equity market.[21]

Privatization of Russian Industry

In order for there to be a Russian securities market, there must be shares of companies that can be bought and sold in a legal fashion according to established rules. The process of privatization was described in detail in Chapter 14. In October of 1992, the Russian government, under the direction of the **State Property Committee** (*Goskomimushchetvso* headed by Anatoly Chubais), began Russia's mass privatization program, the largest privatization program ever attempted.[22] In its first stage, "vouchers," or "privatization checks," were distributed to 148 million Russians, who could use them to buy shares of the 15,000 medium and large Russian companies that were being privatized. In most cases, employees and managers of enterprises were given the opportunity to acquire shares of their own companies, often at preferential prices in **closed subscriptions.** Medium and large scale open-type companies were required to offer at least 29 percent of their shares to the general public in voucher auctions, although in many cases this rule was not observed. Voucher privatization was completed in June of 1994. As a result, major enterprises ended up being owned by previous management in what was perceived as a property grab by the Soviet-period nomenklatura.

The second stage of privatization was governed by the State Privatization Program of July 1994. Under this program, the remaining shares of enterprises to be transformed into open joint stock companies were allocated according to investment tenders, cash auctions, or specialized auctions for the sale of shares. In this phase of privatization, the successful bidders again tended to be the current management or syndicates of managers, banks, and powerful officials.

By the end of 1994, most of Russia's large industrial corporations had been transformed from state enterprises to stock companies. In some cases, the Russian government (federal, regional, and municipal governments) retained the majority of shares. In other cases, private ownership, particularly of managers and their industrial allies, dominated. Table 16.2 shows the 25 largest Russian industrial concerns as of late 1994.

The conclusion of the battle for corporate control shifted property rights to the current owners in the hopes of shifting their interest to long-run profit maximization. Prior to privatization a noted flaw of the Russian economy was the absence of private property rights, which caused management to divert resources from the company to their own pockets in the process of **asset stripping.** Once the management identifies its own fate with that of the company, it will increasingly operate the company in the interest of the shareholders.

Since the inception of the privatization program, more than 100,000 enterprises have been converted, with approximately 15,000 of these being medium- and large-scale enterprises. Most of the market value is concentrated in a very small number of companies. As of October 1994, Russia's ten largest companies had a total market capitalization of approximately $16.5 billion. Certain key enterprises, such as oil and gas, telecommunications, and military enterprises, were either excluded from privatization or privatized according to separate procedures set forth in special legislation. By 1996, most major industrial enterprises had been privatized.

Table 16.2

THE 25 LARGEST RUSSIAN COMPANIES*

	Number of shares	Current stock price	Capitalization
1. Gazprom	23,673,512,900	0.15	3,551,026,935
2. LUK-Oil Holding	95,073,624	33.80	3,213,488,491
3. Unified Energy System	139,989,946	20.27	2,837,596,205
4. Norilsk Nickel	125,999,916	13.77	1,735,018,843
5. Surgutneftegaz (Surgut Petroleum)	5,384,347,600	0.23	1,238,399,948
6. Yuganskneftegaz (Yugansk Petroleum)	53,366,690	21.00	1,120,700,490
7. Rostelekom	186,750,080	4.75	887,062,880
8. Noyabrskneftegaz (Noyabrsk Petroleum)	78,545,000	9.40	738,323,000
9. LUK-Oil Kogalym	14,649,934	46.30	678,291,944
10. Purneftegaz (Pur Petroleum)	111,365,000	5.53	615,848,450
11. Megionneftegaz (Megion Petroleum)	132,209,120	3.80	502,394,656
12. Kondpetroleum	50,509,000	8.90	449,530,100
13. Nizhnevartovskneftegaz (Nizhnevartovsk Petroleum)	18,217,283	19.42	353,779,636
14. Tomskneft (Tomsk Oil)	45,032,112	7.85	353,502,076
15. Komineft (Komi Oil)	33,971,200	9.60	326,123,520
16. Mosenergo (Moscow Power)	2,560,000,000	0.10	256,000,000
17. LUK-Oil Langepas	28,479,308	8.90	253,465,841
18. St. Petersburg Telephone	15,550,000	14.90	231,695,000
19. Varyeganneftegaz (Varyegan Petroleum)	23,022,610	9.70	223,319,317
20. Sakhalinmorneftegaz (Sakhalin Sea Petroleum)	81,241,175	2.18	177,105,762
21. KamAZ (Kama Autoworks)	60,000,000	2.82	169,200,000
22. Chernogorneft (Chernogor Oil)	2,677,100	57.40	153,665,540
23. Krasnoyarsk Aluminum	13,478,400	10.18	137,210,112
24. AvtoVAC (Vaz Autoworks)	21,416,643	5.86	125,501,528
25. Kirishi Oil Refinery	35,180,190	3.35	117,853,637

*Ranked according to market capitalization, October 1994.

Source: *Finansovaya Gazeta*, no. 44 (October 26, 1994).

In sum, the process of privatization created the foundation for equity markets in Russia. It created an ownership structure in which stock shares could be sold to the public, either by selling existing shares (such as selling off state-owned shares) or issuing new shares. Although the corporate governance of privatized Russian companies remained far from ideal, the initial battle for corporate control at least established a partial sense of identification of management with the company.

Russian Stock Markets

Once Russian companies were privatized, with shares in the hands of government bodies, management, workers, and the general public, it became possible to begin secondary trading of securities, or buying and selling existing shares. Immediately after the privatization program began, an active secondary market developed for vouchers. Most vouchers ended up in the hands of *voucher funds,* as private citizens sold their vouchers to investment funds. For many, vouchers offered a cheap way to acquire shares in companies to be privatized. In addition to vouchers, shares in some of the new private companies, especially new private banks, were also traded, since financial information about the banks was generally more available. And a number of investment funds and companies started to issue their own shares.

Once voucher privatization ended, shares could be bought and sold for money, and market prices for the shares of companies were established for the first time. In order for trading in shares to take place, there must be organized exchanges which operate according to established rules and regulations. Russian authorities had to develop the institutions, rules, and regulations for secondary trading in stocks. There had been stock exchanges before the start of the privatization program, but trading was limited. In October 1991, the aggregate volume of trading in the five largest stock exchanges was only 1.3 million rubles ($1.4 m), but it fell even further—to a mere 5.1 million rubles ($35,000)—in June 1992.[23] When privatization began, a large number of stock exchanges and "stock departments" at commodity exchanges were established. Approximately 100 stock exchanges had been licensed by 1993. However, trading in most of them was quite thin.[24]

By the beginning of 1995, the Russian Ministry of Finance had issued licenses to 66 stock exchanges. Regional exchanges trade up to 200 stocks in small volumes. Among the largest Russian stock exchanges are the Central Russian Universal Exchange, the Moscow Central Stock Exchange, the Moscow International Stock Exchange, and the Russian Commodities and Raw Materials Exchange (stock department).

In 1994, Russian stock prices began to rise, as foreign investors sought to buy shares in privatized industrial companies. Although financial information was still scarce, many Russian companies appeared greatly undervalued to foreign buyers. Companies in the energy sector were easier to value than many other industrial enterprises, as their oil and/or gas reserves were known, and the implied value of the reserves was a mere fraction of corresponding Western companies.

Between 1994 and the present, Russian stock prices have been determined by the inflows of foreign investment and by political events. Figure 16.5 traces the course of Russian stock prices from November 1994 to 1996. In 1994 approximately $2.4 billion of short-term capital flowed into Russia, and a large portion of this ended up in equities. Western investment funds alone invested $1.5 billion in Russian equities.[25] Stock prices peaked in September 1994, and by March 1995 prices were down approximately 70 percent from their peak. The ruble crisis in October 1994 scared off many foreign investors, and war in Chechnya reminded investors of Russian political risks. Russian stocks rose in the first half of 1995, after the announcement of IMF agreements and successful renegotiation of Russia's foreign debts. Stocks then fell with Yeltsin's first and second heart attacks in the second half of 1995, and fell again at the end of 1995 (the beginning of the Presidential elections of June 1996), when it appeared that the Communist Party candidate, Genady Zyuganov, would beat the incumbent President Boris Yeltsin. After Yeltsin's recovery from open-heart surgery, Russian stock prices surged again.

TRADING

The trading practices on the Russian equity market are different from Western markets.[26] From the start, the majority of trading has been conducted on a decentralized, over-the-counter (OTC) market. On the Russian OTC, market brokers are in

Figure 16.5 Moscow Times Index, August 1994 = 100

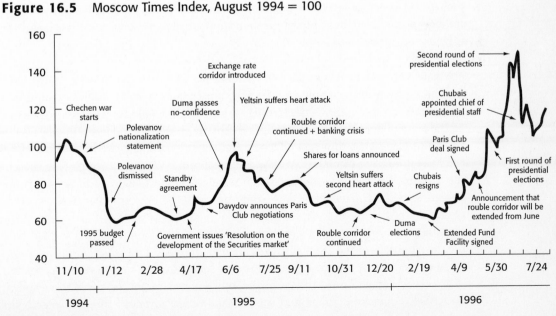

Table 16.3

RUSSIAN EXCHANGES

	1991	1992	1993	1994	1995
Number of exchanges (end of year)	182.0	238.0	180.0	166	56*
Completed transactions (in thousands)	43.9	81.2	137.7	262.1	635.3
Market volume (billions of rubles)	69.9	346.8	1,593.0	31,577	291,869
Market volume by sector:					
Consumer goods	23.6	107.9	215.5	235	NA
Industrial and technical production	45.0	227.0	656.6	1,081	NA
Securities	1.2	6.0	480.0	29,091	NA
Money resources	0.1	5.7	234.6	1,090	NA
Other goods and services	0.05	0.2	6.3	80	NA

* Exchanges licensed by Russian Ministry of Finance.

Source: Goskomstat, *The Russian Federation in Figures, 1993* (1994); Goskomstat, *Russian SocioEconomic Conditions—January 1995* (1995) (preprint); Goskomstat, *Rossiia v tsifrakh 1995*, Table 9.4.1.

contact with each other and with clients; there is no official record of trades; often publicly posted firm bids or offers are not supplied. The actual trading price and volume are negotiated separately.

Russian stock trading may be done in either dollars or rubles, but larger deals are usually in dollars. There have been some attempts to transform the trading system into a more transparent one. In May 1991 some brokers started posting firm bids and offers in an electronic trading system, but the volume was a mere fraction of the total. There are several proposals for more automated settlement systems similar to NASDAQ, to which all stock exchanges would be linked. As of mid-1996 the most promising candidate was the Depository and Clearing Company, owned by the Moscow Brokers' Association, six large Russian banks, and Credit Suisse. If this system were to gain acceptance, it would promote the development of the Russian equity market.

Uncertain practices of registration and custody of equities have also held back the development of the Russian stock market. Transfer of ownership must be registered in a company's share register. Russian securities law said that these registers should be independent of the company, but this was rarely the case. However, by mid-1996, larger companies had set up their share registers to comply with the letter of the law, and many registers were situated in Moscow, not as earlier, at company headquarters (which could be in Siberia). Nonetheless, registering shares is still often inconvenient and time-consuming. If the Russia Registry Company (which is owned by the European Bank for Reconstruction and Development, International Finance Corporation, Bank of New York, and Russian companies LUKoil and UneximBank) attracts enough Russian companies as customers, registering shares in Russia will be simplified, which would mean a more efficient equity market (Table 16.3).

Liquidity

Purchasers buy stock to receive dividends and to benefit from the appreciation of the stock value. In stock markets throughout the world, both dividends and appreciation depend upon current and future profits. Other things being equal, investors prefer to have their investment in liquid stocks, which can be sold freely without risk of driving down the market price. The liquidity of a stock can be seen in its public "float" (the number of shares in public circulation and its trading volume).

From its inception, the Russian stock market has been plagued by "liquidity problems." This means that the vast majority of shares are held either by insiders or by state institutions so that the amount of public float is limited. If there are only a limited number of shares in circulation, a highly liquid market cannot develop for that stock. Significant shareholders are unable to sell their shares without markedly affecting the market price. Large buyers cannot buy large blocs either—they are not available, or such purchases will drive up the price.

Taxation

Stock prices are driven in the long run by after-tax profits. Therefore, to evaluate stocks, potential investors must have clarity about the tax obligations of corporations.[27] Chapter 14 showed that the current Russian tax system is in transition from the old Soviet system, which was based upon sales taxes and on profits taxes of enterprises. The Soviet tax system was arbitrary, in the sense that different retail products had different tax rates and that different enterprises had different tax rates (more profitable enterprises were taxed to subsidize unprofitable enterprises). The Soviet tax system contrasts with those of the industrialized West, which rely heavily on value added taxes and on personal income and payroll taxes, both of which are levied fairly uniformly across branches of the economy. The Russian tax system is summarized in Table 16.4 as of 1996 (p. 374).

Current Russian tax laws create a number of distortions and disincentives. Since the profit tax can equal 33 percent or more, Russian corporations have an incentive to underreport profits. In fact, financial accounting is produced primarily for tax authorities and is the only source of information available to potential investors. Given the high level of taxes, there is an incentive to underreport wage payments and to underreport sales.

Table 16.4

RUSSIAN TAX RATES

Tax	Rate
Profit taxes	13%—federal; 24–30% local
VAT and Special Taxes	
VAT	10%—food and children's goods 20%—all other goods
Special	1.5%—added to VAT for financial support of major branches of the economy
Property tax	Maximum 2%
Payroll pension fund	28% (employer contribution)
Social insurance	5.4%
Employment fund	2%
Medical	3.6%
Other Taxes	
Advertising	5%—paid by advertisers
Dividends	15%
Law enforcement	3%—paid by employer

Source: EBDR MS, 26

Given Russia's complicated system of taxes, corporations are often subject to arbitrary and variable treatment. There are a multiplicity of taxing authorities at the national, regional, and local levels. In many cases, enterprises are treated according to their political clout. Meanwhile, given the declining tax base, tax collectors are under pressure to collect taxes so they focus their attention on what they perceive to be the more successful and liquid companies.

The discussion of tax arrears showed that Russian companies have significant unpaid taxes. Companies often have not paid their taxes because the sum is disputed. Governments may owe them money, or they lack the liquidity. The existence of unpaid and often unknown tax obligations creates substantial accounting problems. Many major Russian companies would be insolvent if they were actually forced to pay their entire back taxes. This uncertainty reduces demand for Russian stocks.

Valuation Issues: Price Discovery

In industrialized market economies, equity markets assist in **price discovery** by setting an efficient price (or value) for companies that are traded. Stock prices provide market valuations of what corporate assets are worth and guide the allocation of capital resources. A rising share price encourages the flow of capital to that company; declining share prices drive capital away by changing the cost of raising capital. In well-functioning stock markets, the prices of individual stocks reflect the expected value of the current and future profits of the corporation. The ultimate test of whether a stock is correctly valued is not the value of its physical assets or of its good will, but its ability to make profits both now or in the future.[28]

The profit potential of a company is typically reflected by its **price earnings (PE) ratio.** The PE shows the share price divided by its earnings per outstanding share. A PE of 5, for example, says that in the last reporting period, the company earned profits equal to 20 percent of the share price. If the stock sold for $10, and its PE is 5, this means that, in effect, the stock yielded a 20 percent rate of return for shareholders, either in the form of dividends or reinvested profits. PEs vary by the economy, by sector of the economy, and by companies within the sector. The higher the PE, the more rapidly the company's profits are expected to grow over time. If one company has a PE of 10 (a 10 percent current rate of return) and another a PE of 5 (a 20 percent rate of return), the market expects the high PE company to experience more earnings growth over time. Otherwise, investors would buy the company with the higher current rate of return.

PE ratios can be calculated for individual companies or they can be calculated for the corporate sector of the entire economy. Figure 16.6 (p. 376) shows that currently Russian PE ratios are among the lowest of all stock exchanges.

Sources of Low Russian PEs   The low PE ratios of the Russian stock exchanges do not necessarily mean that Russian stocks are undervalued relative to other stock markets. Rather, they can suggest either that investors believe Russian companies have limited profit growth potential, that the risks of investing in Russian stocks are too high, or that accounting profits are misstated.

The growth of profits of Russian companies depends upon the success of the Russian economy. Will the transition be completed, will inflation be controlled, will domestic and foreign investment be forthcoming, will the state allow free price formation, or will prices be controlled? When will the Russian economy begin to exhibit positive growth? All of these are unknowns that potential buyers and sellers must weigh.

In addition to the economy-wide risks, there are specific risks, associated with purchasing Russian stocks. The Russian stock exchanges are relatively new and they operate according to an evolving set of rules. How these rules work out will affect the degree of risk. One of the most important aspects of purchasing Russian stocks is the custody of one's stock holdings. If there is a clear record of ownership, where is that record housed? In the early years, publicly traded Russian companies were not required to keep their registry of stock in the custody of an independent organization. These registries were held either by the company (often at a remote location), or by an "independent" organization, such as a bank. That independent organization, however, may have been owned by the company itself. If the company registry of shareholders is not secure, it is possible for investors to purchase shares

Figure 16.6   Price/Earnings Ratios (1996 earnings forecast and 1996 August stock prices)

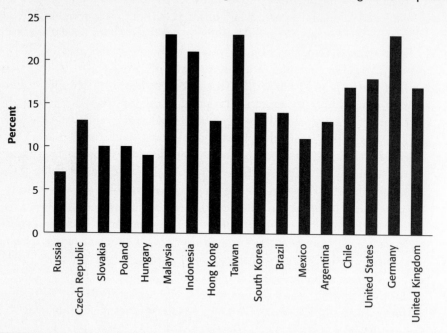

Source: "Bulls in Central Europe Say Markets Are Taking a Breather," *Wall Street Journal*, August 29, 1996.

of stock and have them excised from the registry or find that they are unable to prove ownership. Currently, investors in Russian companies can hold their securities with a nominee of the broker. For foreign clients, brokers can set up nominees in countries such as Cyprus, which has a double-taxation treaty with Russia.

Currently, since most outside shareholders are minority shareholders, and since Russian companies are closely held by their management, there are no guarantees that the current management will not take steps to reduce the voting power of outside shareholders. This could be accomplished by issuing new shares to the existing management, thereby diluting shareholder interests. Most industrialized economies have established protections and provisions to protect the interests of minority shareholders. In Russia, such protections are still lacking.

Procedures for settlement in the case of buying and selling (how are the shares to be transferred, in what period of time, how do sellers get their proceeds?) also remain unclear. If there are substantial and uncertain delays in settlement and transfer of shares, buyers are reluctant to buy and sellers reluctant to sell.

The Russian government has taken steps to resolve the problem of custody of stocks by first requiring that the stock registry be held by an independent organization. In 1996, a Federal Securities Law was passed which requires the Russian Federal Securities Commission (FSC) to solve the problem of custody and settlement in a manner that is consistent with international practice. Companies such as the National Registry Company have been set up to handle the share registries of Russian companies. During the winter and spring of 1995 and spring of 1996, a number of Western companies began offering their custodial services. For example, Chase Manhattan Bank now offers custodial arrangements that satisfy the U.S. SEC requirements for mutual funds and pension funds.[29]

The ADR (American Depository Receipt) is another approach to solving the custody problem. Currently, seven Russian companies can be bought on U.S. stock exchanges through ADRs. ADRs are simply shares of stock of Russian companies owned by large Western banks. These banks allow a portion of their shares to be traded in Western stock exchanges as ADRs. Currently, Western investors can buy shares of large Russian banks and integrated oil companies through exchanges located in the United States.

Accounting Issues   The PE ratio measures earnings per share and is based upon accounting measures of corporate profits. The Soviet system of accounting was quite different from the U.S. or European systems of accounting (GAAP). In the transition, Russian accounting practices reflect a mix of former Soviet and Western accounting practices.[30]

Unlike Western financial statements, which are prepared primarily for company and shareholder use, Russian financial accounting statements are prepared primarily for tax authorities. As Russian companies become more interested in attracting foreign shareholders, their accounting statements will be more geared to providing information for such shareholders. As statements for tax authorities, reporting Russian companies have an interest in minimizing their tax burden. In particular, one of the major Russian sources of state revenue both at the federal and local level is the corporate profit tax—which provides a built-in incentive to minimize their reported corporate profits.

Taxes on the income of the corporate sector in Russia, in particular of the more successful privatized companies, account for a higher percentage of net income than in the West. Chapter 14 showed that the corporate profit tax as a share of tax revenues is three to five times higher than in Western Europe. Corporate taxes are particularly threatening because they can be collected arbitrarily by a multiplicity of tax authorities at the federal, regional, and local levels. Some taxes are not even levied on profits, such as the tax on excess wages, which was purportedly phased out in 1996.[31]

Russian companies have a number of devices they can use to underreport profits. Nevertheless, this does not mean necessarily that Russian corporate profits are naturally understated relative to U.S. accounting practices. For example, Russian accounting rules do not allow Russian companies to deduct a number of social expenditures, such as for employee housing or health. They also do not allow accelerated depreciation of assets, which are simply valued on a historical cost basis adjusted periodically for inflation. Items that are counted as part of enterprise costs in the West must be paid out of enterprise profits in Russia.

Russian companies also have an accounting problem with nonpayments for goods and services. Companies that have delivered goods to other companies and accepted credit in return may be taxed on the basis of accrued revenues, even if their chances of collection are remote. Russian accounting does not allow for the provision for bad debts. Nor does it require reserves for potential future tax liabilities.

RUSSIAN CAPITAL FORMATION

Market Capitalization

A company's market capitalization measures its market price and is calculated as the product of the number of outstanding stock shares times the current stock price. The market capitalization figure indicates the market value that buyers and sellers of this company agree on. The market capitalization of all stocks that are traded on all country exchanges can also be calculated as the sum of the market capitalizations of all publicly traded companies. Figure 16.7 relates the market capitalization of publicly traded Russian companies as a percentage of Russian GDP and compares Russia's "market cap" with that of other countries. As the figure shows, Russia's market capitalization is only a small percentage of the market capitalization rates of other countries.

Russia's low market capitalization can reflect a number of factors: It may suggest that the Russian stock market is still in its infancy and that relatively few of Russia's enterprises are traded on stock exchanges. Therefore, as more Russian companies become publicly traded, Russia's market capitalization will rise as a percent of GDP. In fact, it has been estimated that when Gazprom, Russia's giant integrated natural gas company, goes public, Russia's market capitalization will double, because as Gazprom is currently Russia's largest company. Russia's low market capitalization also can suggest that Russia's stock prices are undervalued. If buyers and sellers place relatively low values on the shares of Russian companies, this will reflect itself in a low market capitalization.

In any case, the low market capitalization suggests that Russia' stock markets will be among the most rapidly expanding (either in volume or in average price) as Russia develops improved securities markets legislation and rules, confidence in Russia's political situation improves, and more information becomes available on the financial statements and corporate governance of Russian corporations.

SOURCES OF INVESTMENT FINANCE

Capital formation must be financed either through the savings of households, businesses, governments, or foreigners. Domestic capital formation is limited to the amount of investment finance generated through these sources. At the beginning of this chapter, we noted that Russian capital formation is going through a transition from government finance to private finance.

The Soviet administrative command economy was noted as a high-investment economy. Throughout the 1980s, the ratio of investment to GDP consistently exceeded 30 percent.[32] Figure 16.8 (p. 380) shows that, at the beginning of Russia's transition process, Russia's investment rate had fallen to 22 percent of Russian GDP. Chapter 15 showed that the collapse of Russian output was concentrated in the area of capital formation. Real investment fell at a much more rapid rate than the other components of output, such as private consumption. Figure 16.9 does show this phenomenon: Between 1990 and 1993–94, the Russian investment rate fell from 23 percent to 17–18 percent of GDP.

Figure 16.9 (p. 381) shows the steep decline of most forms of Russian investment, with the steepest decline in "productive" investment; that is, investment in industry, agriculture, and industrial construction. Whereas productive investment in 1994 was slightly more than 20 percent of 1989, "nonproductive" investment—such as in services, trade, housing, and so on—was almost 60 percent of the 1989 figure. Housing investment (including schools and hospitals) declined by much less than the decline in total investment, and investment in private housing actually rose.

Figure 16.7   Market Capitalization as Percent of GDP (1995)

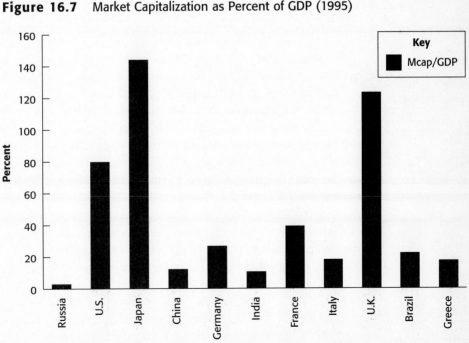

Sources: *Russian Economic Trends* (selected issues); *Statistical Abstract of the United States,* international tables.

Figure 16.8   Russian Capital Formation (percents of total)

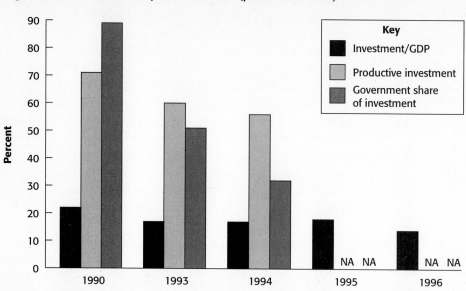

Source: Goskomstat, *Stroitel'stvo v Rossii* (Moscow: Goskomstat, 1995), 9; *Russian Economic Trends* vol. 52, no. 2 (1996), 87.

The pattern of change in Russian capital formation reflects the shift from an administrative command economic structure to a market-oriented economic structure. Once investment decisions began to be freed from central command, capital formation flowed into areas that planners previously scorned, such as private housing, trade, personal services, and financial services.

At the beginning of Russia's transition process, virtually all capital formation was financed by government sources. Investment finance was provided either directly from the consolidated budget or from specialized investment banks, which disbursed funds according to the centralized investment plan. Figure 16.10 (p. 382) shows that, by 1994, government financing of investment (federal, state, and local) had fallen to one-quarter of the total. The major source of enterprises funds (65 percent) was from the enterprises themselves, with another 8 percent coming from individuals, foreign sources, and from investment funds. Figure 16.11 (p. 382) also confirms the limited amount of financial intermediation in Russian capital formation. The overwhelming portion of investment finance comes either directly from the enterprises themselves (65 percent) or from government (26 percent). Less than 10 percent is intermediated through financial institutions or through individual domestic or foreign investors.

One reason for the limited role of financial intermediation in the financing of Russian capital formation is the continued inability of Russian commercial banks

Figure 16.9   Indexes of Investment (1989 = 100)

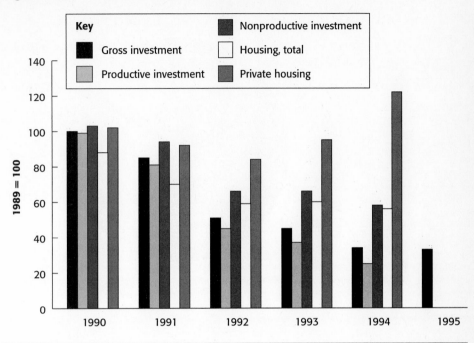

Sources: Goskomstat, *Stroitel'stvo v Rossii* (Moscow: Goskomstat, 1995), 12; *Russian Economic Trends* vol. 52, no. 2 (1997), 156.

and thrift institutions to make the long-term loans required for capital formation. Figure 16.11 shows that in 1995, the overwhelming portion of credit granted in Russian markets was short-term.

SUMMARY

In the past few years, the Russian economy has moved towards a market-oriented economy. To a large extent the allocation of capital has been transferred from planners to markets. Russia's banking system is privately owned, and lending to companies is no longer dictated by government but based on the ability to repay such loans. An emerging equity market has developed, beginning with the trading of privatization vouchers and shares of new banks in 1992. The domestic credit market developed when the federal government started issuing GKOs to finance the large fiscal deficit, which continues to be a problem. In just a few years, Russia has developed a rudimentary financial system that allocates funds according to market criteria. Table 16.5 (p. 383) shows the types of securities traded in the Russian capital market.

Figure 16.10   Sources of Capital Formation (Russia, 1994)

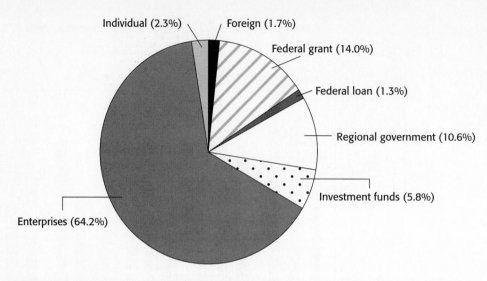

Sources: Goskomstat, *Stroitel'stvo v Rossii* (Moscow: Goskomstat, 1995), 14; *Russian Economic Trends* vol. 52, no. 2 (1997).

Figure 16.11   Short-term vs. Long-term Lending in 1995 (billion rubles)

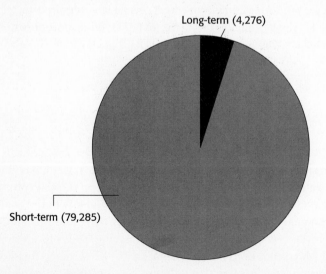

Source: Goskomstat, *Rossiia v tsifrakh 1995*, 174–75.

Table 16.5

RUSSIAN CAPITAL MARKETS: TYPES OF SECURITIES

	1993	1994	1995
Total sales volume	2,046.6	29,329	291,868
Securities	595.1	29,091.0	291,501
Stocks	37.3	218.7	264.5
Government obligations	283.1	27,493.0	288,938
Certificates	0.4	2.6	1.3
Bills of exchange	0.6	2.7	2.4
Options	2.4	18.9	16.8
Futures	0.2	1.3	301.2
Privatization vouchers	270.4	1,333.8	—
Monetary resources	1,445.3	105.0[1]	0.7
Deposits	13.2	10.9	—
Interbank loans	1,429.6	92.9	—
Commercial loans	2.5	1.6	0.7
Currency (in conversion to rubles)	6.2	NA	NA

[1]This figure only includes sales volume data for commodity exchanges.

Sources: Goskomstat, *The Russian Federation in Figures, 1993* (1994); Goskomstat, *Russian SocioEconomic Conditions—January 1995* (preprint; 1995); Goskomstat, *Rossiia v tsifrakh 1995,* Table 9.4.1.

Russia's capital market has yet to develop the ability to make long-term debt capital available; foreign investment remains a low share of capital formation; and Russia's equity markets still account for a modest share of GDP.

Terms and Concepts

working capital   Money capital which is used to facilitate the day-to-day operations of an enterprise.

investment finance   Funds, usually generated though capital markets in a market economy, for the purpose of capital investment, for example in machinery and equipment.

financial intermediation   Creating the link between savers and investors in a market economy through creation of financial institutions.

savings bank (Sberbank)   State-owned savings bank accounting for approximately 60 percent of Russian household savings; insured by the government.

debt market   Market in which debt instruments, for example bonds, can be bought and sold.

Central Bank of Russia (CBR)   The central bank of Russia, created by legislation in the period 1990–92; functions as an independent central bank, a banker's bank, and the lender of last resort in the Russian federation.

directed credits   Bank credits determined not by bank analysis but rather by state directive.

financial depth   The ratio of financial assets (currency in circulation, demand deposits, and time deposits) to GDP.

GKOs   Short-term debt instruments (gosudarstvennye kratkosrochnye obligatsii); similar to U.S. Treasury Bills; discounted notes that pay a face value on maturity.

debt securities markets   A market in which an organization can sell debt instruments.

equity markets   Markets in which equities, for example common stocks, can be bought and sold.

State Property Committee   Formed in October 1992, the committee in charge of state property.

closed subscriptions   Used in Russia to offer shares of enterprises to employees at beneficial prices.

asset stripping   The practice whereby managers of enterprises are able to exercise control over enterprise assets for personal gain.

price discovery   The revelation of value through the functioning of market forces; for example the value of a firm revealed through valuation of shares in the marketplace.

price earning (PE) ratio   The price of a share divided by the earnings per outstanding share.

Bibliography

Bird, Richard M., et al., *Decentralization of the Socialist State* (Brookfield, VT: Ashgate, 1996).

The Economist, Intelligence Unit. *Country Report Russia* (2nd quarter) (London: The Economist, 1995).

Goskomstat. *Natsional'nye schetd Rossii v 1989–1994 gg* [The national accounts of Russia, 1989–1994] (Moscow: Goskomstat, 1995).

———— . *Mezhdunarodnye sopostovleniia valovogo vnuternnogo produkta za 1993 god* [International comparisons of gross domestic product in 1993] (Moscow: Goskomstat, 1996).

Gregory, P., and M. Mokhtari. "What is the Actual Russian Saving Rate?" unpublished paper (January 1997).

———— . "Russian Household Savings During Transition: A Study Based on RLMS," unpublished paper (January 1997).

Ickes, B.W., and R. Ryterman. "The Enterprise Arrears Crisis in Russia," *Post-Soviet Affairs,* vol. 8, no, 4 (1992).

Korhonen, I. "Equity Markets in Russia," *Review of Economies in Transition* vol. 9 (1995).

Lardany, R. Russia—The Banking System During Transition (Washington, DC: World Bank, 1993).

Mirkim, Iq. M. *Tsennye bumagi i fondovyi Rynok* [Securities in Fund Markets] (Moscow: Perspective, 1995).

Rautava, J., ed. *Russia's Financial Markets and the Banking Sector in Transition* (Helsinki: Bank of Finland, 1995).

Robinson, A. *Russia and Its Banking System* (London: 1995).

Smith, J. "Tax and Accounting in Russian Companies," Morgan Stanley Investment Research, UK and Europe: Russia (1996).

Wallich, C.I. *Russia and the Challenge of Fiscal Federalism* (Brookfield, VT: Ashgate, 1996).

World Bank. *Emerging Stock Market Factbook 1996* (Washington, DC: World Bank, 1996).

Notes

1. On this point, see J. Rautava, "Financial Factors and Economic Development—Russian Dilemmas," in J. Rautava, ed., *Russia's Financial Markets and the Banking Sector in Transition* (Helsinki: Bank of Finland, 1995), 35–37.
2. M. Browning and A. Lusardi, "Household Saving: Macro Theories and Micro Facts," *Journal of Economic Literature* vol. 34, no. 4 (December 1996), 1797–1855.
3. The figures on Russian household savings are from Goskomstat, *Natsional'nye schetd Rossii v 1989–1994 gg* (Moscow: 1995), 61.
4. On this, see P. Gregory and M. Mokhtari, "What Is The Actual Russian Saving Rate?" unpublished paper, January 1997.
5. P. Gregory and M. Mokhtari, "Russian Household Saving During the Transition: A Study Based on RLMS," unpublished paper, January 1997.
6. Rautava, 48.
7. The ruble savings figures are from *Natsional'nye scheta Rossii v 1898–1994 gg.* (Moscow: Goskomstat, 1995), 60. The exchange rates are from *Mezhdunarodnye sopostovleniia valovogo vnuternnogo produkta za 1993 god* (Moscow: Goskomstat, 1996), 72.
8. Daiwa Institute of Research, *The Russian Federation: The Economic Turning Point is Expected in 1996* (June 1996), 20.
9. In the aftermath of the banking crisis of August 1995, 130 bank licenses were withdrawn; interbank interest rates rose to 100 percent, thereby destroying the interbank lending market. See *Russian Economic Monitor* vol. 5, no. 2 (1996), 124.
10. Morgan Stanley, "Russian Equity Market: Now for the Hard Part," *UK and Europe Investment Research* (June 6, 1996).
11. Russian banking legislation is discussed in J. Laurila, "Russian Banking Legislation and Supervision," in Rautava, 83–116.
12. Rautava, 41, shows that Russian banks offer quite different deposit rates in Russia's seven main regions. In April of 1995, for example, banks in the Urals region were offering

depositors almost 150 percent per annum, while banks in the Volga region offered slightly more than 100 percent.

13. I. Salonen, "Russian Commercial Banks: A Banker's View," in Rautava, 138.

14. For a discussion of Russia's financial depth, see Rautava, 34–36.

15. Morgan Stanley (June 1996), 2.

16. These figures are from I. Hirvensalo, "Payment Arrears and Russian Reforms," in Rautava, 178, 184; *Russian Economic Trends 1996* vol. 5, no. 2, 43.

17. State debts in the military and state-owned agriculture alone equaled 22 to 25 trillion rubles at the end of 1994—a figure greater than enterprise debts to the state. In 1993, about 35 percent of total indebtedness had accumulated in ministries and state offices. See Hirvensalo, 181.

18. These figures are from Gregory and Mokhtari, "What Is the Actual Russian Saving Rate?" and are calculated for late 1994 and early 1995 from the Russian National Longitudinal Monitoring Survey.

19. Hirvensalo, 185.

20. Gregory and Mokhtari show that Russian workers have an expectation only to collect eventually between 10 and 15 percent of back wages and salaries.

21. Morgan Stanley, 3.

22. For a detailed legal description of the Russian privatization program, see *Prospectus: Templeton Russian Fund, Inc.* (June 15, 1995), Appendix B.

23. R. Larndany, *Russia—The Banking System During Transition* (Washington, DC: World Bank Country Study, 1993).

24. Economist Intelligence Unit, Country Report Russia (2nd quarter, 1995).

25. A. Robinson, *Russia and its Banking System* (London: 1995).

26. This discussion is based primarily on I. Korhonen, "Equity Markets in Russia," *Review of Economies in Transition* vol. 9 (1995), 58–66.

27. This section is based largely upon J. Smith, "Tax and Accounting in Russian Companies," Morgan Stanley Investment Research, *UK and Europe: Russia* (February 1996).

28. I. Korhoven, "Equity Markets in Russia," *Review of Economies in Transition,* no. 9 (1995), 59.

29. A. Berg, *Market Update: Russia* (June 26, 1996).

30. See for example Instructions on the Application of the Chart of Accounts of Financial and Economic Activities of Enterprises (Approved by the Ministry of Finance of the USSR, No. 56 of November 1, 1991 (with Amendments and Additions of December 28, 1994 and July 28, 1995).

31. J. Smith, "Tax and Accounting in Russian Companies," Morgan Stanley, Investment Research, *UK and Europe: Russia* (February 2, 1996), 26–29.

32. *Handbook of Economic Statistics* (1991), 65.

Russia's Integration into the World Economy

THE ADMINISTRATIVE COMMAND LEGACY

As Chapter 9 pointed out, a **foreign trade monopoly** handled virtually all dealings of the Soviet economy in international markets. Soviet exports and imports were part of the material balance plan. Exporting firms were isolated from international markets; dealings with foreign customers were handled by foreign trade organizations, which were a constituent part of the foreign trade monopoly. Importing firms, similarly, were isolated from their suppliers; their purchases were handled by specialized foreign trade organizations. During the Soviet period, Russian nationals and Russian companies were restricted from receiving foreign currency. All foreign currency transactions were managed by a foreign trade bank (at that time called *Vneshtorgbank* and later *Vneshekonbank*).

Trade dealings were directed not by market forces but by bilateral trade agreements at the governmental level, since trade between Russia and other countries had to be balanced country by country. The ruble exchange rate was set administratively. It was by no means a market exchange rate and had no relationship to the ruble's purchasing power. Other than official credits or commercial bank credits (usually backed by government guarantees), there was no flow of private capital from the West into the Russian economy. Restrictions on private property rights prohibited the flow of equity capital into Russia; in the Soviet period, Russian companies and Russian assets were all state owned and were not for sale to anyone either inside or outside the country.

The world economy has become increasingly globalized over the past fifty years. We can now indeed say that we have a globalized world economy with fewer and fewer barriers to trade and to capital flows. The increase in world trade has far outpaced economic growth throughout the world and has served as an important engine of change in the world economy. International companies now encounter few international boundaries; they operate in many countries, and they have markets worldwide. World capital markets are tightly integrated so that we now have a worldwide capital market of interrelated interest rates and interrelated stock markets.

Russia's transition task with respect to world trade is to become integrated into this world economy. It must make the transition from an autarchic economy, isolated by the foreign trade monopoly from world markets, to one in which its exports, imports, capital flows, and currency rates are determined by market forces.

CHANGES IN TRADING ARRANGEMENTS

The foreign trade monopoly had already begun to disintegrate in the late Soviet period, during the era of perestroika. In the late 1980s, enterprises and households were granted for the first time the right to buy and sell in international markets, independent of the foreign trade monopoly. They acquired increasing rights to hold and use foreign exchange. Although the state retained significant controls over the ruble exchange rate, multiple exchange rates were allowed. Some were determined by supply and demand for foreign exchange.

The collapse of the Soviet foreign trade monopoly also brought with it considerable confusion, as inexperienced Russian firms tried to enter foreign markets on their own for the first time. It was during this period of collapse that Russia's foreign indebtedness increased. In the initial confusion, it was unclear what loans and contracts were actually backed by the Soviet/Russian governments, what Soviet/Russian banks could issue state guarantees, and so on.

The period from the final years of perestroika to the present has witnessed a confusing tug-of-war between forces favoring a further liberalization of the Russian foreign trade regime and those favoring continuation of central controls. As a consequence, a series of often contradictory measures have been proposed and enacted.

The tug-of-war centered on several issues, including the convertibility of the Russian ruble. Other questions remained. Should exporters retain foreign exchange or be forced to turn over their foreign exchange earnings to the Central Bank of Russia? Should the ruble exchange rate be pegged or allowed to float? Should companies, particularly raw materials exporters, be permitted to export their goods freely, or should the state control and limit these exports either by licenses or by taxes?[1]

Ruble Exchange Rates

In the Soviet period, the ruble exchange rate was set arbitrarily by the government. Throughout the Soviet period, a black market existed for foreign exchange, and the black market rate was typically a large multiple of the official rate. In 1989, the State Bank (Gosbank) began using a special "tourist rate" and in April 1991 switched over to a currency-exchange ruble rate under the **Currency Exchange Law,** which for the first time authorized currency exchanges and undermined the monopoly of the *Vneshekonbank.*

After April of 1991, although a "market" rate of exchange existed for the ruble, the government continued to maintain "official" or "commercial" rates of exchange for special purposes. These official rates were used for statistical purposes to value Soviet foreign trade and for forced sales of currency to the Russian Central Bank. Then came the failed coup in August of 1991 and the collapse of the Soviet Union. Russia agreed to accept most of the USSR's external debts, but continued an inconsistent policy towards foreign exchange. On the one hand, Russia wished to promote exports to earn foreign exchange needed to meet its debt service. It needed to create policies that gave incentives to Russian companies to earn foreign exchange and to not keep their earnings aboard. On the other hand, the Russian government had to decide between a policy that encouraged exports and thus deprived the domestic economy of goods and policies that discouraged exports to keep domestic production available for the domestic economy.

From March 1991 through 1994, a number of decrees and regulations were passed that required any party earning foreign currency to sell a portion of these earnings to banking authorities at the "official" or "commercial" rates. The main reason for these measures was that central banking authorities required large sums of currency to service, first, the Soviet Union's and, later, Russia's external debt. Obligatory currency sales to the Central Bank were viewed as a way to ensure payment. In late 1990, for example, banking authorities calculated that 40 percent of all perspective currency revenue would be required to meet the USSR's external debt servicing requirements. Accordingly, obligatory sales rates of 40 percent were set for the economy as a whole.

An unintended consequence of these actions was to reduce the overall supply of foreign exchange in Russia because exporters lost the incentive to earn foreign exchange, learned how to conceal foreign exchange by sending it abroad, and engaged in barter transactions that avoided having currency change hands. The government attempted to use its currency retention laws to encourage or discourage exports by sector. For a time, for example, manufacturers and oil producers were formally allowed to keep relatively high portions of their foreign exchange earning, although they were often unable to exercise their legal rights to retain currency.

In a Yeltsin decree "On Liberalization" signed in November of 1991 and effective as of the beginning of 1992, it was decreed that all legal and physical persons were required to sell only 10 percent of their currency revenue to the CBR at the

CBR market exchange rate. However, enterprises selling energy and raw materials abroad were required to sell a further 40 percent of their currency revenue at a new commercial rate of exchange. This was an important exception to the 10 percent rule because the major portion of Russian foreign exchange earnings was earned by raw material and energy exporters. This decree liberalized the holding of foreign currency by both physical and legal persons. Legal and physical persons were allowed to open up currency accounts in domestic banks and were allowed to use the accounts freely. The holding of currency in foreign banks was limited to special cases.

In July of 1992, exporters were forced to sell 30 percent of currency revenue to the CBR currency reserve. Another 20 percent had to be sold to buyers on the foreign currency market.

Flexible Versus Fixed Exchange Rates

When Russia moved to a variable ruble exchange rate at the end of the perestroika period, it entered an era quite different from the artificially **fixed exchange rates** of the Soviet period. As is evident from Table 17.1, Russia has had a **flexible**

Table 17.1

RUBLE EXCHANGE RATES (RUBLES TO THE US DOLLAR)

Fiscal quarter	Rate	Fiscal quarter	Rate
1991		1994	
First quarter	NA	First quarter	1,582
Second quarter	38	Second quarter	1,877
Third quarter	53	Third quarter	2,165
Fourth quarter	110	Fourth quarter	3,194
1992		1995	
First quarter	179	First quarter	4,288
Second quarter	134	Second quarter	4,933
Third quarter	177	Third quarter	4,469
Fourth quarter	398	Fourth quarter	4,556
1993		1996	
First quarter	572	First quarter	4,767
Second quarter	952	Second quarter	4,984
Third quarter	1,028	Third quarter	5,266
Fourth quarter	1,207	Fourth quarter	5,483
		1997	
		First quarter	5,600

Source: *Russian Economic Trends* (selected issues).

(or variable) **exchange rate** throughout the postindependence period. In fact, the Russian exchange rate has depreciated throughout the period, sometimes at breakneck speed, but at other times relatively slowly. The primary reason for the depreciating ruble has been the rapid Russian domestic inflation rate.

Figure 17.1 provides another view of the Russian exchange rate. It shows that Russia's real exchange rate (the volume of foreign goods that can be purchased with a fixed quantity of rubles) has actually been rising in recent years. In other words, Russia's exchange rate has been depreciating at a slower rate than expected, given Russia's more rapid inflation.

As time passed, fewer restrictions were placed on the rights of Russian persons to earn, buy, and sell foreign exchange. But as late as 1996, Russian exporters were still obliged to sell specified portions of their currency earnings to the CBR. Foreign investors must use special types of accounts, which can be monitored by Russian banking and tax authorities. The forced sale of foreign exchange earnings meant a hidden tax on Russian exporters, particularly with a declining ruble exchange rate. On June 1, 1996, the Russian Prime Minister and Chairman of the CBR agreed to fulfill Article 8 of the IMF Charter, meaning the introduction of full convertibility on current account transactions.[2]

Figure 17.1   Russia's Real Exchange Rate (1990 = 100)

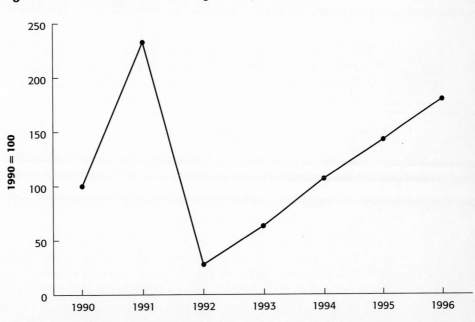

Source: PlanEcon, *Review and Outlook for the Former Soviet Republics* (March 1996), 33.

The rise in Russia's real exchange rate appears puzzling at first glance, but it can be explained by the active demand for rubles in foreign exchange markets. Since the beginning of transition, Russia has had a positive balance on current account in its international transactions, which means that international buyers of Russian goods must acquire rubles on a net basis in foreign exchange markets. As Russia's privatization has been completed and foreigners have increasingly been allowed to purchase Russian equities and Russian bonds, there has been added a new demand for rubles for investment purposes.

Accordingly, Russia appears to be in a strong position to move to full convertibility of the ruble in the near future. If anything, the "strong" ruble has required that the Russian government take steps to prevent the ruble from rising. Given the strong demand for rubles in foreign exchange markets, the Russian government has had to use its own reserves of foreign exchange to buy rubles to prevent the exchange rate from rising.

Under pressure from the International Monetary Fund, Russia expressed an intent to move to full exchange rate convertibility, in which currency transactions and capital transfers could be made without restrictions. Russia even prematurely announced such an intent in July 1, 1992. Although a policy memorandum to the International Monetary Fund in February of 1992 expressed the intention to move to a **pegged (fixed) exchange rate,** this did not happen. Given the continued high rate of inflation in Russia and the limited reserves of foreign exchange (which at one time would have lasted only for 10 days of support), Russia did not feel able to fix its exchange rate without considerable foreign support and use of scarce foreign exchange reserves.

Given the more stable Russian rate of inflation starting in 1994 and thereafter, combined with Russia's positive trade balance, Russia has been able to keep its currency within preset bounds. In fact, it appears that the strength of Russia's inflation performance and trade surpluses may cause appreciation of the rubles value in the upcoming period. At the present time, Russian authorities set a corridor within which they wish the ruble to move. Since 1995, Russian authorities have indeed been able to keep the ruble within the predetermined corridor.[3]

Purchasing Power Parity

One way to judge a currency's status is to compare its market rate of exchange with the hypothetical **purchasing power parity** (PPP) rate of exchange. The PPP rate measures the relative purchasing power of one nation's currency vis-a-vis another's. If a nation's exchange rate is undervalued relative to its PPP rate, this suggests that the country's goods are "inexpensive," since that country's goods can be purchased for less than the PPP rate would suggest.

Figure 17.2 gives Russia's exchange rates and its PPP rates for the transition period. This figure shows that throughout the transition period, Russia's exchange rate has been well below its PPP rates, meaning that Russian goods have been con-

Figure 17.2   PPP Rate Versus Market Exchange Rate in Russia (rubles per dollar)

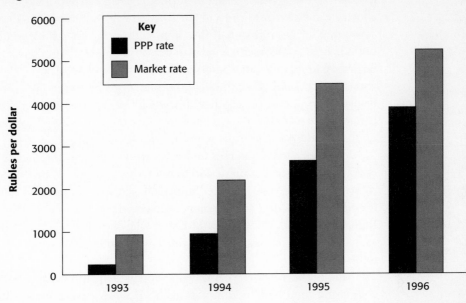

Source: Goskomstat, *Mezhdunarodnye sopostovleniia VNP za 1993 g,* 72.

sistently "inexpensive" for international buyers. As time has passed, however, the gap between the exchange rate and the PPP rate has diminished. Two reasons can be given for this trend. One is that greater political stability in Russia has created increasing confidence in the ruble. The second is that, as inflationary expectations have eased, Russian citizens have been more willing to hold rubles as opposed to hoarding foreign exchange.

TRADE POLICY

In the Soviet period, exports were viewed as necessary evils to obtain imports. In the post-Soviet period, exports have been viewed in a mixed light—on the positive side, as a major source of foreign exchange for keeping up the value of the ruble and for paying Russia's external debt; on the negative side, as a deprivation of the domestic economy of needed supplies and materials. Russian authorities, in particular, have found it difficult to surrender the conception that the Russian economy must continue to supply an economy inefficient in energy and raw materials with inexpensive supplies of these things. It has sought to insure low domestic costs by controlling export licenses, export taxes, and quotas. These techniques have restricted the export of energy and raw materials so that they remain available to the domestic economy at below-world-market prices.

In the late Soviet period, even though enterprises had nominally received the freedom to engage in international trade, central authorities retained the power to allocate the exports of the 15 major Russian energy and raw material exports, which accounted for more than half the value of exports. Since the end of the perestroika period, Russian authorities have relied on a combination of export taxes, quotas, licenses and other extraordinary measures to regulate exports. One of the biggest issues has been whether to allow the market to determine who would be granted licenses and quotas or whether this would be done on the basis of influence and connections. As in the West, a license to export commodities that have lower domestic than world prices creates opportunities for easy profits.

Although various decrees and rules were passed at the end of perestroika and during the early transition period to sell rights to export to the highest bidder, these rights continued to be allocated informally, creating substantial unreported income for officials and influence peddlers, who could control access to these rights. At one time, for example, the Deputy Minister, who allocated oil export quotas and licenses, had to be accompanied by bodyguards to protect him against the various threats to his life.

This tug of war over centralizing versus decentralizing of exports has been a continuing source of friction within the Russian government. After a number of decrees liberalizing Russia's trade regime, in May 1992 the Russian Ministry of Foreign Economic Relations issued a policy paper that backtracked on the path towards trade liberalization for purported national security reasons. The 1992 decree sought to recentralize the exports of strategically important raw materials, arguing that the companies themselves were inexperienced and that trading in raw materials should be in the hands of experienced foreign trade officials. Export taxes were again adjusted and raised for energy products. Barter transactions were subjected to even higher taxes, and import taxes were raised to 10-to-15%. All taxation of these activities had to be paid at the market exchange rate as opposed to the much lower "official" exchange rates.

Gradually, the use of licenses, quotas, and other administrative control of exports has diminished—to be replaced by more subtle controls. Russia has reduced barriers to exports, particularly taxes on raw materials, and has introduced taxes on imports. This switch has been the result of a shift in thinking from a deficit economy to a market-oriented economy concerned with preserving domestic employment. From April 1996, all export taxes were eliminated except on crude oil. In 1996, nontariff barriers to exports were also removed, such as the system of mandatory registration of export contracts, precustoms controls. Centralized trade was limited to sales of arms and defense-related equipment. For example, Russia's most important export, crude oil, remains subject to tight state control via the allocation of 70 percent of Russia's oil export capacity to state needs.[4]

Another major current in Russian trade policy has been to move to protect domestic producers.[5] Under the Soviet system, tariffs, quotas, and nontariff barriers were not formally required. Trade flows were strictly controlled by the foreign trade monopoly. Domestic enterprises were more worried about fulfilling production targets than about losing domestic markets to foreign producers. Workers were guaranteed full employment by the job rights Soviet economy.

During the transition period, Russia has installed a more traditional system of protection of domestic producers via tariffs and quotas on foreign-produced goods. From May 15, 1996, a revised system of import taxes was introduced, which increased the level of import taxation. Commodities, which were previously free of import taxes, were made subject to a mandatory 5 percent fee. The Russian government also experimented with quotas on alcohol imports and on imported textiles. A decree signed by President Yeltsin on April 16, 1996, enabled the Russian government to introduce import quotas on key agricultural commodities, thereby raising the possibility of protecting inefficient Russian agriculture.[6]

RESULTS: TRADE VOLUME

The volume of foreign trade, like the volume of output, fell substantially as Russia began its transition process. The decline is understandable. Russian prices were liberalized. Export/import decisions came to be made more by companies and individual rather than central planners. The Soviet Union with its intricate subsidy schemes collapsed, and more and more sales came to be conducted in market prices. A substantial restructuring of trade was bound to take place. New trading clearing arrangements had to be worked out as new currencies were introduced, while other countries remained in the ruble trading zone.

Moreover, a decline in trade would be expected as the overall production of the economy fell. A whole new set of expertise had to be developed, as previously untrained individuals suddenly became responsible for the external dealings of their companies.

Figure 17.3 (p. 396) shows the best estimates of the volume of Russian trade from 1990 to the present. (Reliable figures are difficult to obtain for this period.) With the currency restrictions and export restraints described above, new incentives developed to conceal both the volume of exports and imports. Russian exporters found ways to underreport trade and hide their currency revenues. Otherwise, they would have to turn their currency earnings over to the government at low rates of exchange. Moreover, if exports escaped notice, one also escaped exports duties and the like. With exports restricted by licenses and quotas, it paid producers to find ways around these restrictions with unreported exports. Even as late as February 1996, with substantial improvements in reporting procedures, it was estimated that slightly more than one quarter of imports went unreported, whereas virtually all exports were officially registered.[7]

Keeping in mind the fact that both exports and imports were underreported during the period 1990 to present, there was nevertheless a substantial collapse of foreign trade during the Russian transition. This collapse affected imports more than exports, although the decline in exports was also precipitous.

Figure 17.3   Volume Index of Russian Trade (in US dollars)

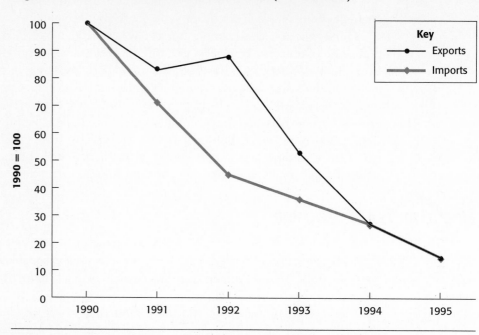

Source: Deutsches Institut für Wirtschaftforschung, *Wochenbericht* no. 3 (1996), 38.

As Figure 17.3 shows, most of the decline in trade took place between 1991 and 1992, as Russia began its transition process. Since then, trade has been recovering as a percent of GDP but still remains well below its level in 1990. Figure 17.4 shows that by the second half of the 1990s, Russia's trade volume (exports plus imports as a percent of GDP) was near 25 percent. As Figure 17.5 (p. 398) shows, this ratio places Russia among the least reliant countries on foreign trade (although low trade ratios are characteristic of large, resource-rich countries such as Russia).

Trade Composition

As Russia discarded its foreign trade monopoly and left more of its foreign trade decisions to individuals, a restructuring of trade was bound to take place. In fact, if left to the market, the expectation was that Russia would export primarily those products in which it possessed a comparative advantage and would import those products in which it had a comparative disadvantage.

In this regard, Russia's **comparative advantage,** which had remained stable for more than 100 years, would be its wealth of natural resources.[8] Its comparative disadvantage—at least during the early years of transition—would be consumer

Figure 17.4   Russia's Foreign Trade Proportions (exports plus imports as percent of GDP)

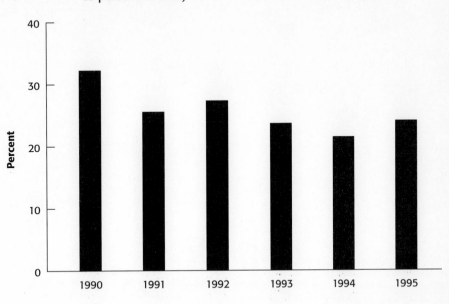

Source: Deutsches Institut für Wirtschaftforschung, *Wochenbericht* no. 3 (1996), 38.

goods (which were deemphasized during the administrative command economy) and advanced technology products. Indeed, if one examines the changing composition of Russian trade, one sees a dramatic shift to Russia becoming primarily a raw-material exporter and an importer of advanced technology and consumer goods. The first wave was the importation of consumer goods, given that they did not require long-term financing or foreign capital. The eventual shift to importing advanced technology will occur when Russia develops its own capital market access to foreign capital.

The shift in trade has been away from the CMEA countries and towards the Western industrialized countries. Table 17.2 (p. 399) shows that, as late as 1991, Russia's primary trading partners were the republics of the former Soviet Union. This is not surprising since until 1991, the 14 other republics of the former Soviet Union were a part of the same market and planning system. The flows of goods and services had changed markedly within just one year's time. A year earlier, in 1991, 67 percent of Russia's exports were to republics of the former Soviet Union. By 1992, this percentage had shrunk to 21 percent. Table 17.2 shows both the shrinkage of Russian trade after 1991 and its changing geographic composition. It shows the relatively rapid growth of Russian exports to the West, the failure of Russian

Figure 17.5   Foreign Trade Proportions (exports + imports/GDP)

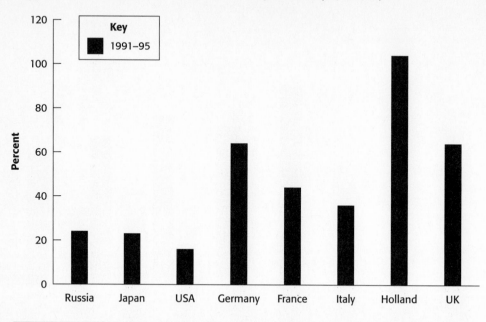

Sources: DIW, *Wochenbericht* no. 3 (1996), 38; *Handbook of International Economic Statistics 1992*, 16.

exports to the former Soviet Union to grow, and the recovery of Russian imports from the West. Figure 17.6 shows Russia's status as a raw materials and energy exporter.

BALANCE OF PAYMENTS

The most widely used measure of a country's balance of payments is the balance on **current account.** It equals the value of exports of goods and services minus the value of imports of goods and services plus unilateral transfers, such as remittances from nationals living abroad or foreign aid. If a country has a positive balance on current account, it is exporting capital (savings) to the rest of the world in the form of net acquisitions of foreign assets such as stocks, bonds, and real estate. If it is running a current account deficit, it is receiving capital from the rest of the world in the form of increased foreign acquisitions of its own assets.

Table 17.3 (p. 400) gives Russia's balance of payments for the years 1994 and 1995. It shows that Russia had a current account surplus equal to about 6 billion dollars (annualized), due primarily to Russia's strong exports (mainly energy products

Table 17.2

RUSSIAN FOREIGN TRADE WITH THE FSU AND THE REST OF THE WORLD *
(billions of U.S. dollars)

	1990	1991	1992	1993	1994	1995
Exports to FSU countries	127	109	11	16	15	16
Exports to ROW**	81	53	42	44	53	66
Imports from FSU	114	83	9	11	14	17
Imports from ROW	83	45	37	33	37	44
Export-import ratio with FSU	13	25	2	5	1	−1
Export-import ratio with ROW	−2	8	4	11	16	22

*former Soviet Union
**rest of the world
Sources: C. Michalapoulos and D. Tarr, eds., *Trade Performance and Policy in the Independent States*
(World Bank: Studies in Economies in Transition, 1994), 33; also *Russian Economic Trends.*

and raw materials). Russia imported more services than it exported and received
some unilateral transfers, but its merchandise export surpluses outweighed its net
imports of services. Table 17.2 shows that Russia had rising positive trade balances
with the West and roughly balanced trade with the Former Soviet Union.

Figure 17.6   Structure of Russian Exports (1995)

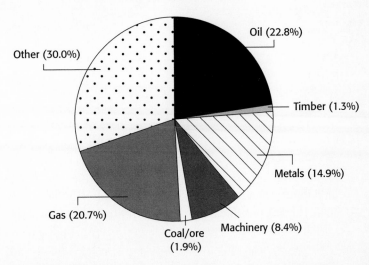

Sources: DIW, *Wochenbericht* no. 3 (1996), 38; *Handbook of International Economic Statistics
1992,* 16.

Table 17.3

RUSSIAN BALANCE OF PAYMENTS
(billions of U.S. dollars)

	1994			1995*		
	FSU	Other	Total	FSU	Other	Total
Exports, merchandise	17.7	51.4	69.1	17.6	56.2	73.8
Oil products	1.7	20.4	22.1	1.8	22	23.8
Imports, merchandise	−15.0	−39.5	−54.5	−14.0	−43.8	−57.8
Merchandise balance	2.7	11.9	14.6	3.6	12.4	16.0
Services	−0.8	−12.0	−12.8	−0.4	−11.4	−11.6
Nonfactor services	−1.1	−7.4	−8.5	−0.8	−6.4	−7.2
Factor services (interest)	0.3	−4.6	−4.4	0.4	−5.0	−4.4
Unilateral transfers	0.9	0.8	1.6	0.6	0.8	1.4
Balance on current account	2.8	0.7	3.3	3.8	1.8	5.8
Government credits	0.4	−12.3	−11.9	0.6	−10.0	−9.8
New credits	−0.2	2.5	2.3	0.0	1.8	1.6
Amortization	0.6	−14.8	−14.2	0.6	−11.8	−11.4
Other long-term capital	0.0	−1.1	−1.1	−0.4	1.6	1.4
Short-term capital	2.6	−9.8	−7.2	−0.4	3.8	3.4
Currency accumulation	0.0	−7.2	−7.2	0.0	−2.8	−2.8
Unpaid interest & amortization	−3.9	2.8	−1.0	0.8	−12.4	−11.8
Debt restructuring	−0.1	12.4	12.4	−5.4	23.6	18.2
Office reserves	0.1	3.9	4.0	0.0	−8.6	−8.4
Capital account	−0.9	−4.1	−4.8	−4.8	−2.0	−7.0
Statistical discrepancy	−1.9	3.4	1.5	1.0	0.2	1.2

*full year extrapolated from first six months
Source: Deutsche Institut für Wirtschaftforschung, *Wochenbericht* nos. 51–52 (1995), 891

If we examine Russia's external **capital account,** we see that Russia increased its net indebtedness to foreigners in 1995 but acquired substantial sums of hard currency holdings. The acquisition of hard currency by private holders is a form of capital flight, even though the currency is held largely in Russia.

Russia's positive balance on current account is explained by a number of factors. First, the Russian ruble has been consistently undervalued (relative to PPP rates as shown above), making Russia's exports "cheap" in international markets. Second, the collapse of Russia's domestic economy has "released" raw materials for export, since they are no longer absorbed by the domestic economy. And third, Russia's terms of trade have improved, especially relative to the CIS countries, which had earlier received Russia's raw materials at below-world-market prices.

FOREIGN INDEBTEDNESS

As the Soviet Union collapsed, the Russian Federation agreed to take responsibility for the Soviet Union's foreign indebtedness. This occurred on April 2, 1993, with the Declaration of the Russian Federation on the Assumption of the Foreign Debts of the USSR.[9] Until the end of the Soviet period, the USSR had accumulated foreign debts that were regarded as reasonable relative to the USSR's hard currency earnings. During the final years, however, Soviet foreign debts increased with the chaos associated with the collapse of the foreign trade monopoly and the worsening Soviet economy. For example, in 1987, the USSR's foreign indebtedness totaled $38 billion. By 1992, this figure was more than double—$79 billion. By 1995, Russia's total foreign indebtedness exceeded $100 billion due not to new borrowing but to the accumulation of unpaid interest and principal payments.

Table 17.4 (p. 402) shows Russia's growing debt burden as measured in dollars. In 1990, Russia's foreign debt was only 10 percent of GDP and 74 percent of annual exports. By 1995, Russia's foreign debt had risen to 33 percent of GDP and to 147 percent of annual export earnings.

Russia's hard currency debt can be divided into two major categories: official credits and commercial credits backed by government guarantees. As Russia became unable to service its foreign debts (as shown in Table 17.5, p. 403), Russia's debts were restructured through negotiations with representatives of Russia's main creditors. The Paris Club of creditors represented Russia's governmental creditors, such as Germany, which had made official loans to the Soviet Union. The London Club represented the approximately 600 commercial banks that had made loans to Russia, often with state guarantees.[10] For example, on May 2, 1993, the Paris Club agreed to restructure its debt for repayment between 1999 and 2003. Another agreement followed on June 3, 1995, to repay between 1997 and 2010. On April 29, 1996, the Paris Club agreed to another debt restructuring.

Russia had not met its interest and principal obligations to the commercial banks represented by the London Club since March of 1992. By the end of 1995, these debts had risen to $33 billion, of which $7 billion was unpaid interest. On November 16, 1995, the London Club agreed to a $26 billion restructuring of commercial bank credits for the period 1998 to 2011. In these restructuring agreements, typically a percentage of unpaid interest was forgiven.

Russia's unpaid debt service on its international debts served as an obstacle to Russia's access to international credit markets. With agreements on debt restructuring reached with the Paris and London Clubs, however, it appears as if Russia will again be able to access international debt markets. For example, in 1996, some 37 percent of the Russian budget deficit was covered by international credits, and the 1996 budget foresaw a $416 billion Eurobond emission. Immediately after the debt restructuring agreement with the Paris Club, the Russian government received a 4 billion DM credit from the German government.

Russia's creditworthiness in the future will depend upon its ability to meet the terms of its debt-restructuring agreements. They require Russia to meet a schedule

Table 17.4

RUSSIA'S EXTERNAL DEBT
(millions of US dollars)

	1989	1990	1991	1992	1993	1994	1995
Medium and long-term debt	35,472	48,017	54,972	64,891	73,108	80,054	8,700
Official credits (IMF, World Bank)	2,252	7,453	11,127	12,648	27,134	36,248	59,400
Private credit, public guarantees	33,490	40,564	43,846	52,243	45,974	43,806	26,400
Short-term obligations	18,200	11,800	12,618	13,112	8,312	9,981	16,800
Overdue interest	500	4,500	4,818	4,412	2,912	5,280	16,600
Official lenders	0	0	0	509	692	1,186	3,200
Private lenders	500	4,500	4,818	3,903	2,219	4,095	13,400
Total	53,942	59,817	67,590	78,992	83,888	94,232	120,400

Sources: Deutsches Institut für Wirtschaftsforschung, *Wochenbericht* no. 2 (1996), 471; *Wochenbericht* no. 4 (1997), 79.

of rising interest and principal payments. In the period 1996 to 1998, these payments will be between 10 and 11 billion dollars per year. After 1999, they will rise to $16–17 billion per year.

The Russian federal government is primarily responsible for meeting this debt service. According to experts, Russia's debt burden of 35 percent of GDP, or 150 percent of export earnings, is not exceptionally high. However, Russia's ability to service this debt depends upon its ability to raise federal revenues. The long-term ability of the Russian government to service this debt (which is denominated in dollars and German marks) depends on two main factors, in addition to the ability of the Russian government to raise fiscal revenues: the recovery of the Russian economy and the ruble exchange rate. If the Russian exchange rate rises in nominal and real value, less government revenues will be required.

FOREIGN INVESTMENT AND CAPITAL FLIGHT

Table 17.6 (p. 404) shows the amount of foreign investment that Russia received during the transition period. By mid-1994, the cumulated sum of direct foreign investment in Russia was only $2.8 billion. After 1994, direct foreign investment accelerated to almost $5 billion in 1995. If we take the year 1995 as an example, the Russian economy received approximately $2 billion of direct foreign investment,

Table 17.5

RUSSIA'S UNPAID EXTERNAL DEBTS
(millions of US dollars)

	1989	1990	1991	1992	1993	1994	1995
Overdue payments	**500**	**4,500**	**4,976**	**11,027**	**10,043**	**19,468**	**NA**
Overdue principal	0	0	158	6,615	7,131	14,187	NA
Overdue interest	500	4,500	4,818	4,412	2,912	5,280	16,600
Official lenders	0	0	0	509	692	1,186	3,200
Private lenders	500	4,500	4,818	3,903	2,219	4,095	13,400
Restructured debt	—	—	—	—	14,498	7,999	NA
Principal	—	—	—	—	9,227	5,312	NA
Interest	—	—	—	—	4,334	2,234	NA

Source: *Wochenbericht* no. 28 (1996), 471.

which is the equivalent of $40 per capita. Compared to Russia's potential as a raw materials producer and as a large consumer market, the sum of direct foreign investment in Russia is patently small. Hungary received almost twice as much for a per capita sum of $663, and Poland received $3.2 billion or $83 per capita.[11] Not only was the volume of gross direct foreign investment in the Russian economy small; Russia itself directed an even larger amount of direct investment abroad, in sums that about equaled the sum of direct investment into Russia through 1995. As might be expected, almost half of Russia's direct foreign investment was in the fuel and energy sector.

Direct foreign investment is only one means to attract foreign savings to Russia. The other form is indirect portfolio investments through purchases of Russian stocks and bonds. According to unpublished reports prepared by the Russian Central Bank, Russia attracted $175 million more of portfolio investment in 1992 than it made abroad. In 1993, the net sum fell to $64 million. In both 1994 and 1995, Russian investors invested more in foreign securities than foreigners invested in Russian securities.[12] In 1995 and 1996, foreign portfolio investment increased as foreigners were permitted to purchase federal government bills (GKOs) and Western companies made substantial purchases of stock of Russian energy concerns.[13]

Earlier, we noted that Russia has been faced with substantial outflows of savings. The above figures for direct foreign investment and for portfolio investment measure the recorded transfer of Russian savings abroad. A more considerable transfer of Russian savings abroad went unrecorded in the form of unregistered

Table 17.6

FOREIGN DIRECT INVESTMENT (CUMULATED TO 1996)
(millions of US dollars)

By Industry		By Country	
Oil industry	1,369	USA	2,041
Trade	1,221	UK	998
Financial	838	Germany	825
Food	782	France	597
Machinery	615	Switzerland	519
Construction	433	Italy	354
Wood, paper	426	Netherlands	354
Other	387	Austria	211
Transportation, communications	342	Belgium	197
Chemicals	286	Canada	196

Source: Daiwa Institute of Research, 19.

capital flight. The total volume of capital flight can be measured as the difference between the inflow of foreign exchange and its recorded uses, such as the increase in official reserves.[14] According to this methodology, capital flight from Russia equaled $8 billion in 1992, $11 billion in 1993, and $7 billion in 1994. For 1995, the capital flight has been estimated at $800 million per month! It should be noted that Russian capital flight typically does not involve the physical flow of foreign currencies out of Russia. Most of it is in the form of accumulation of foreign currencies inside of Russia. If anything, these measures understate Russian capital flight because they do not include false declarations on Russian exports and imports.

Russian capital flight and the limited volume of foreign investment in Russia are two sides of the same coin. The same factors that motivate capital flight—the uncertain political environment, the arbitrary tax regime, and the like—serve also to discourage foreign investment in Russia. The negative impact of capital flight and limited foreign investment on the Russian economy has been substantial. In 1995, gross investment in the Russian economy was approximately $55 billion (250 trillion rubles). With a capital flight of around $10 billion, Russian investment could have been 20 percent greater if this capital had stayed at home. If Russia could attract the same per capita foreign investment as a country like Poland, for example, it would have attracted more than $15 billion—a figure that would have raised Russia's investment another 30 percent.

SUMMARY

Russia's integration into the world economy is still in its infancy. Russia's trade proportions are still small, even when adjusted for the fact that Russia is a large, resource-rich country. Despite the vast profit potential of the Russian economy, Russia is sending as much of its domestic savings abroad as before. Moreover, foreigners are unwilling to commit to the Russian economy.

However, Russia has taken the first steps towards integration into the world product and capital markets. Whereas five years ago the state made trade and foreign debt decisions, now they are made primarily by nonstate organizations. The ruble exchange rate, although traded in a restricted market and with significant government intervention, is set by the forces of supply and demand. Russia's real exchange rate has been appreciating, although the nominal exchange rate has been depreciating. Russia's raw material wealth has allowed it to record strong current account surpluses, which have bolstered confidence in the ruble. The gap between the exchange rate and the PPP exchange rate has narrowed.

Russia assumed responsibility for the Soviet Union's foreign debts at a very difficult time in its history, just as the economy was collapsing and the foreign trade monopoly deteriorating. As a result, Russia was unable to service its foreign debt obligations, thereby destroying Russia's reputation for creditworthiness. Russia's foreign indebtedness rose as unpaid debt service accumulated, but Russia has again reentered the international credit market with the successful restructuring of its international debts.

Russia has taken the first steps to becoming a member in good standing in the various international financial and trading organizations. It is a member of the International Monetary Fund and has signed Partnership and Cooperation Agreements with the European Union. Russia will shortly be admitted to the World Trade Organization (WTO).[15]

In terms of trade policies, Russia is making the transition from a state-directed economy that viewed exports as a necessary evil to obtain imports, to one that is now showing growing concerns for market shares, employment, and protection of domestic producers. Russia has gone from measures that restrict exports to measures that now promote exports and discourage imports. With its potentially powerful agricultural lobby, Russia will probably shortly introduce measures to protect its agricultural sector, much like other countries with powerful agricultural interests.

Terms and Concepts ———————

foreign trade monopoly   Status of foreign trade arrangements during the Soviet era; the state conducted all trade through the Ministry of Foreign Trade and related organizations.

Currency Exchange Law   A law that permitted currency exchanges, an important step towards the elimination of the state monopoly in foreign trade.

fixed exchange rate   Exchange rates among currencies are fixed.

flexible (variable) exchange rate   Exchange among currencies are determined by the forces of supply and demand in the marketplace.

real exchange rate   An exchange rate that is adjusted according to changes in the relative prices of various countries.

pegged (fixed) exchange rate   An exchange rate which is fixed for a given currency against another currency.

purchasing power parity   The theory that in the long run, and in the absence of trade barriers, identical goods will sell in different countries at identical prices and thus exchange rates will adjust accordingly.

comparative advantage   If country A is relatively more efficient in the production of automobiles than trucks compared to country B, then country A has a comparative advantage in the production of automobiles.

current account   That part of a country's balance of payments which includes exports and imports of goods and services, net investment income and net transfers.

capital account   That part of a country's balance of payments pertaining to capital inflows and capital outflows.

Selected Bibliography

Cooper, R., and J. Gács. *Trade Growth in Transitional Economies* (Lyme, England: Edgar Elgar, 1997).

Dallago, B. and G. Pegoretti. *Integration and Disintegration in European Economies* (Brookfield, VT: Ashgate, 1995).

Dezseri, K. *Currency Convertibility* (Brookfield, VT: Ashgate, 1997).

Hillman, A. "The Transition From the CMEA System of International Trade," in M. Keren and G. Ofer, eds., *Trails of Transition: Economic Reform in the Former Communist Bloc* (Boulder, CO: Westview, 1994).

Konovalov, V. "Russian Trade Policy," in G. Michalopoulos and D. Tarr, eds., *Trade Performance and Policy in the Newly Independent States* (Washington, DC: World Bank, 1996).

Pautola, N. "The New Trade Theory and the Pattern of East-West Trade in the New Europe," *Review of Economies in Transition* vol. 6 (1995).

———— . "Trends in EU-Russia Trade, Aid, and Cooperation," *Review of Economies in Transition* vol. 4 (1996).

Russia and East European Finance and Trade (various).

Sheets, N. "Capital Flight From the Countries in Transition," International Finance Discussion Paper, no. 514 (1995).

Smith, A. *Russia and The World Economy: Problems of Integration* (New York: Routledge, 1993).

Sutela, P., and J. Kero. "Russian Trade Policies With the West: 1992 and Beyond," in P. Sutela, ed., *The Russian Economy in Crisis and Transition* (Helsinki: Bank of Finland, 1993).

Tarr, D. "The Terms of Trade Effect of Moving to World Prices on Countries in the Former Soviet Union," *Journal of Comparative Economics* vol. 18, no. 1 (February 1994).

Williamson, J. ed. *Currency Convertibility in Eastern Europe* (Washington, DC: Institute for International Economics, 1991).

Notes

1. The governmental program and decrees described below (through 1992) are most fully described in P. Sutela and J. Kero, "Russian Trade Policies with the West: 1992 and Beyond," in P. Sutela, ed., *The Russian Economy in Crisis and Transition* (Helsinki: Bank of Finland, 1993), 114–41.

2. *Russian Economic Trends 1996* vol. 5, no. 5, 45.

3. For descriptions of the ruble corridor system, see *Russian Economic Trends 1996* vol. 5, no. 1, 34–35; Plan Econ, *Review and Outlook for the Former Soviet Republics* (March 1996), 18–20.

4. "Run for the Border," *Russian Petroleum Investor* (December 1996/January 1997), 24.

5. For discussions of Russian trade policies, see V. Konovalov, "Russian Trade Policy," in G. Michalopoulos and D. Tarr, eds., *Trade Performance and Policy in the Newly Independent States* (Washington DC: World Bank, 1996), 17–22.

6. On this, see *Russian Economic Trends 1996* vol. 5, no. 1, 83–86.

7. *Russian Economic Trends 1996* vol. 5, no. 1, 85.

8. For a discussion of Russia's comparative advantage in the post-Soviet world, see N. Pautola, "The New Trade Theory and the Pattern of East-West Trade in the New Europe" *Review of Economies in Transition* no. 6 (1995), 5–23.

9. DIW, *Wochenbericht 28/96: Russlands Auslandsverbindungen nach der langfristigen Umschuldung* (July 11, 1996).

10. The restructuring of Russia's foreign debt is discussed in DIW, *Wochenbericht 28/96, Russlands Auslandsverbindligkeited nach der langfristigen Umschuldung* (July 11, 1996).

11. DIW, *Die wirtschaftslage Russlands: Integration in die Weltwirtschaft,* 51.

12. The results of this unpublished report are reported in DIW, Table 10.

13. The most substantial single investment was ARCO's purchase of $250 million worth of LUKoil securities, closed in 1995. On this, see Plan Econ, *Review and Outlook for the Former Soviet Republics* (March 1996), 24.

14. N. Sheets, "Capital Flight From the Countries in Transition," International Finance Discussion Paper, no. 514 (1995).

15. For a discussion of these matters, see N. Pautola, "Trends in EU-Russia Trade, Aid, and Cooperation," *Review of Economies in Transition* vol. 4 (1996), 5–20.

Changing Structure: Leading and Lagging Sectors

CORRECTING THE STALINIST MODEL

The Soviet administrative command economy created an **economic structure** that was quite different from **normal structures,** the structures that would have prevailed under a market economy. By the late 1930s, the Stalinist model was firmly entrenched. An administrative command system had replaced market resource allocation; private ownership of the means of production had virtually disappeared; the private peasant had been forced into collective farms. Stalin's economic system for allocating resources was resistant to significant change.

Planners' preferences, dictated by the Communist Party through the planning hierarchy, replaced consumer preferences. As a response to the imposition of planners' preferences, the demand structure was changed dramatically within a brief period of time in favor of selected (priority) heavy-industry branches, in particular, metallurgy, machine building, and electricity. The allocation of resources to light industry and agriculture was severely restricted. These two trends were reflected in prominent structural shifts: The aggregate investment rate rose markedly and rapidly, while there was a fall in the share of GDP devoted to personal consumption. The share of communal consumption (such as public health and education) rose at the expense of private consumption. The rise in public consumption, however, was not great enough to counter the relative decline in total consumption (as a percentage of GDP).

Despite the rise in health and education services, the growth of the service sector was retarded, thereby limiting the flow of resources into "nonproductive" sectors. Development of commerce was especially restricted because the limitations placed on consumer goods retarded the growth of retail trade; the absence of property ownership limited the need for banking, legal, and other commercial services; and the material balance system in large measure replaced the wholesale trade network.

In industry, especially in high-priority branches, highly capital-intensive factor proportions were adopted. In this manner, population movement from the rural to urban areas, though quite rapid, was held down. The result was a below-average ratio of urbanization, relative to the level of development, which enabled planners to restrict the flow of resources into nonproductive municipal services. Urbanization was also held down by encouraging high labor participation rates among the existing urban population, especially women. Authorities used low absolute real income levels and (in later years) laws against parasitism and absenteeism to encourage such high labor participation rates.

Large scale integrated plants were chosen. This gigantomania was sanctioned for reasons of international prestige (having the world's largest dam, for example) and because it was hoped that unit costs would eventually be lower owing to economies of scale.[1] Furthermore, a long planning-time horizon was adopted and interest rate calculations were not used, both of which condoned the long gestation periods involved in such projects. Highly integrated plants were chosen because of the primitive state of the material supply system, a factor that made less integrated plants vulnerable to supply interruptions. Machinery plants, for example, produced their own steel as well as shipping their finished products.[2] This integrated nature enabled planners to limit the size of wholesale trade.

The expansion of transport capacity was limited to restrict investment in social overhead capital. Planners counted on substantial improvements in levels of *utilization*, coupled with the pattern of industrialization, to minimize the need for transport services. To achieve the latter, planners placed strong emphasis on locating industrial establishments at the site of raw materials.[3] A further emphasis on railways as opposed to other forms of surface transportation enabled authorities to avoid highway construction.

A distinctive feature of the Stalinist model was the extent to which the service sector—especially commercial services such as trade, banking, and insurance—was depressed below "normal" levels usually found in the development experience of Western countries. Evidence of a Soviet service gap is found in the fact that the labor force share of services was much below that expected of a market economy at a similar level of development. Thus, the Soviet economy developed without devoting as much resources to services as have "normally" been required in the West.

Structural Change

Earlier chapters examined changes in the institutions of the Russian economy that have taken place during Russia's transition of the 1990s. Our description of the Stalinist model suggests that the economy Russia inherited from the administrative command era was not well suited for a market environment. Some sectors, such as heavy industry and defense, had been arbitrarily promoted to suit the preferences of the Soviet leadership. Others had been deliberately retarded, such as light industry and especially services and transportation. These Soviet or Stalinist resource allocations were reflected not only in the distribution of output but also in the distribution of the labor force. As Russia makes the transition from an administrative command economy to a market economy, we therefore expect to see a "normalization" of Russia's economic structure.

Figure 18.1 compares Russia's economic structure on the eve of transition (1989) with its structure in 1996, some five years into the restructuring process. Figures for the U.S. economy are provided as references to a "modern," large, market economy. Figure 18.1 shows that indeed Russia's economy has transformed itself rapidly, shifting resources away from the "planners' preference" sectors (industry and heavy industry) and towards "consumer preference" industries like trade and services. These changes affected not only the structure of output but also the distribution on labor and its renumeration.

Figure 18.2 (p. 412) illustrates the dramatic changes that took place in the structure of Russian wages. The Soviet administrative command economy gave the greatest rewards to those branches of the economy that produced priority goods for the planning system, by the mid-1990s the Russian economy was rewarding workers

Figure 18.1   The Changing Structure of Russian GDP

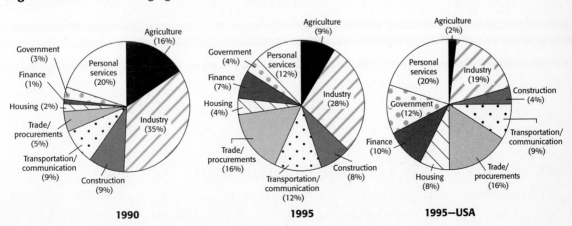

Source: World Bank, *Russian Federation: Report on the National Accounts,* Table 2.1.

Figure 18.2   Changes in Relative Wages from 1990 to 1995

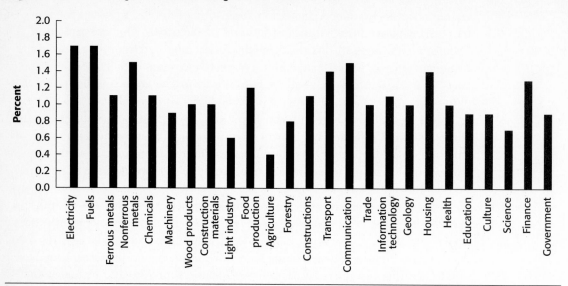

Source: *Rossiia v tsifrakh* (1995).

who produced goods and services demanded by a market economy, such as energy, communications, housing, and finance.

There is no simple formula for the structural change expected in the course of Russia's transition to a market economy. A market economy produces goods and services demanded by the marketplace, both at home and abroad. An economy integrated into the world economy usually specializes in those branches in which it has a comparative advantage. If one goes back to Russia's last market economy, prior to 1917, it is clear that Russia's comparative advantage lay in minerals, raw materials, and agriculture. Russia's ample land and abundant natural resources made it a primary exporter of raw materials, energy, and agricultural goods during the Tsarist period. The previous chapter indicated that in the 1990s, Russia has been primarily an exporter of energy and raw materials, suggesting that the country has retained its comparative advantage in these activities. However, Russia has continued to import food, contrary to its comparative advantage 75 years earlier.

LEADING SECTORS IN ECONOMIC DEVELOPMENT

As economists became interested in economic development in the 1950s, they wondered if a single leading factor could spark the development of an entire economy.[4] A **leading sector** would be one with significant forward and/or backward linkages to other sectors, so its development would push or pull along other sectors of the economy. Leading sectors could also simplify sectoral strategy. The limited amount of investment could be concentrated on the leading sector, whose growth would then facilitate investment in following sectors.

Strategists of Russian economic recovery during the transition have also considered whether certain key sectors of the Russian economy can play the role of a leading sector. At first glance, given the potential of the Russian fuel industry for increased production, as a source of state revenue, as a key input to the rest of the economy, and as a major source of hard-currency earnings, the energy sector appears to have the potential to play the role of a leading sector. In fact, Russian legislators gave priority to the creation of stable energy legislation (discussed in this chapter) for that reason.

In addition to being the engine of recovery, the Russian energy sector can be expected to play a major long-term role in eventual Russian economic growth. As a part of the world economy, Russia will necessarily restructure its output towards those activities in which it has comparative advantage. Given Russia's resource endowments, it is clear that its initial comparative advantage will be in energy production.

Revitalizing the Russian energy sector—specifically oil and gas—requires a number of steps: First, the Russian energy industry must make the transition from a state-planned, owned and operated branch of the economy to a market-oriented business with at least partial private ownership. Second, a climate favorable to long-term investment must be created in Russia. Revitalizing the oil and gas industry requires substantial long-term investments that will pay out over decades. If the investment climate does not promote such long-term thinking on the part of domestic and foreign investors, there can be no real development of the oil and gas industry.

Third, Russian oil and gas reserves must be developed according to the latest technology; advanced technology, however, is only available in the West. Russia must therefore find ways to bring in the latest technology to the Russian energy industry. Fourth, clear property rights to energy resources must be created so that rational economic decisions are made by those who own Russia's underground resources.

Soviet Legacy in the Energy Industry

The oil and gas industry of the former Soviet Union was managed in a highly centralized manner.[5] The powerful Ministry of Oil Industry and Ministry of Gas Industry set production quotas, established delivery plans, and drew up plans for investment and renovation. Oil and gas were produced by regional producer associations under supervision of the ministry. The various departments (glavki) of the Ministry managed different aspects of production, transportation, and sales. For example, the oil pipeline company (Transneft) was in charge of all transportation of oil by pipeline.

At its peak level of production in 1988, the Soviet Union was the world's largest producer of crude oil, at 11.8 million barrels per day, well ahead of the United States

(8.1 million barrels per day) and Saudi Arabia (5.3 million barrels per day). Most of the oil and gas reserves of the former Soviet Union were located in the Russian Republic, which accounted for approximately 95 percent of the Soviet Union's production. At its peak level of exports (1988), the Soviet Union was the world's second largest crude oil exporter (4.1 million barrels per day), slightly behind the world's largest exporter, Saudi Arabia (4.7 million barrels per day). In addition, in 1990 the Soviet Union was by far the world's leading producer of natural gas (817 billion cubic meters per year), well ahead of the second largest producer, the United States (499 billion cubic meters per year). The Russian Republic accounted for a smaller share of the Soviet Union's natural gas production, accounting for 78 percent of the Soviet Union total.

The Soviet Union consumed 7.7 million barrels of oil per year in 1988, which was about half as much as the United States and 80 percent as much as Western Europe.[6] These figures show that the Soviet Union and the Russian Republic were major producers, exporters, and consumers of primary energy products.

In the Soviet administrative command economy, the oil and gas industry was managed like the rest of the economy. Directors of production associations were judged on the basis of quantity plan targets, such as tons of oil produced, volumes of oil or gas transported, gallons of gasoline refined, or numbers of oil wells drilled. Even though oil and gas were sold to the West, domestic producers were paid industry prices that were a small fraction of the world price. Oil exporting enterprises simply received the low domestic price, while the difference went into state revenues. On the other side of the market, Soviet enterprises and consumers paid low domestic prices—so low that energy was considered almost as a free resource. In fact, Soviet and Russian industry were predicated on the notion that energy was readily available at virtually no cost.

Relative Energy Efficiency

The Russian economy was built on the principle of cheap energy during the era of the administrative command system. For a given level of economic activity, Russian industries and consumers tend to use (waste) more energy than industrial and household users in the West. Table 18.1 provides comprehensive measures of relative energy efficiency of the Soviet economy. In its use of oil and primary energy, the Soviet Union was less than half as efficient as Japan and the European Community and is considerably less efficient than the United States, where energy costs are lower than in Europe and Japan. In 1990 the Soviet Union produced, on average, $540 worth of output from one barrel of oil, while the European Community produced $1422 worth of output from one barrel (Table 18.1).[7] These differences illustrate the opportunities for gains from trade: The Soviet Union, by withdrawing one barrel of oil from its domestic economy and selling it to Europe, would allow Europe to transform that barrel—using the imported fuel, capital, and labor—into products worth almost $1000 more than would have been produced by the domestic Russian economy.

Table 18.1

RELATIVE ENERGY USAGE AND EFFICIENCY, SOVIET UNION AND OTHER COUNTRIES, 1990

	USSR	USA	Japan	European Community
Output and Energy Usage				
1. Gross domestic product (billion U.S. $)	$1,423	$5,715	$2,259	$5,292
2. Oil consumption (1000 barrels/day)	7,600	16,990	5,220	10,270
3. Primary energy consumption (1,000 b/day oil equivalent)	26,690	38,670	8,665	21,950
Efficiency Indexes				
4. Output per barrel of oil (U.S. $)	$513	$922	$1,186	$1,412
5. Output per barrel of primary energy consumption (U.S. $)	$146	$405	$714	$661

Sources: Directorate of Intelligence, *Handbook of International Economic Statistics 1992*, Table 7, Table 32, Table 36. At this point, no statistical agency can estimate the gross domestic product of Russia for the early 1990s because of the ongoing disruptions and the impossibility of converting ruble values into dollars. Earlier estimates of Soviet output have been discredited, especially those of the CIA, which apparently grossly overestimated Soviet GDP. For example, the CIA estimated Soviet 1990 GDP per capita at $9,140 — a figure equal to 42 percent of the United States and 62 percent of the UK (*Handbook of Economic Statistics 1991*, Tables 2 and 3). Our approach is to use the more reliable statistics for Eastern Europe and to assume that Soviet (Russian) per capita GDP was equal to the average of Bulgaria and Poland in 1990 (*Handbook of International Economic Statistics 1992*, Table 10). This figure, multiplied by USSR population, gives Soviet GDP for 1990 at $1.4 trillion. Even this figure may be an overstatement.

The difference between the world price and the domestic price of oil provides the most direct measure of the opportunity cost of using Soviet oil for the domestic economy rather than exporting it. The marginal domestic user values the oil (either for industrial use or for consumption) at the domestic price, while the foreign user will value it at the world price. The foreign user will not use the oil for an activity that does not at least equal its price. The difference between the Russian domestic price and the world price approximates the loss of welfare for the Russian economy per barrel of oil.[8]

These figures suggest that Russia has vast unexploited opportunities for energy conservation. Relative to the other industrialized economies, Russia uses more energy resources per unit of output. The lack of energy conservation is a legacy of the administrative command economy and of the continued pricing of energy below its "true" costs for domestic users. Until oil and gas resources are priced closer to their opportunity costs, they will continue to be "overused" by domestic users.[9] Russia, for example, consumes more oil and gas per capita than do its Scandinavian neighbors, who face a similarly harsh winter climate yet have per capita incomes at least five times greater than Russia.

An alternate perspective on the opportunity costs of shifting Soviet fossil fuel from hard-currency exports to domestic markets was the value of production that fossil fuel produced at home versus abroad. We can perform the calculation for the

Table 18.2

EFFECTIVENESS OF FOSSIL FUEL CONSUMPTION BY THE SOVIET ECONOMY (1989)

Industry branch	(1) fossil fuel input (bil. tons)	(2) gross output (bil. rubles)	(3) cost of energy, in world prices (bil. rubles)	(4) gross output per ton of energy (rubles)
Industry	1.363	1,131.1	828.7	830
Metallurgy	.157	92.0	95.5	586
Chemicals	.082	73.6	49.9	898
Agriculture	.095	288.5	57.8	3,037
Transportation and communication	.170	129.3	103.4	761

Source: *Narodnoe khoziaistvo SSSR v 1990 g,* 397. The calculation is done as follows: Fossil fuel energy inputs are calculated by taking the gross ruble value of the fossil fuel sector and dividing by millions of tons of fossil fuel production. This yields a 1989 ruble price per ton of 42.2 rubles. The gross output (in rubles) of each sector is read directly from the input-output table. The 1989 world price of fossil fuel energy (in rubles) is calculated indirectly (and approximately) by taking the market exchange rate for 1989 (5 rubles = $1) and multiplying by the 1989 dollar price per ton ($121.59) from *Handbook of International Economic Statistics 1992,* Table 16.

late 1980s for the former Soviet Union. The 1989 Soviet input-output table shows the inputs and outputs of the various economic branches. It shows the inputs (materials, capital, and labor) used by each sector and the ruble-value outputs produced from these inputs. Table 18.2 shows the physical inputs of fossil fuels (oil, gas, and coal) used by five branches and the gross outputs produced by each sector.

The results in Table 18.2 are striking. They show that if fossil fuels had been valued in world market prices (a direct measure of their opportunity costs), they were being used inefficiently to produce industrial output. In industry, 828.7 billion rubles worth of fossil fuels were used to produce an output (valued in domestic prices) of 1131 billion rubles. In metallurgy, the cost of fossil fuels even exceeded the value of output. In the transportation sector, noted in the Soviet Union for wastage, 103 billion rubles of fossil fuel energy were used to produce an output of 129 billion rubles. (Remember that we are considering only fossil fuel costs and have not yet even counted labor, capital, and the costs of other materials in the above figures.) These calculations are inexact, but they do suggest that Soviet industries used a relatively expensive input (with a clear opportunity cost as reflected by the world price) to produce outputs of limited value.[10]

RUSSIAN ENERGY: THE TRANSITION PERIOD

As noted in Chapter 15, the Russian economy contracted sharply after 1989. The primary energy production of the Russian economy also contracted, but the decline was less severe than in other branches of the economy, primarily due to the fairly stable production of natural gas (Figure 18.3). The decline in crude oil production, however, was as large as the decline in the overall economy.

Despite these declines, the Russian primary energy sector has increased its relative share of the Russian economy. The fuel industry (coal, crude oil, and natural gas) accounted for 7 percent of Russian industrial output in 1991 and for about 20 percent in 1996. Russia's share has increased because of the rise in the relative price of energy products, which were priced at a small fraction of world prices at the start of the transition process, and because declines in the fuel sector have been less severe overall than in other branches. As Table 18.3 (p. 418) shows, since December 1990, Russian energy prices have been rising as a percent of world market prices. The decline of Russian primary energy belies the potential of the Russian oil and gas industry. The Russian Republic accounts for 5 percent of the world crude oil reserves and for 34 percent of proven reserves for gas.[11]

Given its potential, why has Russian primary energy production fallen? Like other branches of the Russian economy, the Russian fuel sector has been damaged by the chaos associated with the collapse of the administrative command economy prior to the creation of the institutions of a market economy. The Russian oil and gas sector has had difficulties in converting from a command system based upon production targets, soft budget constraints, and controlled transportation systems. The Soviet production quota system resulted in poor reservoir management, flooded wells with a high water content, excessive labor staffing, and other typical weaknesses of the administrative command economy.

Figure 18.3   Russian Energy: Production and Exports (oil: million tons; gas: billion cubic meters)

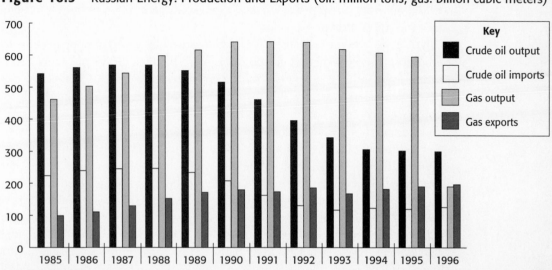

Sources: PlanEcon, *Energy Outlook for the Former Soviet Republics* (selected years); *Russian Economic Trends* (selected issues).

Table 18.3

RUSSIAN ENERGY PRICES AS PERCENT OF WORLD PRICES

	1/94	1/95	10/95	12/96
Crude oil	44.7	33.4	53.2	49
Gasoline	73.3	56.0	79.3	NA
Diesel	54.3	54.3	83.3	124.0
Heating	43.7	34.5	69.9	83.0
Natural gas	22.7	30.2	78.8	34.0

Sources: Ministry of Fuel and Energy; *Russian Petroleum Investor; Russian Economic Trends* vol. 1 (1997), 68.

The Russian oil and gas industry, however, was also hit by a group of problems that did not affect other branches of the economy. Although Russian prices were generally liberalized after January 1992, Russian authorities maintained ceilings on fuel prices, given their importance to Russian consumers and to fuel-inefficient Russian industry. Oil prices, for example, were kept low for domestic consumers although oil exported to the West was sold at world market prices. Low domestic prices were maintained initially by price controls, export quotas, and export tariffs, which reduced the net price to crude oil exporters. As quotas and export taxes were gradually removed in the mid-1990s, they were replaced by transportation and port taxes. The limited export capacity of Russian pipelines also restricted exports and kept domestic prices below world prices. Taken together, these measures served to lower the net price to oil producers and to make them indifferent between selling in the domestic market or exporting.

The Russian energy industry was affected as well by a rash of nonpayments for its products. Although oil and gas products were being sold to consumers and to industrial users, a large percentage of buyers were failing to pay. Instead of payment, oil producers were forced to maintain accounts receivable, for which the probability of eventual repayment was limited.

In addition to the chaos and uncertainty associated with the change in management, the Russian oil and gas industry suffered from a severe collapse in investment spending. Although it is difficult to measure the volume of investment in the fuels industry due to changing prices and statistical practices, key physical indicators suggest a collapse of investment spending. In the 1980s, 3000 to 4000 kilometers of trunkline oil pipelines were either built or reconstructed annually. In 1991 only 300 kilometers and in 1992 only 100 kilometers were built or reconstructed. In 1994, only 20 kilometers were built.[12] Other statistics that speak of the collapse of investment were the rising number of shut-in walls, which had to be shut down due to lack of equipment or capital, and the relatively small number of wells drilled.

The Promise of Russian Oil and Gas

Of the former Soviet republics, Russia, Kazakhstan, and Azerbaizhan are the sites of some of the world's largest unexploited oil reserves. During the Soviet period, with its emphasis on production now, the oil industry was developed in an extensive fashion. Oil fields that required more sophisticated Western equipment and recovery techniques for development remained untapped. Oil and gas located in remote regions had to wait the investment in transportation infrastructure.

The attraction of Russian oil is the substantial reserves that remain to be developed. Although there is dispute about Russian oil reserve figures, currently more than six Russian oil companies claim to have reserves greater than the world's leader, Shell, at 8.6 billion barrels.[13] Whereas international oil companies such as Exxon, Shell, and British Petroleum have current reserves to last for 14–16 years at current production levels, the average reserve life of Russian oil companies is over 50 years. Moreover, with advanced technology these reserves can be developed at a relatively low marginal cost compared to costs in other parts of the world.

Despite hopes of recovery, Russian oil production continued its decline as of 1997, and current hopes are for stabilization as opposed to rapid growth. The impediments to rapid growth are bureaucratic obstacles, the failure to create a positive investment climate, and the resolution of property rights and management issues.

Structure of the Russian Primary Energy Industry   During the process of transition, the management and ownership structures of the Russian oil and gas industry underwent significant and dramatic change. With the collapse of the administrative command system, new organizational arrangements consistent with a market-oriented energy industry had to be developed.

Whereas the Soviet Ministry of Oil Industry micromanaged the production, sales, and transportation of oil, its Russian successor organizations have less power and control over the energy industry. The new Russian Constitution of December 1993 divided the jurisdiction over subsoil resources among the federal, regional, and local authorities. The Law on Underground Resources passed in 1994 also divided authority among the federal, state, and local governments. The Soviet planning structure included republican ministries to assist the all-union ministry in its administration of the energy industry, but the republican ministries exercised little true authority. In place of the all-powerful Soviet oil ministry, the key federal institutions are the Ministry of Fuel and Energy, which supervises all fuel and energy sources (oil, gas, coal, and electricity); the Committee for Geology; and the Committee for Mineral Resources. Figure 18.4 (page 420) presents an organization chart of the Ministry of Fuel and Energy. Whereas their predecessors could exercise tight control, these federal organizations have indirect control, which they exercise primarily through licensing, quotas, influence on legislation, and the regulation of prices and rates. Transneft, the state-owned oil pipeline company that manages the oil pipeline system of the Russian Republic, was formerly a department of the Ministry of Oil Industry. It has achieved more autonomy and is (nominally, at least) a joint stock company but totally owned by the federal and local governments. There continues to be much greater centralization of natural gas. The old Soviet gas ministry has been privatized into a joint stock company, Gazprom, which retains a monopoly over the production, sale, and distribution of natural gas.

The most significant changes in the structure of the Russian energy industry has been the privatization of formerly state-owned enterprises. (The general privatization process has been described in Chapter 14.) The privatization of the Russian oil and gas industry was managed under separate rules because of the industry's strategic importance. The general result, however, was much the same as with less strategic enterprises. Insiders and related groups ended up owning and controlling Russia's oil companies.

At the beginning of the transition process, Russian authorities opted for the creation of vertically integrated oil companies (VICs) patterned after the international

Figure 18.4   Organization of the Russian Federation Ministry of Fuel and Energy

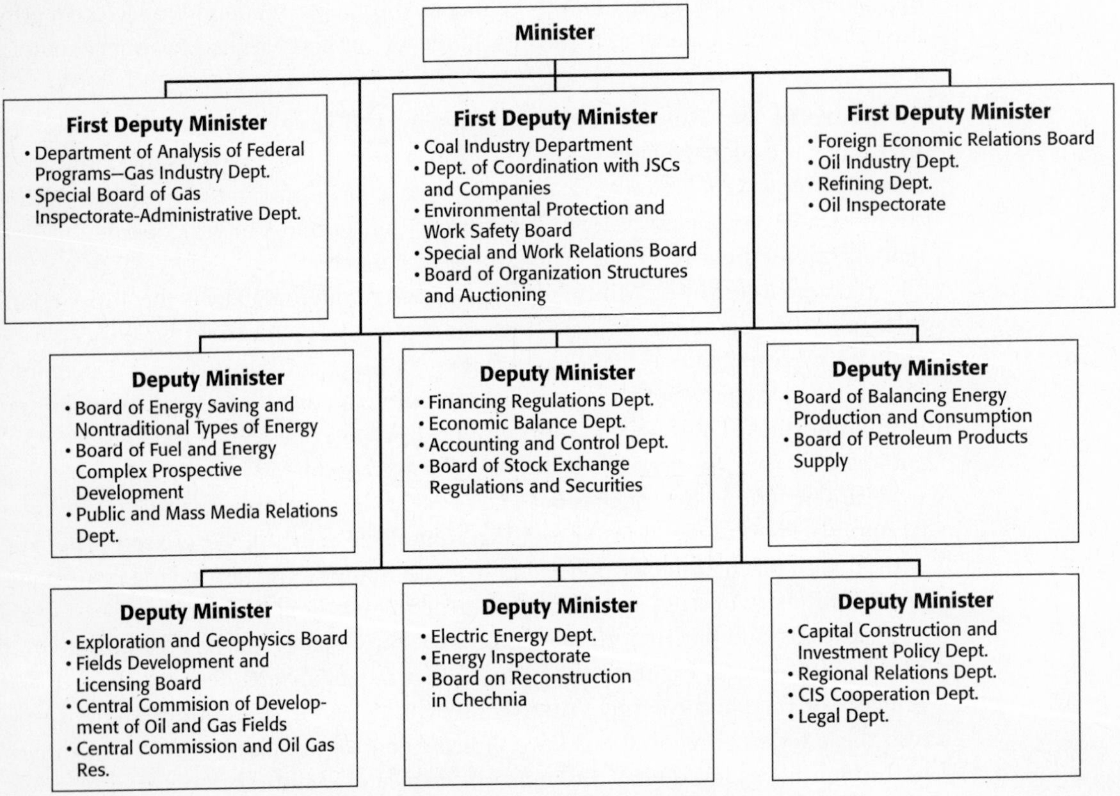

Minister

First Deputy Minister
- Department of Analysis of Federal Programs—Gas Industry Dept.
- Special Board of Gas Inspectorate-Administrative Dept.

First Deputy Minister
- Coal Industry Department
- Dept. of Coordination with JSCs and Companies
- Environmental Protection and Work Safety Board
- Special and Work Relations Board
- Board of Organization Structures and Auctioning

First Deputy Minister
- Foreign Economic Relations Board
- Oil Industry Dept.
- Refining Dept.
- Oil Inspectorate

Deputy Minister
- Board of Energy Saving and Nontraditional Types of Energy
- Board of Fuel and Energy Complex Prospective Development
- Public and Mass Media Relations Dept.

Deputy Minister
- Financing Regulations Dept.
- Economic Balance Dept.
- Accounting and Control Dept.
- Board of Stock Exchange Regulations and Securities

Deputy Minister
- Board of Balancing Energy Production and Consumption
- Board of Petroleum Products Supply

Deputy Minister
- Exploration and Geophysics Board
- Fields Development and Licensing Board
- Central Commision of Development of Oil and Gas Fields
- Central Commission and Oil Gas Res.

Deputy Minister
- Electric Energy Dept.
- Energy Inspectorate
- Board on Reconstruction in Chechnia

Deputy Minister
- Capital Construction and Investment Policy Dept.
- Regional Relations Dept.
- CIS Cooperation Dept.
- Legal Dept.

Source: *Russian Petroleum Investor* vol. 2 (1996).

energy concerns such as Exxon, Shell, and British Petroleum. The VICs were created under the slogan, "From wellhead to gas pump." The idea was to replace administrative management of the Soviet system with integrated companies, consolidating oil operations under one management. Table 18.4 provides production and export figures by Russian VICs.

Legislation

According to the Russian Constitution adopted in December 1993, the statutory responsibility for the Russian energy industry is shared by the federal government and by regional governments. The federal government has the right to make decisions concerning framework legislation, foreign policy, taxation, and defense; the federal government shares with regional governments responsibility for issues such as land ownership, subsoil use, and natural resources generally.[14]

The **Russian Law on Underground Resources** was enacted by parliament in February of 1992 and signed by President Yeltsin in May of 1992 as an umbrella law covering all underground resources. The Law on Underground Resources, in keep-

Table 18.4

OIL PRODUCTION, VERTICALLY INTEGRATED OIL COMPANIES*

	Oil production daily (thousand tons)	Oil exports daily (thousand tons)
Bashneft	44	7
Komitek	10	3
Lukoil	140	21
Onako	22	5
Rosneft	36	15
Sidanco	56	10
Sibneft	50	8
Slavneft	34	7
Surgut	91	22
Tatneft	66	15
Tyumen	59	11
Vostochnaia	31	6
Yukos	96	22
TOTAL	731	153

*The figures are for October 1996.

Source: *Russian Petroleum Investor* (December 1996/January 1997), Appendix.

ing with the later-enacted Russian Constitution, divided ownership of underground resources among federal, state, and local jurisdictions and spelled out provisions for licensing the development of mineral resources.[15]

Although Russian authorities intended to have a Law on Oil and Gas to govern issues such as ownership, licensing, and transportation, a final draft of this law has not been approved by the Duma or signed by the President. In place of a general law on oil and gas, the Russian government and parliament have focused on specifying licensing provisions and on passing production-sharing agreements.

For all practical purposes, the **Production Sharing Agreement** (PSA), signed December 31, 1995, but not approved in final form, currently defines the relationship between the state and oil companies, including foreign oil companies. PSAs have been used by international oil companies to operate in numerous foreign countries. They spell out the manner in which production from a particular venture is shared between the company and the state and how the shares will be distributed over time. For example, if a foreign or domestic company has provided the investment capital to finance a development project, the PSA may allow the investing company first to recapture the investment from an established percentage of revenues. Then the PSA agreement would spell out the distribution of revenues between the state and the company.

Foreign investment is welcomed by some forces in Russia and despised by others, who warn that Russia is "giving away" its natural resources to foreigners. Accordingly, the PSA agreement and the Law on Oil and Gas have been the subject of fierce debate within Russia. In fact, parliamentary revisions to the PSA have added the right of the Duma to approve agreements for strategic areas and to modify PSA agreements in the event of major changes in economic circumstances. Moreover, much of the finer detail of the PSA legislation needs to be worked out in the form of regulatory acts that may affect materially the implementation of PSA agreements.[16] The major foreign investment projects, listed in Table 18.5, currently underway or pending in Russia are all anchored in PSA agreements.

PSA agreements are only one possible approach for international energy company investments in Russia. Several companies have chosen to form joint ventures with Russian companies within the terms of the legislation that already existed, such as the Law on Underground Resources and the licensing regulations. Joint Venture Legislation had been passed already during the era of perestroika (the Law on Joint Ventures of 1987), and subsequent joint venture laws have liberalized these early Soviet laws.

Current Russian joint venture laws are similar to those elsewhere. In an energy joint venture, an international company forms a partnership agreement with a local Russian company concerning capital contributions, responsibilities, management, and other matters. The joint venture is then managed according to by-laws approved by the partners.

Although the PSA agreement was provisionally passed only at the very end of 1995 (with significant provisions still to be determined), existing joint ventures include British Gas's 50 percent interest in Komiarktic Oil and Conoco's joint

Table 18.5

MAJOR AGREEMENTS PENDING PSA LEGISLATION

Project	Companies	Location
Sakhalin 1	Exxon	Offshore Eastern Russia
Sakhalin 2	Marathon, Mitsui, Mitsubishi, McDermott, Shell	Offshore Eastern Russia
Kharyaga	Total	North of Arctic Circle
Timan Pechera	Texaco, Exxon, Amoco	Urals
Sakhalin 3	Exxon, Mobile, Texaco	Sea of Okhotsk

Source: Compiled by authors.

venture with Arkhangelesk Geologia.[17] As of 1995, joint ventures accounted for 8 percent of crude oil production, up from 1 percent in 1992. Joint venture oil production could rise to 20 percent of the total by 2000.[18]

TAXATION AS A DETERRENT TO FOREIGN INVESTMENT

The Russian government has been plagued by declining tax revenue throughout its transition period. Faced with declining tax revenues and collapsing tax discipline, Russian authorities have sought to collect taxes from sources they perceive as being able to pay, such as foreigners or the Russian oil industry. For this reason, the Russian oil industry and its foreign participants have been subjected to a high burden of taxes.[19] Taxes include a 20 percent value added tax (VAT), a 3 percent tax on the value of property, profit taxes levied by both the federal and regional governments. In addition, an array of special taxes, such as export and port taxes, has been assessed. Special tax exemptions have been granted to joint ventures, and special tax treatment is often included in PSA contracts. In theory, the VAT on imported equipment is supposed to be refunded.

Since some Russian taxes on oil are on profits, it becomes important for Western investors that profits are measured correctly. In this regard, Russian accounting differs significantly from Western International Accounting Systems (IAS). In Russian accounting, a number of expenses are not counted in costs but must be covered out of profits. For example, the costs of providing facilities to workers and families in remote locations (often a major expense in the oil industry), interest costs, and tax penalties are not counted in costs. Moreover, oil companies who have not been paid for their sales are not able to deduct their losses due to late collection (or the writing off of bad debts). Depreciation of assets is allowed only on a straight line basis, so that most Western experts would argue that depreciation is undervalued.[20] Russian tax authorities use mountains of regulations to limit allowable expenses and deductions.

The most disconcerting element of Russian taxation of the oil industry is its unpredictability. The tax system has been changed frequently; exemptions from particular taxes have been obtained and then lost. For example, joint ventures given special access to pipelines are sometimes freed from export taxes, while sometimes they are not. In a word, taxation of the Russian energy industry is too arbitrary and unpredictable to justify major Western investment. The new tax code, which is supposed to "normalize" the Russian tax system, will not go into full effect until 1998, at the earliest.

The Debate Over Foreign Investment in Oil and Gas

As noted earlier, the issue of foreign investment in the Russian oil industry in controversial within Russia. Potent political groups within the Russian parliament, in particular the communists and the nationalists, oppose foreign investment and ownership. They argue that Russia should not allow heavy involvement by foreign interests in Russia's crown jewel—its underground resources. Advocates of reform argue that Russia cannot generate domestically the capital formation and technology required to revive and grow Russia's energy industries. The only option is to invite foreign companies to assist in the joint development of Russia's oil and gas industries. A third group opposes foreign participation and ownership because its members are actively competing for ownership of Russia's underground resources with foreign companies. If foreigners can be excluded, their chances of obtaining ownership rights are enhanced. In this third group are included the various banks and industrial/financial combinations that have had success in obtaining shares of some of Russia's major oil companies through the controversial "loans for shares" program of the Russian government.[21]

If Russia's major banks and investment groups gain control of the Russian oil industry, they hope to raise capital independently (perhaps in Western capital markets), thereby creating the necessary capital for the Russian oil industry without sacrificing ownership interests to foreigners. With capital available, they could hire or buy the advanced technology and the management expertise needed to rejuvenate Russia's oil and gas industry.[22]

Foreign investment in Russia's oil and gas industry is therefore limited by domestic opposition by various powerful groups, either for political or economic reasons. An equally serious restriction is the unsure investment climate of Russia, which has been partially described above. Laws are either inadequate, remain to be written, or if written, are poorly enforced. The current tax system is uncertain and based upon complicated special privileges and exemptions that could be arbitrarily withdrawn. The promised new tax system is not expected to go into effect in the near future, and when it does there are no guarantees that it will be more certain than the current system. Although the summer 1996 presidential election seems to have removed the threat of a communist return to power, Russia's political system remains shaky, and the conflict between the presidency and the legislature shows no signs of being resolved.

Major foreign investors have looked to the passage of the Production Sharing Law in 1996 as the legal foundation for proceeding with their major investment projects. However, they must await drafting and acceptance by the regulations government of the implementation of the PSA law, and the communist-dominated Duma has embarked on a counterattack of the PSA Law, with amendments that would discourage foreign investment.[23]

By the end of 1995, the cumulative dollar volume of direct foreign investment in the Russian oil and gas industry reached slightly more than $1.6 billion—an insignificant sum given the size of typical infrastructure investments in the industry.[24] This limited amount of direct investment underscores the uncertain investment environment in Russia, which has retarded foreign investment.

Foreign investors can indirectly invest in Russia's oil and gas industries by purchasing shares of Russian oil and gas companies in equity markets. Such investments leave the current management in place and do not require joint ventures or production-sharing arrangements with foreign partners, and they do create capital funds for field and infrastructure development. Since 1995, there has been one relatively large purchase of blocs of stock by a Western oil company, and individual investors and mutual funds have begun to purchase shares of stock in some of Russia's largest vertically-integrated oil companies.[25] Such stock purchases have been motivated by the argument that Russian oil shares are undervalued when common oil-industry valuation techniques are employed (such as barrels of reserves per share of stock).

It remains to be seen whether foreign participation in the Russian oil and gas industry will be in the form of direct or indirect foreign investment and whether the flow of foreign investment will ever reach a substantial amount. Obviously, the answer depends upon the climate for foreign investment in Russia, a climate that will be created over the next five to ten years.

Export Potential   Foreign investment in Russian oil and gas makes sense only if the resulting production can be exported. Export potential depends upon a number of factors—the overall level of production, the infrastructure for investment, trade and pricing policy, and domestic consumption. Figure 18.3 showed that Russian exports of oil plummeted during the first five years of transition and have not yet begun to increase. Russia still "overconsumes" energy, compared to other industrialized countries—a carryover from the Soviet period. As Russia adjusts to the higher level of energy prices, we can expect it to adjust its energy consumption per capita and per dollar of GDP towards the standards of other countries. As Russia's energy consumption declines, its capacity to export energy will increase.

A major unknown is the reconstruction and expansion of Russia's export pipeline capacity, which is currently operating at full capacity despite the smaller volume of exports. Russia's reduced export capacity is tied to the breakup of the

Soviet Union, which caused the integrated transportation system to disintegrate, and to the lack of investment for maintenance and expansion. Major expansions of Russia's export capacity also hinges upon difficult geopolitical issues, such as agreements to build major pipelines through former Soviet republics, a strategy that might cause the Russian Republic to fear loss of monopoly control over energy exports.

RESTRUCTURING RUSSIAN AGRICULTURE

Although Russia had a comparative advantage in agriculture before Soviet rule, there was little evidence of agricultural success under Soviet rule. Experts agree that while factors such as an inhospitable climate played a role in the problems faced by Soviet agriculture, the dominant causes were organizational arrangements, inappropriate incentives, and lack of appropriate decision-making tools to use resources properly. Although Soviet agriculture was the subject of continuing controversy (as we noted in Chapter 8), nevertheless, in the end, the many attempted reforms, including the injection of major resources into agriculture, failed to stem a continuing decline in total factor productivity. In effect, the inability of expanded resources to solve production problems led to the Soviet Union becoming a major net importer of grains. It would seem that the Soviet agricultural sector suffered from a basic misallocation of resources.

Agriculture in Transition

It is perhaps ironic that during the later years of Soviet rule, Soviet agriculture would be viewed as a sector ripe for change, and yet during transition, it is agriculture the has experienced minimal change. Put another way, Russian agriculture in transition has been given minimal attention, contrary to the attention it received during the Soviet era.

Although privatization of land was very much on the back burner during the Gorbachev era, by the end of 1991, during the early stages of the Yeltsin era, Russia had passed land legislation that spelled out basic options for collective and state farms, with implementation to take place at the local (mostly oblast) level.[26] Farms could be broken up into individual peasant farms, with a service organization or association that would acquire inputs such as fertilizers. A second option was creation of a joint stock company, along lines similar to that in industry. Third, peasants could form a producer cooperative, in which individual farm units belonged to a cooperative but retained a degree of internal independence. Finally, state and collective farms could sustain their existing operations. What has been the outcome?

Specialists observing Russian agriculture in transition argue that while market reforms have had an impact upon production, continuing state intervention has preserved many old ways, making the agricultural sector unattractive to investors and limiting real reform in areas such as land use and marketing.

Since the beginning of the Yeltsin era, the extent of organizational change has been limited. In 1991, about 95 percent of all agricultural land was in state and collective farms. By 1994, this proportion fell to just over 80 percent, although fully 70 percent of these farms were unprofitable in 1995 (even including all state subsidies).[27] As Table 18.6 makes clear, performance trends have been troubling.

Although aggregate output data for Russia would show that the agricultural sector declined less than the industrial sector, nevertheless, the evidence in Table 18.6 shows sharp reductions in the output of major agricultural products. In addition, both direct and indirect state support has been important, though state support of agriculture decreased as a portion of GDP. In 1996, state support was at a projected level of 86 trillion rubles, or 3.8 percent of projected GDP.[28]

The net result of developments in Russian agriculture has been a sharp reduction in the aggregate level of agricultural imports, driven especially by a reduction of grain imports, but a significant increase in the imports of high value products. For example, between 1992 and 1995, Russia's total net imports of meat and meat products more than doubled.

The issue of food consumption has been one of controversy. In broad perspective, household budget survey data shows a decline in the per capita consumption of meat, milk, and eggs, especially noticeable between 1994 and 1995. These surveys show a reduction of calories purchased, with a daily average of 2310 calories in 1995.[29]

Several issues cloud the food consumption issue, however. First, the onset of market forces has raised retail prices, which has, in turn, increased the share of household income devoted to food purchases. This ratio increased in Russia from

Table 18.6

RUSSIAN AGRICULTURE DURING TRANSITION

	Meat (thousand tons)	Milk (thousand tons)	Eggs (million)	Grain* (thousand tons)
1991	9,315	51,886	46,875	116,676
1993	7,513	46,524	40,297	99,000
1995	5,930	39,306	33,714	63,400
1996	5,350	36,000	31,500	69,285

*Total grains (cleanweight). Note that the series present here differ somewhat from those presented on the basis of agricultural rather than calendar year.

Sources: U.S. Department of Agriculture, *International Agriculture and Trade Reports: Former USSR* (Washington, DC: USDA, May 1996 and 1997) and U.S. Department of Agriculture, *Former USSR Update* (Washington, DC: USDA, October 1996).

roughly 36 percent in 1990 to 52 percent in 1995. Second, food consumption comparisons over time are often based upon the questionable consumption norms used in the Soviet Union.

Third, there are important regional differences, for example the extent to which food products are subsidized. Fourth, there is considerable unevenness in the access to food based upon sharp changes in the income distribution in Russia. Not only are high value imports more attractive to high income families, but also families with higher incomes spend a significantly lower share of their income on food than do poorer families.

The prognosis for agriculture in Russia must be considered guarded. Reform of the agricultural infrastructure has been modest, and while it may continue, unquestionably the pace will be modest and the forces acting against change, for example state intervention, will remain, even if at a declining level. Moreover, in the rural sector the availability of human capital capable of promoting change will be a limiting factor. Although the projection of 1996–97 is positive for an increase in grain output, the output of meat and meat products is projected to decline through the end of the century. And a major and yet uncertain role will be played by foreign trade, both in terms of Russian domestic production costs and the terms on which imports are available from the remainder of the former Soviet Union and other countries.

SUMMARY

Development economists have long argued that there is an important relationship between sustained economic growth and economic development and differential (sectoral) rates of economic growth. The Stalinist model was one of unbalanced growth, specifically with major emphasis on sectors such as heavy industry, transportation, energy, and the military. At the same time, much less attention was given to agriculture, the light industrial sector, and consumer services. In a sense, these were, respectively, the leading and lagging sectors of the Soviet economy, albeit functioning under organizational arrangements and policy imperatives that will have a significant impact upon changes attempted in the transition era.

During transition, energy production has fallen due in large part to the difficulties of the transition process, especially those related to pricing and investment policies. Moreover, the privatization of oil and gas production has been difficult, given the strategic nature of the industry. Legislation has been a major part of the story, as have been the controversies surrounding foreign investment.

If agriculture was a lagging sector of the Soviet era, it remains so in transition, influenced greatly by the administrative legacy of the administrative command system. While the formalities of privatization were developed for the rural sector, actual implementation of change has been modest. Output has generally fallen throughout the transition era, with important implications for consumption, though partly offset by imports. While the output of grain has been projected to increase in 1996–97, the output of meat and meat products in projected to decrease through the end of the century.

In effect, change has been modest in the Russian rural economy. Through the end of the century and beyond, the rural sector will be buffeted by a variety of forces, the balance of which will dictate the nature and extent of change. The forces that may stimulate change include domestic demand, state policies, regional policies, trends in international trade, and the attractiveness of the rural economy as an outlet for investment stimulating change.

Terms and Concepts ——————————————

economic structure   Though capable of varying interpretations, used here to denote the development of sectors of the economy (agriculture/industry/services); the shares of these sectors in an economy can be measured over time and in different country settings such that planned socialist structures and market capitalist structures can be compared and assessed.

normal structure   Typically sectoral shares measured in large samples of market economic systems against which planned socialist systems could be compared.

planners' preferences   Generally compared to consumer sovereignty, where planners preferences are associated with planned socialist economic systems in which objectives of the system are developed by politicians and planners, not in the marketplace.

leading sector   An approach to economic growth and economic development in which a sector (such as energy or transportation) might be identified and prioritized (though investment, for example) as a mechanism to stimulate economic growth in the overall economy.

Russian Law on Underground Resources   A law brought forth in the spring of 1992 to govern the use of underground resources in Russia.

Production Sharing Agreement   Subject to agreement on final form, a law dating from late 1995 that spells out the relationship between the state and oil companies, including foreign oil companies.

Bibliography

Growth Strategy: The Big Push

Granick, D. *Soviet Metal Fabricating and Economic Development* (Madison: University of Wisconsin Press, 1967).

Holzman, F. D. "The Soviet Ural-Kuznetsk Combine: A Study of Investment Criteria and Industrialization Policies," *Quarterly Journal of Economics* vol. 71, no. 3 (August 1957).

Katz, B. "'Gigantism' as an Unbalanced Growth Strategy: An Econometric Investigation of the Soviet Experience, 1928–1940," *Soviet Union* vol. 4, no. 2 (1977).

Nurske, R. *Problems of Capital Formation in Underdeveloped Economies* (New York: Oxford University Press, 1975).

Rosenstein-Rodan, P. N. "Notes on the Teory of the Big Push," in H.S. Ellis, *Economic Development for Latin America* (New York: St. Martins Press, 1961).

Woroniak, A. "Industrial Concentration in Eastern Europe: The Search for Optimum Size and Efficiency," *Notwendigkeit und Gefahr Wirtschaftlichen Konzentration* (Basil: Kyklos Verlag).

Energy

Birol, F., and N. Buerer. "Long Term Oil Outlook of Eight CIS Members," *Revue de l'Energie* vol. 47 (January 1996).

Gustafson, T. *Crisis Among Plenty: The Politics of Soviet Energy Under Brezhnev and Gorbachev* (Princeton: Princeton University Press, 1989).

The Russian Petroleum Investor (various issues)

Sagers, M. "The Oil Sector in the FSU: Poised for Recovery?" (Houston: Plan Econ, October 10, 1996).

"Symposium, The Russian Petroleum Legislation Project at the University of Houston Law Center," *Houston Journal of International Law* vol. 15, no. 2 (Winter-Spring 1993).

Agriculture

Braverman, A., and J.L. Guasch. "Agricultural Reform in Developing Countries: Reflections for Eastern Europe," *American Journal of Agricultural Economics* (December 1990).

Brock, G. J. "Agricultural Productivity in Volgograd Province," *Comparative Economic Studies* vol. 36, no. 1 (Spring 1994).

Brooks, K. "Price Adjustment and Land Valuation in the Soviet Agricultural Reform: A View Using Lithuanian Farm Data," *European Review of Agricultural Economics* vol. 18 (1991).

Brooks, K., and Z. Lerman. "Farm Reform in the Transition Economies," *Finance and Development* vol. 31, no. 4 (December 1994).

Brooks, K., et al. "Agriculture and the Transition to the Market," *Journal of Economic Perspectives* vol. 5, no. 4 (Fall 1991).

Clayton, E. "Agricultural Privatization in Transition Economics," *Comparative Economic Studies* vol. 34, no. 1 (Spring 1992)

Foster, C. J. "As U.S. Meat Exports to Russia Reach Record Highs, Trade Barriers Strengthen," International Agriculture and Trade Reports, *Former USSR: Situation and Outlook Series, USDA* (May 1996).

Gray, K. "Changing Consumption, Consumer Sovereignty and Poverty Policies," USDA International Agriculture and Trade Reports, *Former USSR: Situation and Outlook Series* (May 1996).

Johnson, D. G. "Trade Effects of Dismantling of Socialized Agriculture of the Former Soviet Union," *Comparative Economic Studies* vol. 35, no. 4 (Winter 1993).

Liefert, W. M. "Russian Agriculture Could Remain Uncompetitive on the World Market, Even if Reform Continues," USDA International Agriculture and Trade Reports, *Former USSR: Situation and Outlook Series* (May 1996).

Liefert, W. M., R. B. Koopman, and E. C. Cook. "Agricultural Reform in the Former USSR," *Comparative Economic Studies* vol. 35, no. 4 (Winter 1993).

McIntyre, R. "The Phantom of Transition: Privatization of Agriculture in the Former Soviet Union and Eastern Europe," *Comparative Economic Studies* vol. 34, no. 3–4 (Fall-Winter 1992).

Mitchell, J. K. "Production Rebound Projected to Keep Grain Imports Low," USDA International Agriculture and Trade Reports, *Former USSR: Situation and Outlook Series* (May 1996).

Nellow, S. S. "The Food Situation in the Ex-Soviet Republics," *Soviet Studies* vol. 44, no. 5 (1992).

OECD. *The Soviet Agro-Food System and Agricultural Trade: Prospects for Reform* (Paris:, 1992).

RASKhN, Agrarian Institute. *The Program of Agrarian Reform in the Russian Federation for 1992–95* (Moscow: RASKhN, 1992).

Sedik, D. J. "A Note on Soviet Per Capita Meat Consumption," *Comparative Economic Studies* vol. 35, no. 3 (Fall 1993).

———. "Agricultural Policies Mitigate Production Declines, But Have Considerable Cost for the Countryside," USDA International Agriculture and Trade Reports, *Former USSR: Situation and Outlook Series* (May 1996).

Swinnen, J. *Political Economy of Agricultural Privatization and Decollectivization in Central and Eastern Europe* (Brookfield, VT: Ashgate, 1997)

United States Congress, Joint Economic Committee. *The Former Soviet Union in Transition* vol. 2, part IIIB (Washington, DC: U.S. Government Printing Office, 1994).

Van Atta, D. "Declining Soviet/Russian Per Capita Meat Consumption: A Comment," *Comparative Economic Studies* vol. 35, no. 4 (Winter 1993).

Wegren, S. G. "Private Farming and Agrarian Reform in Russia," *Problems of Communism* vol. 41, no. 3 (1992).

Zakony Rossii o Zemle [Russian Laws on Land] (Moscow: 1992).

Notes

1. An empirical study of the costs of gigantism is provided by B. Katz, "'Gigantism' as an Unbalanced Growth Strategy: An Econometric Investigation of the Soviet Experience, 1928–1940," *Soviet Union* vol. 4, part 2 (1977), 205–22. For a statistical comparison of the scale of Soviet industrial establishments with American establishments, see A. Woroniak, "Industrial Concentration in Eastern Europe: The Search for Optimum Size and Efficiency," *Notwendigkeit und Gefahr der Wirtschaftlichen Konzentration* (Basil: Kylos Verlag), 265–84.

2. D. Granick, *Soviet Metal Fabricating and Economic Development* (Madison: University of Wisconsin Press, 1967).

3. Soviet planners long stressed the need for economic development in all regions of the country. The Ural-Kuznetsk Combine was designed to tap the mineral resources of the Ural Mountains and the coal resources of the Kuznetsk area and to be appropriately combined to form a large industrial center. For a detailed discussion of the program, see for example, F. D. Holzman, "The Soviet Ural-Kuznetsk Combine: A Study of Investment Criteria and Industrialization Policies," *Quarterly Journal of Economics* vol. 71, no. 3 (August 1957), 367–405.

4. R. Nurkse, *Problems of Capital Formation in Underdeveloped Countries* (New York: Oxford University Press, 1975); P. N. Rosenstein-Rodan, "Notes on the Theory of the Big Push," in H. S. Ellis, *Economic Development for Latin America* (New York: St. Martin's Press, 1961), 157–81.

5. On this, see T. Gustafson, *Crisis Among Plenty: The Politics of Soviet Energy Under Brezhnev and Gorbachev* (Princeton: Princeton University Press, 1989).

6. The statistics on production, exports, and consumption are from *Handbook of International Economic Statistics 1992* (Washington, DC: Directorate of Intelligence, September 1992), Tables 36, 37, 38, 43.

7. This comparison can be misleading because output is produced not only with energy (which accounts for about 10 percent of the cost of production), but also by capital and by labor, where labor accounts for more than half of the value of output. This comparison reflects directly on the relative efficiency of energy usage, if Russia and the European Community use capital and labor with the same relative efficiency as energy.

8. In early 1993, the highest domestic sales price of Russian oil was approximately $6 per barrel, while the world price was approximately $18 per barrel (figures based upon Ernst and Young, *Russian Tax Structure, 1993*). This means that the marginal domestic user values oil at $6 per barrel versus the foreign exchange value of $18 per barrel. This $12 difference applies at the margin. As more and more Russian oil is sold abroad, the domestic price will be pushed up, and the welfare loss per barrel will decline.

9. An illustration of the overuse of energy resources: Up until the early 1990s, Aeroflot offered flights to remote regions at nominal fares. These flights would burn more than $20,000 worth of aviation fuel (at world market price) while yielding revenue of less than $200.

10. The calculation uses an approximation of the market ruble exchange rate for 1989, as reflected in the market exchange rate of 1989. No one knows the appropriate exchange rate for such calculations. Obviously, ruble holders fortunate to buy undervalued goods had more purchasing power per ruble than the 5 to 1 market exchange rate. However, the fact that rubles were exchanging for dollars at the 5 to 1 ratio tells us that holders of these rubles felt that this transformation rate was appropriate.

11. Morgan Stanley, *Investment Research UK and Europe,* Russia (February 2, 1996), 40.

12. Goskomstat Rossii, *Rossiiskaia Fderatsiia v 1992 godu* (Moscow: Goskomstat, 1993), 534; *Rossiia v tsifrakh* (1995), 254.

13. Morgan Stanley, 46.

14. Morgan Stanley, op. cit., 43.

15. For surveys of these and other regulations, see "Symposium: The Russian Petroleum Legislation Project at the University of Houston Law Center," *Houston Journal of International Law* vol. 15, no. 2 (Winter/Spring 1993).

16. *International Law* vol. 15, no. 2 (Winter/Spring 1993). See for example, "Law in Amendments to the Federal Law on Production Sharing (Draft)," in *Russian Petroleum Investor,* November 1996, 72–73.

17. Morgan Stanley, 45.

18. Mathew Sagers, "The Oil Sector in the FSU: Poised for a Recovery?" Plan Econ Seminar, Texas (October 10, 1996).

19. "Mixed Signals," *Russian Petroleum Investor* (December 1996/January 1997), 30–34; "Better Late Than Never," *Russian Petroleum Investor* (November 1996), 28–31.

20. Morgan Stanley, 47.

21. The "loans for shares" program involved the federal government's auction of significant blocs of shares of major oil companies, such as Yukos to major Russian banks or industrial/financial combinations in 1996. The bidding was restricted to Russian companies, with considerable evidence of bid rigging to ensure a low purchase price. In effect, the winning bidder loaned money to the Russian government with government shares of oil and mineral companies used as collateral. The federal government then used these funds to finance its debt. Upon government default, the winning bidder will receive the collateral shares. For a discussion of this program, see "Take It to the Bank," *Russian Petroleum Investor* (November 1996), 508.

22. To quote a senior official at a Russian government agency dealing with oil and gas issues: "As the Russian banks gain control of the oil industry, the mission of domestic producers will change dramatically . . . Why should a Russian oil company share its oil with a foreign producer when it can hire a foreign contractor much more cheaply to help develop the field? After all, it's not as if the western majors hold any special patents on how to get the oil out of the ground more efficiently." *Russian Petroleum Investor,* November 1996, 8.

23. See for example "The Plot Thickens," *Russian Petroleum Investor* (November 1996), 22–24; "The Speaker Has His Say," *Russian Petroleum Investor* (November 1996), 25–27.

24. Mathew Sagers, "The Oil Sector in the FSU."

25. The largest purchase was Arco's purchases of shares of Lukoil. The shares of a number of Russian oil companies can be purchased as American Depository Receipts (ADRs) in U.S. over-the-counter markets, and Lukoil has undertaken steps to be listed on major U.S. stock exchanges. For a description of the pioneering Lukoil listing, see Bank of New York, "ADR Announcement: Lukoil: The First Russian Level-I ADR" (December 27, 1995).

26. For details, see D. J. Sedik, "Agricultural Policies Mitigate Production Declines, But Have Considerable Cost for the Countryside,: International Trade and Agriculture Reports, *Former USSR: Situation and Outlook Series,* USDA (May 1996); R. McIntyre, "The Phantom of Transition: Privatization of Agriculture in the Former Soviet Union and Eastern Europe," *Comparative Economic Studies* vol. 34, no. 3–4 (Fall-Winter 1992); S. K. Wegren, "Private Farming and Agrarian Reform in Russia," *Problems of Communism* vol. 41, no. 3 (1992).

27. Sedik, "Agricultural Policies," 5.

28. Sedik, "Agricultural Policies," 5.

29. K. Gray, "Changing Consumption, Consumer Sovereignty, and Poverty Policies, International Agriculture and Trade reports," USDA, *Former USSR: Situation and Outlook Series* (May 1996), 27.

CHAPTER 19

Transition of the Former Soviet Republics

The coup against USSR President Mikhail Gorbachev began on August 18, 1991, and collapsed on August 21. A chastened Gorbachev was returned to Moscow, thanks to the President of the Russian Federation, Boris Yeltsin, whose opposition to the coup had resulted in its failure. The involvement of the most senior officials of the Soviet regime in the abortive coup weakened support for the continuation of the Soviet Union and of the Communist Party of the Soviet Union. The balance of power shifted from the USSR to the republics, in particular towards the Russian Republic, under its popularly-elected president, Boris Yeltsin.[1]

After the failed coup, the Soviet Union began to disintegrate. The independence of the Baltic states was recognized on September 6, 1991; Belorussia changed its name to Belarus on September 19; and on September 23, Armenia declared its independence. Although Gorbachev attempted to form a new Soviet administration composed largely of reformers, the Soviet Union continued to dissolve. A referendum on independence passed by a 90 percent majority in Ukraine on December 1, 1991, and Ukrainian independence was recognized shortly thereafter.

The de facto end of the Soviet Union was declared on December 8, 1991, when the presidents of Russia, Ukraine, and Kazakhstan (the three largest Soviet republics) and Belarus formed the **Commonwealth of Independent States** (CIS), stating that the Soviet Union had ceased to exist as a subject of international law and geopolitical reality. Subsequently, all of the former Soviet republics, with the exception of the Baltic states and initially Georgia, joined the CIS, although it never served as more than a loose-knit association. On December 21, 1991, Gorbachev resigned as Soviet president. He departed from the office on December 25, 1991, when he signed a decree divesting himself of authority as Soviet president and transferring his powers as commander in chief to President Yeltsin. The following day, the USSR Supreme Soviet abolished itself and declared that the Soviet Union no longer existed.

The Commonwealth of Independent States (CIS) is the association of 12 former Soviet republics (only the three Baltic states decided not to join) formed at the end of the Soviet Union in December of 1991. The **Newly Independent States** (NIS) is the term commonly applied to all 15 of the former Soviet republics.

CHARACTERISTICS OF THE NIS

In this chapter, we examine the general characteristics of the states that make up the NIS.[2] Figure 19.1 provides a map of the former Soviet Union, showing the 15 constituent republics.

We have spent most of this book describing the largest and most populous NIS state, the Russian Federation, which has a population of 148 million, has the largest land mass of any of the world's states, and has vast energy, mineral, and lumber resources. Over 80 percent of its population is Russian. About 12 percent represent native nationalities within the Russian Federation (such as Tartars, Dagestanis, and Chechens); the rest represent nationalities from other NIS republics (such as Balts and Ukrainians). Three quarters of the Russian population live in cities and one quarter in the countryside. The Russian Federation houses the largest cities of the former Soviet Union—Moscow and St. Petersburg. Russia possesses about one third of the world's known natural gas deposits, accounts for about 5 percent of the world's proven oil reserves, and represents one of the last frontiers for timber reserves. Although Russia is understandably the center of attention, transition in the former republics (NIS) varies considerably from one case to another and deserves our attention.

In this chapter, we divide the NIS into four groups. The three Baltic states of Estonia, Latvia, and Lithuania; the central Slavic Republics of Russia, Ukraine, Belarus, and Moldova; the Central Asian Republics of Kazakhstan, Uzbekistan, Turkmenistan, Tajikistan, and Kyrgystan; and the Caucasus republics of Azerbaijan, Georgia, and Armenia.

The Baltic States: Latvia, Lithuania, and Estonia

The Baltic states are a relatively homogenous geographical and cultural unit. They are small in terms of population (Estonia: 1.6 million; Latvia: 2.7 million; Lithuania: 3.8 million) and are located in the extreme northern part of the former

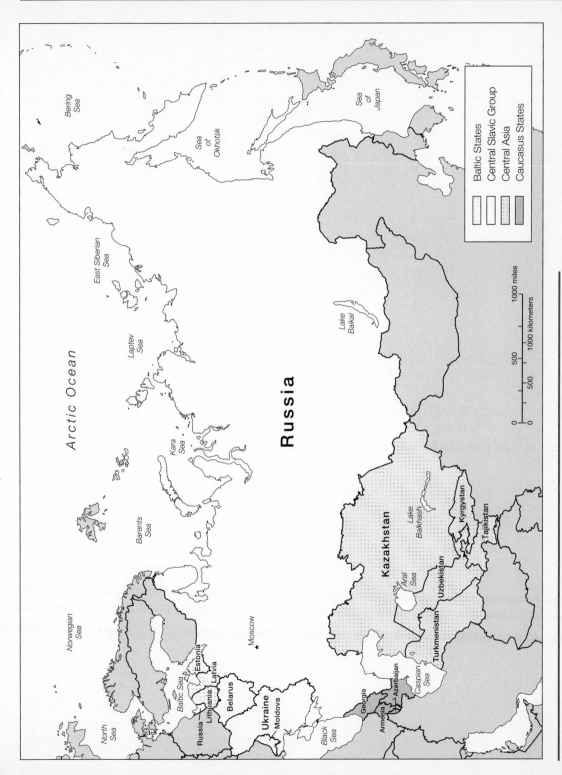

Figure 19.1   Former Republics of the Soviet Union   Source: CIA, Washington D.C., 1994.

Soviet Union. They were a part of the Russian Empire but gained political independence between the Russian revolution and World War II. During this time they developed their own political institutions. When they were forced back into the Soviet Union at the beginning of World War II, they were reintegrated into the Soviet form of governance, as republics of the Soviet Union. Under Soviet rule, there was an influx of Russians into leadership and management positions so that when independence came again they had acquired large Russian minorities. For example, in Latvia, only 52 percent of the population was Latvian at the time of independence. Russians constituted 34 percent. In Estonia, Estonians constituted 62 percent, and Russians accounted for 30 percent.

The Baltic states had to confront the existence of large Russian minorities after independence. One of the most thorny issues has been the issue of citizenship and minority rights, particularly in areas dominated by Russians. Two Baltic states have made knowledge of the local language a condition for citizenship. Moreover, they have largely replaced the Russian ruling elite with local officials. As a potential bridge between Russia and the West, the Baltic states have had to walk a tightrope between their aversion for their Soviet past and the need to preserve good commercial relations with Russia.

The Baltic states speak distinct languages (Estonian is finno-urgic) and all have non-Slavic heritages. They are all resource poor. In the former Soviet Union, they had among the highest standards of living, concentrating on transportation and high-tech and defense industries. They occupied strategic positions in the Soviet transportation system with major warm-water ports and oil terminals. The Baltic states were largely urbanized, with urbanization rates ranging from 66 percent for Lithuania to 71 percent for Estonia.

The Central Slavic Group: Russia, Ukraine, Belarus, and Moldova

The Central Slavic group consists of Russia, Ukraine, Belarus, and Moldova. Moldova's inclusion in this "Slavic" group is a misnomer because Moldovans are a nationality closely akin to Romanians and speak a Romanian language; however we include Moldova in the central group for geographic reasons.

Ukraine was the second largest Soviet republic, with a population of 51 million. It is 73 percent Ukrainian and 22 percent Russian. It boasts the third largest city of the former Soviet Union, Kiev, with 2.5 million people. The Ukrainian Republic is 65 percent urban and 35 percent rural. Historically, Ukraine is the home of the former Soviet Union's best agricultural land—the black earth zone. At the end of the Soviet period, Ukraine produced 53 million metric tons of grain, slightly less than half of Russia's production. Ukraine was also an important transit area for the former Soviet Union. The Druzhba natural gas pipeline to Europe passes through Ukraine, and Ukraine has a number of major Black Sea ports, such as Odessa, Ilchevsk, and Sevastopol. Ukraine has substantial natural resources with its agricultural land, coal and iron deposits, natural gas, and other mineral resources. The country continues to obtain much of its electricity from nuclear power and is still dependent upon electrical power from the Chernobyl facility. Ukraine and Russia contested the Crimean region, ceded to Ukraine by Nikita Khrushchev in the 1950s. However, in May 1997 a friendship treaty was signed including long-term lease arrangements for Black Sea ports.

Belarus has a population of slightly over 10 million, about 1.5 million of which live in its capital, Minsk. Belarus is 62 percent urbanized, and 38 percent of its population lives in rural areas, making it among the more agricultural of the former European Soviet republics. About 78 percent of the Belarus population is Belarussian; 13 percent is Russian. The language of Belarus is very similar to Russian. Belarus is lacking in significant natural resources and is known primarily for its forest lands and peat deposits. In the post-Soviet period, Belarus has failed to develop democratic institutions and has maintained close ties with Russia. There is considerable support for a merger with Russia.

Moldova was one of the poorer Soviet republics. More than 55 percent of the Moldovan population lived in rural areas, and its capital city, Kishinev, has a population of 630,000. Around 65 percent of the Moldovan population is Moldovan; the rest are fairly evenly divided between Russians and Ukrainians. Moldova borders on Romania and has suffered armed conflict with rebel forces, requiring assistance from the Russian military during its period of independence.

Central Asia: Kazakhstan, Uzbekistan, Tajikistan, Turkmenistan, and Kyrgystan

The Central Asian republics vary from large and populous to small and relatively underpopulated. Kazakhstan (which we include in Central Asia) has a population of 17 million and a land mass of 2.7 million square kilometers; Uzbekistan has a population of 21 million and a land mass of half a million square kilometers. The other three Central Asian republics are much smaller and less populous: Tajikistan has 5.5 million population and 140,000 square kilometers; Turkmenistan has a population of 3.6 million and a land mass of a half million square kilometers. Kyrgystan has a population of 4.2 million and a land mass of 191,000 square kilometers. In terms of natural resources, the Central Asian republics vary from being extremely wealthy to very poor. Kazakhstan has enormous energy and mineral resources (oil, gas, coal, manganese, copper, lead, zinc, and bauxite); Turkmenistan and Uzbekistan have considerable natural gas resources and underdeveloped oil resources. Tajikistan and Kyrgystan, on the other hand, are poor in natural resources and are quite dependent on the outside world for their energy. The Central Asian republics are less urbanized than their European counterparts. Kazakhstan is 57 percent urban, Turkmenistan 47 percent, Uzbekistan 42 percent, and Kyrgystan 40 percent. Under Soviet rule, the Central Asian republics produce energy and raw materials along with agricultural products (cotton in Uzbekistan and grain in Kazakhstan).

Like the other former Soviet republics, the Central Asian republics are populated by native populations and by Russian and other nationalities. In Kazakhstan, for example, native Kazakhs represent only 40 percent of the population, being outnumbered by Russians and Germans. In the other Central Asian republics, the native population predominates (with natives accounting for 52 percent in Kyrgystan, 62 percent in Tajikistan, 72 percent in Turkmenistan, and 71 percent in Uzbekistan). The peoples of Central Asia are largely of Turkic origin, with a small proportion of finno-urgic peoples in Kyrgystan. The Moslem religion dominates the Central Asian republics.

The demographic profile of Central Asia is different from the other former Soviet republics. Whereas the Baltic and European republics had birth rates that fell below death rates, the Central Asian republics have birth rates well in excess of death rates. Whereas the European parts of the former Soviet Union had been shrinking in size in the last decades of Soviet rule, the Central Asian republics were growing due to high rates of population growth.

The Central Asian republics were incorporated into the Russian Empire before the Russian revolution, through Tsarist expansionism. Although Stalin and his successors tried to repress local cultures and languages, the efforts were unsuccessful. In the post-Soviet period, much of Central Asian governance has returned to a system where clan relationships dominate. In some cases, the clan system has resulted in political stability (Kazakstan); in other cases, it has led to clan warfare (Tajikistan). Only rarely has a form of democracy arisen (Kyrgystan).[3]

The Caucasus States: Georgia, Azerbaijan, and Armenia

The Caucasus republics of Georgia, Azerbaijan, and Armenia are varied in terms of ethnicity, natural resource endowments, and size. Azerbaijan has a population of 3.3 million of largely Turkic residents in a total land area of 86,000 square kilometers. It is extremely rich in oil and gas resources, with substantial undeveloped resources in the Caspian Sea shelf. The population of Azerbaijan is primarily Azeri, with a relatively small proportion of Russians. Georgia has a population of 5.5 million on 69,000 square kilometers which is primarily Georgian. The Georgians practice an ancient form of Christianity. Armenia has a population of 3.4 million on only 30,000 square kilometers of territory. In the post-independence period, each of the three Caucasus republics has experienced considerable political instability. Georgia has suffered a civil war that caused separation of considerable parts of Georgia. The president of Georgia narrowly escaped an assassination attempt. Armenia and Azerbaijan have fought a bitter war over disputed territory, and the president of Azerbaijan has escaped a number of assassination attempts.

Although Azerbaijan has immense energy resources, they are largely hostage to the former Soviet transportation system that runs though Russia. Large international energy projects have been slowed by the absence of transportation capacity. Armenia and Georgia have few (if any) resources and have suffered extreme shortages of energy and electricity. They have either been shut off or subject to reduced electricity deliveries. Moreover, Armenia has been subject to market blockades from Iran and Turkey as a consequence of its hostilities with Azerbaijan.

The Caucasus republics have different degrees of urbanization. Azerbaijan is 54 percent urbanized, Georgia 54 percent, and Armenia 68 percent. Their demographic characteristics are like those of Central Asia. Their high birth rates well exceed death rates, creating high rates of natural increase.

Table 19.1 provides a snapshot of the former Soviet republics as of 1995. It shows that they varied considerably in terms of output and population size and in terms of per capita GDP. Although all NIS states were poor compared to Europe and Eastern Europe, of the 15 NIS states, only Estonia came anywhere close to a "European" standard of living.

ECONOMIC CONSEQUENCES OF USSR BREAKUP

This chapter describes the transition process in the 14 other independent republics that emerged from the ashes of the Soviet Union. We begin by considering the effects of the breakup on the economies of the region prior to turning to a discussion of the transition process in the separate regions.

Table 19.1

GDP IN THE NEWLY INDEPENDENT STATES, 1995

Country	GDP (billions $, PPP)	Population (millions)	Per capita GDP (1993 $, PPP)
Russia	666.6	148.0	4,501
Estonia	10.3	1.5	6,847
Latvia	13.0	2.6	5,069
Belarus	40.3	10.3	3,898
Lithuania	12.6	3.7	3,386
Turkmenistan	13.4	4.0	3,355
Ukraine	134.0	51.4	2,608
Kazakhstan	40.4	16.7	2,422
Uzbekistan	52.1	22.2	2,348
Armenia	8.3	3.8	2,201
Moldova	9.0	4.3	2,062
Kyrgystan	7.7	4.5	1,716
Georgia	6.1	5.4	1,128
Azerbaijan	10.4	7.5	1,393
Tajikistan	2.4	5.7	449

Source: K. Crane and D. Green, "Overview," Plan Econ, *Review and Outlook for the Former Soviet Republics* (March 1996).

Terms of Trade

Chapter 17 pointed out that the Soviet Union's collapse created 15 national economies where there had been one unified Soviet market. Freed from the Soviet foreign trade monopoly, the 15 former Soviet republics redirected their trade away from what formerly was the unified Soviet market to foreign markets in the West and in Eastern Europe.

The collapse of the Soviet Union also brought an end to intra-Soviet-republic trade conducted in domestic prices that deviated substantially from world market prices. In the former Soviet days, enterprises in Georgia or Lithuania purchased energy from Siberian oil producers at the domestic wholesale price. Buyers from outside the Soviet Union, on the other hand, paid world market prices of energy and raw materials. Intra-Soviet-republic trade therefore involved implicit subsidies from one republic to another, since enterprises received products through the centralized supply system at prices below world market prices. Although those republics that joined the Commonwealth of Independent States continued initially to receive some products from Russia at below-world-market prices, this practice did not continue for long. As time passed, more and more goods traded among the former Soviet republics at world market prices.

Table 19.2 shows that calculated effects on the various republics of the transition from subsidized prices among the republics to world market prices. Two effects are included: The first is the terms-of-trade effect, which measures the change in the ratio of a republic's export prices to its import prices. A positive percentage in

Table 19.2

ESTIMATED INITIAL IMPACT ON THE GDP OF TERMS-OF-TRADE CHANGES
(percentage change in GDP)

	Armenia	Azerbaijan
Interrepublic	−11.1	−6.7
Extrarepublic	3.5	10.5
Total	−7.6	3.7

	Latvia	Lithuania	Moldova
Interrepublic	−11.6	−15.6	−18.8
Extrarepublic	0.2	5.9	2.7
Total	−11.3	−9.7	−16.1

[a] Trade intensity data are based on exports and imports in world prices.

(Continued on facing page)

Table 19.2 indicates the percentage by which that republic's export prices rose relative to its import prices. Such a move is said to be an improvement in the terms of trade. A negative percentage signifies the percentage by which the republic's export prices grew more slowly than its import prices. This is said to be a worsening in the **terms of trade.**

Table 19.2 reveals dramatic changes in the terms of trade of the former Soviet republics. Of the 15 republics, the energy and raw material producers (Russia, Kazakhstan, Azerbaijan, Tajikistan, and Uzbekistan) experienced improving terms of trade, with Russia showing the greatest improvement. The remaining republics experienced worsening terms of trade, with the greatest losses suffered by the Baltic states and by Moldova.[4]

Table 19.2 also presents the percentage loss of GDP caused by a worsening of the republic's terms of trade. Clearly, a worsening of the terms of trade causes a loss of output, since the country must transform its exports into imports at a less favorable rate. Table 19.2 again shows that the republics that experienced improving terms of trade experienced increases in GDP, *ceteris paribus.* The big winners from the terms of trade effect were Russia and Turkmenistan, whose GDPs should have risen almost 20 percent. The biggest losers were the Baltic states (whose outputs would have fallen 10–13 percent and Moldova with a 16 percent loss).

When considering the output performance of the 15 former Soviet republics, we must recognize that they were all subjected to dramatic changes in their terms of trade, changes that affected their economic outputs negatively—with the exception of a few raw material and energy-producing republics. Therefore, the decline in Russian output (discussed in Chapter 15) must be considered in this light. Without improvements in Russia's terms of trade, the loss of Russian output would have been much greater.

Belarus	Estonia	Georgia	Kazakhstan	Krygystan
−11.4	−13.5	−12.1	3.4	−1.3
7.2	0.7	−12.1	4.0	2.6
−4.2	−12.7	0.0	7.4	1.4

Russia	Tajikistan	Turkmenistan	Ukraine	Uzbekistan
4.5	−6.9	15.9	−6.4	−1.9
13.2	8.6	3.6	3.8	3.1
17.7	1.7	19.5	−2.6	1.1

Source: D. Tarr, "The Terms of Trade Effect of Moving to World Market Prices on Countries of the Former Soviet Union," *Journal of Comparative Economics* vol. 18, no. 1 (February 1994), 18–19.

Trade disruption had serious effects, given the close economic linkages that had existed. Studies indicated that in the hypothetical case of total shutdown of CIS trade, Russia would have been able to produce only two thirds of previous output, Kazakhstan 31 percent, Ukraine 15 percent, and Belarus only 4 percent.[5]

Infrastructure: The Problems of Disintegration

As a single market, the Soviet economy was characterized by extreme concentration of production. As noted in Chapter 14, Soviet planners preferred to concentrate the production of specific products among a relatively few producers. Concentrated production meant that the economy was easier to plan because planners did not have to coordinate supplies from a large number of enterprises. The collapse of the Soviet Union meant, therefore, that traditional supply channels were broken, and the concentration of production made such disruptions substantial. The monopoly supplier of submersible pumps was located in Baku, while the monopoly supplier of telephone handsets was located in St. Petersburg. After the breakup, customers would have been left without their traditional source of supply (and with little experience in how to find new sources).[6] Table 19.3 provides some illustrative figures on the degree of concentration within the Russian republic alone.

The breakup of the Soviet economy meant that traditional suppliers were now located in independent countries, often without established means of payment or even communication. New channels of supply and new means of payment and clearing had to be developed in short order.

In addition to the issue of concentrated suppliers, the breakup of the Soviet economy also broke up a formerly unified transportation system into national parts, requiring regulation, direction, and agreement. The oil and gas pipeline system, for example, typically ran from the oil- and gas-producing regions of Siberia or Central Asia to ports located either in Russia or in the Baltic states. Now pipelines crossed national boundaries, and tariffs and taxes had to be paid where none had been collected before. Methods had to be worked out for common maintenance procedures. Transit countries could block access in order to gain political concessions, creating international political problems that had not existed earlier.[7]

For these reasons, the breakup of the Soviet transportation system became a political as well as an economic issue in the post-Soviet period. Projected pipeline expansions are based not only upon project economics but more on political considerations. The breakup of the oil transportation system and the consequent lack of transportation capability, for example, has caused a severe reduction in Russia's export capacity and has prevented the development of Kazakhstan's and Azerbaijan's oil and gas resources. Alternate routes through Georgia, Central Asia, or Turkey have been rejected or delayed because of political considerations.[8] Political uncertainty about rights of way or political stability also prevented constructing and expanding transportation facilities that crossed new national boundaries.

Table 19.3

PRODUCTION OF SELECTED INDIVIDUAL ENTERPRISES

(a) Production of selected product by individual Russian enterprises in 1993 (% of total output)

Enterprise	Type of product	Percent of total Russian output
PO "Kolomenski zavod"	Diesel locomotives	100
PO "Novocherkasski electrovozostroitel'ni zavod"	Electric locomotives	100
Tverskoe PO vagonostroenija	Railway passenger carriages	86
Zavod "Bezhetsksel'mash"	Flax combine	100
Trolleibusni zavod im. Urizkogo	Trolley buses	100
PO "Leningradski metallicheski zavod"	Steam turbines	80
PO "Rostsel'mash"	Combine harvesters	81
AO "Tulamashzavod"	Motor scooters	100
Tikhorezki miasokombinat	Meat goggles for children	100

(b) Concentration of Russian industrial production in 1993

Branch of industry	Share of total Russian output (%)		
	3 enterprises	6 enterprises	10 enterprises
Electrical engineering/electricity generation	11.7	18.5	25.6
Fuel industry	12.3	22.7	34.1
Ferrous metallurgy	26.4	40.2	52.0
Non-ferrous metallurgy	26.2	39.7	48.7
Chemical industry	8.9	13.4	19.0
Mechanical engineering	12.6	16.3	19.8
Timber, wood-processing, and paper industry	5.4	9.4	13.5
Construction industry	4.1	6.2	8.4
Light industry	4.0	7.0	10.1
Food processing	3.9	6.0	8.4

Source: "Review of Economies in Transition, 1/96," *UEEE,* p. 32.

The breakup of the Soviet Union also required the 15 republics to create infrastructure within a short period of time at below-optimal scales of output. For example, each republic had to create its own telephone system, its own airlines, and so on, even if economies of scale were insufficient for the economic operation of such businesses.

Monetary Arrangements

One of the most difficult issues to confront the former Soviet republics immediately after the end of the Soviet Union was the issue of money. Before the breakup, only one currency existed—Soviet rubles, which were in circulation in all of the 15 republics. Each of the 15 republics had regional branch banks of Gosbank with fresh rubles stored in bank vaults. Republican Gosbanks had the authority to grant credits to enterprises, credits that were granted in rubles.

Although all of the former Soviet republics expressed a desire to introduce their own currencies, for the time being, most of them remained in the ruble zone (continued to use the Russian ruble as the means of exchange). Although the Russian treasury retained the sole right to print rubles, banks in other republics could increase the supply of rubles by granting credits. This system created an incentive to issue as many credits as possible as fast as possible. If your republic did not issue rubles faster than another republic, it would be the loser.[9] Therefore, in the ruble-zone countries the competitive expansion of credit during the early years of transition created enormous inflationary pressures, because the money supply expanded at too rapid a rate. Russia moved to resolve this problem by refusing to accept ruble credits as payment and by requiring payments for goods and services in hard currency.

Faced with a shortage of paper rubles as a means of exchange, the various republics began issuing their own currency. The Baltic states issued Latvian, Estonian, or Lithuanian rubles as a precursor to issuing their own currencies (the lat, the kroon, and the lit). By the mid-1990s, each of the former Soviet republics had introduced their own national currency. As will be noted below, they had different degrees of success of controlling the supply of their own currencies. Attempts were made to create new mechanisms for trade among the former Soviet republics, such as the creation of an Interstate Currency Commission in March of 1995, but with little apparent success.[10]

The Soviet Legacy in the NIS

We have examined Russia's transition in previous chapters. We described the immense task of creating there the institutions of a market economy. Each of the other 15 former Soviet republics faced the same daunting task. Each had to undergo privatization, the disruptions of price liberalization, and the task of creating monetary and fiscal institutions. We have described above some of their common difficulties. Most faced sharp declines in their terms of trade as the subsidies of the Soviet period were withdrawn. Only a few raw material and energy-producers benefited. They experienced the shock of disruption of the familiar supply system and were left with monopoly producers in their own countries or perhaps with the prospect of dealing with monopoly producers now located in another country. They even lacked access to a reliable mean of exchange, as they had to convert from a ruble system controlled by another government to their own national currency. All of these disruptions impacted negatively on output and on inflation. In the next section, we look at the manner in which the former Soviet republics addressed the thorny issues of transition and their varying degrees of success.

Capital Flows and the Acquisition of Assets

From 1992 to 1994, Russia's trade surpluses with respect to the CIS countries reached a cumulated total of $10.5 billion. Thereafter, Russia began running insignificant trade deficits vis-à-vis the CIS.[11] The reasons for these surpluses have been discussed above—namely, the change of the terms of trade in favor of Russia and the dependence of the other CIS countries on Russia for raw materials and energy. It is unclear whether these official statistics fully capture the extent of Russia's favorable balance of trade with the CIS. It is difficult to capture fully all the credit arrangements and barter transactions that took place in this period.

Russia's positive trade balance with the CIS countries was financed in a variety of ways: Russian companies extended credit, and substantial credits were extended to countries like Ukraine. It was also financed at the cost of the scarce foreign exchange reserves of these countries when Russian firms increasingly began to demand hard currency payments. Russia also entered into barter transactions, in which CIS country would pay in terms of agricultural or other products.

When a country has a positive trade balance vis-à-vis another country, this means that the country's capital account is negative—the country is acquiring financial and real assets from the deficit countries. These assets could be notes, hard currency, or the direct acquisition of assets of the deficit country. Especially ominous for the CIS countries was the tendency of Russian creditor firms, such as energy and gas suppliers, to arrange payments for arrears in terms of ownership shares of CIS companies. In order to keep energy and raw material deliveries flowing, countries like Ukraine, Latvia, Lithuania, and Belarus had to agree to Russian ownership of their enterprises. Ukraine, for example, blamed their postponement of privatization on the fact that privatization at that stage of recovery could lead to significant Russian ownership of Ukrainian industry.

TRANSITION PATTERNS IN THE NIS

The preceding chapter focused on the transition of the Russian Federation, the largest republic of the former Soviet Union. This attention is appropriate because of Russia's geographic, demographic, and mineral-wealth preponderance among former Soviet Republics. To what extent and in what ways were the transition experiences of the NIS influenced by the Russian case?

The transitions of the 14 other former Soviet republics are of considerable significance in their own right. How quickly and successfully they complete the transition will affect the political and economic stability of the entire region. Transition will determine whether the former Soviet Union might be reestablished as an economic unit, or whether the former Soviet republics will end up in different international political and economic blocs.

Second, the 14 other former Soviet republics provide real-world laboratories for studying the transition process. By the end of this century, social scientists will have had the opportunity to study the transitions not only in the former Soviet block countries of Eastern Europe, but also the transitions of the 15 former Soviet republics and the various reform and transition experiments in the former communist countries of Asia.

Third, the speed with which the former Soviet republics conclude transition will leave a substantial imprint on the European and world economies. The former communist economies of Europe not only represent new markets for Europe and the world economy, they also offer investment opportunities, which, when consummated, can redistribute world labor and capital. New interrelationships will be established as the advanced industrialized countries take advantage of the skilled low-wage labor of the transition countries. If the transitions are successful, capital will flow to the new emerging stock markets located in the former Soviet republics. United States, European, and Asian investors may be able to seek out higher return investments in these new markets.

It is not possible to tell the full transition stories of each of the former Soviet republics. They are too diverse. The politics of each transition experience are different, as are the countries' cultural, demographic, and geographic heritages. We could classify each country's transition experience according to the various abstract models of transition discussed in Chapter 13. For example, we could separate the 15 transitions according to how closely they resemble shock therapy or gradualism. Such a classification would be difficult because of the absence of ready and measurable indicators of transition strategy. The alternate approach, taken in this chapter, is to divide the 15 transition economies into the four geographic/cultural groups—the Slavic republics including Moldova, for geographic reasons, the Baltic republics, the Caucasus republics, and the Central Asian republics. Each grouping includes from three (Baltic states) to five (Central Asian states) countries. Although the various countries in each grouping have not experienced exactly the same transitions, they nevertheless have much in common.

Transition in the Baltic States

The three Baltic states of Latvia, Estonia, and Lithuania represent perhaps the most homogeneous model of transition. Their transition models and experiences have been probably more similar than in the other three groupings.

As relatively small countries that had enjoyed the highest living standards in the former Soviet Union, the Baltic states were the first to engineer withdrawal from the Soviet Union, with Lithuania showing the way. As relatively small, resource-poor countries located close to Scandinavia, the Baltic states had been incorporated into the Soviet Union relatively late after experiencing an interlude of political freedom. Although each country had significant concentrations of Russians in high ranks within the republican governments, the Baltic states consisted of relatively tight-knit ethnic groups, who appeared to share common values and goals.[12]

Geopolitically, the Baltic states understood that they could provide little military resistance if Russia or another major former Soviet republic were to seek to control them. They believe that the most effective guarantee of continued independence would be economic integration into the European economy, in particular economic integration into Northern Europe. The three Baltic states, having withdrawn abruptly from the Soviet Union, also had to undergo the sudden shock of loss of subsidized Russian energy and raw materials before the other former Soviet Republics. The Baltic states also introduced independent currencies earlier than other former Soviet republics and hence withdrew from the ruble zone earlier. Obliged to introduce their own currencies, they were not absorbed in the easy-money policies of the ruble zone.

Left to their own devices, the three Baltic states introduced monetary reform relatively quickly, adopting policies of shock therapy with respect to price liberalization and monetary restraint. Unlike Russia, all three Baltic states moved rather slowly on privatization, preferring to develop market institutions before embarking upon privatization. Moreover, the three Baltic states allowed a greater participation of foreign investors in privatization, with significant concessions being awarded to foreign companies.[13]

The lateness of privatization was also caused by the fact that each country had to deal with significant constitutional issues. Thorny issues, such as citizenship for Russian residents, diverted parliamentary attention away from privatization for the first two to three years of independence. Privatization of nonstate sector, it should be emphasized, did proceed rapidly. Trade, services, and agriculture were privatized rapidly, with little fuss. The privatization of large-scale companies (such as the telephone company, the national airline, and port facilities) proceeded slowly, after each country created their version of a privatization agency. The slow pace of privatization was also dictated by political pressures. Since each country's major companies were being auctioned in an open privatization process, various political factions (some in favor of foreign ownership, others against) had to be given an opportunity to make their case.

In general, one can conclude that the Baltic privatizations, although not without an element of insider manipulation and control, resulted in a fairer and more equitable distribution of ownership than in the other former Soviet republics. As such, it would be expected that a greater political consensus was formed in favor of privatization with a lesser probability of reversal.

The basic results of Baltic transition are recorded in Figure 19.2 (p. 450). It shows a pattern of transition quite similar to the "successful" transitions of Eastern Europe (Poland, Czech Republic, and Hungary). Each Baltic state suffered substantial declines in output beginning in 1991, immediately after independence, but each economy had basically stabilized by 1994, with either a near-zero or a positive rate of economic growth. Inflation spiked in 1992 but was basically stabilized (at least in Latvia and Estonia) by 1993. In 1995, for example, GDP growth ranged from 1 percent (Latvia) to 4.8 percent (Estonia).[14] Although inflation rates remained high by international standards, two Baltic states had reduced their annual inflation rates to 25 percent by 1995, while the third (Lithuania) had reduced its inflation rate to 40 percent. Balanced or near-balanced budgets coupled with relatively slow monetary growth reduced the rate of inflation.

The three Baltic states used different means to stabilize their exchange rates. Latvia used tight money and pegging to the SDR, while Estonia and Lithuania used a currency board approach to stabilize monetary growth and the exchange rate. In each country, the exchange rate remained stable or appreciated relative to major Western currencies and appreciated astronomically relative to the Russian ruble and other currencies of the former Soviet republics. It is unclear whether the Baltic states can continue to have such strong currencies, but they were able to maintain stable and even appreciating currencies during the most difficult years of transition.

The general conclusion concerning the Baltic transition model is that it has been applied successfully. The three Baltic rates have had either positive or zero growth (not declines) of output since 1994, they have reduced inflation to normal levels for emerging markets, and they have maintained stable currencies in international currency markets.

Figure 19.2   Transition in the Baltic States

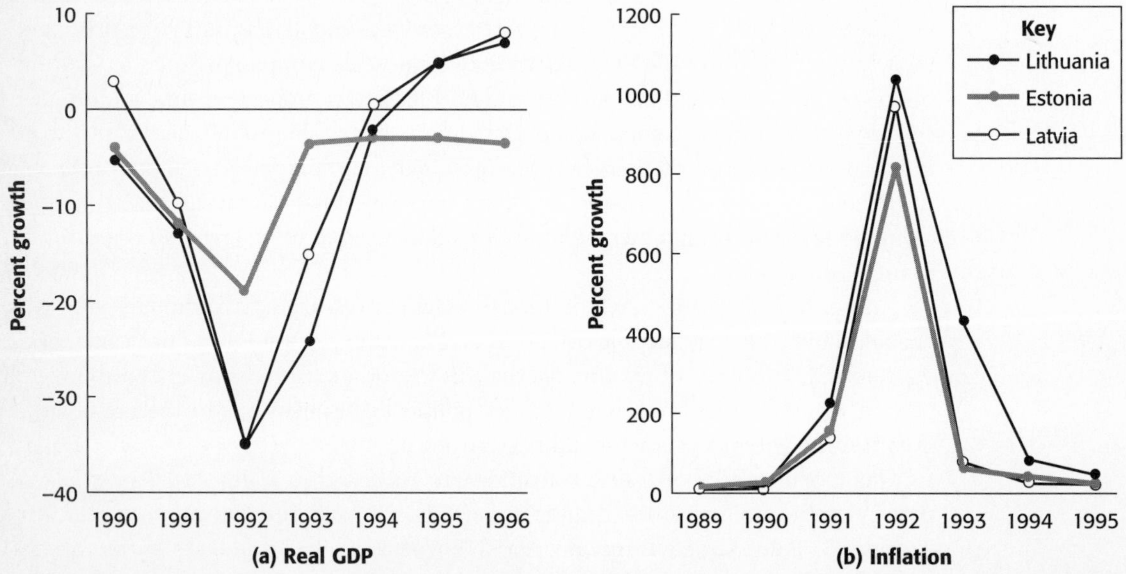

(a) Real GDP

(b) Inflation

Source: PlanEcon, *Review and Outlook for the Former Soviet Republics* (selected years).

Clearly, the Baltic states continue to bank on political and economic integration into Western Europe. They have undertaken the first steps that would eventually lead to membership in the European Union, and they hope to be admitted to NATO in the not-too-distant future. Their trade has become increasingly directed toward Europe, in particular towards the Scandinavian countries and Germany. They had succeeded in attracting cumulative totals of $867 million (Estonia), $675 million (Latvia), and $397 million (Lithuania) by the end of 1996—a total of almost $2 billion for a region that has less than eight million people.

Transition in the European Slavic Republics

The transition stories of the four European Slavic republics—Russia, Ukraine, Belarus, and Moldova[15]—are more varied and hence more difficult to tell. The Russian transition case has been covered extensively above. Whereas, the Russian transition can be characterized at least as partial "shock therapy," the other three Slavic republics followed a gradualist approach. While, reformers took charge of much of the early phases of Russian transition, conservative former communist officials and state enterprise managers took charge of the early phases of transition in the other three Slavic republics. Conservative agrarian interests also opposed significant reform of agriculture and of land tenure. These countries remained part of the ruble zone during the early part of transition, and, although each eventually introduced its own currency, they did so late in the game and were slow to develop the mechanisms to control budget deficits and rapid monetary growth.[16]

The Russian Federation embarked on an ambitious program of privatization, despite its mixed results, that resulted in ownership by the former management elite ("crony capitalism"). The other three Slavic republics were very slow to begin privatization or did not begin at all, as was the case in Belarus. Lacking a meaningful program of privatization and lacking the political will to restrain budget deficits and credit expansion, they succumbed to rapid inflation, which began in 1992 and persisted until 1994 and later. Each country lacked domestic energy and raw material bases (except for Ukraine), and they remained dependent on Russia for energy deliveries. As they were unable to pay, they accrued arrears to Russian energy producers and began to sacrifice ownership of domestic infrastructure to Russian energy companies.

The three European Slavic republics share a number of common transition features: In each case, privatization has been slow and, in some cases, virtually nonexistent (Belarus). The reasons for delays in privatization have been varied: In Belarus, it has been the strong political opposition of the dictatorial president; in Ukraine, it has been fear of Russian takeovers combined with political opposition to privatization from labor, industrial managers, and collective farm managers. The major exception has been Moldova, which, encouraged by the World Bank, embarked on an ambitious privatization program in the period 1993–95. By the end of 1995, 60 percent of the Moldavan economy was in the nonstate sector and over 90 percent of eligible citizens participated in the privatization program.

The three European Slavic republics have been unable to control budget deficits and to restrain the growth of credit, which has led to high rates of inflation. The lack of stable monetary and fiscal policies has caused these countries to lose support of international organizations, which have refused to supply international credits without them. Again the exception has been Moldova, which adopted a stabilization program in 1995 and qualified for significant IMF financial support in March 1995. Also, although Moldova has had a near convertible currency since March 1995, the other republics have had rapidly depreciating and nonconvertible currencies.

Figure 19.3 provides the basic GDP and inflation data for the four European Slavic republics, including Russia. They show the disappointing performance of real GDP, which had not stabilized as of late 1996 and the relatively high and persistent inflation experienced in this region. Only Russia and Moldova had successfully reduced the inflation rate, and Moldova's success came relatively late.

The overall lesson to be learned from the Slavic republic group is that gradualism has not produced superior results to shock therapy. The use of gradualism has not limited the collapse of economic output; it has contributed to higher inflation rates; and exchange rate stability and convertibility have not been achieved.

The political reasons for choosing gradualism vary in this region. In Ukraine a leftist legislature has opposed shock therapy. Although the Ukrainian president may be in favor of reform, he has chosen political stability over a course of crash reform

Figure 19.3   Transition in the European Slavic Republics

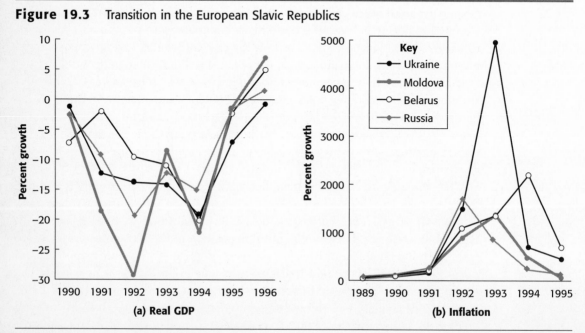

(a) Real GDP

(b) Inflation

Source: PlanEcon, *Review and Outlook for the Former Soviet Republics* (selected years).

to preserve political tranquillity. In Belarus, the president has acted as a dictator, opposing virtually all efforts of a more reform-minded parliament to introduce reforms. Only in Moldova has there been success in forging political support for real reform.

Transition in the Central Asian Republics

The Central Asian republics have the advantage of being energy and raw material producers, whose terms of trade have improved since the breakup of the Soviet Union. Hence, these countries have a growth advantage, along with Russia, vis-à-vis the other former Soviet republics. They vary from resource-rich countries, like Kazakhstan and Turkmenistan, to resource-poor countries, such as Tajikistan and Kyrgystan. Some are large and populous countries, like Kazakhstan and Uzbekistan; others are small with population sizes of five million or less (Kyrgystan and Turkmenistan). One Central Asian republic, Tajikistan, has suffered from armed conflict since the breakup of the Soviet Union.[17]

With the exception of Kyrgystan, the Central Asian republics have adopted a gradualist path to transition, seen in their slowness in introducing a stable domestic currency, in the lack of financial discipline with respect to fiscal and monetary policy, and their ineffective privatization programs. Although some Central Asian countries, such as Kazakhstan have, on paper, privatized much of the economy, the result appears to be formal rather than real. The major energy producers of Central Asia, Kazakhstan and Turkmenistan, have been unable to capitalize on their advantage because of transportation constraints (their energy must still be transported across Russia) and because of nonpayment problems. In these countries there continues to be extensive government (ministerial) interference in the economic affairs of enterprises, which continue to be run much like they were under Soviet rule. Enterprises are still supported, even if they make losses.

Politically, the Central Asian republics tend to be operated as clans, with the president serving as the clan chieftain. This practice has made the Central Asian republics more subject to crony capitalism. In the case of Tajikistan, where warring clans collide, it has resulted in enormous political instability. In Kazakhstan, the president exerts almost dictatorial control over the government (his tenure now runs through the year 2000), so much so that in the past he has dissolved parliament. Although some foreign investors view this dictatorship as a source of stability, in the long run it may actually contribute to political instability.

Kyrgystan represents the major exception to the rule of gradualism in Central Asia. Kyrgystan has created a relatively democratic form of government, has privatized much of the economy, and has implemented a real program of monetary and fiscal restraint. Its actions have won approval and support of the IMF.

Although Kazakhstan was slow to introduce its currency and refrained from monetary and fiscal austerity, it did experiment for approximately one-half year with monetary restraint, which resulted in a significant slowdown of inflation. Unlike other countries that introduced monetary restraint, Kazakhstan backed away from reform and returned to policies of loose credit. Uzbekistan, a large agricultural republic under Soviet rule, has surprised some observers by enacting policies of fiscal and monetary restraint in 1995, thereby driving down the inflation rate.

Figure 19.4 provides information on the growth rates of GDP and inflation for the Central Asian republics. They show Kyrgystan's rather remarkable progress in taming inflation and restoring output to positive growth. They also show the relative success of Uzbekistan's economic policies in 1995. In the other cases, reform policies either have not been adopted or, if adopted, were put in place too late to show up in the statistical charts.

Transition in the Caucasus Republics

The Caucasus republics of Georgia, Azerbaijan, and Armenia have adopted different reform policies and with varying degrees of success.[18] Georgia's economy was so ravaged by civil war that its inflation statistics cannot be placed on the chart below. Inflation was 3100 percent in 1993 and 7380 percent in 1994. After termination of the main hostilities, brokered with Russian assistance and intervention, Georgia adopted a financial austerity program that caused its inflation to drop to an annual rate of 450 percent in 1995. Georgia's output also plummeted in association with its civil war and transition debacle. Its GDP fell about 80 percent in the five years of independence. Without its own energy resources, Georgia is dependent on

Figure 19.4 Transition in Central Asia

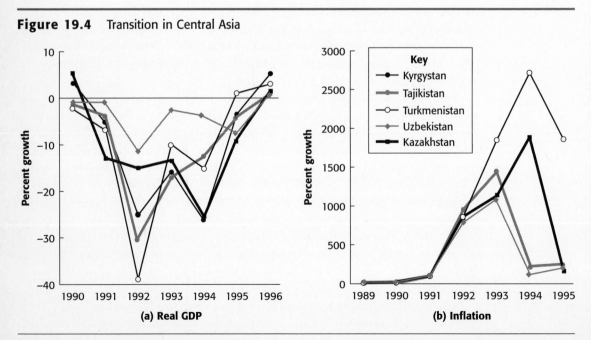

(a) Real GDP

(b) Inflation

Source: PlanEcon, *Review and Outlook for the Former Soviet Republics* (selected years).

other republics for electricity. Turkmenistan, its major supplier of natural gas, has periodically cut off deliveries due to payment failures. The Georgian parliament drafted an economic reform program that won IMF support in July of 1995. In March of 1995, Georgia began a privatization program of industry, services, and agriculture, the latter resulting in the privatization of about one fifth of Georgia's agricultural land. Georgia has granted its national bank full independence from political intervention and has closed about half of its commercial banks for failing to meet capital requirements.

Azerbaijan's economy has shrunk for seven straight years. Its inflation rate was 1780 percent in 1994, which fell to 312 percent in 1995 as a consequence of tightened monetary policy. Damaged by the military conflict with Armenia, Azerbaijan's budget has been in serious deficit, and the Azerbaijan government continues to subsidize industry and agriculture, thus putting additional pressure on the budget. Despite ambitious announced reform programs, Azerbaijan has yet to introduce real privatization. In 1994, the private sector accounted for only 15 percent of GDP.

The slow rate of change may be due to its prospects for substantial foreign investments and the substantial improvements in energy production associated with large energy projects in the Caspian Sea. These opportunities have brought Azerbaizhan considerable foreign investment. However, the consummation of these large energy projects has been thwarted by their dependence on transportation facilities through Russia and by Russia's challenge to Azerbaijan's development rights to Caspian Sea deposits. In 1995 and 1996, efforts were made to solve Russia's objections by including Russian oil companies in the consortiums that have been created to develop Azerbaijan's energy resources.

Armenia, like Azerbaijan, has been seriously harmed by their armed conflict. In addition to the setbacks from war damage, Armenia was slow to recover from its 1988 earthquake, and its trade routes were blockaded by Turkey and Azerbaijan. Its energy supplies have been disrupted, although it has restored some degree of energy independence with the reopening of a nuclear power facility damaged by the 1988 earthquake. Facing blockade, Armenia has sought to develop alternate trade routes via Iran. Fighting between Armenia and Azerbaijan was halted in May 1995. Since then, Armenia has adopted policies of monetary and fiscal austerity and was the sole Caucasus republic to record positive economic growth in 1995. Figure 19.5 (p. 456) shows real GDP and inflation developments for the region.

SUMMARY

Table 19.4 (p. 457) provides another snapshot of the NIS economies as of 1995—three to four years into their transition processes. It shows considerable variation. Although all had introduced their own national currency, they were having quite different results in stabilizing their exchange rates and also in achieving currency convertibility. Some had regained positive growth as of 1995, but most still had

Figure 19.5   Transition in the Caucasus Republics

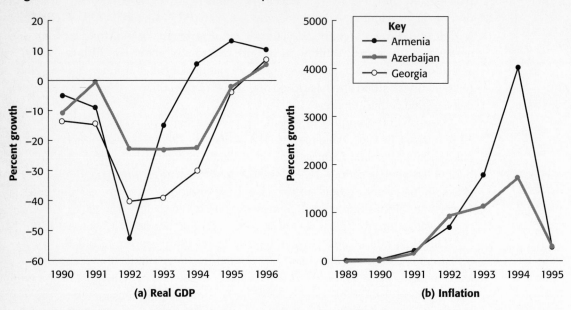

(a) Real GDP   (b) Inflation

Source: PlanEcon, *Review and Outlook for the Former Soviet Republics* (selected years).

declining real output. All were running government deficits; only the Baltic states appeared to have these deficits under control as a percentage of GDP.

Except for the Baltic republics, no former Soviet republic has adopted a true shock therapy program. The overall tendency has been to pursue gradualist programs, in response to pressure from interest groups, such as industrial managers and farm directors. The gradualist approach, it appears, has not spared countries from severe declines in output, and it has definitely contributed to soaring inflation.

Figure 19.6 (p. 458) summarizes the relationship between shock therapy and economic growth in the NIS states. The inflation rate is probably the best proxy for shock therapy. There, we take the average inflation rate for the period 1991 to 1996, and we correlate it with the average rate of decline of real GDP for the same period. If gradualism somehow ameliorates the decline in output (and hence the rise in unemployment), there would be a positive association between inflation and economic growth. In fact, although the association is not strong, there is, if anything, a negative correlation between inflation (shock therapy) and economic growth in the NIS countries. Obviously, much more than financial austerity explains economic recovery. A number of countries experienced the same decline in output while having quite different rates of inflation. In this regard, the experiences of the NIS economies is the same as those of transition countries in general. The general experience has been a negative correlation between economic growth and inflation.[19]

Table 19.4

THE FORMER SOVIET REPUBLICS IN 1995

Country	Currency	Initial exchange rate*	Exchange rate, 1985	Deficit as % of GDP	Foreign investment**	Growth GDP, 1995
Russia	ruble	222.0	4554.0	3.1	$2500 million	−3.8
Armenia	dram	75.0	403.0	15.0	$5 million	5.2
Azerbaijan	manat	1169.0	4311.0	10.0	large	−17.4
Belarus	rubel	4.4	4.0	4.0	insignificant	−16.0
Estonia	kroon	12.1	11.6	1.0	$642 million	4.8
Georgia	lari	102,300.0	1,330,000.0	NA	insignificant	−0.4
Kazakhstan	lei	6.31	63.97	2.8	NA	−8.9
Kyrgystan	som	6.0	10.8	12.6	NA	−6.0
Latvia	lat	0.7	0.54	3.8	$400 million	0.8
Lithuania	lit	4.4	4.0	2.0	$322 million	3.0
Moldova	temge	3.7	6.5	4.5	$42 million	−5.0
Tajikistan	ruble zone	NA	NA	10.2	insignificant	−14.4
Turkmenistan	manat	2.0	100.0	NA	NA	−7.5
Ukraine	karbovanets	35,000.0	180,000.0	8.1	$750 million	−11.8
Uzbekistan	som	1.0	36.0	10.0	NA	−0.5

*Initial exchange rate = rate to dollar when currency introduced.

**Foreign investment: cumulated total of direct foreign investment.

Source: PlanEcon, *Review and Outlook for the Former Soviet Republics* (March 1996), Country tables.

With only minor exceptions, privatization was carried through in a consequent fashion, leaving the system of industrial and farm management basically unchanged from the Soviet period. It is this phenomenon that appears to explain the large drops in output associated with gradualism: the old system has been abandoned, and a new system has not been put in its place, leaving the economy in a state of limbo.

Those former Soviet republics that inherited substantial raw material and energy wealth, particularly those of Central Asia, have been spared to a degree from the worst ravages of gradualism by using their natural wealth to subsidize the economy and its citizens. But even here the opportunities for subsidization are limited, particularly by the inability to export sufficient amounts of natural resources and enterprises' virtually unlimited subsidy demands. To overcome these infrastructure restraints, the resource-rich republics must embark on multibillion-dollar transportation projects, which they cannot finance internally. They must therefore attract financing from the West, which requires the creation of a stable investment

Figure 19.6   Inflation Versus Growth in the FSU Republics

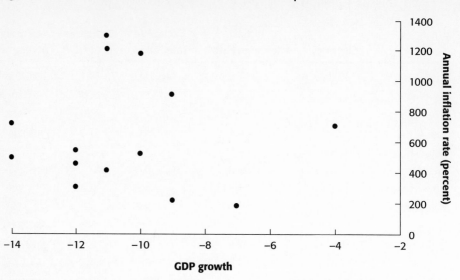

Source: PlanEcon, *Review and Outlook for the Former Soviet Republics* (selected years).

climate. Just as runaway inflation has caused reluctant reformers to reform, so may the need for outside capital eventually force significant reform in the region.

Apparently, the most effective pressure in favor of radical reform has been the pressure of soaring inflation. Reluctant government may be able to postpone privatization, but it cannot postpone runaway inflation. Once it agrees to deal with inflation, it must adapt to stern policies of international organizations like the IMF, which make financial support contingent upon macroeconomic stabilization programs.

The former Soviet republics remain interrelated, even though their trade has shifted from trading with "Near Abroad" countries (the NIS states) to "Far Abroad" countries. Each of the NIS economies remains in a depressed state; although a few are recovering, incomes and outputs are well below levels at the start of transition. One strong reason for the collapsing shares of "Near Abroad" trade has been the economic depressions that have plagued each country. The economic recovery of Russia, therefore, could serve as an engine of growth for the entire region. A vibrant Russia would pull up the other lagging NIS countries.

Terms and Concepts ——————————

Commonwealth of Independent States (CIS)   A loosely knit association of twelve of the former Soviet republics, excluding the Baltic states of Latvia, Lithuania, and Estonia.

Newly Independent States (NIS)   The term applied to the former republics of the Soviet Union, sometimes referred to by Russia as the "Near Abroad."

Terms of Trade   Generally the amount (quantity) of imports that a country receives in exchange for a unit of exports.

Selected Bibliography

General

Artisien-Maksimento, P. and Y. Adjubei. *Foreign Investment in Russia and the Other Soviet Successor States* (New York: St. Martins, 1996).

Bremmer, I., and R. Taras, eds. *New States, New Politics* (New York: Oxford University Press, 1996).

Brzezinski, Z., and P. Sullivan, eds. *Russia and the Commonwealth of Independent States: Documents, Data, and Analysis* (Armonk: M.E. Sharpe, 1996).

Cooper, R.N. and J. Gács, eds. *Trade Growth in Transition Economies* (Lyme, NH: Elgar, 1997).

Dawisha, K., and B. Parrott. *Russia and the New States of Eurasia* (New York: Cambridge University Press, 1994).

Hanke, S., L. Jonung, and K. Schuler. *Russian Currency and Finance* (London: Routledge, 1993).

Murrell, P., "How Far Has the Transition Progressed?" *Journal of Economic Perspectives* vol. 10, no. 2 (Spring 1996).

USDA, Economic Research Service. *Former USSR Update* (Washington, DC: U.S. Government Printing Office, various).

World Bank. *Transition* (Washington, DC: World Bank, various).

The Baltic Countries

Driefelds, J. *Latvia in Transition* (New York: Oxford University Press, 1996).

Gregory, P.M. "Outlook for the Baltics" *Review and Outlook for the Former Soviet Republics* (Washington, DC: PlanEcon, March 1966), 55–90.

Haavisto, T., ed. *The Transition to a Market Economy: Transformation and Reform in the Baltic States* (Cheltenham: Edward Elgar, 1977).

Ministry of Foreign Affairs of the Republic of Lithuania. *Partner in a World Economy* (Vilnius: SIPS, 1994).

Mygind, N., ed. *Privatization and Financial Participation in the Baltic Countries* (Copenhagen: Copenhagen Business School, 1996).

———. "Employee Ownership in the Baltic Countries," in M. Uvalic and D.V. Whitehead, eds. *Privatization Surprises in Transition Economies* (Lyme, NH: Elgar, 1997, 49–79).

Norgaard, O., D. Hindsgaul, L. Johannsen, and H. Willumsen. *The Baltic States After Independence* (Cheltenham: Edward Elgar, 1996).

Sutela, P. *The Baltic Economies in Transition* (Helsinki: Bank of Finland, 1994).

The European Slavic Countries

Crane, K., and D. Green. "Overview," *Review and Outlook for the Former Soviet Republics* (Washington, DC: PlanEcon, March 1996), 1–xxvi.

Drobycky, M., ed. *Crimea: Dynamics, Challenge, and Prospects* (Lonham, MD: Rowman & Littlefield, 1995).

Kushnirsky, F. "Ukraine's Industrial Enterprise: Surviving Hard Times," *Comparative Economic Studies,* vol. 36, no. 4 (Winter 1994), 35–39.

Marples, D.R. *Belarus: From Soviet Rule to Nuclear Catastrophe* (New York: St. Martins, 1996).

Tedstrom, J.E. "Ukraine: A Crash Course in Economic Transition," *Comparative Economic Studies,* vol. 37, no. 4 (Winter 1995), 49–67.

Central Asia

Pomfret, R. *Asian Economies in Transition* (Cheltenham: Edward Elgar, 1996).

Rumer, B. ed. *Central Asia in Transition* (Armonk: M.E. Sharpe, 1996).

Notes ───────────────────────

1. For a description of the end of the Soviet Union, see *The Cambridge Encyclopedia of Russia and the Former Soviet Union* (Cambridge: Cambridge University Press, 1994), 141–44.
2. The statistics on the NIS states are drawn from the following sources: *Handbook of International Economic Statistics 1992*, 55–129; *Narodnoe khoziaistvo SSSR* (selected years); *Cambridge Encyclopedia of Russia and the Former Soviet Union*, Section: Ethnic groups.
3. "Kyrgyz Republic: Sound Policies Yield Economic Improvements," IMF *Survey* (September 9, 1996).
4. D. Tarr, "The Terms-of-Trade Effects of Moving to World Market Prices on Countries of the Former Soviet Union," *Journal of Comparative Economics* vol. 18, no. 1 (February 1994), 1–24.
5. S. Kolchin, "Rossiia-blizhnee zarubezh'e: vzaimootnosheniia, interesy, tsel politiki," MEiMO, no. 4.
6. For information on industrial concentration and its effects, see S. Sutyrin, "Problems and Prospects of Economic Reintegration Within the CIS," *Review of Economies in Transition* vol. 1 (1996), 31–33.
7. *Petroleum Economist,* "Major Pipelines of the Former Soviet Union—Petroleum Economist Energy Map Series No. 31.
8. M. Sagers and D. Green, "Transport Constraints in Crude Oil Pipelines in Russia and in the Other Former Soviet Republics," Plan Econ, *Energy Outlook for the Former Soviet Republics* (June 1955), 91–132.
9. For a description of the ruble monetary system during the early years of transition, see S. Hanke, L. Jonung, and K. Schuler, *Russian Currency and Finance* (London: Routledge, 1993).
10. Sutyrin, op. cit., p. 34.
11. *Russian Economic Trends 1996* vol. 5, no. 2, 97.
12. For general sources on the Baltic transition, see P. Sutela, *The Baltic Economies in Transition* (Helsinki: Bank of Finland, 1994); P. M. Gregory, "Outlook for the Baltics," Plan

Econ, *Review and Outlook for the Former Soviet Republics* (March 1996), 55–90; IMF Surveys (various publications).

13. For example, in Latvia, the national telephone concession was awarded to a consortium headed by Britain's Cable & Wireless, and the national airline franchise was awarded to SAS. In Estonia, the national airline franchise was awarded to a Danish company.

14. Gregory, op. cit., 55.

15. To repeat, the Moldovans are ethnically related to the Romanians and are not a Slavic ethnic group. Moldova is included in the Slavic group for geographic reasons only.

16. For accounts of transition in these countries, see K. Crane and D. Green, "Overview," Plan Econ, *Review and Outlook for the Former Soviet Republics* (March 1996), i–xxvi; Z. Tabernacki, "Outlook for Ukraine," Plan Econ, op. cit., 35–53; J. Glover, "Outlook for Belarus," Plan Econ, op. cit., 91–111; B. Gold, "Outlook for Moldova," Plan Econ, op. cit., 139–50.

17. For information on reform in the central Asia region, see G. Albergo and C. Movitt, "Outlook for Kazakstan," Plan Econ, op. cit., 113–38; P. Murrell, "Outlook for Central Asia," Plan Econ, op. cit., 177–219. Also see "Central Asia's Economies in Transition, Conference Proceedings," *Comparative Economic Studies* vol. 37, no. 3 (Fall 1995).

18. For information on the Caucasus republics, see B. Gold, "Outlook for the Caucasus and Moldova," Plan Econ, op. cit., 135–70.

19. T. Gylfason, "Reforms in Eastern Europe," *Journal of World Trade* vol. 29, no. 3 (June 1995), 107–33.

Russia in the Twenty-First Century

Russia's transition from administrative command to market economy will have been underway almost a decade when the twenty-first century begins. Although a decade is not particularly long in terms of historical time, we should have a much better picture of the outcome of Russia's transition by the year 2000. Whether a success or a failure, Russia's transition is bound to shape the next century.

Russia is currently in the midst of its transition; the course of this transition depends on a myriad of factors, all too complex to predict. All we can do at this point is to summarize the most important events that have taken place so far and to speculate about various possible scenarios for the future.

TRANSITION SUCCESSES AND FAILURES: THE FIRST SIX YEARS

By the middle of 1997, Russia had completed more than half a decade of transition. Judged on the basis of aggregate quantitative indicators, Russia's transition had failed, as of that date, to achieve major identifiable successes. Although we pointed out in Chapter 15 that the decline of the Russian economy after 1991 may be overstated, the Russian economy had, at best, stabilized as of 1997. At worst, its decline was continuing albeit at a much slower pace. The output of oil and gas—a key indicator of economic performance in an economy whose comparative advantage is energy resources—was still declining, although pundits predicted that the industry would resume growth in the near future. There were few signs of the investment boom required to replace and renew the Russian economy's depleted stock of capital and outdated technology. The flood of foreign investment that Russian authorities had hoped for had yet to materialize. The mammoth Russian economy had attracted far less foreign capital than the much smaller economies of Eastern Europe.

In other respects, the five years of transition from 1992 to 1997 had not been wasted. As Chapter 15 demonstrated, the Russian economy had begun the difficult process of restructuring itself from the shape of an administrative command economy to that of a market economy. The relative shares of those economic activities demanded by a market economy—services, finance, and natural resources—had increased, along with the rewards to those who produced them, while the shares of those economic activities desired by administrative planners—heavy machinery, defense goods, and large construction projects—declined, as did the rewards to those who produced them. In a sense, the decline in aggregate output was really a combination of rapid declines in nonmarket-oriented sectors and growth in market-oriented sectors such as housing construction, finance, and services.

Chapter 14 pointed to other signs of movement toward a market economy. Despite its frailties, the Russian democracy survived landmark political elections, which resulted in the reelection of a reform-oriented government under an ailing President, Boris Yeltsin. A new constitution was passed which gave private property equal protection that public property already had and guaranteed basic economic freedoms. Most businesses in the economy were privatized in a highly flawed insider-dominated privatization process, but at least control of the economy was switched out of the hands of the state and of administrative planners. The most significant remaining political problem was the divisive split between the executive and legislative branch, the latter remaining under the control of communist and nationalist deputies. The legislative split made it difficult to pass landmark legislation, such as the Production Sharing Agreement procedures, required to attract foreign investment to the Russian energy industry. The executive-legislative schism also reflected basic differences of opinion on the role of the market, the desirability of foreign investment, and the need for monetary discipline.

Another significant problem complicating the Russian transition as of the second half of the decade of the 90s was the criminalization of the Russian economy. Not only were criminal mafia elements in charge of extortion, murder-for-hire, and entry into retail trade, a nomenklatura mafia had been created by the privatization process. They consisted of powerful officials and their allies who had gained control of leading companies and industries. Although both monopoly rent-seeking and influence-buying permeate all economies, these activities appear to be particularly strong in the Russian transition. In a long-term sense, they represent as great a threat to long-term growth and recovery as do other growth factors, such as capital investment.[1]

Chapters 14 and 16 discussed what may be Russia's greatest achievement of the first half decade of transition: a hard-fought degree of macroeconomic stability. Although the Russian leadership was initially skeptical of the relationship between monetary growth and inflation—preferring to blame monopoly power for inflation—the leaders of the Russian government have accepted the fact that monetary restraint is required to reduce inflation. By the mid-1990s, Russia had reduced its inflation rate to levels more acceptable to an emerging economy and had reduced the possibility of and fear of hyperinflation. The Central Bank of Russia's independence from political intervention is by no means assured, but recent legislation appears to have freed it from the obligation to finance the government deficit. Moreover, pressure from international organizations, such as the International Monetary Fund, to restrain the deficit as a percent of GDP remains a constant fact of Russian political life. Indeed, in the summer of 1997 budget issues, especially curbs on military spending, were the focus of attention.

Chapter 16 discussed the difficult task of converting from state budget finance to private investment finance. Whereas the administrative command economy financed investment through budget surpluses collected from sales taxes and profit taxes, a market-oriented Russian economy must rely on private capital markets to create investment finance. The state's role has, in fact, been reversed. With the federal budget's large deficits, the Russian state now crowds out private investment activities. In the uncertain Russian economic environment, the credit-worthiness of the state is greater than that of private companies. Hence, the state is better able to attract domestic and private credits (via its GKO auctions) than private companies. Despite these drawbacks, there are promising signs. With the impending completion of privatization, both primary and secondary equity markets have arisen to generate equity capital and to create a liquid secondary market in Russian shares. These markets represent an option to direct investments in Russian companies.

In order for Russia to realize an investment boom, there must not only be a supply of investment capital; there must be a demand. The demand for investment depends upon the real investment opportunities available (which are significant in such a resource rich economy) and also upon the investment climate. The investment climate is currently retarded by arbitrary taxation, the criminalization of the economy, and the uncertain legislative support for foreign investment. The Russian tax system faces a dual-edged sword. It must collect taxes to restrain the state deficit, but it must not destroy investment incentives through excessive marginal tax rates or arbitrary taxation. So far, the Russian tax system has not been able to resolve this duality. Its introduction of a "modern" tax system has been delayed to the end of the century.

Chapter 17 discussed Russia's growing integration into the world product and capital markets. In the administrative command era, the Russian economy strived for autarky and sought to cut its companies and citizens off from world markets. The

Russian leadership of the transition era has sought to better integrate Russia into the world economy, although there is still considerable difference of opinion about the need for and desirability of foreign direct investment.

As the transition has progressed, the Russian economy has increasingly become a part of the world economy, although international capital flows remain minimal. Russia's foreign trade proportions are more "normal" for a country of its size and resource endowment. Russia's composition of trade has shifted dramatically toward raw materials and energy and more toward the "far abroad" of Eastern Europe and Western Europe and away from the "near abroad" markets of the former Soviet Union. The Russian Federation assumed responsibility for its share of USSR external debt. Although it has been unable to service this debt, Russia succeeded in renegotiating Russia's external debt with both private lenders and public lenders (the Paris and London Clubs), and has been able to reenter Western debt markets, selling Eurobonds in open markets at rates of interest well below those required by domestic savers.

In sum, although Russia has yet to record positive growth, it appears to have initiated many of the preparatory steps. Chapter 15 used the analogy of a motorist driving through a confusing web of back streets, some of which are one way, to find the entry ramp to the turnpike. Once on the turnpike, the motorist can drive at a high rate of speed. Although Russia still must navigate some additional steps to get on its growth turnpike, an examination of the record suggests progress.

RUSSIAN PERFORMANCE IN PERSPECTIVE

The preceding chapter placed Russia's transition in perspective. It examined the course of transition in the 15 independent countries that once constituted the republics of the Soviet Union. The basic conclusion of this chapter was that transition has been a difficult process in all the former Soviet republics, although some have been more successful than others. Chapter 15 examined the Russian experience in the context of Eastern European transition and concluded that Russia's performance has been modest for a country undergoing the first steps of transition.

Our examination of a relatively large number of countries shows that there is no such thing as a painless transition. The former administrative command economy that underwent transition under the most favorable conditions—the former German Democratic Republic—experienced substantial transition costs, despite enormous financial subsidies from the German government and the almost immediate imposition of German legal and political institutions.

Figure 20.1 examines Russian transition in the context of "successful" and "unsuccessful" transitions in other former administrative command economies. Unfortunately, the successes are rare; the failures more frequent.[2] Figure 20.1 shows the transition path beginning with the year prior to initiation of transition (1991 in the former Soviet republics and 1989 in Eastern Europe). Transition paths are measured by two variables: the average annual growth rate of real GDP and the average inflation rate.

The transition successes suffered, on average, one year of very rapid inflation, after which inflation decelerated to rates acceptable for an emerging economy. The transition failures suffered rapid inflation for four years with an average inflation rate at the end of that period well above an acceptable level for macroeconomic stability. As the figure shows, Russia falls between the successful and unsuccessful inflation paths.

The transition successes restored positive economic growth between the third and fourth years of transition. Moreover, their production declines were less steep than in other transition economies. The transition failures experienced more severe production declines and failed to recover to positive growth rates of output by the end of their fourth year of transition. Russia's production decline was slightly less severe than the average production decline of the transition failures, and Russia was closer to recovering to zero growth of output by the end of the fourth year of transition than the transition failures.

Placing Russia's transition in context underscores the enormous difficulty of transition and the fact that, while Russia's transition performance has not been stellar, many countries have actually performed much worse. Although Russia has had some notable advantages—in particular its vast natural resource wealth—it has had to deal with disadvantages, such as its enormous size and diversity, with which other transition countries have not had to contend.

Figure 20.1   Average Annual GDP Growth Rates—Russia and Other Transition Economies

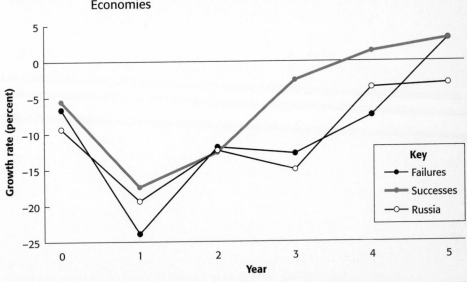

Source: PlanEcon, *Review and Outlook for the Former Soviet Republics* (selected years).

OBSTACLES TO GROWTH

Russia's growth prospects depend upon the removal of the remaining obstacles to growth. Some are political; others are economic. In many cases, economic and political obstacles are intertwined because economic solutions may not be politically feasible. The degree to which they are resolved and the speed of removal will determine whether Russia will be a flourishing economy in the first decade of the twenty-first century or a stagnant one.

Enterprise Restructuring

The enterprises that Russia inherited from the Soviet past were designed to produce the goods required by the administrative command economy, without consideration of the opportunity cost of inputs, such as the real cost of energy. They operated on the basis of the job rights economy, described by Granick (Chapter 8), in which workers belonged to a "kollektiv" and the enterprise's task was to take care of its kollektiv.

Estimates suggest that perhaps one in fifty Russian enterprises will survive with a high degree of certainty in a market context. Perhaps 10 percent have a reasonable chance of survival.[3] Obviously new firms created to react to market needs stand a better chance than those carried over from the Soviet period. Nevertheless, it is in the large Soviet-style enterprises that employment is concentrated.

There are various options for dealing with enterprises that stand little chance of survival in a market context. Their assets can be parceled out into various activities that make sense in a market economy, much like corporate assets are restructured during a bankruptcy proceeding in the West. Although the company cannot make a go of it as a unified company, there may be parts that, if properly valued, can be successful. Restructuring company assets requires bankruptcy laws, financial markets, and entrepreneurial skills. It also requires the political willpower to resist the demand for subsidies, which burden federal or local budgets, to keep the entire enterprise in operation.

In the mid-1990s, enterprises avoided painful restructuring decisions through a variety of means: they could lobby for subsidies, build up arrears to suppliers, lobby local officials for credits, and bribe officials. Russia now has a Federal Bankruptcy Agency and bankruptcy proceedings have become increasingly frequent in the Russian courts.[4] Nonetheless, the ability to delay painful decision making has allowed enterprises to retain workers even when their services are no longer needed.[5]

There are natural market forces promoting rational restructuring. Creditors must at some point collect unpaid debts. They can collect these debts by assuming control of enterprise assets. To recoup their losses, they could either sell these assets to entrepreneurs for use in a market setting or incorporate these assets into their own operations. As enterprises are dissolved or broken up, there will be a period of associated unemployment as hoarded labor is terminated, but in the long run, these labor assets will be reallocated to activities that create profits rather than contribute to losses.

Enterprise restructuring and its associated unemployment present difficult political decisions for local, regional, and national politicians. It remains to be seen how much political will there is in contemporary Russia in favor of restructuring or whether a semipermanent system of costly subsidies will be erected by political authorities.

Corporate Culture

The corporate culture of the Soviet enterprise was discussed in Chapter 7. It was oriented toward meeting production targets at all costs. Managers were not sensitive to costs (which were arbitrarily set), and they were not oriented towards marketing insofar as the supply system automatically took what they produced. The company was owned by the state (by everyone) and hence by no one. Although their careers were dependent upon enterprise success (as judged by quantitative plan fulfillment), managers had little personal financial stake in the enterprise's success.

The Enterprise Law of 1987 (discussed in Chapter 12) set the enterprise free from ministerial control, but it substituted no market discipline in its place. Russian enterprises became (to use the term Russian managers apply) "half pregnant"— meaning that they were free of the old system but had no new system in its place. Sometimes they were allowed to charge market prices; other times they had to sell at state prices. Sometimes they could make their own decisions. Sometimes an arbitrary decision was forced upon them.

In this limbo environment, Russian enterprise managers developed a unique corporate culture. During the early years of transition, the corporate culture prompted managers to use the enterprise for their own benefit. The manager would sign unfavorable contracts in return for payment of a broker's commission or sales fee. Corporate assets were diverted into small businesses that the manager or close associates owned. Hard currency earnings (which were likely to be confiscated by the government) were shipped abroad into the manager's bank account.

Insider privatization changed the corporate control of Russian enterprises. Whereas earlier, no one owned the enterprise and no one cared, after privatization, Russian enterprises were owned by inside management, workers, and by outside shareholders. The issue is whether the new corporate culture will motivate managers and owners to operate the enterprise to maximize profits and hence shareholder value. Management insiders who now control enterprise operations must decide between signing unfavorable contracts on which they can receive "commissions" or contracting in a neutral fashion so that the best interests of the enterprise are served. Studies of Russian privatized firms show that indeed privatized companies appear to be better run than non-privatized companies. They are more willing to restructure their operations. Russian companies that have significant outsider share ownership appear to be the best run of all—outsider ownership appears to ensure a more favorable corporate culture.[6]

Another force in favor of a profit-oriented corporate culture is the growing threat of corporate takeovers. As Russian commercial/financial consortia are formed, they can search for potentially profitable but poorly run Russian companies that can be taken over by purchasing undervalued shares. The threat of an unfriendly takeover can have a firm disciplining effect on Russian managers. In fact, the "loan for shares" program discussed in Chapter 18 is an example of a corporate takeover that threatens the control of existing management.[7]

For the Russian economy to grow, there must develop a pervasive corporate culture that seeks to operate enterprises in the interests of owners; that is, to engage in long-term profit maximization. The search for profit maximization will encourage enterprises to make the difficult adjustment decisions—with respect to such things as excess labor, and collecting debts—that they have not been willing to make to date.

Criminalization and Rent-Seeking

Economists are becoming aware of the depressing effect of widespread criminalization and monopoly rent-seeking on overall economic performance. Countries that are characterized by widespread criminalization, monopoly rent-seeking, and political bribery have been unable to grow, despite favorable underlying economic conditions. We could cite many examples in Africa, Latin America, and Mexico.

The Russian economy is particularly oppressed by criminalization and monopoly rent-seeking. Mancur Olson has offered an explanation for why Russia has been plagued by criminalization. He believes that the Soviet administrative command economy fostered the formation of informal conspiratorial groups, which served to ensure plan fulfillment and to protect local and regional enterprises from central authorities.[8] If Olson's theory is correct, criminalization and monopoly rent-seeking are an endemic force created in the Soviet period and will require time to remove.

Although Russia's commercial legislation has relatively strict anticorruption rules, these standards are not enforced by the legal system. As noted in Chapter 14, Russia's antitrust laws prohibit regulators from ownership shares or economic interests in regulated industries, but press accounts reveal that these prohibitions are not observed.

Solution of Russia's criminalization problem requires a strong and independent judicial system, which does not yet exist in Russia. It may prove easier to deal with overt criminal elements than with the more insidious form of monopoly rent-seeking. Russia would require a strong leader promoting anticorruption and backed by a strong political mandate. Monopoly rent-seeking—bribing officials to receive monopoly privileges—is more difficult for voters to understand. Moreover, the outcome of the presidential election of 1996 was largely dictated by political contributions from powerful business groups, establishing the precedent that political success depends upon political patronage of powerful business lobbies.

Investment Climate and Investment Finance

The collapse of the Russian economy during the first five years of transition was led by a collapse of investment. Investment collapsed because of the disappearance of the budget system of investment finance and deterioration in the investment climate. Chapter 16 described the steps that have been taken to create a private capital market in Russia. Russians and foreigners can now buy Russian stocks; they can purchase government treasury bills, and foreign investors can even purchase Eurobonds denominated in foreign currencies from the Russian government. Despite these promising developments, the Russian investment market continues to have serious weaknesses on both the demand and supply sides.

On the demand side, the most prominent obstacle to investment is the arbitrary tax system. If investors are unable to calculate their after-tax rate of return, they cannot make rational investment decisions. With an arbitrary tax system, future rates of return simply cannot be calculated. The current Russian tax system represents a pragmatic blend of taxation of solvent companies, special privileges, and exemptions, a system that is exceptionally arbitrary and not transparent. A new Russian tax system that relies on predictable income taxes and value added taxes is being devised, but it will take a long time to adopt, given the fact that a large number of preferential tax privileges will be lost in the process. The demand side of investment is also hampered by the weak rule of law and uncertainty concerning the reliability of Russian state decisions. For example, joint ventures in oil were created in the early 1990s, based on promises of tax holidays and preferential access to export pipelines granted by duly recognized Russian officials. However, these ventures have been plagued by government disregard of its earlier commitments (Chapter 19).

The supply side (investment finance) also depends on the investment climate. Although Russia has been desperately short of investment finance, there has been a substantial capital flight out of Russia to safe havens (Chapter 17). This potential supply of savings has been lost because of Russia's unfavorable investment climate, which makes a low-interest deposit in a Swiss bank preferable to a 100 percent rate of return on an investment inside of Russia. Chapter 16 pointed out that Russian households are able to deliver substantial sums of investment finance to capital markets. Prevailing incentives directed this capital into "unproductive" investments such as consumer durables, foreign currencies, and precious metals. A final weakness of the Russian private capital market is the degree to which the federal budget deficit is currently crowding out private investment. Private savers currently prefer notes guaranteed by the Russian treasury rather than in bonds guaranteed by Russian companies. Moreover, the current financial system encourages short-term lending, which is unsuited for long-term industrial investment.

Chapter 18 concluded that foreign investment has been limited to a mere trickle, despite Russia's immense natural wealth. The flow of foreign investment has been restricted primarily by the investment climate, but it has been retarded as well by Russia's ambiguity towards foreign investment. This ambiguity is expressed in political opposition to selling Russia's "wealth" to outsiders. It is also expressed in delays and opposition to legislation and regulations that provide foreign investors with sufficient confidence to invest in the Russian economy.[9]

GROWTH SCENARIOS

Clearly we cannot predict with any confidence Russia's growth path over the next five years and beyond. It depends upon the removal of the obstacles discussed above. Any number of outcomes are possible. Some are more likely than others.

Return to the Administrative Command Model

The scenario of a return to the Soviet administrative command system is a low-probability event. In several elections now, Russia has rejected a return to the communist system. Even if communists were to return to power as a ruling coalition, the heart and brains of the communist system—a highly disciplined and centralized central committee—have long since died. A full restoration of the administrative command system would be comparable to putting the proverbial genie back into his bottle. Moreover, we have the experiences of other former communist countries, in the Baltic states and in Eastern Europe, where communists, returning to a parliamentary majority, have not moved to restore the former system. The communist system is too hated by the population, although some feel nostalgia for some of its features.

A more realistic scenario would be a return of former communists to power on a program of restoring some features of the administrative command economy, such as the social security provisions or subsidization of state enterprises and rigid industrial policy. The growth outcome of this scenario would be disastrous because it would prolong the "half pregnant" status of Russian enterprises, leaving them caught between a planned economy and a market economy.

Continuation of Legislative Indecision

The most likely growth scenario is a continuation of the current rate of progress towards institutional and legislative change. This scenario is the most likely because of the divisions between the legislative and executive branches and because vested interests favor a "go slow" approach. Under this scenario, progress towards removing barriers to growth—such things as improving the investment climate and encouraging improvements in corporate control—would proceed slowly. There would be no forceful campaign to deal with outright criminalization, much less than with monopoly rent-seeking by the mafia nomenklatura. The decline of the Russian economy would cease, but growth would be slow at best. Spontaneous economic forces in the private sector would create growth in services, energy, and raw materials, but the vast former state sector would continue to languish. Agriculture would also languish absent any real efforts to privatize land on a wholesale basis. Investment would continue to flow into activities that yield quick returns, such as trading, and consumer goods and services, but it would be difficult to attract long-term investments for large projects. Russia's energy industry would continue to be undercapitalized, and foreign investors would refrain from significant investments. The Russian oil and gas industry would remain primarily in Russian hands but would not embark on a strong growth path.

Strong Reform Initiative

A third scenario, which is less likely than the second scenario is a renewed drive for rapid reform and change. Macroeconomic policy would become even more restrictive, and Russia would produce an inflation rate similar to those of Western Europe and the United States. The legislative dam would break, and legislation required for foreign investment would be passed in a convincing manner. The Russian leadership would embark on a forceful anticorruption drive which would eradicate the worst forms of criminalization of the economy. Russia's capital flight would reverse as Russian investors, who better understand Russia's opportunities and risk, would direct their investment resource to Russian industry. Russian savers would feel comfortable with placing their funds with competent financial interme-diaries, who would direct investment resources to the highest rates of return.

This scenario could produce results similar to the most successful transition economies of Eastern Europe—Poland, Hungary, and the Czech Republic. Although we have little time series evidence, we do know that such reform pro-cesses can generate relatively high rates of growth and attract large volumes of risk capital. In the Russian case, growth could be higher given Russia's scale and abun-dance of resources.

RUSSIA AND THE OUTSIDE WORLD

Russia's growth prospects also depend upon Russia's role in world politics and in the world economy. If Russia feels that it has become an integral part of the Western world, it will be more willing to take those steps necessary to integrate into world capital markets and to promote foreign investment. A Russia that will eventually join the European Union and perhaps even NATO will adopt different economic poli-cies from one that feels that NATO is its enemy and is denied entry to the European Union.

The Western world must grapple with such weighty decisions in the very near future. It must weigh the advantages of drawing the former Soviet bloc countries of Eastern Europe and the Baltic states into military and political alliances, thereby shielding them permanently from future Russian expansionism, against the dangers of isolating Russia from the West, economically, politically, and militarily.

From a strictly economic point of view, the mutual advantages of drawing Russia firmly into world product and capital markets are obvious. Russia is one of the last frontiers of energy and raw materials that can be developed at low marginal costs; the West has the capital and technology to aid this development. The West has gained substantial economic growth and efficiency increases from globalization. Russia's entry would spur another round of globalization that would benefit all parties.

Russia's full-fledged entry into world product and capital markets can only be assured if Russia is given a level playing field. If Russia does not eventually become a part of the European Union, its playing field will not be level. Russia's potential natural advantages in agriculture may not be realizable if European farmers are protected from the exports produced by a revitalized Russian agriculture.

The battle within Russia about its role in the world economy did not originate in the 1990s. Intellectuals and policy makers debated throughout the nineteenth century whether Russia should remain separate and apart from the world economy to develop according to its own special course. Similar arguments can be heard in Russia today. The appeal of protecting Russia's wealth from marauding Western business persons remains as potent today as it did in Tsarist Petersburg and Moscow.

LESSONS OF THE SOVIET PAST

Some one third of this book was devoted to the Soviet administrative command economy. It should now be apparent that we cannot hope to understand the Russian transition without understanding the Soviet legacy. The Soviet legacy explains the corporate culture, the assemblage of unprofitable companies, the problems of investment finance, the job rights and subsidy mentality, and the arrears crises that plague the contemporary Russian economy. The burden of the Soviet past has been a heavy weight on the Russian economy.

Does an understanding of the Soviet legacy ensure against a desire to return to that system? Writing in the mid-1990s, Joseph Berliner described the reason for abandoning Soviet socialism:

> . . ."When the next century looks back at ours, the first lesson it will learn is that in the 20th century a socialist economy was finally tried and it worked. This will sound perverse to us who are living in the midst of a wholesale rejection of socialism. But the reason for this rejection. . . is that it did not work very well, a proposition that is not at all inconsistent with the assertion that it did work. . . . Twentieth century socialism failed to deliver on one of its major promises—to surpass the productivity of capitalism. . . . Suffice it to say that none of the socialist economies has come near to matching the economic performance of the best of the non-socialist economies.[10]

If the Russian transition continues on a teetering path, there may be a temptation to conclude that the Soviet administrative command system did not collapse; rather it was abandoned because it did not work *as well* as the market system. Additionally, the conclusion may be drawn that it was not the system to blame but those who directed the system. If only the people had been better and had chosen better policies, the result would have been different. Or if the Soviet leadership had used a slightly different variant of socialism, such as market socialism, the result would have been much superior.[11] An unsuccessful transition would give rise to such considerations. A successful transition would bury them for the conceivable future.

FINAL THOUGHTS

We have come full circle in our account of the Russian economy. We began with the last market economy that existed on Russian territory—i.e., the Tsarist market economy—and we end with the difficult task of reestablishing a market economy on that same territory. Our account covered almost 150 years—from the emancipation of the Russian serfs in 1861 to the twilight years of the twentieth century. One-half of these years were lived under the Soviet experiment with the administrative command economy, the greatest social science experiment of recorded history. The Soviet economy was devised by design and was not, like the industrial revolution or the globalization of the world economy, a result of spontaneous forces. The Soviet experiment failed, and we are now witnessing another great experiment: the process of making the transition from the administrative command system back to a market economy.

The eventual outcome in Russia and in other republics of the former Soviet Union is unknown at this point. The outcome depends upon too many variables and too many unknowns. What is probably clear is that we should not expect too much. The highly industrialized countries of North America and Western Europe remain a rarity, governed as they are by well-defined rules backed by powerful enforcement mechanisms. Most countries will probably never reach these standards. The more common cases are countries like Turkey, Venezuela, Mexico, or Pakistan, where the legal rules are less well-defined and where rent-seeking behavior may dominate. We would therefore expect Russia eventually to fall somewhere on this spectrum between Western Europe and the less industrialized economies.

General Bibliography for Russian and Soviet Economies

CIA. *Handbook of International Statistics* (Washington, DC: CIA, annual).

———. *World Fact Book* (Washington, DC: CIA, annual).

East/West Executive Guide (monthly).

"Intelligence Unit, Country Studies" *Economist* (London: Economist, quarterly).

Interfax. *Reports* (Denver: Interfax-America Inc., weekly).

International Monetary Fund. *International Financial Statistics: Supplement on Countries of the Former Soviet Union* (Washington, DC: IMF, 1993).

———. *Survey* (Washington, DC: IMF).

OECD. *Short-Term Economic Indicators: Transition Economies* (Paris: OECD, quarterly).

———— . *National Accounts for the Former Soviet Union* (Paris: OECD, 1993).

———— . *Trends and Policies in Privatization* (Paris: OECD, biannual).

OMRI. *OMRI Economic Digest* (Open Media Research Institute, weekly).

Russian Economic Trends (Lawrence, KS: Whurr Publishers, quarterly).

Shend, J. Y. *Agricultural Statistics of the Former USSR Republics and the Baltic States* (Washington, DC: U.S. Department of Agriculture, 1993).

Vanous, J., ed., *PlanEcon Reports* (Washington, DC: PlanEcon, various).

USDA. *International Agriculture and Trade Reports: Former USSR* (Washington, DC: USDA, quarterly).

World Bank. *Transition* (Washington, DC: World Bank, bi-monthly).

Notes

1. In fact, empirical studies show a strong negative relationship between corruption indexes and economic growth and a strong positive relationship between economic freedom and economic growth. See K. Holmes and M. Kirkpatrick, "Freedom and Growth," *Wall Street Journal* (December 16, 1996). This article discusses "1997 Index of Economic Freedom," copublished by the Heritage Foundation and the Wall Street Journal.
2. We include in the transition success category, the three Baltic states, Poland, Hungary, and the Czech Republic. In the failure category, we include Armenia, Tajikistan, Kazakhstan, Ukraine, and Belarus. The year 0 refers to the year preceding the initiation of transition. For the former Soviet republics, this year is 1991. For the countries of Eastern Europe, year 0 is 1989.
3. S. Linz, "Russian Firms in Transition: Champions, Challengers, and Chaff," forthcoming, *Comparative Economic Studies* (Summer 1997).
4. The numbers of bankruptcy proceedings are as follows: 1993, 74; 1994, 231; 1995, 716; first half 1996, 534. Source: *Russian Economic Trends 1996,* vol. 5, no. 2, 122.
5. In January of 1995, 58 percent of enterprises reported having excess labor. In January of 1996, the percentage had risen to 62 percent. *Russian Economic Barometer,* 1996, vol. 2.
6. J. Earle and S. Estrin, "Privatization Versus Competition: Changing Enterprise Behavior in Russia," *Centre for Economic Performance,* Discussion paper No. 316 (December 1996).
7. See for example the description of the effect of Minatep's takeover of corporate management of Yukos oil company in "Houston, We Have a Problem," *Russian Petroleum Investor* (November 1996), 61–62.
8. M. Olson, "The Devolution of Power in Post-Communist Societies," in R. Skidelsky, ed., *Russia's Stormy Path to Reform* (London: Social Market Foundation, 1995), 9–42.
9. An example would be the interminable delays in passing Production Sharing Agreement legislation and the accompanying regulations.
10. J. Berliner, "Socialism in the Twenty-First Century," in M. Keren and G. Ofer, eds., *Trials of Transition: Economic Reform in the Former Communist Bloc* (Boulder, CO: Westview Press, 1993), 2–3.
11. For such arguments, see J. Adam, *Why Did the Socialist System Collapse in Central and Eastern European Countries?* (New York: St. Martin's Press, 1996).

INDEX